Business Information Systems
Analysis, Design and Practice

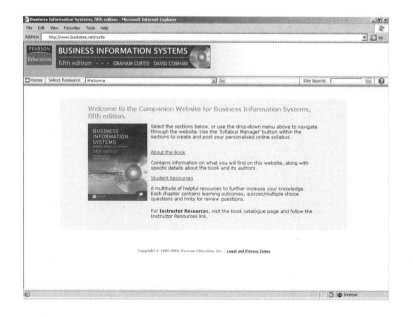

Visit the *Business Information Systems, fifth edition* Companion Website at
www.booksites.net/curtis
to find valuable student learning material including:

- Quizzes to help test your learning
- Hints for review questions

Fifth Edition

Business Information Systems
Analysis, Design and Practice

GRAHAM CURTIS
University of East London

and

DAVID COBHAM
University of Lincoln

 Prentice Hall
FINANCIAL TIMES

An imprint of **Pearson Education**
Harlow, England • London • New York • Boston • San Francisco • Toronto • Sydney • Singapore • Hong Kong
Tokyo • Seoul • Taipei • New Delhi • Cape Town • Madrid • Mexico City • Amsterdam • Munich • Paris • Milan

Pearson Education Limited

Edinburgh Gate
Harlow
Essex CM20 2JE
England

and Associated Companies throughout the world

Visit us on the World Wide Web at:
www.pearsoned.co.uk

First published 1989
Second edition 1995
Third edition 1998
Fourth edition 2002
Fifth edition published 2005

ISBN 0 273 68792 1

British Library Cataloguing-in-Publication Data
A catalogue record for this book is available from the British Library

Library of Congress Cataloging-in-Publication Data
Curtis, Graham.
    Business information systems : analysis, design, and practice / Graham Curtis and David Cobham.— 5th ed.
        p.   cm.
    Includes bibliographical references and index.
    ISBN 0-273-68792-1
    1. Business—Data processing.   2. Information storage and retrieval systems—Business.   3. Management information systems.   4. System design.   5. System analysis.   6. Expert systems (Computer science).   I. Cobham, David P.   II. Title.

HF5548.2.C88 2004
658.4'038'011—dc22   2004053160

10 9 8 7 6 5 4 3 2 1
09 08 07 06 05

Typeset in 10/12pt Sabon by 35
Printed and bound by Ashford Colour Press Ltd., Gosport

The publisher's policy is to use paper manufactured from sustainable forests.

To Julia, Edmund and James

To Christine, Daniel, Matthew and Chloe

Brief Contents

Contents

Companion Website resources
Visit the Companion Website at **www.booksites.net/curtis**

For students
- Quizzes to help test your learning
- Hints for review questions

For lecturers
- Answers to exercises
- PowerPoint slides that can be downloaded and used as OHTs

Also: This website has a Syllabus and Profile Manager, online help, search functions, and email results functions.

Preface

Information technology has permeated the organization at every level. There is a growing need for those interested in business, management or accountancy to understand the nature of this technology and the way it can best be harnessed to provide information for business functions. This text aims to examine and explain:

- the nature of information and its use in managerial decision making;
- the role of the information system within organizational strategy;
- how recent developments in information technology have been accompanied by the rise of end-user computing in business;
- the way that information is organized, stored and processed by modern information technology as viewed from the interests of a business user;
- how developments in networks and the Internet have made an impact on business; and
- the process of analysis and design of a business information system.

Readership

The book is designed as a core text for those undertaking an information systems course as part of a degree or HND in business studies or a related field. It is also recommended for second/third-year undergraduate business information systems modules in computer science courses. The book will be suitable for professional courses run by the major accountancy bodies and the Institute of Data Processing Management (IDPM). It is also appropriate for conversion courses at the Masters level or for MBA-level modules in information systems. It requires minimal prior knowledge of information technology, although an understanding of the basic functions of a business organization is assumed.

Content

It is impossible to appreciate the way that information systems can aid the realization of business objectives unless a basic understanding is obtained both of the information technology, in its broadest sense, and of the way information systems are designed. The level of understanding needed is not to the same depth as that required of a computer specialist. It must be sufficiently comprehensive, however, to enable those in business to assess the opportunities, limitations and major issues surrounding modern business information systems.

Chapter 1 introduces the reader to the idea of information and its relation to management decision making. After covering essential systems concepts, an overview of the structure and purpose of a management information system is explained.

Chapter 2 begins by explaining the central ideas behind business strategic planning. The role of the information system is identified in this process. Various strategic uses of information systems, such as their use as a competitive weapon, are explored.

Chapter 3 explains the basic hardware, software and communications components in a business information system. The reader who is familiar with elementary computer science to A-level may omit most of these sections.

Chapter 4 begins by examining the central notions behind distributed computing and its organizational benefits. The latter part of the chapter examines networks and their position within business. Electronic data interchange and its advantages are explored.

Chapter 5 concentrates on recent developments in global networks and distributed systems. The application of the Internet and the World Wide Web are examined.

Chapter 6 explores the world of e-commerce. It introduces new models for conducting business that exploit the Internet and the World Wide Web.

Chapter 7 explains the central ideas behind decision support systems and their development through prototyping. The relation to and role of end-user computing is examined. Human–computer interaction is treated in later sections of the chapter.

Chapter 8 introduces files and file processing, file organization and access in a business system. The chapter highlights the limitations of a file-based approach to data storage and explains the role of databases and database technology in overcoming these. Major data models – hierarchical, network and relational – are compared.

Chapter 9 looks at the checks, balances and controls in the development, implementation and use of information systems. It considers the rights and responsibilities of individuals, organizations and society as a whole.

Chapters 10 to 15 explain, by use of a case study, the stages involved in the development of an information system. The emphasis is on analysis and overall design of the information system rather than detailed design and implementation. The approach taken is in line with many structured methodologies. Both process analysis and modelling and data analysis and modelling are treated extensively.

Chapter 16 provides alternatives to the linear life-cycle approach and the structured techniques covered in the previous chapters. An introduction to CASE in the development of business systems is covered and rapid applications development is introduced as an important systems development framework. The central concepts of object-oriented methods of analysis and design complete the coverage of 'hard' approaches to systems development. These 'hard' approaches are then critically evaluated and, by way of an alternative paradigm, the 'soft' approaches of Checkland and of the socio-technical school of participative analysis and design are introduced. These are covered because it is felt important that the reader appreciate the scope and limitations of structured methodologies.

Chapter 17 provides an explanation of the core ideas behind expert systems. The storage and use of knowledge in expert systems is described. The central ideas and uses of expert systems are first explained. More detailed aspects of knowledge representation and inferencing are covered in later sections of the chapter.

Structure

Each chapter contains an initial brief summary of the forthcoming chapter content. This is followed by the main body of the text and, finally, a more extensive summary of topics covered. There are numerous questions at the end of each chapter. These fall into two types. First, there are straightforward revision questions, which test the reader's basic understanding of the text; the solutions to these can be found in the contents of the chapter itself. Second, there are problems that require the reader to apply concepts or techniques covered in the text to a described situation, and there are discussion questions where the reader is expected to apply his or her understanding of the text to a wider business or social context. Solutions to these can be found on the instructors' website. Also at the end of each chapter are selected references for further reading. Each

Three different routes to navigate the book's chapters

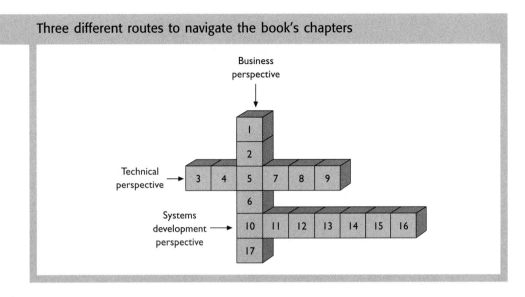

recommended text or article is generally accompanied by a short description indicating the area it covers and the type of reader for which it is most appropriate.

Reader perspectives

Although it is intended that the book be treated as a whole and read in sequence, different readers have different interests:

- *Business perspective*: Those interested in information systems and their development from a business perspective might well read Chapters 1, 2, 5, 6, 10 and 17 first.
- *Development perspective*: Chapters 10 to 16 can be taken as a more or less self-contained section on information systems analysis and design, with the reader being able to dip into previous chapters as is felt necessary.
- *Technical perspective*: For those wishing a technical introduction to business information technology, networks, data storage and control, Chapters 3, 4, 5, 7, 8 and 9 can be approached first.

Mini case studies

The book makes extensive use of mini case studies. These are used, particularly in the earlier chapters, to provide a context for the understanding of key concepts and also to inform the reader about current issues and latest developments. Brief questions prompt the reader to reflect on the content of the mini case study and then apply it to the text.

Longer case studies

Most chapters also conclude with a longer case study. These provide a greater depth of material with which to investigate the topic. They are possible candidates for group activities and can form the basis of productive project work and assignments.

Extended case study

The chapters containing the systems development perspective make use of a more extended case study, Kismet, which is developed progressively. This extended case study introduces a business problem and follows the project through the stages of feasibility, systems analysis and design then implementation and review to provide a realistic context for understanding the systems development process.

Fifth edition changes

This text differs from the fourth edition in a number of ways:

Many topics have been strengthened or rewritten to reflect recent changes and developments. Topics which have been given particular attention compared to the last edition include data mining and data warehousing, the outsourcing of information systems services, enterprise resource planning, the Unified Modelling Language (UML), which has rapidly become the *de facto* standard for object-oriented development approaches, and ethical, legal and social issues in information systems development.

The chapter covering e-commerce and business applications of the Internet has again been updated to reflect the far-reaching changes that continue to take place. The chapter covering networks and distributed systems has been enlarged to accommodate recent developments in the use of the Internet and in mobile computing.

The presentation of current experience and practice and leading-edge developments in technology through mini case studies and longer case studies has been preserved; these have been completely overhauled to continue to provide that current point of reference.

There have also been numerous minor additions and amendments to bring the book into line with technological developments over the three years since the last edition.

Acknowledgements

We would like to thank colleagues at the University of East London, at the University of Lincoln and those elsewhere who have provided useful comments on earlier drafts. In particular, the comments of anonymous reviewers have been invaluable.

Graham Curtis
David Cobham
July 2004

Publisher's acknowledgements

We are grateful to the following for permission to reproduce copyright material:

Mini case 1.2 adapted from *Computing*, July 24, 2003 and Mini case 9.5 adapted from *Computing*, November 27, 2003, by permission of *Computing*; Figure 5.2 reproduced with permission of Robert H. Zakon; Figure 5.3 reproduced with permission of NeoWorx, Inc.; Figures 5.6 and 5.7 reproduced by permission of the Red Cross; Figure 6.5 reproduced with permission of Toys'R'Us; Figure 6.9 reproduced with permission on FedEx;

In some instances we have been unable to trace the owners of copyright material, and we would appreciate any information that would enable us to do so.

Guided Tour

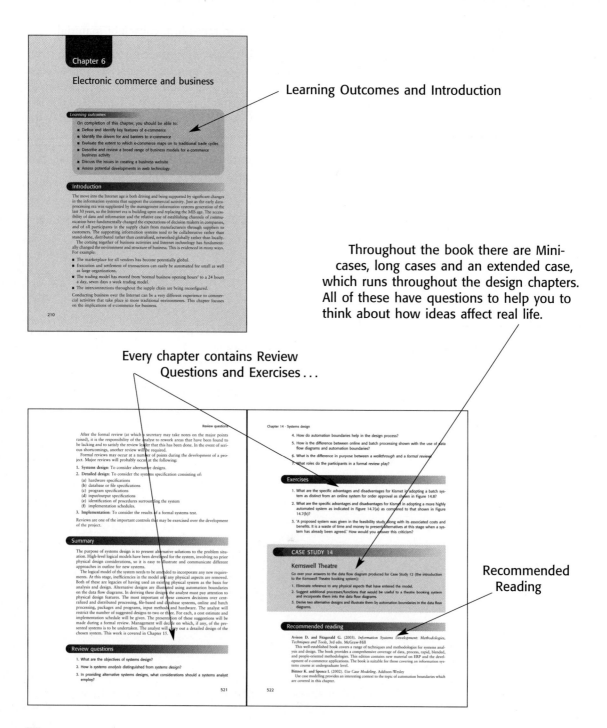

Learning Outcomes and Introduction

Throughout the book there are Mini-cases, long cases and an extended case, which runs throughout the design chapters. All of these have questions to help you to think about how ideas affect real life.

Every chapter contains Review Questions and Exercises...

Recommended Reading

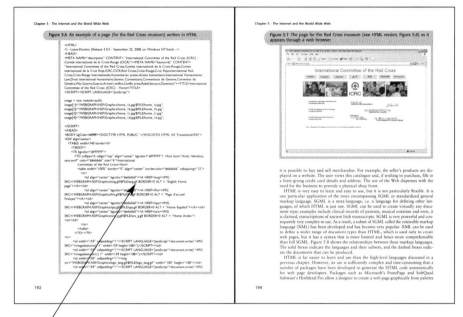

Figures, tables and screendumps help to illustrate ideas clearly.

A free Companion Website with a host of learning and teaching material is available to accompany this book at www.booksites...
Students can access...

Guided Tour of the Website

Learning outcomes

Multiple choice questions

Hints for Review Questions

Chapter 1

Information systems

Learning outcomes

On completion of this chapter, you should be able to:

- Define information, systems and information systems
- Assess the information required to aid business decision making
- Distinguish between formal and informal information
- Contrast models of decision making
- Distinguish the managerial levels at which decisions are made
- Assess the cost and value of information
- Identify the characteristics of systems
- Employ the framework of a systems approach to evaluate the information requirements of more complex systems
- Explain what is meant by a management information system.

Introduction

This chapter covers three interrelated areas – information, systems and information systems. Information is considered in its role of aiding business decisions. By studying the nature of decisions, important characteristics of information can be identified. Models of decision making, the cognitive background of decision makers and the levels of managerial activity associated with management decisions are all considered. Properties of business information are developed in terms of the kinds of decision taken and the types of decision taker involved. The provision of information within an organization has an associated cost. To justify this expenditure the information must be of value. The idea of information value, both qualitative and quantitative, is covered.

The framework of a systems approach is used in understanding the information requirements of a complex organization. Characteristics of systems and a systems approach are explained in the second part of the chapter. The ideas of information and a system are put together in developing the concept of a **management information system** (MIS). This is viewed as a collection of information subsystems interacting with a corporate database. Difficulties in the design of these information systems are considered by outlining five distinct approaches towards MIS design. Finally, the importance of informal information for decision taking within organizations is stressed.

1

1.1 Introduction

The pattern of employment has altered radically in the UK over the last two centuries (see Figure 1.1). There has been a decline in the importance of agriculture as a source of employment brought on by industrialization during the early and middle parts of the nineteenth century. This was followed by a steady increase in the percentage of the workforce employed in manufacturing, which reached a peak in the early decades of the twentieth century. Since the nineteenth century, the decline in manufacturing employment has been taken up by two sectors – the service sector and the information sector. By far the faster growing of these is the information sector.

Many occupations are now almost exclusively concerned with the handling, processing, provision or transmission of information. Included in these would be jobs in insurance, banking, accountancy, and central and local government. Anyone employed in the postal or telecommunications industries is directly or indirectly involved in the transmission of information. Other areas such as travel, retailing, the police and the armed forces all rely on a greater provision of information than at any time in the past. In manufacturing, a declining percentage of the workforce is involved in the production process, and an increasing percentage is employed in the processing of information. The increasing ownership of computers and the phenomenal growth in the use of the Internet and the World Wide Web have accompanied a much greater participation of businesses in the processing of information.

What has led to this burgeoning of the information sector? On the supply side, the development of faster, cheaper and more flexible technology for information processing (computers) and information transmission (telecommunications) has enabled the information sector to grow. More information can now be provided more quickly and cheaply than before. Access to information and to information systems has, particularly with the development of the Internet, become far easier. On the demand side, the complexity and volatility of market forces mean that businesses require more targeted

Figure 1.1 Patterns of employment in the UK

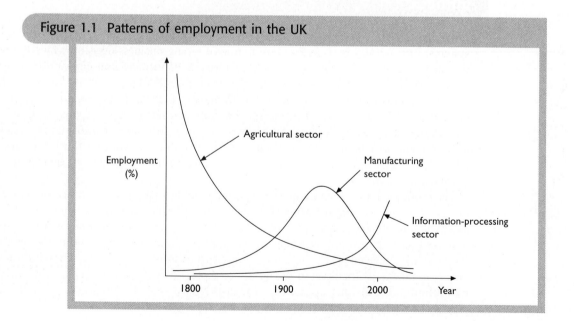

and more current information to gain a competitive advantage and survive. Externally, they need to be up to date with market preferences, competitors' prices, and the supply and cost of finance. Internally, pressures to maintain profitability or efficiency require instant information to monitor and control the continuing functioning of the organization.

This book is about information systems for business. The purpose of this chapter is to provide a general understanding of the idea of information, the concept of a system and, putting the two together, to provide an understanding of the nature of an information system for a business.

1.1.1 Data and information

Before we can understand the idea of a business information system, it is necessary to look at both the concept of information and the concept of a system. In this section and the subsequent two sections, the topic of information and its general characteristics as applied to business are covered.

Many definitions have been proposed for the term **information**. The one that will be used here is that:

Information is data processed for a purpose.

A business deals with a wide variety of data. Some of this concerns financial transactions. An example of an item of transaction data is the record of the sale of a product to a customer by the business. This fact might be recorded on a piece of paper, such as in a sales day book, or as a series of laser-burned impressions on a compact disk. However, it is not information until it undergoes some sort of processing and the results of the processing are communicated for a particular purpose. For instance:

1. The record of the amount of the sale may be aggregated with other sales amounts and the result transferred to a debtors' control account. This in turn will form part of a trial balance sheet and a final balance sheet to be presented to shareholders. The purpose of this processing is to provide a summarized snapshot picture of the state of the assets and liabilities of the business.

2. The sales data may also be classified by customer, aggregated with the current balance of the customer and the result compared with a credit limit assigned to the customer. The purpose is to alert the credit control manager that action may be necessary if the credit limit is exceeded.

Data, as given in the example, is the record of an event or a fact. The information derived from this data is used for making decisions, of which planning decisions and control decisions are the most important.

Mini case 1.1

Census data

The 2001 Census has several significant innovations, including new questions and classifications, postal geography and the use of the web to disseminate data. However, the most radical change is the decision to distribute the statistics free of charge. This will have profound consequences for users and suppliers of value-added services.

3

In past censuses, commercial companies could only get data from census agencies, which were licensed to supply data on the payment of royalties to the government's census offices. In addition, there were restrictive licensing conditions, limiting use of the data to a specified number of computers within a company.

Several consequences will flow from the decision to make data freely available. Store location and customer insight teams in large companies, such as Marks & Spencer, Nationwide, Sainsbury and Whitbread, will exploit the full richness of the geographical and subject detail.

Even more significantly, use will be broadened and new markets created. Start-up businesses and many members of the public will discover census data for the first time on the census offices' websites.

Free data will provide the fuel for the supply of many more software and consultancy services.

This is already providing small area datasets for topics such as crime, education and health, which can be related to census counts of population for small areas. Many new datasets, such as estimates of incomes and access to local services, are planned; these will enable better understanding of local communities and markets.

The new policy of making the census freely available is a bold experiment. The likelihood is that it will illustrate that the benefits to society and the economy of increased use of data will greatly outweigh the costs.

Adapted from: **Free data will transform and create markets: Facts and figures at a keystroke**
By Keith Dugmore
FT.com site: 7 October 2003

Questions

1. List some examples of the data which is collected in Census surveys.

2. Describe how the data might provide useful information for interested parties.

1.1.2 Data processes

Data that is formally handled in a business may undergo complex processing prior to presentation and use as information. However complex, though, the total processing can be broken down into simple steps. The types of basic process are:

- classification of data;
- rearranging/sorting data;
- summarizing/aggregating data;
- performing calculations on data;
- selection of data.

Examples of each are shown in Table 1.1. In as far as these basic processes are governed by rules, they are therefore suitable for a computerized system.

Table 1.1 Examples of types of data process

Type of data process	Example
Classification of data	Transaction data may be classified as invoice data, payment data, order data
Rearranging/sorting data	Data on employees may be ordered according to ascending employee number
Summarizing/aggregating data	Data on the performance of various departments may be aggregated to arrive at a summary of performance
Performing calculations on data	Data on the total hours worked by an employee may be multiplied by the hourly wage rates to arrive at a gross wage
Selection of data	Total yearly turnover data on customers may be used to select high-spending customers for special treatment by sales personnel

1.2 Decisions

Information is data that has been processed for a purpose. That purpose might be to offer the information for sale or could be a statutory requirement, but invariably it is to aid some kind of decision. In order to understand more about the different types of information that are provided in business, it is necessary to look at the area of decision taking and decision takers and the way that information is used in decisions.

No decision is taken in isolation. Decisions are taken by decision takers who have certain organizational objectives in mind, a certain background, and a certain mental way of processing and appreciating information. Moreover, these individuals have personal interests that may affect the decision-taking process. From the corporate point of view, information needs to be supplied to these decision takers in order that the decision taken will be the most effective in the light of the organizational objectives.

1.2.1 Cognitive style and background

'Cognitive style' is a term used in psychology that broadly describes the way that individuals absorb information, process it and relate it to their existing knowledge, and use it to make decisions. Cognitive style and personal background act as filters to the information provided to a decision taker. In outline, one approach to cognitive style (Kilmann and Mitroff, 1976) regards individuals as falling into one of two categories in the way that they absorb information. At one extreme, some people take in information best if it is highly detailed and specific, often quantitatively based. The various elements of information need not be linked as a whole. The other group absorbs information in a holistic way; that is, in a less concrete way, preferring general facts, suppositions and 'soft data' linked as a whole.

After obtaining information the decision must be taken. Once again there appear to be two distinctive styles. One group will involve itself in a high degree of analytic thought in reaching a decision. This group will be capable of providing detailed justifications

Figure 1.2 Four cognitive styles for absorbing information and taking decisions

		Information-absorption style	
		Detailed	Holistic
Decision-making style	Analysis	1	2
	Intuition	3	4

often involving quantitative reasons in support of final decisions. The other group will rely more on intuition, experience, rules of thumb and judgement. There will be a concentration on looking at the situation as a whole rather than parts of it independently. This group will often find it difficult to provide justification for recommended decisions. The combination of these information-absorption and decision-taking styles is shown in Figure 1.2.

It is not claimed here that one or other of these styles of assimilating information or making decisions is superior. The point is that if information is presented in a way that is not conducive to the cognitive style of the recipient then it will not be fully utilized in a decision. When information systems are designed the designer, if at all possible, should take into account the range of cognitive styles of those for whom the information is provided. This important though obvious point is often overlooked or ignored when information systems are designed for business.

The background of a decision taker is also a powerful influence on the way that information is perceived. Differing subject specializations will lead individuals to judge different aspects of information as being more/less relevant or more/less important for making decisions. For instance, accountants will tend to concentrate on numerical information, with which they are familiar. They will require the numerical information to be compiled and presented in a standard manner compatible with their expectations and training. They may ignore details of organizational structure and management styles. It is quite possible that they may even fail to perceive the information when it is presented. In contrast, the organizational specialist may not understand the importance of the numerical, financial and cost aspects of the business organization. This is quite understandable as the specialisms of each only give them a limited model through which to perceive and organize information in a way that is relevant to making decisions.

Personal backgrounds and cognitive styles are not wholly independent of one another. The ability to work best with detailed quantitative information, for example, will not be unconnected with the occupation of an accountant or engineer.

1.2.2 A model of decision making

The process of taking a decision can be described as falling into several stages (Simon, 1965). These stages provide a framework within which decisions can be viewed. To be executed successfully, each of the stages will require different types of information. The stages, shown in Figure 1.3, are:

1. **Intelligence:** The decision maker needs to be made aware of the existence of a problem that requires some sort of decision. Information needs to be presented in a manner conducive to this recognition.

Figure 1.3 Stages in making a decision

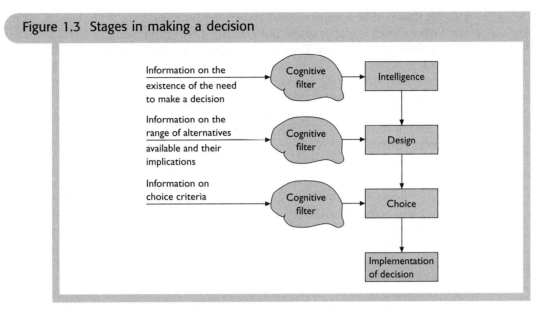

2. **Design:** Alternative solutions to the problem must be considered. This involves the recognition of the range of acceptable decisions and the implications of each. At this stage, information needs to be supplied to aid the decision maker in predicting and evaluating these implications.

3. **Choice:** This involves the choice between the various alternatives investigated in the previous stage. If there has been a full analysis of the options this should be a straightforward stage. Otherwise, the decision maker may have to choose between incomplete and perhaps incomparable alternatives.

4. **Implementation:** The chosen decision is carried out.

The stages are illustrated in the following case. A manufacturing company produces a range of modular kitchen units to supply various retail outlets. These outlets sell and fit the final kitchens for their own customers. The problem is that one of the major retail clients of the kitchen unit manufacturer is becoming dissatisfied with the quality of the delivered kitchen units. There is a problem, which may become a larger problem if nothing is done.

1. **Intelligence:** The decision maker in the kitchen units manufacturing company needs to be aware that a problem exists. This must be a person of sufficient rank to make an effective decision. One way is to wait until a customer complains before taking any decision. Then there is always the danger that notification of the problem will not reach the right level of management before it is too late. A more active form of intelligence gathering is to formally request information from customers on their view of the service that they are getting.

2. **Design:** Once aware of the problem, the decision maker can consider a range of possible options. One is to increase the quality of the product by buying in more expensive fitments. Another is to reschedule production and divert more labour resources to quality control and finishing of the units. Yet another is to do both of these things. The option of deciding to do nothing must always be considered. Each

of these will have implications for costs, profits, the timing of production, what action competitors might or might not take, the order book with the client company, and a range of other areas. The decision maker needs to be able to evaluate each of these. Some implications can be assessed quite easily with the aid of computer support, especially if they rely on internally held quantitative information. For example, the use of a spreadsheet model will yield a fast, accurate and effective picture of the internal cost implications of buying more expensive fitments. Other options are more difficult to assess. This is particularly true where external and qualitative information is needed. The response of competitors may require an analysis of the market and the past history of the firms involved.

3. **Choice:** Once the implications of each of the options have been evaluated, the time will come to make a choice as to what to do. This might not be simple if the design stage is incomplete or has not yielded definite results. Rules of thumb and past experience may be used as a guide for choice. In the case of the kitchen manufacturer, two of the options considered were 'do nothing' and 'buy in fitments of higher quality'. The problems involved with choice can be seen by further investigation of the kitchen unit manufacturing organization. The 'do nothing' option has implications. There will be the possibility that the retail outlet may take its business elsewhere. On balance, this seems unlikely given the long-established trading relationship and the lack of mature competitors for the specific types of unit favoured by this outlet. But then again the retail outlet is advertising for a new purchasing manager. In contrast, the latter decision to purchase high-quality fitments has definite implications for profit and cost, which are to be balanced against the high probability that this will satisfy the customer complaints. Here the decision maker is required to choose between alternatives that have implications in different areas with different degrees of certainty.

In this organization, the power and responsibility to take the required decision rested with middle to upper management. Other types of decision would have been taken at a lower level in the management hierarchy. The levels of managerial decision are explained in the next section.

The classic model of decision making described above defines a strictly linear sequence of stages. Although these stages are clearly essential in arriving at a decision, a more iterative model may be appropriate, particularly where the business environment is changing rapidly. To respond to, or to anticipate, these changes a decision maker might return to an earlier stage and refine or revise his or her view.

1.2.3 Levels of managerial decision taking

Three levels of managerial activity are important in understanding the way organizations take decisions (Anthony, 1965). These are strategic planning, tactical planning and control, and operational planning and control.

Strategic planning

This is carried out by the most senior management and will deal with broad issues concerning an organization's development over the long term. The planning may involve, for example, decisions on what markets to move into, whether to diversify production, how resources should be allocated to major functions or departments within the organization, how to structure the company's finances, or whether to undertake particular major investment projects or accept major contracts with long-term implications. The determination of organizational objectives is also within the scope of strategic planning.

In order to make strategic decisions senior management needs information. Because strategic planning has a long-term time horizon, much of this information will relate to the future rather than the present. The nature of many of the decisions requires information on the development of market forces, patterns of expenditure and the economy as a whole. This requires information to be supplied on matters external to the company from sources such as market surveys, trade publications, demographic studies, government reports and commissioned research from specialist suppliers. The fact that the information refers to external areas outside the control of the organization and that it applies to the future means that it is likely to be highly uncertain and will tend to be of a summarized or general nature rather than highly detailed.

Tactical planning and control

This is a managerial activity normally associated with the middle echelons of management. Tactical planning may involve the allocation of resources within departmental budgets, decisions on medium-term work scheduling and forecasting, and planning medium-term cash flows. Examples of control at this middle managerial level are the monitoring of actual production and expenditure against budgets, the analysis of variances and actions taken in response.

Information for decisions at the tactical level will refer to the medium term, between now and the next few months or a year. It will be mainly generated internally within the organization, although some external information may be necessary. As an example of the latter, it is difficult to set budgets if external raw material prices are the subject of uncertainty or wage rates are set in response to national union negotiations – in both cases external information may be of help. The information will generally be required in an aggregate form – for example, total production for the month of a certain product – though not as consolidated as that for a strategic decision. The internal nature of the information and its time horizon means that it is likely to be subject to less uncertainty than information supplied for strategic decisions.

Operational planning and control

This is concerned with the decisions made in the normal day-to-day operations within a business. Decisions in this area are designed to ensure the effective and efficient use of existing resources to realize budget objectives. These decisions may involve the treatment of personnel (for example, hiring and firing), the control of inventory and production levels, pricing decisions, aspects of credit control over customers and other forms of accounting and cash controls.

Information for operational planning and control is generated almost exclusively within the organization, and it is highly detailed, certain and immediately relevant. For instance, the operational decision as to whether to purchase more of an item that has fallen below its reorder stock level will be based on at least some of the following information:

- the number of requisition orders already placed for the item, the quantities ordered and the expected delivery dates;
- the expected future use of the item, including any outstanding customer commitments;
- the storage and handling facilities available; and
- the range of suppliers of the item, their prices and their expected delivery dates.

Figure 1.4 Information characteristics for managerial decisions

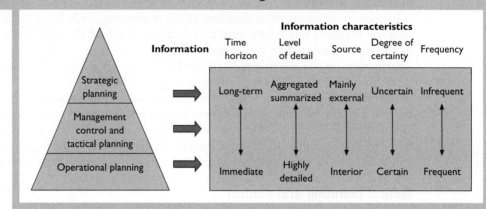

All this information will be held within the organization, and once it is recognized as relevant for the decision it can be retrieved and used. Figure 1.4 shows the characteristics of information supplied for the various levels of managerial activities. These activities need not necessarily be carried out by different people. Indeed, in a very small company decisions at these levels may all be carried out by the same person.

Mini case 1.2

Financial information

The London Stock Exchange (LSE) has expanded its Data-X information services platform by adding new data services for its customers to buy.

The offerings will help strengthen the Exchange's position as a direct provider of financial information, putting pressure on others in the market.

Chief information officer David Lester says the drive to add data services is part of the Exchange's desire to create products and increase revenues, while taking costs out of the industry.

'Information services are helping to expand the revenue base of the LSE,' he said.

The Exchange generates masses of information every day, from data on individual trades and share price movements to company announcements, which it provides directly to the market.

Level 1 Plus, a new market data service, gives customers a range of additional source data, such as buy and sell percentages, money flow per security and time-weighted average spread.

The new information services platform went live this April, adding more data to the real-time price messages the Exchange sends out every day at a rate of up to 300 per second.

Adapted from: LSE takes data supply to the next level
Computing – United Kingdom; 24 July 2003

Question

Provide examples of strategic, tactical and operational decisions that might be supported by the information services of the London Stock Exchange.

1.2.4 The structure of decisions

Simon (1965, 1977) makes a simple yet important distinction between structured (programmable) and unstructured (non-programmable) decisions. **Structured decisions** are those governed by clear rules. The decision procedure can be expressed as a set of steps to be followed, can be incorporated in a decision table or revealed by a procedural logic flowchart. The information that is needed before a structured decision can be made is clearly specifiable and unambiguous, and once it is obtained, the process of arriving at the decision action is straightforward.

An example of a structured decision would be the granting of credit to a customer where this is done on a points basis. The customer obtains points for having a job, the salary associated with it, the time the job has been held, whether they are married, have children, and whether they have other credit cards, loans or a mortgage. The points are assigned mechanically and totalled. If the total is above a certain threshold the customer is granted credit, otherwise not. Because structured decisions are governed by clear rules, they can often be left to low-grade personnel or even be fully automated in some cases.

With **unstructured decisions**, it is often unclear what information is needed and how it should be assessed in relation to the decision objectives. These objectives may themselves be unclear or the subject of disagreement. Unlike structured decisions, there will be no set procedure or rules for arriving at the decision. The use of rules of thumb (heuristics) and 'experience' is characteristic of unstructured decisions.

An example of an unstructured decision is the hiring of supervisory or senior staff. Here information such as qualifications and experience is obviously relevant, but what is not clear is how good qualifications in one candidate are to be measured against experience in a second, and how this is to be offset against the intelligence and adaptability revealed by a third candidate.

Gorry and Scott-Morton (1971) have developed the ideas of Anthony (1965) and Simon (1965, 1977) to provide a useful way of categorizing decisions by comparing managerial activities against the *degree* of structure in a decision. This is shown in Table 1.2. The degree of structure corresponds to the extent to which each of the decision-making stages is structured or unstructured. A decision that is highly structured at the stages of intelligence, design and choice would count as a highly structured decision. A lack of structure during each of these three stages would mean that

Table 1.2 Structure and managerial activity in decision making			
	Strategic planning	Management control	Operational control
Unstructured	Company reorganization	Personnel management	Dealing with customer enquiries
Semi-structured	Introduction of new product	Analysis of performance	Short-term production scheduling
Structured	Financial structure planning	Allocating budgets	Stock reorder decisions

the decision was regarded as highly unstructured. Many decisions lie between these two extremes, being structured in some stages but unstructured in others. These are termed **semi-structured**.

As the type of decision will determine the characteristics of the information that is required to make it, the analysis by structure provides a useful guide for the development of management information systems. In general, the more highly structured the decision the more likely it is that a computer system can provide useful information. In cases where the intelligence, design and choice elements are all structured the computer system may not only be used to provide information but also to automate the decision itself. In other cases, varying degrees of decision support can be given.

1.3   Value of information

Information produced for business purposes has a cost. The costs are associated with collection, processing and storage. These are present whether the information is produced by a manual or a computer system. In order to justify this cost the information must also have some value. The value is generally to be found in better decision making, whether this be in the area of control, planning or in some other area. How then is information to be valued?

1.3.1 Quantifiable value

Sometimes information provided to an organization or generated within it has measurable benefits in monetary terms. These benefits result from two factors. First, the information may reduce uncertainty surrounding the making of a decision. Second, a decision may be taken more quickly, and therefore be more timely, in the presence of the faster provision of information.

Figure 1.5 illustrates the way that information can reduce uncertainty and lead to a measurable financial benefit. Assume that a decision faces a farmer. Should turnips or wheat be planted? The matrix indicates the profits for planting turnips and wheat depending on whether the weather is dry or wet. Past records show that it is as likely to be wet as dry (probability = 0.5). The expected pay-off profits for planting turnips and for planting wheat can now be calculated as 60 and 50 arbitrary units, respectively. If the farmer is risk-neutral, they will go for the higher-yield option and plant turnips with an expected pay-off of 60. Let us now suppose that perfect information can be supplied to the farmer on the future state of the weather. Of what financial value is this information? If the information is that it is wet, turnips will be planted and if dry wheat will be planted. The weather forecast will be as likely to show (accurately) that the weather is wet as it will show that it is dry. Therefore, the expected pay-off profit for the farmer is 90. The value to the farmer of the information is the difference between the expected pay-offs with and without the information. Any rational farmer would be prepared to pay up to 30 for this weather forecasting information.

Although this example is highly simplified, it clearly illustrates the way information can be of aid in a decision. It is necessary to know:

- the range of decision alternatives (plant wheat or turnips);
- the range of factors affecting the results of the decision (dry or wet weather);
- the pay-offs that occur for each decision result (pay-off matrix);

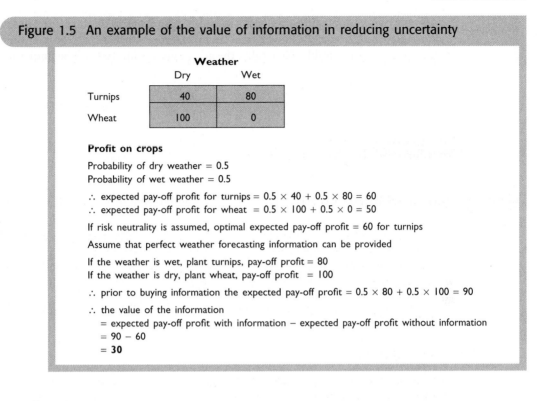

Figure 1.5 An example of the value of information in reducing uncertainty

■ the probabilities that the factors will be operative (past weather records indicating the probability of wet or dry weather); and

■ the reduction in uncertainty surrounding these factors as a result of the information (perfect weather forecast leading to elimination of uncertainty).

The calculations involved are much the same if the range of decisions and conditions is increased and we allow that information only reduces rather than eliminates uncertainty.

Another way that information can prove to be of financial benefit is by being up to date. This enables decisions to be taken more swiftly. Computerized transaction-processing systems and management information systems provide information more quickly than the manual systems that they replace. A computerized system can generate data concerning sales and information on a company's debtors more quickly. This may cut the average time between the sale of a product and the receipt of payment for it. This time is known as the **debtor period**.

Suppose that the average time taken for a customer to pay a debt is six weeks and the amount outstanding from debtors is £6000. If faster processing, such as the immediate generation of an invoice at the time of sale and quicker provision of information on non-payment, can cut the period to four weeks, the average outstanding debt will drop to £4000. This is equivalent to a cash injection of £2000.

Similarly, savings in **buffer stock** may be made. Buffer stock is held to prevent a stockout occurring. Better information can reduce the need to hold such large levels of this safety stock. Often much of this stock is held to counteract the effects of poor and slow stock control. If the levels of stock can be cut from a value equivalent to six weeks' turnover to a value represented by four weeks' turnover then this is equivalent to a cash injection equal to two weeks' turnover at cost prices.

The last two examples illustrate ways in which a computerized information system can lead to quantifiable benefits. However, it is unusual for information to have a total value that is precisely measurable. Generally, the advantages conferred will be unquantifiable. In many cases, it may be difficult or impossible to place figures on the value of information simply because there may be no quantifiable benefits at all. A decision to obtain and provide the information will be based purely on its non-quantifiable value.

Mini case 1.3

The value of information

The government is to spend £2.3bn modernizing the National Health Service's information structure over the next three years.

The figures are below the immediate doubling in IT spending that Derek Wanless, the government's health adviser, said was 'a plausible view' of what the NHS needed to spend to provide patients with booked admissions, an electronic patient record, e-prescribing, digital X-rays and imaging, and the other elements of a health service that took full advantage of modern information and communications technology.

In his first interview since taking up his post in October, Mr Granger, the new NHS IT chief, said that not until later this year, 'when I have bids from suppliers that have completion risk and performance risk clearly attached to their proposals, will I know the exact timetable'.

Adapted from: **NHS information system set for £2.3bn revamp**
By Nicholas Timmins, Public Policy Editor
Financial Times: 20 January 2003

Questions

1. The expenditure described above will lead to the provision of better information in the National Health Service. To what extent is the value of the information quantifiable?

2. Is it possible to estimate the cost effectiveness of a project such as this, considering both the expenditure and the value of the information obtained?

1.3.2 Non-quantifiable value

It is undeniable that information can provide benefits that are not strictly measurable. For example, better information provided to customers on available products and current prices is liable to increase customer confidence, attract new customers and prevent existing customers moving elsewhere. It is impossible to put a figure on this value. Why is this? Many other changes are occurring to alter customer preferences: advertising by the company, competitors, responses, changes in consumer expenditure patterns, and so on. It is difficult to isolate the effect of the provision of better information from these other factors.

Similar observations apply to information provided for internal decisions. It may be thought that the provision of information improves a type of decision, but it is difficult to separate the effect of this information on the decision from all the other influences.

Occasionally, information has other uses than to aid decision making. Performance information on sales representatives, for instance, may be used to motivate them to achieve greater levels of sales. Sometimes information is collected without any clear purpose in mind but merely to build up a background understanding of an area. Strictly this should be called **intelligence**. In both these cases, the information has value or, in the latter case, possible value. In neither is this value quantifiable.

It is a great temptation to restrict attention to the quantifiable benefits associated with the provision of information, especially when taking a decision on whether to undertake an investment in a business information system. However, a limited cost–benefit analysis on this narrow accounting basis would have meant that several information technology projects that have been undeniably successful would not have been given the 'go ahead'. It is important to recognize that even though benefits cannot be quantified this is no reason to ignore them in making investment decisions.

1.4 The idea of a system

We live in a world full of systems. There are central heating systems, telephone systems, computer systems, fuel injection systems and the human circulatory system, to name but a few. As well as these physical systems there are also more abstract systems. Among these would be counted systems of logic and philosophical systems. Social systems containing men and women as social beings constitute a further class that includes, for example, economic systems, social security systems and legal systems. There are also business information systems – the subject of this book. The idea of a system provides a useful framework within which to view business information as it flows within an organization, is used for decisions or is processed by modern information technology. The question that this section addresses is: 'What is it that such a diverse range of things have in common by virtue of which they are all known as systems?' Before we can study business information systems, it is important that we have a clear understanding of the concept of a system.

A **system** can be defined as a collection of interrelated parts that taken together form a whole such that:

- the collection has some purpose; and
- a change in any of the parts leads to or results from a change in some other part(s).

This is a very broad definition. But then the concept of system is itself wide-ranging. The purpose of some systems, such as the solar system, could provide an interesting theological debate! The important point in the definition above is that a system is a collection of interrelated parts – it cannot be a single thing such as a potato but must be perceived as having an internal structure. Moreover, these parts must be dynamically interrelated through change rather than merely being geographically in close proximity. The system must also have some purpose, goal or objective, and the changes or processes in its parts will normally serve that goal. Most systems, and in particular the systems of interest to this book, have several additional characteristics. An understanding of these characteristics will enrich our concept of a system.

1.4.1 Characteristics of systems

The systems model

Most systems can be illustrated by the model in Figure 1.6. Inputs are accepted into the system and outputs are produced by the processes within the system. In many cases, there may be intermediate storage and control over the functioning of the system.

Figure 1.6 A general model of a system

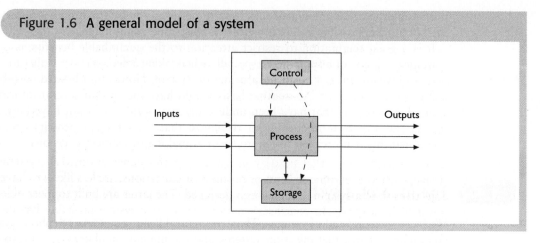

To see how this model is exemplified by a simple familiar system, consider the example of a central heating system. The **input** is gas (energy) at a particular geographical point and electricity (energy) required for the electrical equipment. The **outputs** of the system are heat energy geographically dispersed throughout the house (together with the products of combustion in the boiler such as water vapour). The **process** is the combustion within the boiler, the transfer of the resultant heat energy to the water and the pumping of water through the pipes and radiators. The water within the system provides a temporary **storage** for the heat energy as it becomes geographically dispersed throughout the system. The output heat energy leaves the system and enters the environment by courtesy of Newton's law of cooling. The **control** is provided by the thermostat, which accepts a given standard, say 20 degrees Celsius. The thermostat turns off the input when the sensed temperature rises a given amount above this and turns on the input if it falls below this.

The systems model provides a useful framework within which to view a business organization as it concentrates attention on important aspects of its functioning. Imagine a manual order-processing system in a business. Its objective is to process customer orders accurately and quickly. It will help to increase understanding of this system if the inputs, outputs, control, process and storage aspects are clearly distinguished and identified. For instance, suppose for simplicity that the sole input is a customer order. By concentrating on this input we need to determine:

- the data held on a customer order;
- the source of the customer order (for example from salesperson, mail, phone);
- the frequency with which customer orders are received;
- the peaks and troughs in the volume of received orders (and how the processing element of the system deals with these); and
- controls and checks existing over acceptance of the order.

These are just a few questions suggested by looking at the inputs of the order-processing system. Viewing the manual order processing as a system does not in itself generate these questions but rather directs attention in a way that is helpful in understanding and analysis.

Systems objectives

All systems have **objectives**, and in identifying a system the objectives must be specified. This may be easy in the case of a central heating system. The objective is to convert localized energy (for example, gas energy) into geographically dispersed heat energy in order to maintain the environmental temperature of a building or dwelling within a given range. The objective is clear, and there is a straightforward **measure of performance** that can be applied to establish whether the system is meeting its objective. The measure of performance is the temperature as sensed by a thermometer.

Other systems may have objectives that are less clear, or those objectives may be stated in such a way that no easy measure of performance is obvious. Systems that evolve, such as economic systems or business organizations, are less likely to have clear objectives than a system that has been designed. The latter are built to meet objectives specified in advance. In contrast, a national economic system probably has no clear objectives other than the vaguely stated one of satisfying the economic needs of (some of) those participating in it. Measures of performance are often not agreed. Is it gross national product, the rate of growth of national product, the percentage of the work-force employed, the rate of profit, the distribution of product, or what? Economists and politicians flourish and differ because these issues are not clearly defined. Business systems lie somewhere between these two extremes.

Inputs and outputs of a system

Although the inputs and outputs of systems can be almost anything, each falls into one of a number of distinct broad categories. They are:

- materials
- energy
- labour power
- information
- decisions
- money.

Business information systems are mainly concerned with information/decision inputs and outputs, although they will have others – manual information systems need labour power, computerized information systems need energy.

The inputs and outputs of a system are connected to other systems. This is illustrated in Figure 1.7. The outputs of one system become the inputs to another. It is possible to view the world as being composed of systems. Then there are no outputs that 'disappear'. Of course, a person's interest is always restricted to only some of these systems.

Systems environment and boundary

Inputs come from and outputs are transferred to the **environment** of a system. The environment may be defined as whatever lies outside the boundaries of the system but interacts with the system. If something lies outside a system but does not affect the system's behaviour and changes in the state of the system do not affect it, then that thing would not be in the environment of the system. Environment is not a geographical concept – the central water pumping station is in the immediate environment of a domestic water system, although it is located five miles away, whereas the electrical system in the house next door does not lie in the environment of that domestic water system.

Figure 1.7 Systems connected by inputs and outputs

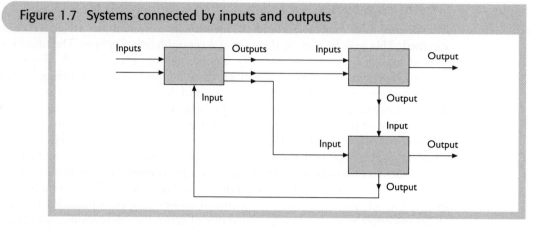

The notion of environment has been defined in terms of the concept of **boundary**. The features that delineate the scope of a system form its boundaries. What is perceived as a system with boundaries by one observer will be determined by what that perceiver identifies as the objectives of the system combined with the area over which that perceiver has interest and control. The idea of a system therefore involves not only 'facts' in the world but also the perceptions and interests of the observer.

To see this, consider the example of a manager whose objective it is to reorganize the stores within a manufacturing company in order to provide the most efficient service. Viewing the stores as a system, the manager will delineate the scope of the system in terms of the control that that manager has to reorganize the stores. The production of stock and its disposal by selling will be seen as lying outside the system. The manager has little or no control over these areas. However, the organization of the stores, their physical layout, personnel, documentation and procedures, will be within the scope of the manager's interest and therefore lie within the system. In contrast, to a member of senior management taking a larger view of the business the stores will be only one part of the system. Others will include production and sales. This manager will see the production and pricing of raw materials, for example, as lying outside the manager's control and so outside the system as perceived.

Closed systems do not have inputs or outputs – they have no environment. Strictly, there are no closed systems (except the universe as a whole), but the term is often used of systems that interact only weakly with their environment. Several command economies in the late twentieth century, such as Albania, were described as closed systems because they had few or no links with the outside world. **Open systems** are those systems that are not closed.

1.4.2 Subsystems and systems hierarchies

Systems are composed of subsystems that are interrelated to one another by means of their inputs and outputs. This gives the system an internal structure. Each subsystem is itself a system with objectives, inputs, outputs, and possibly control and storage elements, and so can be further decomposed into its subsystems. In the example above, the senior manager regarded the stores as a subsystem.

The process of decomposition can continue until the most basic elements are reached. Each of these is called a **black box**. A black box has inputs and outputs, but

Figure 1.8 Hierarchical relations between subsystems in a manufacturing organization

its internal structure is ignored. Whether something is a black box is not an objectively given fact. For most people a TV set is a black box with electrical energy and a signal (coded information via the aerial) as inputs, and variegated light (picture) and sound as outputs. For the TV repairer, however, it is a system composed of many interacting subsystems, which themselves may be composed of elements that to the repairer are black boxes. These are the basic electronic devices. A black box is defined entirely in terms of the relationships between its inputs and outputs. Each black box would be checked to establish which one did not produce the required outputs given known inputs. This faulty part would then be replaced. Although it is a black box for the TV repairer, it would not be so for the electronics expert.

The decomposition of a system into its subsystems may be shown with a **systems hierarchy chart**, as in Figure 1.8. This is a (partial) representation of a manufacturing organization as a hierarchy of subsystems. The subsystems are defined by the functions they perform. The chart gives a clear representation of the hierarchical relations between the various subsystems. At the first level, the system can be seen to be composed of accounts, sales order processing and other subsystems. At deeper levels, the breakdown of each of their constituents is shown. The purpose of decomposition is to break the larger system into its constituent parts. The process continues until the subsystems obtained are of a manageable size for understanding.

Although the hierarchy chart reveals relations between subsystems, it does not illustrate the inputs and outputs to the various subsystems or their interconnection via these inputs and outputs. This is shown by a **flow block diagram**. A flow block diagram for the manufacturing company is shown in Figure 1.9. The subsystems are represented by blocks and the flows of inputs and outputs by directed lines (arrows). The diagram shows the subsystems from the level 1 perspective of Figure 1.8.

Figure 1.9 A flow block diagram for a manufacturing company

Each of these subsystems can be decomposed into further subsystems. Figure 1.10 shows the flow block diagram for the production subsystem. There are four subsystems – material production, operations control, production control and the management subsystems. Each of these is further broken down. For instance, material production contains manufacturing processing, intermediate inventory and product assembly. Two types of input/output flow are distinguished – materials flow and information/data/ decisions flow. Apart from the material production, the other subsystems correspond to information processing and provision at the three levels of decision making and control – strategic, tactical and operational – covered in Section 1.2.3.

There are no hard-and-fast rules to be followed in systems decomposition into sub-systems or in the diagrammatic techniques used. The only rule is that if their use increases understanding of the system and aids communication of this knowledge then the technique is acceptable; otherwise, it is pointless.

1.4.3 Subsystems decoupling

Subsystems can be connected together via their inputs and outputs either directly or through intervening subsystems. The extent of the dependence of the subsystems on one another is known as the **degree of coupling**. Two subsystems are **highly coupled** if a change in the outputs of one causes a substantial change in the state of the other. Two subsystems are **highly decoupled** if changes in the outputs of either have little or no effect on the state of the other. Coupling is a matter of degree.

Figure 1.11 shows two subsystems that are highly coupled. The output of produc-tion is fed directly into sales and distribution, and the demands by sales for products are communicated to production. A change in production will have a direct impact on sales and distribution. For such tightly coupled subsystems to work in harmony it is essential that there is close communication between them.

One way to achieve decoupling is by the insertion of a **buffer** or **inventory** between the two subsystems, as in Figure 1.11(b). The effect of this is to protect the state of

Figure 1.10 A flow block diagram for the production subsystem of a manufacturing company

the sales and distribution subsystems from variations in the output of production. For instance, production may come to a halt but sales need not change its activities, at least in the short term. Goods sold are made up from stock. Another way of achieving decoupling is to ensure that subsystems work with **slack capacity** that can be called upon. In Figure 1.11(c), the production system normally works at less than full capacity and can therefore accommodate a variation in the demand for the product from the sales and distribution subsystem. In each of the examples, the effect of decoupling leads to a greater stability.

Decoupling generally leads to systems stability. Business systems need internal stability to guarantee continued functioning and survival in the light of a changing economic, commercial and financial environment. This is not a free gain, as the mechanisms introduce inefficiency or extra cost. In the example, the cost was the carrying

Figure 1.11 Subsystems coupling and decoupling: (a) highly coupled subsystems; (b) the use of inventory for decoupling; (c) slack capacity as a decoupling mechanism

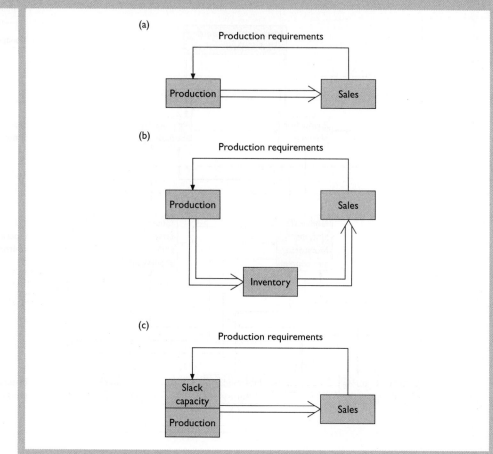

of buffer stock or the maintenance of slack production capacity. Nevertheless, a certain degree of stability through decoupling is usually thought desirable in any system and is often built in at the design stage.

1.4.4 Total systems approach versus piecemeal approaches

The total systems approach is based on the idea that all subsystems are related to one another and cannot be considered in isolation for:

1. the purpose of understanding the behaviour of the system as a whole;
2. the design of a new system.

In understanding systems, certain characteristics of individual subsystems only make sense in terms of serving overall systems goals. In a business system, this translates into the impossibility of making sense of functional subsystems activities except within the context of corporate objectives. The uncritical concentration on subsystems can lead

Figure 1.12 Subsystems optimization versus systems optimization: (a) a case where each subsystem optimizes by minimizing subsystem cost, although the system as a whole suboptimizes on cost; (b) a case where the system as a whole optimizes on cost, even though the production subsystem is not optimal with respect to cost

(a)

	Production during period	Stock held at end of period	Sales during period
Period 0		30	
Period 1	100	60	70
Period 2	100	30	130
Period 3	100	60	70
Period 4	100	30	130
	400		400

Cost of production per item   = 100 per unit
Cost of changing production level = 100 per change
Cost of holding stock   = 10 per unit per period

Production costs   = 100 × 400   = 40 000
Cost of changing production level   =   0
Total production cost   = 40 000

                                                                40 000
Total cost of holding stock   = 10 × (60 + 30 + 60 + 30) =   1 800
Total cost   = 41 800

(b)

	Production during period	Stock held at end of period	Sales during period
Period 0		30	
Period 1	70	30	70
Period 2	130	30	130
Period 3	70	30	70
Period 4	130	30	130
	400		400

Cost of production per item   = 100 per unit
Cost of changing production level = 100 per change
Cost of holding stock   = 10 per unit per period

Production costs   = 100 × 400   = 40 000
Cost of changing production level = 3 × 100   =   300
Total production cost   = 40 300

                                                                40 300
Total cost of holding stock   = 10 × (30 + 30 + 30 + 30) =   1 200
Total cost   = 41 500

to overall systems suboptimization, even though these parts taken individually appear to be performing optimally.

An example of this may be seen in Figure 1.12. Suppose that it is the corporate objective to minimize the total costs (production costs plus storage costs) of supplying a product to meet an externally given fluctuating sales demand. It seems reasonable to expect that if each subsystem functions at the minimum cost compatible with meeting the sales demand then the system as a whole should be optimized and working at minimum cost. Production minimizes its cost by having a constant run of 100 units per quarter, as shown in Figure 1.12(a). This avoids the machine set-up costs of different production runs for different volumes of output. The stock is maintained efficiently at a minimum average cost per unit. However, if the production subsystem can be made to perform suboptimally (with respect to cost minimization) by scheduling a fluctuating production, the extra cost incurred in the change of the production run levels (100 per change) is more than compensated for by the reduced cost of holding stock in the inventory subsystem. This is shown in Figure 1.12(b). Unless a total systems approach is taken, it is difficult to understand why the production subsystem is deliberately avoiding cost minimization in its scheduling.

This is an example that uses simplified figures. However, the general point is that it is not always in an organization's overall interests to adopt a subsystems piecemeal approach and require each subsystem to function efficiently as measured by the same yardstick that is used to measure the system's performance as a whole. The move in organizations towards treating subsystems as financial cost or profit centres in order to remove internal inefficiency in them is in line with this piecemeal approach.

Another equally compelling reason for adopting the total systems approach is related to issues in systems design. A computerized business information system usually augments and sometimes, although increasingly rarely, replaces a manual information-processing system. The formal information in a manual system is conveyed in the form of documents flowing between subsystems. These are demarcated by the traditional functional specializations in the various departments of a business – accounts, purchasing, sales order processing, and so on. Concentration on the information inputs, outputs and processes within each of these subsystems independently of each other will generate a computerized information systems design that mirrors this functional decomposition. Given that all the processing will occur within the central resource of the computer there is no reason why this conventional decomposition should not be sacrificed to a more integrated design that takes into account the information system as a whole. In the later chapters on systems analysis and design, the approach taken is one that allows the development of integrated information systems.

1.4.5 Control

Systems have objectives. In order to ensure that the system's objectives are met, it is important that there is some control operating over the system's functioning. First, this may be needed in order to ensure that a system responds optimally to a change in its inputs or environment. For example, a change in the price of a raw material may lead to its replacement by a cheaper substitute, or a change in a competitor's price may result in a response to ensure a retained market share. Second, the internal functioning of the system may require controls to prevent or to remedy the effects of malfunctions or resource degradation. For example, a labour strike or breakdown of equipment requires an internal response to ensure that systems objectives are not jeopardized.

Controls often work by gathering data on the state and outputs of the system, comparing this with the objectives of the system and taking some corrective measure if necessary. The general model is shown in Figure 1.13. Information on the state of the system or its outputs is collected and compared with some desired standard (**comparator**). The results of this comparison are sent to an element of control, which causes an

Figure 1.13 A general model of feedback control

appropriate decision to be sent to the system (**effector**). This changes the state of the system or its outputs. By continuously monitoring the system and changing it in the light of deviations from standards the system can be controlled to meet its objectives. This form of **feedback control** is common in business and industry. For example, in quality control the output of a process is sampled and its quality established. If this does not meet set standards some decision is made to alter the inputs or process involved. Many forms of regular reporting to management are examples of feedback control.

Feedback control may be automated by computerization. This is most widespread in production processes. More commonly, the computer is used to provide information to management, who then perform the control function and make the decisions. Advances in modern information technology and the increasing use of computer systems have cut the time lag in the provision of information for control purposes. The subject of control is covered extensively in Chapter 9.

1.5   Management information systems

The historical development of these systems is illustrated in Figure 1.14. During the mid-1950s, computers were first used commercially to carry out business data processing. These systems were limited to processing transactions. The most common application areas were payroll, high-volume billing (such as in the electricity industry) and simple ledger accounting activities. The results of this processing were stored. It soon became obvious that this wealth of stored transaction data could provide management with useful information. This information first needed to be extracted and processed to be digestible and useful to management. The early management information systems (MIS) were born when programs were written to do just this. These systems evolved to permit increasingly complex functions, such as *ad hoc* querying and reporting, and thereby support a wider range of decisions. Developments in the desktop computer and in distributed computing then moved the ability to manipulate and even to create these systems away from the centre of the organization and towards the users of these systems. More recently, the advances in Internet technology have seen systems being connected as and when required: across different business sites, between businesses, and between business and customers.

Figure 1.14 Historical development of management information systems

Mini case 1.4

River traffic tracking systems

River transport on the Danube was first disrupted in the early 1990s by the wars in disintegrating Yugoslavia and sanctions against the rump state of Serbia and Montenegro. Then in April 1999, Nato forces bombed three bridges at Novi Sad, in northern Serbia, blocking the river. Navigation has still been only partially restored.

As a result, the Danube, which runs 2,400 km from western Germany to the Black Sea, has largely missed out on east-central Europe's post-Communist economic transformation.

Yet efforts are under way to restore the Danube to its previous role as a key route for freight. River traffic avoids the long border checks that slow down the region's road and rail traffic. From Linz down to Belgrade will take slightly more than two days by river. Even by road, the journey is impossible in less than two days owing to delays at border crossings.

New technology may further enhance the river's attractions. Via Donau is testing its Donau River Information System on a 31 km section of the river near Vienna. The computer tracking system is intended to provide operators and ship owners with up-to-the-second data on the position of vessels and offer information such as whether vessels' cargoes are dangerous.

Adapted from: **Europe's cargo that can go with the flow**
By Robert Wright
Financial Times: 24 February 2003

Questions

1. What information might the Donau River Information System provide?

2. How might an information system like this assist in decision making?

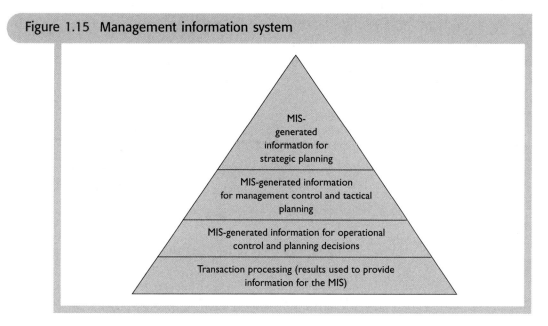

Figure 1.15 Management information system

[Pyramid diagram, top to bottom:]

MIS-generated information for strategic planning

MIS-generated information for management control and tactical planning

MIS-generated information for operational control and planning decisions

Transaction processing (results used to provide information for the MIS)

A **management information system** is, as its name suggests, any system that provides information for the management activities carried out within an organization. Nowadays, the term is almost exclusively reserved for computerized systems. These consist of hardware and software that accept data and store, process and retrieve information. This information is selected and presented in a form suitable for managerial decision making and for the planning and monitoring of the organization's activities.

Today, no one would design a system for processing transactions without considering the way it could also be used to generate information. Figure 1.15 illustrates the reliance of the provision of information at strategic, managerial and operational levels on the transaction-processing base.

The increase in the power of computing technology witnessed over the last two decades, together with its decreasing cost, has meant that computers are used more and more by business organizations to carry out routine data processing. Over this period, there has also been a change in management thinking to accept the importance of the fast, effective provision of targeted information for management planning and control. The combined effect of these two factors has led to an increased growth in management information systems. Specifically, the reasons for this are:

- **Cost:** Once data has been entered for transaction-processing purposes it is within the computer system for the provision of information. The marginal cost of using it to generate information for many different purposes is now low.

- **Speed:** Information can be generated quickly. Even complex reports and statistics on the functioning of a business may take only minutes to prepare if in a standard format. This cuts down the time that management is required to wait for reports once they have been requested. It also means that information provided is up to date and decisions should be more effective.

- **Interaction:** Many modern management information systems provide interactive facilities so that users may request information to be produced online as and when

Figure 1.16 Business information support systems (alternative terminology)

it is needed. This allows end users to be selective about information extracted from the MIS.

■ **Flexibility:** As well as being faced with a predictable set of decisions for which information is required, for example budgeting and performance reporting, management is also faced with new problems. A modern MIS will have some in-built flexibility enabling the manager to decide what information is to be produced.

Alternative terminology

This section has introduced the term 'management information system' as an all-encompassing designation for systems that assist managers of a business in making decisions. However, some authors use the term 'management information system' to define a smaller subset of the systems described above. This alternative terminology is shown in Figure 1.16.

Under this classification, the highest-level information systems are termed **executive information systems** (EIS). These are the systems used by senior management to assist in strategic decision making. Typical examples of their use are in medium- to long-term forecasting and budgeting. The middle layer of systems, used for tactical planning, is divided into two categories: those systems that facilitate routine summarizing and reporting, here called **management information systems** (MIS), and those that allow *ad hoc* queries and analytical reporting, called **decision support systems** (DSS). Examples of the use of the former would be in short- to medium-term forecasting and budgeting and in inventory control. Examples of the latter would be in analysis of sales, pricing and costing, and in the scheduling of production. The lowest layer is then similarly defined as **transaction processing systems** (TPS). Typically, this includes such systems as payroll, order tracking, machine control and employee records. Where this classification is used, it is normal to describe the complete set of layers as computer-based information systems, management support systems or business information support systems. All of these layers of systems are elaborated in this book, but under the single, more generic definition of **management information systems**.

1.5.1 Database

Essential to the idea of a management information system is the ability to retrieve data and use it for the production of targeted information for different purposes. Much data will be stored as the result of transaction-processing operations. It is important that this data is seen as a central resource for the entire management information system and not tied to the application that produced it.

For example, sales transaction data used to update the sales ledger will be stored after the updating process. This data should be available for other purposes. It can be used to provide reports on sales personnel performance as part of the personnel management function. Alternatively, it can be fed into models that use data and information from other sources to forecast cash flows and aid cash management.

In order to achieve the objective of common availability, the data needs to be managed as a central resource. The software that creates this database and handles access to it is called a **database management system**. This ensures that data is controlled, consistent and available to provide information.

Figure 1.17 illustrates this position. Within the organization, materials, energy and labour power are accepted as inputs and processed to provide outputs. Accompanying this will be data recording the transactions and movements involved. This will take the form of records of transactions that the company has with its environment. For example, the sale of a good, the sending of a purchase order to a supplier or the supply of a good will all be accompanied by a record of the transactions involved. Also, records of transactions between the various departments in the organization will be

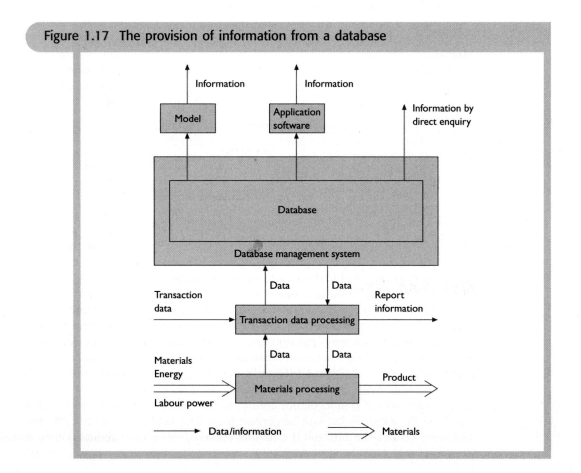

Figure 1.17 The provision of information from a database

generated. An example from a manual system is the requisition of a part from stores for production. This is recorded on a requisition form. Resource use within the organization will also be recorded. Once again, in a manual system the use of individual employee time will be recorded on a worksheet.

The transaction data processing element of Figure 1.17 shows the acceptance of data inputs both from the environment and from internal materials processing within the organization. Transaction outputs are also generated. These may leave the organization, such as an invoice, or be stored in the database, such as the invoice details. This transaction processing is carried out within the computer system.

The database serves as a permanent store for the results of transaction processing, as a temporary store during processing and as a store for the records of the transactions themselves. Interaction between the programs controlling the data processing and the database is handled by the database management system software. This 'protects' the database from direct contact with the applications programs. These carry out such functions as stock control, payroll processing and sales ledger updating. It also maintains consistency of data in the database.

Once stored, this data is available for the production of information to management in its decision-making and control activities. As shown in Figure 1.17, this information may be supplied through a model, may be generated by applications software working on data within the database or may be obtained by direct enquiry using facilities provided with the database management system. Examples of these methods are now explained.

Models

Transaction data on sales and receipts of payments will be processed and stored on the database. This can be extracted along with data on purchases, payment for purchases, wages, the current bank balance and other data that involves cash flows in or out of the organization. The data is then fed into a model. The model predicts the cash flow position of the company over the next six months on a month-by-month basis. This predictive model will also need data that will not be in the database. Data on inflation rates and growth in market sizes fall into this category. This example illustrates the integrating nature of the database. The original data was used in transaction processing for disparate purposes but has now been brought together and used to predict cash flow. Because the modelling element of the provision of the information is designed to aid decisions, in this case on cash management, it is called a **decision support system**.

Applications software

Applications software will also interrogate the database to produce reports for management decision making and control. For example, from the customer sales accounts it is useful management information to know how the total customer debt is aged. If half of the customer debt has been outstanding for a period of more than 60 days, say, then management will respond differently than if one-tenth of the customer debt is over 60 days old. A report on the ageing of debt provides management with information on how successful it is in its debtor control policy. The ageing information will not be stored on the database but will be derived from data held there. Specifically, for each customer account, the date and the amount outstanding on each invoice will be needed to provide a global ageing of debt.

Direct enquiry

Management may also wish to query the database to extract information from it select-ively. An example, once again from customer sales accounts, would be to request the names and balances of all customers with an unpaid balance greater than a given figure.

1.5.2 Management information systems as a collection of subsystems

Although Figure 1.17 shows the *ways* in which information may be produced from the corporate database, it does not illustrate either the levels of management activity for which the data is provided or the functional subsystems of the organization served by the MIS. Figure 1.18(a) superimposes this on the data-processing base. The man-agement information system supplies information for strategic, management (tactical) and operational decision making to all subsystems within the organization. This informa-tion provides an essential part of the feedback control mechanism in these areas and is necessary for the realization of subsystem objectives. Figure 1.18(b) shows how one functional area of the business might operate a number of subsystems. For example, the production department might have separate systems to address inventory management, computer-aided design (CAD), process control and knowledge management systems for office automation such as document management systems.

In the early days of MIS development, it was envisaged that a total systems approach would be taken towards the design of a highly integrated management information system. The reality of MIS development has demonstrated that MIS tend to evolve over time. It is too complex to design the unified system as an initial project. Also, the information needed by different subsystems is markedly disparate and the information required is calculated from differing bases. This has resulted in the develop-ment of individual information subsystems that are only loosely connected. The MIS should perhaps better be regarded as a collection of information subsystems, ideally sharing a corporate database. Each subsystem adapts and is tailored to the needs of the functional subsystem that it serves (Dearden, 1972).

1.5.3 Management information systems and decisions

By providing relevant information, management information systems aid the making of decisions. Where these decisions involve planning, current data is used for predict-ive purposes. This is often associated with using a model to generate future estimates from existing data. This model is used to test the impact of altering the values of para-meters, analysing the effects of alternative plans and testing the sensitivity of predictions to change. Often the model is handled by the user in an interactive way. These decision support systems, as they are known, are an important class of MIS applications, which involve more than just the representation of current information in ways suitable for decisions. In contrast, many control applications require much less – the selection, summary and presentation of information in a manner suitable for exercising control.

Previously (Table 1.2), the structure of decisions was outlined against the different levels of management activities. Those activities of a highly structured operational nature can be replaced by automated computer-based decision making. There is also an area of activities at the strategic unstructured level that require information that is largely external and often subjective. This lies outside the area of relevance for the MIS. However, there is a large band of decisions and activities that can be aided, although not replaced, by the MIS. This is shown in Figure 1.19.

Figure 1.18 The relation between the data-processing and management information systems

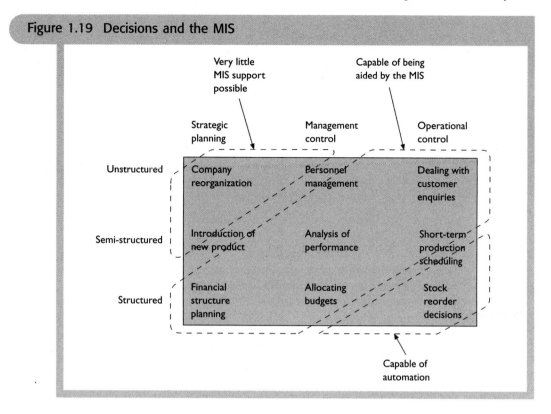

Figure 1.19 Decisions and the MIS

1.5.4 Design of the management information system

The design of the management information system, like the design of any system, needs a methodical approach. A detailed explanation of the stages involved in the analysis and design of information systems is given in subsequent chapters. Here it will be sufficient to note special attributes of information that must be taken into account when designing an information system for management.

- **Relevance:** The information that is generated by the MIS must be relevant to the tasks for which it is provided. The emphasis of the present chapter has been on stressing the importance of information in decision making. An analysis of the decisions taken is required to understand what information is or is not relevant. Information is relevant to a decision if its content potentially affects the decision taken. This is too easily forgotten, and information is provided on the grounds that it might be useful. This is often an excuse for not having carried out a proper decision analysis.

- **Accuracy:** Information should be as accurate as is required for the decision to be taken. Inaccuracy within limits may be perfectly acceptable, especially as increasing the accuracy of information will either increase the cost of its provision or slow its generation, or both.

- **Timeliness:** Information must be presented to the user within the time-span within which it is useful. Late information is not useful. Sometimes accuracy must be sacrificed in order to provide information within the optimum time.

- **Target:** The information must be directed to the correct recipient – that is, the person who takes the decisions for which the information is relevant.

- **Format:** The way in which the information is presented to the user will affect its effectiveness. Traditional attention to clear report formats can now be supplemented by the possibility of producing graphical and chart output. The use of colour and more sophisticated graphics opens up further possibilities in designing output formats. The flexibility of presentation opens the possibility of output designed to match the cognitive style of the recipient.

- **Interactive nature:** Some information is best provided on an interactive basis. This is because further information needs to be called up only if shown to be necessary by current information. To provide all information initially that might be relevant to a decision would be to deluge the decision taker and reduce the effectiveness of the decision process.

- **Control:** Some information may be sensitive or may be of value to competitors. Steps should be taken to ensure that secure procedures surround the MIS.

Dos and don'ts in MIS design

Ackoff (1967), in a now legendary article, stressed some common myths governing MIS projects. These observations are as relevant today as they were over 35 years ago. These myths have a familiar ring to them:

'If only I had more information I would be able to take better decisions,'

says the manager. The reality is often different. It is not that more information needs to be provided but less, and this should be more targeted. Relevant information is being lost in the swamp of large amounts of irrelevant information provided by a poorly designed MIS.

'The best persons to ask in order to establish what information is needed for decisions are the decision makers themselves.'

This is not necessarily the case. The proper starting point is an analysis of the decision. Decision makers will generally attempt a wide specification of information requirements ('if it might be useful let's ask for it').

'Management needs to be supplied with accurate, timely, relevant information for its activities – it is unnecessary for it to know how it is produced.'

In many areas, particularly in management accountancy, what appears to be the same information will have different implications depending on how it is compiled. The management accountant needs not only the information but also knowledge of the way it is produced.

'If information is more freely available then departments can coordinate their activities more closely.'

It should be remembered that departments in an organization may also be in competition with one another. This is especially true if they are profit centres or are attempting to gain as large a slice as possible of the organization's finite resources. Information about one another's activities may mean that departments behave in a way that is dysfunctional to the organization as a whole.

Approaches to management information system design

Although most designers of information systems for management would subscribe to these dos and don'ts and take account of the special attributes of information for decision making described above, there still remains much scope for differing approaches in the design of management information systems.

Here, five approaches towards the development of a corporate MIS are identified. A brief explanation of each of these approaches and their limitations will indicate the minefield of disagreements that still exist on MIS design (Rockart, 1979).

1. The **by-product** approach to the development of an MIS is perhaps the earliest used. The emphasis is on developing a computerized system to deal with all the paperwork that was previously handled within a manual system. Payroll, accounts receivable and accounts payable, stock control, billing and so on are all computerized. Only passing attention is paid to the information needs of management. However, there is a recognition that information is used by management in its activities and that reports can be provided as a by-product of data-processing activities. Little or no analysis of requirements is undertaken. Information produced by the MIS is generally in the form of voluminous reports from which those that need information find it impossible to disentangle what is relevant.

2. The **null** approach is a reaction against the shortcomings of the by-product approach. As its name suggests, the null approach lays little emphasis on the production of formal information for management by means of an MIS. It views the activities undertaken, particularly by top management, as being dynamic and ever-changing. Under these conditions, the production of formal information by an MIS according to static requirements is entirely inappropriate. Supporters of this view also find support in the work of Mintzberg (1973), who showed that as much as 80% of a chief executive's time was spent in verbal communication rather than in absorbing information provided in formal reports. While this view has much to recommend it, one should not forget that the needs of lower management are more clearly defined and are more likely to be properly served by an MIS. Second, the advent of modern interactive systems with user-friendly query and report-generation facilities makes the production of information according to dynamically changing requirements much easier.

3. The **key variable** approach assumes that certain attributes of an organization are crucial for assessing its performance, taking decisions and planning. Examples of such variables might be total cash available, the profit-to-earnings ratio of each plant or the turnover rate of stock. The key variables in an organization are identified and the MIS is designed to provide reports on the values of these variables.

   A variation to the straight reporting of all variables is **exception reporting**. Here the value of a variable is only reported if it lies outside some predetermined 'normal' range. The idea of variance reporting and analysis is familiar to the accountant. Indeed, the emphasis of such systems always tends to favour financial and accounting data at the expense of other information. This is unsurprising given the accountant's propensity for assessing in terms of rates and ratios. The main strength of this approach lies in its recognition that to be effective information must be provided selectively.

4. **Total study** processes concentrate on establishing a comparison between the information requirements of management and the information supply of the current management information system. The IBM business systems planning (BSP) methodology does this by relying on the results of interviewing a large number of managers to determine their key decisions, objectives and information needs. The results of this fact gathering are displayed in matrix form for easy handling and visual

understandability. An attempt is made at gaining an overall understanding of the organization's information needs and identifying just where the current system is falling down. A plan for filling the gaps is then formulated. The total study process is comprehensive and can be useful in identifying shortcomings. However, in common with many total approaches, it is extremely expensive on manpower and the vast amounts of data collected are not easily amenable to analysis. There is also a significant possibility that in attempts at imposing structure on the network of accumulated facts unacceptable biases may occur.

5. The **critical success factor** (CSF) approach is based on the assumption that an organization has certain goals and that specific factors are crucial in achieving these goals. For instance, the general goals of a company in the automobile industry might be seen in terms of maximizing earnings per share, the market share and the return on investment as well as the goal of ensuring the success of new product lines. In order to achieve these goals, the critical factors for success are automobile styling, tight control of manufacturing cost and an efficient dealer network.

As well as general goals and critical success factors for a sector, such as the automobile sector, individual companies will have differing additional goals. These in turn will determine critical success factors based on such influences as geographical position, the past history of the company, local competitors, and so on. These factors are determined by interviews with relevant top managers. By focusing attention on the critical success factors, management highlights those areas where it is crucial to have good management information. Information subsystems can then be designed to serve these critical factors.

The main applicability of this approach is in the design of systems for the provision of control information to monitor the state of the critical success factors. It is less effective at designing MIS for planning. CSF is an active approach to the design of management information systems rather than the passive acceptance of reported information based on tradition and collected historical data. The CSF approach is therefore genuinely information- rather than data-led. Its chief importance is the recognition that the purpose of providing information is to serve corporate goals.

It should be clear from the foregoing that there is no universally accepted approach to the design of an MIS. Nor should it be believed that the few approaches covered above are exhaustive of those available. There are many different methods, each with strengths, weaknesses and areas of applicability. What is becoming quite clear though is that technical issues in the design of a management information system are of secondary importance. The primary aim in design is to establish information needs and requirements. Without success in this area the MIS will be a failure. This is not a simple task, however. It is an area in which the specialist in organizational behaviour, the management scientist and the psychologist as well as the systems analyst can make valuable contributions.

1.5.5 Production of the management information system

It is quite possible for the resources of the IT department of an organization to be devoted to the design, production and implementation of the management information system. In many ways, this appears to be a logical approach as the expertise and knowledge of the organization are readily available. Although this may be the best option in some situations, the trend, particularly for small and medium-sized enterprises, is increasingly towards contracting these services out or purchasing an off-the-shelf solution. Over the last two decades, a large industry has developed in the production of various management information systems. Software vendors and business analysts have built up a range of services and products; some are generic in their application, but others are aimed at very specific sectors of business. Examples of the latter can be found in medicine and health care.

By using a third party to provide the MIS, the organization is purchasing the expertise of the software vendor or analysts and combining it with their own business knowledge. A partnership can then be forged to develop the system to meet the requirements of the business.

1.6 Informal and formal information

Decision control and planning in an organization will be based on available information. If this is produced by standard procedures, is objective and is generally regarded as relevant to a decision the information is known as **formal information**. As well as following organizational procedures in its production, formal information is generally processed from data by known rules and presented in a standard format (see Figure 1.20). The data from which it is produced is usually quantitative and appears on formal documents in the organization. For example, formal information on actual average material costs of production will be generated from document records containing quantitative details of materials purchased and units produced. Formal information is an important component of the total information available to management. Because of its standard representation and its processing by known rules it is easy to generate using a computer system.

Informal information is also used extensively by management in its activities (Land and Kennedy-McGregor, 1987). This is often subjective and passed by word of mouth, and it involves hunches, opinions, guesstimates and rumour. It generally involves explanatory and/or evaluative information. It is most likely to be qualitative in nature. Although an important determinant of decisions, it is less likely to be used in their

Figure 1.20 Formal and informal information

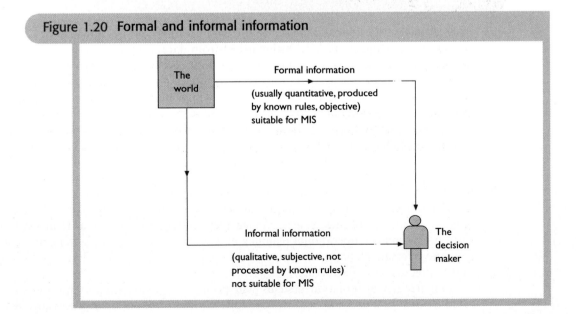

justification. For instance, a decision over job promotion from a junior to a more senior managerial post will be influenced by a variety of information. The candidate's formal qualifications, and the costs and revenues associated with the department over which the candidate has current control, are examples of formal information. The knowledge that the candidate is developing a dependency on alcohol, that the success of the candidate's current department is largely due to an efficient administrator or a competent deputy, are factors that will affect the outcome of the promotion decision. This informal information may even be quite public within the organization. More down-to-earth examples abound. For example, a formal computerized information system will give details of variances from budgets but no explanation as to why these have occurred. This information is precisely what is needed to remedy the situation. Empirical studies suggest that retention of and reliance on a large degree of informal information handling is associated with the more successful organizations (Earl and Hopwood, 1980).

The important point is that although informal information may be subjective, qualitative and not generated by standard procedures or conveyed by usual information channels, it can still be an essential component of effective decision making. Where the managerial activity relies heavily on person-to-person contact, as with top management (Mintzberg, 1973), informal information and its sources are crucial to decisions. By its nature, informal information cannot be readily processed or transmitted by a computer system. There is a great danger that in designing a computerized MIS the role of this other component will be ignored. In particular, where a computerized management information system is installed and much information retrieval and transmission is now handled through terminals, face-to-face contact between individuals will diminish. As a side-effect, this will cut down the informal information flows and may reduce the effectiveness of decision making – just the outcome that the MIS was designed to avoid.

Summary

Information is an essential commodity for the operation and development of a modern business organization. It is distinguished from data in that information has been processed in order to serve some purpose in the business environment. In order to understand the nature of management information, it is important to understand the purposes for which it is provided. Information is used in planning, in monitoring and control of business activities and in making decisions. The first two, planning and control, themselves involve decisions, so the primary purpose of information is to aid decision making.

An understanding of the way decisions are taken and the level of managerial activity involved will cast light on general properties of the information used. The categorization of the decision process into four stages – intelligence, design, choice and implementation – provides a useful framework within which to view decisions. The amount of structure implicit in a particular decision can then be analysed into the degree of structure in each of these stages. Management activity can be seen as falling within three broad bands – operational planning and control, managerial planning and control, and strategic planning. Within each of these, there will be a variety of decisions of differing degrees of structure.

Computerized information systems will primarily provide support for the structured element of a decision because they follow formal rules in their processing. With highly structured decisions, such as in operational control, the computer may replace the decision maker rather than provide information for decision support. As one moves 'up' through the levels of management the types of decision change. At higher levels, there is an emphasis on the need for information that is supplied from sources external to the organization, is highly aggregated, uncertain and future-looking, as well as being less rule-bound. The nature of this information makes it unlikely that computerized information systems relying on internally generated information will be of much value.

The estimation of the value of information is a difficult area. In some cases, a quantitative measure may be placed on the provision of speedier information, as in debtor control, or in the reduction of uncertainty. However, there are intangible benefits. It is difficult, if not impossible, to analyse the contribution of more effective information to a better decision, or to isolate the impact of greater information availability to customers on their purchases. It is a great mistake to ignore the intangible, non-measurable benefits in assessing the overall benefit to the firm of a proposed information system.

The provision of information in a business needs to be looked at in a systematic way. A useful perspective from which to operate is to view the organization as a system and apply systems concepts to the design of its information system. The general characteristics of systems were covered in the chapter. It was emphasized that in order to facilitate understanding of the business it is helpful to decompose the total system into its components. These subsystems and their relations to one another can be shown by means of a hierarchy chart. Flow block diagrams provide an alternative method of representation illustrating the flows between subsystems.

Although a system can be understood by analysis into its component subsystems, it should not be forgotten that this piecemeal approach to analysis may mask systemic properties that apply to the system as a whole. For example, subsystem optimization may occur at the expense of system suboptimization. The concept of control if viewed from a systems perspective is particularly important in understanding the role of the information system within the organization.

Management information systems are computerized systems that provide information for managerial decision making. These systems rely on extracting and processing data from a commonly shared corporate database that stores the results of transaction processing. Information may be provided via a forecasting model, as the result of the activity of a specially designed applications program or package, or by direct enquiry using powerful database query languages (see Chapter 8).

Designing an integrated, total management information system for an organization is a complex task and one that may lead to a final product that falls short of expectations. Instead, the MIS is better regarded as a grouping of information subsystems that are designed (or evolve) more or less independently to meet the information needs of the subsystems they support. This collection of information subsystems is unified by the shared database. In the design of an MIS, the presentation of information, its timeliness, levels of accuracy and the person to whom the information is delivered must be taken into account as well as the information content. No single approach towards the design of an MIS is accepted as standard. The chapter outlined several approaches to illustrate the wide diversity of differences. The information systems requirements can be developed by the company itself or contracted out to a third party. Finally, informal and formal information were distinguished and the importance of the former to effective decision making stressed. No MIS should block the use of informal information, as this will impair the effectiveness of decision making.

The advent of cheap, powerful microcomputers has added a new dimension to the provision of information. Together with versatile packaged software, designed for use by non-specialists in computing, these have led to the mushrooming of alternative information centres. They may not rival the sophistication of the traditional MIS that is centrally controlled and developed, but their ability to respond to local information requirements has been both an attraction to their users and a threat to the power and importance of the centralized computing resource.

Review questions

1. Distinguish between *data* and *information*.

2. What are the differences between strategic, tactical and operational levels of management activities?

3. What are the major differences in the types of information needed for each level of management activity?

4. What influences affect the decision-making process of a decision maker?

5. What problems are there in assessing the value of information for decision making?

6. Outline the main features of a system.

7. What is a management information system?

8. Outline the ways that information may be processed from a database and presented to management.

9. How is the structure and level of management activity related to the level of support given by a management information system?

10. Give basic guidelines that should be followed in the development of a management information system.

11. Outline *five* approaches to management information system design and explain some of the advantages and disadvantages of each.

Exercises

1. Give examples of *four* business decisions and specify the information needed for each.

2. Outline a model of decision making and illustrate this with a business example.

3. What is the difference between a programmable and a non-programmable business decision? Give two examples of each from business.

4. Apply the basic systems model to an inventory system, explaining how each of the parts of the model is exemplified in the inventory system.

5. Define *subsystem decoupling*. Give three examples of how this may be achieved in a business system. In each case, state the advantages and disadvantages of the decoupling.

6. What advantages do modern computerized management information systems have compared with their manual predecessors?

7. What are the differences between *formal* and *informal* information? Give examples of each that you encounter in your college or work routines.

8. How have technological developments affected the provision of information over the last decade?

9. What are the similarities and differences between the field of information systems and the field of management accounting?

10. 'The information needs of managers are varied and change quickly in today's dynamic business environment. The lack of flexibility in computer systems implies that if managers rely on these for the provision of information then the effectiveness of their decision making will be diminished.' Do you agree?

11. What criteria do you suggest to assess the success or failure of a management information system?

CASE STUDY 1

Supply chain event management

Despite the vast amounts that companies have invested in complex planning and forecasting software, unexpected events, such as a production delay or late shipment, are part and parcel of logistics. Supply chain event management (SCEM) aims to anticipate, manage and rectify these exceptions, increasing the granularity of information at weak points in the existing infrastructure, notably between manufacture and delivery.

SCEM works by monitoring information across the supply chain and sending an alert to operations personnel when conditions fall outside pre-defined parameters. It has been described as an 'electronic tap on the shoulder' that warns the company and its suppliers about potential problems and recommends a course of action to help resolve the issue.

The UK supermarket company J Sainsbury recently implemented an SCEM system from Eqos. 'Working closely with suppliers is a business imperative,' explains Diane Carter, supply chain operations director at the company. 'We believe this new investment will help us work with them more effectively, irrespective of their size, and enable us to be more responsive to customer demand by jointly identifying problems earlier and proactively managing issues through to resolution.'

The essence of SCEM technology is the ability to share data across multiple organizations, or within an individual organization, and extract relevant information from a number of different systems, explains Steve Wilson, from the supply chain practice at Accenture. 'Based on these data feeds, the system is then able to provide status information, or raise alerts to recognize certain activities – the delay to a shipment, for example. Some of the more advanced technologies are trying to develop mechanisms to suggest alternatives to assist with resolving issues as they arise,' he says.

Mark Mahara, managing director and vice-president of EMEA at Silvon Software, a business intelligence provider, describes the kind of scenario that SCEM is designed to address. 'Say a company launches a new product with an initial forecast that underestimates demand. Then, it finds it has no time to procure more supplies and make more

▶

products within client delivery requirements. Throw in some other product launches in multiple markets for numerous customers to add to the supply chain complexity, and process breakdown becomes a snowball expanding in size and gaining speed as it barrels downhill.'

SCEM should enable companies to cope more effectively with this kind of eventuality. 'Visibility is SCEM's greatest benefit,' Mr Mahara continues. 'Seeing a problem is 90 per cent of fixing it.' For example, SCEM might be able to interpret early individual events as indicators that a runaway situation threatens, providing the opportunity to rectify problems before it develops fully. 'A very simple example would be the ability to create a purchase order or requisition request automatically when inventory falls short of a certain threshold. This would be done from the SCEM system and integrated back into the business system so the user can resolve the issue quickly and effectively in a single process,' says Mr Mahara.

Visibility across the supply chain is one thing, but being able to act upon new information is another thing entirely. Eddie Capel, vice-president of trading partner management at Manhattan Associates, points out that companies must be able to manage and execute supply chain operations to reap the benefits of SCEM. For instance, factories have to be able to create advanced shipping notices (ASNs) electronically, or carriers must be able to provide automatic shipment status updates. 'The output of the analysis and event management will result in required responses by parties throughout the supply chain,' he says. 'The creation of an ASN may result in a cross-docking operation at a warehouse based on demand at a store. A late shipment could drive the transportation system to switch selected carriers to an expedited parcel service. Thus, it is not just the visibility that benefits the enterprise, but also the ability to respond to the information revealed in a quick and efficient manner.'

When this can be made to work in practice, the benefits are considerable. Consider the case at Ford Parts & Logistics. With more than 2,000 suppliers using multiple supply chain networks, Ford found its existing information systems offered limited visibility with no ability to identify product shortages. This has been rectified with a system from Teradata that comprises an enterprise data warehouse to consolidate existing supply chain information and the Supply Chain Intelligence software package to provide SCEM.

The system measures and monitors the supply chain continuously, analysing events and changes in supply and demand, and then converting that data into actionable information. For example, all information about every Ford part is continuously updated in the company's data warehouse. Staff can drill down to find out exactly how many of these parts are available and pinpoint their precise location. If the part is in transit, the system can even indicate the whereabouts of the vehicle that is carrying it. This data is correlated with demand information from the service centres. The data warehouse then runs event-based and predictive analytics on top of this information to balance inventory with demand and predicted demand. Ford says that the new system paid for itself five times over in six months, with 20 per cent reduction in inventory costs, 30 per cent reduction in overall supply chain cycle times and 40 per cent improvement in ability to replenish.

However, SCEM should not be considered as a panacea for a company's every supply chain problem. As with all kinds of system, if bad data is entered, bad information comes out. In other words, if it is to be successful, SCEM must come as part of a comprehensive supply chain strategy.

Adapted from: **Better visibility helps plug the information gap**
By Mark Vernon
FT.com site: 25 November 2003

Questions

1. Define the terms 'data' and 'information' in the context of the supply chain event management systems described above.

2. Using the model of decision making, describe the stages that J Sainsbury might go through in deciding whether to switch from one supplier to another.

3. From the case study, list examples of strategic, tactical and operational decision making that might be supported by supply chain event management systems.

4. Does the case study focus on structured or unstructured decision making? Provide examples to support your answer.

5. Supply chain event management systems can provide valuable feedback control. Explain how, and provide examples based on the case study.

6. How would you define the level of systems coupling in the Ford Parts and Logistics system? How does the information system assist in the functioning of this system?

References

Ackoff R.L. (1967). Management misinformation systems. *Management Science*, **14**(4), B140–56

Anthony R.N. (1965). *Planning and Control Systems: A Framework for Analysis*. Cambridge, Mass.: Harvard University Press

Dearden J. (1972). MIS is a mirage. *Harvard Business Review*, January–February, 90–9

Earl M. and Hopwood A. (1980). From management information to information management. In *The Information Systems Environment*, Lucas H., Land F., Lincoln T. and Supper K. (eds), Amsterdam: North Holland

Gorry G.A. and Scott-Morton M.S. (1971). A framework for management information systems. *Sloan Management Review*, **13**(1), 55–70

Kilmann R.H. and Mitroff I.I. (1976). Quantitative versus qualitative analysis for management science: different forms for different psychological types. *TIMS Interfaces*, February 1976

Land F.F. and Kennedy-McGregor M. (1987). Information and information systems: concepts and perspectives. In *Information Analysis: Selected Readings*, Galliers R.D. (ed.), Wokingham: Addison-Wesley

Mintzberg H. (1973). *The Nature of Managerial Work*. New York: Harper & Row

Rockart J.F. (1979). Chief executives define their own data needs. *Harvard Business Review*, March–April 1979

Simon H.A. (1965). *The Shape of Automation for Men and Management*. New York: Harper & Row

Simon H.A. (1977). *The New Science of Management Decision*. Englewood Cliffs, NJ: Prentice Hall

Recommended reading

Dearden J. (1972). MIS is a mirage. *Harvard Business Review*, January–February, 90–9
Worth reading for an alternative 'pessimistic' approach to the possibility of design of an integrated management information system.

Frenzel C. (2003). *Management of Information Technology*, 4th edn. Thompson Course Technology

An extremely thorough book full of illustrations and adopting a very academic approach. The text is an excellent one; the sections on tactical and operational considerations, controlling information resources and preparing for IT advances are particularly worth reading.

Hussain D.S. and Hussain K.M. (1997). *Information Management: Organizations, Management, and Control of Computer Processing*. Hemel Hempstead: Butterworth-Heinemann

This is a straightforward, highly readable text suitable as an introduction for non-specialists at final-year undergraduate or postgraduate levels. The text is divided into four sections dealing with the structure of computing resources within the organization; the control of information processing, including quality control, privacy, security, performance evaluation and auditing; the management of processing, including standards and resistance to change; and future areas of information systems development, including global information management. Each chapter contains a list of exercises.

Liebenau J. and Backhouse J. (1992). *Understanding Information: An Introduction*. London: Macmillan

An interesting text for those who wish to enlarge their understanding of the concept of information from a narrow technical definition. The book brings together material from a variety of disciplines, including sociology, semiotics, management, philosophy and anthropology.

McNurlin B. and Sprague R. (2003). *Information Systems Management in Practice*, 6th edn. Prentice Hall

This covers the management of information technology in modern organizations. The book gives a thorough description of information and information systems in setting a context for a deeper analysis of knowledge management. It uses case studies of organizations' use of information and technologies.

Chapter 2

Strategy and information systems

Learning outcomes

On completion of this chapter, you should be able to:

- Appreciate the need for businesses and other organizations to plan strategically
- Differentiate between information systems planning and information technology planning
- Identify models for determining the effects of internal and external factors on business information systems development
- Analyse external factors and forces as a guide for the development of information systems strategy
- Describe stages in the development of an organization's information system and the process of moving effectively from one stage to the next
- Describe how information systems can provide competitive advantage for an organization and how IS needs can be identified.

Introduction

In Chapter 1, the central idea of a business information system was developed by initially exploring the concepts of 'system' and 'business information'. Any introduction or expansion of an information system in a business will require:

- the allocation of large resources;
- a recognition that the firm's activities will change as a result of the information system; and
- the intention to improve the organization's services or increase its profits.

Such important decisions should be taken in the light of the business strategy. The subject of this chapter is to expand on the relationship between strategy and information systems. Initially, the need for a business strategy is explained together with a suggested overview of the strategic business planning process. The way in which this necessitates an information systems strategy is covered. There are many frameworks within which information systems strategy can be viewed. One framework is outlined in the chapter, and its various components are explained. Each emphasizes a different perspective on the issues that a firm may wish to take into account when formulating strategy. They all have one feature in common though – they acknowledge the need for an information systems strategy to be determined by the business needs of the organization, not by the functions of available technology.

2.1 The need for a business strategy

A business will function on a day-to-day basis without the obvious need for a business strategy. Orders will be taken from customers, goods despatched, invoices sent and payments from customers acknowledged. Where stock runs low, purchase orders will be drafted and sent, goods will be received, stock stored and inventory records updated, and when the invoices arrive from the suppliers these will be authorized for payment and payment made. Work will be scheduled and products manufactured. Payroll will produce payslips and instruct banks to make automated payment of wages and salaries at the end of the month. Sales reps' cars will be put into garages for maintenance, bills received, and so on. This is the day-to-day functioning of business.

A business, or any other organization, may continue to function in this way for some period of time without reference to any strategy. However, a business under these conditions is analogous to a ship under way without a destination or without reference to the environment in which it is voyaging.

There needs to be a strategy and strategic planning for a business for several reasons:

1. As was seen in Chapter 1, the individual departments in an organization (subsystems within a system) may function well in terms of their own objectives but still not serve the objectives of the organization. This is because of a lack of coordination between departments, because departments themselves have specific objectives counter to those of the organization, or because subsystems optimization may on occasion lead to total systems suboptimization. It is therefore important that there be an agreed and communicated set of objectives for the organization and a plan on how to achieve these.

2. The organization will on occasion need to make major resource allocations, especially for the purchase and development of new plant, property and machines. Information systems will need expensive hardware and will incur design costs. They will need large resource allocations. These allocations can only be made against an agreed direction for the organization – a strategy for the future.

3. The organization will have responsibilities to a number of different groups. Included among these would be the owners, whether it be the shareholders or the public, the employees, the customers and those that provide finance, such as banks. These parties will have a particular interest in the corporate strategy as their interests will be served or otherwise by the extent to which the strategy takes into account their interests and the success of the organization in meeting these interests.

2.2 Strategic business planning

There is no *one* accepted method that a business should adopt in its strategic planning. However, there are a number of different steps that would normally be taken in the development of a business strategy (see Figure 2.1).

Most large organizations will already have strategies currently formulated. These strategies are often for a future period of five years. This is a convenient time horizon. If it was longer, then future uncertainties would render the planning process for the later

Figure 2.1 Developing a business strategy

stages of little value; if it was shorter, then many developments could not be planned through to fruition. For some organizations, the planning horizon will need to be extended significantly – national defence and the nuclear industry are two such examples. In some very dynamic and fast-changing environments, a shorter period of say three years might be more appropriate – some high-technology industries might fall into this category.

The business strategy is not frozen into the operations of the business but is evaluated and redrafted from time to time. This often occurs on a yearly basis, when the strategy for the next five years will be decided. The strategic business planning process then yields a five-year rolling plan. Unless there are serious problems within the organization or it is undergoing major internal change, it is likely that changes to strategy will be incremental. The following sections expand on Figure 2.1.

2.2.1 Determine the business mission and objectives

The mission of the organization will be a general statement of its overall purpose and aims. It often consists of a number of individual aims. Examples might be (for a chemical company) 'to become a major supplier of agrochemicals to the farming sector through the research and development of new and more effective fertilizer and pest controls' or (for a chain of hi-fi shops) 'to expand the number of retail outlets and diversify into the sale of all electronic leisure goods'.

The objectives, both medium- and long-term, should support the organization's overall mission. Each objective should have a measurable performance indicator, which can be used to determine the success of the organization in meeting the objective. In the above, an objective could well be 'to increase the number of retail outlets by 35% within three years and the area of floor space devoted to sales by 50% within the same period'.

2.2.2 Identify the likely future performance against objectives

The organization should be continuously monitoring and evaluating its performance against its current objectives. Part of this monitoring process will involve forecasts of future sales, cash flows, materials requirements and profitability based on the current situation. In other words, when developing business strategy the current operations of the organization will have an implied future scenario, which can be compared with desired objectives.

As an input into the assessment of future performance, it is common to identify internal and external factors that will have a significant impact. This **SWOT** (strengths, weaknesses, opportunities, threats) **analysis** will identify internal strengths, such as a highly trained and flexible workforce, and internal weaknesses, such as a poor internal information system, together with external opportunities, such as the opening up of trade through a common European market, and external threats, such as low economic entry barriers to the industry.

Given the predictions and the identified strengths, weaknesses, opportunities and threats, it will be possible to estimate the extent of the gap between future objectives and forecast future performance. The business strategy should determine a series of measures and plans that will remove this gap.

2.2.3 Develop the business strategy

The business strategy will be the set of plans that the business will implement in order to achieve its stated objectives. These plans may involve new projects or the continued operation of existing activities.

Most businesses are modelled and managed in a functional way. Human resources, information systems, marketing, financial management and production are examples of common functions. The business strategy will have as components a human resource strategy, an information systems strategy, a marketing strategy, and so on. These strategies will support the business strategy and interact with one another. The information systems strategy is taking on a key role as more businesses rely increasingly heavily on their computerized information systems for all aspects of their business functions.

2.3 Business information systems strategy

The previous section identifies, in broad terms, the steps taken in strategic planning, but it provides no insight into what specific factors should be taken into account in business information strategy development. In particular, it does not give any framework within which to answer the questions as to which information systems should be developed and why. This section will be directed at these issues.

First, it is important to distinguish between a business information systems strategy and a business information technology strategy.

The **business information systems strategy** is focused on determining what information systems must be provided in order that the objectives of the business strategy can be realized. The concentration is therefore on determining information needs and ensuring that the information systems strategy aligns with the business strategy.

The **business information technology strategy** is focused on determining what technology and technological systems development are needed in order that the business information systems strategy can be realized. The concentration is therefore on how to provide the information, not on what information is required. The strategy will also cover how the information resource and information systems development is to be managed.

There is a close interaction between the information systems strategy and the information technology strategy. It is important, however, to make a distinction between them given that the information systems strategy should be led by the needs of the business, not by technology.

There has been a considerable debate as to how best to develop a strategy for information systems/information technology. The urgency of this debate has been fuelled by the speed with which information technology continues to change and by a recognition that information technology is being used less in a support function in the business but is increasingly integral to the business operations and development itself.

Many models have been put forward to guide the strategist in formulation. An important selection is explained in the rest of this section. They have different approaches and objectives and cover different aspects of the strategy formulation process. The framework in Figure 2.2 indicates that some models address the area of information systems strategy, whereas others can be seen as more relevant to information technology strategy. Within the former (information systems strategy), there is a division between those approaches that concentrate on internal aspects of the business compared with those that focus on areas within the environment of the organization. It should be noted that many of the models discussed in the following sections were developed as generic models of strategy that have since been adapted to provide models for the development of information systems strategy.

Figure 2.2 A framework for the interrelation of influences on information systems strategy and information technology strategy

(Adapted from source material, Susan Gasson, Warwick Business School)

Mini case 2.1

Business information systems strategy

Ever since the introduction of interactive executive information systems (EIS) nearly two decades ago, the IT industry has been striving to give boards of directors increased visibility of their organization's performance and early warning of potential problems.

For 20 years the industry has been wrestling to bridge the gap between strategic management processes and technology. In a changing world, management's focus is constantly shifting between problem areas.

'Software is being marketed to give potential users the impression that it is a marvellous idea that they can pick it off the shelf and put it into practice,' warns Tim Jennings, research director at Butler Group, the analyst.

'It glosses over the fact that it has to be built on firm foundations. The vendors are starting to understand that they need to provide an end-to-end solution that has data quality and metadata [data about data] management facilities built in.'

A fully-integrated performance management solution will help companies to improve their performance by frequently re-forecasting non-financial drivers, evaluating alternative actions and avoiding subsequent financial variances. It will combine all planning, budgeting, consolidation, analysis, reporting and control processes. However, there is still some way to go.

Adapted from: **Struggling to provide a solution**
By Rod Newing
FT.com site: 4 June 2003

Questions

1. Why is it important for an organization's information systems strategy to be led by the business strategy?

2. If businesses only look for technological solutions which facilitate the fulfilment of their own business strategies, what role is there for software vendors such as those referred to above?

2.3.1 Competitive forces within an industry – the five forces model

Modern technology is increasingly being used as part of an information systems strategy that yields competitive advantage for the organization. One way in which a business can gain a **competitive advantage** is by using information technology to change the structure of the industry within which it operates.

The five forces model (Porter and Millar, 1985) views a business operating in an industry as being subject to five main competitive forces. The way in which the business responds to these forces will determine its success. These forces are illustrated in Figure 2.3. Information technology can aid a business in using these competitive forces to its advantage. In this way, information technology can be seen as a strategic competitive weapon.

Suppliers

The suppliers provide the necessary inputs of raw materials, machinery and manufactured components for the firm's production process. The suppliers to a business can exert their bargaining power on that business by pushing up the prices of inputs

Figure 2.3 An industry and its competitive forces

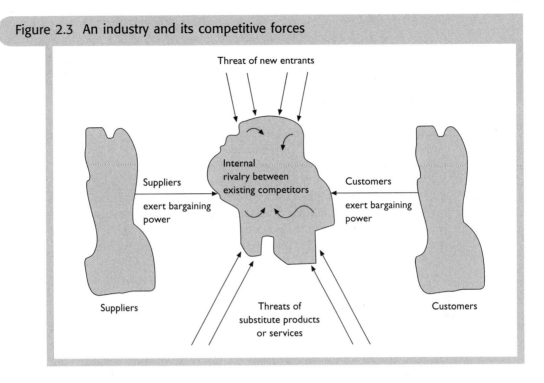

supplied using the threat of taking their supply goods elsewhere to a competitor business in the same industry. It is in the interests of the business to make alternative rival businesses who would purchase the supplier's goods seem less attractive to the supplier.

One way of achieving this is by creating good relationships with the supplier by using **electronic data interchange (EDI)**. EDI requires that there is an electronic connection between the business and its suppliers. When supplies are to be ordered this is accomplished by sending structured electronic messages to the supplier firm. The supplier firm's computer decodes these messages and acts appropriately. The advantage of this for both partners is:

- reduced delivery times;
- reduced paperwork and associated labour costs; and
- increased accuracy of information.

For the business that is purchasing supplies, EDI can be part of its just-in-time approach to manufacturing. This yields benefits in terms of reduced warehousing costs.

Creating links with suppliers is becoming increasingly important in the manufacturing sector, especially between car manufacturers and the suppliers of component parts.

Customers

Customers can exert power over a business by threatening to purchase the product or service from a competitor. This power is large if there are few customers and many competitors who are able to supply the product or service.

One way in which a business may reduce the ability of a customer to move to another competitor is by introducing switching costs. These are defined as costs, financial or otherwise, that a customer would incur by switching to another supplier. One way of achieving switching costs is to allow the customer to have online ordering facilities for the business's service or product. It is important that customers gain a benefit from this or there is little incentive for them to put themselves in a potentially weak bargaining position.

For instance, with electronic banking the belief is that once a customer has established a familiarity with one system, gaining advantage from it, there will be a learning disincentive to switch to another. Another example is American Hospital Supplies. It has improved its competitive position by allowing online terminals into customer hospitals. These allowed the swift order/delivery of supplies by using less skilled personnel compared with more expensive purchase agents. Once established, it became very difficult for a hospital to change suppliers.

Recent developments in providing businesses with the information and processes necessary to understand and track customers' behaviour has been termed **customer relationship management (CRM)**. Analysis techniques and sophisticated software tools have been developed to exploit the potential information contained in databases of customer details and activity. CRM is often refined into customer profiling, developing categories of customer and attempting to predict their behaviour. One of the goals of CRM is to prevent **churn**, the gradual wastage of customers to competitors.

Substitute products

Substitute products or services are those that are within the industry but are differentiated in some way. There is always the danger that a business may lose a customer to the purchase of a substitute product from a rival business because that product meets the needs of the customer more closely. Information technology can prevent this happening in two ways. First, it can be used to introduce switching costs as stated above. Second, the technology may be used to provide differentiated products swiftly by the use of computer-aided design/computer-aided manufacturing (CAD/CAM). In this latter case, the business produces the substitute product itself.

New entrants

Within any industry there is always the threat that a new company might enter and attract some of the existing demand for the products of that industry. This will reduce the revenue and profit of the current competitors. The traditional response has been for mature businesses in an industry to develop barriers to entry. These have been:

- exploiting economies of scale in production;
- creating brand loyalty;
- creating legal barriers to entry – for example patents; and
- using effective production methods involving large capital outlays.

Information technology can assist a business in developing these barriers. In as far as information technology makes a firm more productive, for instance by reducing labour costs or by speeding up aspects of the production process, any firm attempting to enter the marketplace will be competitively disadvantaged without a similar investment in capital. If expensive CAD/CAM equipment is common for the production of differentiated products speedily then this will also act as a barrier to entry.

Competitor rivalry

Unless it is in a monopoly position, any business in an industry is subject to competition from other firms. This is perhaps the greatest competitive threat that the business experiences. Information technology can be used as part of the firm's competitive strategy against its rivals, as illustrated in the preceding sections. Close linkages with suppliers and customers produce competitive forces against rivals, as does the investment in technology allowing product differentiation and cost reductions.

In some cases, the investment in information technology will be necessary to pre-empt the competitiveness of other businesses. The major investment by the banks in automated teller machines is just one example of this.

Mini case 2.2

Competitive advantage

The UK cinema market has never been so competitive, with many of the key operators fighting for a decreasing number of prime sites. Location decisions have to consider a range of complex factors in order to arrive at some estimate of trading level. These factors relate to the proposed site in question (quality, accessibility, size, and mix), the competitive offer in the local market, and the satisfied and unsatisfied levels of demand – especially the number of 25–34-year-olds – in the market. Geographical Information System (GIS) software, data and modelling techniques can help to make sense of such intricate local markets and predict the level of customer trips.

The basic system itself comprises the GIS software usually coupled with a demographic reporting tool and any externally available data. The external data usually consists of: background context mapping (roads, rail, urban sprawl, locations); census or demographic information by small area (census counts, geo-demographic or lifestyle profiles); administrative geography (postcodes, postal sector boundaries, TV regions); and competitor locations (quality and location of competitive outlets, open or planned), and if possible, trading levels.

The main source of competitive advantage in such a system is that of internal data – the information held by an organization that is not generally available to competitors. One significant source of internal data is that about the company's own customers. Odeon Cinemas generate a large amount of local market knowledge from the collection of customer information through their call centre or by box office surveys. For example, gathering postcode information allows Odeon to quantify the 'distance decay effect' – the decreasing propensity to attend as one lives further away from a venue. This effect differs by geographic location and is governed by the transport infrastructure as well as the location of competing offers.

For Odeon these models are useful in predicting sales or admissions, the likely impact on own or competitor outlets, and market share by small area. Odeon have applied the use of GIS to help in site openings, campaign analysis at the local, regional or national level, and in customer acquisition and retention.

Adapted from: **Cinema site planning**
By Simon Briscoe
FT.com site: 7 October 2003

Questions

1. Apply the five forces model to Odeon Cinemas.

2. Given that Geographical Information Systems are available to all cinemas and other entertainment providers, how can Odeon Cinemas maintain a competitive advantage?

2.3.2 Environmental influences on the organization – PEST analysis

Porter's five forces model considers the industry sector within which the business operates. However, in formulating strategy there are other external factors that the strategist needs to take into account. This is the function of a PEST (political, economic, socio-cultural, technological) analysis.

The questions to be asked are:

Which environmental factors are currently affecting and are likely to affect the organization?

What is the relevant importance of these now and in the future?

Examples of the areas to be covered under each heading are given below:

- **Political/legal:** monopolies legislation, tax policy, employment law, environmental protection laws, regulations over international trade, government continuity and stability.
- **Economic:** inflation, unemployment, money supply, cost of parts and energy, economic growth trends, the business cycle – national and international.
- **Socio-cultural:** population changes – age and geographical distribution, lifestyle changes, educational level, income distribution, attitudes to work/leisure/consumerism.
- **Technological:** new innovations and development, obsolescence, technology transfer, public/private investment in research.

At a minimal level, the PEST analysis can be regarded as no more than a checklist of items to attend to when drawing up strategy. However, it can also be used to identify key environmental factors. These are factors that will have a major long-term influence on strategy and need special attention. For instance, included in the key environmental factors for a hospital will be demographic trends (increased percentage of older citizens in the population and decreased percentage of those who are of working age), increases in technological support, government policy on funding and preventive medicine. These key factors are ones that will have significant impact on strategy and must be taken into account.

PEST analysis may also be used to identify long-term drivers of change. For instance, globalization of a business may be driven by globalization of technology, of information, of the market and of the labour force.

In general, a PEST analysis is used to focus on a range of environmental influences outside the organization and (perhaps) outside of the industry that are important to longer-term change, and therefore strategy, but may be ignored in the day-to-day decisions of the business.

As has been seen in Chapter 1, where the characteristics of information needed for decision making were covered, the information needed for strategic decisions partly comes from outside the organization, is future-looking and may be highly uncertain. This is clearly true of some of the areas considered by the PEST analysis. This contributes towards the difficulty of the important task of drawing up strategy.

2.3.3 Internal stages of growth

The preceding two sections explain the way that factors external to the organization will need to be taken into account when developing an information systems strategy. However, factors internal to the organization will also need to be introduced into the strategy. The introduction, development and use of computing information systems cannot be achieved overnight. It requires the organization to undergo change and a learning process internally. This concerns not only the technological factors of information systems but also the planning, control, budgetary and user involvement aspects.

Over the last 30 years, several influential approaches have been developed that look at the development of information systems in an organization as proceeding through several stages of growth. In the following sections, two of these models will be considered.

The Nolan stage model

The earliest of these models, developed by Nolan, explains the extent and type of information systems used in an organization as being determined by the maturity of growth of information systems within that organization.

It was Nolan's original thesis that all organizations went through four stages of growth. This was later refined by adding two intermediate growth stages. The six-stage growth model (Nolan, 1979) was used to identify which stage of growth characterized an organization's information systems maturity. This in turn had further implications for successful planning to proceed to the next level of growth. The model has been used as the basis in over 200 consultancy studies in the USA and has been incorporated into IBM's information systems planning (Nolan, 1984). Before considering any planning implications of the model, the stages will be briefly explained.

The Nolan stage model purports to explain the evolution of an information system within an organization by consideration of various stages of growth. The model is based on empirical research on information systems in a wide range of organizations in the 1970s. Expenditure on IT increases with the stages (see Figure 2.4).

Within each stage of growth, four major growth processes must be planned, managed and coordinated:

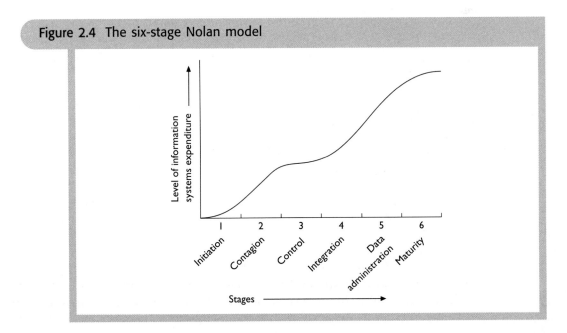

Figure 2.4 The six-stage Nolan model

1. **Applications portfolio:** The set of applications that the information systems must support – for example financial planning, order processing, on-line customer enquiries.

2. **DP organization:** The orientation of the data processing – for example as centralized technology driven, as management of data as a resource.

3. **DP planning and control:** for example degree of control, formalization of planning process, management of projects, extent of strategic planning.

4. **User awareness:** The extent to which users are aware of and involved with the technology.

The stages have different characteristics (see Figure 2.4).

1. **Stage 1 Initiation:** The computer system is used for low-level transaction processing. Typically high-volume data processing of accounting, payroll and billing data characterize the stage. There is little planning of information systems. Users are largely unaware of the technology. New applications are developed using traditional languages (such as COBOL). There is little systematic methodology in systems analysis and design.

2. **Stage 2 Contagion:** The awareness of the possibilities of IT increases among users, but there is little real understanding of the benefits or limitations. Users become enthusiastic and require more applications development. IT is generally treated as an overhead within the organization and there is little check on user requests for more applications. Budgetary control over IT expenditure and general managerial control over the development of the information system are low. Technical problems with the development of programs appear. An increasing proportion of the programming effort is taken up in maintenance of systems. This is a period of unplanned growth.

3. **Stage 3 Control:** As continuing problems occur with the unbridled development of projects there is a growing awareness of the need to manage the information systems function. The data processing department is reorganized. The DP manager becomes more accountable, having to justify expenditure and activities in the same way as other major departments within the organization. The proliferation of projects is controlled by imposing charges on user departments for project development and the use of computer services. Users see little progress in the development of information systems. Pent-up demand and frustration occur in user departments.

4. **Stage 4 Integration:** Having achieved the consolidation of Stage 3, the organizational data-processing function takes on a new direction. It becomes more oriented towards information provision. Concurrent with this and facilitating it, there is the introduction of interactive terminals in user departments, the development of a database and the introduction of data communications technologies. User departments, which have been significantly controlled in Stage 3 by budgetary and organizational controls, are now able to satisfy the pent-up demand for information support. There is a significant growth in the demand for applications and a consequent large increase in supply and expenditure to meet this demand. As the rapid growth occurs the reliance on computer-based controls becomes ineffective. In particular, redundancy of data and duplication of data become a significant problem.

5. **Stage 5 Data administration:** The response to the problems of Stage 4 is to introduce controls on the proper administration of data. The emphasis shifts from regarding data as the input to a process that produces information as an output to

the view that data is a resource in an organization. As such, it must be properly planned and managed. This stage is characterized by the development of an integrated database serving organizational needs. Applications are developed relying on access to the database. Users become more accountable for the integrity and correct use of the information resource.

6. **Stage 6 Maturity:** Stage 6 typifies the mature organization. The information system is integral to the functioning of the organization. The applications portfolio closely mirrors organizational activities. The data structure becomes a data model for the organization. There is a recognition of the strategic importance of information. Planning of the information system is coordinated and comprehensive. The manager of the information system takes on the same importance in the organizational hierarchy as the director of finance or the director of human resources.

The Nolan model – implications for strategic planning

The Nolan stage model was originally intended to be a descriptive/analytic model that gave an evolutionary explanation for information systems development within an organization. It identified a pattern of growth that an organization needed to go through in order to achieve maturity. Each stage involved a learning process. It was not possible to skip a stage in the growth process. As such, the model became widely accepted. On the Nolan analysis, most organizations will be at Stage 4 or Stage 5.

However, the model has also come to be used as part of a planning process. Applied in this way, the organization identifies the stage it is currently occupying. This has implications for what has to be achieved in order to progress to the next stage. Planning can and should be achieved, it is argued, in the areas of the applications portfolio, the technology used, the planning and control structures, and the level of user awareness and involvement. Managers should attend to planning, which will speed the process of progression to the next stage and the accompanying organizational learning.

The Nolan model – critique

The model is based on empirical research in the 1970s. It cannot therefore incorporate recognition of the impact of more recent technologies. In particular, its concentration on database technology ignores the fact that:

- the growth of desktop computers has significantly increased the extent to which users have been able to use information technology and to become autonomous of the computer centre;
- there have been important developments in the area of communications and networks, especially local area networks linking desktop computers and other technologies together; and
- new software development tools and decision support tools have shifted the emphasis to the user as development agent.

Despite these limitations, the Nolan stage model still provides a way of viewing the development of information systems in an organization by recognizing:

- that growth of information systems in an organization must be accompanied by an organizational learning process;
- that there is an important interplay between the stimulation of growth involving the presence of slack resources together with the need for control;

Figure 2.5 Earl's model of multiple learning curves

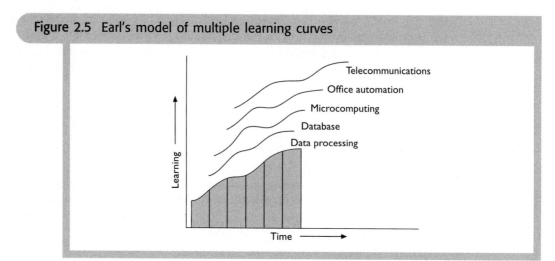

(Adapted from Galliers and Sutherland, 1991)

- that there is a shift of emphasis between the users and the computer centre in the process of growth; and
- that there is a move from concentration on processor technology to data management.

The Earl model

Earl (1989), along with others (e.g. Hirscheim *et al.*, 1988; Galliers and Sutherland, 1991), takes seriously the idea of maturity through stages of growth. For Earl, it is of particular importance to note that stages of growth apply to different technologies. The S-curve represents cycles of new technological developments where there is a sudden increase in understanding leading to a new plateau; this process of further developments and improvements and a higher plateau is a perpetual feature. This pattern is reflected for each technology, with the relationship existing between the degree of organizational learning, the technology and time (see Figure 2.5). It is also acknowledged that different parts of the organization may be at different points in the stages of growth.

Earl's model concentrates not on the interplay between expenditure and control but rather on the task and objectives of planning at each stage. The view taken by Earl is that the early focus in information systems development is around the extent of IT coverage and the attempt to satisfy user demands. As the organization develops along the learning curve the orientation of planning changes. Senior managers recognize the need for information systems development to link to business objectives and so take a major role in the planning process. During the final stages of growth the planning of information systems takes on a strategic perspective, with planning being carried out by teams consisting of senior management, users and information systems staff (see Table 2.1).

2.3.4 Dynamic interaction of internal forces

Nolan and Earl were interested in the various internal stages of growth through which organizations progress in the use of information technology, together with the implications of this for strategic planning. The current section takes a different perspective in

Table 2.1 Earl's stage planning model (Galliers and Sutherland, 1991)

Factor	Stages					
	I	*II*	*III*	*IV*	*V*	*VI*
Task	Meeting demands	IS/IT audit	Business support	Detailed planning	Strategic advantage	Business–IT strategy linkage
Objective	Provide service	Limit demand	Agree priorities	Balance IS portfolio	Pursue opportunities	Integrate strategies
Driving force	IS reaction	IS led	Senior management led	User/IS partnership	IS/executive led: user involvement	Strategic coalitions
Methodological emphasis	*Ad hoc*	Bottom-up survey	Top-down analysis	Two-way prototyping	Environmental scanning	Multiple methods
Context	User/IS inexperience	Inadequate IS resources	Inadequate business/IS plans	Complexity apparent	IS for competitive advantage	Maturity, collaboration
Focus	IS department			Organization-wide		Environment

that it concentrates on internal organizational forces and how these must be acknowledged in the derivation of a business information systems strategy.

It has long been recognized that there is an internal organizational interaction between people, the tasks they perform, the technology they use to perform these tasks and the structure of the organization in which they work. This derives from organizational psychology and has influenced strategy formulation and, among other areas, approaches to the analysis and design of information systems (see Section 16.5.2 on socio-technical analysis and design).

Following this theme, an organization may be viewed as being subject to five internal forces in a state of dynamic equilibrium (as well as being subject to external influences and forces). This is illustrated in Figure 2.6. It is the central goal of the organization's

Figure 2.6 The dynamic interaction of internal forces

59

management to control these forces and their interaction over time in order that the organization may meet its business objectives and its mission. Scott Morton (1994) takes this model as the basis for research into the likely impacts that changes in IT will have on organizations, and to provide theories of management on how these changes may be steered to the benefit of the organizations concerned.

1. **Technology** will continue to change. The effect of this will be to cut down 'distance' within the organization as geographical separation is rendered less important. This will be aided through the development of telecommunications and will be evidenced by new applications such as e-mail, intranets, video-conferencing and shared data resources. The organizational memory and access to it will be improved through more effective classification of data and its storage.

2. **Individuals and their roles** will change as information technology provides support for tasks and increases interconnection within the organization. This will require significant investment in training and the reclassification of roles. The nature of jobs will change as IT facilitates some roles, makes some redundant and has no effect on others.

3. The **structure** of the organization will change as roles vary. The greater interconnection brought about by information technology will lead to integration at the functional level.

4. **Management processes** will be assisted by the provision of easy access to fast, flexible, virtually costless, decision-relevant internal information. This will enable new approaches to operational planning and control within the organization.

5. The key to effective planning and to the benefits of new information systems enabled by information technology lies in the proper use of **strategy**. This will ensure that information systems/information technology developments are aligned with the business strategy.

2.3.5 Exploitation of IT through the value chain

Continuing developments in information technology, together with decreasing costs, have enabled businesses to exploit new opportunities to change the nature of competition. In a series of publications (Porter, 1980, 1985; Porter and Millar, 1985), Michael Porter has developed a model of a business organization and its associated industry by focusing on the value chain and the competitive forces experienced (five forces model). This allows an understanding of the way competition affects strategy and the way information provision, in its turn, affects competition.

Central to Porter's analysis of the internal aspects of the business and the strategy for its exploitation of IT is the value chain. The **value chain** identifies those activities that the firm must carry out in order to function effectively (see Figure 2.7). The value chain consists of nine **value activities**. Each of these activities adds value to the final product. In order to be competitively advantaged, the business must carry out these activities at a lower cost than its competitors or must use these activities to create a product that is differentiated from those of its competitors and thereby be able to charge a premium price for the product. The nine activities are divided into two categories: **primary activities**, which are concerned with the direct generation of the organization's output to its customers; and **support activities**, which contribute to the operation of the primary activities.

Figure 2.7 The value chain

Support activities	Organizational infrastructure						Margin = Value Added – Cost
	Development product/technology						
	Human resource management						
	Procurement						
		Inbound logistics (receipt/ warehousing of input)	Operations (manufacture of product)	Outbound logistics (distribution of product)	Sales and marketing	Customer service	

Primary activities

- **Primary activities**
  - *inbound logistics*: activities that bring inputs into the organization, such as receipt of goods, warehousing, inventory control;
  - *operations*: activities that transform the product into its final form, whether it be physical good or service;
  - *outbound logistics*: activities that despatch products and distribute them to clients;
  - *marketing and sales*: activities concerned with locating and attracting customers for the purchase of the product – for example advertising;
  - *service*: activities that provide service and support to customers – for example maintenance, installation.

- **Support activities**
  - *firm infrastructure*: activities that support the whole value chain – for example general management, financial planning;
  - *human resource management*: activities concerned with training, recruitment and personnel resource planning;
  - *technology development*: activities that identify and develop ways in which machines and other kinds of technology can assist the firm's activities;
  - *procurement*: activities that locate sources of input and purchase these inputs.

As well as having a physical component, every value activity creates and uses information. The competitive advantage of the organization is enhanced by reducing costs in each activity as compared with its competitors. Information technology is used to reduce the cost of the information component of each activity. For instance, inbound logistics activities use information technology to provide information on goods received and use this to update inventory records. Financial planning, an infrastructure activity, will use information technology to collect information provided by many of the firm's activities to generate forecasts on future performance. Information technology may also

Figure 2.8 Information technology in the value chain

Support activities	Organizational infrastructure	Financial planning models Space optimization		Administrative information Building management systems	**Margin = Value Added − Cost**
	Development product/ technology	Computer-aided design Market analysis/modelling			
	Human resource management	Optimization of distribution of personnel			
	Procurement	Electronic procurement e.g. electronic data interchange (EDI)			
		Automated warehousing	Customization of manufacturing process	Processing orders (through EDI) and automated distribution	Telemarketing	Online monitoring and servicing of equipment. Scheduling servicing
		Inbound logistics (receipt/ warehousing of input)	Operations (manufacture of product)	Outbound logistics (distribution of product)	Sales and marketing	Customer service

Primary activities

be used to increase product differentiation for specific customer needs. For instance, operations can use information technology to control the production process to generate tailor-made output for customers.

Where previously the organization relied on the manual production of information, it is now more common for information technology to permeate its entire value chain (see Figure 2.8). The greater the extent to which this reduces costs or enables product differentiation the greater the competitive advantage conferred on the business.

The organization's value chain is composed of a set of interdependent activities that are linked to one another. These **linkages** need to be coordinated in order to ensure that the activities are carried out in the most effective way. Information is necessary to manage these linkages. One way that this may occur is in **just-in-time (JIT) manufacturing**. JIT is an approach to production that requires the output of each stage of the production process to be fed into the following stage without undergoing an intermediate storage stage of indefinite length. The benefits of JIT are that it removes intermediate inventory storage costs for personnel and space and prevents the organization's working capital being tied up in goods waiting in the production process. JIT can also be extended outside the organization to include the purchase of inputs that are delivered just in time for the manufacturing process, which in turn produces an output just in time to meet the specific needs of a customer. **Automated billing systems** or **electronic data interchange (EDI)** can be used for the external linkages. The application of JIT can be viewed as an increase in the degree of systems coupling, as described in Section 1.4.3. The goal is to reduce the necessity for the inventory illustrated in Figure 1.11 and introduce more effective linkages between the systems. For

JIT to work the effective management of these linkages is imperative, and it is here that information technology can provide the necessary information – accurately and on time. Hence cost reductions in the organization's value activities are achieved and the business can gain a competitive advantage.

In summary, information technology is at the basis of information systems in business, which increase the competitive advantage of that business over its competitors by:

- reducing the cost of the information component of value activities;
- allowing product differentiation; and
- providing information for the effective management of linkages.

The importance of this approach is that it views information not merely as a support for the tasks that a business undertakes but rather as permeating the entire set of business activities. As such, its correct provision can give the organization a strategic competitive advantage over its rivals in the industry.

Mini case 2.3

Managing information systems

Business intelligence software is a classic product for the post-bubble era. Many companies that spent heavily on new technology in the late 1990s have been left with a problem: much of their corporate information resides in different software applications and on different computer systems, none of which were built to talk to each other.

How best to dig for and analyse information that would give a fuller picture of a company's operations? The answer to that question could unlock more of the value from the vast sunk cost that has gone into existing systems, prompting companies to buy even at a time when most new IT developments have been put on hold.

According to research group IDC, the market for business intelligence software is already worth more than $7bn worldwide and could double by 2006.

Aside from bulking up and broadening out, the specialist software makers are trying to persuade companies to think of their products as a completely new class of software – a classic tactic of tech entrepreneurs, who have always strived to set themselves apart from established industry leaders.

According to Jeffrey Rodek, chairman and chief executive of Hyperion, business intelligence software, by its nature, has to stand apart.

Since it taps into different database formats, it cannot be provided by rival database makers such as IBM, Oracle or Microsoft. And since it draws on a wide array of software applications, it cannot come from application makers such as SAP and Oracle.

'The aim is to create the category clearly in customers' minds,' says Mr Rodek.

Adapted from: COMPANIES THE AMERICAS: Fighting with giants for the business intelligence market
By Richard Waters
Financial Times: 15 August 2003

Questions

1. Over a period of time an organization might install a number of different information systems across the value chain. What advantages might accrue from combining these systems?

2. What problems do you envisage in employing business intelligence software as referred to above?

Figure 2.9 The strategic grid

(Adapted from McFarlan and McKenny, 1983)

2.3.6 The strategic grid

The strategic grid (McFarlan and McKenny, 1983; McFarlan, 1984) assists the organization to determine in which of four categories it finds itself with respect to the impact of IT and its information systems (see Figure 2.9).

The grid plots the extent to which the **existing** applications portfolio has a strategic impact against the likely strategic impact of the **planned** applications development. The four possible resulting positions are:

1. **Support:** The role of the information system is to support the transaction-processing requirements of the organization. Information technology is utilized to bring about cost reduction, and information is produced as a by-product of the process.

2. **Factory:** The current information systems are an integral part of the strategic plan of the organization. Few strategic developments are planned, and the focus of IT activity is on improving existing systems.

3. **Turnaround:** This is a transitional phase. Organizations move from the 'support' category to this as a result of internal and external pressures. Internal pressures result from the confidence of management in the support systems together with the recognition of the strategic benefits of information technology as a competitive weapon. The external pressures come from improving technology acting as an enabler for development together with the increasing use of information technology by competitor firms in the same industry. If the firm continues with strategic innovation it will enter the 'strategic' category, otherwise it will revert to the 'factory' category.

4. **Strategic:** This category requires a continuing development of information systems through the exploitation of information technology at a strategic level. It can only be accomplished with the commitment of senior management and the recognition of the integral part played by the information system within the entire fabric of the firm's activities.

These categories aid managers in identifying the role and importance of information technology in their business. It plots 'where we are now' rather than 'where we want to go' or 'how we get there'. This is not unimportant, since each of the categories implies a strategy for the management of the information system. The 'support' and 'factory' positions are essentially static. They concern the more effective and efficient use of the existing applications portfolio and as such do not require an extensive senior management involvement. The 'turnaround' and 'strategic' categories imply a dynamic strategy that must, if it is to be successful, involve senior management in an active way in the implementation of strategy. An organization moving from one category to another should be prepared to adopt the appropriate involvement of senior management.

2.3.7 Critical success factors

The critical success factor (CSF) approach was developed initially by John Rockart (Rockart, 1979). Critical success factors are those limited areas of a firm's operations that if satisfactory will ensure that the objectives of the business are achieved. They are thus critical to the competitive performance of the organization. In order to ensure that the critical success factors are satisfactory, it is important to have appropriate information identifying their performance. This is a guide to which information systems should be developed, namely those that give information on the critical success factors, and the consequent implications for the information technology strategy.

For example, consider the case of a mail order supplier of clothes:

Objective: To increase market share by 5% per annum.

CSFs: Effective advertising; faster customer order processing; faster distribution service.

Information systems applications: Market research database and analysis; web-based order processing; computerized delivery scheduling.

Each objective taken from the strategic business plan will yield a set of CSFs. In order to identify the CSFs, which will be different for different organizations and different sectors, it is recommended that a consensus be achieved among senior managers. This can be achieved in special workshops using an outside facilitator. Not all CSFs will demand information systems support in tracking their performance. However, for those that do the method acts as a valuable way of focusing the development of information systems, particularly the applications portfolio. The strength of using CSFs is that they provide the important link between the business strategy and the information systems strategy, with the consequent impact on the information technology strategy.

The CSF approach has since been extended (Henderson *et al.*, 1987). The extended approach recognizes that critical success factors determine three distinct areas. First, each critical success factor remains critically based on only certain assumptions, and information is required on these assumptions. Second, the performance of each critical success factor must be monitored. This requires information (as explained above). Finally, each critical success factor will entail decisions that can be aided by information systems providing decision support. These three areas determine the information systems development.

2.4 Information systems strategy today

This section considers some of the developments of recent years that have challenged the accepted tenets of business and IS strategy.

2.4.1 Business strategy and IT strategy

The debate over business strategy and IT strategy has in the past focused mainly on the need for the former to precede and inform the latter. The business strategy has been perceived as the driver, while the IT strategy has guided the identification of resources and been the enabler. As information systems have become embedded into the operation of companies it has become clear that an IT strategy is a fundamental and integrated component of the overall business strategy.

The development of the Internet and electronic business has largely challenged this perceived wisdom. It has become evident over the last few years that developments in IT can be a driver for business strategy. For organizations in the Internet age, new threats and opportunities have emerged. Fundamental questions about the nature of the business, the appropriateness of business models and the structure of the organization have been asked. In these circumstances, organizations have been obliged to revisit their business strategies and reconsider the IT requirements.

The traditional approach has been one of alignment, i.e. bringing the IT strategy into line with the business strategy. Many see the future more in terms of integration rather than alignment. Creating a business strategy that recognizes the electronic business world also accepts that IT can be an input to as well as an output from the strategy formulation process. Changes in IT strategy can lead to new opportunities for business development.

A further factor is the pace of change in the business world. To reflect this rapid change, an almost continuous reassessment of IT and business strategy is needed. The traditional setting of IT strategy to meet business objectives does not recognize the rapid real-time responses necessary in the modern economy.

One school of thought divides IT investment into two pools: the mainstream and the innovative. The mainstream IT investment represents the traditional approach to developing and then implementing a well-constructed strategy. Innovative IT investment is the equivalent of the military 'rapid response unit', anticipating developments and being flexible enough to adapt to an environment or shape a new environment. As projects become embedded and established they move from the innovative to the mainstream pool. In this model, the integration model of strategy clearly has resonance with the innovative pool and the alignment model of strategy with the mainstream.

2.4.2 Enterprise resource planning (ERP)

Enterprise resource planning (ERP) systems are computer-based business management systems which integrate all aspects of a business's functions – for example, planning, manufacturing, inventory, sales, marketing, personnel and accounting.

ERP systems were developed in the late 1990s. ERP grew out of the manufacturer resource planning (MRP) of the 1980s which sought to integrate manufacturing and business functions. The effective planning of resources for a manufacturing company involves the integration of sales, operations, production scheduling, materials requirement planning and inventory, with financial reports. ERP takes this a stage further in extension to all businesses, and integrates the remaining functions using relational database and object-oriented approaches to software.

The driver for the development of ERP was the recognition by organizations that they were disadvantaged in a global marketplace if their total information system consisted of different departmental functions being supported by different non-communicating computer systems. This led to many systems being involved in the handling, say, of a customer's order, as it went through the stages of placing, manufacturing, dispatch and invoicing. Moreover, merged corporations often still held independent systems for each of the components involved in the merger. The resulting set of systems could not be accessed easily to provide overall high-level business information needed for strategic development of the entire corporation.

The above ideas and concerns were not new. However, the trigger for the expansion of ERP systems came with the need to deal with the millennium (Y2K) bug. This led many organizations to consider replacing their existing legacy systems with new systems and to capitalize on the integrative opportunities offered by ERP. The later development of the World Wide Web and the possibility of greater online interactivity with customers further stimulated the search for an integrative approach.

The purchase of an ERP system often led to a reconsideration of the structure of the organization and the way it carried out its processes. In some cases this was beneficial, but quite often the exact nature of the purchased off-the-shelf ERP system placed constraints on the way the organization should be structured, and it was not clear that this was optimal.

In summary, the advantages of ERP leading to a single system were:

- one software vendor to deal with;
- reduced maintenance and other ongoing costs;
- a unifying and integrating strategy for the organization; and
- greater comparability between systems within the organization.

However, many systems have not lived up to their (promised) potential and have resulted in high costs, lengthy delivery times and disappointing functionality. In summary:

- Systems required high initial costs and development or tailoring, requiring long lead times.
- The software required the business to re-align itself (rather than the business changing itself as a result of a more extensive business process engineering).
- The inability of the software to respond to changes in the business.

The expenditure on ERP systems is beginning to decline. It leaves several large ERP vendor companies which have grown with, or reoriented themselves to, enterprise resource planning systems. Five companies dominate the world supply of ERP products, generating over 90% of world revenues in 2000. SAP, with over 40% of the market, is the largest of these.

Mini case 2.4

Enterprise resource planning

The concept of agility is creating something of a stir among manufacturers. New techniques and technologies, it is said, will enable companies to steal a march on their less nimble rivals.

Agile manufacturing underpins the success of the Smart car, DaimlerChrysler's city car brand. Thanks to its agile processes, Smart has been able to respond rapidly to customer demands. There are now five Smart car variants, including a not-so-small roadster, introduced last month.

The Smart car is made in a purpose-built plant in Hambach, France, which is also home to the suppliers of its main parts. The production system is unusual: suppliers are given greater responsibility (Smart prefers to call them 'partners'); processes are shorter and thus more reliable; and buffer stocks are kept to a minimum, in accordance with the 'just-in-time' model.

A key feature of the plant is its 'flexibility funnel': the system holds three weeks of orders and a sequencing tool allows the plant to optimize production of the variants according to the orders in the system.

Surprisingly, there is no fancy software powering the plant – just an off-the-shelf enterprise resource planning (ERP) product from Baan, the Dutch software vendor. For simplicity, Smart chose not to develop customized software but to adopt a standard package, customizing it where necessary. For the same reason, it used established electronic data interchange (EDI) networks to communicate with its suppliers.

An important feature of the IT system is its flexibility to handle changes in existing processes and the development of new ones within a very short period of time. Smart has already put this flexibility into practice with its new Roadster model. Instead of the pure 'just-in-time' model, this car is made using a hybrid process: some stock is held in warehouses run by an external partner.

Agile and lean are not synonymous terms. Lean manufacturing dates back to an era of mass production and unchanging processes. Agile manufacturing accepts that there are things that manufacturers cannot control. So, they should adopt technologies and processes that enable them to adapt to change.

In an agile world, customers increasingly call the tune. They require more specific products and shorter lead times. Design, manufacturing and procurement have a greater tendency to be customer-driven.

Adapted from: **Customers in control**
By Geoff Nairn
FT.com site: 7 May 2003

Questions

1. What advantages did the manufacturers of the Smart car gain from using ERP software?

2. What difficulties might other organizations face in trying to emulate the experience of DaimlerChrysler?

2.4.3 Business process re-engineering

In the early 1990s, much attention was given to **business process re-engineering** (BPR). This strategy demands a fundamental rethinking of how business processes are executed. It aims to bring about dramatic improvements by redesigning core activities such as production or sales order processing.

The origins of BPR are in the failures of organizations beset with rigid functional structures. Innovation and flexibility are often not encouraged in a strongly demarcated environment. BPR involves the consideration of particular core business processes and analysing them from start to finish. Existing structures such as departmental roles or responsibilities are ignored in an attempt to identify the key features of the business process. For example, a purchase might be followed from initial customer interest, through enquiry, order, delivery, settlement and after-sales service. Many different departments and personnel might be involved in the entire business process. By analysing the process like this, it might be possible to see why, for example, orders are delayed, delivery is made to incorrect locations or after-sales service does not meet expectations. Individuals are often too close to the process or have their own vested interests and agendas, which impede the effective completion of the process.

The evaluation of BPR has been varied. The early BPR projects took place in the difficult atmosphere of 'downsizing' in the early 1990s. The lessons of implementation were often learned 'the hard way', and the resulting effect on companies, and more so their employees, left bitter memories for many.

The critics of BPR point to its very high failure rate, with only about 30% of BPR projects clearly delivering the expected results. Their case is backed up by numerous examples of companies that effectively re-engineered themselves into liquidation. The strategy is clearly one of high risk. Fundamental change is rarely going to be readily accepted.

The proponents of BPR would say that the need to change is often inevitable. Leaner, fitter organizations, they claim, can only be produced through fundamental review and change, and failure to do so could lead to a more rapid and pronounced slide towards failure. They also point out that the critics of BPR have often characterized its use as mere 'downsizing', implying a straightforward shedding of staff and breaking up of business units. Supporters of BPR claim that it involves a much more philosophical review of the business.

Recently, the language of re-engineering has become more tempered, and many companies are considering business process improvements. This implies a more gradual and incremental strategy of looking at core processes, but perhaps just one at a time, thereby minimizing the disruption to the organization as a whole.

Mini case 2.5

Business process management

The fact that legal staff at Birmingham-based law firm Martineau Johnson are no longer drowning in the 3,500 paper documents generated each week is largely thanks to its business process management (BPM) system. Installed in autumn 2002 to accelerate the approval and processing of forms (particularly client cheques), BPM has significantly reduced internal bureaucracy and made the company more competitive.

▶

In the year since Ken Agnew, IT director at Martineau Johnson, installed the system, he has recouped the original £40,000 purchase cost.

'We recognized common processes between different charities and in one week built a proof of concept working system for one charity which demonstrated what could be delivered by BPM,' he explained. 'We then replicated the process throughout the other charities and in eight weeks had all 43 charity clients fully automated on the system.'

A new digital dictation system uses e-Work to smooth out the peaks and troughs in the typing load, ensuring that clerical staff are neither overburdened nor underworked.

Financial information is now keyed into the right part of the system at the start, thereby reducing duplicated effort, manual errors and the need for paper documents.

'BPM allows the company to see the whole picture, cuts down the amount of traffic on the network and builds in the flexibility to direct work accurately,' explains Mr. Agnew. 'Ours is an internally built, bespoke system that does what our users want it to do.'

Adapted from: **Martineau Johnson: a BPR Case Study**
By Priscilla Awde
FT.com site: 5 November 2003

Questions

1. In what way does business process management challenge the traditional departmental view of an organization?

2. What improvements did Martineau Johnson make in business processes management? To what extent can these improvements be applied to other organizations?

2.4.4 Outsourcing

The first business information systems tended to be developed and supported using in-house expertise. Project teams were set up to establish the needs and requirements and to specify the solutions. Consultants were often used to facilitate this process but the ownership was usually clearly located with the initiating organization. As the system was implemented, systems support and user support was provided by IT or computer services staff working for a department with its own line management structure. This model still prevails, particularly in many larger companies.

Over a period of time the concept of outsourcing has gained credence. Under this strategy a separate budget is established to finance the information systems requirements and then tenders are invited for the provision of the required services. The costs, risks and the associated research and development implications are transferred to the outsourcing agent thereby freeing the initiating organization to concentrate on its own area of business expertise. Specialist IT providers can reduce the cost of these services due to economies gained through specializing in this one activity. Recently there has been an increasing trend in outsourcing provision to economies such as India and the Far East where skill levels are high but wages are lower than in the West. Both routine systems maintenance and new project developments are increasingly being outsourced adopting this strategy.

There are several reasons for adopting this approach:

- Businesses will not necessarily have the technical expertise to develop and support systems.
- In all but the largest organizations there may not be a sufficient IT requirement to justify or to retain the best technical and support staff.
- Outsource providers can specialize in their field and gain extensive sophisticated knowledge which an individual business in a non-computing-related sector could never achieve.
- Unlike an in-company IT department, outsourced service providers can seek economies, such as contracting staff overseas, to carry out functions at a reduced cost.

There are, however, some disadvantages:

- There is an inevitable loss of immediate control over the outsourced service.
- Although the initial contracting process might establish a lower cost solution, many organizations retain the services of the outsourcing company for long periods, vesting the outsourcer with an invaluable, almost unique understanding of the organization. This renders difficult any termination of the contract. In this situation the cost saving can be lost.
- There may be ethical issues concerning the employment contracts of workers in low pay economies.

A number of services can be outsourced. Some examples include:

- system development, particularly coding software from a specification;
- system maintenance, such as hardware support, helpdesk provision;
- data entry and data conversion;
- document management such as scanning, OCR, OMR (discussed in the next chapter);
- Web site design and web hosting;
- back office operations, including call centres.

One way that organizations can outsource their software requirements is to make use of an **application service provider** (ASP). These are third-party businesses that manage software systems and services. Unlike a software vendor, an ASP will usually maintain a central access point to their services and will distribute their software over a wide area network, often using the Internet. Costs to the customer can be reduced as the expense of, for example, purchasing a mainframe computer, or an enterprise-level database solution such as Oracle is passed on to the ASP who can distribute it over its customer base. The charge can be made on a per-usage basis or can be by subscription. ASPs might specialize in a particular sector of the economy, such as local government or health care, or might focus on clients by size, such as high-end enterprise solutions or pre-packaged mass-volume solutions. One of the most widely used applications is that of web hosting where the ASP provides expertise in the service along with web servers and other networking hardware, software, high bandwidth, backup and maintenance services.

Mini case 2.6

Outsourcing

Jack Welch, GE's former chief executive, was one of the first western business leaders to recognize the importance of business process outsourcing and India's potential as a cost effective offshore outsourcing centre. About 48 per cent of GE's software is now developed in India.

For most Indian software and services companies, breaking into the GE account was an important milestone – even if the work was mundane maintenance work or more recently, mainframe migration projects. That is because GE's projects typically stretch over a period of several years, ensuring a regular flow of revenues.

GE has also been growing its outsourced back office operations in India rapidly in recent years. GE's massive consumer finance division saves between 30 and 35 per cent by outsourcing services such as analytics, collections, help desk and e-learning to India.

Overall, GE now employs 22,000 people in India including 13,000 working in call centres that handle about 40 per cent of GE's total call centre traffic. Offshore outsourcing like this has enabled GE to transform its cost structure and provide an improved service to its customers.

GE has gone a step further setting up a $80m multi-discipline research and development site in Bangalore, the southern city at the centre of India's rapidly expanding IT software and services industry. It employs 1,600 scientists and technicians and supports GE's 13 business sectors which assign projects on the basis of each centre's expertise.

Adapted from: **GE: Trailblazing the Indian phenomenon**
By Paul Taylor in New York
FT.com site: 2 July 2003

Questions

1. What benefits does a company like GE obtain from outsourcing?
2. What ethical implications are raised from this business strategy?

Summary

There is a general recognition that businesses must plan strategically in order to ensure that individual operating units act in a coordinated way to support the business objectives of the organization, that those objectives are realizable given the internal resources within the business and the external environment, and that current and future resource allocation is directed to the realization of these corporate objectives. Although there is no one accepted method of strategic planning, central themes are commonly accepted. Specifically, there must be a determination of business objectives, an identification of future performance against these objectives and the development of a plan to close any identified gap.

Businesses are commonly viewed as being composed of various functions. Each of these will require information in order to plan, operate and monitor performance. The function of the provision of information is thus key to an organization's success. The development of an information systems strategy to support this function recognizes the priority of information systems planning over information technology planning. The latter supports the former.

There are many frameworks within which one can develop an information systems strategy. The one provided in this chapter distinguishes the information systems strategy from the information technology strategy and within the former recognizes both the influence of factors external to the organization and those internal to it.

Factors external to the firm include the forces exerted on it, depending on the structure of the industry within which it operates. These competitive forces may be exerted by suppliers, customers, existing competitors or new entrants, or through differentiated products. An analysis of these forces can provide a guide to information systems strategy. A PEST analysis takes into account other political, economic, socio-cultural and technological influences.

Emphasizing internal factors, the work of Nolan suggests that organizations undergo a series of discrete stages of development in their evolution. By identifying the current stage, an organization can plan the most effective and swift route to the next. Although this research was based largely on the evolution of mainframe systems, there are striking similarities with the development of microcomputers and local area networks. This approach has been extended by Earl. As well as the internal evolution of the information system within the organization and its connection with technological development, it is important to recognize that the technology will have an impact on the work of individuals and the roles they fulfil. Management control may be significantly affected, along with the internal structure of the organization. This must be taken into account in the formulation of strategy.

The work of Porter and Millar views the firm as being composed of a linked value chain consisting of nine primary and supporting activities. If an organization is to be competitive then each of these must function at a cost advantage over similar functions within its competitors or help to produce a differentiated product. The way in which information technology can be used as a competitive weapon and support these activities and coordinate their linkages was examined. The strategic grid of McFarlan and McKenny identifies the strategic impact of existing computer-supported applications as compared with planned applications. The firm broadly falls into one of four categories – support, factory, turnaround or strategic. Different information systems strategies are suggested depending on which category best fits an organization currently and which best fits its likely development.

Critical successful factor approaches view an organization as being crucially dependent on certain factors to meet its objectives. In order to keep the organization on its planned course in reaching these objectives, information on the workings of the factors needs to be supplied by the information system. In this way, the strategic information system needs of an organization can be identified and information technology planned to support them.

This chapter looks at a selection of the more influential approaches to information systems strategic planning. Other approaches, for example the information engineering approach, attempt to provide a methodology for the complete planning and development process from strategic information systems through to the implementation of designed systems. The emphasis of this chapter has been that business information needs should determine strategy, not the characteristics of the various technologies. Recently, some authors have challenged this view, citing developments in the Internet and e-commerce as evidence of technology driving business strategy.

Review questions

1. Why do businesses and other organizations have to plan strategically? What factors affect the timescale of the strategic plan?

2. How does information systems planning differ from information technology planning?

3. Outline the main characteristics of the following models and frameworks for analysis of strategy:

   (a) The five forces model
   (b) PEST analysis
   (c) Nolan's stage model
   (d) The Earl model
   (e) Internal forces model
   (f) The value chain
   (g) The strategic grid
   (h) Critical success factors

Exercises

1. Consider the business, organization or university in which you work. Does it have:

   (a) a strategic plan?
   (b) process for developing and reviewing this strategy?
   (c) an information systems strategic plan?
   (d) a process for developing and reviewing the information systems strategy?

2. Explain and apply the *five forces* model to:

   (a) a bank
   (b) a holiday travel company.

3. By considering the business, organization or university in which you work, apply the Porter value chain analysis. To what extent is it appropriate? To what extent are information systems used in supporting the activities and linkages? To what extent could information systems be further used?

4. Analyse the applicability of the Nolan stage model to your organization.

5. How does the Nolan stage model differ from the Earl model, and what are the likely implications for planning?

6. What are the objectives of the organization in which you work? What are the factors critical to the success of meeting these objectives? To what extent do computerized information systems play a role in the provision of information on these factors?

7. Outline factors along the lines of a PEST analysis specifically related to:

   (a) a bank
   (b) a university
   (c) a motor manufacturer.

CASE STUDY 2

Information systems strategy and business value

The current pace of innovation in information and communication technologies, coupled with competing projects and shifting business priorities, no doubt presents business leaders with a number of paths in the road toward business value.

Information technology, in particular, continues to simplify and decrease the cost of interactions with both customers and suppliers. With these developments, businesses face new opportunities to restructure their value chains by focusing on core competencies and spinning off or outsourcing non-crucial business capabilities. At the same time, IT groups are expected to deliver increasing service levels and deliver more cost-effective support for the business priorities.

The context above raises the question about the changing role of IT within the enterprise and the IT levers that can be employed to deliver value. A global A.T. Kearney study conducted by Harris Interactive asked executives how they manage and use IT to create measurable business value and position their companies for future competitive advantage. We found that the leading performers consistently master the following:

- Move toward integration of business, technology and investment strategies.

- Manage IT as a portfolio of business elements from operational costs to innovative opportunities.

- Invest in leading-edge, innovative IT as an organisational activity aimed at delivering business value.

Companies can integrate IT and business strategies by viewing IT planning and execution as an integrated process, based on a partnership between the business and IT executives. Rather than passing the baton like runners in a relay race, business and IT executives need to move together toward the finish line. Most firms that create value from IT go a step further by incorporating their investment strategy as part of this mix. The result is a coherent IT investment plan that delivers the appropriate level of IT sophistication for the different business capabilities, depending on how each capability is expected to contribute to customer value and competitive differentiation.

But today's organizations are rarely structured to realize the benefits that such a model can deliver. The study reveals that although companies believe that IT adds value to their business, their planning and governance models do not allow the organization to capture full benefits from their IT investments. According to the study, 91% of executives say IT enables business strategies, and almost all state that IT creates value relative to their competition.

Yet, only one-third say that their IT planning is fully integrated with their business strategy. And although business value wields increasing influence in IT project sponsorship, IT executives often lack access to the boardroom. Only 35% of the companies surveyed involved IT in the overall capital planning process.

There are many reasons for the prevalent divide. At a structural level, changes can be made to increase collaboration and accountability. Just as technology executives should be held accountable for business results, business managers should be responsible for realizing results from IT investments.

Along with structural changes, business and IT executives must also support and lead the charge toward integration. In leading organizations, the chief information officer (CIO) operates as a business leader who understands technology. Today's CIO must be able to articulate to top management, business unit leaders and line employees how new technology can help achieve the business goals.

One survey respondent, Lands' End, represents an example of effective integration. The executive team, consisting of the CIO and other senior leaders, formulates business strategies and initiatives. Key strategic and technology initiatives are communicated to all employees to ensure that everyone is aware of the strategic direction. An IT steering committee, made up of business vice-presidents and the CIO, prioritizes IT initiatives and approves its technology blueprint. The CIO summarizes four key roles that he needs to perform in order to be effective: strategist, business partner, architect and executive.

Today's businesses face a constantly changing landscape that will force closer collaboration between the business and IT areas. IT has moved beyond support status to become a key contributor to value. A solid partnership will not happen overnight as too many changes in strategy, culture, organization and process are involved. Yet, this shift cannot be avoided. Companies that begin strengthening IT and business partnerships and move strategically toward more integrated strategies will be well positioned for continued success and growth.

Adapted from: **The role of IT in business value**
Bangkok Post – Thailand: 27 November 2003

Questions

1. Business strategy and information systems and technology strategies should be aligned. Which themes from the case study above support this assertion?

2. What analytical tools can organizations employ to 'simplify and decrease the cost of interactions with both customers and suppliers'?

3. Why is it important for organizations to focus on the value chain within their area of business?

4. Why is it important to consider 'spinning off or outsourcing non-crucial business capabilities'?

References

Earl M. (1989). *Management Strategies for Information Management*. Hemel Hempstead: Prentice Hall

Galliers R.D. and Sutherland A.R. (1991). Information systems management and strategy formulation: the 'stages of growth' model revisited. *Journal of Information Systems*, 1, 89–114
   This article explains the most important stages of growth models together with critiques. It also develops the authors' own variant.

Henderson J., Rockart J. and Sifonis J. (1987). Integrating management support systems into strategic information systems planning. *Journal of Management Information Systems*, 4(1), 5–24

Hirscheim R., Earl M., Feeny D. and Lockett M. (1988). An exploration into the management of the information systems function. In *Proceedings Information Technology Management for Productivity and Strategic Advantage*, IFIP Conference, March 1988

McFarlan F.W. (1984). Information technology changes the way you compete. *Harvard Business Review*, May–June, 98–103

McFarlan F.W. and McKenny J.L. (1983). *Corporate Information Management: The Issues Facing Senior Management*. Homewood, Ill.: Dow-Jones-Irwin

Nolan R.L. (1979). Managing the crisis in data processing. *Harvard Business Review*, March–April, 115–26

Nolan R. (1984). Managing the advanced stages of computer technology: key research issues. In *The Information Systems Research Challenge*, McFarlan F.W. (ed.), pp. 195–214. Boston: Harvard Business School Press

Porter M.E. (1980). *Competitive Strategy*. New York: Free Press

Porter M.E. (1985). *Competitive Advantage*. New York: Free Press

Porter M.E. and Millar V.E. (1985). How information gives you competitive advantage. *Harvard Business Review*, July–August, 149–60

Rockart J. (1979). Chief executives define their own data needs. *Harvard Business Review*, March–April, 81–92

Scott Morton, M.S. (ed.) (1994). *Information Technology and the Corporation of the 1990s*. Oxford: Oxford University Press

Recommended reading

Frenzel C.W. (2003). *Management of Information Technology*, 4th edn. Thompson Course Technology

A comprehensive book covering the development of IT strategy and IT planning. The book adopts a distinctive flavour by considering alternatives to traditional approaches and change management.

Galliers R.D. and Leidner D.E. (2003). *Strategic Information Management*, 3rd edn. Butterworth-Heinemann

Many of the leading academics in the area have contributed chapters on information systems and management to this book which is aimed at the MBA market. Information systems strategy and planning, and the relation between business strategy and information systems strategy is covered, as is its relation to the organizational environment.

Grindley K. (1995). *Managing IT at Board Level: The Hidden Agenda*, 2nd edn. London: Financial Times Prentice Hall

This is a readable, 'punchy' non-technical coverage of how management is coping/not coping with the problems of IT. It contains references to many practical examples.

Johnson G. and Scholes K. (2003). *Exploring Corporate Strategy*, 6th edn. Hemel Hempstead: Prentice Hall

This is a standard text on strategic analysis, choice and implementation. It is aimed at students on BA business studies and MBAs. It covers many of the major themes on strategic choice together with examples, exercises and case studies and has a European orientation, although some US cases are covered. Although it is not specifically aimed at IT, there is much of relevance to the strategic use of IT. There is also an accompanying 'text and cases' book.

Klepper R. and Jones W.O. (1998). *Outsourcing Information Technology Systems and Services*. Prentice Hall

A comprehensive coverage of outsourcing, including useful sections on contract negotiation and managing the outsourcing process.

McNurlin B.C. and Sprague R.H., Jr (2003). *Information Systems Management in Practice*, 6th edn. Hemel Hempstead: Prentice Hall

A standard comprehensive text covering the strategy and management of all aspects of information systems. Each chapter has exercises and discussion questions.

Mintzberg H., Quinn J.B. and Ghoshal S. (2003). *The Strategy Process*. Hemel Hempstead: Prentice Hall

Although not particularly directed at information systems or information technology, this major text has a very clear explanation of the entire strategy formulation process. It is readable, with many well-worked case studies. The length of the book, over 1000 pages, makes it a comprehensive reference.

Robson W. (1997) *Strategic Management and Information Systems: An Integrated Approach*, 2nd edn. London: Pitman

This is a comprehensive text covering all aspects of information systems strategy and the management of information systems. It covers strategic management, management of information systems and risk management of corporate information systems. It is also useful as a reference text.

Sahay S., Nicholson B. and Krishna S. (2003). *Global IT Outsourcing: Software Development across Borders*. Cambridge University Press

This traces the management of software development across international boundaries by using case studies from North America, Europe and Asia. The latter chapters analyse the challenges facing the management of global software alliances.

Ward J. and Peppard J. (2002). *Strategic Planning for Information Systems*. Wiley

A very well-written account of the effect that information systems have had on organizations, in particular focusing on their strategic development. The book discusses tools, techniques and management frameworks and emphasizes the importance of information systems in implementing a strategic plan.

Chapter 3

Business information technology

Introduction

In Chapter 1, the areas of information, systems and business information systems were approached from the perspective of information provision for business needs and in particular for decision support. Little emphasis was placed on the role of technology. In order to understand how computers can be used in the provision of business information, and their scope and limitations, it is important to have a basic understanding of the technological concepts. This chapter achieves this by first placing current technology within the historical context of its evolution over the last 50 years. The functional components of a computer are then explained, together with the way each function is performed by various types of hardware. The concept of a program is central to understanding the provision of computer-generated information. Various categories of programming language, including fourth-generation languages and their role in prototyping, are compared. Finally, organizations have a choice between applications packages and specially commissioned software. The advantages of each are outlined.

3.1 Historical development of computing technology

Electronic computers are a comparatively modern invention, although their manual predecessors go back several centuries. The mathematicians Pascal and Leibnitz developed some of the first primitive calculating machines in the seventeenth century. It was not until the mid-nineteenth century, however, that Charles Babbage designed his 'analytical engine'. This was to be a mechanical device incorporating a punched card input, memory, calculation section, automatic output and, importantly, a series of instructions that would control its operation.

3.1.1 The first generation

Progress in electronics allowed the first *electronic* computer to be built in the early 1940s. This was centred around the electronic valve. The valve is a device about the size of a small domestic electric light bulb. The valve is responsible for regulating and amplifying flows of electricity.

The first computers were seen mainly as pieces of research or military equipment, but by the mid-1950s, the possibility of using computers for business data processing was realized. In 1954, the first commercial computers, were produced. They were used for simple repetitive tasks that, until then, had been labour-intensive. Examples were payroll, billing and simple accounts processing. All the earliest computers were based on the valve. Unfortunately, valves are unreliable, consume a great deal of power, generate much unwanted heat and are large, expensive and slow in operation. In short, the development of the computer was limited by the operating characteristics of the electronics from which it was built.

3.1.2 The second generation

The reason for the increased interest and use of computers in the late 1950s and early 1960s was the development of the **second generation** of computers. These were based around the new technology of the solid-state transistor. Compared with the valve, the transistor:

- is faster in operation
- is more reliable
- uses less power
- is smaller in physical size (about the size of the head of a match)
- generates less heat
- costs less.

Not only had the hardware technology improved, so had the software. Instead of writing programs using instructions coded in 1s and 0s (or simple mnemonic translations of these instructions), programs were now written in specialized languages such as COBOL. This increased the productivity of programmers and enabled them to write more sophisticated software for business data processing.

3.1.3 The third generation

The miniaturization of transistors and their integration on circuit boards ushered in the next generation of computers. During the 1960s and early 1970s the cost of computers dropped. This was accompanied by an increase in their power. Smaller computers were now being built, and a number of firms entered the market specializing in these **minicomputers**. Businesses were beginning to use computers for a larger variety of purposes than previously. They were used not only for transaction processing but also for the provision of information for managerial decision making – MIS had been born. Computing equipment was now becoming cheap enough for medium-sized companies to purchase their own computing facilities. The technology of disk storage was also improving, becoming cheaper and more reliable, and providing larger storage capacities and faster access.

3.1.4 The fourth generation

The fourth generation of computers was stimulated by the dramatic developments in microchip technology. A **microchip** is a flake of silicon, smaller than a fingernail, on which millions of transistors have been etched in a mass-production process. Once again, compared with the previous technology the microchip was very much faster, cheaper, more reliable and smaller. As well as carrying out calculations, computers need to have a memory from which data and the program can be quickly retrieved. Microchips could also be used as the hardware for this fast-access memory storage. Developed in the 1970s, microchips became used in computers in the middle to late years of the decade. Firms such as Intel and Motorola have established leading positions in the worldwide production of microchips.

One of the major impacts of the microchip was that it at last became feasible to build small, cheap **microcomputers**. This potential was first exploited commercially by Apple Computers and later by IBM which entered the market in the early 1980s and rapidly established an industry standard with the IBM PC. The comparatively high price of IBM hardware has allowed cheaper copies (or 'clones' as they are called) of the IBM series to be built using the same types of microchip. These function like the IBM microcomputers and can all use the same software. These are often described as a personal computer (PC) or desktop PC. There are two further categories, or **platforms**, of microcomputer: the Apple Macintosh (Mac) and the workstation.

The Mac has a fundamentally different and unique philosophy in terms of ease of use and extensibility. It has a different architecture and employs a different operating system. Designers and publishers often have a particular affinity for the Mac.

The workstation, such as the Sun SparcStation, is a high-powered microcomputer often employed in engineering and computer graphics environments.

Although many software packages are available for all three microcomputer platforms, they need to be programmed specifically for the operating system used by that platform. The categorization 'microcomputer' is less fashionable now, and often the term 'desktop computer' or PC is used in its place.

More recent developments include highly portable microcomputers such as a **laptop**, or **notebook** and **tablet PCs**. These weigh five or six pounds, are the size of A4 paper and are about an inch thick. The performance of these machines approximates that of their more bulky desktop brothers but because they are small enough to be carried in a briefcase, they bring genuine portability to business computing.

Mini case 3.1

Tablet PCs

A year ago, a handful of the biggest names in personal computers launched the tablet PC at a razzmatazz event in New York. The launch was designed to prove that innovation was still thriving in the PC industry.

Tablet PCs come in two types. Some are 'slate' devices designed to be used mainly with a pen-like stylus device. Others, dubbed 'convertibles', feature keyboards and ingenious hinges that enable them to be configured like a traditional 'clamshell' notebook PC. Typically these sell for more than comparably configured traditional notebook PCs.

From the outset, the tablet PC has stirred strong emotions. Proponents insist it is the future of portable computing and will eventually be accepted by the mass market. Critics say it fails to answer any real computing need, costs too much and will always be confined to niche markets such as healthcare, insurance and field sales operations. Sales in some markets, particularly Europe, have failed to live up to even modest expectations.

Another barrier has been the lack of packaged software designed specifically for tablet PCs. There are a few exceptions, including MindManager, an application designed to help tablet PC users organize ideas. Tablet PC makers insist that more off-the-shelf applications are on the way.

It may well be premature to write tablet PCs off as another IT industry failure, though for some critics that may be a bitter pill to swallow.

Adapted from: **Tablets give PC makers a sales headache**
By Paul Taylor
FT.com site: 4 November 2003

Questions

1. What are the advantages and disadvantages of using Tablet PCs?
2. Which devices do you think the Tablet PC will be competing with in the mobile computing marketplace?

The most recent examples of miniaturization are the hand-held devices. The **palmtop** computer has a small LCD screen and a pen for data entry. The processor is similar to that of a low-specification microcomputer and has several megabytes of RAM (see section 3.2.7). A range of packages such as word processors and spreadsheets are available, and information can be exchanged with a desktop computer. Palmtops are sometimes referred to as **PDAs** (personal digital assistants). The miniaturization of technology has allowed mobile telephones to incorporate many of these features. Internet access and voice recognition are now possible on the most recent generation of **WAP** (wireless application protocol) telephones.

For businesses, the development of the desktop computer has had a major impact on the way computers are used. Medium-sized and large organizations usually still have a larger computer (minicomputer or mainframe computer) for their major data-processing and management information provision. This installation will require a computer centre of trained technical staff to operate the company's information resource. However, the presence of cheap desktop computers has enabled individual departments and sections to purchase their own equipment. They typically use this for word processing, spreadsheet modelling, small database applications, electronic filing and desktop publishing. Because desktop computers are so cheap, they can often be purchased using departmental budgets without seeking central approval. This has a number of effects. First, the resulting greater autonomy and control possessed by the department is likely to stimulate computer use. Second, the power of the central computing resource is diminished. Traditional computer centres often view the mushrooming of desktop computers with alarm. This is not only jealousy but is also based on a real fear of a lack of standardization of hardware and software throughout the organization. Finally, there may also be a duplication of data and applications development effort on the part of staff in separate localities unless coordination is achieved.

The proliferation of local desktop computers in large organizations is one impact of the development of the microchip. Another is the wide variety of businesses that are able to use desktop computers in their day-to-day transaction processing, office work and decision support. A very large number of small businesses can afford to computerize their standard business functions. This has been stimulated by the production of cheap software that is easy to use by personnel who have not had formal technical computer training.

The explosion of desktop computers reflects the breakdown in **Grosch's law**. This states that the computing power of a computer is proportional to the square of its cost. In other words, it was always more cost-efficient for an organization requiring computing power to purchase a large (and therefore centralized machine) than several smaller microcomputers or minicomputers.

Mini case 3.2

Personal computers

In August 2000 Lou Gerstner, the chairman and chief executive of IBM, declared 'The personal computer is dead.' The warning sounded absurdly exaggerated, but it does reflect the evidence that although sales of PCs are not actually falling, the rate of growth in sales is slowing.

There are a number of reasons for the slowdown. One problem is that most consumers who want PCs already own one, certainly in economies such as the USA. There is a real concern that the PC market may be reaching saturation point. In the past, sales have been pushed by PC users upgrading machines every three years or so as ever more sophisticated software was offered that required ever-faster processing power. Increasingly, the main frustration of home PC users is not their hardware but the speed of their connection to the Internet. What is holding them back is bandwidth – slow access to the Internet. Who needs faster chip speeds when you are using a slow 56K modem?

Companies are also becoming more reluctant to keep upgrading PCs in the office. They are increasingly put off by the loss of productivity involved in deploying new technology. PC makers have reacted to the slowdown with a variety of strategies, including designing sleeker models and monitors in various translucent colours. Others are placing more emphasis on hand-held machines. Moves into new markets are extraordinarily difficult to execute. Very few of the mainframe makers succeeded in minicomputers, hardly any minicomputer makers moved successfully into PCs, and almost none made it from PCs to laptops. The record of transition is dismal.

▶

Many companies that have depended on PC growth for their fortunes are now wondering what they will have to do to prosper in a new era of technology. The PC may not be dead but, with the outlook for sales growth uncertain, these are dangerous days.

Adapted from: **Speeding to a halt**
Financial Times: 1 December 2000

Questions

1. Why has the chairman of the company that pioneered the introduction of the personal computer now stated that the personal computer is dead?

2. What factors are making companies reluctant to upgrade their office computers?

3. Carry out some research to provide evidence of the difficulty for computer manufacturers to transfer into new markets.

The power of the desktop computer has been further enhanced by the development of **local area networks**. These link various pieces of hardware, including desktop computers, together in order to communicate with each other and to share resources.

The rapid increase in performance and decrease in price can be seen by consulting Table 3.1. No other form of technology can boast such rapid performance and price developments. If a luxury motor car of the 1940s, for example a Rolls-Royce, had demonstrated changes on the same scale it would cost about a pound sterling, travel at one thousand million miles per hour at ten million miles to the gallon of fuel. It would also be the size of a matchbox yet, paradoxically, have ten thousand times the luggage capacity of the 1940s' Rolls-Royce!

Table 3.1 An indicative summary of the effects of technological advance on the performance of computers

Date	Generation	Technology	Number of instructions executed per second	Storage capacity (number of characters)	Cost (for a typical large computer)	Average time between breakdowns
1950s	1	Valve	1000	10,000	£5m	hours
1960s	2	Transistor	100,000	100,000	£2m	hundreds of hours
1970s	3	Integrated transistor circuit board	10,000,000	10,000,000	£4m+	thousands of hours
1980s	4	Micro-integrated circuit (microchip)	1,000,000,000	1,000,000,000	£2m+	years
1990s			5,000,000,000	100,000,000,000	£1m+	years
2000s			10,000,000,000	10,000,000,000	£100,000+	years

3.2 Hardware

The terms 'hardware', 'software' and 'firmware' occur frequently in any literature concerned with computers. It is important at the outset to have some understanding of their meanings:

- **Hardware** is the physical components in a computer system. Circuits, keyboards, disk drives, disks and printers are all examples of pieces of hardware.
- **Software** is a set of instructions, written in a specialized language, the execution of which controls the operation of the computer. Programs are examples of software.
- **Firmware** is the permanent storage of program instructions in hardware. It is usually used to refer to a set of instructions that is permanently encoded on a microchip. The term 'firmware' is used because it is the inseparable combination of hardware and software.

3.2.1 Functional components of a computer system

A computer system is a system that accepts data as input and produces information as output. Information, as will be recalled from Chapter 1, is data that has been processed to serve some purpose. In producing this, the intermediate products of this process may be stored. The process of transformation of inputs into outputs is carried out by electronic circuitry. The process is controlled by a sequence of instructions – the program – that is stored in the computer.

Computer systems fit the common systems model explained in Chapter 1. Figure 3.1 illustrates the basic organization of a computer system.

1. **Input:** The purpose of the input component of a computer system is:
   - (a) to accept data in the required form;
   - (b) to convert this data to a machine-understandable form;
   - (c) to transmit this data to the central processing unit.

   Examples of input devices to be explained later are keyboards, magnetic ink character readers, bar-code readers, optical character readers and the mouse.

2. **Central processing unit (CPU):** This is made up of three components: the control unit, the arithmetic and logic unit, and the main memory.
   - (a) The purpose of the **control unit** is:
     - to decode and execute the program instructions one by one;
     - to control and coordinate data movements within the CPU and between the CPU and the other components of the computer system.
   - (b) The purpose of the **arithmetic and logic unit** (ALU) is:
     - to carry out arithmetic operations – for example, to add two numbers together;
     - to carry out logical operations – for example, to compare two numbers to establish which is the larger.
   - (c) The purpose of the **main memory** (synonyms – fast memory, immediate access memory, core store, direct access memory) is:
     - to store programs during their execution;
     - to store data that is being used by the current program;

Figure 3.1 Functional components of a computer system

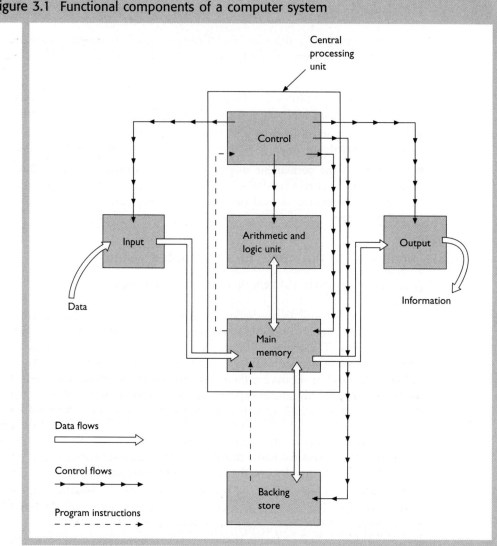

- to store the operating system (this is an important program in the control of the computer; details are covered in a later section of the chapter).

Currently, the main form of hardware for carrying out the functions of the central processing unit is based on the microchip.

3. **Secondary storage (backing store):** The purpose of secondary storage is:

   (a) to maintain a permanent record of data and programs when not being used by the CPU;
   (b) to maintain a store for the program and data currently being used if the main memory is not large enough to accommodate the entire program and data;
   (c) to maintain a copy for security purposes of data held in the main memory;
   (d) to act as a secondary input/output device when the input is in magnetic form or the output is required in magnetic form.

Examples of secondary store hardware to be covered later are magnetic and optical disk devices, magnetic tape machines, and tape streamers.

4. **Output:** The purpose of the output component of a computer system is:

   (**a**) to accept information/data from the CPU;

   (**b**) to convert this information/data into the required output form.

   Examples of output devices are printers, monitors, machines for producing computer output on microfilm and voice synthesizers.

In the next sections, each of these functional components is treated in some detail. In particular, the various ways in which each may be physically realized in a modern computer system are explained and evaluated.

3.2.2 Input devices, media and data capture methods

The purposes of input devices are:

- to accept data in the required form;
- to convert this data to a machine-understandable form; and
- to transmit this data to the central processing unit.

Keyboard

The most common keyboard device used is the QWERTY keyboard. It is called a 'QWERTY' keyboard because these are the first six letters on the top left of the keyboard. The keyboard is derived from the old typewriter standard to which some extra keys have been added for specific computer-based functions. Unfortunately, the standard typewriter layout was not designed to be the most efficient from a data input point of view. Rather, the key layout was organized in the nineteenth century so that old mechanical typewriters were least likely to jam when typing occurred. Modern computers and electric typewriters do not suffer from this deficiency and so the standard is outmoded. Keyboards have been designed that allow a trained typist to input text at the rate of about 180 words per minute. This compares with the QWERTY norm for an input of about sixty words per minute. Why are all standard typewriter keyboards based on this old-fashioned inefficient layout? The answer is partly to do with inertia in the computing industry but also because there is now a huge investment in QWERTY-based equipment and QWERTY-trained staff. This does not make it feasible, in the short run at least, for any organization to change.

Key presses are converted into character code consisting of **bits** (binary digits) which can be either 1s or 0s. There are a few internationally recognized coding systems for computers. The two most used are the **American Standard Code for Information Interchange** (ASCII) and the **Extended Binary Coded Decimal Interchange Code** (EBCDIC). The former code is most commonly used for desktop computers and data communications. The EBCDIC code is used in IBM mainframe computers. Within a coding system, each different keyboard character is coded as a separate binary string. For instance, in the ASCII 7-bit code C is coded as 1000011.

Keyboard data entry is almost invariably accompanied by a monitor or screen on which the characters input to the keyboard are displayed.

Using a keyboard for data entry is common to a wide range of applications. They fall into three main categories:

1. The entry of data from a source document such as an invoice or an order. Controls must ensure that all the data is copied correctly and completely. Data entry controls are covered in the later chapter on controls.

2. Interactive use of the computer by a user. Here there is no source document but the user is inputting commands or queries into the computer system.

3. The entry of text data, as in word processing.

Advantages: Keyboard data entry has a number of advantages over other forms of data input:

- There is a low initial cost for purchase of the equipment.
- The method is extremely flexible as it relies heavily on the person entering the data. People are flexible.

Disadvantages: There are also a number of disadvantages:

- For efficient use, training of personnel is needed.
- It is a slow form of data entry. People are slow.
- It is costly in operation as it relies on people. People are expensive to employ compared with the capital cost of equipment.
- Unless there are adequate controls, using a keyboard will lead to high error rates. People are error-prone.

Where data is input by keyboard, invariably a **mouse** is used as a supporting device. A mouse is a small hand-held device about the size of a bar of soap. It contains a ball on its lower surface and selection buttons on its upper surface. As the mouse is moved over a desk the ball-bearing moves and controls the positioning of a pointer (often an arrow) on the monitor. The pointer can be moved to a position on the screen to select an item such as a menu option or position a cursor, such as the text insertion marker (called a caret) in a word processor. Alternatively, in graphics applications, the movement can be used to trace out lines and draw and colour shapes.

Multimedia input devices

- **Digital camera:** A digital camera is similar in appearance to a normal camera and captures still images. Rather than using photographic film, the images are stored in memory inside the camera and later transferred to a computer. The digital camera has the advantage that pictures of poor quality can immediately be deleted and replaced.

- **Webcam:** A webcam is similar to a digital camera in that it digitally captures images. Webcams are low-cost devices that are connected to a desktop computer system and usually placed on top of the monitor. Images are not usually stored but are communicated in real time using a local network connection or the Internet to another computer user.

- **Video capture:** Moving images, from either a digital video camera, a television transmission source or a prerecorded video disk or cassette, can be input directly into a computer with a video capture card installed. These images can then be edited or enhanced in a variety of ways and then either stored or output for immediate display.

- **Scanner:** A scanner is a desktop device used to capture a document image. The document is placed on a glass plate and an image is optically captured by passing a bright light across the source document. The image is converted into a digital bitmap, an array of 1s and 0s, and transmitted to a computer, where it can be stored in memory and later edited, if required, and saved. A particular application of scanning is in optical character recognition, which is described below.

■ **Voice data entry:** Voice data entry consists of the reception of speech data by a microphone, the conversion of the data into electronic signals, the recognition of the data and its final conversion into textual form.

A difficulty for the designers of speech recognition software is that two people represent the same word verbally in different ways, the same person represents the same word verbally in different ways on different occasions, and two people may speak different words in a similar way. There is, however, massive investment in developing voice recognition facilities. This is because the potential financial rewards are great. These will occur in two main areas. First, the need for typists (as distinct from secretaries) will disappear. Text will be dictated into a microphone and instantly displayed on a screen for voice-controlled editing. There will be no need for a person to be employed to take down shorthand, which is then converted into printed text for correction. Hundreds of thousands of typists' jobs will rapidly disappear. Second, voice data input will enable people to interrogate computers remotely via the telephone system with miniature mobile transmitter/receivers connected to the public telecommunications network. This will enable the information-providing power of computers to become fully portable. Output might be provided by a synthesized voice or connection to a traditional output device.

Currently, voice data entry systems are already used in telephone-based information provision and order-processing systems. Software for the acceptance of speech that is then turned into text has become more readily available. These programs run on standard PCs and interface with standard word-processing packages. In order to work effectively the user must undertake a period of training on the computer – training, that is, of the computer in order to allow it to recognize the particular voice patterns of the user. This typically takes a few hours. Accuracy rates of 95% with speech input at over 100 words per minute are claimed as standard at the current level of development.

The main advantage of voice data entry then lies in the possibility of remote interrogation of computers for information and the preparation of text documents by unskilled personnel rather than in high-volume business data entry.

Mini case 3.3

Speech recognition

A range of entertainment and 'driving oriented' technologies is on offer to modern drivers, including in-car DVD players, navigation systems, mobile computers, web browsers, MP3 music players, voice-recognition-based electronic mail, messaging systems and more.

IBM researchers suggest that its technology, which places heavy emphasis on the use of in-vehicle voice recognition technology, eliminates the problem of drivers having to take their hands off the wheel to interact with in-vehicle devices.

Jonathon Connell, an IBM researcher, says IBM has developed an 'audio visual speech recognition' system that involves adding a camera into the mix. 'Whether it is navigation information, faxes, phone calls, or web content that a driver requires, this will eliminate the need to shift eyes to dashboard screens,' says Mr Connell.

The use of information from an in-car camera, when combined with speech information from a microphone, sharply increases speech recognition accuracy and could help further reduce the need for a driver to take his or her hands off the steering wheel.

Mr Connell also suggests the technology could 'monitor for drowsiness' by looking at whether the driver's eyes were open or closed and then prompt the driver with an 'interactive response', such as 'wake up or we'll all be killed'.

Meanwhile, Harold Goddijn, chairman and chief executive of TomTom, a Dutch-based navigation system producer, says telematics should be seen more as an aid to safety than a threat or a further driver distraction. Mr Goddijn suggests that it would be premature for any government to legislate against the use of such systems at this stage. 'My feeling is that [authorities] want to see how the technology is developing before they interfere. In Europe, the general perception is that car navigation systems, provided they are implemented properly, can make a positive contribution to road safety.'

Adapted from: **Controversy shifts into higher gear**
FT.com site: 6 August 2003
Safety issues by Geof Wheelwright

Questions

1. What advantages can be gained from using the technology of voice recognition as part of 'in-car telematics'?
2. Identify other applications which can make use of this method of data input.

Optical character readers

Optical character recognition (OCR) entails the reading of preprinted characters on documents. These documents are passed through an optical character reader, which optically detects the characters on the document and converts them to code, which is sent to the CPU.

Many large public utilities, such as gas, electricity and water, use OCR, as do the major credit card companies. The method is for the billing company to prepare a turnaround document with billing details and an attached counterfoil for payment. The customer returns the counterfoil with their payment. As well as details of the required payment being printed on the counterfoil, a special section is reserved for the characters that are to be optically read. This section is generally at the bottom of the counterfoil and appears below a printed warning such as 'do not write or mark below this line'. The characters will give the account number of the bill receiver together with other details. These may include the postal area, the type of customer, the amount of the bill and other management information.

A number of standard character fonts are capable of being read by commercial optical character readers. OCR-A is a standard American font that is used by about three-quarters of US applications. OCR-B is a standard British font. Examples of these fonts are shown in Figure 3.2.

The characters may be preprinted on the documents using a standard printing technique such as litho. However, it is more usual for the character data to be produced using a computer-driven printer. Optical character readers have now been produced that will read carefully produced handwritten numbers and letters. This extends the

Figure 3.2 Examples of optical character fonts: (a) OCR-A; (b) OCR-B

(a)
ABCDEFGHIJKLMNOPQRST
UVWXYZ
1234567890 .,;:&

(b)
abcdefghijklmnopqrstuvwxyz
ABCDEFGHIJKLMNOPQRSTUVWXYZ
1234567890 .,;:&!?

use of OCR beyond the limitations of turnaround documents, as data can be entered by hand between the stages of document production and document reading. A common application of this form of data input is in hand-held PDAs. Many of these devices allow the user to write characters with a stylus into a particular area of the screen. These are converted immediately into printable characters and redisplayed on the text entry portion of the screen.

OCR has a number of advantages and disadvantages over keyboard entry:

Advantages: The advantages of OCR as opposed to keyboard entry are:

- It is cheap in operation for high-volume activities, such as billing, which can include preprinted characters.
- It has low error rates.
- It is fast. Up to 500 characters per second can be read.
- The fonts are easily readable by people (unlike magnetic character fonts).

Disadvantages: There are two main disadvantages:

- The equipment is expensive to purchase.
- It is easy to corrupt the characters; this can often be achieved by small pieces of dirt or smudges.

Magnetic ink character readers

Magnetic ink character recognition (MICR) is a method of data entry widely used in the banking system for customers' cheques. Each cheque has identifying information (cheque number, account code and bank sort code) printed in magnetic ink in the lower left-hand corner. On depositing a cheque at the bank, the following process takes place. It is passed to an employee, who prints the amount of the cheque using a special machine; this appears on the right-hand side of the cheque. The cheque is then passed under a magnet, which magnetizes the iron oxide particles in the ink. It is finally sent through another machine, which detects the centres of magnetization and converts these into the codes for each character, representing the amount of the cheque.

Figure 3.3 Examples of magnetic ink character fonts: (a) E13B; (b) CMC7

The style of typeface, called the **font,** used by the British banking system is E13B. Another internationally recognized standard font is CMC7. This has characters as well as numbers and is used by the Post Office in its postal order system. Examples of both fonts are shown in Figure 3.3.

A cheque is an example of a **turnaround document**. This is defined as a document that is:

- machine-produced
- machine-readable
- readable by human beings.

Because of their machine-readability, turnaround documents allow the fast entry of data with low error rates.

Advantages: The advantages of MICR as opposed to keyboard entry are:

- It is cheap in operation for high-volume activities such as cheque processing.
- It has very low error rates. This is of crucial importance in the banking system.
- The magnetic characters are resistant to corruption by the folding of cheques or smudges of dirt.
- It is fast – for example, up to 1000 characters per second can be read.

Disadvantages: There are two main disadvantages:

- The equipment is expensive to purchase.
- The fonts are not easily readable; this limits the use of the method to applications where this is unimportant.

Both MICR and OCR suffer from the same limitation in that they are inflexible methods of data entry. Keyboard entry allows a large amount of 'intelligent preprocessing' by persons before data entry. This implies flexibility in the interpretation of handwritten data entered on documents between their production and final data entry of their contents.

Bar-code readers

Bar-codes are now familiar as part of the printed packaging on supermarket products. A bar-code consists of a series of thick and thin black bars divided by thick and thin

Figure 3.4 A bar-code – EAN standard

5 000243 925103

spaces printed on a light-coloured background. These bars correspond to digits, which are also printed underneath the bar-code.

There are two common systems of bar-codes. The earlier Universal Product Code (UPC) is used in the United States. In Europe, the standard is the European Article Number (EAN). EAN consists of thirteen digits, represented by twenty-six lines. The digits have a standard interpretation. Two digits indicate the country of origin of the product, five digits indicate the manufacturer, five digits indicate the product, and the remaining digit is used for checking that the other digits have been read correctly by the device reading the bar-code. Figure 3.4 is a bar-code.

The bar-code is machine-read either by passing a 'light pen' over it in either direction or by passing the bar-code over a reader machine. The second method is more flexible as the bar-code can be passed over at any angle as long as the code is pointing towards the sensitive screen of the machine. The latter type of machine is common in supermarkets.

Bar-codes are suitable for data input where it is important to maintain a record of the movements of material goods. This occurs at the point of sale in a supermarket, at a library loan desk and in stock control systems.

As mentioned previously, a common use for bar-codes is at checkout points in supermarkets and other retail outlets. The bar-code is read at the point of sale and so such a system is known as a **point-of-sale** (POS) system. The way these systems typically work is that the code for the product, having been identified by the bar-code reader, is sent to the computer. There, the relevant record for the product is retrieved. The product price and a short description of the product are then sent back electronically to the point of sale, where the details are printed on the till slip. At the same time, the computer records of the quantity of the item held are decreased by one unit.

Advantages: The advantages of a bar-code point-of-sales system over the more traditional manually controlled checkout till are:

- Better management information: management has up-to-date information on stock levels and can thus sensibly plan purchases and avoid stockouts. The records of sales are also date- and time-stamped. This enables analysis of sales data to identify fast- and slow-moving items and peaks and troughs in the sales of items. It is also important to be able to have information on consumer patterns of expenditure. It may affect shelving policy if it is discovered that purchases of smoked salmon are often accompanied by white wine, whereas peanuts are associated with bottles of beer.

- Better customer service: there are lower error rates than for manual checkout tills. This is because operators have little scope for incorrect data entry. Itemized bills provide customers with the ability to check their purchases against till slips. Certain types of checkout fraud are also rendered impossible with the system.

- Easier implementation of price changes and special offers: because prices are held in computer records, a change of price merely requires a single data change in the item record and a replacement of the price card in the shop display. Individual pricing of items is no longer necessary (but see *Disadvantages*). Offers such as 'three for the price of two' can be easily implemented and detected at the till.
- Staff training time to use the systems is minimal.

Disadvantages: The two main disadvantages are:

- The necessary equipment is expensive to purchase and install.
- Unless there is an adequate manual backup system, a breakdown will immediately stop the retail sales of the organization. A typical manual backup is to revert to the old system. This requires that the practice of individually labelling each item is maintained.

Optical mark readers

Optical mark recognition (OMR) is a common form of high-volume data entry where the application requires the selection of a data item from various alternatives. In its most common form it consists of a printed document on which the various options are displayed, together with a box, or field, for each. To select an option, the person entering data puts a mark in the relevant box. Part of a typical document is shown in Figure 3.5.

Once marked, the document is passed through an optical mark reader. This machine optically scans the boxes and determines those in which a mark has been made – a 1 corresponds to a mark and a 0 to the absence of a mark. The computer,

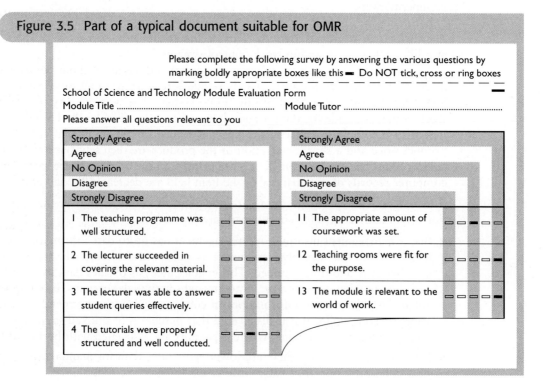

Figure 3.5 Part of a typical document suitable for OMR

Please complete the following survey by answering the various questions by marking boldly appropriate boxes like this ▬ Do NOT tick, cross or ring boxes

School of Science and Technology Module Evaluation Form
Module Title .... Module Tutor ....
Please answer all questions relevant to you

Strongly Agree
Agree
No Opinion
Disagree
Strongly Disagree

Strongly Agree
Agree
No Opinion
Disagree
Strongly Disagree

1 The teaching programme was well structured.

2 The lecturer succeeded in covering the relevant material.

3 The lecturer was able to answer student queries effectively.

4 The tutorials were properly structured and well conducted.

11 The appropriate amount of coursework was set.

12 Teaching rooms were fit for the purpose.

13 The module is relevant to the world of work.

which has been preprogrammed with the meanings of the boxes, then interprets the binary code sent from the optical mark reader.

Typical applications are market research surveys, multiple-choice examination questions, time sheets for the entry of start and stop times for employees, and order forms for the selection of stock.

Advantages: OMR has a number of advantages over keyboard entry, MICR and OCR:

- Data can be entered on to a document not only by data entry personnel at the data entry stage but also by other people at any stage between the production of the document and its reading. This is a distinct advantage over OCR and MICR, which have a basic 'data out equals data in' limitation.

- No knowledge or skill is necessary to enter data on to the document other than the ability to read and use a ballpoint pen. This is to be compared with skills needed to operate a keyboard.

- It is less susceptible to erroneous machine reading than an OCR document.

- It is cheap and fast in operation compared with keyboard entry.

Disadvantages: There are also a number of disadvantages:

- There is a high initial cost for the purchase of the equipment.

- Its use is limited to those applications where selection from a few presented alternatives is required. It is therefore not appropriate for applications where character data is required. For instance, to enter a person's surname consisting of up to fifteen characters would need fifteen rows, each with twenty-six options for selection. Not only would this use much document space, it would not be easy to enter the data.

- It is not suitable where the printed documents need to be changed frequently as a result of flexible data requirements. Each document change necessitates the reprogramming of the optical mark reader.

Remote data entry using network technology

Increasingly, customers and businesses are being encouraged to make requests and enquiries or to place orders by establishing a data communications channel and, for example, completing an electronic form held on a web page. In other cases, electronic invoices are produced, which also cut the cost of handling paper and data entry.

Web page forms have similar advantages to their paper counterparts in that they direct the user to fill in data in a predefined and structured format. In addition, the accuracy of the data can be checked. For example, important fields can be made mandatory and thus cannot be left blank. Validation checks, where required, can be performed on key items of data. The data on the form is then uploaded to the host computer and can be input directly into their system.

Advantages: Remote data entry has several advantages:

- Data can be entered at the convenience of the user of the system, for example when the receiver is closed for business.

- The validation checks ensure that data is provided in a format that can be readily accepted.

- It is a cheap and fast method to accept data as the user is carrying out the inputting tasks.

Disadvantages: There are also disadvantages:

- There is a high initial cost in creating the website and pages to allow the data entry to be performed.
- The system requires a level of both computing equipment and expertise of the user. This minimum specification will be changing over time.

Swipe cards

These are in the form of plastic cards incorporating a magnetic stripe that contains identifying information. The magnetic stripe can be read by a machine, which converts this into code to be sent to the main body of the computer. They are most commonly used as identification for cash-dispensing machines or point-of-sales systems for credit card sales.

Smart cards

The smart card contains information encoded in a microchip built into the structure of the card. They are harder than swipe cards to copy, can contain much information and can be programmed to self-destruct if incorrect identifying information is keyed into the machine reading them. The use of smart cards is predicted to increase over the coming years.

Touch screen

A touch screen enables the selection of an item from a screen display by pointing to it with a finger, or touching with a stylus. It is used in some business applications such as stock dealing and in information kiosks, and is a common form of data input for hand-held devices such as PDAs.

Magnetic tapes and disks, and optical disks

These are often regarded as input and output media utilizing corresponding devices, such as disk drives, as input and output devices. In a sense this is true. A name and address file can be purchased on magnetic disk and read into the computer for use. However, here these media and devices are regarded as secondary, not because of their importance but rather because data held on them must previously have been entered through one of the other entry methods or be the output of computer processing. They are discussed in the next section.

Mini case 3.4

Hospital data input devices

The paperless office may still be a distant dream but the paperless hospital is close to becoming a reality, at least in Spain.

'This hospital will be paper-free in one and a half years,' says Iñigo Goenaga, chief information officer at the Clínica Universitaria de Navarra, a prestigious hospital in the northern Spanish city of Pamplona.

In 1999, CUN embarked on an ambitious project to eliminate paper and improve access to hospital data using one integrated clinical system. According to Mr Goenaga, this is an important goal because hospitals often have a significant number of IT systems, but they do not always provide an integrated view of data. Nor are the disparate systems able to exchange data easily.

CUN chose a system from Picis, which specializes in IT systems for intensive care units. The system, CareSuite, aims to eliminate one of the most time-consuming and error-prone tasks in an ICU, namely the manual recording of data from anaesthesia machines, monitors and the other medical equipment. By automating the collection process and storing the data in a database, ICU staff cannot only document the care process more efficiently but, hopefully, detect potentially life-threatening 'events' sooner – before the alarm bells start ringing.

The most recent developments in CUN's IT strategy have focused on boosting productivity and improving bedside care with wireless handheld devices, allowing doctors to access and enter information at the bedside rather than having to walk down the corridor to use a workstation.

Notebooks were rejected for being too cumbersome while PDAs were discarded because the screen is too small. CUN settled on the SIMpad, a tablet-sized device from Siemens Medical Solutions that uses the Microsoft Windows CE operating system.

The roll-out of wireless LAN connections to all wards means doctors can use the SIMpads throughout the hospital. Even doctors' prescriptions – the last bastion of paper-based processes – have been largely eliminated at CUN. The details of the prescription can be filled in on the SIMpad and the order sent electronically to the hospital pharmacy.

Adapted from: **CUN, Spain: Moving towards a paperless hospital**
By Geoffrey Nairn
FT.com site: 21 May 2003

Questions

1. What advantages does the use of the data entry tablet provide for the hospital?
2. What problem might be encountered in introducing this new system?

3.2.3 Factors involved in the selection of data entry devices, media and methods

The data entry methods mentioned earlier have different characteristics and therefore will be appropriate for different types of data entry application. The main features that determine the data entry method are as follows:

- **The type of application:** This is perhaps the most important factor. Some applications allow turnaround documents to be used, while others do not. Some applications need only allow selections from a limited range of choices, which would suggest OMR, while others require the addition of a wide variety of data. Interrogation generally requires data entry personnel to interact with the computer, so a keyboard is required. It is impossible to specify in advance the range of applications, together with the most suitable data entry method and devices. Each application needs to be matched against the characteristics of the data entry methods before a choice can be made.

- **Costs:** In particular the difference between operating costs and initial costs. Most methods that are low in initial costs, such as keyboard entry, are high in operating costs, and vice versa.

- **Speed and volume of input:** Some methods are only applicable to high-volume applications.

- **Error tolerance:** All errors are undesirable, but in some applications it is more crucial to prevent their occurrence than in others. The banking sector, for instance, is one that places a high priority on preventing error. There are many controls that minimize erroneous data entry. These are covered extensively in Chapter 9 on control. For the purposes of this chapter, it is worthy of note that those data entry methods that involve less human skill, such as MICR, are less prone to error than, for example, keyboard entry.

Over the last two decades, the cost of processing hardware has dropped considerably. The costs of producing software are also likely to diminish over the coming years. With the increasing power of computers to process data and the ever-demanding needs of management for information based on this data, the importance of cutting data entry costs will be emphasized. It is likely that automated compared with manual data entry will increase in the future.

3.2.4 Secondary storage devices

The purpose of secondary storage is:

- to maintain a permanent record of data and programs when not being used by the CPU;

- to maintain a store for the program and data currently being used if the main memory is not large enough to accommodate the entire program and data;

- to maintain a copy for security purposes of data held in the main memory; and

- to act as a secondary input/output device when the input is in electronically readable form or the output is required to be stored in electronic form.

All computers need permanent secondary storage facilities, because the main memory store within the central processing unit is limited in size, and in the event of a power failure or the machine being switched off the contents of this main memory disappear.
The factors to be looked at when considering secondary storage technology are:

- **Speed of data retrieval:** Given a data retrieval instruction executed in the CPU, the quicker the desired data can be loaded into the main memory the better.

- **Storage capacity:** The larger the amount of data stored and accessible to the storage device the better.

- **Cost of storage:** This is usually measured in terms of the cost to store one byte of data (one byte – eight bits – of space is sufficient to store one character).

- **Robustness and portability of the storage medium:** The more secure the data storage medium is against corruption or 'crashes' the better.

Storage devices are often classified according to the type of access to data permitted by them. In general, there are **sequential-access storage devices** and **direct-access storage devices**. The difference between the two is that with the former, access to data begins at a given point on the storage medium, usually the beginning, and the entire storage medium is searched in sequence until the target data item is found. With direct-access storage devices, the location of the required data item can be identified. The target data item can then be retrieved from this location or addressed without the need to retrieve data stored physically prior to it; in other words, access is direct. Generally, all direct-access storage devices also allow sequential retrieval if required.

From a business information and business data processing perspective, these differences in access lead to differences in suitability for business applications. In particular, sequential-access storage devices are suitable for only those applications that require sequential processing. Here would be included routine data-processing operations such as the billing of customers, the production of customer statements and the production of payrolls. Many applications, including all those concerned with the selective retrieval and presentation of information for decision making, require direct access and thus direct-access storage media and devices. The increased use of computers for decision support, forward planning and management control has led to the increased use of direct-access storage devices as the more important form of secondary storage. Where the store of corporate data is centralized and held for access by many applications, then it is imperative to have direct-access storage.

This is not a text on the more detailed aspects of hardware. However, it is important to understand the basic principles underlying modern storage devices. Without this knowledge, it is difficult to appreciate why the types of business activity impose restrictions on the forms of appropriate storage. The following are common types of storage media.

Optical disks

Optical disk technology consists of encoding data on a disk that is covered with a transparent plastic coating. The data can then be read by means of laser light focused with great accuracy on to the spinning disk; this is illustrated in Figure 3.6.

The storage capacity of such disks is huge: for a 5-inch disk it is typically 650 megabytes. The trend is towards increasing this capacity. Because the disks are protected by a transparent plastic cover and there is no danger of the optical head coming into accidental contact (head crash) with the surface of the disk, optical systems are very robust.

There are three main types of optical system. **CD-ROM** was the first to be developed. The data is stored as a series of microscopic pits, which are burned into the surface of the disk. These disks are capable of read-only access but have very large storage capacities. The read rate of CD-ROMs has increased rapidly over the last few years – CD-ROM drives with read-in rates of over fifty times early read-in rates are now common. The costs of production of CD-ROMs is small for large production runs, and the cost of CD-ROM drives has dropped from several thousands of dollars to less than 50 dollars. CD-ROMs have three main uses:

Figure 3.6 Reading data from a CD-ROM

1. **Software provision:** Most software is too large to be stored on floppy disks, and it is now usual that purchased software is provided on CD-ROM. This has paralleled the trend for the inclusion of CD-ROM devices in modern business PCs.

2. **Multimedia provision:** Modern PCs have the software and hardware capacity to display graphics, audio and video, as well as text. The storage capacity needed for the data for these is very large. CD-ROMs can meet this requirement. This ability has led to the development of multimedia disks, which intersperse text with graphics, audio and visual output. This is particularly common with the multi-billion dollar business of computer games. Also, businesses often produce marketing materials on CD-ROM for easy distribution.

3. **Mass storage of reference material:** Where reference material seldom changes, CD-ROM is ideal for cheap, easy-to-handle storage. Examples are accounting data of UK companies, telephone directories and permanent components details of manufactured products. Text archives of newspapers and academic journals are now commonly provided on CD-ROM for easy access in libraries.

A second type of optical system is the **WORM disk** (write once, read many times). These disks are often referred to as CD-recordable, or CD-R. This system allows data to be written once to any part of the disk. The data is written on to the disk by burning into a layer of sensitive dye. Once written, the data cannot be altered, although it can be read many times. WORM disk systems are thus more flexible than CD-ROMs for business purposes. The inability to remove data once encoded opens up the possibility for the permanent archiving of transactions. This is of importance from an accounting perspective in that a complete history of a business transaction's life is held permanently on record. Known as the **audit trail**, it can be used to establish the authenticity of accounting balances.

Finally, there is the full **read/write optical disk**. These are often referred to as CD-rewritable, or CD-RW. These provide mass, flexible, direct-access secondary storage at a low cost per byte of information stored. The material used in the recording layer of the disk adopts different properties depending on the temperature applied to it. These changeable states allow the recorded data to be amended by heating those parts of the disk to a different temperature. Optical disks are rivalling magnetic media in larger systems as the main form of secondary storage.

The latest technology in optical storage is the **DVD** (digital video disc, or digital versatile disk). These disks have the general appearance of traditional CDs but can contain a much larger volume of data. This is achieved by using a more precise laser, a narrower track width and smaller pits to store the 1s and 0s; the difference between the density of data stored on CDs and DVDs is illustrated in Figure 3.7.

In addition, a disk can be read from both surfaces and, by refocusing the laser beam, data can be read from more than one layer on each surface. This, combined with improved algorithms for error detection and data compression, allows up to 17 gigabytes (Gb) of data to be stored on a single DVD. Popular applications of DVD are for video and audio data, such as feature films and interactive training packages. The large potential storage capacity makes DVDs an attractive alternative for all forms of commercial data storage, and for large software suites that would otherwise require several CDs. Inevitably, the development path of DVD is mirroring that of the CD in that WORM and erasable DVDs are already becoming available commercially.

Figure 3.7 Storage of 1s and 0s on optical media

(a) Typical DVD architecture   (b) Typical CD architecture

Figure 3.8 A typical magnetic disk

Magnetic disks

A magnetic disk has a magnetizable surface on which data is stored in concentric rings called **tracks** (Figure 3.8). These tracks are not visible to the eye. Each track is accessed by a movable read/write head. The number of concentric tracks on a disk is determined by the disk drive manufacturer and the program controlling the movement of the

101

disk head. A disk typically ranges from forty tracks to over 200. The disk is divided logically into a number of pie-shaped sectors. There are eight or more sectors on each disk. Once again, the number is determined by software.

The combination of a track number (track #) and a sector number (sector #) is called an **address**. The read/write head can be sent directly to an address by rotation of the disk and movement of the read/write head over the radius of the disk. The content of an entire address is the smallest unit that can be transferred between the CPU and the disk in one operation. The fact that (1) the disk is divided into addresses and (2) the read/write head can be sent to a designated address means that provided the address of a piece of data is known or can be calculated, direct access to the data is possible. This characteristic of a disk is the most important in distinguishing it from sequential media such as magnetic tape. Disks can also be read sequentially if required, by first reading one track and then the next, and so on.

There are several types of disk:

1. **Floppy disks** or **diskettes:** A floppy disk is, as its name suggests, floppy and is contained within a firm plastic envelope. Floppy disks are $3^1/_2$ inches in diameter. In most drives, both upper and lower surfaces of the disk can be simultaneously employed for storage (double-headed disk drive). As well as having a track and sector the address will then also have a surface number. Floppy disks typically store 1.44 megabytes (Mb) as standard. They can easily be inserted and removed from their drives and are portable. Floppy disks rotate at about five revolutions per second and so access to an address takes less than a second.

2. **Hard disk:** In order to increase the storage capacity of a disk and decrease its access time it is necessary to use different technology. Hard disks are inflexible magnetic disks sealed within their own drives. This provides an environment protected from dust. They can rotate at faster speeds than floppy disks and rather than the read/write head being in contact with the surface of the disk it floats just above it.

   Hard disks have significantly larger storage capacity than floppy disks, with access speeds significantly faster. Eighty gigabyte (80,000 Mb) hard disks are common, with the trend being towards larger storage capacities. Floppy disks are used for archiving data files, maintaining secure data files (floppy disks can be locked up easily), and for transferring data from one desktop computer to another. Although it is possible to take backup copies of the hard disk on floppy disks, it may take thousands of floppy disks to back up a complete hard disk. Unless backups of selected parts of the disk are made by using special software (known as archiving software) it is common to use tape streamers, specialized cartridges known as zip drives, optical disks or even other hard disks.

3. **Exchangeable disk packs:** Larger computers use exchangeable packs of hard disks. These are usually 14 inches in diameter and come in packs of up to ten disks, which are double-sided except for the two outer surfaces. The disks are read by means of a movable arm with read/write heads for each surface (see Figure 3.9). Tracks that are directly above and below one another on the disk pack are said to constitute a **cylinder**. A large mainframe system may have many disk drives and so can have massive direct-access secondary storage.

The trend in hardware is towards developing disk technology that is cheaper, has greater capacity and faster access times, and is more robust. Ultimately, however, the storage efficiency and access speeds for magnetic disk systems are limited by the moving mechanical parts, in particular the read/write head, and by the density with which data can

Figure 3.9 An exchangeable disk pack

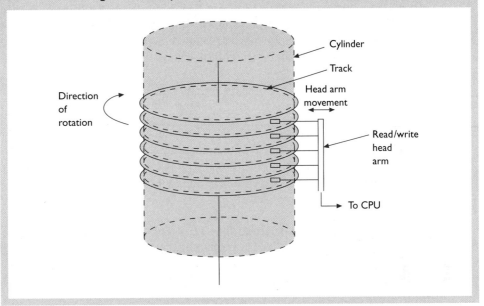

be packed on to the magnetizable medium. These limitations put magnetic storage devices at a significant disadvantage compared with optical disk technology.

RAID

Reliability and speed of data transfer are two essential aspects for effective hard disk drive utilization. Where two or more disk drives can be combined it is possible to address either or both of these concerns by creating a Redundant Array of Independent (or Inexpensive) Disks, commonly abbreviated to RAID.

To increase reliability, copies of data are written across several disks. This disk mirroring means that in the event of one disk failure, files can easily be restored from their mirror copy.

To increase reliability further, check bits (see later section on parity checks) can be added to the data so that in the event of data corruption it may be possible to repair the corrupted item without user intervention.

To increase performance, individual files can be split into blocks which are then spread over a number of disks. This is known as striping. When accessing a file, it may be possible to read the disks containing the required information in parallel, thereby reducing the overall disk access time.

A number of RAID levels have been established, allowing users to choose the level of reliability and speed which is most appropriate for their application. See Figures 3.10 and 3.11.

Magnetic tape

Standard magnetic tape stores data in the form of **records** (Figure 3.12). Several records are collected together and stored in a **block**. Between these blocks of data there are parts of the tape on which no data is stored. These are called **interblock gaps**. The

Figure 3.10 **RAID Level 2.** Six files (numbered 1 to 6) are stored, each with a mirror copy (file 1 on both disk a and disk b, file 5 on both disk c and disk d etc). Data reliability is improved as in the event of an error in data transfer the mirror copy can be used to restore the file. Data access times may be improved as disks can be read in parallel allowing multiple reads on the same file from different source disks

Figure 3.11 **RAID Level 3.** Three files (1, 2 and 3) are written in stripes across four hard disks (a, b, c and a disk for parity checking). Data reliability is improved as the parity bits can identify, and in some cases correct, errors in data transfer. Data access times are improved as disks can be read in parallel making data from the various stripes more readily available when required

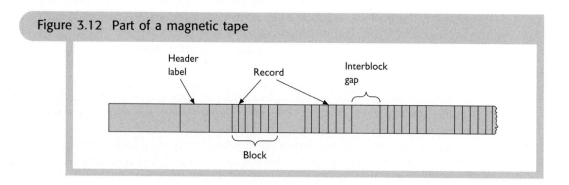

Figure 3.12 Part of a magnetic tape

header label gives information such as the name of the tape, the name of the program that is used to update it and the last date of update.

Data is transferred between the tape and the CPU by means of a tape drive (Figure 3.13). This device passes the tape from reel to reel over a read/write head, which either reads the data into the CPU or writes data from the CPU on to the tape. In order to allow the tape-reading device to rest while the computer processes data previously read, the tape machine always stops on an interblock gap. The block is the smallest unit of data that can be read into the machine at one time.

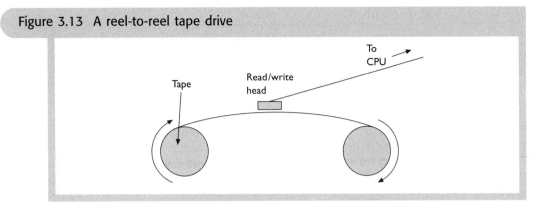

Figure 3.13 A reel-to-reel tape drive

Tape drives are used on larger machines for high-volume transaction processing. To update a payroll file requires at least three tapes and tape drives – one to read the current pay details for each employee, one to read the time-sheet data for the current period and one to write the updated details on to the new tape.

Standard magnetic tape is 4 inches wide. A typical tape might be 2400 feet long. The speed at which the tape can be passed over the read/write head varies from manufacturer to manufacturer, but a common speed is about 10 feet per second. Data is packed on the tape and, ignoring interblock gaps, a standard density is 1600 bytes per inch. If one byte is needed to store one character this is slightly less than 20 kilobytes per foot (1 kilobyte is 2^{10} bytes, which is just over 1000 bytes. 1 megabyte is 2^{20} bytes).

Advantages: There are a number of advantages to using magnetic tapes as a storage medium:

- It is an extremely cheap storage medium – a tape costs about £15.
- Tapes are highly portable and can easily be transferred from place to place.

Disadvantages: The disadvantages are:

- No direct access is possible to records; all access is sequential. Using the figures given, it is easy to calculate that the average time to search for and retrieve an individual record on a fully packed tape is of the order of a minute or two. This implies that tapes are unsuitable for applications that require the selective retrieval of records on a random basis. Tapes are only suitable for those functions where each record on a tape is used in sequence. An example is the preparation of the payroll, where employee records are processed in the order they appear on the tape.
- It is not possible to read and write to the same tape in one operation. It is often necessary to have many tape drives for standard operations.

Although the use of tapes has been diminishing over the last few years, they are still employed for some sequential processes as mentioned earlier. Their cheapness and portability makes them ideal as a security backup and archiving medium. Copies of data held on other storage media may be made on tape for transport to a secure location. This is known as **dumping**. Special devices known as **tape streamers** facilitate the fast copying of data on to tape for security reasons.

Flash memory

Flash memory, or flash RAM, is a non-volatile form of storage. In a computer, flash memory is used to hold the essential control code which is required to start the booting-up process. This information occasionally needs to be updated, such as when new hardware is installed. The data held in flash memory can be overwritten; this is normally done in blocks, contrasting with the individual byte-level addressing in normal RAM.

Recent developments have made flash memory a popular alternative form of portable storage. Many devices such as cell phones, digital cameras, MP3 players and games consoles make use of flash memory for data storage.

3.2.5 Output devices

The purpose of the output component of a computer system is:

- to accept information/data from the CPU;
- to convert this information/data into the required output form.

Broadly speaking, there are two important categories of output. **Soft copy** is output that does not persist over time. Examples are the visual output from a monitor or speech from a synthesizer. **Hard copy** output such as printed paper or microfilm persists.

Monitor

Monitors are a common form of output device because they provide a fast output of information that is practically costless and does not yield vast amounts of waste product such as paper. Applications are of course limited to those where no permanent record of output is required.

Modern monitor screens are colour and high-resolution, allowing a fine-grain representation of the output. This is not only important for the display of graphics but is also essential for operators who may spend many hours each day studying screen output. Screens are designed to be minimally tiring to those using them. As well as being high-resolution, modern monitors provide steady, non-flickering images on anti-glare screens. There is some evidence to suggest that the emissions from monitors lead to a higher likelihood of miscarriage in pregnancy. There is also evidence to indicate that prolonged work periods in proximity to monitors cause stress and related illnesses.

Liquid crystal display (LCD) output

This screen output does not use a cathode-ray tube. Its quality rivals that of the CRT screen, and it has the advantage that the screen is flat. This is particularly important for machines with a high degree of portability, such as notebooks and palm devices. The development of flat-screen technology for both mono and colour has been one of the key factors in enabling portable computer technology. Modern flat screens are becoming a popular alternative to monitors for desktop PC output as they occupy a much smaller space (sometimes referred to as its footprint). The highest quality screens use thin film transistor (TFT) technology to generate the output.

Voice output synthesizer

Voice output from computers is becoming increasingly popular. It is chiefly employed where visual output is undesirable, such as on-board computers in cars, or unhelpful, such as systems used by blind people. Voice output is also used extensively in telephone answering systems where callers are guided through a series of menu options. Prerecorded digits and words can be conjoined on an *ad hoc* basis to make dates, times or simple phrases.

Mini case 3.5

Voice output

If you've ever wanted to hurl abuse at the person that invented those telephone systems that ask you to 'press 1 for your current balance, press 2 for . . .' then feel free to flame-mail me.

The system is called interactive voice response (IVR) and I work for Intervoice, the company responsible for it. Back in July 1983 we cooed over the beautiful, healthy baby that bounced out of the delivery lab. IVR would save companies billions and give customers direct access to vital information. We cheered as it cut the cost of the average customer/company interaction by 88 per cent.

Fifty-five million telephone calls now get routed through these systems daily. So apologies for all the wasted hours you've spent pressing buttons in a fruitless search for the information you want. And mea culpa for the dreadful hold music, the premium call rates and all the 'your call is important to us' lies.

The next 20 years will see IVR at the peak of its power, delivering precious intangibles such as natural language questions and answers, while voice authentication provides more security than your mother's maiden name and a memorable address.

IVR is better technically, is more understood and – with marketers' help – will become more powerful and appreciated as the voice of an organization.

Adapted from: **Press 1 for an apology**
By Simon Edwards
FT.com site: 28 July 2003

Questions

1. How can voice output 'cut the cost of the average customer/company interaction'?
2. To what extent do you believe that voice output will increase in usage? What factors might encourage the development of applications which employ voice output?

Printers

Printed output persists and so is important for permanent records. Printed output is also portable and can, for instance, be posted to customers. The main disadvantage of printed output is its bulk and the expense of paper involved. The benefits of permanent, readable records and portability must be offset against these shortcomings. There are a large range of types of printer, all offering a different mix of:

■ speed
■ quality of output
■ range of print fonts
■ graphics abilities
■ cost of purchase

- cost of operation
- associated noise levels.

The choice of printer will be dependent on how each meets the desired mix of these features.

It is not the purpose here to cover the technology of printers in detail. The interested reader is directed to the references at the end of the chapter. Rather, the main categories are outlined, together with their most general characteristics.

Laser printers

Laser printers generate a page at a time. Using the light of the laser, the page image is directed on to a rotating drum. This leaves an image area, which attracts ink through which the drum is rolled. The image is then transferred to paper. Page printers for large computers can cost over $10,000. They can produce output of high quality at up to fifty pages a minute. Smaller laser printers aimed more at the desktop PC market cost less than $200 and produce a page about every 4 to 6 seconds.

Serial printers

Serial printers produce one character at a time. The two most common types are the inkjet and the dot-matrix printer.

Inkjet printers eject a stream of special ink through a fine nozzle to form the characters. These are 'painted' on to the paper. Inkjet printers provide good-quality output. They can also provide a variety of typefaces and produce diagrams, logos and other graphical output. Modern inkjets can also produce high-quality multicoloured output. Inkjet printers are quiet in operation. Typical speeds for an inkjet would be approximately ten pages a minute. Improvements in technology have made inkjet printers a serious rival to laser printers for certain office purposes, particularly low-volume colour printing.

The **dot-matrix printer** has a movable print head, which consists of a matrix of pins. For example, a head may contain 252 pins in a matrix of 18×14. In printing, the set of pins corresponding to the shape of the character to be printed is impacted on to the ribbon, which then leaves an inked image on the page. Dot-matrix printers print at a range of speeds – 400 characters per second would be typical. Because they are not limited to a particular set of typefaces, dot matrix printers can produce a wide variety of typefaces, fonts, spacings and symbols. Dot-matrix printers have largely been replaced by laser printers for business use and by inkjet printers for home use. The most common use for dot-matrix output now is in the production of documents such as receipts, where carbonized copies are produced for both the customer and the business.

Other less common types of printer include **thermal printers**, which burn away a coating on special paper to leave a visible character.

Line printers

The two most common sorts are **chain printers** and **drum printers**. These are both printers that rely on the impact of type on a ribbon, which then marks paper. Line printers are high-speed and can produce between five and thirty lines a second, depending on the particular type of printer chosen. Line printers are more expensive than serial printers, and their speeds mean that they are more suitable for a larger computer, usually a minicomputer or a mainframe computer. The quality of output is low, and there is little flexibility in type styles. Line printers are the output workhorses of a large computer system. Because of their low-quality output, they are generally used for internal reports or high-volume output activities such as printing customer account statements for a large company.

Output to optical disk, magnetic disk or tape

Rather than producing an output that is directly understandable visually or aurally, it is possible to produce output on a magnetic medium such as disk or tape or an optical medium. This is done if the output is being generated for eventual input into another computer system. Alternatively, it may be used where the disk or tape is employed at a later stage or at a different geographical location to supply output information based on one or other of the other output media.

Output on disk or tape is popular as a persisting medium because it is very cheap and fast to produce. The tape or disk itself is highly portable, requires little storage space and is even capable of being sent through the post. The obvious drawback of this output method is the need to possess a computer to understand its magnetic or optical contents.

3.2.6 Factors involved in the selection of output device and medium

The following features must be taken into account:

- **The type of application:** This is crucial when considering output. It is important to establish whether permanent copy is required or not, and whether the output is to be distributed or not, and whether receivers have access to special machinery such as microfiche readers or computers.

- **Costs:** Initial costs for the output devices vary enormously. The chief components of running costs will involve sundries such as paper, film ribbons, and so on. Depreciation and maintenance must be allowed for those output devices that involve mechanical parts.

- **Speed and volume of output:** Estimates must be made of the requirements under this heading and suitable devices chosen that match them.

- **Quality of output:** Internal documents generally require less high-quality output than external documentation used for clients or marketing purposes.

- **Storage of output:** Bulky output cannot be stored and retrieved easily.

- **Environmental considerations:** This is particularly important for output devices that would normally be located in an office. Many printers produce noise, which causes stress and other complaints. Manufacturers have responded to this need by emphasizing quietness, where applicable, to their advertising and naming of products.

Although aspects of technology have been emphasized in this section, it should never be forgotten that the first, and most important, consideration with respect to output is its content and format. Unless attention is paid to the selection of relevant information and its proper presentation at the right time and at the desired level of detail the output will be of little use. This area is covered in the chapters on systems analysis and design.

Mini case 3.6

Output by text message

Forget being sacked by text message. Jobcentre Plus, which manages the national network of state employment and benefits offices, plans to text the mobiles of unemployed people with news of suitable jobs.

David Anderson, the new chief executive of Jobcentre Plus, told the *Financial Times* of plans to match listed employer vacancies with jobseekers' CVs automatically through a computer system. By 2006 everyone on jobseeker's allowance will be able to see a list of vacancies that match their skills and experience at job centre screens, on the Internet, and by checking messages on their phones.

The news will help to destroy mobiles' nascent reputation as bearers of bad tidings. When the company behind Accident Group, the personal injury business, went into administration in May a text message was sent asking employees to call a number where a recorded message told them of their redundancy – a technique that has passed into trade union folklore as an exemplar of heartless capitalism.

Jobcentre Plus's high-tech plans form part of a strategy to devote more time to those who are hardest to help into work by devoting less time to those who are more capable of finding work.

A more automated system will allow personal advisers who help people into work to reduce time spent on routine tasks, in favour of intensive practical and moral support for people who face severe barriers to finding a job. Pressures on staff time are particularly severe since the number of job centre staff has been cut by about 10 per cent in recent months.

Jobcentre Plus plans to use text messaging for sending vacancy alerts.
By David Turner, Employment Correspondent
Financial Times: 29 July 2003

Questions

1. What alternative method of output could be used to communicate with the clients of Jobcentre Plus?

2. What factors might have been considered by Jobcentre Plus in choosing the text message method of output compared to alternative approaches?

3.2.7 Central processing unit

The central processing unit is often described as the 'nerve centre' of the computer. It is a term that has been defined in many different ways. These include:

- a conceptual view of the functional units individually called the control unit, the ALU, the main memory and the register set (all defined below);
- the 'processor' i.e. the control unit and the ALU but not including the main memory;
- a proprietary chip such as one of the Intel Pentium series of processor chips;
- the entire base unit case containing fans, disk drives, chips, cables etc. (as in 'I keep my CPU on the floor rather than on my desk').

In this text, the first definition has been adopted. A general outline of the component parts of the CPU is now given (see Figure 3.14).

Figure 3.14 The components of the central processing unit

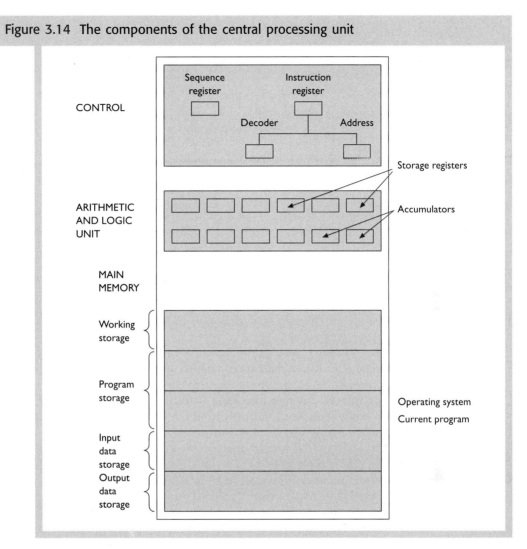

Main memory

Synonyms are fast memory, immediate-access memory, random-access memory, direct-access memory and primary storage. The purpose of the main memory is:

- to store programs during their execution;
- to store data that is being used by the current program; and
- to store the operating system.

Main memory nowadays is exclusively based on silicon microchip storage. The unit of storage is the byte, and the declining costs per byte of store can be seen in Figure 3.15. Memory space is divided into separate storage locations. Each storage location is assigned an **address** and holds a certain number of bits of information. It is common for computers to hold one byte (eight bits) at each location. The contents of these locations can be directly recovered using the address of the location. The contents of other addresses do not have to be searched in order to retrieve a piece of data from a given address.

Figure 3.15 The declining costs of silicon-based microchips

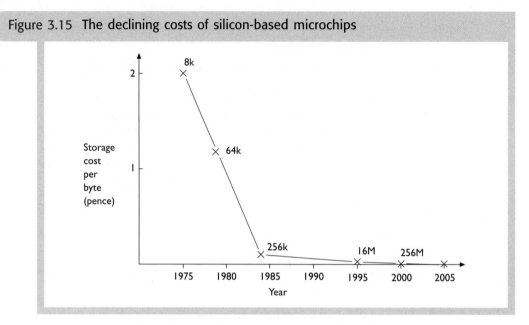

Because the time taken to recover the contents of an address is independent of the address, main storage is called **random-access memory** or **RAM**.

The contents of RAM disappear when the power supply is disconnected, so RAM is said to be **volatile**. Another important feature of RAM is that not only can data be read that is copied from a memory location but data can also be written to that memory location. In doing this, it erases any previous contents.

As shown in Figure 3.14, main memory is divided into several areas depending on the function that is served.

One part of the memory is used to store the current program being executed. In a large computer, there may be many 'current' programs, which are programs somewhere between their initiation and completion. The operating system, or a large part of it, is also stored in main memory. The functions of an operating system are covered in a later section in this chapter. Other parts of the primary storage are reserved for holding input data coming from either an input device or secondary storage, for holding output data that is to be transferred to an output device or secondary storage, or for holding working data that is being swapped in and out of the arithmetic and logic unit.

A typical size for main memory in a modern business desktop computer is 512 megabytes. Each couple of years sees the doubling of average desktop computer RAM. For a mainframe, the primary store will run into many megabytes.

Computers also have **read-only memory (ROM)**. ROM, as its name suggests, will not allow the data stored in its memory locations to be written to or changed. The data is permanent, even when the electrical power is removed. ROM is used to store the initial instructions in a computer's start-up routine. ROM is also used for the storage of **microprograms**. These are series of instructions that carry out commonly used routines.

Arithmetic and logic unit

The purpose of the arithmetic and logic unit (ALU) is:

- to carry out arithmetic operations – for example, to add two numbers together;
- to carry out logical operations – for example, to compare two numbers to establish which is the larger.

The arithmetic and logic unit consists of electronic circuits made with transistors. Many program instructions involve a logical or arithmetic operation of the type outlined above. The operation is carried out by the ALU, its exact nature being governed by the circuitry triggered by the program instruction. Typically, the items of data being operated upon are stored in special-purpose **data registers** and the result placed in a special register called the **accumulator**. Any specific outcomes of the operation, such as an overflow caused by a calculation result that is too large to be represented in the registers, are stored in a register called the **processor status register**.

Control

The purpose of the control unit is:

- to decode and execute the program instructions one by one;
- to control and coordinate data movements within the CPU and between the CPU and the other components of the computer system.

Inside the control unit are important registers dealing with the execution of a program. One register, called the **sequence register**, contains the address of the current instruction being executed. The **instruction register** contains the current instruction being executed. There are two parts to this instruction. The **operator** stipulates the type of instruction, such as **ADD**, **GET**, **MULTIPLY**. This is decoded by circuitry in the decoder. The **operand** contains the address or addresses of the data items on which the instruction must work. Having carried out the program instruction, the contents of the instruction register are incremented, and this provides the address of the next instruction to be executed.

Data must be moved around the computer. An example is the need to print the output of a program where the output is currently held in main memory. The CPU works by carrying out many millions of instructions every second. In contrast, the printer may print only a hundred characters a second. In order to make efficient use of computing resources, this speed difference must not be allowed to tie up the fast CPU while waiting for the slow printer to finish its task. What happens is that the CPU instructs the printer to produce output, and while it is doing this the CPU can carry out other activities. When the output device has completed its task it **interrupts** the operation of the CPU, which then continues to service the device. Handling these interrupts is a function of the control unit.

3.2.8 Current issues involved in CPU design

The control unit and arithmetic and logic unit are together called the **processor**. These two components are generally held on one silicon micro-integrated circuit (microchip). The immediate-access memory is held as several microchips, which are accessible to the processor. Each memory chip may hold up to 512 megabytes of memory, depending on its type. Technological developments of the CPU concentrate on two major areas:

1. speeding up the operation of the CPU, so that programs run more quickly;
2. making larger amounts of cheaper RAM available to the processor, so that a larger number of more complex programs may be held entirely in main memory during

execution. This saves the lengthy task of loading parts of programs in and out of secondary storage and main memory during a program run.

In order to achieve these objectives, several development strategies are adopted by microchip manufacturers and designers.

1. The speed of the CPU is partly determined by the **clock cycle time**. There is a clock in the CPU, and operations can only occur in time with the beat of this clock. If the clock is speeded up then more operations can occur per second. This is one strategy – to design microchips capable of operating with faster clock speeds. Clock speeds are measured in terms of the number of operations per second and are commonly expressed in terms of **megahertz**. One megahertz (MHz) is equivalent to one million operations per second. A business desktop computer might be expected to operate at over 1000 MHz.

2. Increasing clock speed is not the only possibility. All processors are designed to be able to decode and execute a determinate number of types of instruction. This is known as the **instruction set**. It is well known that a majority of these instructions are rarely used. Microchips can be designed to operate more quickly if the set of instructions is reduced to those that are most basic and commonly used. If one of the more rarely used instructions is needed it can be carried out by combining some of the more basic instructions. These microchips are known as **RISC** (reduced instruction set computer) chips.

3. The ALU and control unit are designed to carry out each operation with a chunk of data of a standard size. This is known as the **word** length. The earliest microchips worked with a word length of 8 bits, or one **byte**. If this is increased, then clearly the computer will be able to process more data in each operation. Word sizes of 32 bits are now common in business desktop computers and 64-bit processors are beginning to create interest. Mainframe computers have traditionally used longer word lengths compared to PCs. The trend is to develop processors that handle longer words.

4. Data is transferred between main memory and the processor frequently. The processor will be slowed in its functioning if it has to wait for long periods for the transfer of the data needed for an operation. Data is transferred in parallel along data lines. For an early 8-bit processor (word length equals 8 bits) there were eight data lines in and eight data lines out of the processor. Clearly, one byte of data could be transferred in one operation. This coincides with the word length. Modern processors can transfer several bytes of data in each operation.

5. The speeds of operation of processors and memory chips are so fast now that, relatively speaking, a major delay occurs because of the time the electrical signal takes to move from the memory to the processor. One way to shorten this period is to decrease the distance of the processor from the memory. This is achieved by building some memory on to the processor chip. This memory is called **cache memory**.

6. The single processor is based on the von Neumann model of the computer. In an application, although some of the tasks must be carried out in sequence, many can be performed in parallel with one another, provided that the results of these tasks are delivered at the right times. There is considerable research and development interest in **parallel processing** using several processors, each working in parallel with the others. This can increase the rate at which the computer can carry out tasks.

7. All the developments mentioned so far are directed at increasing the speed of processing. There is also a need to increase the amount of RAM available to the processor. This cannot be achieved simply by plugging in more RAM microchips. Each RAM location needs to be separately addressable. Memory address lines fulfil this function. If there are twenty memory address lines associated with a processor, then a maximum of 2^{20} bytes or 1 Mb of memory can be addressed directly. Modern desktop computers may have over 512 Mb of RAM and processors are able to address increasingly large amounts of memory.

8. At the leading edge of developments, new technologies based on laser-light switching and biochemically based processors are being investigated. These are currently in an early stage of research.

Over the last two decades, chip manufacturers have produced families of processor chips incorporating successive improvements. For instance, Intel, a major international microchip manufacturer, has produced a series of chips that are widely used in business desktop computers. The set consists of the 80X86 and Pentium processors. The later chips are improvements over the earlier ones, having faster clock speeds, larger word sizes, more data lines and more addressable RAM.

Mini-case 3.7

Processors

Do not take this personally, but the microprocessor that powers your personal computer is pretty dumb. While the sliver of silicon can crunch gazillions of numbers per second, it can do only one thing at a time.

Until now, computer scientists have worked round this limitation using a technique known as time slicing. The processor devotes itself for a few milliseconds to, say, surfing the Internet, then moves on to burning a compact disc, then does a few of the calculations that allow you to play Grand Theft Auto III.

This happens with such speed and slickness that to the user it feels seamless. The computer appears to be multi-tasking even though it is not.

But time slicing is no longer enough to satisfy the demands of users. The technology to enable microprocessors to multi-task has been around since the mid-1990s.

In contrast to time slicing, with each job dealt with in strict rotation, a 'simultaneous multi-threading' (SMT) processor can work at any time on whatever requires attention. It does not need to wait for the next time slice in order to change jobs.

What is more, the really big performance gains come only when the applications that the computer is working on are easily divisible into sub-tasks or 'threads'.

This last point means that some jobs lend themselves more naturally to multi-threading than others. Serving up web pages to consumers, where each request for a page can be treated as a new thread, is the kind of application at which SMT processors excel. The order in which threads are executed is not usually critical.

In contrast, complex scientific calculations that require numbers to be crunched in strict sequence are less susceptible to the SMT treatment.

When will this technology reach consumers?

It already has. Intel's newest Xeon chips for servers and Pentium IV chips for personal computers, launched late last year, are each capable of running two simultaneous threads.

▶

IBM's newest PowerPC processors have similar capabilities and can switch between single-threaded and multi-threaded modes as circumstances dictate.

It is Sun Microsystems, however, that is placing the biggest bet on SMT. The company says that by 2006 it aims to be building computers based on chips that incorporate no fewer than eight processors on a single chip, with each processor capable of running four threads simultaneously.

Adapted from: **TECHNOLOGY: From soloist to symphony orchestra**
By Simon London
Financial Times: 26 November 2003

Questions

1. How does the SMT processor improve system performance?
2. Which applications are particularly suited to the multi-threading processor approach?

3.3 Software

'Software' is the general term for instructions that control the operation of the computer. This section deals with the basic sorts of software and the various languages in which it may be written.

3.3.1 The concept of a program

In order to be able to serve any useful purpose, the operation of the computer must be controlled by a program. A **program** is a set of instructions, written in a specialized language, the electronic execution of which controls the operation of the computer to serve some purpose.

Software is the general name given to programs or parts of programs. There are two types of software. **Systems software** carries out functions that are generally required in order to ensure the smooth and efficient operation of the computer. Examples are the operating system (explained later), a program for copying the contents of one disk to another or a file reorganization program. **Applications software** performs functions associated with the various needs of the business (as distinct from the needs of the computer). Examples are programs that carry out accounting tasks such as sales, purchase and nominal ledger processing, a modelling program for forecasting sales figures, or a word-processing program.

Programs are stored in immediate-access memory while being run. The instructions are executed in sequence starting from the first instruction. They are loaded one at a time from immediate-access memory into the control unit of the CPU, where they are decoded and executed. Broadly speaking, there are four types of instruction:

1. **Data movement instructions**, when executed, cause data to be moved around the computer. The movement may be between the CPU and the input, output or backing store, or within the CPU itself.

2. **Arithmetic and logic instructions** lead to the transformation of data in the ALU.

3. **Program branching instructions** alter the sequential execution of the program. An unconditional branch instruction leads to the execution of a specified next

instruction rather than the instruction immediately after the one being currently executed. This is achieved by putting the address of the desired instruction in the sequence register in the control unit. Conditional branch instructions lead to a change in execution order only if a specified logical condition is met: for example, if $x > 19$ then branch to instruction 1200.

4. **Start, stop and declaration** instructions commence the execution of the program, terminate the execution of the program and make declarations, respectively: for example, that a certain area of memory is to be known by a particular name.

3.3.2 Applications packages and programs

When faced with the need to obtain software for its business information, decision support or data-processing systems, an organization may either commission specially written software or purchase a standard applications package.

An **applications package** is a piece of software designed to carry out a standard business function. It is usually produced by a computer manufacturer or software house intending to sell many copies of the package to different organizations. Purchasers of the package do not own the copyright and will usually have clearly specified limited rights to make copies or alterations. Applications packages are common in the following business areas: all accounting, payroll and stock control functions, word processing, electronic spreadsheets, critical path analysis, financial modelling, and statistical analysis, being described as 'off the shelf' or 'shrink-wrapped'.

In contrast, **specially commissioned software** is designed and written for the *specific* business needs of an organization. It may be written 'in house', if the organization is large enough to have a computer centre with a team of programmers, or it may be produced by a third-party software house. In either case, the commissioning organization usually owns the copyright. The software can be written in a high-level language, such as C++. The specification of the business needs of an organization and the translation of these into program specifications is often preceded by a considerable period of analysis and design. Specially commissioned programs are often described as being 'tailor-made'.

There are several benefits and limitations associated with purchasing applications packages as compared with commissioned software.

Benefits

In summary, the benefits are:

- **Cost:** Applications packages are intended for sale to many purchasers, therefore the research and development costs of the software are spread among many organizations. This lowers the cost to purchasers. For instance, a quality accounts package for a desktop computer may cost £2000 and for a mainframe £20,000. This compares favourably with the costs of specially commissioned software, which would be many times greater.

    From the supplier's point of view, when enough packages have been sold to break even with production costs, the profit margin on each additional copy sold is immense. For instance, on a £500 desktop computer-based package, after subtracting the costs of the disk and manual, it is not uncommon for there to be £490 gross profit. However, if there are few sales the software house can suffer a very large loss.

- **Speed of implementation:** A package can generally be purchased and installed on the hardware very quickly compared with a specially commissioned program, which requires much time to write and debug.

- **Tried and tested:** A successful package has been tried and tested by many previous purchasers. This means not only that various errors that may have occurred in earlier versions will have been remedied but also, more importantly, that the package will be one that is known to satisfy the general business function for which it was intended. However, a tried and tested package will not be 'state of the art' software but will reflect what was new several years ago.

- **New versions:** New, improved versions of a successful package are brought out from time to time. These updated versions are often made available to existing customers at a lower rate. This is one way the customers are assured that their software follows what the market is currently offering. From the supplier's point of view, it encourages 'brand loyalty'.

- **Documentation:** Packages often have clear, professionally produced documentation. This is a marketing point for the software house. It also prevents customers encountering difficulties that would otherwise involve the software house in answering time-consuming enquiries. Specially commissioned programs generally do not have such good documentation.

- **Portability:** Packages may be portable from one type of computer to another. As important is the portability of the user interface. For instance, a company that currently uses a particular word-processing package on a certain type of hardware may wish to change its hardware. If it can purchase another version of the package on the new hardware that presents the same screens and uses the same files it will not have to retrain its staff or convert files.

Although these reasons are persuasive in opting for packaged software, there are some limitations.

Limitations

In summary, these are:

- **Lack of satisfaction of user requirements:** This is the most important drawback of purchasing a package. A large business is likely to have specialized information and data-processing requirements. It is common that no package fits these needs exactly. Large businesses can afford to commission software. The situation is different for small organizations. However, their needs are simpler, and it is more likely that a package can be found that suits them. Also, they are often not able to afford the extensive costs involved in writing programs.

- **Efficiency:** In order to appeal to as wide a market as possible packages build in flexibility (for example, many report options) and redundancy (for example, the ability to handle many accounts). For the purchaser, much of this may not be needed and will cause the package to run less efficiently on the computer.

- **Compatibility with existing software:** It is unlikely that packages will be compatible with existing specially commissioned software. If interfacing is required it is usually necessary for further software to be commissioned.

The desktop computer market is more heavily package-based than the minicomputer or mainframe market. From the demand side, this is because there are more desktop computers, and in particular more small businesses with desktop computers, than larger computers. Small organizations are forced for cost reasons to purchase packages to meet their software needs. On the supply side, the desktop computer market presents more opportunities for very high volumes of sales of package-based software.

The price of the standard business desktop computer has dropped over the years. This can be explained partly by the decrease in hardware costs and partly by the development of cheaper versions of the IBM PC range by other manufacturers. The numbers of machines has expanded and so, therefore, has the market for software.

As the number of business desktop computers has increased, package software suppliers have produced more specialized packages. For instance, as well as many standard accounting packages for small businesses, there are now specialist packages for the general professions such as solicitors, insurance brokers and general practitioners, and for the more unusual needs of veterinary surgeons, funeral directors and others. As business desktop computers become more powerful in the future and competition between software houses more intense, the packages themselves are likely to become more sophisticated.

Office suites

Early applications packages in the desktop computer marketplace usually competed by product rather than by vendor. Each product type was promoted highlighting the unique features compared with its rivals. This often resulted in companies selecting their word-processing package, spreadsheet and database from different vendors to exploit these differences. More recently the trend has been towards package integration, with vendors putting together suites of packages for a range of business solutions. The emphasis is towards consistency in user interface, in features and functions and in file formats. Customers have usually selected the product of one vendor to gain the benefits of this consistency.

A typical suite such as Microsoft Office will comprise a word processor, spreadsheet and database, a presentation and graphics package, an e-mail package and possibly other items such as accounting software. The consistency is reinforced by the interconnections between the packages. For example, a spreadsheet can be embedded inside a word-processed document, and a database can be converted into a spreadsheet. A graphical image can be scanned in using a scanner, edited in a graphics package and then placed on to a slide as part of a presentation. The integration provides a valuable additional level of functionality while maintaining the loyalty of the customer across the range of packages.

Usually, the word processor is designed to integrate fully with the communications software, allowing a document to be e-mailed or faxed to another user from within the package. A spelling checker, which once found its home only in a word processor, is now a fully integrated part of the other packages.

3.3.3 Operating systems

An operating system is a piece of systems software that handles some of the housekeeping routines necessary for the smooth and efficient operation of the computer. Its relation to hardware, users and applications programs is shown in Figure 3.16. The operating system is loaded into main memory and run when the power is supplied to the computer. It is usually held initially on disk and is loaded by means of a short ROM-based 'bootstrap' program. The operating system has many functions. The main ones are:

Figure 3.16 The relation between the operating system, users and hardware

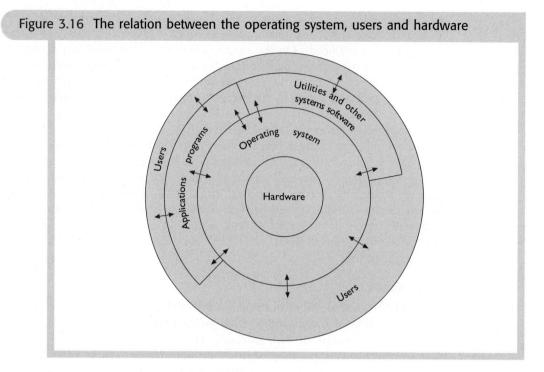

- **Handling input/output:** All applications programs require interchange of data between the CPU and input/output devices. This could be controlled by instructions within the applications program, but as, say, sending output to a printer is common to most programs it makes more sense to produce the controlling instructions once and make the code available as part of the operating system, to be called upon as necessary.

- **Backing store management:** Data and programs need to be loaded into and out of main memory from time to time. It is important that this be done without over-writing existing files and in such a way that later retrieval is possible.

- **Main memory management:** Similarly, main memory must be allocated to programs and data in such a way that they do not overwrite one another. If the program is too large to fit into main memory, then the relevant parts are **paged** into and out of main memory. It 'appears' to the applications program that the computer has an indefinitely large **virtual** memory.

- **Handling job scheduling, multiprogramming and multiprocessing:** To meet the processing requirements of a business organization needing many 'jobs' performed by its hardware, it is necessary to prioritize these jobs and ensure that the CPU acts on them according to this priority. **Job scheduling** is controlled by the operating system. To make more efficient use of the hardware it is often necessary to run more than one program simultaneously so that the fast CPU can carry out operations on one program while waiting for a slow output device to handle the output from another program. The programs are not strictly simultaneous but rather interleaved in their execution. The operating system ensures this efficient **multiprogramming**. In larger computers with more than one central processor the activities of the processors need to be coordinated. The operating system controls this **multiprocessing**.

Mainframe manufacturers either produce their own operating systems in house or commission a software company to do this. With desktop computers, the main operating systems are produced by Microsoft and Apple. The former produces the set of operating systems for the PC, while the latter produces an operating system for its own Apple computers. Microsoft produced the operating systems MS-DOS for the early PCs. These primitive operating systems have now been superseded by the Windows set of operating systems.

Developments within the Windows set of operating systems include the ability to hold, run and pass data between many programs simultaneously within the CPU and to display this with sophisticated screen graphics. Windows ensures that the same graphical interface is consistent from one application to the next. It is possible to pass text, data, spreadsheet model output, graphs and images from one application to another. For instance, the output of a spreadsheet can be pasted into a word-processed document. Essential to this approach is the idea that the interface presented to the human being should be more than the ability to type in text commands at a prompt. Rather, the use of **windows, icons, menus and a pointing device (WIMP)** increases the ability of the user to interact with the machine (see Figure 3.17). The **graphical user interface (GUI)** has become a common feature in most software applications.

Another development in operating systems is the UNIX range. UNIX is a multi-user operating system containing many features useful for program development. It comes in several versions and runs on a range of microcomputers, minicomputers and mainframe computers. The original intention was that software developed in a UNIX

Figure 3.17 An example of a Windows XP interface

environment on one type of machine would be transportable to another. This is not now as straightforward as the original intention assumed, with different 'dialects' of UNIX being developed for different machines.

More recently, the Linux operating system has been developed as a virtually cost-less alternative to UNIX. A number of interested programmers have combined in the project to produce and distribute the code for the system. A popular application for Linux is to provide the systems software for web servers, which require a robust multi-tasking environment for their operation. Linux and the many applications designed for the Linux environment are referred to as **open source software**. This is because the code is mode freely available for developers to inspect, amend and recompile.

Mini case 3.8

Open source software

OSS can give businesses the ability to create standardized working practices and tai-lored business ecosystem models that allow industry vertical markets to collaborate in a way that hasn't been possible before. The quality of open source efforts has certainly increased and it is no longer perceived a radical idea, but a trend and a method of software development that has produced good work and has sometimes surpassed its commercial alternative in terms of robustness.

The basic idea behind OSS is very simple. Programmers can read, redistribute, and modify the source code for a piece of software in an 'open' environment. The software can therefore evolve rapidly, and more people can use it as a 'standard'. As more people use the code, it becomes richer and evolves to become the choice for even more people to use. If you're used to the slow pace of conventional software development with limited numbers of developers, the speed of development and the deployment of capabilities across the Internet that OSS can support is astonishing. For these reasons OSS is likely to become the normal approach for many web services offerings.

The quality of OSS is usually very high, as the creation process applies strong peer pressure. Many professional programmers work in their own time on OSS code, where they feel freed from constraints of commercial management structures that demand 'good enough' results or even compromises. There is a serious code of conduct that OSS pro-grammers adhere to around truth, and to the production of quality, that leads to acclaim for good work, as well as the kudos of seeing their name forever associated with the code they have produced. This perpetual linkage is a strong incentive to make sure it is a good advert for their skills!

In summary, OSS is not a magic bullet, and cannot be used for every type of soft-ware development project. Selecting to use OSS where the conditions are right will prove to be successful not only in the functionality provision but in the cost and time benefits too. However, it still needs to be managed in the same way as any other project, includ-ing licensing terms, and may have to be integrated with existing software.

Adapted from: **Open source software – friend or foe**
By Andy Mulholland
FT.com site: 10 November 2003

Questions

1. What are the benefits to organizations of adopting open source software?
2. An IT manager might have a view that 'I only buy Microsoft – I know where they are when things go wrong'. Evaluate this strategy.

3.3.4 Low-level, high-level, object-oriented and the fourth generation of languages

A program is always written in a specialized language. There are a number of categories of language, each exhibiting different characteristics.

Machine code

Each CPU has its own particular basic set of instructions; a CPU can only 'understand' an instruction if it is taken from this set of instructions. These instructions, known as machine code, consist of strings of 1s and 0s. A typical instruction might be 0110 1010 0110 1011. The first programs were written in machine code in the 1940s. Writing in machine code is extremely difficult. Not only must the programmer think in terms of 1s and 0s when writing code, it is almost impossible to understand code once written. This leads to further difficulties if the program does not perform as intended – that is, has a **bug**. Programs are rarely written in machine code nowadays. Assembly language is used.

Assembly language

Assembly language overcomes some of the difficulties of programming in machine code. The instructions use mnemonics such as 'ADD' or 'STO' (store) instead of binary. A typical instruction might be 'ADD R1,R2,R4' – add the contents of registers 1 and 2 and put the result in register 4. References to memory locations are replaced by reference to named memory areas. The use of binary to represent numbers is replaced by decimal or hexadecimal (a number system having a base of 16). Groups of instructions that are to be repeated many times in a program can be defined and named. These are called **macros**.

These differences mean that programming with assembly language is much easier than with machine code. Assembly languages were developed very early in the history of the electronic computer. Once written, an assembly language program needs to be translated into a machine code program. This is achieved by an **assembler** program. This straightforward program takes the original **source program** and translates it instruction by instruction to become the final machine code **object program** capable of being run on the computer.

Assembly languages are an improvement on machine code in terms of the ease of program production, but they do have some drawbacks:

■ Each different type of processor has a different set of instructions and a different assembly language. Assembly language programs are therefore not portable from one type of machine to another.

■ The assembly language is machine-oriented. Reference is made to registers in the ALU and memory locations. In writing an applications program, a programmer would prefer to concentrate on the task to be coded rather than physical aspects of the machine on which the program is to be finally run.

■ Because each task must be specified in detail, programming is very time-consuming. Assembly languages are context free; they do not provide specific instructions for writing programs in particular problem domains such as business or scientific situations.

The main advantage of programs written in assembly language, as distinct from programs written in high-level languages covered in the next section, is that operations can be specified in detail, making the most efficient use of the machine. This leads to the production of programs that run quickly on the computer. Assembly language programming is used for systems software, where high-speed program execution is required.

High-level languages

High-level languages were developed to increase the productivity of programmers. These languages are task- rather than machine-oriented. This means that instructions in them are more suited to the types of application on which the programmer is employed than to the machines on which the programs will finally run.

Different types of application have spawned different types of high-level language. Well-known languages include:

- **COBOL** (*CO*mmon *B*usiness-*O*riented *L*anguage): COBOL was developed in 1960/61 as a general-purpose business data-processing language. It is particularly suitable for processing large numbers of records. COBOL was a widely used commercial language. It conforms to standards set by ANSI (American National Standards Institute) and CODASYL (*CO*nference of *D*ata *SY*stems *L*anguages). Although versions do exist for desktop computers, COBOL is used most extensively for business applications running on minicomputers and mainframes.

- **FORTRAN** (*FOR*mula *TRAN*slator): FORTRAN is a language developed in the 1950s specifically for the purposes of scientific and mathematical work. It is rich in its ability to handle formulae.

- **BASIC** (*B*eginners *A*ll-*P*urpose *S*ymbolic *I*nstruction *C*ode): BASIC was developed in 1963 and 1964 at Dartmouth College as a language that could be learned and understood very quickly by students. It is now embedded in Microsoft's Visual Basic programming environment.

- **C and C++:** The C programming language has always been popular with experienced programmers. It allows for the construction of very terse code that can, if required, control the machine at a very low level. By accessing registers and memory locations directly, programs can be highly optimized for speed of execution. Code is arranged into functions, with each function performing a logically cohesive task. There is a clear specification of what data is allowed to flow between functions. The aim is to ensure that programs once written are easily understandable, testable and amendable. C++ is a development of the C language. It provides additional programming constructs and structures that allow for the creation of object-oriented programs.

- **Java:** The growth in the Internet and developments in web page construction have led to a sudden increase in interest in the Java programming language. Java has a similar set of instructions to C++ and a number of additional features that make it well suited to developing programs for web pages. Small blocks of code called Java applets can be stored on web servers. When a client requests a web page containing applets, the applet code is transferred to the client and run inside the client's web browser.

- **Ada:** The Ada programming language is named after Ada Augusta, daughter of Lord Byron. It is sponsored by the US Department of Defense for use in military applications.

- **PROLOG:** PROLOG is a language specifically designed for writing programs that require reasoning as distinct from record processing, text handling or number crunching. It is therefore used in artificial intelligence applications. Unlike other languages previously covered, which are all based on writing code for procedures to carry out tasks, PROLOG is designed to be able to declare states from which implications are then derived. PROLOG and another popular artificial intelligence language, LISP, are playing a large role in the development of future intelligent business applications.

The languages discussed constitute a selection of some of the more important high-level languages in current use. There are many more. There are several advantages to using high-level languages compared with low-level assembly languages:

- It should be clear from the descriptions that high-level languages are task-oriented, and there are different types of language for different types of programming requirement. This increases programmer productivity.

- High-level languages also increase programmer productivity because each high-level instruction will eventually be relatively straightforward to learn, often using expressions that are near English. Some, such as BASIC, are so straightforward that simple programs may be written after an afternoon's study of the language. Training times for programmers are reduced and programming requires less qualified personnel.

- Programs written in high-level languages should be portable from one type of machine to another. In practice, this is unlikely because of differences in dialects. However, changes that are necessary are often minor.

In order for a source program in a high-level language to run on a computer it needs to be translated into a machine code object program. This translation may be by **interpreting** or **compiling**. In each case, the translation is carried out by software. When a program is interpreted, as each line is translated into object code it is immediately executed. In contrast, when a program is compiled a compiler program translates the entire source program into object code. The object program can then be executed.

Once compiled object code is produced, it can be used again and again without the need for the source program. Applications software producers prefer to release their packages as compiled code. Compiled code is difficult to understand and so is difficult to alter. This prevents unauthorized tampering with programs. In contrast, no permanent object code is produced when a source program is interpreted. Moreover, the interpreted program will run less quickly than the compiled version. This is because of the necessity for the translation as well as the execution of instructions each time the program is run. Interpreting is popular in the writing of programs because there is no need to compile the entire program each time an alteration is made to it.

Compared with assembly language programs, high-level language programs, whether interpreted or compiled, always run more slowly. This is partly because inefficiencies occur in the process of compiling or interpreting, even though optimization procedures are used. It is also partly because the machine-independent nature of high-level languages prevents programmers using their knowledge of the internal structure of the CPU to increase run-time efficiency. These shortcomings are not enough to deter the use of high-level languages in business applications, where the increases in programmer productivity and the other advantages outweigh the run-time considerations.

Object-oriented languages

Since the 1980s, object-oriented approaches have become important in the design of information systems. This has led to the development of object-oriented analysis (OOA) and design methods (OOD), object-oriented databases (OODBs) and object-oriented programming languages (OOPLs). The ideas behind object-oriented analysis are treated later in this book. Given here is a brief summary of the essential ideas behind an object-oriented programming language.

In conventional programming languages, primitive procedures are combined by the use of the language to perform complex operations – the more high-level the language the more similar these primitive procedures are to real-world tasks and the more distant from machine structures. However, we study the world not in terms of operations but in terms of objects that have properties, stand in relationships with other objects and take part in operations. If a programming language is used to mirror the world, then these features should be deeply embedded in its structure. Object-oriented languages do this by enabling software to be constructed representing objects that have properties and take part in operations.

Three essential ideas lie behind object-oriented languages:

1. Early programming languages usually refer to only a limited number of types of data, such as integers and strings (a string is a collection of ordered characters). These **data types,** as they are known, are defined in terms of the operations in which they can take part. For instance, integers can take part in the operations of multiplication and addition, whereas strings cannot. In later languages, programmers were able to define their own data types. For example, in C an enumeration type can be created: enum summer-month {June, July, August}. Relations such as 'earlier than' could then be defined for this data type. **Abstract data types** as used in object-oriented programming languages are an extension of this principle. An abstract data type, or **class**, is a data type representing a type of object, defined by the programmer in such a way that the data structure is defined along with the named operations in which it can take part. Moreover, the exact details can be kept private from the user of the class. The user has access only to the name of the class and the names of the permitted operations.

2. Object-oriented languages allow for **inheritance**. For example, a pig, as well as having various properties characteristic of a pig, also inherits certain properties, such as suckling its young, from the larger type, mammal, of which it is a subtype. Object-oriented programming languages enable this inheritance to be achieved easily and automatically.

3. Once a system has been developed, a user has only to specify the name of an object and the name of an operation to be carried out and the system will select the appropriate method for carrying out the operation. **Method selection** is a feature of object-oriented programming languages. Object-oriented languages allow for **polymorphism,** so the same operation might cause a different result depending on the type of object to which the message was sent. For example, the same 'draw' instruction sent to a circle object and a rectangle object will produce different screen images.

Object-oriented programming languages have borrowed ideas from other languages, particularly Ada and Simula. The first genuine object-oriented language to be developed was **Smalltalk**, dating back to the 1970s. C++ is the most commonly used commercial language.

It is claimed that software developed using object-oriented techniques and written using object-oriented programming languages has certain advantages:

- Being similar to the way in which users view the world it is a more natural way of mirroring the world with software.
- Program code, once written, is more likely to be reusable. This is because it relies heavily on the definitions of the object types, which can be reused.
- In terms of measures of program complexity (for example, the number of loops nested within loops) object-oriented software is simpler than programs written in other languages and therefore less likely to contain errors.

Object-oriented techniques are influencing many areas of information technology. Many CASE (computer-aided software engineering) tools are based on object-oriented techniques. In artificial intelligence, frame-based approaches (essentially an object-oriented approach) are establishing success as a way of representing knowledge. Object-oriented databases are also gradually becoming more popular. It is likely that object-oriented approaches and languages will have a significant long-term impact on the development of information systems.

Fourth-generation languages

Although it is difficult to derive an agreed standard against which programmer productivity can be measured, it is generally recognized that significant advances have been brought about over the last 30 years by the use of high-level languages. It is also generally accepted that with modern, cheap and powerful micro, mini and mainframe computers, together with the increasingly sophisticated programs required by business, these productivity increases are insufficient to meet the extra demand placed on software production. There are three separate but interrelated problems:

1. **High costs of software production:** High-level languages have reduced costs by increasing programmer productivity, reducing the training required for programmers and increasing the reliability of programs. However, as hardware costs drop, the cost of software production as a proportion of a company's total expenditure on its information system has been increasing over time. The production of versatile software packages to carry out standard business functions has gone some way towards reducing this cost burden. But for an organization that has special needs there is no alternative to commissioning purpose-designed software.

2. **Need to produce systems quickly:** Traditional high-level language programming is still a lengthy business. It cannot be easily speeded up by employing more programmers on the project. The man-month attitude to programming ('if it takes four programmers six months it will take twenty-four programmers one month') has been shown to be a myth. Project control and communication problems between programmers increase rapidly with the number of programmers. Modern project control and the use of structured techniques in programming have gone some way towards diminishing this problem, especially with larger systems. However, small systems are often needed quickly to meet fast-changing requirements, so some alternative to conventional programming must be found.

3. **Need to produce systems that meet user requirements:** The history of business information systems has many examples of systems that are technically efficient but do not serve the needs of users and so are underused or misused. Because traditional

programming involves a long and expensive development by programming experts, much emphasis has gone into methods and techniques that ensure the correct identification of user needs. Another approach is to develop quick, cheap versions or prototypes of systems that users can test for their adequacy before revision and improvement. An extension of this is to develop languages so straightforward and powerful that users themselves can develop their own systems. **End-user computing**, as it is known, requires a different sort of programming language.

Fourth-generation languages (4GLs) attempt to overcome these shortcomings of the previous generations of languages (see Table 3.2). There is no agreed definition of what constitutes a fourth-generation language. It may be a sophisticated language aimed at improving professional programmer productivity by the provision of a range of facilities and routines commonly needed in programming applications. Alternatively, it may be a much more straightforward language designed for end users to construct their own systems. A number of features, though, are common to many fourth-generation languages:

- They are often centred on the storage and retrieval of data in a database, most often a relational database. Although database ideas are covered extensively in the chapter devoted to databases, it is sufficient here to understand a database as a centralized, integrated store of commonly shared data for an organization.

- There is an emphasis on instructions to specify what applications are to do rather than how to do them – that is, utilizing **declarative** rather than **procedural** instructions. These instructions often closely resemble their English equivalents.

- There is a powerful interface with the user of the language, enabling interactive dialogue in the development of applications, the specification of input and output screens and reports, the specification of record contents, the use of defaults, and the use of graphics.

- There are interfaces to conventional programming languages for writing special procedures not covered within the 4GL.

- There are often special facilities for the development of models.

Table 3.2 The generations of languages

Generation	Typical languages	Capabilities
1st	Machine code	Machine-oriented, each language specific to a processor type, programs not portable
2nd	Symbolic assembly language	Easier to use than machine code, although still machine-oriented, each language specific to a processor type, programs not portable
3rd	For example, COBOL, C, BASIC, LISP	Procedurally oriented, task-oriented, increase in programmer productivity over 2GL, portable programs
4th	For example, SQL, FOCUS, NOMAD, RAMIS	Designed for fast applications development, some end-user oriented, integrated for interactive applications development around a database, programs generally not portable

■ The use of these very high-level instructions reduces the total number of programming instructions needed in the development of the system compared with conventional code.

It should be clear from these features that a 4GL is not a conventional language in the sense that say BASIC or COBOL is. The speed, cheapness and ease with which applications can be developed has had impacts in two main areas.

First, the traditional development process for a new system need not be followed. This traditional process involves the progression of a project from its feasibility study through the stages of analysis, detailed specification and implementation. Because the time and costs involved in implementation are great, it is important to ensure that an adequate and final design to meet users' needs is achieved during the specification stage. This linear development process, or rather how a structured analysis and design methodology is appropriate to it, is covered extensively in later chapters. Fourth-generation languages allow the speedy and cheap development of applications software. The importance of this is that a **prototype** version can be developed comparatively quickly and cheaply. This can be tested for its acceptability to users and its appropriateness in the provision of facilities. The prototype can serve either as an integral part of the process of final specification or as a first attempt, which is successively refined over time to make improvements or changed to meet evolving user needs. In both cases the ability to deliver a working prototype quickly and cheaply has changed the development strategy to be adopted.

Second, 4GLs have been developed specifically with the intention of **end-user applications development** in mind. One of the problems of the traditional approach to programming to meet user requirements is that these requirements must be translated into a form suitable for a programmer to be able to write a program. It would ease any communication difficulties if users could translate their information requirements directly into the satisfaction of those needs by programs. Fourth-generation languages oriented towards end-user computing allow this and are simpler than the 4GLs aimed at increasing programmer productivity. Some are designed specifically for the development of desktop computer applications. There is a good reason for this. Purchasers of cheap desktop computers often cannot or do not wish to undertake the expenditure of commissioning lengthy programming in conventional high-level languages. If they cannot find an existing package for their application then writing their own software using a 4GL or development tool is often an acceptable middle-ground approach.

In summary, the main advantages of fourth-generation languages are:

■ It is possible to develop new applications quickly and cheaply.

■ It is possible to maintain and update applications quickly and cheaply.

■ Prototyping is therefore facilitated.

■ Some fourth-generation languages are designed for end-user applications development and so remove the need for a separate body of experts (programmers) in applications development.

From the foregoing, it might be wondered whether fourth-generation languages spell the end of conventional programming for business systems. This is unlikely, not least because there is a large investment in current programs and programming skills involving third-generation languages. These will need continual maintenance and updating. There are, however, other drawbacks and limitations to fourth-generation languages:

- Although 4GLs provide a fast development time for software, the eventual code generated requires more processing power than applications written in third-generation languages such as COBOL. There is a current debate about the trade-off between the costs saved by the short development time in the use of 4GLs and the extra expenditure necessary on hardware to obtain similar performance characteristics in finally developed systems.

- The use of 4GLs particularly by end users can lead to lack of standardization of systems development in an organization because centralized standard setting and control tends to be diminished.

The most widely used 4GL by a large margin is SQL. This language has been used for the prototyping and, in many cases, the subsequent development of a very large number of data-processing applications. SQL is built into most database development tools like Microsoft Access and Oracle. SQL will continue to have a major impact on the development of business information and decision support systems in the future.

Summary

The last five decades have seen the rapid improvement and extensive use of the computer in business data processing and information provision. Successive generations of computers have incorporated technological advances enabling faster, cheaper and more reliable processing. The development of the microchip, as well as improving performance and decreasing the size of computers, has added a new dimension to business computing with the cheap, powerful desktop computer. This has not only extended the user types to include businesses of all sizes but has also enabled a 'leap to freedom' for users in larger organizations from the control of the centralized computer centre.

As a basis for appreciating the ways in which technology can support business information requirements and decision making, it is important to have a background understanding of the hardware and software aspects of technology. In this chapter, the functional components of a computer system and the ways these are implemented with hardware were explained. This was linked in the case of input devices to their suitability for various applications.

Hardware improvements have increased the demand for sophisticated software. Basic software was also examined in the chapter. In particular, the functions of an operating system were covered. Modern operating systems use graphical interfaces and exchange text, data and images between applications. High-level languages, procedurally based around the types of task for which they were suitable, were designed to increase programmer productivity and program reliability to meet this demand. Structured high-level languages are to be viewed within the context of a structured methodology of systems analysis and design. Object-oriented languages have been designed in conjunction with object-oriented analysis and design methods to lead to a richer and more natural means of capturing data-modelling and -processing requirements. The recent development of fourth-generation languages is an alternative to the traditional linear approach to programming through specification, coding, testing and maintenance stages. They are intended to be employed, often by end users, in prototyping. Despite having limitations, prototyping is seen as a way of quickly developing systems meeting user requirements that can easily evolve over time. The area of end-user computing and prototyping is investigated extensively in a later chapter. Small organizations, or those with standard business functions, can avoid the cost of specially commissioning software by purchasing applications packages. These have many advantages. The increasing sale of desktop computers has led to a substantial market for packaged software that is particularly user-friendly.

Review questions

1. What specific advantages did advances in electronics provide for the development of computer systems?

2. What are the factors that influence the selection of data capture method, input method, input devices and media for an application?

3. Explain the distinction between *hardware*, *software* and *firmware*.

4. What characteristics of a business application make it appropriate for computerization?

5. Explain why high-level languages have superseded assembly languages in the production of applications software.

6. How do fourth-generation languages differ from earlier generations and what benefits do they offer over traditional languages?

7. What are the advantages of adopting a package approach to the acquisition of software?

8. Give *four* reasons why packaged software is more common for the microcomputer market than for the mainframe market.

9. Outline the functions of an operating system.

Exercises

1. Why has there been a movement towards the use of desktop computers in large organizations rather than relying wholly on centralized mainframe resources staffed by experienced and highly trained personnel?

2. Why is it not feasible to include a code for the price of a product in the bar-code associated with its packaging?

3. A large TV rental company has high-street branches throughout the UK. Customers typically sign contracts for TV and video rental. Payment is monthly. The majority of customers pay by direct debit through the banking system. However, a significant minority pay at the high-street branches each month. Customer account records are held on a mainframe computer at the head office and require regular updating with customer payment details. Suggest *two* suitable methods of data capture and input for those customers paying at branch offices. Comment on the advantages and disadvantages of your proposals.

4. It is often claimed that programmer productivity has increased over the years. How would you measure programmer productivity?

CASE STUDY 3

Processor power

Today Hewlett-Packard takes a huge step in a computing strategy that not only carries great risks to its future viability but also exposes its large corporate customer base to rivals Sun Microsystems and International Business Machines.

HP is announcing its first commercial corporate computer systems based on a new version of Intel's Itanium 2, a 64-bit microprocessor – called the Integrity family. It ranges from huge supercomputers with hundreds of microprocessors, to speedy servers with one or two microprocessors.

Although Itanium systems have been available from HP and others before now, those were experimental test systems, not ready for serious commercial applications.

The launch of the Integrity Itanium systems marks a critical point in HP's business strategy. Carly Fiorina, chief executive of HP, is betting that the 64-bit computer market will be rapidly commoditized, in the same way as the personal computer market. Gone will be the pricey proprietary 64-bit systems based on Sparc, from Sun Microsystems, Power, from IBM, and HP's own Alpha and PA-Risc chips.

Instead, Itanium chips, available to any computer-maker, will create dynamic price competition, driving down system costs, as in PCs. Computer-makers will make money on software and services, rather than on selling boxes.

Ms Fiorina intends that HP will lead and accelerate that trend towards commoditization. If all goes to plan, HP's huge bet on Itanium will allow it not only to convert its own large Alpha and PA-Risc customer base but also to win substantial business from Sun and IBM users converting to 'industry standard' Itanium systems.

The risks, however, are that commoditization of 64-bit computing will develop far more slowly. And by abandoning its own chips, HP could lose customers to Sun and IBM, whose 64-bit systems offer many more business applications than are available for Itanium.

For HP there is no turning back. And its Integrity Itanium systems appear impressive. The company claims customers can save as much as $1m in costs over three years, compared with IBM's Power-based systems, because of better price performance – a compelling proposition. HP claims similar cost advantages over Sun's Sparc-based systems.

For Intel, HP's success will be critical in its goal to displace Sparc and Power microprocessors with Itanium. Intel dominates PC markets but those have been moribund for more than two years; 64-bit microprocessor markets offer higher prices and profits.

But establishing Itanium has been a hard slog. After nine years in development and three years in production, and HP's and Intel's tireless promotional efforts, Itanium has made hardly any impact. Early versions suffered from poor performance. They had bugs and there were large holes in the supporting infrastructure that every microprocessor needs: software tools, applications and operating systems.

This time it is different, it seems. 'We now have all the elements in place,' says Mike Fister, executive vice-president at Intel. 'We have Microsoft and Linux operating systems, we have increasing numbers of key corporate applications that run on Itanium and the price performance is far ahead that of IBM or Sun.'

But Intel still needs lots more business applications for Itanium and they are slow in coming. It is the problem that faces every new computing architecture: software developers will not create applications for a new type of computer system unless there is a large number of users. Customers will not buy that computer unless lots of applications are available.

The challenge facing HP and Intel is compounded by the fact that potential customers face substantial costs to move from their current 64-bit Risc systems to Itanium. This is because their applications have to be adapted to a new computer system – always expensive. With IT budgets tight and a relentless focus by managers on cutting costs, Itanium can be a hard sell. 'There is clearly no sense in persuading customers to move to Itanium if there is no good reason,' says Tom Iannotti, vice-president of strategy and business development at HP Services. 'But we are confident that for many customers there are proven substantial cost savings.'

One cost-cutting trend within companies is the scrapping of hundreds – sometimes thousands – of servers common in many IT systems. It takes a lot of people to maintain and operate them and staff costs are by far the largest item in IT budgets. By consolidating low-end systems into one or two powerful systems such as HP's Integrity systems, the savings are large and easy to document.

However, in other areas, especially when it comes to converting HP's large customer base to Itanium, cost savings are less apparent. And because HP has stopped developing Risc microprocessors, HP Risc system users will eventually have to move to a different computing platform.

'We hope that customers will switch to Itanium but we know that they will be obligated to look at all other options,' says Mr Iannotti.

Sun, in particular, sees this as a huge business opportunity. 'We love the fact that HP has adopted Itanium,' says Larry Singer, head of competitive strategy at Sun. 'Before, it would have been extremely difficult to target that market but now HP customers face the same costs in migrating to Itanium as they would to Sun. But there are far more applications that run on Sun; and future Sparc microprocessors will easily match Itanium performance.'

IBM, too, is expecting a bounty. Even though it says it will build Itanium systems for customers, it is heavily promoting its competing Power systems. It will also offer customers the opportunity to outsource their IT operations, thereby avoiding the problems of having to migrate to a new computer platform.

Adapted from: **HP gambles on a future with greater power**
By Tom Foremski
Financial Times: 30 June 2003

Questions

1. What is meant by a '64-bit processor'? How does a 64-bit processor deliver improved performance compared to a 32-bit processor?

2. The super computers referred to above contain a large number of processors. How does parallel processing further improve performance?

3. The case study refers to RISC chips. How does the size of the instruction set affect the operation of the processor?

4. What are the risks for HP in moving towards the 'commoditization' of 64-bit computing?

5. The case study indicates that Microsoft and Linux operating systems both run on the Intel Itanium processor. What are the main functions of an operating system? In what ways does the Windows operating system differ from Linux?

6. Applications might be off-the-shelf or tailor-made. How does this distinction affect the ease with which customers might switch between computer platforms?

7. The case study refers to 'consolidating low-end systems into one or two powerful systems'. This reverses the earlier trend of replacing mainframes with networks of servers and desktop PCs. Why has this change come about?

Recommended reading

Chalk B.S., Carter A.T. and Hind W.R. (2004). *Computer Organisation and Architecture: An Introduction*, 2nd edn. Palgrave Macmillan

This is a concise introduction to the way computers work. It explains with straightforward detail the various hardware components, the way they are organized and interconnected, and the way that programs can be executed upon them. It is suitable as a more detailed introduction for those seeking a greater understanding of hardware.

Englander I. (2002). *The Architecture of Computer Hardware and Systems Software Science*, 3rd edn. Wiley

An extremely comprehensive approach to the subject illustrated with numerous examples.

Hennessy J.L. and Patterson D.A. (2003). *Computer Architecture: A Quantitative Approach*, 3rd edn. Kaufmann Academic Press

This is a highly detailed text for students who wish to extend their knowledge of computer architecture well beyond the current text. It adopts a quantitative approach to all aspects of computer systems architecture. It uses illustrations of design from consumer electronics, multimedia and web technologies, and high performance computers, as well as a standard coverage of microprocessors. It is aimed at the computer science student.

Ritchie C. (2003). *Operating Systems Incorporating UNIX and Windows*, 4th edn. Continuum

This is a clearly written and straightforward text intended to give an overview of operating systems with specific reference to UNIX and Windows. The book is aimed at those doing a diploma or degree in computer science. The earlier chapters provide a clear introduction to operating systems accessible to those studying more generally.

Stallings W. (2003). *Computer Organization and Architecture*, 5th edn. New York: Macmillan

This is a detailed text presenting the structure and functions of a computer in much greater depth than the current chapter. It is more than an introductory text. The 2003 edition includes a section devoted to RISC technology.

Chapter 4

Distributed systems, networks and the organization

Learning outcomes

On completion of this chapter, you should be able to:

- Define a distributed system
- Analyse the organizational benefits and drawbacks of distributed systems
- Appraise the degree of distribution in a system in terms of processing power and data
- Describe basic techniques used to transmit signals across networks
- Compare and evaluate techniques for creating communications channels across networks
- Describe topologies for local area networks
- Outline the OSI model and cite issues relating to standards in networking
- Discuss EDI communications between organizations and evaluate the benefits of EDI.

Introduction

Major developments over the last 30 years have been achieved in information technology. It is not uncommon to view this purely as the advent and development of computer systems. However, this ignores the significant impact that improvements and innovations in telecommunications have had as an enabling technology for information systems.

This chapter begins with a consideration of the way in which centralized and distributed systems can be seen as alternatives for handling information provision. The impact of a distributed system on the organization, its benefits and its acceptability, are analysed. In order properly to appreciate issues in networks and distributed computing it is necessary to have at least a basic understanding of the underlying technology. The 'language of networks' is explained, various types of public and local area networks are examined, and the way that issues concerning standards bedevil the full integration of systems is covered. The Internet and the World Wide Web are important enough to merit chapters on their own (Chapters 5 and 6, respectively), although concepts key to their understanding are covered in this chapter. Finally, the impact of electronic data interchange and its effect on the competitive position of the firm in the marketplace is assessed.

135

4.1   Networks and distributed systems

In the last two decades, many organizations have adopted the policy of installing several geographically distinct computers within their organizations and linking these using telecommunications. The computers may be desktop computers linked together locally in one site or even one office. Or it might be the linking of minicomputers or mainframe computers across large geographical distances. As well as these traditional network connections, the growth of the Internet has introduced a simple and relatively inexpensive way for users to establish temporary connections between computers. The issues involved in this distribution of computing power and the linking networks are the subject of this section.

It used to be believed that computing benefited from economies of scale. The previous chapter introduced **Grosch's law**; this stated that the computational and data-processing power of a computer increases with the square of its cost. It therefore made financial sense for an organization to centralize its computer systems in order to get the most power for its money. Under centralization, an organization that is located on several geographically distant sites would then incur a large communications cost. Terminals at each site needed to interchange data constantly with the centralized central processing unit.

With the development of much cheaper computing hardware and, in particular, the development of the microchip, Grosch's law has broken down. There are no longer the same economies of scale to be gained by centralization. Local computers can carry out local processing needs, and the need to communicate between different sites in an organization is reduced to those occasions where data held at one location is needed at another. This is called **distributed computing**.

An example of a distributed system is shown in Figure 4.1. A tyre and car battery manufacturer purchases materials and produces goods for sale throughout the country. The headquarters, factory and a warehouse are located at one site. In order to cut

Figure 4.1 An example of functions in a hierarchical distributed system

distribution costs and satisfy retail orders quickly, the organization maintains two other warehouses in different parts of the country to which the manufactured goods are distributed for storage prior to sale. The headquarters' mainframe computer takes care of centralized accounting, purchasing, production scheduling, wages and salaries, local stock control and local sales order processing. Each of the two warehouses has a small minicomputer to handle its own local stock control and local sales order processing. These two minicomputers are connected to the mainframe computer so that an enquiry can be made to the other warehouses for products not held in the local warehouse that are needed for local retail outlets.

Most of the stock control enquiries and updates will therefore be on the locally held data stores. On the occasions when the local warehouse cannot satisfy a customer demand, the data held at the other warehouses is interrogated via the telecommunications links. As the accounting is carried out centrally, although the sales order processing is local, it is necessary to ensure that sales order and delivery details are exchanged between the local computers and the mainframe. As this is not required immediately on a sale then the data can be transferred at the end of each day in one operation. Although accounting, wages and salaries are handled centrally in this organization, an organization with a different structure might grant greater independence to its branches. These functions would then be the responsibility of each site, and headquarters would receive consolidated accounting reports.

Compare this with a centralized system, as shown in Figure 4.2. Here all the functions are carried out centrally at headquarters. Each time there is a need to access the data store or carry out any processing the interaction between the local sites and headquarters will involve a telecommunications link – even though the processing of data only concerns stock held at the local site. This involves a heavy telecommunications cost. Moreover, unless the links involve high-speed connections the response times in the interaction will be slow. At the headquarters, the mainframe will need to be able

Figure 4.2 An example of functions in a centralized system

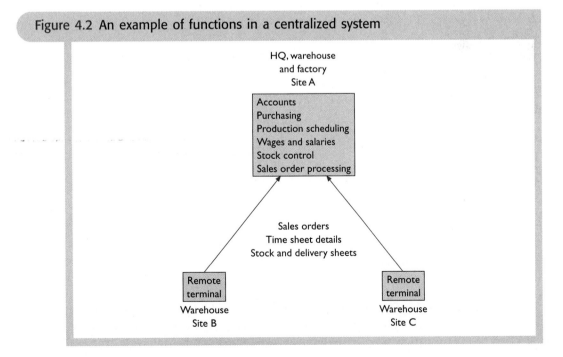

137

to accept transactions from many sites and will need to give over some of its processing time to the maintenance and servicing of queues. This problem will be larger the greater the number of sites and the greater the traffic. In this scenario, it is unlikely that computer personnel will reside at each of the sites. It would be more common to have a centralized team at the headquarters responsible for applications development and the day-to-day running of computer operations. It is easy for users at the local sites to feel isolated – particularly if help is required or difficulties are encountered with the operation of the system. As can be seen from the two treatments of essentially the same set of functions, a distributed approach has much to commend it.

However, it would be simplistic to suggest that there were only two possible approaches – distributed or centralized. In the above case there is a hybrid. In the 'distributed' example certain functions are in fact centralized: the distribution of the stock control system, particularly that component dealing with the update of stock data relating to another warehouse held at another site, involves considerable technical complexity as the database itself is distributed. A variation on this is to hold copies centrally of the stock data on each of the sites. Downloading to each site of all the stock data on all of the sites occurs early in the morning. Local processing of data on stock held locally occurs during the day. However, information on stocks at other warehouses is obtained by interrogating the early morning copies received locally. These may be out of date – but only by a maximum of 24 hours. Requests for stock from other sites together with the end-of-day copy of the local stock data are transferred to the central mainframe at the end of the day. The central mainframe carries out overnight processing and produces up-to-date stock data for each site, which is downloaded the following morning. This escapes the complexity of requiring a truly distributed database at the expense of forfeiting the immediate update of all stock transactions.

It should be clear from the above that the simple idea of distributed versus centralized does not apply. Rather the question that is addressed nowadays is to what extent and how should the organization decentralize its functions and data?

4.2 The idea of a distributed system

The term **distributed system** has been used to cover many varieties of computer system. A computer system is said to be distributed if:

> *it consists of hardware located at least two geographically distinct sites, connected electronically by telecommunications, where processing/data storage occurs at more than one site.*

In a distributed system, there are a number of important features to be considered:

- the locations of processing and the types of interaction between them;
- the location of data storage and the way data is presented to users;
- the nature of the communications links between the various locations; and
- the standards governing the nature of the communication.

These are introduced here and covered in more technical detail later in this chapter.

1. **Distributed processing** can occur in several ways. At the simplest level (and hardly justifying the term 'distributed processing'), individual computers may carry out their own processing but send messages to one another in an electronic mailing system.

A more integrated connection occurs with **cooperative processing**, where processing is handled by two cooperating geographically distinct processors. One processor sends the output of its processing to another for completion. The situation becomes more complex if the operating systems of both machines are different. **Cooperative operating systems** are then needed as well.

2. **Distributed databases** occur when data is not held at one central site but is held at various locations. Broadly, this can happen in one of two ways. 'Master' data may be held at a designated site and copies downloaded via telecommunications to other sites to be held locally. When data is needed at a site it consults its own copy of the master data. With such systems it is usually not permissible for a site to change its locally held copy of data relating to another site, otherwise the various copies of the data held throughout the organization would become inconsistent. If data changes are to be made, data is uploaded to the master database, which is then updated, possibly overnight. New copies of the database are sent to all sites the following morning.

   However, truly distributed databases distribute the data over several sites without duplication. Any user wishing to access the data does so and the data is recovered from the database at the relevant site using database and communications software. As far as the user is concerned it is transparent as to where the data is held. In both cases of distributing data, common data definitions and standardization of data operations are crucial.

3. The **nature of the communications links** between the various locations concerns the topology of the network and the technology of its implementation. The ways in which sites may be connected – their topology – are shown in Figure 4.3. Different topologies serve different purposes. For example, the hierarchical topology often characterizes the arrangement in organizations that have a centralized mainframe (the top) connected through a **wide area network** to minicomputers at local sites, which in turn have PCs connected to them. The ring and bus topologies are common methods of connection for groups of PCs that need to communicate with one another and with other devices. These **local area networks** are treated more extensively later in the chapter. Finally, many systems may be connected together, yielding hybrid topologies. As well as the topology, the nature of the hardware – cabling and network cards in machines – and software controlling communications are major determinants of network characteristics.

4. The **standards** governing the way in which devices 'talk' to one another and the principles governing the way in which users can communicate are currently being specified through internationally agreed standards such as the **Open Systems Interconnection (OSI)**, treated later in the chapter.

4.3 Organizational benefits of distributed systems

Distributed systems were first introduced in the 1970s and have become increasingly common ever since. This is partly because of technological advances in telecommunications, distributed databases and communications software, and partly because of the recognition of the benefits conferred on an organization by the use of such systems. This is one area in which IT developments have responded to user needs as well as being driven by them.

Figure 4.3 Various network topologies: (a) hierarchical; (b) star; (c) ring; (d) bus; (e) hybrid

Organizational benefits are as follows:

- **Increased user satisfaction:** As stated above, users can feel remote from the computer centre, its expert staff and the development of applications if geographically separated from the source of the computing power. User needs are often not taken into account, and assistance may be slow or at 'arm's length' through the computer terminal. Local computer centres serving local needs solve this problem by ensuring that users have greater autonomy. However, from a central organizational perspective, it is important that dispersed sites be connected to one another and the centre. This is not only for reasons of data sharing but also to ensure that, although autonomy may be welcomed, local sites act congruently with corporate goals. Distributed systems ensure that data transfer and connectivity with the centre occur while encouraging local autonomy and user satisfaction.

- **Flexibility of systems development:** An organization that is growing can add to its computer power incrementally in a distributed system by the purchase, installation and connection of new nodes to the network as the needs arise. With a centralized system, flexibility is reduced by the inability to grow incrementally. Growth typically involves the overloading of the current system, which is then replaced by a more powerful computer. If further growth is planned this will need to be taken into account by building in redundant computing power in the current system to cope with future growth in requirements. This is expensive.

- **Lower telecommunications costs:** In a distributed system, it is usual for most of the local computing to take place locally. The network is accessed only when data or processing is required elsewhere. Telecommunications costs are reduced compared with a centralized system, which requires transmission of local transactions for central processing.

- **Failsoft:** With a centralized system, if a breakdown occurs in the computer all computing functions in the organization come to a halt. This is an unacceptable state of affairs. Backup facilities, such as a duplicated computer or reciprocal agreements with other companies to use their computers in times of breakdown, are expensive and often not satisfactory. However, with a distributed system breakdowns will be limited to one computer at a time. The remaining machines in the network can continue to function and perhaps also take over some of the work of the failed node. What can be achieved depends on the particular network topology and the communications software.

- **Transborder data flows:** Many multinational corporations maintain separate computer systems in each country in which they operate. These are connected via networks. Only limited transborder data flows may be allowed by legislation. Thus it is important to ensure local processing while retaining the possibility of transnational data flows. Data protection legislation on the holding and processing of personal data (data on persons) is often different in different countries, and this is particularly restrictive on transnational data flows.

- **Response times:** Centralized systems can, at peak loading, give poor response time for users.

Persuasive though these organizational benefits may seem, there are potential drawbacks and costs associated with distributed systems. These should be taken into account when assessing the overall systems strategy:

- **Loss of centralized standard setting and control:** In a distributed system, where processing, data storage and computing staff are located at many sites, it is common for local practices to evolve, local alterations and 'patches' to software to be carried out to meet specific user needs, and local adjustment to data representation and storage characteristics to occur. All these can lead to non-standardization across the organization and to difficulties in data communications and security.

- **Complex networking software is needed:** This controls data communications.

- **Possibility of replicated common data at several sites:** If the same portion of data is used by all sites it is common for the data to be held as copies at each of the several sites rather than be held once and accessed through the network when needed. This cuts down data communications costs and increases response times. However, it may lead to inconsistencies if the data is updated or changed.

- **Loss of career paths for computer centre personnel:** A large centralized computer centre provides more opportunities for staff development and promotion. Distributing staff leads to smaller numbers of personnel at each site. A move towards decentralization will also require changes in work practices and significant staff retraining for some employees.

Figure 4.4 Typical hierarchical organizational structure

4.4 Organizational levels and distributed systems

It is not usual in a distributed system for each node to be directly connected to each other node. Nor is it common, if data is to be distributed, that it is spread over all nodes in the distributed network. It is more likely that the structure for the distributed system reflects the organizational structure it is meant to serve.

A typical organization structure is shown in Figure 4.4. This is a traditional hierarchical structure, which exemplifies many large industrial and service organizations. There is a headquarters for the organization. The organization has several local plants or sites that carry out many of the functions of the organization itself at a local level. Examples are the functional departments of production, stock control and order processing. In each functional department, there are work groups reflecting groupings of employees that perform much the same function in that department – an example might be customer enquiry handling in a sales order-processing department. Finally, there are the individual employees, who are the simplest 'processing unit' (i.e. unit that may require a computer for support) in the organization.

Where there are distributed systems in an organization, one possible architecture for the distribution is to ensure that where data is distributed and computers are networked this occurs at the level reflecting the organizational structure. For example, within one work group the network ensures that connections and data needed by that group are spread over the entire group. The various levels will also be connected together and if required will effect data transfers.

The larger the organization the more likely it is to have large numbers of personal computers, minicomputers and mainframe computers. In this case, it is also more important that the distributed architecture is planned to reflect the needs of the organization.

4.5 The extent of distribution

In the early 1980s, one of the uppermost questions in the minds of those involved in long-term strategic planning of information systems was whether to employ distributed systems or whether to rely on centralized mainframes. The issue has now shifted to decisions on the extent to which the organization should embark on distributing its information systems for future information provision.

There are technological determinants governing the distribution of data and computers, especially those to do with communications. However, as has been stressed in early chapters, technology is designed to support the organizational information requirements, not to drive the development of information systems. Technological factors must be considered in deciding on the extent and nature of the distributed systems, but other features are equally significant. Central among the other important characteristics are the following:

- **The corporate culture and employee behaviour:** Managerial assumptions about human behaviour will have implications for the amount of control that is exercised over employee activities. A traditional model characterizes attitudes in two distinct groupings. Theory X perspectives hold employees as inherently unwilling to work and needing to be controlled by incentives and discipline in order to ensure that their activities align with organizational goals. In contrast, Theory Y perspectives hold employees as self-motivated and willing to ensure that their activities are congruent with organizational objectives. In an organization where Theory X views are the dominant culture there will be an unwillingness to relinquish central power. This will be mirrored in a hierarchical organizational structure and a pressure towards centralization of information systems, where standards and control are easier to implement. The local autonomy that accompanies distributed systems fits a managerial strategy of decentralization of control within a Theory Y culture.

- **The location of decision making:** Closely linked to the points raised above is the issue of who makes the key decisions. The further decision making is decentralized in an organization the more likely it is that the resources follow. Decentralization of resources and decisions over their commitment with respect to information technology is most compatible with a distributed system.

- **Interdependent activities:** Where one type of activity is very closely related to another it is more likely that the processing associated with both will occur in one location. Distribution of processing between two activities tends to lead to a lack of connectivity, which should only be allowed if the activities are themselves not connected.

- **Homogeneous activities:** In some cases, activities may be independent of one another but there is a case for centralized planning of distributed systems. For example, franchises may involve local franchisees in carrying out completely independent activities from each other. Yet their operations are so homogeneous that it makes sense that each has the same type of system. This can be achieved only if there is centralized planning and control over the development and purchase of the information systems.

4.5.1 Client–server computing

Most modern information systems are constructed following the client–server model of computing. This involves using desktop computers as the clients, which make requests for data or applications. The requests are passed to servers, which are the centralized stores of data and applications. Computer processing power is spread throughout the organization; some is available centrally at the servers, some is available locally at the clients. Clients and servers can run on the same or on different machines, use different languages and operate on different platforms. Typically, there will be a number of servers, each dedicated to a particular task. Examples are:

■ file servers
■ application servers
■ database servers
■ print servers
■ mail servers.

An example of an application of client–server computing is that of a corporate e-mail system. Normally, e-mail is distributed via a designated computer called a mail server. Employees of an organization will be assigned an e-mail account, and any mail sent to that account is held on the mail server. In order to read the mail the client will need to run a mail application on their local computer; this collects the mail from the server and makes it available to the user. There is no permanent connection or shared application between the client and the mail server. Any compliant mail application can be used by the client to carry out this task.

The major advantage of the client–server approach is that the sharing of resources between clients and servers can be balanced to suit their particular environment. Typically, the server, a more powerful computer, will store both the data and the applications that can be run to update and interrogate the data. In certain situations, however, it may be desirable to locate more of the data at the client computer. Similarly, it is also possible to store the applications locally. In the example of the e-mail system, the client mail software might be stored on the local disk drive of the client or may be downloaded from the server then executed locally.

A typical decision for the designers of client–server systems might be as follows. A database holds a very large number of records. A client computer user wants to make a number of requests interrogating the data store. Should the entire file of records be copied to the client to allow fast searching by software at the client end? Or should the searching be carried out by the server and only the results passed to the client? Similarly, should an entire set of records matching the search criteria be copied to the client to allow fast access to the results at the client end? Or should the searching be carried out by the server and the matching records be passed to the client one at a time as they are perused?

Clearly, there are several factors which influence the balancing of resources between client and server:

Figure 4.5 Models of client–server computing: (a) two-tier with thick client; (b) three-tier model with thin clients

1. **System performance:** Generally, applications will execute faster if stored locally. Similarly, data can be interrogated more quickly if located locally.

2. **Consistency:** Applications and data can be more easily maintained if held centrally. Upgrades to applications and updates to data can be made more easily if held at the server and distributed as required.

3. **Bandwidth:** The capability of the network must be such that it can support the volume of network traffic between clients and servers.

4. **Volume of data/size of application:** It may not be possible to hold some massive databases locally. Similarly, programs that are too large for local storage will need to be stored centrally.

Clients are categorized as **thick clients** or **thin clients** according to the extent to which applications and data are held and executed locally. A thick client will undertake a larger proportion of activity. Figure 4.5(a) shows a two-tier model of client–server computing where the application logic is held and executed by a thick client. In the three-tier model, seen in Figure 4.5(b), there is a separation into three activities: formatting and presenting results, the logic for querying and interrogating, and storage of data. In this model, a thin client might be responsible for only the input and output of data.

An extreme example of a thin client is the **Net PC**. These are low-cost computers designed to have minimal memory and disk storage and are dependent on servers for most applications and data.

<table><tr><td>4.6</td><td>The distribution of data</td></tr></table>

In a distributed system, it is likely that, as well as processing occurring at many sites linked by telecommunications, data will also be distributed. This can happen in a number of ways. These reflect the extent to which the organization wishes to relinquish control over its data as well as over technological issues.

1. A centralized repository of data may be downloaded each day to local nodes in a network. This typically happens when these nodes are separated geographically by large distances. The downloaded data can then be interrogated locally. During the day, transactions occur at local sites, which require update of the central data store. The transaction details may be transferred to the central site for processing immediately or held and uploaded at the end of the day. In either case, a new copy of the central repository is downloaded the following morning.

The effect of this approach is to cut down on expensive enquiry traffic between the local sites and the central store of data. The disadvantage is that the information is up to 24 hours out of date. Whether this is acceptable or not will depend on the nature of the application.

For instance, it is likely to be permissible in a situation where data on stock at local sites was held centrally and downloaded each morning provided that the number of update transactions was relatively small compared with the number of enquiries, and ample buffer stocks were held. In this case, the savings on telecommunications costs would compensate for the loss of immediate accuracy of the data. However, if the ratio of update transactions to the number of enquiries is high and the stock holdings are volatile with little buffer stock being held, then this method will be not appropriate.

This approach to distributing data is little more than a fast electronic version of printing out the database each day and sending the hard copy to the local sites.

2. A variation on the above, which overcomes some of the problems concerning lack of immediacy, is to download data from a centralized repository each day but allow update transactions to be made on records held locally and applying to local events immediately the transactions occur. The local data is uploaded at the end of the day along with other transactions in order to update the central data store. If most update transactions apply to local data then this method will yield high accuracy of data.

3. In order to ensure full immediacy of data but at the same time distribute it to gain the benefits of local data storage and processing, a fully distributed database must be used. Each piece of data is stored at one or other of the nodes in the network either with or without duplication. Distributed database and communications software ensures that when users interrogate or update the data it is transparent to them as to where the data physically resides.

Mini case 4.1

Distributed vs centralised data storage

Sabah is a Malaysian state, located on the island of Borneo. The Sabah Credit Corporation (SCC) is a financial institution fully owned by the State Government and under the portfolio of the State Ministry of Finance. Its mission is to encourage economic development through the strategic issuing of loans. Its main premises are in Kota Kinabalu, the capital, and there are several regional offices in towns across the state.

The Corporation is divided into two divisions, administration/finance and operational. The latter oversees the evaluation process for arranging loans in a range of situations: agricultural loans, bridging finance, hire purchase loans etc.

The Corporation is supported by a Management Information System; this provides support for a range of decision-making activities at the operational, management and strategic levels. The MIS has evolved with the Corporation. Within the system a number of sub-systems cater for functional areas such as personnel, property management, training and legal issues. These complement the core system activity of recording customer details and repayments and have been progressively added and augmented over time.

The borrower system records all transaction activity, including customer repayment details. Customers can check this information by logging onto a password-protected website. Managers can use the system to obtain reports on core indicators such as cumulative profits, liabilities and tax paid.

All data is held in electronic files at the head office. Regional offices use network connections to the head office to access or update the data. Although customers may deal with a regional office for making payments, obtaining advice etc. the records are stored at the head office and can only be obtained through the network communications channel to those centrally held files. It would be possible for data to be held at local branches but it would make reconciliation and reporting for the whole corporation far more difficult. By keeping multiple copies of the same data as there is always the danger of inconsistency when one copy is updated.

Further details about the Sabah Credit Corporation can be found at http://www.sabah-credit.com.my

Questions

1. Data is held centrally. What advantages does this provide for the corporation?
2. An alternative model would be for data to be distributed throughout the regional branches. What benefits does this alternative model bring? Why do you think that this approach has not been adopted?

4.7 Networks and communications

The development of computer technology and applications software has been accompanied by a corresponding growth in telecommunications and the need to link computers together. Earlier sections have demonstrated the reasons for the distribution of data and computing power and the benefits it confers. The remaining sections investigate the technologies and standards governing the connections.

In the early years of data processing, corporate computing power was concentrated in the organization's mainframe computer. Where remote sites needed access to the computer, this was usually achieved through the public telephone network. A link was established between the dumb terminal and the central computer. The nature of the interaction between the two was controlled entirely by the centralized mainframe in a **master–slave** manner. If the amount of data to be exchanged was high and spread throughout the day (as compared with short bursts) it was cheaper to lease a direct line from the relevant telephone company. This also had the advantage that the connection carried a less distorted signal and was subject to less interference. Signal distortion and interference were lower because the connection between the terminal and the computer did not form part of a temporarily connected circuit through a number of telephone switching exchanges. With leased lines, data communication speeds were thus able to be higher.

Over time, the increased need to provide more extensive computing support for an organization – often at many sites – put a significant burden on the ability of the telecommunications network to carry the volume of data at costs the organization was willing to bear. The advent of local minicomputers for local processing was part of a solution to this problem. These would be linked together via the telecommunications network to form a distributed network. Another part of the solution was the introduction of more effective and cheaper means of transmitting a message from A to B across the public network – the use of digital transmission, packet switching and new types of physical link (see below).

Even within one site the explosion of demand by users for computing power, both caused by and enabled by the growth of user-friendly personal computers and applications packages, produced a requirement for communications between them that could not easily be satisfied by channelling all traffic through the site mainframe or minicomputer. Local area networks were designed to provide the necessary communications.

What had been experienced a decade earlier in the 1970s was a drive to distribute computing over many sites in an organization connected by a network of communications. In the 1980s, this was repeated in a microcosm and experienced as the need to distribute computing within one site connected by a local network. There were differences, especially the fact that in networking between sites a third party – the telecommunications company or data carrier – was involved, but many of the issues and pressures had a familiar ring to them.

The evolution of distributed computing has been, and still is, bedevilled by the problem of standards. Standards are needed because different types of machine are used to send messages to one another across different types of network. Nowadays, this may also involve machines running under different operating systems cooperating with one another to carry out work. Standards problems are particularly noticeable in the area of communications across the public network. The public carriers have often appeared to regard themselves, particularly in the early years, as electronic postal services – their purpose was to ensure that a neatly packaged message was transmitted reliably, swiftly and cheaply between a sender and receiver. The concept was neutral as to whether the package consisted of an electronic message rather than one written on paper. Nowadays, the need is for computers not only to connect with one another but also to work with one another. This has led to the development of standards to avoid the proliferation of confusion in communications.

4.7.1 Communications – the basics

Communication involves the transmission of a **message** from a **sender** to a **receiver**. The physical line over which communication is established is known as the **communications channel**.

Where it is possible to send data simultaneously in both directions between two devices the type of communication is called **full duplex**. If transmission is possible between both devices, but not simultaneously, then the communication is called **half duplex**. The remaining case, where transmission is possible in one direction only, is known as **simplex** communication.

Transmission signals

Data in a computer is encoded digitally. The two discrete states correspond to 0 and 1 – the two values for the binary digit. This is transmitted in the computer by means of a digital signal where, for instance, 0 corresponds to a low voltage and 1 corresponds to a high voltage (see Figure 4.6(a)).

Transmission through the public telecommunications network has in the past been through communications channels that were designed for carrying voice (voice-grade channels). This involved the sending and receiving of analogue carrier signals (Figure 4.6(b)). In order to ensure that 0s and 1s could be communicated across

Figure 4.6 Data transmission by signals: (a) digital transmission; (b) analogue carrier signal; (c) amplitude modulation; (d) frequency modulation

voice-grade lines, the carrier signal needed to be varied. This was achieved by altering either the amplitude of the wave formation – **amplitude** modulation (Figure 4.6(c)) – or the frequency of the wave (increasing the frequency involves decreasing the wavelength, and vice versa). This is known as **frequency modulation** (Figure 4.6(d)).

Under these circumstances, transmitting digital signals between one computer and another across the public telephone network required a device to modulate and demodulate the carrier signal at either end. The use of a **modem** (*mo*dulate–*dem*odulate) device is illustrated in Figure 4.7. The modem is a device that is either housed inside the computer's covering or is plugged into the computer.

Bandwidth

The **bandwidth** of a communications channel is the range of electrical or electromagnetic frequencies that can be used for the signal transmission.

Figure 4.7 A modem link

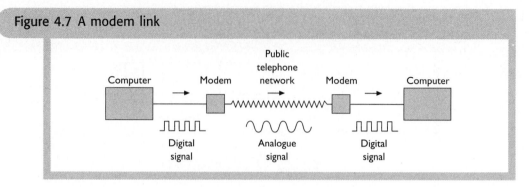

In a **baseband** channel, the entire channel is given over to the transmission of a digital signal. Baseband channels may have high transmission speeds – for example, transmission of data at up to 10 megabits per second over a limited range (a few kilometres). With baseband communication, only one signal may be transmitted at a time.

A **broadband** channel uses different ranges of frequencies carrying different signals at the same time. Each range of frequencies is modulated to represent the digital signal. In this case, the physical link will be carrying many messages simultaneously – the larger the bandwidth the greater the number of signals.

Multiplexing

Most physical communications channels would be underused if restricted to convey-ing one message between a sender and a receiver in a given period. Instead, several messages are amalgamated. The amalgamation and subsequent decomposition of all the signals is known as multiplexing (see Figure 4.8(a)). The device that accomplishes this is a **multiplexer**. A multiplexer enables a single communications channel to carry several messages in the same time period.

Even with a baseband channel it is possible to give the appearance to many senders and receivers that they are simultaneously sending messages to one another down one physical communications link. This is because transmission speeds are high and the transmission time is being divided between the various senders and receivers. In order to do this the signals from the senders must be amalgamated, ensuring that a part of sender A's message is followed by a part of sender B's message, followed by part of sender C's message, and so on. An illustration of this **time-division multiplexing** is given in Figure 4.8(b).

With broadband channels, many messages are sent simultaneously at different fre-quencies. It is the role of the multiplexer to assemble and decompose these. This is known as **frequency-division multiplexing** (see Figure 4.8(c)).

Parallel and serial transmission

Information is transmitted from sender to receiver translated into one of the major bit-coding schemes (usually ASCII). In **serial transmission,** the data is sent in a con-tinuous stream with one bit followed by the next. **Parallel transmission** involves all the bits in a character being transmitted simultaneously along parallel transmission lines. Serial transmission is therefore slower, but parallel transmission requires many physical channels. Voice transmission over the public telephone network is usually via a twisted pair of wires and is serial. High-speed connections between computers and computers,

Figure 4.8 (a) Multiplexing; (b) time-division multiplexing (baseband); (c) frequency-division multiplexing

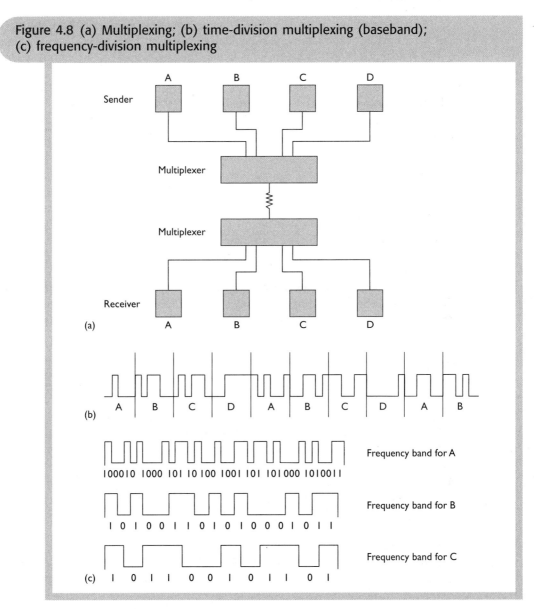

or computers and peripherals such as printers, are nowadays usually via parallel transmission. Recent improvements in serial transmission, for example Universal Serial Bus (USB), have ensured that serial transmission remains a realistic alternative method of transmission.

Synchronous and asynchronous transmission

Under **asynchronous transmission**, the receiver is alerted to the arrival of an encoded character by a front-end signal. This is known as the start bit. A similar signal is placed on the line at the end of transmission of the character. This method is used for the transmission of each character in turn. It is relatively slow, transmission rates rarely being able to exceed 2400 bits per second.

151

For the faster transmission required in computer-to-computer links, both sender and receiver operate at the same rate by synchronization of their clocks. Data is interspersed with synchronization characters, which alert the clocks and cause them to synchronize. This is known as **synchronous transmission**.

Transmission media

The physical medium over which signals are transmitted is an important determinant of the speed, reliability and number of messages that can be sent simultaneously.

Twisted pair

A twisted pair consists of two insulated wires twisted around one another. One wire is for the send signal and the other the return. It is common for twisted pairs to be twisted with one another in a spiral configuration to improve the reliability of the signal (see Figure 4.9(a)). The individual wires and/or the whole cable can be shielded by insulation. This is the typical telephone cable, where each pair is a dedicated line for a private household. Typical data transfer rates are up to 10 megabits per second. The popular standard for connecting a desktop computer to a local area network is a generic telecommunications cabling system known as CAT5 ('CAT' being an abbreviation of category). This uses unshielded twisted-pair (UTP) wiring, normally terminated by a

Figure 4.9 Alternative forms of cabling: (a) twisted pair; (b) coaxial cable; (c) optical fibre

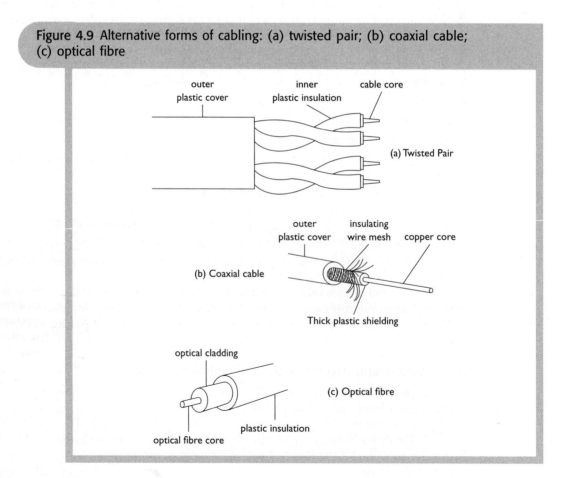

telephone-style jack plug. CAT5 allows data transmission at speeds up to 100 megabits per second with a bandwidth of 100 MHz.

Coaxial cable

Coaxial cable is made up of a central wire insulated and surrounded by a further conducting wire. This in turn is surrounded by insulation (see Figure 4.9(b)). Coaxial cable is used for the transmission of TV signals – either by cable to the home or from the aerial to the set. This type of cabling is common in local area networks such as the Ethernet (see below). The cable can conduct large quantities of data – up to 200 megabits per second – with very low error rates.

Fibre optics

An optical fibre cable consists of thin strands of glass, each about the thickness of a human hair. Messages are transmitted via a pulsating laser beam that is sent down the centre of the fibre. The light beam is reflected internally by the outer cladding around the fibre (see Figure 4.9(c)). The bandwidth of fibre optic transmission is large – for instance, one optical fibre can transmit half a million telephone calls simultaneously. The data transmission rates are several hundred megabits per second. Fibre optic cabling is becoming commonplace for the transmission of public data, with common carriers beginning to install fibre optic systems for the transmission of voice, data, text and images. It is also being used for the transmission of data within a single organization in local area networks. Typical data transfer rates are up to 10 gigabits per second.

Fibre optics has the following advantages:

- high capacity for message transmission;
- insensitive to electrical or electromagnetic interference;
- as cheap and easy to install as coaxial cable;
- low error rates;
- low power consumption;
- secure against illicit interception (as this requires physical breaking of the cladding, which results in signal breakdown).

Microwaves

Data can be transmitted using waves from the electromagnetic spectrum. Whereas fibre optics uses light in the visible wavelengths, microwave transmission uses radio signals of short wavelength. Microwaves may be used for satellite transmission or terrestrial links. Typical data transfer rates are up to 100 megabits per second.

With a **satellite link**, a microwave beam on which the data has been modulated is transmitted from a ground station to a satellite. The satellite remains in a constant position with respect to the Earth (geostationary orbit). The beam is then retransmitted to the destination receiver. Geostationary satellites typically orbit about 22,000 miles above the Earth's surface to enable them to synchronize with the Earth's rotation. The microwave channel has a very high bandwidth and may handle more than 1000 high-capacity data links. Microwave satellite transmission can relay both analogue and digital signals. Unlike a beam of light, the microwave beam is not interrupted by cloud or affected by adverse weather conditions. It has a reliable straight-line transmission distance of approximately 30 miles at the Earth's surface. As most of the transmission to and from a satellite is through empty space, this is sufficient.

Mini case 4.2

GPS tracking

Advertisers are clamouring for ever more sophisticated methods of accurately targeting their audiences in order to make their investments count. VNU, the Dutch business information group, is stepping up tests of technology that will allow outdoor advertisers unparalleled access to the movements of potential customers.

Nielsen Media Research, VNU's US-based media measurement unit, has developed a device that can track consumers' movements and relate that information to the positioning of billboard advertising campaigns.

The outdoor monitoring technology comprises a cellphone-sized device that uses global positioning satellite (GPS) technology from Seattle-based RDP Associates to track and record the movements of volunteers. That information is relayed to NMR's database outside Tampa, in Florida, where it is overlaid with a map of advertising billboard sites.

The GPS device also provides data, such as gender and age, critical to the effective targeting of advertising campaigns. The technology has been tested in South Africa and a pilot project will be launched in Chicago in the next few months.

Adapted from: **VNU to boost billboard technology**
By Ian Bickerton in Amsterdam
Financial Times: 18 August 2003

Questions

1. What form of network technology would facilitate the accurate and effective positioning of advertising billboards?
2. How might VNU gain a competitive advantage by using this technology?

Terrestrial microwave links are used when line-of-sight data transmission is needed over short distances (less than 30 miles) and it is inconvenient or impossible to lay cabling. This may occur because of physical difficulties such as ravines or rivers, or because high-bit-rate links are needed between buildings in sight of one another and where cabling cannot easily be laid.

Wireless technology

Much interest has been generated recently in facilitating wireless connections to both internal (private) and external (publicly available) networks. Both business and home users are benefiting from the ability to connect a laptop, PDA or other portable device to their existing network which itself may be wired or wireless. This adds great flexibility in the positioning of devices and in the ease of connectivity. In addition, mobile users are now able to access so-called wireless hotspots; these are publicized locations which provide wireless access to the Internet via a service provider. The service provider offers connectivity and recoups costs through advertising and other services.

The main wireless protocol used is a standard known as 802.11b. This employs radio frequencies to effect a connection. Line of sight between connecting devices is not required but the signal does degenerate with obstructions and with increasing distance. One implementation of this standard is **Wi-Fi**. Using this, data transfer rates of up to 54 Mbps (Mega bits per second) are possible.

Another radio wave technology gaining popularity is **Bluetooth**. This is a short range radio technology standard. Unlike Wi-fi it does not support TCP/IP and wireless LAN applications very well. It is more commonly used for connecting PDAs, mobile phones and PCs across short distances for short intervals. Typical data transfer speeds are around 2 Mbps.

Mini case 4.3

Bluetooth and Wi-Fi

The short-range radio standard Bluetooth has often been described as a solution waiting for a problem, but one potential application is as the medium for delivering broadband Internet capacity around a vehicle. Unlike, for example, infra-red transmission, Bluetooth does not need line-of-sight to work. Content could also be downloaded before a journey, while a car is in a garage. But Bluetooth is not the only game in town: another alternative is 802.11b (or Wi-Fi). This does not work when you are moving in relation to the Wi-Fi hotspot transmitter, and you have to be in range. But that may not be the disadvantage it appears to be, and Wi-Fi is beginning to appear in automotive settings. For example, Fiat and 3Com (Iberia) have announced that Wi-Fi is to be embedded in the Lancia Phedra, giving passengers high-speed Internet access at wireless hotspots in service stations, car parks, or in urban environments.

Adapted from: In-car IT
By Geoffrey Nairn
FT.com site: 23 June 2003 and 6 August 2003

Questions

1. How does Bluetooth allow broadband Internet usage inside a vehicle? Can it be used to send an e-mail from a vehicle?
2. How does Wi-Fi differ from Bluetooth?

4.7.2 Public transmission links

The transmission between one device and another across common or public places is carried out in each country by one or more organizations licensed by the government of that country to provide these communication services. These are known as **common carriers**. Examples of common carriers are the telecommunications giants AT&T in the USA and British Telecom and NTL in the UK.

Leasing

Where a large volume of data traffic is to be exchanged between two sites, an organization may decide to lease a line from the common carrier. This is a physical link between the two sites that is dedicated solely to the leasing organization. Leasing a line has the advantage that the physical link does not require temporary circuit connections to be established between various telephone exchanges. These temporary circuit connections make the signal much more open to distortion and interference and result in generally lower transmission speeds. In cases where there are large amounts of data to be exchanged, leasing is also a much cheaper alternative than establishing 'dial-up' links. However, if a large number of nodes need linking over long distances then costs

Figure 4.10 Circuit-switched telecommunications network

generally prohibit inter-site leasing. Because the data travels across a permanent physical channel any network made up of such links is called a **non-switched network**.

Public switched telephone network

In cases where a channel connection is made for a temporary period during the time of the data exchange but is then discontinued after exchange the connection is known as switched. Devices that can be connected in this way are said to be part of a **switched network**. In the case of the public switched telephone network (PSTN), the exchange of data between two sites requires establishing a temporary voice-grade circuit link through the public network of exchanges (see Figure 4.10). As soon as the required data has been exchanged the circuit is broken. This is known as a **circuit-switched network**.

The advantage of this type of connection is that the public switched telephone network allows data exchange between any two points that are connected to the telephone system. This gives great versatility. The disadvantages are that transmission speeds are low, distortion and interference probabilities are high, and costs are high for long periods of connection. Transmission speeds are being increased and the period taken to establish the connection (dial-up time) is being decreased by the introduction of digital networks (see below). Finally, with a circuit-switched network the circuit link is dedicated to the sender–receiver connection until broken. It may be the case that during much of this time there is no traffic in either direction and the circuit is 'waiting' for data exchange. The physical links between the exchanges making up the circuit are nevertheless 'tied up' and cannot be used for other purposes. This is an inefficient use of the network.

Packet-switched network

With a **packet-switched network** a message to be sent from a sender to a receiver is split into a number of self-contained packets a few hundred bytes (characters) long by a packet assembler/disassembler (PAD). These packets are routed through the network by being passed from node to node. Each packet may follow a different route through the network. At each node, the packet is stored temporarily before being forwarded

Figure 4.11 Packet-switched telecommunications network

PAD = packet assembler/disassembler

to the next node in the network. Once it has reached the destination in the correct order the message is reassembled by a PAD (see Figure 4.11).

The sender and receiver are oblivious of the assembling/disassembling process and of the routing. It appears to them that a dedicated circuit is established between them. Because no actual circuit link exists, the connection is known as a **virtual circuit**.

The route for each packet through the network is computer-determined to ensure that the network is being used most effectively. Clearly, many messages broken into packets will be passing through the system simultaneously. Another advantage of packet switching is that data exchanges between two devices along the virtual circuit may involve considerable periods of waiting between a receiver receiving a message and sending out a reply. Because no physical circuit link exists continuously, valuable network transmission potential is not being wasted.

Many countries have now installed public packet-switched networks. International packet-switched network data transmission is possible between countries that have developed their own systems, provided that they follow certain standards in the way they represent data. A commonly used standard is known as **X25**.

Integrated services digital network

Most public telecommunications systems are being upgraded to be integrated services digital networks (ISDNs). All switching, networking and transmission is then by means of digitized signals.

In order to ensure that compatibility will exist between different national systems and that equipment can be connected to the system, an ISDN standard exists. The basic transmission speed for this system is 64 kilobits per second. A typical domestic user with basic access would have two transmission channels at this speed plus a control channel at 16 kilobits per second. Businesses are offered primary access with twenty-four channels, each running at 64 kilobits per second (one channel being used for control purposes). This is a substantial improvement over typical speeds for voice-grade lines, which are up to 9.6 kilobits per second.

Under an ISDN, transmission of voice, data, text and images will be fully digital. This will allow faster transmission speeds and much faster dial-up times for circuit connection (milliseconds compared with seconds).

ADSL and cable

Asymmetric Digital Subscriber Line

The potential for sending data over traditional copper telephone lines has been further expanded by the introduction of Asymmetric Digital Subscriber Line (ADSL). By employing a special ADSL modem, this technology supports data transfer of up to 9 Mbps when receiving data and up to 640 Kbps for sending data (hence the asymmetry in the title).

Cable connection

Even greater bandwidth can be exploited where coaxial cable is available. A cable modem connected to the lines also used for transmission of cable television provides very fast access to the Internet. Data transmission speeds of 2 Mbps are possible.

Although extremely popular, there are limitations to this approach. One problem is the availability of a cable connection. Until now this has been limited to urban areas of the more developed economies. In addition, the asymmetry issue persists; the TV infrastructure is primarily intended to transmit in one direction.

4.7.3 Local transmission links

Local area networks

As well as having minicomputer or mainframe computer facilities, most large and medium-sized organizations will also possess a large number of desktop computers, printers and other information technology. The desktop computers can be used for single-station word processing, spreadsheet modelling, data management and other applications. Frequently, though, it is important for desktop computers to be able to communicate with one another, communicate with the organization's larger computers, share scarce resources such as printers or communicate with the outside world.

In order to achieve this a **local area network (LAN)** may be used. An LAN consists of:

- high-speed cable, such as coaxial cable, connecting the various devices;
- a network card for each device that is connected to the network, which is a printed circuit board that manages the transmission of data across the interface between the device and the network cabling;
- network software, such as Novell Netware or Windows Server 2003, that manages data transmission around the network cabling.

An LAN is owned by a single organization and does not run outside the confines of that organization. It allows the following types of facility:

- downloading of data from the corporate database held on a mainframe computer for local processing – for example in spreadsheet models;
- communication of the personal computer with the 'outside world' and other networks via a **gateway** with the public telephone network;
- access to the Internet;
- use of a centralized shared data and program store held on a **file server**, which is a high-capacity disk storage device that is attached to the network;
- sharing of scarce resources by many users connected on the network;
- the use of electronic mail to send messages, memos and electronic letters to other nodes on the network;
- use of electronic calendar and diary facilities to schedule meetings.

The use of a file server reduces the need for, and therefore the cost of, a large hard disk for each computer on the network. Separate parts of the file server can be allocated for use by each node on the network. Programs for common use are stored on the file server rather than on individual hard disks. Smaller organizations that do not have a mainframe normally use a file server as a shared database. For instance, most of the major accounting packages for small businesses have a multi-user version to allow this (see Figure 4.12).

LANs vary in their topologies and in their transmission speeds. Examples of typical topologies are shown in Figure 4.13. Because LANs are non-switched networks the communications links are shared by all devices. Many devices may wish to transmit on the network simultaneously – the devices are in contention for the services of the network. As it is impossible for two devices to share the network literally at the same time, techniques have been devised to handle the situation. Two are examined here.

Figure 4.12 Devices connected to a local area network

Figure 4.13 LAN topologies

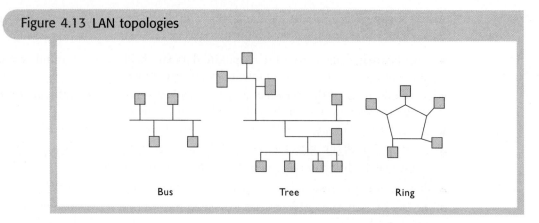

Bus   Tree   Ring

Carrier-sense multiple-access collision detection (CSMA/CD)

This is used on bus and tree networks. When a message is being transmitted from one node to another all nodes read the message and do not transmit while it is on the line. Only when no messages are on the network can a node initiate a transmission. If two nodes attempt to transmit simultaneously the collision is detected, the transmission is blocked and the nodes are forced to wait for a random time interval before retransmitting.

Ethernet is a commonly used type of LAN that employs CSMA/CD. The standard derives from its introduction by the Xerox Corporation. Ethernet systems are tree configurations using coaxial cable. Several hundred devices may be connected in one LAN.

Token passing

This can be used in ring or bus networks. If a device wishes to transmit on the network it removes a transmitted token before sending its message. After transmission the device retransmits the token. If the token is not available, it means that the network is being used and the device needs to wait until the token is retransmitted.

The **Cambridge ring** type of network is one using token passing. In it there is a continuously circulating packet of binary digits. If a sender node wishes to transmit, it alters the contents of the packet (takes the token) and puts the message on to the network combined with the address of the node to which the message is to be sent. When it has finished transmitting and has received acknowledgment that the data transfer was successful, the sending node puts the token back in the ring ready for another sender to take. No nodes other than the current token holder can transmit on the ring.

Local area networks have been designed primarily for the transmission of text data. However, the increasing use of audio and video presentations, video-conferencing, and more general multimedia applications require LANs to support much richer services. These **broadband multiservice networks** can accommodate the high transmission rates associated with data, speech and video. This has involved a new method of transmission and switching known as **asynchronous transfer mode (ATM)**. ATM LANs have now been developed to accommodate this. Also, a new generation of ATM wide area networks, known as **metropolitan area networks (MANs)**, have been produced to link ATM-based LANs.

Grid computing

Oracle will next week unveil the latest version of its flagship database in an attempt to regain leadership of an industry that Oracle founded but where it has recently lost market share.

Oracle 10g, as the new database is code-named, is being promoted as one of the most significant technological developments in the 25-year history of the Oracle database. The 'g' stands for grid computing, which many see as the biggest trend in computing today.

Grid computing is essentially a new blueprint for corporate computing in which servers, networks and storage can be coupled together, accessed and managed as if they were a single system.

Chuck Rowzat, Oracle's executive vice president of server technologies, describes grid computing as 'a more flexible and cost-effective way to manage enterprise information and applications.' It should appeal particularly to Oracle's largest customers, as grid computing allows lots of low-cost computers, such as blade servers, to be linked together to simulate expensive symmetric multiprocessing systems – the traditional way to run big databases.

Adapted from: **Oracle to unveil database**
By Geoffrey Nairn
FT.com site: 3 September 2003

Questions

1. What form of network topology is required to facilitate grid computing?
2. In what ways might grid computing be 'a more flexible and cost-effective way to manage enterprise information and applications'?

4.8 Standards

Users and purchasers of information technology would like to be able to connect different technologies easily. These, once connected, should be able to cooperate in carrying out applications by exchanging information and, where appropriate, by sharing the workload of the application between many devices. Unfortunately, too often the following problems arise:

- The technologies cannot physically be connected. The devices just will not 'plug in'.

- Once the devices are connected the information passed from one device to another is packaged and formatted in a way that is not 'recognized' as information by the receiving device.

- Once recognized as information, the information cannot be 'understood' with respect to the applications software of the receiver.

These problems are increasingly being resolved by the take-up of 'plug and play' hardware technology, which automates the installation process, and by the use of 'hot plugging' where devices can be connected and recognized without restarting the computer.

4.8.1 The scope of the problem

The problem identified above is not an easy one to solve. There are several reasons for this:

1. The range of the different types of device that handle information and the many media through which the information is channelled would require a significant effort in global standardization to ensure compatibility. There are, for instance, keyboards, processing units, printers, fax machines, telephones, monitors, optical scanners, voice recognition devices and bar-code readers. Different media include coaxial cable, optical fibres, twisted pairs of wires, and microwave and infrared links.

2. Considering one type of product or transmission medium from the above, there will be many suppliers, each of whom may develop their product in what they regard as the most appropriate way. There is no guarantee that each supplier will regard the possibility of substitution of a rival's product as a benefit.

3. Even with one type of product and one supplier it may not always be possible to carry out full interconnection. Products develop over time and respond to the market environment. All companies attempt to standardize interconnections between their products as this encourages brand loyalty. However, advances in technology and the need to respond to competitor developments may on occasion preclude this. The problem is to try to develop the technology so that it looks backwards, forwards and sideways (to competitors) at the same time.

4. As well as competition between suppliers selling the same types of product, there is also rivalry between sectors. In particular, there has been rivalry between the suppliers of mainframe computer technology and the suppliers of telecommunications services (the public carriers). This is evidenced in the development of different approaches to communications protocols (agreements over the way information is to be packaged and transmitted). IBM developed its own synchronous transmission protocol (**synchronous data link control, SDLC**) and its own network standards (**systems network architecture, SNA**). The two together, SDLC/SNA, defined IBM's product development for the future. The public carriers, acting independently of IBM (and probably as a response to it), identified their own synchronous transmission protocol through their standards-setting body (**Consultative Committee of the International Telegraph and Telephone, CCITT**). This protocol is called **X25**.

In summary, everyone can realize the usefulness to the user of having the highest possible degree of interconnectedness and interworking between products. However, the independent interests of the suppliers, the need to develop and change to improve technology, and the diversity of the product field place severe difficulties on obtaining agreements on standards. This is most obvious in the area of network communications.

There are several standards-setting bodies that have influence over the development of new technology. The **International Standards Organization (ISO)** has developed a model for standard setting for devices engaged in communication across a network. This is known as the **Open Systems Interconnection (OSI) reference model**.

4.8.2 The Open Systems Interconnection model

The OSI model is intended to be a reference model for the development of protocols. It views exchange of information between two devices operating across a network from

Figure 4.14 The seven-layer OSI model

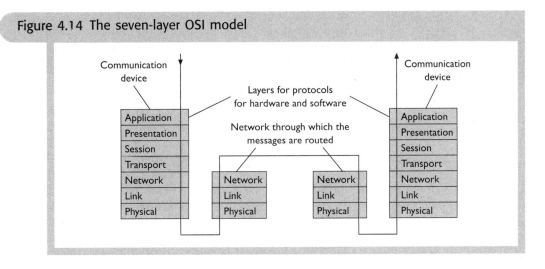

a number of levels of abstraction. These are known as **layers**. The seven-layer model is shown in Figure 4.14. The various layers correspond to different functions that must be carried out to ensure smooth and cooperative interconnection:

1. **Physical layer:** Standards for this layer govern the transmission of electrical signals between devices. Specifications would include the physical media, and the shape and size of plugs and sockets.

2. **Link layer:** This ensures that bits carried across the physical network have an agreed structure. Specification of packet structure and error detection and correction occur in this layer.

3. **Network layer:** This ensures that packets find their way across the network. Specifications for ways of handling address identification and routing are made here.

4. **Transport layer:** Specification of the way that multiplexing occurs and of the way that packets are assembled and disassembled is handled at the transport layer. This layer is responsible for ensuring that reliable two-way communication is established.

5. **Session layer:** This ensures that the two-way communication, once established, is coordinated between the communicating devices, and that protocols for information exchange are agreed.

6. **Presentation layer:** Specifications here deal with the way that data is encrypted and the way that data is formatted for processing or display in the receiving device.

7. **Applications layer:** This ensures that the information is in the right format for recognition and processing by the receiving application.

It may at first sight seem to be unnecessarily complicated to assume that each of these layers is involved in effective communication and that therefore there need to be standards at each layer. However, if a simple case of postal communication is considered it will be clear how some of these layers are already implemented in a familiar application. It is only a short step to realizing that the added complexity of electronic communication yields the need for extra layers.

Imagine that a manager at one organization wishes to order goods from another organization. The manager will need to know the name of the supplying organization and the sorts of information that are required to place an order (item to be ordered, quantity, and so on). This is accepted as standard information for the application of 'making an order' (applications level). The order needs to be presented in a way that can be understood by the receiver. This is written in English, although it need not be for foreign orders (presentation layer). At a lower level, to ensure that the order message is routed through the system properly, a recognized address for the carrying network, i.e. postal service, must be added. The standard agreed here is usually the post code or ZIP code (network layer). The order message, just like any other message through the system, has to be packaged in a way that the carrier network can handle. The standards agreed here involve encoding the message on paper, placing it inside an envelope and writing the address on the outside of the envelope (link layer). Finally, it is agreed that the letter will be taken to a post box, from which it will be physically picked up and carried through the system. Here the order message is treated just like any other (physical layer). Because the postal example does not require two-way interaction, the session and transport layers are missing. There is a certain artificiality in the example, but the point should be clear that the placing of an order for goods via the postal service can be viewed from various layers in which standards have to be agreed if communication is to be effective.

The OSI model was intentionally defined in a loose and all-embracing language in order to capture the full richness and variety of distributed applications. Although the OSI model was widely received by most vendors, it failed to provide sufficient detail for universal implementation and has been maintained more as a reference model to describe good practice.

4.9 Electronic data interchange

Electronic data interchange (EDI) can be defined as:

> *the transfer of electronic data from one organization's computer system to another's, the data being structured in a commonly agreed format so that it is directly usable by the receiving organization's computer system.*

What distinguishes EDI from other electronic communications between organizations, such as fax, electronic mail, telephone and telex, is that in these latter cases the information is intended for consumption by a human being, who needs to understand it before any action can be taken. With EDI, the received electronic data can be processed immediately by the receiver's computer system without the need for human interpretation and translation before action.

4.9.1 An example

To see how EDI can be used in the context of significant in-house automation, consider the following example. It is important for many manufacturing companies that assemble final products to be assured of the supply of components from their stock. When the stock of a particular kind of component runs low the manufacturer orders replacements from the supplier. The supplier then despatches these and invoices later.

The whole process can take a long time, particularly if the manufacturer's purchasing department needs to draw up a paper order that is posted to the supplier. At the supplier's end, this needs to be processed by the accounts and dispatch departments. The production of paperwork by the manufacturer and the supplier, together with the transfer of this between organizations, can lead to costly delays and errors. It may be necessary for the manufacturing company to maintain larger stocks to take account of the lead time in ordering. This in itself will be a cost. If the supplier is also low on stock of the component, it may take several days for the manufacturer to be notified. This scenario can occur even if both organizations are fully computerized as far as their own internal transaction processing is concerned.

In the context of full automation and EDI, this situation could be handled in the following way. As soon as the manufacturer's component stocks fall below a minimum level, a computer-based list of possible suppliers is consulted and the most appropriate chosen. An electronic order is generated on the manufacturer's computer system. This is then transmitted to the supplier's computer system (EDI), where it is matched electronically against stock records of the item held. A stock decrement is effected, and an instruction to despatch the goods with full delivery details is sent to the supplier's despatch department. An electronic acknowledgement of order satisfaction is transmitted to the manufacturer, along with an electronic invoice, which will await receipt of the goods before payment is made.

In the above EDI-automated version, there need be no paperwork exchanged at all. Human beings need only limited involvement – for instance, in the loading and distribution of the goods, or in the authorization of the placing of the purchase order by the manufacturer and agreement to satisfy the order by the supplier. These human authorizations can be by entry into the computer system, although it would be possible to automate the process of authorization entirely as well. The advantages for both companies are:

- the speed with which the order is satisfied;
- the lack of paperwork involved;
- the low cost of processing the transaction, as the involvement of costly human labour on both sides is minimal; and
- the lack of human error.

There may be further organizational advantages if the trading relationship between the two companies is altered. This point will be expanded fully later in the chapter.

4.9.2 EDI – the method

EDI may be introduced where a group of organizations wish to ensure that electronic transactions are passed between one another. One of the earliest EDI groups was set up to allow international airlines to process bookings electronically worldwide (IATA). SWIFT (Society for Worldwide International Financial Transfers) is another EDI group. This handles the transmission and processing of international financial transactions between banks.

EDI groups require EDI services in order to effect the data exchanges. These are often provided by a third-party organization. The service provided by the third party is more than merely the transmission of the data. It is customary for added facilities, especially mailbox facilities, to be offered. An electronic mailbox for a client is an electronic storage location for messages or data that are sent to the client by other organizations.

Figure 4.15 EDI network

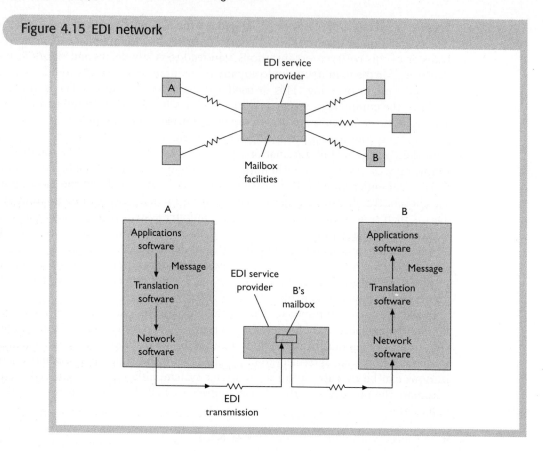

The client (addressee) can read the data or messages, which are usually held on an identified area of the service provider's disk space. By providing these services, the third party adds value to the data transmission and is thus said to run a **value-added network**.

A typical configuration for EDI transfer is illustrated in Figure 4.15. The message produced by the sender's applications software is translated into the agreed EDI format and placed on the network by the network access software. This electronic data is sent to the mailbox facility of the EDI service provider. Here it is stored until retrieved by the receiver organization using the retriever's network access software. The received electronic data, in the agreed format, is then translated by software into a form directly usable by the receiver's applications programs.

It is clear that a group of organizations needs to agree on standards for message representation and communication in order to take part successfully in EDI. For instance, the banks agreed on standards for SWIFT. It is becoming more common though for groups to come together to agree international standards for EDI. This has prompted the United Nations to set up a standards body for the commercial application of EDI. This group – UN/EDIFACT (United Nations/EDI for Administration, Commerce and Transport) – has produced a set of standards, known as EDIFACT, for the electronic transmission of data in relation to commerce in goods and services.

4.9.3 The benefits of EDI

Some of the benefits of EDI are clear from the examples in previous sections. In particular, EDI ensures that:

- The speed with which an inter-organizational transaction is processed is minimized.
- The paperwork involved in transaction processing is eliminated.
- The costs of transaction processing are reduced, as much of the need for human interpretation and processing is removed.
- Reduced human involvement reduces error.

These are benefits experienced by both sender and receiver in an EDI relationship. Of course there is a cost – the cost of purchase and installation of the technology. However, there are more strategic advantages associated with the introduction of EDI.

First, by increasing the speed of processing of transactions between an organization and its suppliers and between an organization and its customers it enables the supply chain to the customer to provide a faster service. This gives the companies in the supply chain a competitive advantage over other companies in the same sector.

Second, the speed of response to requests for component parts in the manufacturing process enables all participants in the supply chain to reduce their holding of buffer stocks. This reduces the need to tie up a company's assets in unproductive materials and is compatible with the organization of production on 'just-in-time' principles. The whole chain, therefore, gains a competitive advantage within the industry sector.

Finally, it is in the interests of an organization to 'tie in' both many suppliers and many customers through EDI. For example, a motor car production manufacturer will gain a significant competitive advantage by linking in many suppliers of substitutable component parts through EDI. While EDI benefits each supplier for the reasons stated above, its own position of dominance over the manufacturer in these circumstances is weakened by other suppliers participating in EDI. Similarly, it is in the interests of the supplier to link up with as many manufacturers through EDI as possible. The supplier's competitive position is then strengthened because it is no longer dependent on one customer manufacturer.

From the above it can be seen that the presence of EDI in the supply chain increases the competitive advantage of that chain over others in the sector. But, depending on the exact nature of the supplier–customer relationship, individual organizations in the chain may have their competitive advantage weakened or strengthened by EDI.

Mini case 4.5

EDI

The American pharmaceuticals company McKesson began linking in its customer pharmacies in the USA through EDI by the installation of terminals. Pharmacies were then able to input orders for products directly. This saved McKesson the cost of employing sales personnel to take drug orders and reduced the number of paperwork errors. From the customer point of view the system, called ECONOMIST, enabled a speedy and error-free response to ordering stock, especially when late orders were required. ▶

McKesson could fill and deliver an order overnight, ensuring that the drugs would be on the shelves the following morning.

Stage two of the involvement occurred when McKesson also offered software through the terminals to assist pharmacists in the preparation of accounts and the improvement of shop layout. This provided an additional source of revenue for McKesson.

Finally, McKesson was then able to provide a service to pharmacists in processing the millions of medical insurance prescriptions put through pharmacists each year. This was achieved by electronically passing on the details to the identified medical insurance company. The effect was to save the pharmacist a great deal of time and expense. Once established, it was difficult for a rival pharmaceutical company to compete in the same arena.

Questions

1. How did EDI give McKesson a competitive advantage?
2. How sustainable is the competitive advantage gained from the introduction of EDI?

4.10 The effects of the Internet on business

The whole topic of the Internet and the World Wide Web is developed in subsequent chapters. However, at this point it is important to acknowledge the massive changes that the Internet has brought about in businesses and in the way that business is carried out. The proliferation of computing power through business and home users has provided many more opportunities for interchange of information and for business transactions to be carried out. Using the five forces model introduced earlier it is clear that competitive advantage can be gained through the successful development of a company website. Relations with suppliers (often referred to as business-to-business or B2B) can be greatly enhanced. Similarly, new opportunities for reducing the costs of goods and services to customers are introduced (reflected in the business-to-customer or B2C relationship).

The technology of the Internet can also be applied within the confines of an organization. An **intranet** of locally devised and accessed pages distributed over the company's own local area network can improve information sharing and communications within the organization. All these topics are dealt with in more detail in following chapters.

Summary

The last decade has witnessed a dramatic increase in the extent of use of distributed systems. Distributed computing may be defined as occurring when hardware located at two or more geographically distinct sites is connected electronically by telecommunications so that processing/data storage may occur at more than one location. The network may involve many organizations or the connection of several remote sites within one organization. These wide area networks use transmission services provided by licensed third parties known as common carriers.

The benefits of distributed systems include increased user satisfaction and autonomy – users do not need to rely on a remote computer centre for the satisfaction of their needs. Telecommunications costs are lower, as local processing will not involve expensive remote links. Distributed computing also allows for flexible systems development in that computing power can be expanded incrementally to meet demand. Although there are substantial advantages, an organization needs to be aware that unbridled distribution may lead to problems of standard setting and loss of control. If data is distributed then duplication of data may lead to inconsistency.

Although technological features will be operative in determining the extent of the use of distributed systems, it is important to remember that other features are also significant. In particular, the corporate culture and location of decision making need to be compatible with distribution, which, by its nature, involves devolution of resources and power. The type of activities undertaken by the organization must also be considered – distribution is more likely to be recommended the less dependent computerized activities are on each other.

There are several ways in which data may be treated in a distributed system. These range from electronic downloading of copies of data to various sites, to the development of a fully distributed database system with minimal duplication of data. Although there are still problems in distributing data, advances in software and telecommunications make this an increasingly attractive option for organizations.

In order to understand issues related to the implementation of distributed computing and the influence of networks, a basic understanding of technical issues is required. Transmission of data will be achieved through digital or analogue signalling, will involve parallel/serial and synchronous/asynchronous transmission, and may involve the use of high-bandwidth techniques and multiplexing. Media used are likely to be twisted-pair or coaxial cable, although, increasingly, fibre optics is being employed.

Transmission through the public network has traditionally required the leasing of special lines or the use of the public switched telephone network. Packet-switched networks and integrated services digital network transmission systems are also now in operation. These latter provide faster, more reliable services suitable for the transmission of large quantities of data and enabling the integrated transmission of image, data, voice and text.

Local links are usually via local area networks. These optimize the use of scarce resources. They are compatible with the implementation of a client–server approach in the satisfaction of user needs. Local area networks usually exhibit tree, bus or ring structures. They are used to provide commonly shared program and data files, printer services, communications with the corporate mainframe or the public networks, electronic mail, calendaring, and other facilities. Different topologies have different approaches to contention handling.

One of the major factors inhibiting the progress of networks and distributed computing is the difficulty in agreeing standards. The reasons for this largely reside in the variety of products and the commercial structure of the supplier market. Early attempts to set standards include SNA from IBM. Currently, an important influence on standard setting is the Open Systems Interconnection reference model for standards. This identifies seven layers as requiring standards for full distributed cooperation.

Electronic data interchange (EDI) is one area where developments in telecommunications and networking are having an impact beyond that of merely passing messages between computer systems. EDI is understood as the exchange of formatted data capable of immediate computer processing. Various benefits derive from EDI, including cost saving and speedy processing of transactions. In particular, though, EDI affects the nature of the trading relationships between organizations in a sector and, by way of influencing the supply chain, can considerably enhance the competitive advantage of a company.

Review questions

1. What important features need to be taken into account when considering introducing a distributed system?

2. What costs and benefits can an organization expect from using a distributed system for its information provision?

3. What benefits are likely to be gained by an organization if it uses a local area network to connect its separate computing devices?

4. Under what circumstances would it be desirable to distribute data and under what circumstances would it be desirable to centralize it?

5. What are the advantages and disadvantages of using a leased line compared with the public circuit-switched telecommunications network? Under what circumstances would it be recommended?

6. How do packet-switched networks differ from circuit-switched networks?

7. Explain the difference between *frequency modulation* and *amplitude modulation*.

Exercises

1. The same features that led to the advent of distributed computing and wide area networks between sites operated a decade later to provide the need for local area networks. Discuss.

2. What is meant by saying that the structure for a distributed system mirrors the organizational structure it is required to serve – and why should it?

3. Why has it been so difficult to obtain agreements on standards for interconnecting devices through networks?

4. What is EDI?

5. How can the effects of EDI be analysed within the terms of Porter's competitive advantage and competitive strategy approach?

6. Consider a large organization with which you are familiar (e.g. your college, your employer organization, your bank).
   (a) To what extent does the distributed structure of its information systems mirror its organizational structure?
   (b) How important have organizational characteristics such as corporate culture been in determining the extent of distribution?

7. ABC Co. is a medium-sized company manufacturing and installing office furniture. Manufacturing and installation are located in seven sites spread throughout the UK. Each site also runs its own sales team, which promotes and sells ABC office furniture by providing a concept design service for organizations wishing to refurbish their offices.

Currently, all computerized information provision and transaction processing is by way of ABC's mainframe computer located in London. Local sites possess terminals connected to the mainframe by public telecommunications. Local site managers are arguing for more autonomy in responding to the needs of local customers. They claim that the central computer services, for which they are charged internally, provide poor and non-targeted information. As a group, individual site managers have put a case for abandoning the company's central mainframe system – which is due for review with respect to significant upgrading – and replacing this with local minicomputers that would communicate, if necessary, through the public carrier system. All functions appertaining to the local sites would be processed locally. Advise the managing director on this issue.

8. A large regional college is extending its network and IT infrastructure to support all its academic and administrative functions. Currently, the network infrastructure is used for internal personnel, payroll, accounting, student registration, administrative and financial functions. Academically, it is used by students following computing and engineering courses. It is the long-term intention of the college to ensure that all staff have a PC connected into the college network and that all students have IT skills training, especially in the use of word-processing and spreadsheet packages. Laboratories are gradually being upgraded under the direction of the computer centre. For some years, the Computer Science and Engineering Departments have been unhappy with much of the service provided by the computer centre. These departments have already implemented their own laboratories of desktop computers separately, cabled and networked for students on their courses. Staff in these departments have also been networked using a physically separate cabling system, as the respective department heads believe that with computing students there is a danger that their knowledge will allow them unauthorized access to staff data traffic. The college principal is concerned that there is an absence of strategic planning and control and is unhappy about the current situation. Advise the college principal on a course of action.

CASE STUDY 4

Call centres

A call centre provides the public with a point of contact to an organization. Telephone calls are routed to a department, often located away from the organization itself, which acts as a first-stage filter for calls. Simple enquiries can either be dealt with automatically, using computer-generated messages, or can be fielded by operators who have a basic understanding of the business and are aware of frequently asked questions. They may also place orders or make reservations for customers.

Call centres were traditionally operated by companies in the financial sectors and offered products such as insurance and mortgage services. Now it is becoming increasingly common for many large companies, including cinemas, travel operators and local authorities, to use a call centre to handle first-line enquiries.

Call centres would not be possible without the technological advances of the last few decades. Developments in information and communications technology, especially advances in telephony, have seen telephone switchboards being replaced by much smaller and less expensive computerized systems. These systems are easily tailored to suit the

▶

organization's requirements and require much less human supervision and intervention. As well as computerized speech output, many systems also employ voice recognition software.

The immediate effect of establishing a call centre is for the organization to gain a competitive advantage over its rivals. The cost of dealing with customer enquiries falls, and if set up with care, the quality of customer service and satisfaction is raised.

The work flow through the call centre is largely controlled by the system itself. The agents who take the calls are allocated tasks and their daily activity is closely monitored by the system. A number of indicators can be generated to monitor the performance of the agents in this way. These statistics can be used to ensure that the quality of service is maintained.

The agents are clearly pivotal in the call centre as they are the customer's first point of contact. To gain any competitive advantage it is important that they are effective in their work. The automated distribution of tasks leads to a very intense working atmosphere, and rates of pay are relatively low. Call centres have historically demonstrated low staff retention rates and high levels of absenteeism. The careful management of the agents is therefore an important consideration.

Questions

1. In order to answer customer enquiries, agents in a call centre need access to the company database. Explain how this might be achieved. What potential problems does this create?

2. Computers in a call centre will be connected to a local area network. Describe the different topologies of LAN that could be used. What criteria could be used to establish the most appropriate?

3. Explain the role of 'standards' in ensuring that different devices can be connected.

Recommended reading

Cole M. (2002). *Introduction to Telecommunications: Voice, Data and the Internet.* Prentice Hall

A very readable introduction to telecommunications topics. The book has a technical focus and is very well illustrated.

Harasim L.M. (ed.) (1994). *Global Networks: Computers in International Communications.* Cambridge Mass.: MIT Press

This is a collection of articles by a range of authors with differing backgrounds that looks at the global aspects of networks and communications. For example, included are articles on social and cultural aspects of international communications, global education and computer conferencing. The book should be of interest to those who wish for more than a technical treatment of networks and communications.

Harle D. and Irvine J. (2001). *Data Communications and Networks: An Engineering Approach.* Wiley

A technical look at the subject of networks. The book focuses in particular on the Internet as the context for discussion of data communications techniques.

Hodson P. (1997). *Local Area Networks.* Letts Educational

The text is restricted to LANs and interconnections with wide area networks. Although not assuming any initial knowledge the text takes the reader into technical areas of LANs and communications. It is designed for the student and has many exercises and self-help questions.

Peng Z.-R. and Tsou M.-H. (2003). *Internet GIS: Distributed Geographic Information Services for the Internet and Wireless Networks.* Wiley

This provides the background to basic network architecture and then moves on to explore how geographical information systems have become a popular feature of the Internet. The book combines theory with applications and also discusses the importance of standards in network developments.

Peterson L. (2003). *Computer Networks: A Systems Approach*, 3rd edn. Academic Press

A thorough coverage of networks with an interesting chapter on congestion control, resource allocation and network security.

Stallings W. (2003). *Data and Computer Communications*. Prentice Hall

This provides an encyclopaedic coverage of the topic. Includes end of chapter review questions.

Chapter 5

The Internet and the World Wide Web

Learning outcomes

On completion of this chapter, you should be able to:

- Define the Internet and explain the historical developments that have led to the Internet of today
- Illustrate how a connection to the Internet is effected and how nodes in the Internet are named and addressed
- Describe the various services that the Internet provides
- Evaluate the role of the World Wide Web and explain how web pages are constructed and made available over the Internet
- Define and contrast the Internet with intranets and extranets.

Introduction

Over the last three decades, the Internet has developed from a useful facility for the exchange of academic, scientific and military information to become a major force in information exchange globally. This explosion has been driven by the increased use of personal computers in the workplace and at home, and by the involvement of business on the Internet as a way of reaching trading partners and customers. This chapter sets the foundation for understanding how the Internet can assist businesses in reaching their objectives. It is important that the reader understands the background and basis of the Internet and its facilities. The earlier sections address this. The most important contribution to business activity (along with e-mail) is the World Wide Web. The latter part of the chapter introduces the World Wide Web as an easy-to-use and consistent interface to the Internet. Finally, intranets and extranets are introduced and the rationale for their use by an organization is outlined.

5.1 The evolution of the Internet

In order to understand the basis of the Internet, it is instructive to cover the history of its evolution.

During 1956, the United States set up the Advanced Research Projects Agency (ARPA) to assist it to gain increased military competitive advantage and to stimulate advances in science and technology. In the late 1960s, the US Department of Defense set up the **ARPANET** group to develop a secure network between computers. This was to develop stable methods by which computers could be connected to one another for military and scientific purposes. It had long been recognized that with the increasing reliance of the US military on computers and computer control of its defence systems it was imperative to ensure that in a 'hostile environment' when parts of a network were not working (or were destroyed) the remaining network should continue to function. Thus from the early days it was assumed that networks were unlikely to be stable but still had to function effectively. The connecting network between such computers became known as the ARPANET. In 1972, ARPANET connection was demonstrated between forty geographically dispersed machines in the United States. By 1973, the UK had become connected to the ARPANET. During the 1970s, various facilities that are used today were developed initially for the ARPANET. These are covered later in the chapter and include e-mail, USENET (an electronic bulletin board) and various methods for transferring electronic files across the network.

For computers to communicate effectively across a network they need to ensure that they transmit and receive information in a standard way. These transmission standards are called protocols. During the 1980s, the International Standards Organization (ISO) was in the process of developing a comprehensive layered approach towards all computer communication through the development of the Open Systems Interconnection (OSI), which was covered in Chapter 4. However, progress was not fast enough for ARPANET members, and in 1982 the development of the transmission control protocol (TCP) and the Internet protocol (IP) established the standard for computer network transmission across the ARPANET and became the foundation of the Internet communication standards.

During the 1980s, local area networks (LANs) were being installed in businesses and other organizations for internal communication based around PCs. Organizations desired these internal networks to be connected to the ARPANET, which now had a much wider function that its original military/scientific objectives. In the UK, **JANET** (Joint Academic Network) was set up in 1984 to provide connections between universities, and scientific and major government organizations. Internal networks in each of these organizations had connections to JANET. JANET itself was linked to ARPANET.

One of the important new US networks commissioned by the National Science Foundation (**NSFNET**) involved the development of five supercomputers located at five major universities. These were to be connected together, and each was to be the centre of a regional network with links through the telephone network to local schools and colleges. The philosophy was to provide universal educational connection to the network. This network was to be connected to ARPANET. But as the number of networks had risen so had ARPANET bureaucracy, and it had become increasingly difficult to deal with the increased requirements on it. The NSFNET rapidly became more important, and connections to it increased rapidly in the United States. The late 1980s saw the serious commercial interest of the telephone companies in the interconnection of computers. MCI took over the management of the telephone connections within NSFNET. In 1989, the electronic mail provider CompuServe linked up with what was now becoming known as the Internet by a connection through Ohio State University. ARPANET had ceased to exist by 1990.

The Internet as it was known by the late 1980s was a collection of networks that could communicate with each other running under TCP/IP. Its use was still largely confined to educational, government and scientific organizations. Two developments led to the explosive growth of the Internet in the 1990s. The first was the rapid increase in the ownership of PCs, both privately and in businesses. This was most obvious in the United States but was a worldwide phenomenon. PCs were becoming cheaper and much more powerful. Modems, the devices needed to connect the PC through the telephone network, were becoming much faster in operation, thus allowing the possibility of graphics and sound being communicated to the PC as well as text. The other major development was the design and development of the **World Wide Web**. This was introduced in 1990. It allows users to retrieve information in text and graphic form easily from the Internet. Extensive use is made of **hypertext** and links to information held on other computers. These links make information readily available, and navigation around the Internet is easy. The World Wide Web is covered later in this chapter.

By 1992, over one million users had become connected to the Internet and the World Wide Web via linked networks. In 1993, The White House, the UK government, the United Nations and the World Bank all went online with the provision of information on the World Wide Web. Throughout 1993 and 1994 business use of the World Wide Web grew, credit card transactions were established over the Internet, and television commercials increasingly made reference to websites. During 1995, sophisticated software **browsers** were developed (in particular Netscape Navigator and Microsoft's Internet Explorer). These enabled advanced use of the World Wide Web to distribute and view video and sound as well as text and graphics. Developments in operating systems such as Windows XP and the free availability of the browser software made access even easier. Connection to the Internet, particularly for private use, was further accelerated as the number of Internet service providers (ISPs) increased and the cost of service fell. The introduction of broadband Internet connection has had a massive impact on both business and home usage. Rapid transfer of data, easy transfer of large files and 24-hours-a-day connection are all possible. It has also moved the charging model towards a flat rate subscription and away from a per-use basis. Membership and use have continued to grow at an exponential rate. By 2000, there were over 20 million websites spread over 150 countries. The Internet and the World Wide Web have now become established globally as a major source of information and entertainment to businesses and private individuals.

Mini case 5.1

Broadband

Broadband is regarded as necessary to prevent the populations of developing countries falling behind economically and socially. But is that true, and should broadband therefore be a priority for developing countries?

Broadband Internet began a few years ago and has now reached 6.9 per cent of the population in America and 2.3 per cent in the UK. Several countries, most notably South Korea, have higher penetrations (21.4 per cent).

Politics and economics are about choices. Of course it is preferable to have an Internet connection rather than a slow dial-up service. But such an upgrade costs about $250 of new investment and labour per existing Internet subscriber. Is this money well spent? At the same time, few people in poor countries have phone connectivity of any kind. Two-thirds of the world's population live in countries with fewer than 10 phone connections per 100 people. It costs about $1,000 to wire up a new user; wireless can bring down the cost somewhat. Thus, the money for about three broadband upgrades could instead support one basic connection of a new user to a network.

There are few things one could not do on narrowband outside its use for music and video. Yes, there are important applications, such as tele-medicine and distance education. For those, broadband may be justified in institutional settings, and they could grow into shared community high-speed access points. But that does not mean that broadband is essential as a residential service.

It may be comforting to declare that one can do it all, widening service as well as deepening it. This might be true one day. Until then, universal connectivity rather than broadband is the better but more boring strategy for development.

Adapted from: **Let them eat megabits**
By Eli Noam
FT.com site: 26 November 2003

Questions

1. What issues affect the choice of broadband over dial-up connection?

2. Do you think there will continue to be a place for dial-up networking in the Internet of the future?

5.2 How the Internet works

5.2.1 Connection to the Internet

A computer may be connected to the Internet and transmit and receive information from the Internet in a number of ways:

1. If the computer is part of a local area network then it is quite likely that the computer will be connected through that network to a gateway, which will itself be linked to another network. This is linked to other networks, and so on. It is usual for the link to the first network to be a leased (as distinct from a dial-up) line. The links to other networks will also be via non-dial-up links.

2. Another method of connection is to utilise an **Internet service provider** (ISP). An ISP is usually a commercial organization that provides access to the Internet for a private user or a small business. The ISP has a high-speed machine(s) and a fast link into the Internet. Connection might be established by dialling a number to create a link using a normal telephone connection. Alternatively, a cable connection to a cable modem provides a constant broadband connection to the Internet; ready when required. The cost of the provision varies according to the service provided. The user might be charged a monthly rental and, for a dial-up connection, may also pay a usage charge while connected. At the other end of the spectrum, a so-called free service ISP might make no charges at all, leaving the user with just the cost of the phone call to the service provider. The level of service is normally reflected in the charges levied. Many free service providers will disconnect users after a short period of inactivity on the Internet (often 10 minutes), or after a longer period (usually a couple of hours) regardless of usage. Similarly, an account with an ISP might be

Figure 5.1 Connections and the Internet

frozen or discontinued after a period of dormancy (often three to six months). The ISP, as well as providing access to the Internet, will usually provide news and other information services, e-mail and the management of a small website for the subscriber. This last is an important service if the subscriber is a small business.

Figure 5.1 shows how different users of the Internet might effect the necessary connections to communicate with other Internet users. Two companies, ABC and XYZ, each have a local area network. From a computer attached to the ring network in company ABC it will be possible to access pages from the ABC corporate website and send internal e-mail messages. Similarly, users of the bus network in company XYZ will also have access to their own internal e-mail system and web pages stored on their corporate web servers. Each of the companies has a computer identified as providing a gateway to the global Internet. If company users want to make a connection to an external computer user, e.g. to view pages hosted on an external web server, the gateway computer provides the interface through which that connection can be set up. Mary, a home computer user, can use Internet services, such as e-mail, but must first dial up her Internet service provider. The ISP then acts as her gateway to the Internet. Many ISPs provide space for private users to create their own website, and these pages will become part of the globally accessible World Wide Web. Employees working at companies ABC and XYZ and Mary from her home computer can all now communicate with each other, whether it be exchanging e-mails, transferring files between computers or viewing designated web pages.

5.2.2 Addresses and domain names

Each computer attached to the Internet is given an address. This consists of a 32-bit number. Conventionally, this is expressed as a sequence of four decimal numbers, for example 128.146.16.5. Each number is less than 256. For ease of understanding to humans these host computers are known by more meaningful names. For example, *dc.lincoln.ac.uk*. The name gives information as well as being a formal address. It can be read as the computer identified as *dc* (the Department of Computing) located at Lincoln University (*lincoln*) which is an academic site (*ac*) located in the United Kingdom (*uk*). It is convention that each country has an identifier, although it is also convention that the United States does not use a national identifier.

The host computer names are translated into the relevant 32-bit addresses by means of the domain name system (DNS). This is a worldwide hierarchical system of assigning names. Each name is allocated by a name server. This server is responsible for allocating all names within its domain. For example, a domain might be non-governmental organizations. This authority is derived from the next higher level. There is a set of two-letter domains that correspond to the highest domain in each country on the Internet. For example, *uk* stands for the United Kingdom and *nl* stands for the Netherlands. Within each country, the domains are broken down into lower-level domains. For example, Table 5.1 illustrates the original high-level domains in the United States.

Table 5.1 High-level domains in the United States

Domain	Area
com	commercial organization
edu	educational organization
gov	governmental organization
mil	military organization
org	non-governmental organization
net	network resource

Mini case 5.2

Domain names

After more than a decade of debate, the Internet is set to be given seven new top-level domain names to compete with the ubiquitous 'dotcom'. The Internet's ruling body has chosen the following:

- .name will be for personal websites;
- .pro will be for professionals such as lawyers and doctors;
- .museum, .aero and .coop will be for speciality museum, airline and cooperative business websites;
- .biz will be for any business organizations; and
- .info will be a generic tag for any website.

▶

The move is aimed at eliminating the so-called 'John Smith problem' and will give a broader range of alternatives to individuals or organizations whose names are already being used with a .com suffix by someone else. If approved, the seven new suffixes will mark the first additions to the Internet's naming regime since the late 1980s.

China's Internet authority now allows Internet domain names to be registered in Chinese characters. Experts believe that there could be more than 300 million Chinese speakers on the Internet by 2005. Network Solutions, the US company that registers the rapidly dwindling supply of English-character Internet addresses not already taken, also plans Chinese characters to be used to the left of the .com termination.

Adapted from: **Seven new domain names chosen by ruling body**
FT.com site: 17 November 2000

Questions

1. What is the 'John Smith' problem referred to in the mini case?

2. What factors limit the number of Internet addresses? Is there a danger of demand for Internet addresses outstripping the available supply?

The worldwide growth in the number of users of the Internet has been exponential. There are many ways of quantifying this growth: it could be measured in terms of the number of users of the Internet, the number of computers connected to the Internet, the geographical zones where Internet access is possible, the number of websites, and so on. The graphs in Figure 5.2 chart the growth of the Internet in terms of the number of hosts (where a host is defined as a machine with its own IP address) and the number of domains (where a domain is defined as a registered domain name). Although the exponential nature of the growth is evident, there are signs that the rate of increase in the number of hosts is beginning to fall, possibly providing evidence of a plateau of saturation.

5.2.3 Connection through the Internet

Network connection concepts were introduced in the previous chapter, and the reader is referred to that chapter for a more extended coverage than here. Connection between one computer on the Internet and another computer on the Internet is not like the connection of one telephone to another via a circuit link through the public-switched telephone network. In the case of a phone link, a circuit connection is established through the network at dial-up and exists for as long as the telephone call exists.

In the case of an Internet connection, the information that passes between one computer and another is divided into packets, with different packets taking different routes through the network. There is thus only a virtual circuit connection. This process is known as **packet switching** and was illustrated in Figure 4.11.

In order to ensure that information proceeds from the transmitter computer to the correct receiver computer, and that the information that is received in different packets is assembled in the correct order at the receiving computer, two important standards (protocols) are used.

Figure 5.2 Growth in use of the Internet

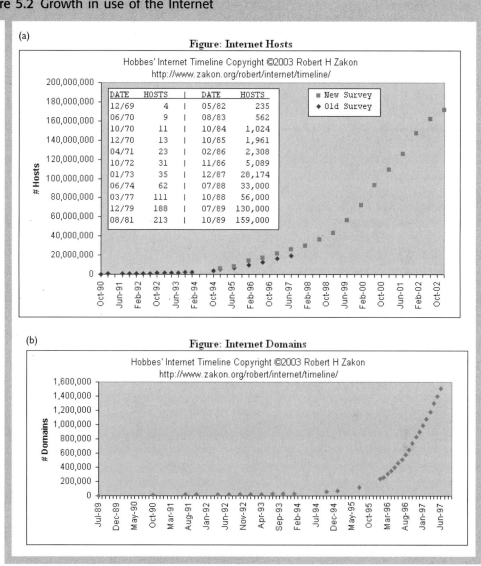

(a)

Figure: Internet Hosts

The **Internet Protocol (IP)** ensures that a packet of data arrives at the correct address (the destination computer) after transfer through the Internet. As the packet passes through the Internet, onward transmission from one network to another is handled by computers known as **routers**.

Because a packet of data contains the equivalent of only about 1500 characters, it is usual for the information sent between one computer and another to be divided into several packets. Ensuring that these packets arrive at the correct address is the job of the Internet protocol. However, having arrived:

- the information held in the packets needs to be reassembled in the correct order;

- the receiving computer must determine whether the data has been altered in error during transmission; and

Figure 5.3 (a) A virtual network connection (produced by NeoTrace); (b) Nodes used to establish the network connection

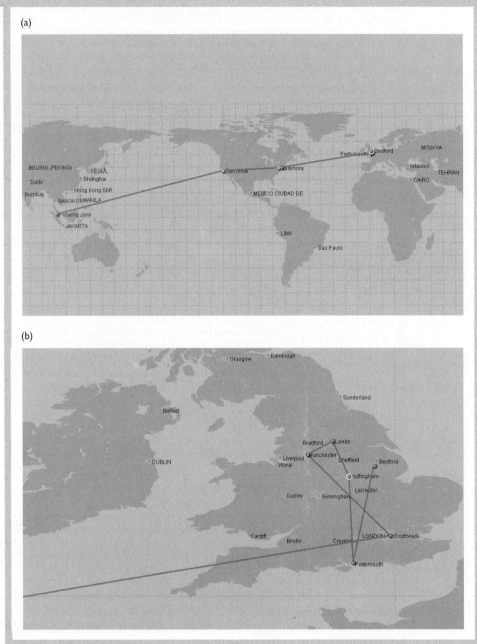

Figure 5.3 *(cont'd)*

(c)
NeoTrace Version 3.25 – TRIAL Trace Results
Target: www.sabah-credit.com.my
Date: 04/01/2004 (Sunday), 16:41:48
Nodes: 19

Node	IP Address	Location	Time (ms)	Node Name
1	123.321.11.11	Lincoln	0	LAPTOP
2	10.175.231.254	Unknown	24	
3	80.4.47.181	Portsmouth	26	nott-t2cam1-a-ge-wan52-135.inet.ntl.com
4	80.1.79.61	Nottingham	86	not-t2core-a-pos41.inet.ntl.com
5	62.253.188.33	Leeds	26	lee-bb-a-so-200-0.inet.ntl.com
6	62.253.187.186	Leeds	25	lee-bb-b-ae0-0.inet.ntl.com
7	62.253.185.193	Manchester	34	man-bb-a-so-700-0.inet.ntl.com
8	62.253.187.178	Manchester	34	man-bb-b-ae0-0.inet.ntl.com
9	213.206.159.245	Southwark	46	sl-gw11-lon-8-0.sprintlink.net
10	213.206.128.58	Southwark	39	sl-bb21-lon-11-0.sprintlink.net
11	144.232.19.69	39.617N, 74.383W	272	sl-bb21-tuk-10-0.sprintlink.net
12	144.232.20.132	39.617N, 74.383W	101	sl-bb20-tuk-15-0.sprintlink.net
13	144.232.20.122	Baltimore	215	sl-bb21-rly-14-3.sprintlink.net
14	144.232.7.254	Baltimore	276	sl-bb22-rly-13-0.sprintlink.net
15	144.232.20.186	San Jose	269	sl-bb22-sj-10-0.sprintlink.net
16	144.232.3.210	San Jose	276	sl-bb25-sj-12-0.sprintlink.net
17	144.232.3.114	San Jose	279	sl-gw8-sj-10-0.sprintlink.net
18	144.228.110.130	San Jose	495	sl-telec3-1-0.sprintlink.net
19	210.187.19.36	Petaling Jaya	----	www.sabah-credit.com.my
		Total	2523	

- the receiving computer must be able to request the sending computer to resend any packets not received or determined to have been received in an altered state.

All of the information required to do this is inserted into each packet along with the information to be transmitted. The standard protocol that determines how this is done is known as **transmission control protocol (TCP)**. The combination of IP and TCP occurs so regularly that it is known as **TCP/IP**. Most operating systems (e.g. Microsoft Windows) contain software to handle these protocols.

Figure 5.3(a) shows a snapshot in time of the route taken by packets of data transmitted from the University of Lincoln in the UK to an information website in Sabah, East Malaysia. The packets can be seen travelling through London, the USA and onwards to Malaysia using a combination of satellite and land line connections.

The connection and route taken has been tracked using a software package called NeoTrace. Although the user of the system might assume that a direct route is followed, the enlargement in Figure 5.3(b) shows that a more idiosyncratic path is taken, particularly at the earlier stages.

Figure 5.3(c) shows a more complete trace and identifies nineteen nodes that are involved in the data transfer. A more complete picture emerges, with the data being sent from a laptop computer in Lincoln through various cities in the UK until reaching a relay station in Southwark, London. From there (node 10) the time intervals increase dramatically, representing the switch from wired cables to satellite transmission. The message is then passed across North America and on to South East Asia and its destination in Kota Kinabalu, Sabah.

The process is dynamic and, if repeated, would produce a different trace with different time intervals. At the moment when this image was captured the longest time interval between nodes was 495 milliseconds (approximately half a second), with the total time to make the trace between the sender in the UK and the recipient in Malaysia being approximately two and a half seconds.

If all the data that is being sent can be fitted into one packet, an alternative protocol known as the **user datagram protocol** (UDP) may be used. It has the advantage of being less complex and swifter in operation than TCP.

Some users will be using a telephone connection and modem for the first part of the connection into the Internet. For example, an employee might connect to the Internet from home or while travelling on business through the employee's organization's local area network. The first part of the connection will often be made using a protocol known as **point-to-point protocol** (PPP). This protocol allows a computer to use a modem and telephone line to establish TCP/IP connection to the Internet.

Mini case 5.3

Internet connection

The Internet allows you to trawl foreign stores without having to speak foreign languages. But while the Internet can cater for the more globally minded, it also has offerings for the more parochially focused consumer. The www.expatshopping.com site offers high-tech confirmation that armies of British expats march on their stomachs. The site has more than 1500 items, 'all British and all ready for delivery to you' through its association with Parcelforce Worldwide.

While not every country is listed, hungry expats in regions from Aruba, Azerbaijan, Barbados and Bhutan – assuming that they can get an Internet connection – can order an array of nostalgic foodstuffs, from Marmite and Heinz baked beans to Ovaltine. If you are in Dubai, don't expect to be able to order whisky: the site automatically bars you from buying goods that are illegal in the country from which you are ordering.

The category *par excellence* is beverages, with thirteen variants of Brooke Bond and twenty-four selections of Twinings teas. For expats struggling with foreign languages there are *Beano* comics and *The Economist*. There are also dozens of varieties of Fray Bentos tinned pies, sausages and corned beef.

Adapted from: **Home thoughts**
Financial Times: 13 September 2000

Question

Outline how an Internet order for goods placed by a hungry British ex-patriot living in a remote part of Sweden might be transmitted to a company based in Great Britain.

5.3 What the Internet offers

Connection to the Internet makes available a number of facilities that are useful to business and private users (who may also be customers of businesses). Some of these are more important than others. For business, undoubtedly the two most important are e-mail and the World Wide Web. The full range of facilities are covered in the current section, although the World Wide Web is mentioned only briefly as it is covered extensively later. The application of the Internet to business is covered in the next chapter.

5.3.1 E-mail

Electronic mail (**e-mail**) is the sending of an electronic message or memo from one person to another. The messages are sent and received through the use of e-mail software running on a computer.

In local area networks, e-mail software enables users within a company to send and receive messages to and from one another over the network. These packages work by reserving part of the hard disk of a file server on the network for each person. Each user has an individual address, which corresponds to the disk storage location. This is known as the user's **mailbox**. Messages sent to the person are stored electronically prior to (and after) being read in the mailbox. Users can access their mailbox through the normal procedure of identifying themselves by logging on to their network account and then running the e-mail software. Alternatively, employees may be able to access their mailbox from a remote (off-site) location. Generally, e-mail packages are user-friendly and have a large number of facilities for users such as filing messages, constructing distribution lists and linking to a calendar for diary-based activities.

Private users of e-mail have a mailbox located at their Internet service provider (ISP). The user sends and reads their e-mail by connecting to the mailbox, which is maintained by the ISP.

An e-mail message typically consists of a header and text (see Figure 5.4). The address consists of both the address of a host machine (the part after @ in the example) and the address of the person's mailbox at the host machine (the part before @ in the example).

When the message is sent over the Internet, it is sent by the **store and forward** method. This means that during its progress from sender to receiver the message is not

Figure 5.4 The format of an e-mail message

To:	receivername@receiveraddress	*inserted by sender*
From:	g.a.curtis@uel.ac.uk	*inserted automatically by sender's package*
Organization:	University of East London	*inserted automatically by sender's package*
Date:	5th September 2004	*inserted automatically by sender's package*
cc:	copyreceivername@copyreceiveraddress	*inserted by sender*
Reply to:	g.a.curtis@uel.ac.uk	*inserted automatically by sender's package (usually the same as From address)*
The message text is inserted here and can be of any length.		*inserted by sender*

Table 5.2 A comparison of e-mail, post and telephone

	E-mail	Post/memo	Telephone
Speed	fast	slow	instant
Security	moderate	high	low
Interactivity	moderate	low	high
Formality	moderate	high	low
As record	moderate	high	low
Multiple recipients	possible (cheap)	possible (costly)	limited

continuously in electronic transit but may be stored at a computer(s) on the Internet prior to being forwarded on the next part of its journey. This implies that e-mail transmission over the Internet is not instantaneous. Messages may take a few seconds to several hours.

The use of e-mail provides several advantages (and disadvantages) over the telephone and the postal system. These comparisons are outlined in Table 5.2. E-mail is increasingly used in organizations in preference to paper-based memos because:

- it is faster to transmit (almost instantaneous);
- it is more convenient and environmentally friendly (no paper);
- there is an automatic record of when the e-mail is read; and
- it is possible to send the same e-mail to a number of recipients for no extra effort.

The use of e-mail over the Internet is also increasing. It is preferred to the postal system because:

- it is faster than post (and unlike telephone messages time differences are unimportant);
- it is more convenient and environmentally friendly (no paper); and
- it is possible to send the same e-mail to a number of recipients for no extra effort.

Typically, e-mail packages provide several facilities:

1. **Notification of receipt/reading:** On receipt/reading of the e-mail the receiver's package automatically replies with an acknowledgement. It is often useful to know if a recipient has received and (particularly) read a message.
2. **Mailing and distribution lists:** The e-mail package enables a user to build up several lists of e-mail addresses, which can be called up and inserted with one key stroke, for example all departmental heads, or all client contact names.
3. **Forward or reply:** A message may be forwarded or replied to. Typically, this can be accompanied by the reader's comments (editing) and be with or without the original text.
4. **File attachments:** Files, for example word-processed document files and spreadsheets, can be attached to messages and loaded into receiver software.
5. **Folders:** Received messages can be automatically stored in different electronic folders.
6. **Filters:** Filter facilities allow mail to be selectively read and stored depending on whether the messages meet some rule (filter rule) specified by the user. It might be the case that mail from a certain organization is filtered out to a particular folder, or only mail with certain key words in the headings is read.

Figure 5.5 An example of a screen from an e-mail package

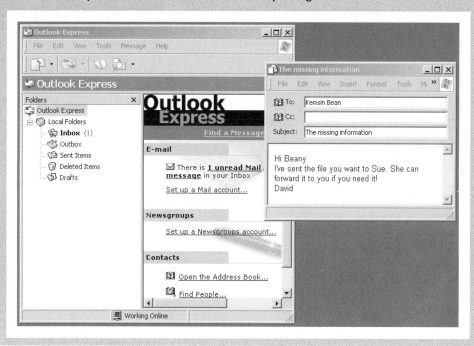

An example of a typical interface provided by an e-mail package is shown in Figure 5.5.

In order that different e-mail packages can send and receive information other than standard ASCII text e-mail messages to one another it is important that there be a standard way of representing the structure of these messages. This standard is called **MIME** (multipurpose Internet mail extension). As well as specifying the structure of the messages, the MIME standard also specifies how video, graphics and audio files can be sent as attachments to e-mail messages along with standard ASCII text. The MIME standard ensures that non-text files are converted into text – although the resulting text is not readable. Also, as well as specifying the type of file being sent, the MIME standard specifies the method that needs to be used by the recipient in order to convert the file to its original form. If two different e-mail packages can be used to send and receive non-text files to one another according to the MIME standard, these packages are said to be MIME compliant.

It is clear that e-mail is now an essential means of communication. This is especially so within a business, where e-mail together with intranets (covered in a later section) are rapidly replacing paper-based communications in an organization.

5.3.2 The World Wide Web

The **World Wide Web** has dramatically increased the accessibility of information on the Internet and the private and commercial use of the Internet. The World Wide Web, together with software that enables a user to browse, ensures that text, graphic, video and audio information is available globally in a standard manner. The Web is treated extensively in the following sections (5.4 and onwards) of this chapter.

5.3.3 TELNET

In an organization, a PC located on the organization's local area network will be able to run the organization's application programs in one of two ways. The program may be run off the hard disk on the PC, or it may be run over the LAN from a server. The PC is effectively acting as a terminal and as a client to the server. This client–server relationship was explained in Chapter 4. A similar relationship can exist between two computers over the Internet. A client computer can remotely log on to a server computer across the Internet. The protocol that governs this remote login is known as **TELNET**, and the process is known as **telnet**. An organization may wish to allow telnet access to (part of) its computer systems for a number of reasons. Chief among these is that the organization is providing a public service. For instance, it is common for libraries to allow telnet access to their library catalogue. The reader logs on to the library computer and runs the accompanying library software necessary to read the catalogue. Businesses may wish to allow telnet access for specified clients or for their own employees if remotely located (for example the travelling sales person). The telnet access that an organization allows to its own computer system is usually the subject of a high level of security restriction and password control.

5.3.4 File transfer protocol (FTP)

Rather than logging on to a remote computer as a telnet session and using that computer's software to access and run applications, it may be desirable to obtain a copy of a file that can then be stored on the client's computer for later use. In order that this can be achieved over the Internet a protocol – **file transfer protocol** (FTP) – is used. As with telnet, there may be security levels allowing access to files only by a login account and a password. Some organizations may allow open access for transfer of files, for example public service or research organizations. FTP is a popular method of transferring web pages that have been developed on a local computer across to the website that will host them and is located on a remote system.

5.3.5 Newsgroups

The Internet has since its earliest days provided many newsgroups. Newsgroups may be set up to deal with any topic that is of particular interest to a group of people. These can be to do with a hobby, a social issue, a scientific area, a football team, a product, jobs offered – in fact anything. By joining a newsgroup, the member has the right to add text that is read by other members of the group and to read text provided by other members of the group. Membership is usually open and free. Members of a newsgroup may be located anywhere in the world and place and read their news through connection to the Internet. They are thus able to take part in a global debate on their area of interest. The information held by each newsgroup will be administered by a newsgroup administrator. This information will be held on one server (although this may be duplicated). Groups tend to have names that identify themselves – for example *alt.atheism* or *misc.forsale*.

5.3.6 Internet relay chat

Internet relay chat (IRC) was first developed in 1988. It enables a group of users to interact with one another over the Internet in much the same way that a group of people talk to one another in a social situation or at a meeting. At a meeting, anyone can talk to anyone else in the group, although everyone in the group can hear the conversation of others. Unlike verbal interaction at a meeting, interaction over an IRC is usually by way of typed text. Each can 'view' the conversations of the others. Internet relay chat groups are called channels. Each channel has one or more operators responsible for managing the channel. These conferencing channels usually concentrate on specific subjects. The main feature that distinguishes IRCs from newsgroups is the immediacy of the interaction between participating members.

5.3.7 Instant messaging

Instant messaging (IM) is a rapid and simple way for two online users to communicate, normally by using text. Although the concept is similar to e-mail, IM provides a far more immediate transmission and simplifies the process where an extended exchange of messages takes place. As cell phone text message services have moved into the mainstream, IM has gained the interest of businesses who have realized commercial potential from using the technology.

5.3.8 Internet telephony

The Internet provides an alternative to traditional telephone services. With appropriate software and hardware installed on their systems, Internet users can make telephone or videophone calls, send faxes and leave voice mail or paging messages. The sound and picture quality might be lower than that achieved with a permanent circuit connection, but the cost is that of the normal Internet service provision (which regardless of the location of the participants could be just that of a local or free call).

5.3.9 Electronic conferencing

Tools for electronic conferencing provide a further medium of communication and facilitate collaborative working. Members of work groups can meet to share ideas in real time even though geographically dispersed. A number of alternative models exist:

- **Voice-conferencing:** This technology replaces the traditional method of using conference telephones to realize a meeting. Participants use the Internet telephony described above combined with browser-based software such as Microsoft's NetMeeting or Netscape's Conference to conduct a meeting.
- **Data-conferencing:** A browser package or specialized software tool is used collectively by participants to display, edit and revise text documents or graphical images in a technique known as whiteboarding.
- **Video-conferencing:** Groupware software packages called electronic meeting systems (EMS) can be used to offer the full range of voice, data and interactive video to provide a comprehensive virtual meeting. Document editing, whiteboard facilities and voice input are enhanced by the addition of video images of the participants and other audio or visual data content. Where conferences are dispersed over a number of sites, the term 'teleconferencing' is often used to describe this activity.

5.3.10 Collaborative work management tools

Many tools exist to help groups to accomplish a task or manage an activity. These tools include project management and resource scheduling software, calendar and diary systems, and work flow systems. The generic description of these tools is that of group support systems (GSS). The proliferation of networked computing has made all these tools far more accessible in a more distributed environment. They are evaluated further in Chapter 7.

Mini case 5.4

Linux

Today, market ecosystems exist in many industries already, such as utilities, financial services, logistics etc., where market value lies in exchanging data, or even access to pooled data. These ecosystems are very different from internal enterprises, being based more on protocols than on extensive transaction logic. Web services are intended to enrich the interchanges much in the way that the TCP/IP protocol acted as the starting point for the Internet to develop steadily richer services. Interestingly, the effect of being able to interact and collaborate in this manner within the market ecosystem will result in an increased need within the enterprise for commercial software offering new forms of business logic that can provide competitive advantage from these new information sources.

Linux is increasingly hard to ignore, as shown by the extensive press coverage it's recently received. It effectively extends the Internet revolution from Linux web servers, to form the basis for 'the Internet of Things', where many different forms of devices will communicate, collaborate and transact together. To support this requires the use of non-differentiated standardized software that can perform many, many more tasks than the relatively simple task of content management performed by the open source software that created the World Wide Web.

The link with Linux is important, as it was the first, almost only choice available for web servers when the World Wide Web exploded. Linux is growing out of this role as more and more commercial organizations are using it. Most hardware vendors now support a Linux version, as they increasingly understand operating systems are as much a cost as a profit today. As Linux becomes a more mainstream operating system, it will be used with Open Source Software (OSS) in generic areas of an enterprise, with sensible management, where the need for standardized 'utility' software is based on cost.

The Internet of Things that will require this approach is already emerging, usually referred to under the generic description of 'Mobility'. An example is radio frequency identification, or RFID, the addition of 'tags' to objects that allow 'readers' in the proximity to identify the item. By 2002, this is said to have become a $960m market with many global leaders conducting pilots. Using RFID, the retail and logistics market can create a 'pool' of data that tracks loads, or goods. Members of the 'ecosystem', such as shippers and receivers, carriers and retailers will all require access to elements of the data pool for different reasons. The data pool belongs to everyone, and standardized ways to interact, collaborate, and eventually automate transactions must be built. OSS is likely to prove the most effective mechanism in these circumstances. Higher-level functionality between individual partners evoked on the basis of the information provided may well continue to be the province of commercial software providing the complex business logic.

Adapted from: **Linux and the 'Internet of Things'**
By Andy Mulholland
FT.com site: 10 November 2003

5.4 The World Wide Web

In 1989, CERN (the European Laboratory for Particle Physics in Switzerland) proposed the development of the World Wide Web (now commonly known as the Web) in order to enable high-energy physicists across the world to collaborate through the easy provision and accessibility of information. Through CERN, the National Center for Supercomputing Applications (NCSA) at the University of Illinois, USA, soon became involved. Certain key features of the Web rapidly became established. Broadly speaking, these are:

■ a standard way of providing information on web pages stored electronically on a host computer – this would include text, formatting, graphics, audio and video;

■ the use of hyperlinks to direct a web page reader to other web pages on the same website or to a different website; and

■ easy-to-use software that would enable users to transfer quickly between pages on a website or between different websites at the click of a mouse.

In 1993, the NCSA released a web browser program, **Mosaic,** which allowed easy and powerful access to the Web. At the time there were only about fifty websites worldwide. The facilities offered by Mosaic and particularly by its successor software browser, **Netscape Navigator,** led to an explosion in the development of websites and the accessing of these by users. (The author of Mosaic, Marc Andreeson, left NCSA to author the Netscape browser.) There are now over 20 million websites across the world. In order to understand the World Wide Web it is important to understand the basics of hypertext, browsers and the way websites are addressed.

5.4.1 The World Wide Web – basics

Hypertext and hypertext markup language

The concept of **hypertext** goes back to the 1940s. The idea is that when reading a piece of text, at certain points terms may need greater explanation, or related information may be helpful to the reader. Where this happens the reader should be able to call up directly the explanation or related information via a link within the text. Of course, these explanations are text and may themselves contain terms that need further explanation. These will be linked to other explanations, and so on. This system is known as hypertext.

Pages stored electronically on the Web have these hypertext links within them so that readers of a web page may click on a link and proceed along it to another web page (possibly at another website). In order to do this, the structure of the web page and its related links are designed in a special language called **hypertext markup language** (HTML). An example of a page specified in HTML is given as Figure 5.6. It leads to the

Figure 5.6 An example of a page (for the Red Cross museum) written in HTML

```
<HTML>
<!-- Lotus-Domino (Release 5.0.5 - September 22, 2000 on Windows NT/Intel) -->
<HEAD>
<META NAME="description" CONTENT= "International Committee of the Red Cross (ICRC) -
Comité international de la Croix-Rouge (CICR)"><META NAME="keywords" CONTENT=
"International Committee of the Red Cross,Comite international de la Croix-Rouge,Comite
internacional de la Cruz Roja,ICRC,CICR,Red Cross,Croix-Rouge,Cruz Roja,International Red
Cross,Croix-Rouge internationale,Humanitarian action,Action humanitaire,International Humanitarian
Law,Droit international humanitaire,Geneva Conventions,Conventions de Geneve,Convenios de
Ginebra,War,Guerre,Guerra,Armed conflict,Conflit arme,Relief,Secours,Detention"><TITLE>International
Committee of the Red Cross (ICRC) - Home</TITLE>
</SCRIPT><SCRIPT LANGUAGE="JavaScript">

image = new makeArray(4);
image[1]="/WEBGRAPH.NSF/Graphics/home_1a.jpg/$FILE/home_1a.jpg";
image[2]="/WEBGRAPH.NSF/Graphics/home_1b.jpg/$FILE/home_1b.jpg";
image[3]="/WEBGRAPH.NSF/Graphics/home_1c.jpg/$FILE/home_1c.jpg";
image[4]="/WEBGRAPH.NSF/Graphics/home_1d.jpg/$FILE/home_1d.jpg";

</SCRIPT>
</HEAD>
<BODY bgColor=#ffffff><!DOCTYPE HTML PUBLIC "-//W3C//DTD HTML 4.0 Transitional//EN">
<DIV align=center>
  <TABLE width=740 border=0>
    <TBODY>
    <TR bgcolor="#FFFFFF">
      <TD colSpan=5 valign="top" align="center" bgcolor="#FFFFFF"> <font face="Arial, Helvetica,
sans-serif" color="#666666" size="6">International
        Committee of the Red Cross</font>
        <table width="100%" border="0" align="center" bordercolor="#666666" cellspacing="12">
          <tr>
            <td align="center" bgcolor="#e0e0e0"><A HREF=/eng><IMG
SRC=/WEBGRAPH.NSF/Graphics/eng.gif/$FILE/eng.gif BORDER=0 ALT = "English Home
page"></A></td>
            <td align="center" bgcolor="#e0e0e0"><A HREF=/fre><IMG
SRC=/WEBGRAPH.NSF/Graphics/fre.gif/$FILE/fre.gif BORDER=0 ALT = "Page d'accueil
Français"></A></td>
            <td align="center" bgcolor="#e0e0e0"><A HREF=/spa><IMG
SRC=/WEBGRAPH.NSF/Graphics/spa.gif/$FILE/spa.gif BORDER=0 ALT = "Home Español"></A></td>
            <td align="center" bgcolor="#e0e0e0"><A HREF=/ara><IMG
SRC=/WEBGRAPH.NSF/Graphics/ara_g.gif/$FILE/ara_g.gif BORDER=0 ALT = "Home Arabic">
</a></td>
          </tr>
        </table>
      </TD></TR>
<tr>
      <td width="159" cellpadding="1"><SCRIPT LANGUAGE="JavaScript">document.write("<IMG
SRC="+imagealeatoire() +" width=159 height=108>");</SCRIPT></td>
      <td width="159" cellpadding="1"><SCRIPT LANGUAGE="JavaScript">document.write("<IMG
SRC="+imagealeatoire1() +" width=159 height=108>");</SCRIPT></td>
      <td width="100" cellpadding="1"><img
src="/WEBGRAPH.NSF/Graphics/logo_lang.gif/$FILE/logo_lang.gif" width="100" height="108"></td>
      <td width="159" cellpadding="1"><SCRIPT LANGUAGE="JavaScript">document.write("<IMG
```

Figure 5.6 (cont'd)

```
SRC="+imagealeatoire2() +" width=159 height=108>");</SCRIPT></td>
    <td width="159" cellpadding="1"><SCRIPT LANGUAGE="JavaScript">document.write("<IMG
SRC="+imagealeatoire3() +" width=159 height=108>");</SCRIPT></td>
    </tr>
  <TR>
    <TD width=159> </TD>
    <TD width=159> </TD>
    <TD width=100> </TD>
    <TD width=159> </TD>
    <TD width=159> </TD></TR>
  <TR>
    <TD colSpan=2>
      <BLOCKQUOTE><!-- ENGLISH TEXT -->
        <P><FONT face="Arial, Helvetica, sans-serif"><B><FONT
        size=-2>International Committee of the Red Cross<BR>
          </FONT></B></FONT><A

href="/HOME.NSF/060a34982cae624ec12566fe00326312/125ffe2d4c7f68acc1256ae300394f6e?Open
Document"><FONT face="Arial, Helvetica, sans-serif"><B><FONT
        size=-2><font color="#003399">The mission of the ICRC</font><FONT
        color=#ff0000> </FONT></font></b></font></A></P>
        <!-- FRENCH TEXT -->
        <P><FONT size=-2><B><FONT face="Arial, Helvetica, sans-serif"><BR>
          Comit&eacute; international de la Croix-Rouge<BR>
            </FONT></B></FONT><A

href="/HOME.NSF/060a34982cae624ec12566fe00326312/b0b420c039178308c1256ae30043e89d?Open
Document"><FONT size=-2><B><FONT face="Arial, Helvetica, sans-serif"><font color="#003399">La
            mission du CICR</font></font></b></font></A></P>
        <!-- SPANISH TEXT -->
        <P><FONT size=-2><B><FONT face="Arial, Helvetica, sans-serif"><BR>
          Comit&eacute; Internacional de la Cruz Roja<BR>
            </FONT></B></FONT><A

href="/HOME.NSF/060a34982cae624ec12566fe00326312/8b8b90a08361b20dc1256ae300476983?Open
Document"><FONT size=-2><B><FONT face="Arial, Helvetica, sans-serif"><font
color="#003399">La misi&oacute;n del CICR</font></font></b></font></A></P>
        </BLOCKQUOTE></TD>
        <TD colSpan=3><img src="/WEBGRAPH.NSF/Graphics/keywords_15-07-
03.gif/$FILE/keywords_15-07-03.gif" width="400" height="145"
align="top"></TD></TR></TBODY></TABLE>
       </DIV>
</BODY>
</HTML>
```

page (as viewed through a browser) for the International Committee of the Red Cross, as shown in Figure 5.7.

Later versions of HTML allow for the specification of forms that the viewer of the web page may fill in and send back to the site on which the page is located. This facility allows interactivity over the Web. Once interactivity is fully and securely established

Figure 5.7 The page for the Red Cross museum (see HTML version, Figure 5.6) as it appears through a web browser

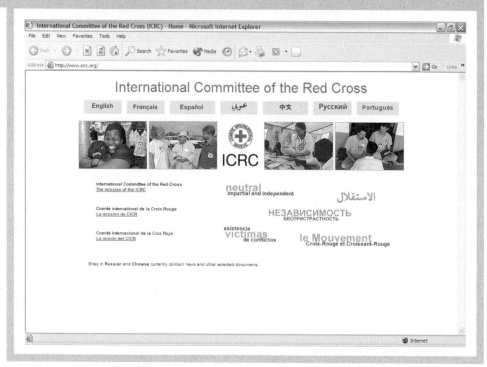

it is possible to buy and sell merchandise. For example, the seller's products are displayed on a website. The user views this catalogue and, if wishing to purchase, fills in a form giving credit card details and address. The use of the Web dispenses with the need for the business to provide a physical shop front.

HTML is very easy to learn and easy to use, but it is not particularly flexible. It is one particular application of the more encompassing SGML or standardized general markup language. SGML is a meta-language, i.e. a language for defining other languages, of which HTML is just one. SGML can be used to create virtually any document type; examples include clinical records of patients, musical notation and even, it is claimed, transcriptions of ancient Irish manuscripts. SGML is very powerful and consequently very complex to use. As a result, a subset of SGML called the extensible markup language (XML) has been developed and has become very popular. XML can be used to define a wider range of document types than HTML, which is used only to create web pages, but it has a syntax that is more limited and hence more comprehensible than full SGML. Figure 5.8 shows the relationships between these markup languages. The solid boxes indicate the languages and their subsets, and the dashed boxes indicate the documents that can be produced.

HTML is far easier to learn and use than the high-level languages discussed in a previous chapter. However, its use is sufficiently complex and time-consuming that a number of packages have been developed to generate the HTML code automatically for web page developers. Packages such as Microsoft's FrontPage and SoftQuad Software's HotMetal Pro allow a designer to create a web page graphically from palettes

Figure 5.8 Markup languages

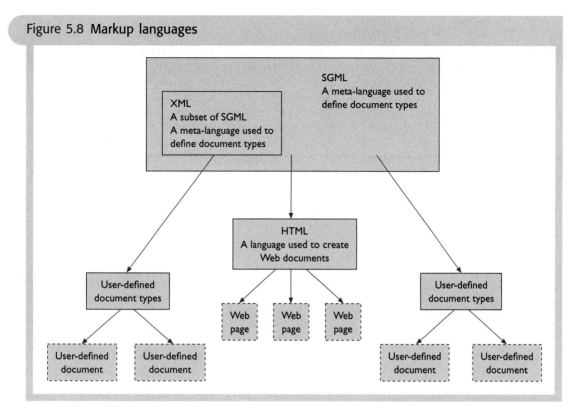

of predefined background styles, images and controls. The HTML produced can then be stored and executed directly or can be edited 'manually' in a normal text editor to make minor alterations. Many word-processing packages also have a facility for saving a document as a web page. The package attempts to preserve the appearance of the document by generating HTML code that mimics the style of the original.

Objects and mark-up languages

For most people soap is used in the bath, but not in IT. Simple Object Access Protocol makes it easier to get computer systems to talk to each other at a high level across the Internet.

Using existing Internet standards, Soap defines a set of specifications for encoding 'rich' communications between different computer platforms. While the basic Internet standards enable easy access to data, Soap makes it possible to activate processes across the World Wide Web (which is what web services is all about).

If, for example, a retailer wants to run an independent credit check on a new customer, it could use Soap to pass the request to a credit checking agency's system, without knowledge of the computer system at the other end of the line. As long as it is 'Soap-enabled', the agency's system can respond to the request.

How does Soap work?

Soap uses hypertext transmission protocol (HTTP), the basic Internet communications 'language', to pass messages to other systems on the web. But instead of a request for access to a web page, a Soap message carries a specially coded request to start a process – a so-called remote procedure call (RPC). Soap uses the eXtensible mark-up language (XML), another important Internet standard, to specify the details of the RPC. Because it is based on two widely accepted standards, use of Soap is spreading quickly. The two main web server systems, Microsoft's Internet Information Server (IIS) and Apache, both support Soap.

Why is Soap important?

Soap's ability to handle high-level communications makes it ideal for building web services and it is expected to play an important part in the growth of this new market. But Soap also transforms the Internet from a 'publish and subscribe' data distribution network into one that can process transactions.

Adapted from: **Soap**
By Philip Manchester
FT.com site: 1 October 2003

Questions

1. Explain the functions carried out by HTTP and XML.
2. What advantages does 'SOAP' offer to users of the Internet?

Web browsers

A **browser** is a software package that runs on the user's (client's) computer. It is able to display the contents of a web page (for example written in HTML) held on another (server) computer. In order to achieve this, the browser must be able to retrieve the contents of the page over the Internet. To make sure that this is carried out a standard for data transfer called the **hypertext transfer protocol** (HTTP) is used.

The two main browsers used are Netscape Navigator and Microsoft's Internet Explorer. An example of a web page viewed through a browser is given in Figure 5.9.

Browsers typically provide useful features to enable the Web user to retrieve the desired information as easily as possible. These may include:

- **bookmarks:** these enable the web address of a web page to be stored and called up again later – particularly useful if the same site is visited often;
- **history:** this provides the user with a list of websites visited in a session – useful as it is often necessary to go back to a previously visited site;
- **e-mail:** most browsers incorporate an e-mail facility;
- **file/print:** this facility allows the user to store the web page(s) as a file, or print it out, which may be either as seen through the browser or as source HTML;
- **find:** find enables a user to search through a web page(s) in order to locate the position of a word or phrase;
- **format options:** these provide a range of colour, typeface and other possibilities affecting the presentation of the web page.

Figure 5.9 The United Nations home page (as seen through Internet Explorer)

Uniform resource locator

Each page on the Web is on a website, which is itself located on a computer attached to the Internet. As has been explained earlier, each computer attached to the Internet has an address. The **uniform resource locator** (URL; note that some people call this the universal resource locator) identifies the location of a resource on the Web (type of resource, site and position or path to the resource at the site). It is useful to think of the URL as the web page address.

The current format for URLs is:

scheme://path

The scheme identifies which protocol is to be used to retrieve the resource and is normally followed by a colon (:). The protocol normally used for web documents is HTTP. The path is taken to be a host identifier, conventionally preceded by a double forward slash (//). The remainder of the path usually gives the location within the host. This is often hierarchical, each stage being separated by a single forward slash (/). An example is given below:

http://www.un.org/overview/origin.html

This states that information may be retrieved using the HTTP at the website with the address *www.un.org*. Within that website, the page retrieved is a subpage, called *origin.html*, of the main page, *overview*.

Pages are usually organized as tree structures, with the top node known as the **home page**.

Web search engines

In order to display information from a website it is necessary to:

1. achieve connection to the Internet (either through an Internet service provider or through a local area network located at one's employer or university);
2. load web browser software;
3. input the URL (website address) of a desired resource.

The HTTP working through the web browser then displays text, graphics, audio or video from the website on the user's screen. If the URL is not known, for example when the user wants to search the web for a particular topic, a web search engine can be employed to find sites with the relevant information.

There are several web search engines. Examples are Alta Vista, Yahoo! and Google. The **web search engine** is a program that, when running, makes connection to many thousand of websites a day, retrieving and indexing web pages from these sites. Web search engines will have visited and indexed millions of web pages. This index will be stored at the website associated with the search engine. A user accesses the website at which the search engine is located and enters, via a form on the screen, a word or words (known as the search string) of search interest. The web search engine then displays at the user's terminal the URLs of all sites at which the search string is located. The search string may be sophisticated, indicating that two or more words must be present (AND), or any of them could be (OR), or some words should not be present (NOT). An example of a search string might be:

Jackson AND president AND NOT (Michael OR music OR five)

A typical search engine page is shown in Figure 5.10.

Recent developments in web search engines have included simplified panels into which the search criteria can be entered ('include all of these words . . .', 'include any of these words . . .', 'exclude these words . . .', etc.). Also, the results of an enquiry are being presented in ever more innovative ways, classifying the findings and suggesting further places to look if more information is required.

Plug-ins

Plug-ins are (usually) small programs that are 'loaded into' a larger program in order to add some function. The plug-in may be produced by a (third party) organization different from the publisher of the larger program. Web browsers may have plug-ins associated with them that allow them to carry out extra functions. The following are examples of plug-ins for browsers that extend their functionality:

- **Internet telephone tools:** These allow telephone conversations to be made over the Internet. These usually incorporate facilities such as audio-conferencing, a telephone answering machine and the ability for all participants to view common graphics on the screen as well as participating in discussion.

- **Interactive 3D viewers:** These **virtual reality modelling language** (VRML) viewers allow 3D to be viewed over the Internet, with the possibility of navigation through the scenes depicted.

- **Audio and video viewers:** Audio and video viewers are plug-ins that allow the user to view/hear video/audio files transferred over the Internet. Most of these allow viewing to occur before the data transfer has been completed.

Figure 5.10 An example of an enquiry in a search engine

- **Streaming audio and video viewers:** These allow the viewer to have online viewing of audio or video as it is streamed to the user's browser software through the Internet. Thus live events may be viewed as they occur.

Browser software has developed very rapidly, and the various offerings of the Internet listed in Section 5.3 have gradually been incorporated as standard elements in a web browser. Today's plug-in often becomes tomorrow's standard feature.

Java

Java, which was introduced in an earlier chapter, is an object-oriented programming language similar to C++ that can be used to produce machine-independent portable software. Programs written in Java can be downloaded over the Internet and run immediately on the user's computer. Small Java programs, known as **applets,** may be embedded in HTML in a web page. This may be downloaded across the Internet with the web page and the program executed from within the user's browser program. Security is maintained as the executed program cannot have access to the user's resources such as files, printers and other computers on the same network. In theory, this should prevent the infection of the receiving computer by a virus. An applet loaded over the Internet may only create a link to the host computer from which it was downloaded. The execution of applets allows web browsers to have more interactive areas and thus extends their functions.

5.4.2 Organizational control of the Internet

There is no organizational control over the Internet. However, there are a number of organizations with influence. First, there are the businesses that are providers of either hardware or major software items used on the Internet. These operate a *de facto* steering direction via the products they produce. However, three organizations are recognized as having authority over coordination of developments on the Internet. The **Internet Engineering Task Force** (IETF) is a large, loosely connected group of designers, researchers and vendors who influence the development of the standards governing the architecture of the Internet. They achieve this through setting up working groups. The IETF is chartered by the **Internet Society** (ISOC), which is a professional member organization of Internet experts that oversees policy and practice. The Internet Society also charters the **World Wide Web Consortium** (W3C), which is a consortium of voluntary member organizations that funds developments on the Web. There is much common membership between the IETF and the W3C.

5.4.3 The World Wide Web and business opportunities

As has been mentioned earlier, the ease of accessing documents over the World Wide Web together with the rapid increase in personal computers has been a major factor in the burgeoning use of the Internet for business. This is discussed more fully in the next chapter.

5.5 The Internet and copyright

Copyright law has historically developed to ensure that an author had the exclusive right to copy his or her work and distribute those copies to the public. The author could also assign this right to others. Copyright law was originally designed for the printed word but has been adapted to deal with broadcasting, software and satellite television.

Copyright protects the expression of an idea – not the idea itself. It comes into existence when the expression is fixed on some medium, such as paper or disk. In some countries it may be essential to register the material as copyright. Generally, copyright applies to classes of work – for example, literary, sound recordings, films. The **Berne Convention** is an international treaty to which approximately 160 member countries belong. An infringement of copyright in any one of these countries of work produced by a foreign national from one of the others is protected in the country as though the infringement were of locally produced material within the country. In this way, the level of protection in each of the countries is standardized for home or foreign publications. In countries not signatory to the Berne Convention, the infringement of copyright needs to be enforced in the country of the alleged infringement and is dependent on the law of that country and not of the country in which it originated.

Copyright applies to the Internet. In UK law, for instance, copying, even if only temporarily into RAM in order to display on screen, is a potential infringement of copyright. It is not necessary for the material to be printed or stored to disk. Since the only way of accessing material on the Internet involves the temporary storage of material in RAM in the recipient machine, it seems to imply that a copyright holder, in placing material on the Internet, authorizes this level of copying. However, the law is at present unclear on this. It is therefore advisable for businesses to establish copyright in much the same way as for printed material, by seeking permission, rather than assuming that the presence on the Internet grants copying permission. There is another important issue. Material on the Internet may already be in infringement of copyright and be held and distributed without the permission of the author. Finally, it is common for businesses to hold copies of popular websites on their own servers to prevent excessive employee use of Internet connection. **Mirror sites**, as these are called, are also held in different countries in order to cut down international Internet traffic. It is quite clear that unless permission has been granted these will infringe copyright.

For any business to copy works from the Internet it is safest to seek permission to copy, to distribute the work and to authorize others to do so. This applies to text, graphics, video and audio and, in some cases, synchronization of audio and video and graphics.

5.6 The Internet and financial transactions

In the early days of the Web it quickly became clear to businesses that the Internet would be not only a vehicle for dispersing information but also a shop front for the sale of goods and services. This would entail commercial transactions being conducted electronically. As a result, 'cybercash' has now become an accepted way of payment over the Internet and particularly over the World Wide Web. It is likely that with increased use of the Web the use of cybercash will become more common. There will be many more transactions. Also, there will be a large increase in the number of small transactions – for example, attachment to a news service based on time connected. With a large volume of small transactions the cost of processing the transaction becomes important and needs to be minimized.

Three forms of electronic payment or electronic cash substitute are currently being used.

1. **Electronic credit card transactions:** This form of payment had already become acceptable prior to the Internet with card swipe and electronic transfer from points of sale. Equally, the quotation of a credit card number over the phone will often secure purchase of goods and services. In this respect, the Internet poses little that is new. The credit card number and other verifying information will be input and the transfer of liability for payment of goods will move from the purchaser to the credit card company, which will then take over responsibility for the transfer of funds to the seller and recovery of money at the end of the month as part of a consolidated bill from the purchaser. No real issues arise that are new – although security (see below) will continue to be a concern. The seller will still be able to gain information concerning the purchaser and purchaser's credit card number, so anonymity of purchasers will not be guaranteed. The costs of processing the transaction are still high relative to the purchase of goods through electronic cash.

2. **Electronic cash or e-cash:** With electronic cash a sum of e-cash is purchased from a 'money merchant' and is held electronically in an account. When a purchaser of a good makes a purchase then the merchant is informed electronically and the e-cash is transferred from the purchaser's account to the seller's account at the merchant (or the seller's account at some other merchant who accepts the e-cash). The entire transaction is conducted electronically over the Internet. The anonymity of the purchaser (and of the seller) can be maintained. This is a relatively new form of payment. It requires the acceptance of e-cash, which has no intrinsic value, by both

purchaser and seller. In some ways this mirrors 'paper money'. Paper money has no intrinsic value and only works as a medium of exchange because it is backed by the government and is difficult to reproduce (counterfeit). Governments have no plans to back e-cash in the same way. E-cash will work only if there is confidence in its exchange value, and this will be unlikely unless there is confidence in the organization 'backing' it. It is likely that well-established major financial institutions will need to be involved with e-cash before it becomes readily acceptable. There are security issues (see below) but also the need for confidence in the accuracy of the software that handles the accounting aspects. E-cash has one major advantage in that the transaction cost is minimal. Governments will need to take a regulatory interest in e-cash, since it is easy to see how repetitive and transnational flows of e-cash could be used for money laundering and tax evasion purposes.

3. **Electronic cash substitutes:** Air miles, supermarket points and other forms of non-cash rewards are becoming increasingly prevalent. These may be earned by a purchase on the Internet, recorded electronically and redeemed electronically for goods, air tickets, etc. These, therefore, become e-cash substitutes.

Electronic payment generates two different types of major security issue. First, all transactions over the Internet require the transmission of electronic data. The data is publicly accessible. This may be a credit card number, e-cash or an electronic cash substitute. The normal way to prevent this information being identified and copied for fraudulent purposes is to encrypt it. It is also important that no corruption of the information occurs, and this will need to be handled by devices such as error-checking codes.

The second major security issue surrounds the businesses that operate on the Internet. Businesses may appear to be providing legitimate investment opportunities, for example, but actually deceive the would-be investor into parting with money. There has always been a problem with unscrupulous companies, but what gives rise to additional concerns with the Internet are:

- it is largely unregulated;
- it crosses international boundaries;
- the business is not tied to some place that the purchaser/investor can visit that is relatively stable, such as a building; and
- the credibility of the company is largely dependent on the web page presentation.

These concerns over security are not seen as preventing the use of the web for commercial transactions but rather viewed as problem areas that should and will be addressed.

Mini case 5.6

Electronic patient records (EPR) and XML

Healthcare experts have been preaching the benefits of electronic patient records for at least two decades. But adoption has been slow and even in the US, most healthcare institutions still maintain the majority of patient records on paper.

Today, patient information is typically dispersed in a collection of paper records that are often poorly organized, illegible and not easy to retrieve. Even if a particular hospital has computerized some records, the information it holds on a patient will typically be incomplete.

Using electronic messaging standards such as XML and HL7 – a standard developed for messaging in healthcare – it is now feasible for different healthcare providers to exchange information, thus leading to better diagnoses and avoiding the duplication of treatment and tests.

'XML is a very powerful force for change in healthcare IT and HL7 is now widely accepted,' says Dr Fickenscher.

Healthcare providers increasingly recognize that EPR can not only cut paperwork, but is also essential to support other initiatives, such as computerized physician order entry, clinical decision support and process improvements.

A recent HIMSS survey found that 46 per cent of US healthcare organizations have or are implementing computerized patient records. Another 23 per cent are currently developing plans.

Adapted from: **Better prognosis after slow start**
By Geoffrey Nairn
FT.com site: 21 May 2003

Questions

1. Could electronic patient records be constructed using HTML? Explain the essential differences between these two languages.

2. Once an EPR has been created in XML, what advantages can be exploited by users of the information?

5.7   Intranets and extranets

The software and technology used by an organization to develop web pages and to access them over the Internet is equally suitable for the development and access of web pages designed purely for consumption by employees and clients of that organization.

This system is known as an **intranet**. It is a privately accessible network, constructed using Internet technology and tools. Businesses quickly recognized that the richness of media (text, graphics, audio, video) for presenting information on the Web, and the use of hyperlinks to other web pages, was ideal for the development of an organization-wide information system. This has now been extended to cover direct access from outside of the organization.

Businesses are using intranets for the internal display of:

■ company manuals covering employment and other procedures;

■ easily updatable internal news and information services;

■ company catalogues; and

■ project notice boards (to which project participants can add information and comments to be seen by all).

Intranets are replacing historical paper-based information systems because they are both cheaper and more easily updatable. Software specifically aimed at supporting intranet functions is now readily available.

5.7.1 Intranet construction

An intranet is created by using the normal network infrastructure existing in an organization. The standard features of Internet applications are used: software such as web browsers, web protocols such as TCP/IP and HTML hypermedia documents. The use of the intranet is limited to those in the company who are given access rights. The adoption of the same standards as those used for Internet-delivered systems and the World Wide Web means that the applications created are available throughout the organization on a variety of hardware platforms, and the look and feel is that of any other Internet-based application.

Public access to an intranet is prevented by channelling all external connection through a **firewall**. This is normally a dedicated computer or computers running specialized security software. The packets of data that arrive are inspected and depending on the contents of the address information are either accepted and passed on or rejected.

5.7.2 Intranet usage

Intranets have a variety of business uses, which fall largely into two categories: those involving the management and running of the business; and those relating to communications and group working. The business applications of the intranet include systems such as stock control, order processing, which might interface with existing core data, and enterprise-wide applications. The communications applications relate to the range of collaborative and group-based applications discussed earlier.

Intranets have potential applications for most functional areas of a business. Accounting and finance staff might use the local intranet to perform *ad hoc* queries on financial data, to access standard summary reports or to produce consolidated reports taken from different legacy systems.

Sales and marketing staff might use the intranet to track and manage the activities of their sales force. Latest promotions, price details or information about customers can also be made readily available.

The personnel department might display details about financial packages available to the staff, or advertise current vacancies. It could also use the intranet to inform staff about training opportunities or forthcoming staff events.

Mini case 5.7

Intranets and portals

A corporate intranet is an internal network architecture based on Internet standards. Users access it through the same browser software that they use on the Internet to access sites on the World Wide Web. They can use the browser to search internal websites for information they need to find to solve problems. It is essentially a static information delivery system.

A 'personal' or 'workspace' portal creates a single, coherent, integrated interface to the corporate intranet.

It is interactive and designed to present users with access to all the information and services they need to carry out their jobs. It provides them with access to management information and decision support tools to improve their decision making.

It also gives them all the daily services they need, such as contacts, calendar, scheduling, electronic mail, word processing, news, stock quotes, employee self-service applications, workflow and collaboration. Lastly, it can provide the powerful search and document management functionality that gives access to all the organization's knowledge on the corporate intranet.

Eventually, users will be able to customize their own portal themselves, until it is so comprehensive they never need to leave it. It will change the way you work, but unless your organization has properly addressed the many cultural implications of portals, the opportunity could be wasted.

Adapted from: **Intranets and portals**
By Rod Newing
FT.com site: 15 October 2003

Questions

1. What advantages does the provision of a portal provide for users of a corporate intranet?

2. What limitations might a portal impose? How could these be addressed?

5.7.3 Extranets

Intranets have become such a valuable and integral part of information systems that many organizations have seen the benefits in widening their availability and access to users who are located outside the scope of the local area network. When access to an intranet is extended outside the organization, the resulting system is referred to as an **extranet**. The connection to the organization's intranet can either be by secure leased line, creating a **virtual private network**, or by using the less secure Internet. In the latter case, the security is enforced by the firewall and by using access codes, passwords and data encryption. In addition to providing employees with an external method of accessing the company intranet, an extranet can be used to forge strategic links with trading partners and customers. They provide a medium for collaborative ventures such as product development.

Information systems strategy is moving increasingly towards the development of integrated systems that provide fast and effective methods of communication, support for decision making and ways of sharing information and working collaboratively. Extranets fit into that strategy by widening the scope of the in-company systems to include a selected subset of all Internet users. As the success, or even just the survival, of businesses becomes increasingly dependent on their ability to communicate effectively between employees and with other partners, it is clear that extranets will have a decisive role to play in that success.

Summary

The Internet has evolved over the last decade from being a small set of interconnected networks for the exchange of scientific information to a highly sophisticated set of publicly accessible networks for the global provision of information and services to business and private individuals. The key to this development has been the agreement of protocols for information exchange (TCP/IP) and the exponential growth in the use of technologically advanced microcomputers in business and for personal use. E-mail is now a recognized method of cheap, fast, secure information transmission either across a local area network or globally across the Internet. Other facilities provided by the Internet are telnet, enabling remote login to host computers over the Internet, and file transfer protocol for the transmission of all forms of files. Newsgroups and Internet relay chat allow the development of particular areas of interest globally over the Internet – the latter in interactive real time. Access to stored information held on remote computers has been enabled by the Internet and a number of applications have, over time, progressively simplified access to this information. However, the most significant development has come in the 1990s with the growth of the World Wide Web.

The World Wide Web allows pages to be written and stored in hypertext mark-up language (HTML) in such a way that they can be accessed over the Internet using hypertext transmission protocols (HTTP). What is particularly important is the ability to use hypertext links to other websites or pages for greater amplification of information obtained. The World Wide Web protocols also allow graphics, audio and video information to be stored and retrieved as well as text. The development of web browser software, especially Netscape Navigator and Internet Explorer, has enabled inexperienced users to retrieve and display information easily. The ability for users to find information has been increased by the development of web search engines, which index millions of web pages. Recently, software plug-ins have enhanced the presentation of information.

Recently, there has been very rapid development in both intranets and extranets. Intranets use the technology of the Internet internally within an organization to present corporate data and to host applications to employees. The extranet extends an organization's intranet by giving access to a restricted group of users who are based outside the company. This extends the scope of the intranet and provides further opportunities to work collaboratively with partners and to distribute more widely the access to data and applications.

Review questions

1. Explain the following terms:

hypertext	browser
Internet service provider	domain name
TCP/IP	routers
point-to-point protocol	file transfer protocol
HTML	XML
HTTP	URL
search engine	intranet and extranet

2. Explain the difference between the Internet, intranets and extranets.

Exercises

1. Which factors drive and which factors limit the growth of the use of the Internet for business?

2. Compare and evaluate the three mark-up languages SGML, HTML and XML in terms of ease of use, flexibility and comprehensibility.

3. Define what is meant by 'electronic cash' and discuss the extent to which it may become the *de facto* trading currency of the Internet.

4. Should the Internet be regulated, and if so by whom and how?

5. To what extent is e-mail leading to a more paperless office, given that many e-mail users print their e-mails on to paper?

6. 'Searching for something on the web is like looking for a needle in a haystack. Even hunting through the search results of a query can be like looking for a needle in a haystack.' What tools and techniques are available to aid web searches? How can they be made even more efficient?

CASE STUDY 5

Networks

Mexican cement manufacturer Cemex has become one of the Internet-generation companies (IGCs) using network technologies to reorganize its business activities. As it discovered, the model of industrial organization established over the past century is fast becoming obsolete. A superior model that organizes work around deeply networked communities is emerging, and the race is on to convert existing business operations to these more efficient, web-based infrastructures.

Managers of IGCs recognize the transforming and organizing potential of the Internet and employ network technology to connect everyone involved in the supply and purchase of their products or services. They view the Internet as more than an electronic brochure through which customers order, or a medium merely permitting employees to communicate via e-mail. For them, it is the most important integrating device of the company, and no facet of business is excluded.

Established in 1906, Cemex's transition began in 1985. New chief executive Lorenzo Zambrano began by building a telecommunications infrastructure to connect Cemex's plants. With fewer than twenty PCs, an unreliable state telephone service and postal delays, Zambrano was unable to get the facts from plant managers.

So the company bought satellite capacity over Mexico, and a centre was established in Texas to permit toll-free calls to the headquarters in Monterrey. Later, Mexican operations were connected to other parts of Latin America, and fibre optic lines and microwave networks connected operations in Europe and the USA. Short-wave radios linked plants in Venezuela. In less than 10 years and for under $200 million, a network of 300 servers, 7000 PCs and eighty workstations was built.

With connectivity established, Cemex turned to office and factory automation. A customized system was built to feed an executive information system and the company's intranet. Zambrano no longer relies on employees for data. Instead, he logs on to check ▶

company-wide sales for the previous day, or to review the chemical composition of clinker in a furnace in Venezuela.

In the company's flagship Tepeaca plant, quality control is automated: samples flow automatically into a laboratory, where clinker paste is dried into wafers and checked by laser. The plant is wired with sensors and process control computers, so operators can run close to capacity and still improve efficiency. Operating margins are double the industry average.

Cemex then used networks to drive innovation. In the company's second major business (the supply of ready-mix concrete) margins are high, but business is difficult. Concrete must be poured within 90 minutes of loading to avoid spoiling. In Mexican cities, traffic congestion, unexpected roadworks and weather make deliveries a nightmare. Yet by analysing the volatile nature of orders and deliveries, the company was able to develop a system based on chaos theory that predicted concrete order rates by day, hour and location. Fleets of trucks were equipped with dashboard computers and satellite global positioning systems to relay pouring status and location. The closest loaded trucks filled orders immediately. Within six months, 98 per cent of deliveries made in the congested Guadalajara test market arrived within 10 minutes of the promised time, prompting an on-time guarantee and a 5 per cent rebate on orders more than 20 minutes late. Maintenance and fuel costs plummeted, truck deliveries rose from four to ten a day, and loading was more uniformly distributed across plants. Irate customers no longer clog Cemex telephones, freeing people for calls from customers.

To make the transition to the Internet generation, a company must first build bandwidth, then automate and Web-enable existing operations. Finally, the freed-up people will do only what software cannot do: create innovations that transform the market in a way that competitors cannot replicate and customers value. To prevent copying and so enhance sustainability, the innovation is embedded in the networked infrastructure.

Over the next decade, much of the business and operations infrastructure of the industrial world will be Web-enabled. What will IGCs look like? They will not be the rigid hierarchies of industrial capitalism that pay fixed salaries for repetitive, mechanistic work. They will be flexible networks of entrepreneurial capitalism that unite communities around beneficial and automated productivity exchanges.

Adapted from: **The challenge of the Web-enabled business**
Financial Times: 27 November 2000

Questions

1. Explain the technological changes that Cemex was required to make to become an Internet-generation company.

2. Describe the business benefits that can accrue following the changes referred to in 1. above.

Recommended reading

Bickerton P., Bickerton M. and Pardesis U. (2000). *Cybermarketing: How to Use the Superhighway to Market Your Products and Services*. 2nd edn. Oxford: Butterworth-Heinemann

This book is intended for those who wish to use the Internet for marketing their products and services. It is published on behalf of the Chartered Institute of Marketing. It is useful as it emphasizes and develops marketing concepts and techniques in an easily accessible fashion. Intended for practitioners, it is practical rather than academic in orientation.

Keogh J. (2001). *The Essential Guide to Networking.* Prentice Hall

A comprehensive coverage of LANs, WANs, the Internet, intranets and extranets, and interesting sections on Internet security, privacy and reliability. The book is written in a non-technical style and is easy to read.

Newcomer E. (2002). *Understanding Web Services.* Addison-Wesley

This book describes and evaluates web services in a way that is accessible to both managers and technicians. Topics include SOAP, XML, UDDI.

O'Mahoney D. *et al.* (2001). *Electronic Payment Systems.* 2nd edn. Artech House

A thorough coverage of different methods of electronic payment such as credit card systems, electronic cheques and cash.

Porter D. (ed.) (1997). *Internet Culture.* New York: Routledge

This is a collection of essays that sets out to examine the Internet and its effects on communication between social groups. The perspective taken is to examine a cultural phenomenon from the point of view of psychology, sociology and politics. Although the contributions are not technical (from a computing point of view), they are saturated with the culture of the disciplines from which they emanate. Several are highly interesting, although not recommended for the casual reader.

Sterne J. (2002). *Web Metrics: Proven Methods for Measuring Web Site Success.* Wiley

This book provides a range of techniques for measuring the success of a website. It includes a number of interesting examples and applications.

Chapter 6

Electronic commerce and business

Learning outcomes

On completion of this chapter, you should be able to:

- Define and identify key features of e-commerce
- Identify the drivers for and barriers to e-commerce
- Evaluate the extent to which e-commerce maps on to traditional trade cycles
- Describe and review a broad range of business models for e-commerce business activity
- Discuss the issues in creating a business website
- Assess potential developments in web technology.

Introduction

The move into the Internet age is both driving and being supported by significant changes in the information systems that support the commercial activity. Just as the early data-processing era was supplanted by the management information systems generation of the last 30 years, so the Internet era is building upon and replacing the MIS age. The accessibility of data and information and the relative ease of establishing channels of communication have fundamentally changed the expectations of decision makers in companies, and of all participants in the supply chain from manufacturers through suppliers to customers. The supporting information systems tend to be collaborative rather than stand-alone, distributed rather than centralized, networked globally rather than locally.

The coming together of business activities and Internet technology has fundamentally changed the environment and structure of business. This is evidenced in many ways. For example:

- The marketplace for all vendors has become potentially global.
- Execution and settlement of transactions can easily be automated for small as well as large organizations.
- The trading model has moved from 'normal business opening hours' to a 24 hours a day, seven days a week trading model.
- The interconnections throughout the supply chain are being reconfigured.

Conducting business over the Internet can be a very different experience to commercial activities that take place in more traditional environments. This chapter focuses on the implications of e-commerce for business.

6.1 A brief introduction to e-commerce

E-commerce is certainly not a new phenomenon. Electronic data interchange has been available for over 25 years and has had a number of very successful applications in that time. The range of EDI applications includes such diverse activities as the issuing of student examination results from central examining boards to schools and the registering of investors who are interested in purchasing new issues of shares in companies. However, the major concentration of EDI activity has been in heavy manufacturing industries and in high-volume and routine restocking.

In the last 5 to 10 years there has been explosive growth in e-commerce developments. The reducing cost and complexity involved in establishing electronic connectivity is clearly a prime factor in this growth. In addition, the Internet has opened the door to different ways of trading; it supports the traditional system-to-system trading seen in EDI but also allows for computer-mediated trading between otherwise unconnected companies and between companies and individuals.

The development of websites

There are many advantages to an organization in developing a website. These include:

- **Reduction in cost of advertising:** Organizations, particularly those selling products or services, rely on providing information and advertising to a marketplace in order to attract new customers and retain existing ones. The cost of this is considerable, especially if achieved through the media – newspapers, magazines, television, radio, advertising hoardings. Alternatively, mailshots may also be used. These are also very expensive unless target mail groups are tightly defined. However, running a website is comparatively cheap. Computer hardware, the design of the site and maintenance seldom take a start-up cost of more than a few thousand pounds or dollars. Once running, the website provides 24-hour access daily across the world. Nowadays, the content of advertising on the web is sophisticated in relation to that provided a few years ago. The move towards regarding the design of website material to be the province of the creative rather than the computing media has ensured that the approaches towards advertising commonly seen on television are now becoming more prevalent on the Web.

- **Cheaper and easier provision of information:** Some organizations, particularly public services, provide information. These traditionally have been by way of paper-based publications or through recorded telephone messages. Putting such reports on a website to provide electronic access offers a cheaper way to disperse information for the host organization and a faster and more convenient method of access for the public (at least the public with access to the Internet). Governments, and non-government organizations that are not commercial, now provide extensive information services on the Web.

- **Ease of update:** An organization can easily update its product range, list of services, list of prices or any other information if provided on a web page. This compares with the costly resending of catalogues and other paper-based information through the postal system.

- **Lack of need to maintain a shop front:** When viewing an organization's supply of information, or list of products and services, the web user does not need to enter the organization's premises – there is no need therefore for the organization to maintain a costly shop front. Indeed, the view of the organization is largely determined by the impression given by its web pages, unless the organization is a household name. For a business this is important as it can overcome the limitations of capital investment in the provision of expensive buildings to impress clients. Importantly for the business, the web user has little idea whether they are dealing with a large multinational or a small business. In this way, the small business can compete with the large. From the perspective of the customer, however, it is difficult to make judgements about the status of the business behind the web page.

■ **The ease of crossing geographical boundaries:** Because the Internet provides global access the business has a worldwide audience through its web pages. If the business is selling a product, provided that postal or shipping services are reliable, even a small business is able to market and sell its products globally. If the product is information, this can easily be dispensed electronically.

■ **The absence of the middleman:** A business that needs a distributor and a retailer to ensure its goods are sold and delivered to a customer can now dispense with the need for these middlemen. Direct marketing to the customer is possible. It should, however, be pointed out that in many cases retailers provide a service over and above that of merely being point-of-sale seller. Advice and other services may also be provided. But if the customer is in need of no such help, then the shop front becomes superfluous.

Multi-channel commerce

For most existing businesses the issue is not about e-commerce being a new or alternative way of conducting business but about providing an additional complementary avenue for trade. The challenge here is to align the electronic business with existing channels, such as the traditional so-called bricks and mortar business, tele-sales, catalogue business, and so on. This requires a strategic approach that looks holistically at the business and fits e-commerce into the overall structure of the organization. Recent evidence suggests that the most successful e-commerce ventures are those with a traditional business background or infrastructure; these multi-channel organizations are sometimes called 'clicks and mortar' businesses.

6.2 E-commerce – key features

E-commerce can be defined as

any exchange of information or business transaction that is facilitated by the use of information and communications technologies.

Although the popular perception of e-commerce is that of individuals buying goods and services over the Internet, the parties involved are more likely to be small and large companies and public authorities or other not-for-profit organizations rather than home computer users. The variety of systems used to facilitate e-commerce is huge, and it is helpful to attempt to categorize them. Whiteley (2000) classifies e-commerce systems as falling into one of three categories:

1. **Electronic markets:** These are information sources that can be used to search for a particular service or product. Rail travel operators might provide timetables of services, details about seat types and other services, and various ticket options. In such an electronic market, customers can examine the alternatives and make comparisons

between the services and prices offered before making a purchasing decision. In addition, the Internet allows for the provision of other information services, such as after sales service, technical support and the sharing of expertise.

2. **Electronic data interchange:** Companies, in their regular dealings with other trading partners, such as suppliers and retail outlets, might establish electronic communications to process the volume of transactions carried out. These lines of communication might be permanent, using leased telephone connections, or established temporarily for the duration of the transactions, using the Internet to establish the connection. EDI provides a standard protocol for encoding this data exchange.

3. **Internet commerce:** This category of e-commerce incorporates the popular image of home computer users making purchases over the Internet. In fact it includes a much broader range of trading. In Internet commerce, goods and services are advertised and individual transactions are executed. The participants might both be businesses, leading to a business-to-business (B2B) transaction, or might involve a private individual, in which case the transaction is described as business-to-customer (B2C).

Mini case 6.1

Weather forecasting

Germans, according to Manfred Klemann, are almost as obsessed by the weather as the English. And Mr Klemann should know: he is managing director of wetter.com, Germany's leading online provider of weather information.

Wetter.com is already an established website, but last year it launched a mobile version of its service, running via i-mode on the e-plus mobile network.

The i-mode service allows e-plus subscribers to access localized weather information, either in graphical form, through a mobile-optimized version of the wetter.com site, through multi-media messaging (MMS) and through simple text messaging.

'We are in the top 10 most requested services on i-mode. But it is not just offered over i-mode, but also SMS and MMS over mobile phones. When people are, say, talking to friends about taking a trip, they can call up weather information there and then.'

And the mobile service has another important advantage over the wetter.com website; it knows where you are.

Using a technology known as 'cell ID', developed by the US mobile software company Openwave and the Swedish company ENEA, wetter.com can offer very localized information.

If a user in Berlin wants the weather forecasts for that city, all he or she needs to do is select the link for local information and wetter.com will send the most appropriate pages, with a forecast for up to the next five days.

Cell ID can work out a user's location down to the nearest 500 metres in metropolitan areas, although this extends up to 5 km in rural areas or on roads. However, even a 5 km range is sufficient for weather information.

Adapted from: Wetter.com: No grey clouds for forecasting service
By Stephen Pritchard
FT.com site: 26 November 2003

Questions

1. How does wetter.com fit into the categorization of e-commerce described above?

2. What benefits are offered to customers of wetter.com?

6.3 Conducting business over the Internet

Trading over the Internet creates challenges and opportunities. As has already been stated, business can be conducted at any time of the day. Markets become globally accessible, whether on the opposite side of the world or, possibly just as important, in the locality of the company itself. Small operators discover new-found access to large companies, and vice versa. In addition, e-commerce pays no attention to time differences between countries.

In many market sectors, the introduction of e-commerce has changed the nature of the business itself. In the music distribution and software industries, the medium adopted for creating and storing the product has evolved progressively using advances in the hardware (from tapes through CDs to DVDs). Now the distribution of the product is being revolutionized with Internet releases and online product updates.

The features that make a product more likely to be able to be sold over the Internet are:

- browsing over a range of products where touch prior to purchase is not needed;
- no advice is needed from the seller;
- the desired choice is known unambiguously by a title or specification;
- the range of products is large (and difficult to accommodate under one shop front);
- the products can be despatched easily (ideally non-bulky, high-price products);
- there would not be differences in the quality of the product between one seller and another.

The economic comparison of retailing through a shop front and through the Internet are given for a typical outlet in Figure 6.1.

The expansion of e-commerce brings about associated benefits. The participants become members of virtual communities in ways that are not possible through traditional trading. Marketplaces have become more open and trading activities more diverse. In addition, e-commerce allows businesses to gain competitive advantage in a number of ways:

- **Price competitiveness:** Reduced transaction costs in automated ordering and invoicing systems can lead to lower prices.
- **Timeliness:** Faster ordering, delivery and invoicing can reduce the time to market for suppliers.
- **Knowledge of market:** Trading electronically provides additional methods for companies to acquire knowledge of the market in which they operate. Customer information and profiling can improve the trading relationship and lead to new marketing opportunities.

6.3.1 The drivers for using the Internet for business

A number of factors are promoting the adoption of e-commerce:

- **Cost:** For a business, the entry costs for participating in e-commerce are relatively low. Systems can be designed and implemented and a web presence can be established relatively cheaply. The systems therefore offer a potentially fast return on the investment.

Figure 6.1 A comparison of Internet and traditional retailing margins

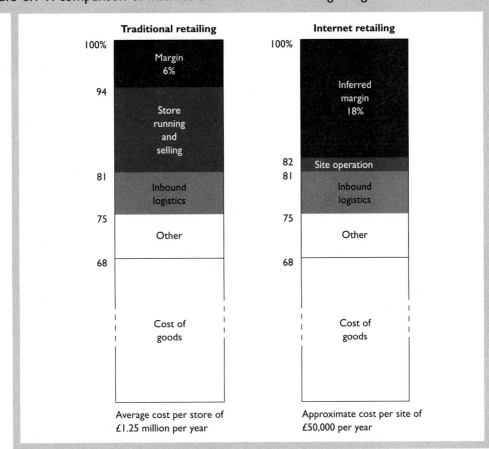

Source: Hoskyns Gemini

- **Flexibility:** Organizations can select the appropriate level of participation from simple access to the Internet through the creation of a Web presence to full-blown transaction-handling systems. The systems can be developed incrementally to add this additional functionality.

- **Protecting investment:** In the Internet world, many common and open standards are employed. The switching costs incurred when a business selects an alternative system are, as a result, relatively low.

- **Connectivity and communications opportunities:** Buying into Internet technology brings an accompanying range of opportunities, such as creating a local intranet or establishing video-conferencing links.

- **Low risk:** A critical mass of e-commerce participants already exists, and the technology, although constantly developing, is well understood. In addition, there are many government initiatives aimed at promoting e-commerce, and there is a significant level of activity in educational institutions to provide additional backup.

- **Improved customer service:** Although essentially a medium that promotes relationships at a distance, the Internet does also provide opportunities for businesses to work more closely with customers. For example, many techniques of directed, or focused, marketing are made easier when trading over the Internet.

6.3.2 Barriers to entry

Despite the many drivers persuading businesses to venture into e-commerce activities, there are nonetheless several concerns that might induce caution.

- **Uncertainty over business models:** The technology has developed at such a pace that businesses have had little time to reflect on the most appropriate structures to facilitate e-commerce. This concern could lead to a reluctance of some businesses to commit themselves to e-commerce solutions. Business models are discussed further in Section 6.5.

- **Telecommunications costs:** In many geographical areas, particularly outside the USA, the cost of telephone communications is a significant factor. This situation is changing rapidly, as local calls in particular are becoming much cheaper, if not completely free, in many countries. The cost of leased lines, while an expensive option for smaller enterprises, is also becoming less prohibitive.

- **Bandwidth:** The multimedia content of the traffic on the Internet can create bottlenecks and slow down other forms of Internet access. The managers of many organizations fear that providing a facility for employees to access online sports updates and events, radio and TV broadcasts on their PCs might interfere with the normal running of the business. Continuing improvements in hardware, software and network infrastructure, along with the increasing uptake of broadband connectivity, are helping to alleviate the effects of increasing volumes of data transfer requests.

- **Security:** Several notable breaches of security have caused organizations to be cautious about implementing e-commerce solutions. Major problems have been caused by recent violations of confidentiality such as the customers of Internet banks being shown the account details of other customers, by virus attacks, and by unauthorized intrusion (e.g. Microsoft source code being stolen).

- **Lack of clear standards:** Although the Internet operates on largely open standards some tensions remain, for example the battle between Netscape and Microsoft to produce the *de facto* web browser.

- **Law and legal frameworks:** The global Internet environment poses many questions over legal issues, particularly when disputes occur. Trading may cross national boundaries, and the appropriate contract law must be employed. This can be difficult to establish where customer, vendor and web server are all located in different countries.

- **Preparedness:** Many businesses foresee the 'crest of the wave' effect of participating in e-commerce and are cautious about entering this global marketplace until completely prepared (for example, Fedex competitors).

6.4 Trade cycles and e-commerce

This section considers the three modes of e-commerce identified in Section 6.2 and investigates how they map on to more traditional business trade cycles.

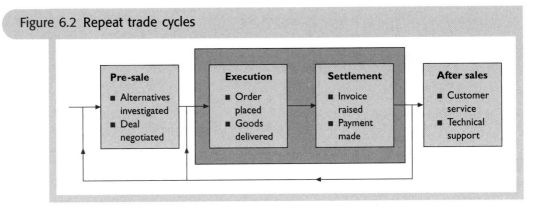

Figure 6.2 Repeat trade cycles

6.4.1 E-commerce and traditional trade cycles

Business transactions have traditionally fallen into one of three so-called trade cycles. These cycles reflect the participants, the frequency of the transactions and the nature of the transactions involved.

Repeat trade cycles

This pattern of trading is characterized by companies that are closely linked in the supply chain. A typical example might be a manufacturer selling components to an assembly plant, or a regional warehouse supplying stocks to a supermarket. Often the restocking follows the just-in-time approach of maintaining minimal stock levels. In repeat trade cycles, orders are placed at regular intervals, invoicing is carried out periodically, and settlement is often automated.

Transactions that feature in repeat trade cycles are most suited to an EDI e-commerce solution. The placing of orders, raising and issuing of invoices and transfer of funds electronically (represented by the shaded area in Figure 6.2) can all be carried out using EDI technology. Once the initial negotiations have established the specification of product or service and price, the trading cycle iterates around the execution and settlement phases. Changes to the initial contract are shown by the feedback loop to the pre-sale phase. Once renegotiated, the business falls back into a new iteration of execution and settlement.

Irregular invoiced transactions

This form of trade is normally characterized by business-to-business transactions. One company might search for the best price or trading arrangements from a number of competing suppliers before placing an order. Settlement is often achieved through an invoice relating to the particular order placed, and payment is made at a later date. An example of this sort of trade is an estate agent locating a property on behalf of a customer, based on a set of criteria.

The search described above reflects the category of e-commerce that was classified as electronic markets. An estate agent might use a property management system to compare details such as location, number of bedrooms and price. The focus of the interaction is usually only on the investigation (highlighted in Figure 6.3), although in other situations, such as a travel agent locating a particular journey, it may follow the

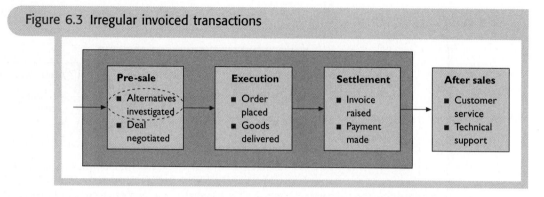

Figure 6.3 Irregular invoiced transactions

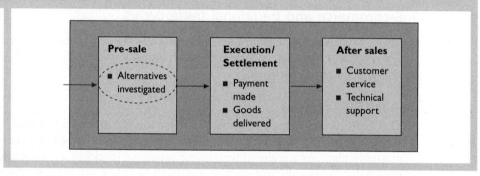

Figure 6.4 Irregular cash transactions

transaction through to payment. The e-commerce trade cycle in the former case is unlikely to cover all stages of the transaction, as the estate agent is acting only as an intermediary. The settlement and after-sales components are more likely to be dealt with by traditional business methods.

Irregular cash transactions

The third type of trade cycle is that of irregular cash transactions. This equates to a one-off purchase of a service or product by an individual or a company. The settlement is normally made at the point of sale. The term 'cash' is therefore misleading, as payment may be by a variety of methods, such as a credit card. However, the principle is that mechanics of payment are established and commenced.

The best-understood aspect of e-commerce is that of individual 'home shoppers' purchasing goods and services over the Internet. However, the model does also apply to business-to-business transactions. As with the previous example, the Internet-based component may only comprise the search for and investigation of alternative products (highlighted in Figure 6.4). This again is characteristic of the electronic market classification of e-commerce. More often, however, the search leads to an online purchase with settlement and execution being combined into one phase and, in the case of software and music, delivery may be instantaneous. After-sales service may also be provided through access to a website with e-mail contact. In this case, the full activity of Internet commerce occurs with the entire transaction from pre-sale through to after-sales being conducted electronically.

Mini case 6.2

Business to business

Squeezing more efficiency out of the supply chain is like reducing crime. Every right-thinking person is in favour of it. But just like criminal acts, unsatisfactory logistics are always with us and continue to defeat the attentions of experts in the field. Just what is it about getting goods from A to B that is so difficult?

Business-to-business Internet marketplaces, known generically as B2B, also enjoyed a brief but spectacular rise before falling from grace. B2B promised to cut intermediaries out of the supply chain altogether and generate huge economies of scale as suppliers and customers communicated directly via online exchanges. It was ultimately doomed by poor business models and a general reluctance to share key business data with competitors in order to flatten trading structures.

All interventions in the supply chain involve a trade-off between service and costs. French software house Ilog sells suites of software that maximize the visibility of items for customers. One program, Dispatcher, is used to plan vehicle schedules, producing the best sequence of addresses for a delivery driver to visit. Linked to geographical information systems and global positioning system locator beacons, the software can optimize transport plans and reduce mileage, fuel costs and overtime.

But the final decision on whether to exploit the information generated by systems like this rests with a manager who must weigh how and when the customer expects goods to be delivered against the saving generated by shifting items to earlier or later in the day. Sarah Taylor, an international director at Lawson, a US software company that concentrates on reducing stock levels for customers with complex supply chains, sums up the challenge for her colleagues and customers alike. 'Getting the right level of the right product at the right time is very easy to talk about but incredibly difficult to do.'

Adapted from: **In search of the missing link**
By Michael Dempsey
FT.com site: 25 November 2003

Questions

1. Apply Porter's model of the supply chain to the B2B commerce described above.
2. What is the objective of systems such as Ilog?

New variants on the trade cycles

An e-commerce solution provides additional business opportunities and creates variations on the traditional trade cycles described above. Customers participating in irregular transactions may undertake only a pre-sales enquiry or use only the after-sales facilities such as 'frequently asked questions'.

Once the lines of communication between participants in e-commerce have been established, it is possible to distribute a company newsletter or marketing mailshot. In other situations, it may be desirable to implement an order and delivery tracking service.

6.4.2 Porter's five forces model and e-commerce

The model of competitive forces introduced in Chapter 2 can usefully be applied to the e-commerce marketplace.

Threat of new entrants

Competitors considering adopting e-commerce may not need to match the IT infrastructure of the existing players. Indeed, because of the rapid development of new technology, it may be possible to by-pass existing technology completely and establish a new 'leading edge' by employing fresh ideas. This has been the case in the rise of Internet bookshops and banking.

Threat of substitution

E-commerce solutions may lead to the introduction of substitute products. An example is seen in the introduction of alternative methods of product delivery, not always through legitimate channels, such as in the software, books and recorded music businesses.

Bargaining power of buyers

The role of intermediaries may be reduced where e-commerce is adopted. An example of this is seen in airline ticketing, once the preserve of specialized agencies. The introduction of cheap online flight ticketing has segmented the market. Increased information to customers poses similar threats to suppliers who may have faced much less intense competition in traditional markets.

Bargaining power of suppliers

As has been stated previously, the adoption of e-commerce may be a requirement of the suppliers. This is the case in some industries where EDI is a precondition to engaging in trade.

Competition with rivals

E-commerce solutions can reduce transaction costs, reduce stockholding, increase the reliability of supply and help to differentiate the company's product or service.

6.5 E-commerce business models

There are many different models for conducting business. The introduction of e-commerce has brought a revolution in some markets, with accompanying new business models being introduced. Traditional business models coexist, alongside these new models for e-commerce. In other cases, the traditional model for business has been modified but not overhauled by the introduction of new electronic trading relationships.

Business models

A business model is the theoretical design for an organization that describes how it makes money on a sustainable basis and grows. Business models take on many forms, including:

■ straightforward industry classifications, such as heavy industry, service sector;

■ methods of trading, such as shop, supermarket, auction;

■ structural definitions, such as functional responsibilities, 'everyone does everything'.

Table 6.1 Business models for electronic commerce

Type	Features	Examples
E-shop	Business-to-business Business-to-customer	www.cisco.com www.amazon.com
E-mall	Diverse range of products and services	www.fedcenter.com
E-procurement	Supply chain operations on the Internet	www.sap.com
E-auction	Electronic bidding for goods and services	www.letsbuyit.com
Specialist services	Online provision of goods and services	www.nortonweb.com
Market segmenters	Differentiated markets	www.buzzaway.com
Content providers	Information services	www.ft.com
Internet infrastructure	Trust services, electronic payments	www.verisign.com

The following section introduces a number of business models for conducting e-commerce. These models are summarized in Table 6.1.

6.5.1 E-shops

An e-shop is a virtual store front that sells products and services online. Orders are placed and payments made. The logistics of delivery are usually accomplished by traditional methods, although some electronic products can be downloaded directly. Examples of electronic delivery can be seen at the site for recorded music company SonicNet (www.sonicnet.com), and the image and photographic services provider Photodisc (www.photodisc.com). An example of a business-to-consumer e-shop is shown in Figure 6.5. Toys'Я'Us, the children's toy retailer, offer a range of items which

Figure 6.5 A business-to-consumer website

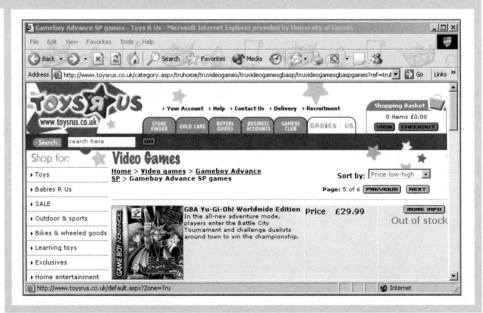

Figure 6.6 A business-to-business website

customers can order and have delivered to their home. An example of a business-to-business e-shop is shown in Figure 6.6. Ladybird is a brand label for children's clothing and distributes its products via a network of franchised retail businesses.

E-shops are a convenient way of effecting direct sales to customers; they allow manufacturers to bypass intermediate operators and thereby reduce costs and delivery times. This is referred to as disintermediation.

Mini case 6.3

Internet retailing

In the UK, there is considerable competition between the large supermarkets over the consumable food and drink market. The main competitors are Tesco, Sainsbury, Asda and Safeway. Each has embarked on a number of competitive strategies that seek to extend their markets by the sale of alternative products, for example the sale of clothing (Tesco), or by offering alternative services (both Sainsbury and Tesco offer simple banking services at attractive rates for savers). Each supermarket is also attempting to attract custom away from its competitors. It is known that price and quality of product are features that will attract customers. It is also known that many customers regard the traditional supermarket shopping at weekends as less than desirable. There is a target group who would be willing to pay for the extra service of selection, packing and delivery of goods. The Internet is a key factor in this. The supermarket that provides the most reliable and user-friendly system is likely to attract larger numbers of customers.

Tesco is operating a scheme whereby customers can order goods over the Internet. The user logs on to the Internet shopping centre, having previously registered. Goods are provided in a number of categories, such as vegetables, bakery, wine. The user navigates a menu system and selects a desired item for a virtual 'shopping basket'. At the end of the session the customer pays by means of a credit card and goods are packed and delivered to the customer's home address within a customer-defined time slot of a couple of hours on a customer-defined day. In order to speed up proceedings the customer can save the 'shopping list' for the next session and just add or subtract items. Given that there is much commonality between the shopping list from one week to the next this is a considerable saving on time. The cost to the consumer is a flat rate delivery and packaging charge of £5. Tesco reports continued interest in the scheme and is expanding it. The scheme itself is not likely to make extra profit on a given Tesco's customer (although reports indicate that customers shopping in this way will tend to order larger 'shopping baskets'). However, it is being used to attract customers away from competitors.

Question

What are the strengths of this alternative form of supermarket shopping? Can you identify any limitations?

Mini case 6.4

Legal services

The provision of legal services over the Internet is becoming increasingly widespread. Examples include the writing of wills, support for the purchase and sale of property, and online quotations.

Traditionally, in the UK, the buyer of a property instructs a solicitor to act on their behalf. If the client also has a property to sell the same solicitor will often take on this additional role. The solicitor acts on behalf of their client by liaising with the solicitor of the vendor of the desired property, with local authorities, with the land registry and other interested parties. They also collect and hold the deposit paid on the property and ensure that the exchange of contracts occurs smoothly and moves through to the completion of a sale.

Fidler and Pepper are a UK-based partnership of solicitors comprising six partners and fifty staff distributed over three offices in the Nottinghamshire area. They have been operating a website (www.fidler.co.uk) since 1995 that offers a range of services to clients, including an online matter progress report to inform their clients about the latest developments in the sale and purchase of their properties. The system also preserves confidentiality by assigning a unique case number to each property purchase or sale and by using a system of passwords to prevent unauthorized access.

'The system has made a huge difference,' says Mat Slade, the partner responsible for conveyancing. 'From the client's viewpoint there is up-to-the-minute notification about all issues. The system cuts out those frustrating switchboard delays and telephone transfers. More importantly, it gives 24-hours-a-day access to information that previously could only be obtained by speaking to a solicitor and thereby incurring additional expense. It also makes us accountable to the client in that if any piece of work hasn't been done the client will see that it hasn't been done on the online reports.'

▶

'From a company perspective,' said Slade, 'it provides an internal tracking system across our intranet whereby we can trace and monitor work flow and, if necessary, share work loads between us. Another useful advantage is the reduction in low-priority phone calls from clients which, although well intentioned, could slow down progress.'

The latest improvements to the system include a facility to communicate case matters on the website to clients using the mobile phone short message service (SMS). Slade says: 'With over 50% of the population having mobile phones we believe that this is a huge step forward in providing clients with up-to-date information at what is a very stressful time. As soon as an important step is progressed on a file, for example exchange of contracts or the local search is received, a short text message is automatically sent to the client's mobile phone telling them what has happened.'

'We definitely believe we have gained a competitive advantage from using the system,' added Slade. 'Solicitors are notoriously slow at adopting new technology. Our client base has opened up, taking us from being essentially a regional service to becoming an international operation.'

Question

Outline the advantages of web-based support for legal services. In a customer-focused environment such as this, could the Internet eventually replace the personal contact traditionally offered by solicitors?

6.5.2 E-malls

The retailing model of a shopping mall, a conglomeration of different shops situated in a convenient location, is mirrored in e-commerce by the development of electronic malls or e-malls. The e-mall provides a common interface to the range of participants. This amalgamation of different businesses produces a virtual community with associated benefits such as shared costs and mutual advertising.

The iMegaMall e-mall, shown in Figure 6.7, is an electronic marketplace offering a wide range of products and services.

Another type of e-mall development comes about where an individual e-business diversifies to the extent that it presents itself as a virtual shopping arcade. E-companies such as Lastminute.com present customers with a wide range of products and services, all hosted from a single website providing a common interface.

6.5.3 E-procurement

Procurement is the whole process of obtaining services, supplies and equipment from identifying a business need through to fulfilment of contract. With the continuing trend in globalization of business the management of the supply chain has become an increasingly complex activity. An operation that has traditionally been controlled by specialists has now been largely automated. The ease of establishing connections using the Internet and web browsers rather than a costly infrastructure of dedicated private networks enables suppliers to open up their catalogues and product ranges at significantly reduced costs. The provision of information to customers thereby improves, and alternative methods of tender specification become possible. In addition, delivery times are reduced, leading to lower stock holding and further cost savings.

Figure 6.7 An e-mall website

Mini case 6.5

E-procurement

Airbus says 15,000 suppliers have registered to use its new epurchasing system.

The aircraft manufacturer has gone live with the 'sourcing' module of its Sup@irWorld electronic collaboration initiative, a EUR50m (GBP34.8m) project to introduce web-based interaction between the company and its suppliers.

Airbus is using technology from Ariba to operate the system, which will eventually process the bulk of its purchases.

'This application is intended to support any kind of products or services within our company,' said esourcing manager Frederic Geoffrion.

'It covers flying and non-flying materials and processes, strategic data as well as non-strategic.'

Sourcing is one of four domains that make up Sup@irWorld. The others are buy-side, supply chain and foundation.

Buy-side will comprise an online catalogue of general procurement items.

The supply chain domain, which uses technology from i2, will allow Airbus to exchange information with its suppliers.

The foundation domain will look after information and data about suppliers.

Sourcing is the only domain that has gone live, but Geoffrion says the rest of the project is on course to be fully operational by the end of the year.

Adapted from: **Eprocurement takes off at Airbus**
Computing – United Kingdom; 27 November 2003

Questions

1. What advantages does e-procurement offer?
2. Are there any drawbacks to adopting this approach?

Figure 6.8 A web auction site

6.5.4 E-auctions

The e-auction business model is based on the traditional auction concept of a bidding mechanism where the customer making the highest offer secures the purchase. The multimedia nature of e-auctions allows the supplier to make a more attractive presentation of the product offered. Figure 6.8 shows the popular E-Bay auction website. This is the longest running and most successful of the web-based electronic auction sites.

Highly interactive e-auctions can operate like clearing houses, where the prices of goods fluctuate in real time as the stocks vary. Revenue for the auctioneer is derived from transaction fees and from associated advertising. The potential global audience for an e-auction makes the sale of low-cost, small-margin items a more viable proposition. Business-to-business auctions may offer additional services, for example guaranteed payment for the seller or a warranty for the buyer. As described before, membership of an e-auction leads to the development of a virtual community, with accompanying benefits for all participants.

An alternative model for the e-auction is for a number of buyers to make a communal bid for an item. As more buyers are persuaded to participate in the purchase, the web company can strike a better deal and thereby reduce the price. An example of an e-auctioneer is LetsBuyIt.com.

A novel twist to the concept of an auction is the **reverse auction**, where buyers submit their proposed price to multiple suppliers in an attempt to secure the best deal. An example of a reverse auction specialist is Priceline.com, which offers a range of products such as airline tickets, cars and hotel rooms. The customer supplies key information (in the case of airline tickets the dates, cities and desired price), along with a credit card number. Priceline locates possible matches from a range of suppliers and, if successful, books the ticket at up to the price desired and charges the credit card automatically. The customer has to be flexible and is not allowed to be too prescriptive about times of travel or particular hotels in a given city.

In addition to the models above, there are an increasing number of more innovative business models for e-commerce.

6.5.5 Specialist service providers

Many companies engaged in e-commerce specialize in a particular market function. An example is the provision of logistics support, where Federal Express is a leading player (www.fedex.com), and in postal services, where the UK Royal Mail offers a range of delivery and tracking facilities. Another example of specialist services is the online computer support offered by companies such as NortonWeb (www.nortonweb.com). This service provides software updates, technical support and tools to tune and enhance the performance of a personal computer.

Mini case 6.6

Jobs and Google

Many Silicon Valley-based technology companies have instituted hiring freezes or are laying people off. But even in the midst of a recession, Google, the search engine, continues to expand.

The company employs about 800 staff and has been hiring steadily since its inception in 1998. Last week the Jobs section of the Google website was advertising around 100 positions, for everything from software engineers to real estate project managers.

Because the search engine attracts so many eyeballs, it is no surprise that the company receives 95 per cent of its job applications via the online Jobs section.

Google has created an automated applicant tracking system (ATS) to help human resources staff and their colleagues handle the myriad *curricula vitae*. Developed in-house by Google engineers, the ATS filters applications as they are received and files them in a database by job title. Each application is read and evaluated manually, with the computer system gathering and storing feedback and ratings about each candidate to help the hiring committee evaluate applicants and reach their decisions.

When it comes to hiring experts in a particular field, however, the Internet can be a very useful tool. Google's HR team frequently relies on its own search engine to source individuals with specialist skills.

Adapted from: **Google: Search engine is link to new staff**
By Chloe Veltman
FT.com site: 16 July 2003

Questions

1. What are the advantages to Google of adopting a web-based human resource strategy?
2. What additional elements are required in addition to the web interface?

Mini case 6.7

Parcel-tracking services

The parcel-tracking sector of the commercial World Wide Web was the first sector to reach maturity. The largest courier services in the world provide tracking facilities for their customers at no customer cost. Each of the companies claims to be saving money as it cuts down the staff needed to answer telephone enquiries on the location of packages. In order to use the facilities, customers enter their parcel reference number through a form on the company's web page as viewed through a standard web browser. The carrier's computer system is then searched and the latest information on the parcel retrieved – when and where it was picked up, its current location, or, if it has already been delivered, the time of delivery and the receiver's name will be displayed. The main courier companies register hundreds of thousands of 'hits' on their web tracking pages each week. The service is expanding. Companies are placing foreign-language interfaces on their sites. It is now possible to arrange pickup of parcels over the Internet with each of these carriers.

The stimulus has come from the pre-emptive introduction of the first service and the reactive introduction of the others in following it (see Figure 6.9). It is also possible that the service has reduced telephone answering costs.

Question

The provision of parcel-tracking services does not appear to have increased the demand for courier services and has done nothing to enhance the total courier requirement of the companies involved. What advantages do you think have accrued to these companies?

6.5.6 Market segmenters

The immediate and accessible nature of electronic business has enabled some large companies to engage in market fragmentation in ways that would not otherwise have been possible. For a period of time large airlines identified electronic markets as a way of offering the same product, an airline ticket, at a lower price to certain sectors of the market. By creating e-businesses to handle these cut-price sales they successfully separated these alternative markets from traditional business customers, who continued to purchase tickets at a higher price through more conventional channels. Examples of these e-market segmenters were KLM's offshoot company Buzz and the equivalent British Airways company Go.

6.5.7 Content providers

The developments in digital storage media, particularly optical media, have led to the creation of e-businesses whose function is purely to maintain electronic archives. Newspapers have traditionally been archived in paper and microfiche formats. Now dedicated websites such as FT.com maintain archives of news reports and press releases and provide search facilities to extract the desired content. Other content providers are creating a niche as information specialists. Search engines such as Altavista provide an increasing range of search facilities and post-search links and services to enrich the information provided.

Figure 6.9 **An example of a shipment tracking page**

Mini case 6.8

Wimbledon website

Superficially, there would seem to be little to link the Wimbledon Lawn Tennis Championships with research into protein structure. Both, however, are supported by the same IBM computers. When the machines are not powering Wimbledon's newly redesigned website, they grind away at calculations and simulations needed by IBM scientists to determine how amino acid chains become folded into specific proteins.

'We want to be at the forefront of sports technology,' says Bob McCowen, Wimbledon's marketing director. Since 1995, his principal weapon has been the Internet. Wimbledon claims to have been the first major sports event in the UK to use its website as a promotional and marketing tool. This year, new features include a match ticker providing up-to-the-minute highlights, access to the site from personal digital assistants over GPRS networks and a subscription service including match commentaries streamed over the web.

To run the website for the two weeks of the championships requires six months of planning and three months of design and implementation. The site claims 2.8m unique users, each spending an average of two hours nine minutes on the site, a degree of 'stickiness' that most commercial organizations would kill for.

▶

The match analysis is delivered to the website scoreboard, TV and radio broadcasters and to players anxious to study the weaknesses of their opponents.

This year, for the first time, the length of each rally will be recorded in addition to the usual 'speed of service' radar system. And 'Hawk-Eye', the ball-tracking equipment that is used in international cricket, will be on Centre Court and No 1 Court for the first time, although it will not be used for umpiring decisions. The idea is to help viewers' understanding of the game by modelling the bounce, speed and swerve of the ball during matches.

And, again for the first time, IBM is installing a WiFi wireless local area network so officials and the media can log into the internal information system.

Adapted from: **Game, net and match**
By Alan Cane
FT.com site: 24 June 2003

Questions

1. What features does Wimbledon's website offer to enhance the Wimbledon Championships?

2. Explain how the website might fit into a larger information system that provides both real-time and archive facilities.

6.5.8 Internet infrastructure providers

Electronic commerce requires its own infrastructure. E-businesses are being created to fulfil those facilitating roles. Examples can be seen in companies that offer trust services, which provide facilities to enable secure transactions and communications. These companies provide certified authority that the service provided is reliable and secure. One such company is Verisign (www.verisign.com), which offers facilities to make secure a website, intranet or extranet to enable secure payments and to protect program code from being tampered with or corrupted.

6.5.9 Push and pull marketing strategies

A number of the business models above feature highly interactive participation. A key marketing decision for an e-business is to decide whether a proactive strategy to marketing will be adopted. The passive activity of customers or clients accessing and downloading pages from the Internet is termed **pull marketing**. The information is made available by suppliers, and customers search for and request, or pull, the pages from the server. Once a supplier has stored details about its customers, it could then develop a more active strategy of distributing information. This is known as **push marketing**. Particular benefits can be gained when push marketing is targeted at selected users. However, much of the activity in push technology is of a broadcast nature, with suppliers sending streams of information relating to recent developments such as price changes or new products. The information can be broadcast globally or sent to a select group of interested individuals. The recipients can receive the information in many different ways:

■ For general release of product information, e-mails can be composed and distributed to those identified.

■ Details of software upgrades, such as the latest version of a web browser, can be transmitted when the user logs on for a new session.

- If the user runs special software in the background on their computer it becomes possible for the information to be transmitted in real time, for example across a scrolling banner or as an update on a screen saver.

6.6 The development and management of a business website

As has been explained earlier, a business may choose to develop and maintain a website for a number of reasons. Most commonly, these are (some of) the following:

- to advertise services and products;
- to sell services and products;
- to promote the corporate image;
- to provide information (especially public services).

Three main areas must be considered in the development and maintenance of a corporate website. These are **connection**, **publication policy** and **presentation of materials**.

Connection

Strictly speaking, a business could develop a website purely for access by its own employees through its own local area network (LAN). It might wish to create an intranet like this in order to provide a better and more cost-effective internal information service. The remaining sections on publication policy and presentation of materials apply to this, although the observations on connection do not.

However, it is more common for a business to use a website for public access. In order for the website to be publicly accessed over the Internet it must be permanently connected to the Internet. This can be achieved by the organization connecting its own host computer (or LAN) containing its website pages on a permanent connection to the Internet, either through ISDN lines or through connection to one of the established wide area networks. An alternative is to allow a third-party organization to handle the provision of the access to the business website by placing the business website pages on that organization's computer systems. This is common for smaller businesses, which may wish to use the disk space and web access service provided by Internet service providers (such as CompuServe or America On Line). This still requires the business to design and maintain its own web pages, which is partly a technical and partly an editorial/creative operation. Nowadays, third-party organizations are providing services to business that involve not only the provision of public access websites for the business but also the development and maintenance of the content of the website.

A final factor taken into consideration by a business in deciding on the method of connection of its website to the World Wide Web is the security aspect. If the public-access website is held by a third-party organization then it is impossible for unauthorized access to be made to the business's own computer systems – at least by way of the World Wide Web. However, update and maintenance of the website contents are not as easy or immediate as when the website is under the direct control of the business itself. On the other hand, if a business runs its own website on its own host computer/local area network it incurs a risk of unauthorized access and must take precautions to ensure that security is maintained.

Generally speaking, large businesses will prefer to run their own websites and incur the costs of extra computers, permanent connection to the Internet and the need for security. They do this for the convenience of maintaining easy control over the content and update of the website, together with the ability to allow a high volume of public access. Small businesses may have neither the finances nor the trained personnel to do this; nor would the volume of public access justify that level of expenditure. These small businesses are likely to opt for a third-party provision.

In all cases where possible, it is desirable to have a web address that is meaningfully connected to the organization, then those wishing web access will be able to intelligently guess the address. For example, the web address of CNN is *www.cnn.com*, not *www.cablenetworknews.com*.

Publication policy

Once an organization has decided to develop its website it will need a policy governing the publication of material. This should cover the following areas:

- **Objectives of the website:** It is usual to state clearly the objectives of the website. This acts as guidance to the overall development.

- **Responsibility:** The policy must specify those with responsibility for the development and maintenance of:
  - the pages
  - the information
  - the computer support

  In a large organization, many departments may have the right to provide material for pages governing their activities. The policy must be clear on this matter, and the individuals with responsibilities must be identified. The more centralized, hierarchical and authoritarian the organization the less responsibility and authority will be devolved to departments. It is instructive to observe that organizations such as universities, for which individual autonomy is an important cultural aspect, often allow staff and students the right to develop personal web pages with little or no control over their content – save the requirement to remain within the confines of the law.

- **Public relations and consistency of presentation:** It is usual for a policy to lay down guidelines for the level of consistency that must be contained within the presentation of each one of its pages. This may cover fonts, the way graphics are presented, layout and the presence of the corporate logo. The pages are what the organization presents to the world, and it is imperative that the correct corporate image be conveyed. It is therefore likely that the appearance of the home page (the first page to be accessed at the top of the hierarchy) and subsequent pages may have their style and content closely specified by the corporate public relations department.

- **Accuracy:** The organization will have a view on the need for the maintenance of accuracy of information on its website. It is likely that those with the responsibility for the provision and maintenance of the information will also have the responsibility for accuracy.

- **Security:** As has been mentioned above, security aspects over unauthorized access from outside the organization need to be established. It is also important that within the organization those with rights and responsibilities for page development and maintenance have procedures developed that allow them appropriate access, while those that do not have such rights and responsibilities are denied access.

■ **Audit:** It is important that the organization checks whether its publication policy, as outlined above, is being observed and so will specify the internal audit (procedures for checking) on this.

Presentation of materials

In the early days of the Web, the material presented on a website was:

■ largely text;

■ aimed at the provision of factual information;

■ written in source HTML;

■ developed by programming/technical personnel.

More recently, there has been a shift in orientation, and now material for a website is likely to be:

■ a mixture of text, graphics and (possibly) audio/visual using plug-ins;

■ aimed partly at the provision of a corporate image and advertising objective;

■ developed using a mixture of high-level web development tools;

■ developed by end users or those specifically charged with website development.

The contents of the website of today are more likely to be the province of the advertising and publicity and public relations departments of an organization than of the computing department. This shift in emphasis acknowledges the role of websites in the corporate image and as part of the business interface with the organization's marketplace. The development of high-level tools for the design of web pages has removed the focus of the developer from programming aspects to end presentation issues. These tools will generate HTML and XML code as their output.

Decisions on website development and approach are now considered to be of strategic importance to the organization in the presentation of itself to its market. Once developed, it is important that the business website be accessed. This will only be the case if the website address is known. There are a number of ways in which the web address may be publicly available:

■ by inclusion of the web address in TV and other media advertising;

■ by selection of a web address that is self-explanatory – for example, *www.ibm.co*;

■ by advertising the web address on other websites using hypertext links;

■ by inclusion in the catalogues of large indexing websites such as Yahoo! or Lycos.

Web presence

An organization contemplating an involvement in e-commerce must consider which type of Web presence is most appropriate. A simple Web presence might have no interactive component and just consist of a website hosting pages of information; the communication with the company in this case might be by conventional methods. The site could be developed further to include a facility for the client to e-mail the company. At a more involved level of Web presence still, clients would use the website to place orders for goods and services. This can be enhanced by the inclusion of the settlement stage, where either the method of payment is established or more usually, payment is actually made. For some electronic products, delivery might also be carried out through the website.

Increasing sophistication in Web presence might lead to the provision of online and real-time information relating items in stock or latest prices. Alternative methods of customer contact such as regular or *ad hoc* marketing mailshots can also be incorporated.

Website awareness

In the above cases, the customer needs to know of the fact that the business or organization in question has a website and that the business is a seller of a product or service that is desired by the customer. This is handled in a number of ways:

- The business will conventionally advertise on television or in the press and place the website address on the advertisement.
- The business will ensure that the home page contains key words that make it easy for a searcher to use a web search index produced by a search engine.
- The organization will attempt to have its link placed on another website so that visitors to that website may click on a hyperlink to the organization's website.

The last method is important and can be achieved in different ways:

- **Reciprocal arrangements:** The organization may have a reciprocal arrangement with another so that both websites cross-link.
- **Web communities:** The organization may be part of a group or community that provides a website for a particular interest area (see below on web communities).
- **Commercial advertisement:** The organization may pay to have an advertisement and hyperlink on a frequently visited website. For example, web search indexes are visited by millions of clients per day. If a company has a corporate logo and link advertised on the web search site then only one-tenth of one per cent of readers need to click on the hyperlink to ensure that thousands of potential customers are in touch with that company's products or services.

The business trend is to make more extensive use of websites for the provision of information and the exercise of business operations. This will be fuelled by improvements in telecommunications, the increasing proportion of the population owning PCs and the economics of the Internet as a medium for information provision.

6.7 Trends in e-commerce

Although e-commerce has now been established for some time, the models for electronic business are still fairly immature and the underpinning technology is constantly evolving. However, some trends are already discernible.

6.7.1 Structural developments

There appear to be two strands of divergent development in the more innovative e-business models. The first is a move to greater integration in business activity, the second a specialization into business services and function.

The increase in integration can be evidenced by the reinforcement of linkages along the supply chain. This is demonstrated by specific arrangements such as EDI and in the integration of transaction support in the electronic sales functions.

The specialization into business services is seen in the growth of third-party arrangements such as trusted services and electronic transaction settlement.

6.7.2 The reliance on advertising

The business plans of many e-businesses are framed with a built-in reliance on advertising revenue. In recent years, the advertising revenue generated by these dot.coms has been less than was originally predicted. Alternative sources of revenue can be found in subscription or transaction fees, but these in turn lead to strategic implications for the organization.

6.7.3 Maintaining competitive advantage

A constant desire of companies is to sustain any competitive advantage gained, particularly where the company has been first to market with a new technology. The first mover takes the risk of testing the market and also incurs the higher development costs associated with the pioneering technology. However, they do take the initiative upon launching the product. The challenge is then to maintain that advantage. This can be accomplished, for example, by associating the brand image with the new development, as was achieved initially by the FedEx parcel-tracking system and by Amazon.com booksellers. The advantage can be further reinforced by enhancing the website and augmenting the range of services that it provides.

It is far harder to achieve this degree of competitive advantage with EDI. Here it is relatively easy for competitors to establish the systems required and imitate the first mover. With EDI, it is more a case of producing a competitive disadvantage for those not following the first mover.

6.7.4 Intelligence on the Web

Intelligent agents

It is becoming increasingly common for software products to exhibit a degree of 'intelligence' in their activities. Familiar desktop artefacts include organizers that suggest layout changes while text is entered, spelling correctors and other 'wizards' that suggest the best time to carry out system maintenance such as defragmenting the hard disk of a PC. The intelligence comes from an ability to learn from and adapt to the environment in which the software is operating. The software might, for example, monitor the user's responses and incorporate that newly acquired knowledge into future suggestions to the user.

Electronic business can provide many opportunities for the use of intelligent agents. Customers are often persuaded to take up membership or become a registered user of a Web-based facility. Having stored these details, the business can build up a profile of customers and their behaviour and use the information for targeted marketing activities. An online bookseller might use an intelligent agent to store information about previous choices and make suggestions about future purchases, or notify users when selected new books become available.

Bots

A **bot** (a shortened form of the word 'robot') is a piece of software that trawls through vast numbers of websites searching for particular items of data and gathers the results into massive data stores. They are commonly used by sites that offer shoppers comparative price information. The bot searches in much the same way as an individual uses a search engine, but it issues the query repeatedly in a relentless search through sites on the Web. An example is the bot used by Bidders Edge, which targets e-auction sites, collecting product price information. The bot is not always a welcome visitor to a website. Apart from using up valuable processing power and bandwidth, it can instantaneously rank the price of a product against that of competing brands. Although this information is in the public domain, once gathered by a bot it can be made much more readily available to the public at large. A further possible concern to suppliers is that once posted in a comparative format, the information might rapidly become out of date, giving customers a misleading impression. A number of sites attempt to detect and block an incoming bot and attempt thereby to restrict access to the information to private individuals. There have also been legal actions taken, such as that brought by E-Bay against Bidders Edge, to attempt to deny access to sites by bots.

Another application of bots is in the creation of animated advertising banners. As the average take-up rate on most banner advertisements is less than 1%, companies are looking for innovative ways to increase user participation. Companies such as Artificial Life have developed Banner Bots, which allow natural-language conversations with users. They are intended to enhance an advertiser's online presence by entertaining, educating or leading users where they want to go by responding to questions instantaneously. These bots are also valuable market research tools that store and analyse conversation logs between consumers and the bots.

One of the more innovative uses of bots is in providing a virtual human interface. The interactive division of the Press Association in Britain has developed Ananova, a virtual newscaster who acts as the front end of the PA's online news services. Other human-like incarnations include Eve, the customer service advocate of eGain of Sunnyvale, California, and German retailer net-tissimo.com, whose bot is an exclamation mark dressed in a tuxedo!

Summary

Businesses have been swift to realize the opportunities provided by the Web and have developed websites in order to:

- advertise services and products;
- sell services and products;
- promote corporate images;
- provide information (especially public services).

As the various mini case studies indicated, advantages in using the Web include a reduction in the cost of advertising, cheaper and easier provision of information, the lack of a need to maintain a shop front, the ease of crossing geographical boundaries, and the absence of the middleman. Issues, including the security of electronic communications, particularly commercial transactions, will need to be tackled before the Internet becomes a stable environment for business operations.

It is likely that the use of the Internet and the Web will continue to grow in importance for business as new applications are exploited and the number of people able to access the Internet increases. The activities of e-commerce can be classified into the three areas of electronic markets, EDI and Internet commerce. These activities are embodied in the traditional business trade cycles: EDI represents an example of a repeat trade cycle; electronic marketplaces are extensively used in the pre-sale phase of irregular transactions; and full Internet commerce takes place in irregular transactions, particularly where there is cash settlement.

A number of business models for conducting electronic business have emerged. The most commonly found are:

- e-shop (business-to-business and business-to-consumer)
- e-mall
- e-procurement
- e-auction

In addition, there are companies providing specialist online services, information archives or tools for developing Internet infrastructure.

Trends in e-commerce are likely to include greater integration into business activity, with stronger linkages through the supply chain and a specialization into business services and functions such as trusted services and electronic transaction settlement.

Review questions

1. Provide a definition of e-commerce.

2. In what ways does e-commerce allow businesses to gain competitive advantage?

3. What factors encourage participation in e-commerce? What are the barriers to entry for businesses?

4. List *eight* business models for e-commerce. Give an example of the type of business that might adopt each model.

5. Give *two* examples of intelligence as seen in Web-based business activity.

Exercises

1. Using Porter's value chain and five forces model (Chapter 2), analyse the strategic impact of the use of the World Wide Web for the following business areas:

   - food and grocery retail
   - courier parcel tracking
   - property agency
   - banking
   - equity and stock trading
   - news and publishing.

2. Provide three different definitions of e-commerce, giving a justification for each.

3. How would a business identify the cost-effectiveness of its website?

4. Search the World Wide Web for a range of different business websites and analyse these with a view to answering the following:

- What are the objectives for the business of the website?
- How effective has the business been in meeting these objectives?
- Which features of the website should be added to or removed?

5. To what extent do traditional business trade cycle models help us to understand the way in which e-commerce is carried out?

6. 'If the Internet is a lawless frontier, then the service providers are the new marshals in town' (Spar and Bussgang, 1996). Is this the case?

CASE STUDY 6

Europe's top 150 corporate websites

A recent piece of published research entitled 'Europe's top 150 corporate websites' provides invaluable information and makes fascinating reading. If you want to pick up tricks on what to do, and not to do, on your website, this ranking is an excellent place to start. I have been trawling through some of the top and bottom performers, and have found a host of lessons.

It is important to be clear what the list is and is not. It is heavily biased towards financial information – the criteria were developed after interviewing analysts – so it cannot be seen as more than a proxy for a full 'what's best and what's worst' ranking.

On the one hand that is fine: websites are so complex that it would be almost impossible to create a table that looked at every aspect. And anyway, sites that are brilliant in investor relations are likely to be pretty good at everything. On the other hand, it does mean that companies which use their sites as working tools tend to be marked down, because corporate and IR material will inevitably get second billing.

So Tesco, the UK supermarkets group, should not be too distraught that it comes in 100th. Its site fronts a highly successful online retailing operation, and I would guess that is what counts most at Tesco Towers. Conversely, at least one company's site scores well here but is a nightmare if you attempt to buy anything from it.

Anyway, back to the lessons, most of which are of detail rather than broad theme. What is so special about the website of Stora Enso, the Finnish paper company? It looks nice, works well but what marks it out is its use of clever online tools. Tiny icons trigger pop-up windows with interactive calculators built into them: they range from the general, such as currency and imperial/metric converters, to the industry-specific: calculate the postage saved by changing paper weight. In the reports section I found a technical, environmental and financial glossary and a 'My notes' tool. Click this and you can write notes in a pop-up box, either for your own use or to e-mail to someone else.

None of this is world-changing stuff, but it shows a nice attention to detail, and also makes use of what the web is good at (interactivity, mostly). UBS, the top-scoring bank, also has neat icons triggering downloads of financial Excel files, charts or pdf documents.

UBS, and also ThyssenKrupp, are, however, most interesting for their work on 'journeys' – leading visitors through their sites with a minimal chance that they will get lost or distracted (something few sites, even e-commerce ones, manage successfully). UBS's

Service Finder is a Flash-powered system that lets you drill down to the right page with great ease. This is an excellent use for Flash – a tart of a technology that has been seeking respectability for years – though UBS should provide an alternative, which it doesn't. The ThyssenKrupp 'Base' is even more impressive: it lets you locate companies or products by criteria that range from customer sector to production site.

Hallvarsson & Halvarsson says there are no truly bad sites in this year's list. From those I have looked at, I would agree. Bottom-placed Banco Popular Español has a site that is old-fashioned, rather than bad: its financial reports are in PDF, which is not very user-friendly, and it is short of bells and whistles. But the main use of the site is as a provider of Internet banking – an area where Spain has been among the leaders of the field – and none of its national rivals score too well either.

Lloyds TSB should perhaps be more worried. Its corporate site is weak, with PDFs by the bucketful and, strangely, no attempt to promote the services of its registrar Shareview (proprietor: Lloyds-TSB). Although fellow Brits HSBC and the Bank of Scotland do not do much better, Abbey (National) shows them all up with a comprehensive site that has separate areas for private and institutional shareholders as well as an excellent large-type section for the visually-impaired. It will be interesting to see if there is catch-up across the sector: given the nature of this survey and the professed love of shareholders by UK PLCs, there certainly should be.

After all this detail, there is one theme I would like to highlight: reputation management. BAT, the top-ranking UK company, has five of its main navigation links broadly in this area. Its material on Smoking and Health treads a careful line between defensiveness and self-flagellation. It needs space to do that, which the web provides.

But you don't have to be subtle to defend your reputation. Look at www.yukos.com, a site that has been turned into a fighting machine. A 'Target Yukos' banner leads to a special section headed 'Your support for Yukos is support for all of Russia'. There follows a day-by-day account of developments since 'the attack' started, along with a clutch of western press articles. Yukos may rank modestly in the table, but this is an excellent use of the web: lots of material, kept up to date and broadcast round the world. How else could you provide that?

Adapted from: **Winners exploit what the web is good at**
By David Bowen
FT.com site: 26 November 2003

Questions

1. Which factors does the survey highlight as contributing towards a successful website?

2. Are there any other factors which you consider to add to the success of a website?

3. What are the negative features highlighted in the survey (e.g. excessive use of PDF downloads)? Hosts of these websites might claim that these features are unavoidable. Can you advise them whether this is so?

4. How can a company develop 'web presence' and 'web awareness'?

5. What are bots? Investigate some ways in which bots are used as an intelligent agent for web exploitation.

6. The survey implies that the business model adopted might affect the position in the ranking.

   (a) Identify a number of business models for e-commerce.
   (b) Evaluate a mismatch between the business model and the criteria used in the survey which might lead to an over- or under-estimation in the league table.

References and recommended reading

Barnes S. and Hunt B. (2001). *E-Commerce and V-Business: Business Models for Global Success.* Oxford: Butterworth-Heinemann

This book takes a business-focused look at Internet trade, virtual organizations and disintermediation.

Bickerton P. and Bickerton M. (2000). *Cybermarketing: How to Use the Internet to Market Your Products and Services*, 2nd edn. Oxford: Butterworth-Heinemann

This book is intended for those who wish to use the Internet for marketing their products and services. It is published on behalf of the Chartered Institute of Marketing. It is useful as it emphasizes and develops marketing concepts and techniques in an easily accessible fashion. Intended for practitioners, it is practical rather than academic in orientation.

Boon M. (2001). *Managing Interactively: Executing Business Strategy, Improving Communication and Creating a Knowledge Sharing Culture.* McGraw-Hill

This book looks at informing and engaging people, sharing knowledge and practical strategies for 'smart' communication.

Bressler S. and Grantham C. (2000). *Communities of Commerce.* McGraw-Hill

This book contains a collection of case studies and looks at the business climate of Internet communities and the effect of putting a community online.

David W.S. and Benamati J. (2003). *E-Commerce Basics: Technology Foundations and E-Business Applications.* Addison-Wesley, Pearson

This is a comprehensive introduction to all aspects of e-commerce. Later chapters also cover cybercrime, cyberterrorism, security and ethical issues. Chapters contain summaries, review questions and exercises.

Fellenstein C. and Wood R. (2000). *Exploring E-Commerce: Global E-Commerce and E-Societies.* Prentice Hall

This text focuses on many issues, including the management of the supply chain, e-societies, e-governments and techniques for anticipating customers' needs.

Lawrence E. *et al.* (2003). *Internet Commerce: Digital Models for Business*, 3rd edn. Wiley

An excellent book packed full of examples, illustrations, mini cases and case studies that takes a business-focused look at e-commerce. As well as the expected chapters on business models and technology basics, it also includes sections on taxation, legal and ethical issues.

Liautaud B. and Hammond M. (2001). *E-Business Intelligence: Turning Information into Knowledge into Profit.* McGraw-Hill

This book looks at the new enterprise business intelligence, information governance, customer care and the supply chain.

Lucas H.C. Jr. (2002). *Strategies for Electronic Commerce and the Internet.* MIT Press

This is an accessible book intended for those with a business background who wish to learn about strategy, business models and the Internet. It provides a good introduction to business models and shows how these are used in strategies adopted in the introduction of Internet business by established organizations and by new businesses.

Raisch W.D. (2001). *The E-Marketplace: Strategies for Success in B2B E-Commerce.* McGraw-Hill

A readable book covering business models, the dynamics of the e-marketplace, community and commerce strategies, and value trust networks.

Spar D. and Bussgang J.J. (1996). Ruling the Net. *Harvard Business Review*, May–June

A thought-provoking paper comparing the use of the Internet to the lawless frontiers of the Wild West. The authors highlight the contrast between the lack of a legal framework for the Internet, making e-commerce unpredictable and unstable, and the tremendous opportunities for business.

Timmers P. (2000). *Electronic Commerce: Strategies and Models for Business-to-Business Trading.* Wiley

This well-written book provides an excellent coverage of the subject, with numerous examples and illustrations.

Turban E., King D., Lee J. and Viehland D. (2004). *Electronic Commerce 2004: A Managerial Perspective.* Prentice Hall, Pearson

This is the latest edition of an established undergraduate text and contains new material on launching successful online businesses, an extended coverage of the digital economy, e-marketing, e-supply chains and market mechanisms. There are role-playing exercises, summary and discussion questions at chapter ends.

Whiteley D. (2000). *E-Commerce: Strategy, Technologies and Applications.* McGraw-Hill

A good all-round overview of electronic commerce written with a business focus. The book contains a large amount of material relating to EDI.

Decision support and end-user computing

On completion of this chapter, you should be able to:

- Describe the features of a decision support system
- Categorize decision support systems
- Evaluate the role of a range of tools, particularly spreadsheets, in decision support
- Discuss the development of end-user computing and evaluate its contribution to applications development
- Evaluate the importance of human–computer interaction in business information systems.

Introduction

In Chapter 1, information, decisions and the use of information in decision making were examined. This was achieved without recourse to discussion of any technology involved. Earlier chapters have introduced aspects of technology. This chapter covers how technology supports decisions in systems for planning, control and management. These are known as decision support systems. The chapter analyses the characteristics and classes of decision support system, including those systems that support group decisions – group decision support systems.

The influence of modern technology and, in particular, the role of fourth-generation languages, spreadsheets, expert systems tools and model generators in their development are emphasized. The role of end users in the specification and development of applications, especially decision support systems, is introduced. The phenomenon of end-user computing, its benefits and its challenge to management, are examined. Prototyping as a method of developing decision support systems within the context of end-user computing is explained. The focus on decision support and end-user computing has emphasized the need for a theory of the role of the user in the total system. Approaches to this area in the context of human–computer interaction are covered.

7.1 Features of decision support systems

Although the term **decision support system** (DSS) is a general one used to cover virtually any computerized system that aids decision making in business, most DSSs share certain features.

DSSs support decisions

One of the important characteristics of a decision support system is that it is intended to *support* rather than replace decisions. The Gorry and Scott Morton framework relating the structure of a decision to the level of managerial activity involved in the decision was covered in Chapter 1. Computerized systems can replace the human decision maker in structured decisions but are of little help in completely unstructured situations. There is, for instance, a large group of decisions taken by personnel in business organizations that have a structured computational and data transformation element to them as well as an unstructured non-rule-governed component. It is just these decisions that can be aided but not replaced by decision support systems.

Examples of semi-structured decisions are planning a mix of investments for a portfolio, looking at the financial implications of various ways of financing a short-term cash flow deficit, consideration of alternative production and pricing policies, assessing the impact of potential future changes in exogenous variables such as interest rates, analysis of the creditworthiness of corporate clients, and assessing the likely impacts of departmental reorganization.

DSSs involve flexible interactive access to data

Decision support systems are designed with an understanding of the requirements of the decision makers and the decision-making process in mind. This has implications, two of the most important being:

1. **The need for interactive support:** Typically, many of the semi-structured decisions for which DSSs are relevant involve the decision maker in asking questions that require immediate answers. As a result of this, further interrogation is made. Examples are:
   - **what if** – as in 'what would be the effects on profits if we were to be subject to a 5% material cost rise?'
   - **goal seeking** – as in 'what would be the required mix in the liquidation of short-term and medium-term assets to reduce a projected cash deficit to zero over the next six months (the goal)?'
   - **optimization** – as in 'how do we ensure optimum utilization of our machines?'

2. **Flexible access to data:** Many semi-structured decisions are only possible if the decision maker has immediate access to *ad hoc* data retrieval and report-generation facilities. For internal decisions this generally means that access by powerful query languages to existing data held in a corporate database is required.

Modern decision support systems meet these requirements by ensuring easy and quick availability of access to decision makers. This can be supplied by PCs placed on the desks of managers. The use of local area networks of PCs and the connections between these networks and mainframes, coupled with increasingly easy access to the Internet, have enabled easier data access to decision makers.

The use of spreadsheets, database management systems and other modelling packages together has provided the necessary modelling and data retrieval facilities. The standardized web page interface to the Internet and local intranets has further simplified the problems surrounding presentation of information to decision makers. Although data may be collected from a range of different systems and sources, the acceptance of a standard document structure for the Web simplifies the presentation of this information.

DSSs are fragmented

In Chapter 1, we saw that the totally integrated corporate management information system designed as a single project is extremely unlikely to be successful. Information systems are more likely to be loose federations of subsystems evolving separately to serve the information needs of the individual functional subsystems of the organization. This pattern is also exhibited with decision support, where the trend is towards development of models to provide support for individual decisions or types of decision. No attempt is made to develop global comprehensive decision support models for entire organizations.

DSS development involves end users

This is reinforced by the involvement of end-user decision takers in the development of models for computerized support. Nowhere is this more pronounced than in the use of local PCs and spreadsheet modelling. The purchase of PCs and the development of models are often carried out independently of any knowledge or aid from the central computer department. The use of fourth-generation languages in general has increased the influence of end users over decision support design.

In summary, the trend in modern decision support systems is towards end-user involvement in the development of simple fragmented models targeted to aid, rather than replace, the kinds of decision to be made. Easy and flexible interactive access to data and modelling facilities is as likely to be provided by PCs and networks as by the more traditional large central computers.

Mini case 7.1

Decision support systems

Aspen Technology, Inc. today announced that China Petroleum and Chemical Corporation (SINOPEC Corp.), the largest integrated petroleum and chemicals company in China, has signed a new licence agreement to standardize on AspenTech's solution for fuels marketing to optimize the secondary distribution of its petroleum products.

The company will also begin the implementation of AspenTech's solutions for petroleum primary distribution, polymer supply chain management and pipeline scheduling. These new initiatives represent the next stage of the long-term cooperation agreement between SINOPEC and AspenTech that was signed in September 2002.

SINOPEC operates over 29,000 retail service stations in China. Aspen Retail will enable SINOPEC's petroleum company to calculate the most economical way to transport petroleum products to each gas station based on accurate demand forecasts, thereby optimizing replenishment schedules and ensuring the stations receive timely deliveries. The solution will be implemented in a series of regional deployments, beginning with the first phase of projects in Shandong province, Beijing, Shanghai, Shenzhen, Zhejiang province and Guangdong province.

In a separate agreement, SINOPEC has also decided to implement AspenTech's petroleum primary distribution solution, and to pilot AspenTech's solutions for polymer supply chain management and pipeline scheduling.

The primary distribution solution for SINOPEC is designed to maximize the overall profitability of the company's primary distribution system by optimizing the key operations, including purchasing, sales, exchanges, and inventory management.

The solution will provide a production planning and scheduling system based on market demand, enabling the companies to increase their response to market change, improve customer satisfaction, lower inventory and production cost, and obtain a better balance between supply, production and demand. In addition to optimizing the supply chain, the systems will also increase the value of SINOPEC's ERP system by providing accurate production and supply chain data.

Adapted from: **SINOPEC selects AspenTech's solution for fuels marketing to optimize secondary distribution of petroleum products**
Business Wire: 10 September 2003

Questions

1. In what ways can this new system assist in decision support?
2. What barriers are there to implementing a system such as this?

7.2 Types of decision support system

Decision support systems can be divided into a number of categories, depending on the type of processing of data and information involved and the type of decision made.

1. **Data retrieval and analysis for decision support:** These systems rely on interaction with an existing database:

   (a) **Simple entry and enquiry systems:** These support decisions by providing immediate interrogation of a database for specific enquiries. Examples are stock enquiry systems, airline booking systems and account enquiry systems. They are used to aid operational decisions – for instance, whether to reorder stock.

   (b) **Data analysis systems:** These provide summaries and selected reports of data held on the database. An example is a system to provide information on the rate at which sales orders are being satisfied.

   (c) **Accounting information systems:** These are very similar to the last category as accounting information is provided as an analysis of accounting transaction data. However, because accountants commonly need the same types of report – for example, aged analysis of debtors, summary balance sheets, cash reports, profit and loss reports – and such information is prepared according to professional accounting standards, much of this information is supplied by accounting applications packages.

2. **Computational support for structured decisions:** These involve using existing general data held on a database and computation together with details of individual

cases to arrive at information for a decision. An example would be a motor insurance quotation system. This accepts data on an individual, searches a database of insurance companies' terms and computes a set of calculated premiums, which optimize on some group of variables such as low cost, maximum protected bonus or minimum excess.

3. **Decision support involving modelling:** These systems rely on the use of existing data from a database or user input data, which might be hypothetical. Using this data, its consequences are calculated using a model. The model reflects relationships that the decision taker believes to hold between the variables relevant for a decision.

   (a) Spreadsheet models are used to represent accounting relationships between numerical accounting data. They are used to take the tedium out of budget preparation and forecasting. The sensitivity of the organization to changes in the values of accounting data is then easy to estimate by hypothetical 'what if' changes.

   (b) Probabilistic models incorporate elements of probabilistic reasoning and risk analysis in their modelling calculations.

   (c) Optimization modelling involves mathematical computation of optimization or goal seeking based on constraints.

Many decision support systems in this category exhibit all three characteristics.

Mini case 7.2

Decision support through modelling

MEDai, Inc., a leading provider of predictive modelling solutions to the healthcare industry, develops a Clinical Decision Support System (CDSS) for healthcare providers that uses artificial intelligence (AI) to predict the probability, severity, effective treatment and outcomes of specific diseases and the costs associated with their prevention and control. The company also serves payor markets with a unique High Risk Predictor System (HRP), which identifies high-risk, high-cost individuals allowing proactive intervention to improve healthcare quality and reduce costs.

Steve Epstein, president and co-founder of MEDai, said the healthcare market relies more heavily on accurate, scientific predictive modelling aided by sophisticated AI applications to produce improved outcomes.

'The healthcare system is becoming more stressed and resources are being stretched,' Epstein stated. 'This kind of technology can make a critical difference for providers and payors as they seek to provide high quality health care in an efficient and cost-effective manner.'

Adapted from: **MEDai experiences growth; Predictive modeling firm moves HQ to new offices**
Business Wire: 1 July 2003

Question
What benefits does modelling offer for decision takers?

7.3 The development of decision support systems

The development of a decision support system is determined by the types of information and the facilities needed for making the decision. In this sense, DSS development is decision-led. Because an intimate knowledge of the decision-making process is needed it is important that end users – that is, the decision makers – are involved in the process of design. They may carry out the development and design themselves, as is common with spreadsheet modelling, or it may be undertaken by analysts and programmers.

Decision support systems are developed using programming languages or produced by packages specifically incorporating decision support development tools. These methods will now be considered. In all approaches, it is generally considered advisable to develop prototypes initially.

7.3.1 The use of very high-level languages

Conventional high-level languages such as C++ and COBOL can be used to develop decision support systems. They are extremely flexible. However, decision support systems using these languages involve a lengthy analysis and design phase. They are not suitable for prototyping. It is now not common to use them, especially as technical efficiency considerations, which may be important with transaction-processing systems, are not so important for decision support.

Fourth-generation or very high-level languages are more appropriate. They are particularly useful as they are generally database-oriented. This is important for those systems that rely on data retrieval and analysis for decision support. An example of a prominent fourth-generation language is SQL, which can be used on many relational database systems, such as IBM's DB2 and ORACLE. The advantages of using them are that:

- applications development is more rapid;
- many are end-user oriented; and
- they are more likely to be declarative rather than procedural.

Fourth-generation languages are covered more extensively in Chapter 3.

7.3.2 The use of spreadsheets

Of all the computerized productivity tools made available to the decision maker in business organizations over the last decade, the electronic spreadsheet is among the most powerful, widely employed and user-friendly.

Spreadsheets are a particularly suitable tool for the accountant, although they may be used for many general business modelling tasks. A popular area is the development of cash flow forecasts. A firm's cash flow position can be crucially affected by changes in average debtor or creditor periods, in the pattern of expected future costs and sales, and the charge incurred in remaining in overdraft, which is particularly sensitive to interest rate changes. Model building and 'what if' analysis enable the accountant to keep an up-to-date and changing view of the firm's current and future cash flow position without the laborious need to recalculate in the light of unexpected changes.

To understand the idea of a spreadsheet, imagine a large sheet of paper divided into many rows and columns. Through the keyboard the user may enter text, a

Figure 7.1 The output of a spreadsheet for profit forecasting

	1	2	3	4	5	6	7
1	Compact disc players TYPES CD-A and CD-B						
2	6 months projections from January						
3							
4	SALES	Jan	Feb	March	April	May	June
5	units CD-A	43	43	44	44	45	45
6	units CD-B	121	109	98	88	79	71
7							
8	price CD-A	123	121	118	116	113	111
9	price CD-B	278	306	336	370	407	448
10							
11	sales revenue CD-A	5289	5235	5182	5129	5076	5025
12	sales revenue CD-B	33638	33302	32969	32639	32313	31989
13		----	----	----	----	----	----
14	TOTAL	38927	38537	38150	37768	37389	37014
15							
16	COSTS						
17	labour CD-A	1075	1086	1097	1108	1119	1130
18	labour CD-B	5203	4683	4214	3793	3414	3072
19							
20	materials CD-A	2795	2823	2851	2880	2908	2938
21	materials CD-B	21296	19166	17250	15525	13972	12575
22		----	----	----	----	----	----
23	TOTAL	30369	27758	25412	23305	21413	19715
24							
25	GROSS PROFIT	8558	10779	12738	14463	15976	17299
26							
27	TABLES	Jan price	Price	January	Sales	Material	Labour
28		per unit	growth	sales	growth	cost per unit	cost per unit
29	CD-A	123	0.98	43	1.01	65	25
30	CD-B	278	1.1	121	0.9	176	43

number or a formula into each cell; a cell is the 'box' at the intersection of every row and column. Spreadsheet software running on a computer provides a computerized equivalent of this grid-like worksheet. The entry in each cell is made by moving a highlighted box, called a cursor, to the required cell. This is achieved by means of cursor control keys on the keyboard or the use of a mouse. The cell entry is displayed on the screen. For example, in row 35 column 19 the text **SALES** or the number **100.23** might be entered. Or again the formula (**ROW 23 COLUMN 2 + ROW 14 COLUMN 3**) × 2 might be added. In the last case, the resulting number calculated from the formula would be displayed on the screen in the cell position. Any cells referred to in a formula may themselves contain numbers or other formulae. Cells may be linked together in this way.

The example in Figure 7.1 concerns the projected sales, sales income and costs for two types of compact disc player, CD-A and CD-B. Figure 7.1 would be displayed on the screen. Figure 7.2 shows the logic behind the model from rows 4–30 and columns 1–3 as it would be entered at the keyboard. Text is clearly shown as enclosed by quotation marks. Note that **R29C4** means 'row 29 column 4' and **R(–6)C** means '6 rows prior to the current row, same column'. The separation of data in rows 29 and 30 from the logic of the model makes it easy to carry out 'what if' analysis. Suppose that

Figure 7.2 The logic part of the model in Figure 7.1

	1	2	3
4 "SALES"		" Jan"	" Feb"
5 " units CD-A"		R29C4	RC(–1)*R29C5
6 " units CD-B"		R30C4	RC(–1)*R30C5
7			
8 "price CD-A"		R29C2	RC(–1)*R29C3
9 "price CD-B"		R30C2	RC(–1)*R30C3
10			
11 "sales revenue CD-A"		R(–6)C*R(–3)C	R(–6)C*R(–3)C
12 "sales revenue CD-B"		R(–6)C*R(–3)C	R(–6)C*R(–3)C
13		"------------------"	"------------------"
14 "TOTAL"		R(–3)C+R(–2)C	R(–3)C+R(–2)C
15			
16 "COSTS"			
17 "labour CD-A"		R29C7*R(–12)C	R29C7*R(–12)C
18 "labour CD-B"		R30C7*R(–12)C	R30C7*R(–12)C
19			
20 "materials CD-A"		R29C6*R(–15)C	R29C6*R(–15)C
21 "materials CD-B"		R30C6*R(–15)C	R30C6*R(–15)C
22		"------------------"	"------------------"
23 "TOTAL"		SUM(R(–6)C:R(–2)C)	SUM(R(–6)C:R(–2)C)
24			
25 "GROSS PROFIT"		R(–11)C–R(–2)C	R(–11)C–R(–2)C
26			
27 "TABLES"		"Jan price"	" Price"
28		" per unit"	" Growth"
29 " CD-A"		123	0.98
30 " CD-B"		278	1.1

the managing director of the company wanted to know the impact of an increase in material cost of components for CD-A compact discs. After the estimated figure has been entered in row 29 column 6 the spreadsheet program will automatically recalculate all cells that are affected by the change. The managing director can carry out as many 'what ifs' as required.

As well as standard arithmetic functions, most spreadsheets have the ability to calculate financial ratios such as internal rates of return and net present value, along with common statistical functions such as standard deviation.

A feature of many spreadsheet packages is that the individual spreadsheet models may be linked together so that figures in one spreadsheet can be fed into another. For instance, the cost side of the production of CD players would be modelled by the production department. The responsibility for developing the sales forecasting part of the model in Figure 7.1 might lie with the sales department. Selected parts of each of these separate spreadsheets, saved on disk, can then be linked to a third spreadsheet, which produces the projected profit/loss forecast for the next six months. Changes, or 'what ifs', in the subsidiary spreadsheets feed through to the main spreadsheet by way of the linking.

Because spreadsheet packages represent information to the user in rows and columns, they are particularly suitable for tasks that require report production. They can therefore be used to produce profit and loss, balance sheets and other reports.

Most modern spreadsheets also provide the facility to present information in other forms, such as charts, diagrams and graphs.

Spreadsheet packages also enable the development of models that interact and extract data stored in a database. This is important where future rolling projections based on current rolling figures are needed.

Modern spreadsheet packages incorporate their own very high-level programming languages. Although limited, these enable the user to write various application programs that interact with the spreadsheet model or that control the interaction of the spreadsheet with the user.

The use of spreadsheets as an interactive modelling tool is limited by the matrix nature of the model representation and data input. Only applications that are high in number handling as distinct from text handling are suitable for spreadsheet applications.

There are other drawbacks to the use of spreadsheets. Spreadsheet model design, although capable of being carried out by end users, is time-consuming. Unless much 'what if' investigation is to be carried out or the same relationships used again and again it may be quicker and more flexible to use pen and paper. Spreadsheet package developers are conscious of this limitation and are constantly adding new facilities to speed up complex model building. It is also now becoming obvious that spreadsheet model development cannot be carried out in an *ad hoc* manner if reliable, testable and amendable models are to be built. It is necessary to follow good modelling practice.

Another limitation of spreadsheets is in their ability to display only a small part of the spreadsheet at a time on the screen. Package manufacturers have attempted to overcome this by the provision of **windows**. Windows show several selected rectangular sections of the spreadsheet simultaneously on different parts of the screen. A facility is often provided to split a window into two panes, allowing the user to freeze one pane, for example a section containing the headings, and manipulate the other.

Despite these limitations, spreadsheet packages will continue to be used widely in business, especially accounting and decision making, not least because models can be built using them by those without technical computing skills. The trend in the future is to make these packages more user-friendly and able to interact more with other standard commercial packages. Although these packages will have other facilities, such as built in word-processing and database facilities, they will continue to be based on the same philosophy of the electronic matrix worksheet.

Mini case 7.3

End-user systems

For many years managers have been encouraged to move away from basing decisions on historical monthly management accounts and a fixation with the 'fast close,' which was described as 'like driving by looking only in the rear view mirror.'

Instead, they were encouraged to look at the leading indicators that drive performance, such as customer satisfaction, brand strength, market share, productivity and innovation, which are all non-financial. This requires integrating summarized historic and forecast financial and operational data from many sources.

A technology solution needs to address a number of linked management processes that all share the same data. These include statutory consolidation, analysis, modelling, reporting, planning/budgeting/forecasting, activity-based costing and management, tax planning and treasury management.

Unfortunately, these diverse, but inter-related, requirements have been met by different specialist software packages. This has resulted in the widespread use of bespoke spreadsheets. But these are cumbersome, costly to build and operate, and prone to errors.

The specialist software vendors are attempting to provide an integrated solution through a process of mergers and acquisitions. Hyperion, Comshare and SAS Institute have their origins in financial consolidation applications that use a relational database.

The online analytical processing (Olap) vendors provide a generic tool, based on a multidimensional database, that can do everything required, but has to be built from scratch.

The enterprise resource planning (ERP) vendors have produced their own suites, drawing data from their own systems and providing links to external data.

Except for spreadsheets, they all share the same basic approach of taking data from ERP and other systems into a dedicated decision support database. Various end-user tools are available for users to access the data.

The industry consolidation aims to produce a single solution, variously called business performance management (BPM), corporate performance management (CPM) or enterprise performance management (EPM).

'The different products are only integrated at the PowerPoint level,' warns Nigel Pendse, lead author of the Olap Report. 'Either they have to re-engineer the products to make them link, in which case they often destroy the value of the acquired product and the people involved in it leave, or they have to leave them loosely coupled. You end up with individually spinning wheels not linked together – with the odd rubber band trying to connect them.'

The fragmented nature of the solution becomes more evident in independent research. Coda Group, the accounting systems vendor, found that 66 per cent of European companies still used spreadsheets for month-end reporting and 77 per cent used them for budgeting.

In the US, CFO Research Services interviewed more than 250 senior finance executives on behalf of Comshare. Sixty per cent were unsatisfied with the amount of time it took to create an annual performance report. Half were not satisfied with the speed and accuracy of plan re-forecasting, only one-third were able to do rolling forecasts and only one-third were satisfied with their ability to test the impact of the proposed changes.

Only one-quarter of those surveyed said their budgets focused on key business drivers. As a result, 71 per cent planned to overhaul their performance management systems to get better visibility into current results.

Adapted from: **Financial reporting**
By Rod Newing
FT.com site: 4 June 2003

Questions

1. What benefits can be gained from using spreadsheets for month-end reporting?

2. Why have many organizations moved away from using spreadsheets for month-end reporting?

7.3.3 Spreadsheet design

Spreadsheets may be very large, containing several different sheets, each comprising several hundred rows and columns. Data may be entered directly on to the sheet or into a 'form' that encapsulates the contents of a single row of the sheet. The results may be displayed on the sheet in numerical form or may be converted into a textual equivalent, a graphical representation or a summary report. In all these cases, the development and presentation of a spreadsheet should be in accordance with a systematic method. If this is not done, individuals may have difficulty in using the spreadsheet – data entry, report and logic functions may not be clearly distinguished. Also, the process of building the spreadsheet can, as with software, yield errors, and these must be capable of discovery and identification before rectification.

A well-designed and robust spreadsheet should distinguish clearly the data input, working formulae and output aspects of a spreadsheet model. Other areas should be reserved for general information for the user and for the reporting of error conditions. The main areas can be developed in a diagonal formation on a single sheet (see Figure 7.3(a)), or on separate sheets within a workbook (see Figure 7.3(b)), to ensure that operations on complete rows or columns do not affect the contents or display of entries in other main areas. Spreadsheets have the facility to protect cells or blocks of cells. This prevents the contents of the cell being altered without first disabling the protection. Once a model has been designed, all cells except for data input cells are protected as a precaution against inadvertent alteration. The five main areas are:

1. **User information:** When the spreadsheet is loaded the user should automatically be placed in this area of the spreadsheet. The information area gives essential information about the purpose and limitations of the spreadsheet. Users may not be designers. If so, their knowledge of the spreadsheet may be minimal and this area is essential.

2. **Data input:** Users should only be able to alter the contents of the spreadsheet by inputting data in this area. The data input area contains no formulae. It is the only area of the spreadsheet not covered by protection. It may be implemented by using data entry forms. Data validation checks and routines may be included to ensure for example that the items entered are within specified ranges, types or prescribed lists.

3. **Logic:** This area contains the formulae to carry out the calculations of the spreadsheet. It should contain no data.

4. **Report:** The output of the logic area is taken and displayed in the correct format. This may include graphical display. The design of the report area is based on considerations of the optimum way to present information for user needs.

5. **Error:** Spreadsheets contain some functions that are suitable for error checking. Others can be built into the design of the spreadsheet. For instance, certain data inputs may require a set of percentages to be entered, which should total 100. A simple check and display of error in the error section is an aid to data input.

A spreadsheet is a decision support tool. In order that decisions may be supported properly, the output of the spreadsheet should present information in the most helpful way. It is therefore good practice to design the report area first. The data requirements and finally the logic are then determined.

Good spreadsheet design methods ensure that the model performs operations correctly and that users, who may not be builders, are presented with information organized in the most beneficial way.

Figure 7.3 The five main areas of spreadsheet design

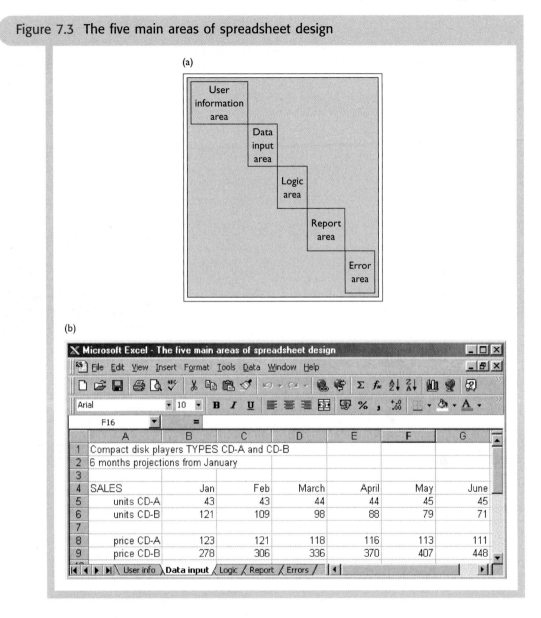

Spreadsheet reporting

Lockheed Martin is an advanced technology company that employs 125,000 people worldwide. Prior to 1997, it used a specialist financial consolidation package and transferred the results to spreadsheets for reporting.

It had a vision for a central database to provide a single source of information at the corporate level. It built this database using Khalix from Longview Solutions, a small privately-owned software company.

'It has increased confidence that the financial consolidation process is accurate and complete and that the information is presented in an appropriate manner,' says Michael Gabaly, Lockheed Martin's director of enterprise performance management.

At its heart is a multi-dimensional database that draws data from several heritage general ledger systems and other operational systems in the business units and performs the financial consolidation.

The existing spreadsheet formats were transferred into Khalix, with individual cells linked to the database. Spreadsheet templates are used to create new reports.

The same set of data is used for monthly financial reporting; long range planning; forecasting to individual contract level; and tax reporting.

Management uses a list of standard reports to access the database. 'When we need to amend our reporting requirements we can easily change the current reports,' says Mr Gabaly.

Because the different applications are integrated and use the same data, it is possible to produce an instant report that compares the long-range plan with actual, to date and forecast figures. 'What if?' scenarios are used to model potential declines in the market or in revenue.

'It provide us with the accountability and trust that data is accurate and complete and enables management to access the information much more quickly. It gives more visibility to the information and allows us to analyse it more frequently,' says Mr Gabaly.

'We have seen the elimination of a lot of waste caused by duplicate systems,' says Mr Gabaly. 'We didn't expect to achieve the efficiencies we have received so far, so that has been a very pleasant surprise.'

In conclusion, he says the system has given the company an easier way to report and assess financial performance and to alert management to any potential issues in performance.

Adapted from: **Lockheed Martin: Single source for all spreadsheets**
By Rod Newing
FT.com site: 4 June 2003

Questions

1. What problems might have arisen under the previous reporting system at Lockheed Martin?

2. Is it advisable to allow end-users to prepare their own spreadsheet templates for financial reporting?

7.3.4 The use of expert system tools and shells

Systems involving data retrieval, analysis and computation do not exhaust the range of systems for decision support. Decision makers often seek advice from human experts before taking action. For example, the doctor seeks additional expertise from a specialist for diagnosis and prescription for an ailment with which the doctor is not familiar. The accountant recommending a business plan for a client will seek specialist advice from a tax consultant. Before embarking on a major contract with another company, a business executive will require expert advice on that company's financial health.

All of these cases involve consultation with an expert prior to decision taking. The expert provides decision-relevant information not purely by analysis or computation but by applying the facts of a particular case to a body of knowledge possessed internally by that expert.

Expert systems are computer systems that mimic the expert in being effective consultants in a particular knowledge area or domain. In common with experts they can provide explanation for their advice and conclusions. They are distinguished from other decision support systems by possessing general knowledge in a specific domain of expertise. This knowledge is often represented in the form of interconnected rules. An example of a rule from a system designed to aid a bank manager on whether to grant a loan to a client might be:

If the client is a home owner then establish:

1. the amount of the mortgage;

2. whether there have been any payment defaults.

Many similar rules would be incorporated into such a system. The aim of the system would be to provide a recommendation, based on the bank's standard lending policy, on whether to lend to the client, the size of the loan and any other conditions attaching to it. It is decision support rather than decision replacing because it is just one of the factors that the bank manager would take into account. There may be other circumstances, not covered by the system, that the bank manager finds relevant. Using discretion, the manager could 'overrule' the advice of the expert system.

Expert systems are used where *reasoning*, as distinct from computation, is important in providing advice. These systems are particularly suitable for handling vague and uncertain reasoning under situations of incomplete information and data. This is also an important characteristic of an expert.

Not all expert systems are used for decision support. Other uses include training personnel, archiving important knowledge in an organization and aiding a person in a complex procedure such as registration of a company under the Data Protection Act. Their use in all these spheres is increasing and will continue to increase over the coming decade. Expert system decision support for business will be an important area of artificial intelligence.

Expert systems can be developed in a conventional programming language such as Pascal, BASIC, C++ or using a language more suited to artificial intelligence such as PROLOG or LISP. These approaches, though flexible, are time-consuming and costly. Expert systems can be built using **expert system shells**. In essence, these are expert systems from which all domain-specific knowledge has been removed. All that is left is the shell, comprising the user interface, the programmed reasoning strategies and a knowledge entry module through which the expert's knowledge is initially input into the system for later reference. Expert system shells allow speedy prototyping of expert systems – often by end users. There are a large number of shells on the market for use with PCs, minicomputers and mainframe computers. Examples are Expertech Xi Plus, Leonardo and Savoir.

Shells that are used to prototype decision support systems suffer many limitations. The chief one is that they are not very flexible in the ways that they allow knowledge to be represented and the ways in which reasoning can be carried out. **Expert system tools** provide a middle ground of increased flexibility over shells while avoiding the time-consuming and costly design of an expert system using conventional languages. Among other features, these tools provide:

■ control over ways of representing knowledge;

■ control over the reasoning strategies adopted by the expert system;

- the ability to use interactive graphics in the development of the system; and
- the ability to customize the user interface.

Expert system tools are suitable for a prototyping approach to the development of expert decision support systems. They are often sophisticated and require extensive training to use. They are not associated with 'casual' end-user development, as for instance spreadsheets are.

Examples of commercial expert system tools are KEE, ART and Goldworks. Expert systems are covered in more detail in Chapter 17.

7.3.5 The use of model generators

Spreadsheet packages are designed primarily for use with PCs. Although their facilities are now extended to include graphical presentation and they have their own languages, often called macro languages, they are still based around the concept of the grid-like worksheet. Model generators are more extensive packages, often mainframe-based, that enable speedy development of a wide range of models using interactive design techniques.

All packages provide model generation facilities. Individual packages differ in the additional features offered, but the following are common:

- sophisticated report generation facilities
- capacity to carry out complex statistical analysis
- capacity to carry out time series analysis, linear programming and solutions to linear equations
- Monte Carlo risk analysis simulation
- sensitivity analysis
- sophisticated financial and mathematical functions
- consolidation of different models
- interaction with a database.

Model generators incorporate many of the features of very high-level languages, spreadsheet packages and statistical packages. Because of the complexity in the range of features offered, they are not suitable for use by casual end users.

7.3.6 The Internet and decision support

The information searching and retrieval facilities of the Internet have added a further dimension to the range of decision support tools available. As has already been discussed, the exploitation of search engines, intelligent agents and bots has enabled desktop computer users to trawl the massive contents of the World Wide Web more efficiently. The data uncovered can be used in isolation but becomes much more valuable when aggregated with data from other sources. The resulting systems are sometimes referred to as **heterogeneous information source systems** (HISS). Singh (1998) describes the challenge to the designers of these systems of integrating data that may be derived from a number of different but complementary sources. The sources may vary greatly. Some may provide data that is very structured in nature, such as that extracted from databases. Some may contain completely unstructured data, such as word-processed documents. Unstructured data will need to go through a process of indexing to facilitate its incorporation into the system. The middle ground contains those sources that are semi-structured in nature, including web pages and e-mail. The formatting information contained in data from these semi-structured documents and files can assist in its aggregation with structured or semi-structured data from other sources. The richness derived from combining these complementary sources offers many benefits; as a result, a great deal of current research (such as Fielding *et al.* (1998)) is being undertaken to find effective ways of integrating data from heterogeneous sources.

The growth in adoption of XML is helping to address these problems as data from widely differing sources can more readily be assimilated into systems.

Another effect of the growth of the Internet has been the increasing interest in and availability of group decision support tools. This is the topic of the next section.

7.4 Group decision support

The decision support systems considered so far have been concerned with computerized support for an individual taking a decision characterized as semi-structured or unstructured. Many decisions taken in an organization will be taken not by a single individual but as a result of group deliberations. **Group decision support systems** (GDSS) provide computer-based support for group decisions.

Groups typically consist of fewer than twenty people, who arrive at decisions through communication. The communication serves to share information and implement the decision-making process. The decision may be taken by vote but is more often by negotiation, consensus or preference ranking.

Three types of computer-based support are available:

1. **Decision networks:** This type allows participants to communicate through networks with each other or with a central database. Applications software may use commonly shared models to provide support. The commonest implementation is using a local area network and PCs. The technology filters out many of the typical group dynamics of a participative meeting.

2. **Decision room:** Participants are located in one place – the decision room. The purpose of this is to enhance participant interaction and decision making by computerized support within a fixed period of time using a facilitator. Specific computer-based tools are provided (see below).

3. **Tele/computer conferencing:** If groups are composed of members or subgroups that are geographically dispersed, tele/computer conferencing provides for interactive connection between two or more decision rooms. This interaction will involve transmission of computerized and audiovisual information.

Whereas decision networks can be viewed as the use of local area networks, for decision making involving groups the decision room is an entirely new development.

The decision room is used by an organization to create an environment in which groups may enhance their decisions. The decision-making process is guided by a **facilitator,** who is usually not from within the organization but a trained professional in group dynamics brought in for the decision-making sessions. There will also usually

Figure 7.4 A typical layout for a decision room

be a computer controller, whose responsibility it is to maintain computer communications and software support within the room.

The decision room (an example of which can be seen in Figure 7.4) consists of a table with networked workstations for the participants and workstations for the facilitator and controller. The screen of any node of the network can be projected on to the wall screen. The facilitator can also ensure that, if required, any participant's screen can replace some or all of the other nodes for demonstration or interactive purposes. Breakout rooms, used for smaller discussions, are also equipped with similar networked machines. A combination of overhead projector, flipchart, photocopier and other presentation devices is also provided.

The software may take many forms but will always consist of tools that aid group decision making, are easy to use and are interactive. Examples of software (as well as spreadsheet and statistical/graphical packages) are:

- **Brainstorming:** Brainstorming software may be used at any stage of the proceedings but is particularly valuable in the early stages, when members of the group need to think and converse freely on issues. A problem or statement can be entered for comment. This will appear on all screens. Each individual may then produce comments, which are consolidated and displayed anonymously. The tool increases creativity and lateral thinking.

- **Voting:** It is frequently important to obtain a swift view on the acceptability of proposals from a group perspective before proceeding. Voting software enables this to happen. It is not merely restricted to yes/no but will also enable different formats for expressing preferences, including multiple choice and 1–5 scales.

- **Policy formation:** Software can aid policy formation by allowing decision makers to identify connections and relations between issues and communicate this to all present for comment.

The software will be used as part of a methodology followed by the facilitator in arriving at decisions. Much work is still to be done in the area of development of tools to support decision rooms.

Decision rooms are expensive to equip, and all but the largest organizations would find it difficult to justify the expenditure, particularly as the use of the decision room is not regarded as an everyday occurrence. It is becoming more common for establishments, especially academic institutions, to hire out these facilities to organizations when needed.

It is difficult to analyse the effectiveness of these group decision support systems, although it appears that they are most likely to be beneficial (and to be regarded as beneficial by participants) for larger group sizes (eight and above). Participants are aware of the need to impose some structure on groups of this size and welcome the direction given by the decision room and the facilitator.

7.5 End-user computing

End-user computing generally refers to a situation in which the target users of an information and decision support system are involved extensively in the specification, development and use of the system and its applications.

This is to be contrasted with the more traditional approach, where analysis, design and development of computer systems are carried out by a team of analysts and programmers affiliated to a centralized computer department. In this case, the final users of the system are likely to be involved at only two stages. First, they may be required at the early stages of specification for interview to establish the nature of the activity to be computerized, together with the information required. Their next involvement is likely to be at the stage where the system is tested.

In end-user computing, those that use the system will be expected to play a leading role in most, if not all, of the following:

- the identification of the need for a system or application;
- the specification of the type of system and/or software to satisfy that need;
- the purchase/resourcing of the hardware/software;
- the development of the application according to corporate standards;
- the use of the application for business purposes;
- the management of security/backup for the application.

7.5.1 The rise of end-user computing

The growth of end-user computing began in the late 1970s, and is now seen as an important component of the strategy of many organizations for their information and decision support provision. The trend was stimulated by demand considerations and facilitated by supply developments.

First, the backlog of computer applications developments that accumulated in many organizations meant that users were becoming increasingly frustrated with the computer centre. When applications were finally delivered they were often over budget and disappointing in that they did not meet user expectations. Although end-user computing was not the only response to this situation (another was the design of more appropriate methodologies for systems analysis and design), it can be seen as one of the reactions to problems with the traditional approach to information systems development and management – problems that had been building up throughout the previous decade.

Second, the introduction of microcomputers placed computing power within the reaches of departmental budget holders and users of information systems. The rapid increase in the power of microcomputers, together with the decrease in costs, was supplemented by the production of software specifically designed for the end user. End users wanted the autonomy provided by PCs. Software suppliers responded to this by designing programs serving end-user requirements. This in turn stimulated the growth of end-user computing.

Third, there was a general increase in computer literacy among business users. This was an essential prerequisite for the full growth of end-user computing. The improvement in computer literacy can be partly put down to the stimulus of the reasons mentioned above – the demand for more independence from the computer centre and the availability of the means of establishing that independence. However, it should be remembered that the growth in computing in universities and colleges was also turning out computer-literate graduates who were able to utilize computer support in their work.

7.5.2 Types of end-user computing

End-user computing as a category involves a range of individuals with differing types of skills, access to and relationships with the computer system. End-user computing may be at varying stages of maturity of development in different organizations. If end-user computing is going to be managed well in the organization then an understanding of the types of end user is essential so that proper training, control, resourcing and applications development can be undertaken, and an understanding of the stage of development will determine appropriate strategies for management of the process.

Categorization by skills of end users

One categorization, by Rockart and Flannery (1983), distinguishes end users in terms of the type of computer skills they possess and the way this interacts with the types of information the end user requires. There are six categories, and end users may 'progress' from one category to another. Each is distinguished by a different type of skill and information requirement. Recognition of this will aid end-user management.

1. **Non-programming end user:** This is the 'traditional' end user. In this category the user is not involved in the systems development process. The non-programming end user responds to prompts and menus on screens, inputs or extracts data. Typically, the user will have little understanding of the way the application is built. The data entry clerk, the shop assistant using computer-based checkout facilities and the airline reservation clerk are examples in this category. Improvements in the interfaces to the World Wide Web have greatly increased the number of non-programming end users. The ease of use of browser software and search engines has encouraged even those with very few IT skills to take advantage of the Internet.

2. **Command-level end user:** Users in this category have a greater understanding of the way the application is handled. Typically, individuals will be able to form database

query commands or interact with the operating system using commands. This level of user is generally responsive to training if their systems level knowledge is in need of upgrading.

3. **Programming-level end user:** This category refers not to the traditional programmer in the computer centre but to personnel usually working in one of the functional business departments, such as accounting, who have a deep understanding of the use of 4GLs or development tools in building applications. An example would be the management accountant who, with a thorough understanding of both spreadsheet software and management accounting, can develop spreadsheet models to support management accounting decisions.

4. **Functional support personnel:** Users in this category are technically skilled information systems developers located in functional departments within the organization. The difference between this category and the previous category is one of perception. For example, accountants who develop models for decision support would primarily view themselves as accountants (programming end user), whereas computer-trained systems developers in an accounting department will need to know about accounting in order to develop systems. These latter personnel would nevertheless regard themselves as information systems professionals (functional support personnel).

5. **End-user support personnel:** End-user support personnel usually reside in the computer centre. They will be specialists in the technicalities of a range of applications development software packages. Their understanding, though, will be limited to the software aspects, not to an understanding of the business nature of the applications developed. They will provide support on development, from a technical point of view, choice of software and installation services.

6. **Data-processing programmers:** Although the term is slightly archaic now, this category of users is composed of highly trained computer centre personnel. The data-processing programmer is likely to be computer trained (not business trained) and to take creative decisions using the full power of the array of software available. This breadth and depth distinguishes the data-processing programmer from the programming-level end user.

As can be seen by examination of the different categories, there are a wide range of skills and approaches associated with end users. All categories represent end users in the sense of persons who use the computer system for business purposes or take part in the applications development process. However, the term 'end-user computing', as introduced at the start of this section, is restricted and generally understood to involve only categories 3 and 4 – programming-level end users and functional support personnel. The different categories in the Rockart and Flannery typology provide insights into what activities are appropriate for what types of personnel, what training must be provided in order to develop end users from one category to another, and how an organization might decide to spread its approach to applications development using 4GLs between different types of user. As with any categorization, its chief purpose is to enhance understanding and to differentiate what was previously undifferentiated.

Categorization by maturity of end-user computing

Chapter 2 dealt with the Nolan stage model for the evolution of information systems in an organization. Huff *et al.* (1988) have adapted this approach to consider the development of end-user computing specifically. As with the Nolan model the importance lies in identifying the stage of growth associated with the organization. This provides a guide to obtaining the most effective management strategy for the process of growth to the next stage of maturity. The model has five stages, in which the degree of integration of the applications is taken as the measure of maturity:

1. **Isolation:** Applications are developed in an individually uncoordinated way. There is no exchange of data between applications. The developments are more associated with learning than with enhancing productivity.

2. **Stand-alone:** Applications development takes place at a greater rate. These are still 'stand-alone' applications developed and used generally on personal computers. There is no exchange of data between applications. Individuals come to depend on their own applications development support to enhance their productivity. Data, if shared with other applications, is rekeyed in.

3. **Manual integration:** The next stage is where the need for significant exchanges of data is recognized. This may occur through the physical exchange of disks or through the downloading of files over a local area network. Issues of standards in hardware, software and communications become more important.

4. **Automated integration:** This stage differs from the previous one chiefly in that the trend towards automation of data exchange increases. Integration and the need to exchange data are now considered in applications development and design. End-user exchange of data still requires substantial knowledge of the location of data, and exchange is only effected by transfer commands.

5. **Distributed integration:** Here the physical location of data becomes transparent to the user. Network or other software handles the data supply. The application serving the end user may use data fully distributed across a network.

If organizations are to proceed in their growth towards maturity in end-user computing, then management must plan to move smoothly from one stage to the next. It is particularly important to emphasize standardization issues in order to achieve the integration necessary in the later stages.

7.5.3 The benefits of end-user computing

End-user computing confers many benefits on an organization. Among those most commonly identified are the following:

■ End users are now able to satisfy their own requirements in many cases. This cuts the waiting period resulting from the backlog of applications awaiting development in the computer centre.

■ Innovation and control over one's own information provision stimulated by end-user computing encourages autonomy and responsibility in users.

■ End users are able to translate their information requirements into applications without the need to transfer these via an analyst/programmer, who will not in general be an expert in the application area. This reduces one of the main difficulties in systems development – that of designing a system that meets user requirements.

- End users are able to release analyst/programming staff for other uses. In particular, centralized resources such as the corporate database will not be developed or controlled by end users.

- End users are able to adapt their systems to their needs as they evolve.

7.5.4 The risks of end-user computing

Its liberating impact has undoubtedly been a major force in the growth of end-user computing. However, there are risks and pitfalls that can easily remove corporate advantages or create corporate problems. These may occur even if the benefits to the performance of the individual are realized. Many risks concern proliferation without standardization. Among these, the following are the most important:

- Quality assurance may be diminished in end-user applications development as compared with centralized systems analysis and design. Centralized control, combined with the knowledge that a lack of quality control would revisit the programmers and analysts at a later date, meant that quality issues have always been accorded a high priority in traditional computing centres. The potential anarchy, especially at the earlier stages of the growth to maturity of an organization's end-user computing, can yield problems. This may be revealed in a number of ways:
  - poor development methodologies, which yield error-prone applications;
  - incomplete testing;
  - inadequate or non-existent development documentation and user manuals – both may make it difficult for anyone but the developer to use the system;
  - inadequate access control, backup and archiving.

- Computer centre analysts are used to making complete systems specifications. The end-user developer is far more likely to be interested in a swift development without the need to produce a complete specification. The familiarity that users have with their own requirements can be a drawback. The systems analyst may be able to provide insights with a more general questioning approach.

- At the later stages of mature growth, when end-user applications involve the manipulation of shared data, the absence of controls on data may yield data integrity problems.

- Unless there are mechanisms in place for directed growth, unrelated applications in different areas of the organization may be created that duplicate each other. Although this can create waste, it should be borne in mind that other benefits, such as the creation of user autonomy and responsibility, must be offset against this.

- Costs of hardware and software need to be monitored. If the growth of end-user computing does not proceed in parallel with central policies on purchase standardization and bulk purchase discounts then the benefits will be jeopardized.

- End-user applications are likely to service local needs and objectives. This is only beneficial to the organization if these are congruent with and support global corporate objectives.

- There is a risk that users produce private and informal information systems that run counter to company policy or against the law. Compliance with data protection legislation is one known area of difficulty.

Mini case 7.5

Instant messaging

It is free and in recent years it has spread like wildfire. Instant messaging (IM) began life in the mid-1990s as a text-based, pop-up window chat service beloved by teenagers.

Since then, IM has grown by leaps and bounds and has penetrated the highest echelons of corporate life – often without IT support or sanction. 'IM provides the immediacy of the telephone without the interruption, and the convenience of e-mail without the delay,' notes Ipswitch, a US-based IM software vendor.

Many participants are 'stealth users', using consumer IM systems on an informal basis without the knowledge or approval of their IT department, noted the analysts.

Inevitably this makes IT departments and a growing number of corporate managers very nervous. They fear that these unmanaged consumer-based IM services pose a number of potential risks.

In particular they worry that confidential or sensitive data could 'leak' out past the corporate firewall during online chat sessions. In addition IT departments in particular argue that unmanaged IM services represent a security threat in terms of both hackers and viruses.

Advocates argue that aside from being fun to use, IM can be a valuable business tool enhancing productivity, encouraging collaboration and enabling employees to improve relationships with customers and conduct business online.

Another key benefit of hosted IM services is their ability to detect online 'presence' – whether or not someone in a user's 'buddy list' is online. This feature is exploited in the latest version of Microsoft Office – Office System 2003 – to help facilitate collaboration between co-workers.

Adapted from: **Headache or instant cure?**
By Paul Taylor
FT.com site: 26 November 2003

Questions

1. In what ways might instant messaging be a valuable business communications tool?
2. Why might IT departments be nervous about this use of information systems?

7.5.5 End-user applications development and management

If the corporate benefits from end-user computing are to be realized then ultimately the organization must proceed to the final stages of the Huff model – that is, to distributed integration. This requires a responsible role to be taken both by the computer centre and by the end users themselves.

The role of the computer centre

- **Standard setting:** Standards need to be set, monitored and maintained for end-user computing. These will apply to hardware, software, systems analysis and design, documentation, data structure definition, data communications, access, security, and the privacy of personal data. It is not an easy task for the computer centre to ensure that these standards are adhered to and at the same time create the necessary climate of autonomy within which end-user computing can flourish.

- **Communications and networks:** As well as maintaining standards for communications and networks, it is likely that the computer centre will be responsible for the provision and maintenance of a cross-organizational local area network. This is key to successful integrated end-user computing as well as bringing benefits such as electronic mail and the sharing of scarce resources.

- **Training:** The computer centre is usually responsible for training end users in the use of development packages. As well as providing end users with the necessary skills, this is also an important mechanism for developing a culture of standards following.

- **Data administration:** The computer centre will also be responsible for defining the corporate data structure so that it meets the needs of the organization, including those of end users.

- **Research:** End users will rely on the computer centre to be continually aware of developments in the software and hardware market. The mature computer centre is providing a research service to ensure that the needs of end users are satisfied.

The role of end users

- **Applications portfolio identification:** One of the benefits conferred by end-user computing is the autonomy granted to the development of applications meeting user requirements. However, this should not be done independently of corporate objectives; nor should it be done in isolation from similar or complementary developments in other departments. It may be the case that cross-departmental applications are implemented. This coordination facility is not easily established.

- **Applications development and implementation:** End-user departments are responsible for applications development. This must be in accordance with policies and standards set out by the computer centre.

- **Applications operation:** As the end user is responsible for the application the end user is also responsible for security. This includes following procedures for secure access, backup and recovery. Once again, it is usual that standards in these areas will be set by the computer centre.

Influences on end-user computing development

Managerial approaches to end-user computing should be designed to create effects in accordance with the information systems strategy of the organization. The aims will always attempt to maximize the benefits and minimize the disadvantages of end-user computing. Two important influences on end-user computing need to be managed (Munro *et al.*, 1987):

1. the rate of expansion of end-user computing;
2. the level of control over end-user computing activities.

The rate of expansion is managed by (1) making hardware and software easier/more difficult to obtain; (2) making information easier/more difficult to obtain; and (3) imposing/relieving the end-user departments of the costs of end-user computing. The level of control over activities is managed by (1) more or less restrictive standards over the purchase of hardware/software; (2) the level of requirement of mainframe use compared with PC use for applications; and (3) restrictions on access to data.

In general, the organization can manage the rate of expansion to yield a high or low rate of growth of end-user computing. Similarly, by using the above levers the

Figure 7.5 The expansion/control matrix for end-user computing

organization can ensure a high or low level of control over end-user activities. The matrix of possibilities that this yields is shown in Figure 7.5. High expansion strategies are associated with forcing the growth of end-user computing in order to obtain its benefits. High control strategies are aimed at limiting the disadvantages of end-user computing, particularly those associated with lack of standards, duplication and waste. As can be seen, there are four broad possible mixes of strategy:

1. *Laissez-faire*: This is the 'no policy' situation. End-user computing is neither encouraged nor controlled. This state typifies the early stages of the organizational growth path – either the isolation or the stand-alone stage in the Huff growth model.

2. **Containment:** Here the organization concentrates its strategies on channelling any end-user activities. The growth of end-user computing is not organizationally encouraged by its policies, yet it is recognized that where such activities occur they must be controlled lest organizational disadvantages result.

3. **Acceleration:** The policies adopted by an organization wishing to 'kick start' end-user computing will stimulate growth of activity without emphasis being placed on control. An organization adopting policies within this quadrant will be risk-taking. This is unusual, as it is consonant with a planned diminution of computer centre control.

4. **Controlled growth:** Policies are in place to encourage expansion and at the same time to ensure a directed effort at the organizational level. This is a characteristic of a mature level of organizational end-computer development and activity. It corresponds to a situation in which the roles of the end users and of the computer centre as identified in the previous two sections are fully realized.

In summary, the essence of the analysis of Munro *et al.* is that there are just two dimensions to manage with respect to end-user computing: the rate of expansion and the level of control over activities. Depending on how these are managed, the organization's end-user computing will fall broadly into one of the four categories (although in reality these categories shade into one another).

Generic management strategies for end-user computing

Gerrity and Rockart (1986) defined four generic management strategies for end-user computing. These offer a different perspective on the management of end-user computing from that of Huff *et al.* in the previous section, although one that is not necessarily in conflict with it. The four generic strategies are examined below.

1. With the **monopolistic approach**, the computer centre attempts to block the development of end-user computing. This is not so much a strategy for management as a strategy for prevention. It can only succeed for a short time. The pressures, mentioned earlier, fuelling the growth of end-user computing eventually make this policy untenable. In particular, the combination of the backlog of applications waiting for development, the increasing computer literacy of end users and the decreasing cost/increasing power of desktop computers and software ensure that this policy ultimately fails.

2. The *laissez-faire* approach involves doing nothing to stimulate, prevent or interfere with the growth or control of end-user computing. Once again this is not so much a policy for the management of end-user computing as the absence of one. With *laissez-faire*, end-user computing may initially flourish, but the problems associated with lack of control soon start to arise. In particular, the inevitable lack of standards causes difficulties. In addition, the duplication of end-user effort, poor selection of inappropriate (and often expensive) hardware and software, and the lack of training make this an untenable generic policy in the long run.

3. The **information centre approach** offers both support and control. The computer centre designates specific groups of staff who are assigned to respond to the needs of end-user computing. These needs could be for training, package support and installation, analysis of needs, production of user support documentation, or applications development. The emphasis is on creating an organizational culture of support for end-user computing. The identified support groups are decentralized from the computer centre. However, because these groups are organizationally linked to the computer centre and are themselves computing professionals they will ensure that proper standards are maintained over the development and use of end-user applications. This is a common approach in many organizations. However, its very strength – the presence of computer professionals in a support role, thus ensuring standards – is also a weakness. The support personnel will still not have the requisite knowledge of the business activities they support.

4. In the **management of the free economy approach,** the relationship between the computer centre and the end users is altered. This approach recognizes the importance of providing end users the freedom to define their own needs while providing the skilled support needed to guide development and ensure standards. The balance is achieved by following a number of guidelines:

    (a) A clear statement of the strategy for end-user computing is needed. This should be a senior management function, which must identify the role of end-user computing within the information systems strategy and the business strategy.

    (b) Balance between the responsibilities of the computer centre and of the end users must be clearly articulated.

    (c) The provision of end-user support should be by an information centre independent of the computer centre. In this way, end users will be assured of their autonomy.

    (d) Identification of a range of critical end-user applications must be made. These are then given a high organizational priority.

    (e) There is a continuing emphasis on improvement, growth and autonomy for end-user computing through the use of education.

The management of end-user computing is regarded as important, yet there is no received wisdom on the most appropriate strategy. For other views, see Galletta and Hufnagel (1992) and Clark (1992).

Mini case 7.6

Customizing personal portals

A corporate intranet is an internal network architecture based on Internet standards. Users access it through the same browser software that they use on the Internet to access sites on the World Wide Web. They can use the browser to search internal websites for information they need to find to solve problems. It is essentially a static information delivery system.

A 'personal' or 'workspace' portal, in comparison, creates a single, coherent, integrated interface to the corporate intranet.

It is interactive and designed to present users with access to all the information and services they need to carry out their jobs. It provides them with access to management information and decision support tools to improve their decision making.

It also gives them all the daily services they need, such as contacts, calendar, scheduling, electronic mail, word processing, news, stock quotes, employee self-service applications, workflow and collaboration. Lastly, it can provide the powerful search and document management functionality that gives access to all the organization's knowledge on the corporate intranet.

Eventually, users will be able to customize their own portal themselves, until it is so comprehensive they never need to leave it. It will change the way you work, but unless your organization has properly addressed the many cultural implications of portals, the opportunity could be wasted.

Adapted from: **Intranets and portals**
By Rod Newing
FT.com site: 15 October 2003

Questions

1. Define the terms 'personal portal' and 'corporate intranet'. What are the main differences between these concepts?

2. What advantages and disadvantages can be gained from allowing end-users the freedom to tailor their personal portal?

End-user applications development – prototyping

One method of developing an application is to carry out the process of development through a series of linear stages. In this approach, the computer centre is heavily involved at all times. The process can be summarized in the following way:

A user department identifies a need satisfiable by a computerized system. The computer centre will investigate and provide a feasibility study and report. If this report and its cost implications are accepted by management then computer centre personnel carry out a detailed analysis of the data and activities and specify a systems design that will satisfy these. Upon acceptance of the design, the computer centre develops software, purchases and installs hardware, tests the system and finally hands it to the end users for ongoing use.

The previous paragraph summarizes a linear approach to systems development. Each stage of the project is completed before proceeding to the next. Clear specifications and reports are provided at each stage. The computer centre is responsible for managing and working on what may be a very large project, involving many staff, with a large budget, to be developed over a lengthy period. This approach is at odds with the type of end-user development examined in the preceding sections. In the linear approach, end users have no involvement at most stages in the development process. The linear approach has had numerous significant successes (and some failures!) in the design and delivery of large, well-defined systems. The approach is covered extensively in later chapters on structured process and data analysis, design and implementation. However, it may not be the best way forward for the development of decision support systems, where end-user knowledge and involvement are important and there are applications development tools and 4GLs. In this case, **prototyping**, involving end users, may be the most appropriate development method.

Prototyping is the approach where systems are developed swiftly, without having undergone a complete analysis and specification. The system that is developed is known as the **prototype**. The process relies on the prototype system itself being an aid to the specification – by consideration of the prototype and identification of its weaknesses an improved version can be developed. Prototyping also relies on the presence of software tools to produce prototypes quickly. Typically, users take part in the prototyping process either with or without the aid of the computer centre. The process is thus heavily user-oriented. There are two types of prototype:

1. **Discardable prototypes:** In this situation, the prototype is produced and assessed as to its suitability in meeting user needs. An operational version of the system is then written, usually in a third-generation language such as C++ or Java, and is used for ongoing work. Discardable prototypes are developed when there is a need to produce a final version that is technically efficient in the way it uses computing power. This is most common if a large volume of data needs manipulation. The discardable prototype written in the 4GL may have been produced quickly and is unlikely to use code that is efficient. Other features, such as error-checking routines and security, will need to be added to the final operational system.

2. **Operational prototypes:** In the development of a system using prototyping, it is not uncommon for a first prototype written in a 4GL to be refined and replaced by a second. This in turn may undergo successive alterations until a final version that satisfies the user is good enough to become a working version. At the various stages of development and use, the prototype is always thought of as being the current version open to change as needs arise. The approach is only possible through the use of fast systems-building tools and 4GLs. The process of development is one of iteration.

Advantages of prototyping

- By using prototyping, it is possible to obtain working versions of a system very quickly, often within days. This is particularly important where decision support systems are involved. With these systems, as dictated by the varying information needs of management in making decisions, the type of computer-based support needed may vary within a short period of time. It is not easy for linear methods, with their long lead times, to be so responsive.

- Often it is difficult to provide clear, detailed specifications for the requirements of a system. This may be because these requirements are not readily understood. With a linear approach, it is assumed that there is a clear understanding of both the current set of operations and those that need to be computerized. Unless this condition is met, developers may be forced into some type of prototyping, which can, among other advantages, be viewed as a systems specification method.

- Prototyping is end-user driven. It should therefore meet the requirements of end users. Involvement in the development of a system is one of the ways in which a user gains confidence and understanding of the system. This in turn increases the likelihood of a system being successful. Many of the benefits of end-user computing are realized with the prototyping approach to development.

- A system developed through operational prototyping is capable of easy adaptation.

Disadvantages of prototyping

- Because of prototyping's iterative nature, there is no clearly defined deliverable or completion deadline. This may give rise to considerable management concern. One of the guidelines of project management is to specify deliverables, deadlines and budgets. None of these clearly fits the prototyping approach.

- As has been stated above, the prototyping approach is aimed at obtaining speedily working systems meeting user requirements in terms of functionality. Code inefficiencies may be a drawback.

Prototyping is most appropriate in the following situations:

- The user finds it difficult to define the requirements of the system clearly.
- It is important to develop a system quickly – this is often the case with systems needed for decision support.
- User satisfaction, understanding and confidence are important considerations.
- Appropriate development tools are available.
- Users are committed to being involved with applications development.
- End-user autonomy is regarded as important.
- Low-volume transaction processing is involved.

Prototyping is least likely to be appropriate when:

- Appropriate development tools are not available and not understood by the users/computer centre.
- End users are unwilling to commit the necessary development time to prototype development.
- High-volume transaction processing is required.
- Technical efficiency in the use of computer-processing resources is a high priority.

Prototyping has become an increasingly important element in applications development. The nature of decision support systems and their relation to end-user computing has contributed to this growth. Prototyping is also an important component of approaches such as rapid applications development (RAD) using CASE tools. These are covered in Chapter 16.

7.5.6 Desktop applications and programming languages

At the time when the personal computer first became a significant factor in business computing there was a clear distinction between the programming environments available for developing software and the desktop packages employed in end-user computing. Programming was a separate activity leading to the development of unique products tailored to meet particular user requirements, whereas desktop applications such as spreadsheets and databases were largely purchased and used without modification.

The development of desktop applications

The arrival of desktop computing packages such as word processors, spreadsheets and databases put computing power onto the desktop. These packages eliminated the need for many areas of development that had traditionally been carried out through the use of high-level languages. Desktop computer users, however, still wanted the facility to tailor their systems to perform job-specific tasks. The early desktop applications usually included facilities to create **macros**; these are collections of instructions that can be recorded as a single named sequence of activities, then replayed to automate a particular task. Gradually, the macro facilities became more sophisticated and became more like programming languages in their own right.

Programming for a graphical user interface

The rapid growth of graphical user interfaces such as Windows as a standard environment for the desktop PC required extensions to high-level programming languages or the creation of new languages to build the new interfaces. The extensions to some languages, such as C++, resulted in a very complex range of programming tools and libraries, putting the development of Windows-like software clearly in the hands of experienced software developers only. Other programming environments, such as Microsoft's Visual Basic, provided a simple language and an easy-to-use set of tools, which made it possible for end users to construct desktop applications with potentially mission-critical importance. Several large organizations began to question traditional methods of systems development, which were proving to be costly and unreliable, and consider a move to applications development using these new end-user approaches. This is discussed in more detail in later chapters.

The merging of end-user packages and programming environments

The demand for more sophisticated tools to be provided in desktop applications has continued to grow. The traditional macro has not proved powerful enough to enable end users to produce the solutions they require. Software vendors have now, as a result, incorporated the power of the visual programming language into the desktop application. This allows users to enhance the built-in facilities of the application, whether word processor, spreadsheet or database, by building a front end or interface and some application logic to meet their own particular requirements.

This blurring of applications packages and programming environments is likely to continue as applications development for the Internet becomes a more prevalent programming activity. End users are now looking for their desktop packages to be 'Web-enabled' to allow, for example, access to database tables over the Internet. Similarly, programming languages that are used to create Web applications are constantly being enhanced to provide stronger integration with desktop applications. This strategy has been adopted in Microsoft's .NET approach.

7.6   Human–computer interaction

Early in the development of business information systems, it was realized that the way the screen or printed output was designed influenced the ease and accuracy with which users understood the information supplied by the computer. It was also recognized that input screen design was also crucial to input performance and accuracy.

Attention was given to the design of the **man–machine interface** (**MMI**), as it was then called, in order to ensure maximum effectiveness of the information system. Concerns concentrated on presenting information that was necessary and sufficient to user needs and to present that information in the most uncluttered way. Determination of what information was necessary and sufficient was achieved through a careful analysis of the task for which the user needed the information. (The reader's attention is drawn to the section on input/output design in Chapter 15 for further coverage of related issues.)

It is now recognized that this approach is no longer sufficient, for the following reasons:

- The development of decision support systems has brought with it a recognition of the change of emphasis from information supplied in order to perform a task to information supplied in order to support a decision. As has been stressed earlier in the chapter, and in Chapter 1, the use of the computer for decision support involves not only an analysis of the decision but also the decision maker's cognitive style, the objectives of the decision and the organizational setting within which the decision is taken. The focus on screen design is no longer sufficient.

- The increase in end-user computing, particularly the involvement of end users in applications development, has meant that designers of development tools are required to take into account the background, skills and objectives of these end users. Without attention to this point, development tools could well turn out to be technically powerful but unusable.

- Developments in computing power and the sophistication of software, particularly dealing with graphics, have led to a range of pictorial screen possibilities. This has made possible a much richer set of methods of communication with the user. It is easier to take into account the vastly increased range of people using computers and the purposes for which they use them.

- Failure of computers to achieve the business objectives for which they were designed has often been put down to user resistance and a failure to take into account user needs (as distinct from the information a user requires to perform a task). Several studies on the introduction of new technologies, including information technology, suggest that designers need to extend their focus beyond the narrow technical system to be designed. They should also take into account the interrelationship between the technical system, the tasks to be performed, the people involved in these and the organizational setting.

All of the above has shifted the emphasis from the man–machine interface as the focus of design to a consideration of the interaction of the human with the computer systems in an organizational setting. This is the study of **human–computer interaction** (**HCI**).

The phrase 'human–computer interaction' appeared in the mid-1980s. There are many definitions. The following gives a picture of the scope of the term:

Human–computer interaction is a discipline concerned with the design, evaluation and implementation of interactive computing systems for human use and with the study of the major phenomena surrounding them.

(ACM SIGCHI, 1992, p. 6)

It is important to realize that what distinguishes human–computer interaction is the last phrase – 'the study of the major phenomena surrounding them'. This goes far beyond the scope of input/output screen design.

The major features of human–computer interaction design for computerized information systems are:

- The approach is user-centred. End users are involved as much as possible in the design process. Involvement may occur through users building systems with user-oriented development tools or by participation in the analysis and design process.
- The approach integrates knowledge from a wide range of disciplines. The major influential disciplines in the area of human–computer interaction are shown in Figure 7.6.
- Rather than the development of a system occurring in a linear fashion (analysis through design to implementation), the process of design involves iteration of various stages. Often this involves the building of prototypes, which can be used to test the efficiency of the human–computer interaction.

Figure 7.6 Influential disciplines on human–computer interaction

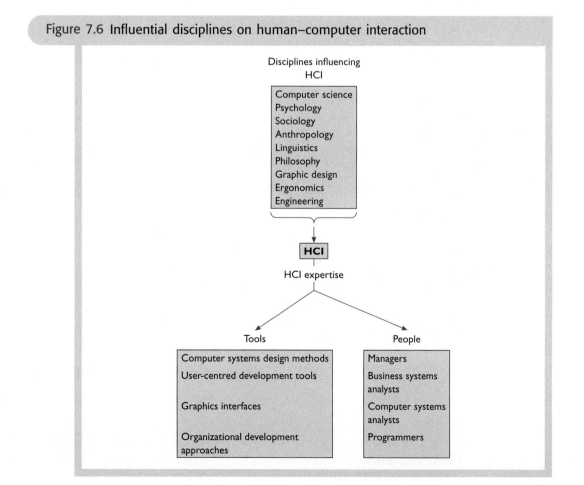

In order to account properly for the human in human–computer interaction design, it has been necessary to utilize a model of the human within the process.

Mini case 7.7

HCI and website design

'There are 20 million sites on the Web, and nearly all of them are awful.' So says Jakob Nielsen, perhaps the best-known design and usability guru on the Internet. When people design websites, he complains, they rely too much on their own perceptions of style and aesthetics without giving enough thought to how the average user, dialling up on a slow connection and lacking the sophisticated aesthetic sensibilities of a design professional, will explore the site.

As a result, users get frustrated with their surfing experience, get bored with trying to fight their way through the pretty graphics to find what they really want, and become more and more ruthless in their judgement of sites. If a site has not delivered what the user wants in a few seconds, one click and they're off to a competitor. Which means lost profits to the website owner.

Nielsen aims to bring the neglected disciplines of user testing and proper design to the Internet.

How can it be that so many commercial websites, often costing hundreds of thousands of pounds to design, turn out to be so awful? Easy, says Nielsen: they are built not for the end user but for the designer's boss – often the marketing department or the chief executive of the client company.

'Too many sites are there to make the hierarchy happy. They are judged only from the inside, and that is no good – users are coming from the outside. Insiders think: how are we presenting ourselves? Outsiders think: how do I get the information?'

However well-designed your site, though, remember that most sites today can only be viewed on PCs, cautions Don Norman. In the near future, other technology platforms, like mobile phones and hand-held computers, will be used to access the Internet. These hardware platforms themselves are poorly adapted to the Internet, he believes, and will have to be redeveloped.

'A lot of this technology was not designed with the end user in mind – it's not human-centred design,' says Norman. Today's WAP phones, for example, are far from ideal, with their clunky, alphanumeric keyboards and cramped screens.

As examples of good hardware design, he points to the Internet radio from Kerbango, which looks like a normal radio but actually tunes in to broadcasts on the Internet. Psion's hand-held computers are also excellent, he says, as are some of the new MP3 players, portable devices that play music files downloaded from the Web.

Nielsen and Norman have a simple piece of advice for this Christmas: set yourself the goal of buying half of your presents online this year. 'And,' Nielsen chuckles, 'learn about design through personal suffering.'

Adapted from: **Simple is best when it comes to website design**
FT.com: 28 November 2000

Questions

1. Why does Jakob Nielsen believe that most websites are, in his words, awful?
2. What steps can be taken to ensure that the HCI is better designed?

Figure 7.7 The human information processor model

7.6.1 The human information processor model

One of the most influential models derives from the area of cognitive psychology, in which the human is treated as an information processor. The human information processor model starts out from the basis that information enters via the senses through the processes of attention and perception. Decoding of information takes place and comparison of the internal representation of the information is made with the internal representations in the memory. A response is selected, executed and output. In the model, information is processed in a linear manner (see Figure 7.7). By concentrating on the sequence of operations and their timing, a proper account can be taken of the human in human–computer interaction. Areas of general interest, among others, would be:

- how information is perceived and encoded;
- how information/knowledge is represented in memory;
- how comparisons are made;
- how information is stored and retrieved from memory;

and specifically on:

- how humans represent models of familiar objects to themselves;
- how users learn to use computer systems.

The human information processor model has been profoundly influenced by the development of computing itself. More sophisticated versions of the simplified model outlined here have included, for example, analogues of serial and parallel processing, and of buffer stores.

7.6.2 The distributed cognition approach

The human information processor model has recognized that the human is more than merely the provider of information to, and receiver of information from, the interface with a computer system. The user has a task to perform and will process information internally for the execution of this task. The basis of the approach assumes that an understanding of the internal processing in the mind of the user will enable the design of a better interactive system.

Later approaches to human–computer interaction recognize that the human information processor model is too limited. Its concentration on the individual, the computer and the task leaves out important dimensions of human–computer interaction. Specifically:

- Users do not carry out individual information-processing tasks in theoretical settings. Rather, the user performs part of a complex function involving many interrelated tasks for a purpose.
- This function occurs in a real organizational setting.
- Users interact with one another, particularly in teams.

Distributed cognition is an evolving theoretical framework for human–computer interaction that takes account of these points. The approach goes beyond the individual to viewing activities as involving the interaction of people, technology and tasks in an organizational setting (see Figure 7.8). The emphasis is on the study and design of functional systems that concentrate on the way information is transmitted and processed through the various components of the system in order to perform a function such as accounting control. The components will include computers and humans. This and similar approaches have influenced the development of systems design methodologies. See, for example, the socio-technical approach and soft systems analysis – both covered in Chapter 16.

Figure 7.8 Human–computer interaction in an organizational setting

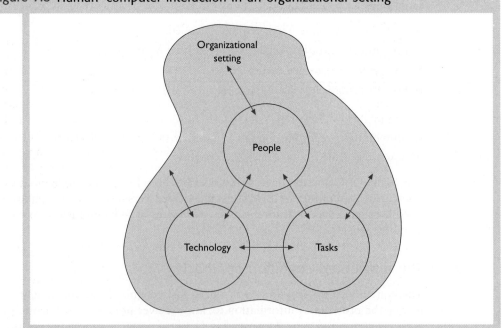

Human–computer interaction involves concepts that pervade many aspects of the analysis, design and use of information systems. The reader is referred to other parts of this text, particularly input/output design, Windows interfaces, socio-technical design, soft systems analysis, knowledge representation techniques, group decision support and prototyping.

Summary

The last four decades has seen the rapid improvement and extensive use of the computer in business data processing and information provision. Decision support systems make use of many of these aspects of modern technology. They aid, rather than replace, decision making. They may involve the selection and analysis of data from a corporate database, the use of models for predicting outcomes, optimization techniques, or the application of details of particular cases to general rules in order to support decisions. Decision support systems allow flexible access to data and the interactive use of models. These systems supply information to managers for semi-structured problems.

In the design of decision support systems, the emphasis is on stand-alone systems rather than the grand design of the total integrated decision support system. Because the development of a decision support system is driven by the type of decision-making process and the information needs of the decision, end users play a prominent role in design. Fourth-generation languages, spreadsheets, expert system shells and tools, and model generators are all used in decision support system (DSS) design.

Group decision support systems are a more recent development that takes account of the fact that many decisions are taken in group situations. The group decision support system involves not only standard technology for decision support but also specific software to aid group activities such as brainstorming, voting and policy formation. Group decision support takes place in carefully constructed environments with an experienced facilitator to enhance the decision process.

End-user computing has been fuelled by the need to develop systems, particularly decision support systems, that speedily meet the needs of users. This has been facilitated by the presence of easy-to-use enabling software. 'End users' is a term covering a wide range of individuals, involving different types of skill and different information requirements. The growth of end-user computing progresses through several stages in an organization, depending on the level of integration of applications. At all stages, to be successful it is necessary to manage the process. The computer centre is expected to set standards and also to take on the role of the provision of training, education and technical support to end users in the development of their own systems. There are several different approaches to the management of end-user computing. One emphasizes the importance of managing the balance between control and expansion. Another concentrates on the role of end-user support and examines the information centre concept.

The traditional linear development process for systems, where progression is through a number of stages culminating in final implementation, may not be appropriate for the production of decision support systems. Prototyping is an alternative that is compatible with the need to develop systems quickly in situations where a clear specification is not available, when there is a need to involve users in development, and there is a desire to create adaptable responsive systems. Discardable prototyping is the approach that views the role of the prototype as the specification of the functionality of the desired system. The final version is written to ensure greater technical efficiency in computer processing. In operational prototyping, the prototype is successively and interactively refined until it becomes the final version. Prototyping has been made possible by the design of 4GLs and applications development tools.

Developments in decision support systems, the rise of end-user computing and prototyping have emphasized the need for a theory on the way in which the user interacts with computer systems. The study of human–computer interaction provides this. Approaches that look merely at input/output screen design have been superseded by those that regard the user as an information processor in performing a task (human information processor model). Later approaches have attempted to remedy the limitations of this approach by concentrating on the functions performed by users and technology in a real organizational setting.

Review questions

1. Why has there been a movement towards the use of microcomputers in large organizations rather than relying wholly on centralized mainframe resources staffed by experienced and highly trained personnel?

2. Identify characteristics of a decision support system and explain how these distinguish decision support systems from the more general notion of an information system.

3. What classes of decision support system are there? Give examples of each.

4. What are the risks associated with end-user computing? How can they be reduced?

5. What is the difference between a *computer centre* and an *information centre*?

6. What are the main features and benefits of prototyping?

7. Distinguish between *input/output design* and *human–computer interaction design*.

Exercises

1. In Chapter 1, decision making was divided into four stages. The first three were intelligence, design and choice. By selecting an appropriate example, illustrate how decision support systems can be used in each of these stages.

2. Why are there many different types of aid and approach to the development of decision support systems?

3. What special advantages do spreadsheets confer over the use of pen and paper in accounting modelling?

4. Why is it important to have a facilitator in group decision making using a decision room?

5. What characteristics of group decision making distinguish it from individual decision making? How could these be supported by a GDSS?

6. By considering the classification of types of end user, identify the types of training and support needed for each.

7. As a senior manager working in an organization that can best be described as adopting the monopolistic approach to end-user computing, what policies would you wish to see adopted in order to transform the management of end-user computing to a managed free-economy model?

8. You have been commissioned to conduct a third-party investigation into decision support systems as used in ABC Co. This has revealed that many departments are developing their own applications independently and without the knowledge of the computer centre. The computer centre has traditionally taken a very strong line against end-user computing and has been unwilling to provide support for end-user applications development. In the current situation, the proliferation of end-user decision support systems involves duplication of resources, data and applications. The culture of senior management is one of centralized control. How would you advise the company to proceed?

9. For each of the disciplines mentioned in Figure 7.6, discuss how these may be of use in HCI design.

10. Outline the main differences in approach between the human information processor model and the distributed cognition model to understanding human–computer interaction.

CASE STUDY 7

End-user computing

Fusty, Dusty and Crusty are a partnership of solicitors specializing in property work such as probate and conveyancing. Eleven solicitors are employed, supported by eight secretaries, an accountant and an IT manager.

The practice is well equipped with IT facilities, and most employees are IT literate. All employees use a desktop computer; these are linked on a local area network, which provides access to a file server containing the applications software and all of the details relating to clients and cases.

To assist work flow each case is identified by a unique case number. All work in the practice, including invoicing and payments, revolves around the use of this case number.

Letters arriving in the daily post are scanned electronically by a secretary and stored in the designated file locations. Partners are notified by e-mail of newly scanned postal items and access them by the case number. A separate directory, named using the case number, is created on the file server for each case. This provides shared access to the information about cases for all partners and secretaries in the practice.

Once working on a particular case, solicitors and their clerks might need to access a number of other electronic documents. Examples of these might be standard word-processed template letters notifying clients of recent developments in the case, or requests for further information. When a standard letter is used for a particular client, the amended version is saved in the directory for that particular case, thereby joining the history of documents issued.

Recently, a problem has been identified in terms of work flow. The secretaries are fairly well skilled at scanning and storing the daily post, but occasionally they will misread a case number and store a scanned item in an incorrect directory. More frequent problems are created by the partners. It is common for a solicitor searching for an item to look in the wrong directory. Being less well versed in IT, they often abandoned the search and

►

Figure 7.9 Dialogue boxes for work flow system: (a) 'Safe Open' Dialogue box; (b) 'Safe Save' Dialogue box

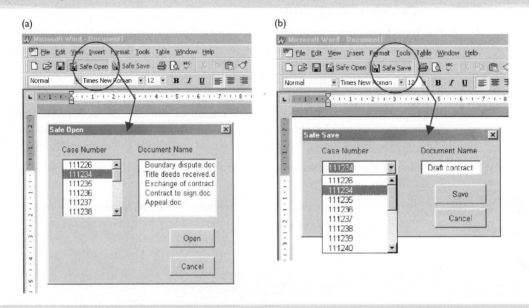

sent a note to the secretarial team asking for assistance. The most common and potentially most damaging problem of all is in the use of standard letters. A solicitor will often locate and amend a standard letter correctly but will then either save the new document back into the directory of standard documents, or on to the local hard disk, or to the wrong case number. These 'lost' documents lead to countless difficulties, particularly when a client telephones and requests advice on the status of their case.

One of the partners has devised a potential solution to some of these problems. Using the programming facilities built into the word-processing package, she has devised a new dialogue box for opening and saving documents. Rather than allowing the user a free choice of where the document is stored, a pull-down list of directories is provided. When a document relating to a case is opened the case number is 'remembered' by the system; later, the correct case number directory is offered automatically as the location for saving the work.

Figure 7.9 shows the new dialogue boxes in operation. Once the user clicks on the 'Safe Open' button, a dialogue box appears offering a pick-list of case numbers. The correct case number is selected, and the list box on the right is then populated by all the documents relating to that case. The desired document is selected and the 'Open' button is clicked.

Once the user has finished using the document, the 'Safe Close' button is clicked. A dialogue box appears with the case number and document name already selected. If the document had been loaded from the list of templates then the case number would be chosen from the list, or a new case number entered if appropriate. While not completely foolproof, the system limits the possibility of operator error by shielding the user from the entire range of networked and local disk drives and other directory structures available for storing documents.

Questions

1. What are the advantages of scanning the daily post electronically? What additional steps would need to be taken to ensure that documents were safely and permanently archived?

2. Describe how the proposed 'Safe Open' and 'Safe Save' features could promote effective work flow through the solicitors' practice.

3. The example above illustrates how the development of end-user computing can lead to solutions to problems in information systems. What issues arise from this method of development? Should it be encouraged, regulated, restricted or prohibited? Is it an effective way of developing information systems within an overall IT strategy?

4. The system developed could be viewed as a prototype for a more sophisticated solution. Evaluate the approach of investing more resources in developing this prototype further, compared with treating the work done as a throw-away model that forms the basis of a new system being created in a more traditional approach.

References

ACM SIGCHI (1992). *Curriculum for Human–Computer Interaction*. ACM Special Interest Group on Computer–Human Interaction. Curriculum Development Group, New York

Clark T. (1992). Corporate systems management: an overview and research perspective. *Communications of the ACM*, February, 60–75

Fielding R. *et al.* (1998). Web-based development of complex information products. *Communications of the ACM*, August

Galletta D.F. and Hufnagel E.M. (1992). A model of end-user computing policy. *Information and Management*, 22(1), 1–18

Gerrity T.P. and Rockart J.F. (1986). End-user computing: are you a leader or a laggard? *Sloan Management Review*, 27(4), 25–34

Huff S.L., Munro M.C. and Martin B.H. (1988). Growth stages of end-user computing. *Communications of the ACM*, 31(5), 542–50

Munro M.C., Huff S.L. and Moore G. (1987). Expansion and control of end-user computing. *Journal of Management Information Systems*, 4(3), 5–27

Rockart J. and Flannery L. (1983). The management of end-user computing. *Communications of the ACM*, 26(10), 776–84

Singh N. (1998). Unifying heterogeneous information models. *Communications of the ACM*, May 1998

Recommended reading

Chaffey D. (1998). *Groupware, Workflow and Intranets*. Digital
    An interesting overview of the design issues in collaborative applications.

Dix A. *et al.* (2003). *Human Computer Interaction*. Prentice Hall
    A very readable book investigating the usability of computer technology. The book takes a multi-disciplinary approach. Many examples are provided, in particular from web applications.

Edwards J.S. and Finaly P.A. (1997). *Decision Making with Computers: The Spreadsheet and Beyond*. London: Pitman
    Aimed at the reader with existing knowledge of the use of computers and spreadsheets, the book is intended to explain new decision-making techniques that will enable the most effective

use to be made of the spreadsheet facilities. It also contains chapters on the methodology of good spreadsheet design. It is aimed at the business person rather than the computer scientist.

Galitz W. (2002). *The Essential Guide to User Interface Design: An Introduction to GUI Design Principles and Techniques*. Wiley

This describes the fundamentals of good interface design. The book covers a range of GUI applications, including design for the web.

Isaacs E. (2002). *Designing from Both Sides of the Screen: A Dialogue Between a Designer and an Engineer*. Sams

This is equally relevant to software engineers and designers. It covers the principles of good interface design and provides many examples of good and bad practice. An extended case study provides the context for much of the theory.

Marakas G.M. (2003). *Decision Support Systems in the 21st Century*. Prentice Hall

This book covers decision support systems, modelling decision processes, group decision support, knowledge engineering, data warehouses and data mining. It also covers implementing and integrating decision support systems.

Mo A.M. (2003). *Advanced Topics in End User Computing*. Idea Group

This offers a more theoretical and in-depth approach to issues in end-user computing.

Preece J. (1998). *A Guide to Usability: Human Factors in Computing*. Wokingham: Addison-Wesley

This book provides a clear and concise account of the human factors in computing.

Regan E. and O'Connor B. (2001). *End User Information Systems: Implementing Individual and Work Group Technologies*. Prentice Hall

This is written in a style that would be easily accessible to both general managers and those involved in technical support. It covers help desk management, office automation, and a vast range of end-user issues. It also provides techniques in managing projects in this area.

Shneiderman B. (1998). *Designing the User Interface*, 3rd edn. Wokingham: Addison-Wesley

This book provides a straightforward, thorough and relatively jargon-free exposition of the development of effective interactive software.

Thomsen E. (2002). *OLAP Solutions: Building Multidimensional Information Systems*. Wiley

An interesting text covering the technical aspects of data warehousing, data mining, and online analytical processing. Using case studies, it also attempts to explain how these tools and techniques can inform the decision-making process.

Turban E. (2000). *Decision Support and Intelligent Systems*, 6th edn. New York: Macmillan

This is a comprehensive textbook covering all aspects of DSS and expert systems from the perspective of a manager wishing to know about management support technologies. It has several case studies and chapter-end questions.

Chapter 8

File organization and databases for business information systems

Learning outcomes

On completion of this chapter, you should be able to:

- Describe the physical and logical characteristics and structures of computer files and records
- Compare and contrast file-based and database approaches to data management
- Describe alternative approaches to data modelling and database design
- Explain the concept of a data warehouse and describe techniques for extracting data from a data warehouse.

Introduction

This chapter covers the organization, storage of and access to business data held in files and databases. It introduces key concepts in the representation of data at both a logical and a physical level. The central ideas behind files and file access are explained. Files and file-based approaches to data storage are important, but they suffer from limitations. Database systems were developed as a response to these shortcomings. File-based and database approaches to data storage are compared. The central ideas underlying databases and database management systems are explained. As well as highlighting the facilities offered by database systems, the importance of data models is stressed. Three main types of database model are covered – network, hierarchical and relational. The analysis of an organization's data requirements, the development of a data model for that organization and database design techniques are left to Chapter 13 on data analysis and modelling, part of the sequence of chapters on systems analysis and design.

8.1 Files and file structures

The survival and successful growth of a business organization depends crucially on the data it keeps. Whether the business is computerized or not, much of this data will be held in files. A manufacturing company will keep files on its employees, customers, stock supplies, plant and many other items. These files will be updated by data on employee

Figure 8.1 Producing a wage slip by consulting a manual file

hours worked, customer sales and payments, and stock transactions. The files will be searched and sometimes sorted.

Simple concepts used in the operation of manual files are often a good guide to computerized data processing. Figure 8.1 is an illustration of the process of producing a wage slip. Time-sheet data on an employee is taken from a file. The relevant employee record is then found in the employee file. Data from this record is used to produce a wage slip, and the employee record is updated. Exactly the same description could be applied in a computer-based system. The only difference is that the files would be held on tape or disk and the process of producing a wage slip would be handled by a computer program.

Document files in manual systems contain records. For instance, an employee file will contain records on employees. These records are often collections of employee data prepared on preprinted company documentation. Other documents, old references and the like are kept in an individual employee's record. A cursory glance through document files may indicate that there is little organization in them.

By contrast, a **computer file** is more structured. It contains records of the same **record type** rather than a mixed collection of data held in different formats. An example of a simple employee file is shown in Figure 8.2(a). For each employee, data such as the employee # (# is the symbol that commonly abbreviates number), name, date of appointment, salary and sex are held. This data will be used in a number of activities, such as preparing the payroll and establishing the length of service of employees.

Each record is a collection of **data items** on each employee. These data items are also sometimes known as **field values**. For instance, in Figure 8.2(a) the field values are 1234, Yorke, Jones, 14500, etc. The **fields** themselves correspond to the types of data held on the employee and are *employee#, family name, first name, date of appointment, salary* and *sex*.

Figure 8.2 An employee file example: (a) contents of a simple employee file; (b) illustration of the record structure

Figure 8.3 The relation between the world and data

	World	Corresponds to	Data	
Example				**Example**
Thomas Yorke	Object	⟶	Record	1234 Yorke Thomas...
Employee	Object type	⟶	Record type	(employee#, family name...)
Sex	Attribute	⟶	Field	sex
Male	Value of attribute	⟶	Field value or data item	M

The record type (or structure as it is often called) is shown in Figure 8.2(b). Saying that a file contains records of the same record type means that all records in the employee file exhibit that structure. It is important to realize that we know that Yorke is the family name of the employee and Thomas is the first name *not* because of our knowledge of typical family and first names but rather because of the positions of the data items in the record structure.

The distinction between data and the objects in the world on which the data is kept is important. It is necessary to keep this distinction in mind in order to understand some of the modelling ideas covered in Chapter 13 on data analysis and modelling. This is summarized in Figure 8.3.

The **key field** of a record type is an important concept. It is the field that uniquely identifies a record. The key field in the employee record would be *employee#*, because a value such as 1234 will occur in only *one* record. This is the reason that employers are given employee numbers – to identify them and their records. If there are two key fields in a record type, one is called the **primary key**. This is the one that is most likely to be used to pick out the record. For instance, in an employee record the National Insurance number of the employee would also be a key, but the *employee#* would be the primary key.

Obviously, the record structure in Figure 8.2(b) has too few fields to be realistic for an employee file. It is left as an exercise for the reader to list the fields that he or she would expect to find on an employee record type. Think of the processes for which a business might wish to use an employee record. The data needed for these will give a clear indication of which fields should exist.

Records and record structure

A simple record structure consists of a fixed number of fields of a fixed length. The record structure in Figure 8.2(a) is an example of this. A file comprised of records with this simple structure is often referred to as a **flat file** as it can be pictured as repeated rows of identically structured data. There are shortcomings associated with restrictions such as these. An important problem arises with the desire to have many occurrences of the same field in a record. For example, in an employee file it may be useful to hold, not only the current position, date of appointment and salary but also the history of the employee with the organization. One way of achieving this is to have a fixed number of fields set aside for the past history. This may not be satisfactory. An employee may have held only one position with the firm, in which case several fields will be blank, or may have had more positions than can be accommodated by the number of repeated fields. In the latter case, only the most recent history of the employee can be held. The solution is to allow a field or group of fields to be repeated. Figure 8.4(a)

Figure 8.4 (a) A two-dimensional record structure; (b) a three-dimensional record structure

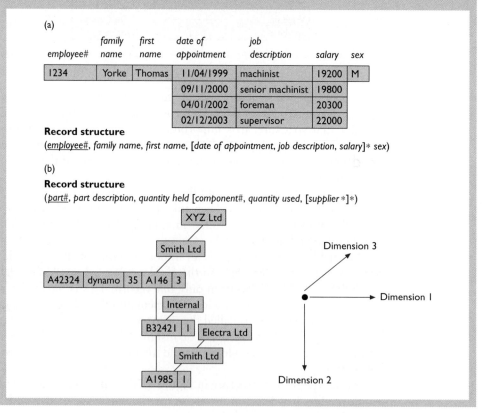

(a)

employee#	family name	first name	date of appointment	job description	salary	sex
1234	Yorke	Thomas	11/04/1999	machinist	19200	M
			09/11/2000	senior machinist	19800	
			04/01/2002	foreman	20300	
			02/12/2003	supervisor	22000	

Record structure
(employee#, family name, first name, [date of appointment, job description, salary]* sex)

(b)
Record structure
(part#, part description, quantity held [component#, quantity used, [supplier *]*)

XYZ Ltd

Smith Ltd

| A42324 | dynamo | 35 | A146 | 3 |

Internal

| B32421 | 1 | Electra Ltd |

Smith Ltd

| A1985 | 1 |

Dimension 3

Dimension 1

Dimension 2

gives an example of this. Note that the key is underlined and that the repeating group of fields is indicated by [field1, field2, . . .]*. The asterisk indicates repetition. The employee record shown is regarded as two-dimensional.

A record structure can have repeating fields within repeating fields. For instance, a record of stock held by a manufacturing company may contain a variable number of fields for the components and for each component a variable number of fields for the suppliers. This is shown in Figure 8.4(b). It is called a three-dimensional record structure.

Record structures can be multidimensional, but details of the number of repeating groups and groups within groups must be held somewhere in the record. When programs are written to obtain information from these files the programmer's task is made considerably more complex. They now need to pay particular attention to the structure of the record as well as to the task for which the obtained data is to be used.

8.3   Physical and logical views of data

An important concept in data processing and systems analysis and design is the difference between a physical and a logical view of data. Broadly speaking, a **logical view** is concerned with the nature of the data or information as viewed independently from the physical details of storage or presentation. In contrast, a **physical view** involves physical aspects of the storage and presentation. The difference is important. A business computer systems analyst will be interested in the nature of the data stored and in what forms it needs to be retrieved. Exactly how this data is stored will be of less interest. Technical details on, say, disk sector division and blocking factors are not needed. The analyst is concerned with the use made of data in the functioning of the business. The technical systems analyst and the programmer, though, must pay attention to physical detail in order to design technically efficient storage and write programs that access data in stored files.

In the present context, the difference between a logical and a physical view of files and record structures can be summarized as follows:

8.3.1 Records

Physical and logical record structures

A logical view of a record structure consists of the names of the record fields, including repeating groups. A logical view of a record (logical record) is the set of data items filling that structure.

A physical view of a record structure shows how the logical view of the structure is implemented. The following, from Figure 8.2, illustrates physical details:

- The *employee#* consists of up to six characters preceded by leading blanks.
- The *family name* and the *first name* consist of characters, the two fields being divided by a *.
- The *salary* consists of a binary number 16 bits long.
- The *date* consists of eight characters representing the year/month/date in that order – for example, 6 February 2003 is represented as 20030206.

A **physical record** is the minimum chunk of data that is transferred between the storage medium and the CPU in the course of data processing. It is sometimes called a block. The physical record may contain many logical records or, if the logical records are large, several physical records may be spanned by one logical record.

Fixed-length and variable-length records

A decision to be taken at the physical level of record design is whether the record structure should be of a predetermined size – a fixed-length record – or whether it should be allowed to expand and contract to accommodate the size of the actual field items stored in it – a variable-length record.

A comparison of fixed- and variable-length records is shown in Figure 8.5. There are advantages and disadvantages to each.

If a variable-length record is used, it is apparent that the storage locations occupied are all gainfully employed, with the small addition of some markers to indicate the end

Figure 8.5 (a) Fixed-length records; (b) variable-length records

(a)

FORENAME	SURNAME	DEPARTMENT	SALARY
Mike-----------	Davies-----------------	Accounts------	–33000
Oliver----------	Smee------------------	Sales---------	–24000
Myra----------	Cottesmore-------------	Marketing------	–45000
Ajay-----------	Yousef-----------------	Finance--------	–45000
Kosoladevi-------	Thirugnansampantamoorthy	Director-------	103000
Ukay-----------	Amponsah--------------	Production----	–64000

Each record shown occupies 55 characters of data storage. The six records require 330 (6 × 55) characters of data storage space. 162 of the characters (almost 50% of the file) are redundant space characters (represented by the – character to make them visible here).

(b)

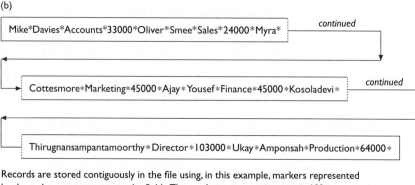

Records are stored contiguously in the file using, in this example, markers represented by the * character to separate the fields. The total storage requirement is 192 characters (including the markers which occupy less than 13% of the file).

of each field. Where a fixed-length structure is operated, the field lengths default to the size of the largest expected item. A large amount of storage space is thus potentially wasted using fixed-length records.

When a query is carried out a record must be located. If all records are of the same length, a simple arithmetic calculation (such as *record number* × *record length*) may lead directly to the position of the required record in the file. Where the records have a variable-length structure a sequential search through all preceding records is required to reach the required record. Searching through a file comprised of variable-length records can therefore take much longer than for fixed-length records.

8.3.2 Files

A **logical** view of a file is the representation of the logical records together with the order in which they are represented for storage and retrieval purposes. For instance, an employee file might have its records arranged in ascending order of employee#, as they were in Figure 8.2.

A **physical** view of a file consists of the way in which the physical records are stored. For example, an employee file can be stored on several disks, with an index stored on a different disk from the disks on which the records are stored. The records can be stored physically adjacent to one another in ascending order of employee#. Once one track is filled, the next track inwards contains the next record. When records are deleted they may not be removed from the disk but merely marked with an X in the delete field of each physical record. These are all physical details of a file.

When programs are written, the programmer will need to be aware of some of the physical structure of the records and the way that the files may be spread across tracks. However, the analyst who is designing the file structure for a system need concentrate initially only on the logical aspects of the files to ensure that the data held is sufficient for the task for which it is required. Later, the analyst will decide on how the file is to be arranged physically. The distinction between logical and physical views is never as clear-cut in practice as has been suggested. Rather, there is a spectrum ranging from logical to physical on which a particular view will lie. As will be demonstrated in Chapters 10–15 on systems analysis and design, the distinction between logical and physical views of data, although difficult to grasp at first, is important because it runs right through the process of analysis and design.

8.4 Data storage – files, records and lists

There are many ways of categorizing files, but in data processing there is an important division of files in terms of their usage: files may be master, transaction or backup files.

1. A **master file** consists of records that contain standing data on entities that are of a permanent nature and are of importance for the successful operation of the business. For example, an employee master file holds the employee name, address and date of birth, all of which need little or no change, together with data on gross pay to date and tax paid to date, which would be regularly updated. Master files can be logically organized in a number of ways. For example, an employee master file may be in employee # sequence or with an index on employee name, or both.

2. A **transaction file** contains records, each of which relates to a single, usually dated, event or fact. These files are source data and are used to amend or update master files. For example, a timesheet transaction file contains records, each of which has data on the number of hours worked by a particular employee.

3. **Backup files** are copies of transaction files and master files held for security purposes.

Files may be physically stored on disk in the following ways:

- **Sequentially:** Records are physically ordered by some field such as employee number.
- **Randomly:** Records are stored at a physical address computed by an algorithm working on a field value such as the employee number.
- **Indexed:** Records are physically stored randomly with a sequentially ordered index field (e.g. by customer name) and a pointer to the physical location of each record.
- **Indexed-sequential:** Records are physically stored sequentially ordered by some field together with an index, which provides access by some, possibly other, field.

If files need only be processed sequentially, then they can be stored sequentially. The sequential update of an employee master file by timesheet data is an example. However, if individual records need to be accessed from time to time by some field, for example employee name, then one of the other storage methods must be used.

In the files considered so far, the individual records have not been connected to one another in any way. With a simple **list structure**, each record has one field in it that points to (has the address of) another record in the structure. Thus a list could be linked by pointer fields that point from one record to another in ascending order of customer name alphabetically. Insertion and deletion of records merely involves the readjustment of pointers. Sequential processing involves passing along the list. List structures may be extremely complex, with many pointer fields in each record, so that records can be accessed sequentially in many ways. Also, indexes may be attached to list structures to allow maximum flexibility in data access. If all the fields of a record that can take values have indexes, the file is said to be **fully inverted**.

Because pointer organizations allow data to be retrieved in flexible ways, list structures are among those used in databases. Access to the database and the insertion and deletion of records are controlled by specialized software called a database management system. This is covered extensively in later sections of this chapter.

8.5 File-based and database approaches to data storage

A central feature of a database approach is the recognition that data is an important resource of an organization. Data is not regarded merely as the input and output of the data-processing department but as a valuable asset that requires careful planning and management.

The database is a store of data that may be used for many applications in the organization. It must be designed to service these and future needs. In particular, it must allow extraction of information for management information requirements in as flexible a manner as is needed for management decision making. For this reason, the database is at the heart of a comprehensive and evolving management information system.

The main characteristics of a modern database are:

- It is an integrated store of shared data for servicing the requirements of many users and applications.

- It is structured in a manner that is logically meaningful to the organization. For example, if data was held both on employees and on the company projects on which they work, then in the database there would be a link between the data on each employee and the data on the projects on which they work.

- There is minimal redundancy of data; this means that as far as possible the same item of data will not be repeated in the database.

Modern databases are usually held online on disk. Databases require careful design because they hold information that is structured for the organization. An important aspect of management is the use of software to handle all data access to the database. This software, the **database management system**, interfaces between users and user applications and the database itself, so enabling centralized control over the data. The main characteristics of a modern database management system (DBMS) are:

- It is software that handles all read and write access by users and application programs to the database.

- It is capable of presenting users with a view of that part of the database that is relevant to their needs.

- It presents a logical view of data to users – details of how this data is stored and retrieved by the database management system software are hidden.

- It ensures that the database is consistent.

- It allows authorization of different users to access different parts of the database.

- It allows the person in control of the database to define its structure.

- It provides various facilities for monitoring and control of the database.

The differences between a file-based and database approach towards data can be seen in Figures 8.6 and 8.7. Three application programs are considered in this example. In

Figure 8.6 An illustration of an application-led, file-based approach

Figure 8.7 An illustration of a database management system interfacing user programs and a database

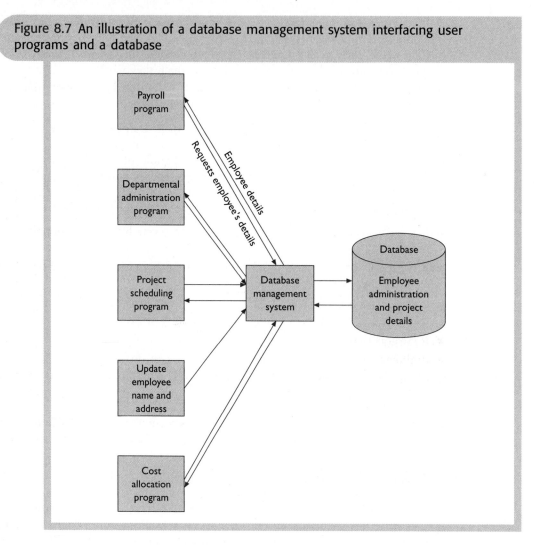

Figure 8.6, the company runs a payroll program that uses a payroll master file for employee details. The data on this payroll file is the responsibility of the payroll department. The company also runs a program for handling various departmental administration routines to do with staffing and staff locations. This was developed later and has its associated file, the administration file. Each department has an official who is responsible for forwarding data changes for this file. The company also has a program to aid the scheduling of staff to the various projects on which they work. Ensuring that project details are up to date is the responsibility of each project leader. This example typifies characteristics of the file-based approach:

- Files are developed in a piecemeal fashion to service the data needs of an application and are associated with that application.
- The same data may be repeated on many files – for example, *employee address*.
- The same data may be held under different names – for example, *employee name* and *staff name*.

- The physical characteristics of storage of the same data on different files may be different.

- The responsibility for data is dispersed.

Two main problems arise with this approach. First, amendment of data is likely to lead to inconsistent data being held by the organization. In the example, if an employee changes his or her address, unless this is notified to all persons responsible for files on which this data is held, updates will be haphazard and inconsistency will result. Second, the retrieval of data for new applications is difficult. Suppose it is required to develop a program that allocates costs against projects (for pricing purposes) and allocates costs against departments (for internal budgeting and management accounting). All this data is present but is spread over three files and is not easily accessible. It may be difficult to retrieve as it is not stored in a manner convenient for this new application.

The central weakness of the application-led approach is that files are tied to applications, not to the objects or entities to which those files refer. Another way of viewing the position of the data needs of the organization in the example is to recognize that three types of entity are involved – **EMPLOYEES**, **DEPARTMENTS** and **PROJECTS**. Not only may details be held on these entities but there are also relations between them. **EMPLOYEES** *work* on **PROJECTS** and are *members* of **DEPARTMENTS**. These relationships are ignored in the file-based approach, only being recognized when needed for an application. Databases and database management systems manage to encode these relationships.

In Figure 8.7, the database approach overcomes the difficulties experienced by the applications-led, file-based approach by storing all the organizational data in an integrated manner, which is accessible to all applications. Access to this database is always through the database management system. This ensures that consistency is maintained if data is altered, such as an employee address. The DBMS also provides data in the form required for new applications – for example, a cost allocation program.

8.5.1 The advantages of using a database approach

- **Data redundancy is reduced:** In the application-led, file-based approach, data such as *employee name* may be unnecessarily duplicated in various files. This is a waste of storage space and can be reduced, if not entirely eliminated, in a database system.

- **Data consistency can be maintained:** A corollary of the elimination of redundancy is that update inconsistency is reduced. Some inconsistency may result unless care is taken in database design, because some duplication of data is not eliminated.

- **Independence of data and programs is possible:** In the file-based approach considered earlier in this chapter, the application programs are closely interdependent with the file structure. For example, the payroll programs will need to 'know' how the employee file is organized in order to access records. It makes a great deal of difference whether the file is organized sequentially by *employee#* or organized with an *employee#* index. At the level of the record, the order of the fields and the length of each will probably need to be 'known' by the program. It is not possible to change the file organization or change the record structure without changing the program or programs that access it. The program is dependent on the data.

  In a database system, many programs will share the same data. It is not desirable to require each program to be changed when there is a change in the physical form of storage of data. (Changes in physical storage can be made for reasons of technical efficiency.) The database management system maintains the same view of the data to the accessing program no matter how the data may be reorganized physically on the disk.

- **A logical view is presented to the user or user programs:** Following from the last point, it is clear that the view of data presented to users or user programs must be independent of the physical storage details – it must be logical. Many database management systems allow different logical views of the same data to be presented to different users or programs. This is important as it frees programmers from a need to pay attention to the physical details of storage and allows them to concentrate on the applications to be coded. In the example covered earlier in this chapter, it is much easier for programmers to develop the cost allocation program if it is not necessary to consider the physical details of data retrieval. Programmers can concentrate on *how* to do a task, not on how to obtain the data to do it.

- **Applications development is enhanced because data sharing is possible:** The ability to use the database management system to retrieve data across the database in any required form once it has been stored opens up the range of applications for which the existing data can be used.

- **Standards can be enforced:** The fact that all access to data occurs via the database management system allows the individual responsible for this, the database administrator (DBA), to ensure that applications standards are followed in the representation of data.

- **Security is more easily implemented:** The DBA will control access to the database. The DBA can ensure that authorization codes for users are set restricting their access to only those parts of the database and for only the functions (read, write, copy) that are legitimate to their data purposes. Databases allow more effective control over access than the dispersal of responsibility associated with file-based systems. However, a breach of security may lead to a greater risk, as more data is accessible than with a traditional file-based system.

The advantages of a database approach can be summarized in that it leads to a system where:

- data management and control are more effective; and
- the ability to share data is increased.

8.5.2 Disadvantages of a database approach

Databases have become more common in recent years, but they still have limitations, and there are circumstances that might suggest a file-based environment is more appropriate.

- **Database design involves time and cost:** When an organization opts for a database approach it is necessary to pay considerable attention at the outset to the design of the database structure. This involves a study of the entities on which the organization wishes to hold data, the types of data to be held on these entities and the relationships and links between them. In comparison, a file-based approach leads to a piecemeal design of files for applications as they are required. This both simplifies design and spreads the cost over time as applications arise.

- **Database hardware and software costs need to be taken into account:** The database management system for a mainframe computer system is a complex piece of software costing many thousands of pounds. It is usual to use a standard package such as IDMS or ORACLE. As the entire database must be online all the time, it is also essential to purchase large amounts of disk storage.

- **Database access is slower than direct file access:** Recovery of data from a database using a DBMS involves another layer of software over and above an application program directly reading a file. The database may be physically implemented using large numbers of pointers, which will slow down access. These two considerations imply that database access is considerably slower than reading files.

Over time, disk technology has become cheaper and faster, which diminishes the importance of some of the disadvantages and partially explains why there is a drift towards business databases. In general, a file-based approach will seem more appropriate (as compared with a database) if:

- Different applications require different data.
- Fast, repetitive transaction processing in high volumes is to be undertaken.
- The application needs of the organization are unlikely to change over time.
- Information production is according to standard formats – little flexibility is required.

For these reasons, it is common to use file-based systems for accounting purposes, particularly financial accounting and book-keeping, where heavy transaction processing occurs. The flexible requirements of internal management accounting and the provision of information for tactical and operational management decisions are best served by database systems supplying data through management information systems.

Mini case 8.1

Databases

Databases are becoming commodities and while vendors fight the trend, not even Oracle's Larry Ellison can create much excitement around the topic any more. IT managers aren't interested in so many features and functions. Instead, they want to reduce the cost of running databases – hence the interest in Linux and MySQL, an open source database. But there is a bigger trend at work. The database dates back to an era when companies processed data; today, they handle information. The success of US retailer Wal-Mart, for example, is partly due to its massive data warehouse. Data mining and business intelligence applications have transformed the database from data manager to a strategic analytic data store. But in doing so the focus has shifted from the database to the tools and applications on top. Stellar growth rates are a distant memory – database sales dropped 7 per cent in 2002 – and former high-fliers such as Ingres and Informix have thrown in the towel. More worryingly, the supremacy of the relational database model is now being questioned. New-fangled XML databases, for example, are being used to manage product data as the texts and diagrams cannot easily be stored in the rigid rows and columns of a relational database. The growth of the Internet has led to a proliferation of richer content and further shown the limitations of the relational model. The industry is in no danger of disappearing, but the database is now just an element in a broader information management strategy. The news that Oracle has launched an ▶

audacious bid for enterprise software rival PeopleSoft suggests Mr Ellison has seen the writing on the wall.

Adapted from: **Databases in the enterprise**
By Geoff Nairn
FT.com site: 23 June 2003

Questions

1. What problems did the database model originally address?

2. The traditional database model is being radically enhanced. Note the key points that are raised in the mini case above. These issues are the topics of the remainder of this chapter. As you work through the chapter, refer back to see how current developments are changing the concepts of database management.

8.5.3 Database users

The corporate database is an important resource and may be needed by several types of user. These generally fall into one of three categories. Each has differing levels of understanding of the database and differing requirements.

The database administrator

The database administrator (DBA) is an experienced and senior member of the computer centre staff. The post requires involvement with different categories of user as well as extensive technical knowledge. The dependence of the organization on the smooth and effective management of its data resource ensures that the DBA's post is one of considerable responsibility. The DBA is typically involved in:

■ assisting the development of the database during the analysis and design life cycle of the information system;

■ achieving and maintaining an acceptable level of technical performance of the database;

■ attaining a satisfactory level of security, including:
  – ensuring that authorization codes for database access are implemented according to the rules of the organization;
  – ensuring that backup and recovery facilities in case of database failure are adequate;
  – establishing integrity constraints within the database;

■ monitoring use of the database from the point of view of accounting and the efficient utilization of the data resource;

■ reorganizing the physical structure of the database when necessary;

■ setting standards for documentation and data representation in the database;

■ liaising with users of the database to ensure that their data requirements are satisfied;

■ educating the organization on the use and availability of the database.

Applications programmers

Applications programmers are responsible for developing and maintaining programs for the functions required by the organization. Many of these programs will involve manipulation of data held in the database. Major programming languages contain instructions that enable calls to be made on the database via the database management system. This **data manipulation language** (DML) typically contains instructions governing the handling of data such as **STORE**, **RETRIEVE**, **MODIFY**, **DELETE** and **INSERT**. The programmer needs to know enough of the structure of the database to provide correct data-handling instructions in the host language.

Casual users

These are management and clerical personnel who make specific data enquiries of the database. This is an important group of users who are able to make *ad hoc* requests for information reports in a flexible way. They use simple query languages (see Section 8.5.4) to frame their requests. This group of users has been greatly liberated by the presence of online database systems. Previously, reports they required needed to be extracted in standard form and often produced at standard times. By being able to target their requests for information to what is relevant and obtaining speedy online responses, their decision making has become more effective.

8.5.4 Database utilities

In order to aid the DBA and other users in their tasks concerning the database, utility programs or modules are commonly used.

Query languages

Query languages are designed for casual users making enquiries of the database. Unlike data manipulation commands embedded in a host programming language such as COBOL, these languages can be used for *ad hoc* queries of the database. They are easy to understand and use and generally consist of near-English expressions. An example might be:

DISPLAY ALL EMPLOYEE.*employee-name* **FOR** EMPLOYEE.*employee-age* > 60

meaning 'display on the screen a list of employee names for all employees who are over 60 years old'.

It is easy to combine conditions in data enquiries. In the case of the employee/project/department example used earlier in this chapter, a typical request might be 'display all employee numbers and names for employees from any department located in London and working on more than two projects'. Such a request is easy to frame using a query language. It would be virtually impossible to extract such information from the file-based system. Examples of simple enquiries using actual query languages on databases are given in Sections 8.9 and 8.10.

Data dictionaries

A data dictionary may be defined as a store of data about data. The data dictionary will keep information on the record types, field names and types, and other information on the structure of the database. Data dictionaries are useful for the development and maintenance of the database structure. Nowadays, data dictionaries are often part of the database itself.

Accounting and monitoring utilities

These are used by the DBA to determine the extent of use of the database by individuals, departments and other cost and use centres. This is useful information for charging the database to the various user departments.

Report generators

It is sometimes necessary to produce output data in a special format. This may be desirable for reasons of clarity or standardization in the company. Alternatively, there may be accepted and required formats for certain types of report. Common examples are balance sheets and profit and loss statements. Output data from a database is printed or displayed on the screen in a standard form. This is generally just a list of the data items produced by the database management system. Report generators are utilities that allow different formats to be defined for the data. They are generally powerful and easy to use.

Backup and recovery

In order to make sure that data is not lost irretrievably after a database failure it is common practice (from time to time) to dump or store the database on to a secure medium. Between these dumps, a record is automatically kept of every transaction that affects the database (insertion, deletion and modifications). This combination of the saved database plus the log file of these transactions allows the state of the database before failure to be recovered.

Concurrency control

Databases contain data that may be shared between many users or user applications. Sometimes there may be demands for concurrent sharing. An example is the simultaneous access to inventory data in a multi-access system by two different users. No problem arises if each demand is to read a record, but difficulties occur if both users attempt to modify the record at the same time. The database utility responsible for concurrent usage then 'locks' one user out until the modification by the other has been effected.

Physical reorganization

These aid the DBA with the efficient restructuring of the physical database when necessary. This restructuring is necessary as data modification, addition and deletion of records change the physical characteristics of the stored data, resulting in long access times or inefficient storage of data across many disks.

8.6 A three-level architecture for databases

Some of the key reasons for the use of a database have been illustrated in terms of:

- the separation of the data from the applications that use it;
- the presentation of a logical view of the data independent of the physical details of storage; and
- the restriction and presentation of only relevant data to users and application programs.

Figure 8.8 A three-level model of a database architecture

Central to the understanding of the way a database and DBMS works in achieving these aims is the concept of schemas and views. This is shown in Figure 8.8 (derived from the ANSI/SPARC Study Group's report in 1978).

In overview, the conceptual schema provides the logical view of the entire database, the external schemas provide 'tailored' views of the database for each application or user, and the internal schema provides information on the detailed aspects of data storage, which have little to do with the logical content of the data.

Conceptual schema

The conceptual schema is the logical view of the entire database. Among other details it will contain a specification of:

- The types of data held on each entity of interest to the organization. For example, the following might be held on a supplier:
  - *supplier#*:numeric(6)
  - *supplier-name*:character(15)
  - *supplier-address*:character(30). . . .

This is similar to the specification of a record type.

- Any relationship between the entities. For example, suppliers *provide* products.
- Any restrictions on data – for example, *item-quantity* > 0.
- Authorization codes applicable to various items of data. For example, employee salary data may only be read by a user with authorization codes 5,6,9 and modified by a user with code 9.

The conceptual schema will be defined in a special language, the **data definition language** (DDL). This language is specific to the DBMS used. The schema can be regarded as derived from a model of the organization and should be designed with care as it is usual for its structure to remain relatively unchanged.

External schemas

An application program or user is uninterested in large sections of the database and is best presented with a view of the relevant sections. This is the external schema, and it exists in a subset of the conceptual schema. There may be a different external schema for each user of the database.

For instance, it is usual for a user to require only certain types of record and logical relationships between these. In these records, the user may need access to only a few selected fields in order to perform the specified user tasks. The external schema supplies just this window on the conceptual schema.

Internal schema

This describes how the database is implemented in terms of pointers, hashing functions, indexes, stored record sizes, and so on. It is concerned with storage details that are not part of a logical view of the database.

Mappings between schemas

As well as maintaining these views, the DBMS needs to keep a record of how each view is connected to (that is, maps to) each other. For instance, components of the internal schema will be represented at a logical level by components of the conceptual schema. It must be possible to reorganize the physical database without altering the logical content of the database (conceptual schema) or to alter the conceptual schema without altering the existing external schemas. The presence of mappings enables this.

For instance, it may be necessary to add extra fields to hold details on an employee's health where health details were not held before. This alteration to the conceptual (and internal) schema should not affect existing external schemas that have no need of this data. Again, it may be decided to reorganize the storage characteristics of the database for efficiency reasons. Although this may affect the internal schema, it should not affect either the conceptual or external schemas.

8.7　Models and schemas

It was stated in Section 8.6 that the conceptual schema was derived from a model of the organization. It is important to be clear that a conceptual schema is defined in a data definition language that is particular to the DBMS used. Each DBMS imposes different restrictions on what can and cannot be defined. Some database management systems severely limit what can be specified within the conceptual schema for the benefit of providing fast data access times. Others are very flexible, at the expense of slow access speeds.

Most database management systems fall into one of three types, depending on what restrictions are imposed. These types correspond to three distinct models of data structures: network, relational and hierarchical data models. The data model, then, is the type of data structure that is most appropriate for a DBMS. A conceptual schema is the definition of that model within the DBMS data definition language.

The three main types of data model surveyed here are important as they have influenced the development of commercial database software. Many other types of data model exist, although they have not had the same impact on the industry. For each type of model, what constitutes the basis of an external, conceptual and (particularly) internal schema cannot be properly explained without reference to general or specific characteristics of database management systems exemplifying the model.

8.7.1 Data structures and occurrences

One of the main differences between a file and a database is that the former is simply a collection of records of the same type, whereas the latter consists of:

- different types of record;
- collections of records of each of these types; and
- links between the records, depending on whether there are relationships in the world between the entities for which the records stand.

The database has structure that is absent from files. The most important structure from the point of view of the data models is the allowable links or relationships that exist between records of different types.

1:*n* relationships

Figure 8.9(a) shows the 1:*n* relationship existing between departments and the employees attached to them. The relationship is 1:*n*, or one to many, because each department can have many employees, but each employee can be attached to *at most* one department. The arrowhead is attached to the *n* side of the relationship. Occurrences of this structure are shown in Figure 8.9(b).

Figure 8.9 (a) A 1:*n* relationship; (b) occurrences of a 1:*n* relationship

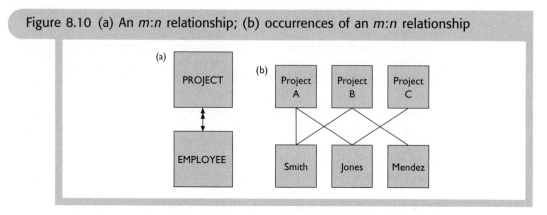

Figure 8.10 (a) An *m:n* relationship; (b) occurrences of an *m:n* relationship

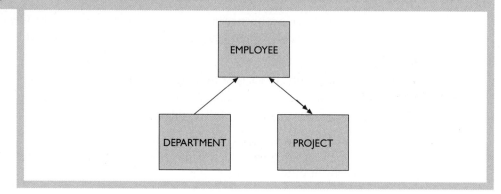

Figure 8.11 The DEPARTMENT/EMPLOYEE/PROJECT model

m:n relationships

Figure 8.10(a) shows the *m:n* relationship existing between employees and the projects on which they work. The relationship is *m:n*, or many to many, because each employee may work on many projects, and each project may be worked on by many employees. Occurrences of this structure are shown in Figure 8.10(b).

The three main data models for databases are covered in the subsequent sections. The simple example model in Figure 8.11 is used to illustrate the restrictions of each of the models.

8.8   Network models

The network model allows the representation of all 1:*n* relationships existing between records. The treatment here is in line with the recommendations of the Database Task Group (DBTG) report on the Conference on Data Systems Languages (CODASYL) in 1971 and following years. It is often referred to as the CODASYL model. The treatment follows the spirit of the approach, although CODASYL terminology is avoided where possible.

The use of the term **network** in this context has no connotation of the interconnecting of computers; rather, it refers to the network of linkages between data items within files.

8.8.1 The model structure

A major restriction on databases following the network model is that no many-to-many relationships are allowed. To see why this is limiting, consider the projects/departments/employees example used earlier. As well as having employees attached to departments, the organization also runs projects on which employees work. Each employee may work on many projects, and each project has many employees working on it. This cannot be directly represented in the network model. Instead, a dummy or **link** record type is used to translate the many-to-many relationship into two one-to-many relationships. This is shown in Figure 8.12(a) and 8.12(b). Each employee works on many assignments, and each project is served by many assignments. The link records need not contain any data and may represent nothing meaningful to the organization. It is just a trick to stay within the constraints of the network model. In Figure 8.12(b), there might be data inside each **ASSIGNMENT** occurrence recording the number of hours each employee works on each project.

The occurrences of this treatment are shown in Figure 8.13. It is clear that each **EMPLOYEE** can work on many **ASSIGNMENTS**, although each **ASSIGNMENT** is

Figure 8.12 Treatment of an *m:n* relationship in the network model: (a) disallowed in the network model; (b) representation of an *m:n* relationship using link records

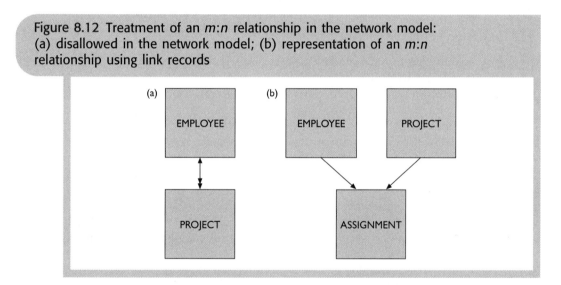

Figure 8.13 Instances of the use of link records

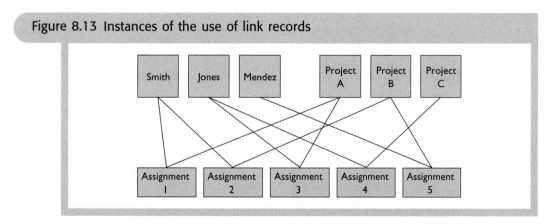

Figure 8.14 The logical pointed structure associated with the EMPLOYEE/PROJECT relationship

connected to only one **EMPLOYEE**. Similarly with the relationship between **PROJECT** and **ASSIGNMENT**.

Connections between records in a network model are maintained by **pointers**. Figure 8.14 illustrates the logical pointer structure associated with the record occurrences for the network treatment of the many-to-many employee/project relationship. The **ASSIGNMENT** link records used here are not purely dummies. They contain, as shown in parentheses, data on the number of hours each employee is assigned to each project.

It is easy to see that, given an employee, it is possible to determine on what projects that employee works and for how long on each. The database is navigated following the pointer structures to obtain the information.

Figure 8.15 illustrates another feature of the network model. It allows many 1:n relationships between records – two records may have more than one relationship between them.

As well as disallowing the direct representation of m:n relationships the network model also forbids involuted relationships. An example of this and its treatment is shown in Figure 8.16. In many companies, a hierarchical management structure implies that some employees supervise other employees, who in turn supervise others. So an employee may be both supervised and a supervisor. The network model will not allow direct representation of this involuted relationship. Instead, a dummy record type, **SUB-ORDINATE**, is used. The relationship is used to refer back to those employees who are the subordinates. The way individual occurrences are related can be seen in Figure 8.17.

The way the network model represents the relationships between projects, departments and employees is shown in Figure 8.18. A complete definition of the schema would define:

■ for each record type, its name and a list of fields in the record;
■ for each relationship, the name of the relationship and the record types at both the 1 and the n ends of the 1:n relationship (**set, owner,** and **member** in the CODA-SYL terminology);

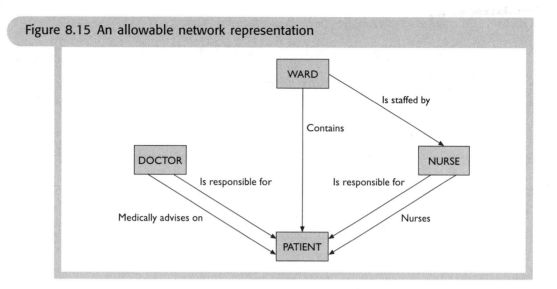

Figure 8.15 An allowable network representation

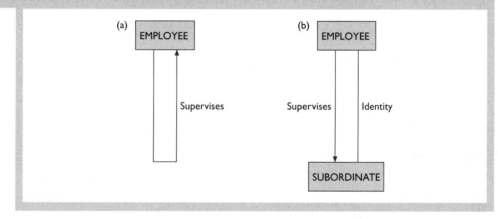

Figure 8.16 Treatment of involuted relationships in the network model:
(a) disallowed in the network model; (b) representation of an involuted relationship
using dummy records

Figure 8.17 Occurrences of the treatment of involuted relationships in the network
model

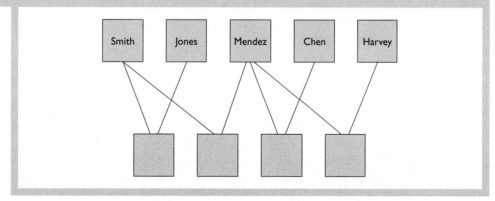

Figure 8.18 Network representation of the EMPLOYEE/PROJECT/DEPARTMENT example

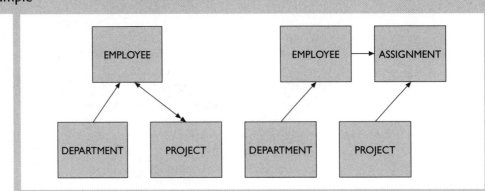

- the logical order in which records on the *n* side of a 1:*n* relationship can be retrieved – this amounts to a statement of how the pointers are organized;
- certain restrictions on whether records are obliged to be within relationships.

8.8.2 Data manipulation

Data can be inserted into and retrieved from databases exhibiting a network structure in very flexible ways. Resetting the pointers if a record is inserted or deleted is complicated, but this is handled automatically by the database management system. However, commercial systems, while allowing flexible record retrieval, require the user to have an understanding of the pointer organization in order to navigate around the database. This implies that the user is not presented with a truly logical view of the data. This is one of the main weaknesses of databases based on the network model.

8.9　Hierarchical models

Databases and database management system software based on hierarchical data structures were the first to be developed. IBM's Information Management System (IMS) is one of the most commonly used systems.

8.9.1 The model structure

Hierarchical data models, in common with network models, do not allow direct representation of many-to-many relationships. They also have a further restriction that distinguishes them: the allowable structures are in the form of trees.

Figure 8.19 shows a hierarchy for part of a college database. The top record type, **DEPARTMENT**, is known as the **root**. The links between the various record types (or **nodes** as they are sometimes known) represent the relationships.

Each department may run many courses, but each course is run by only one department. This relationship is represented by the downward-pointing one-to-many link between the **DEPARTMENT** and **COURSE** record types. Each course consists of many

Figure 8.19 A hierarchical structure

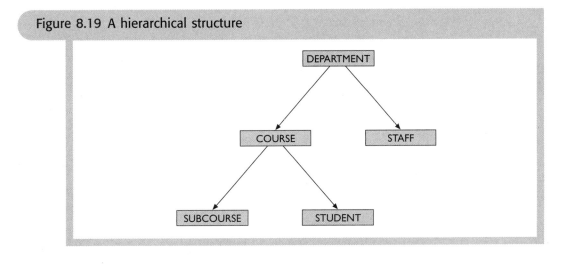

Figure 8.20 Disallowed structures for hierarchical models

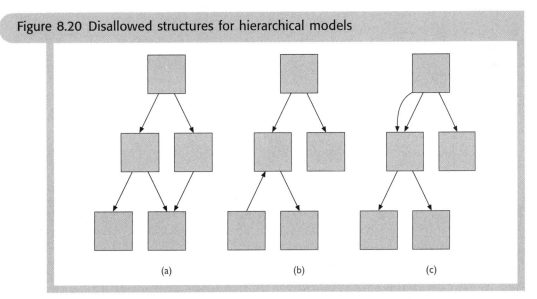

subcourses, and each course has many students registered on it. **COURSE** is a **parent** record type and **SUBCOURSE** and **STUDENT** are dependent record types at lower levels. They are all the **children** of **COURSE**. The tree consists only of downward-pointing one-to-many links.

Figure 8.20 illustrates three structures that are disallowed within the limitations of the hierarchical model but which would be representable within a network structure. Structure (a) is not a tree structure but a network. If there is more than one path between any two record types then the structure is a network. Structure (b) contravenes the requirement that all relationships should be downward-pointing. Structure (c) has more than one relationship between two record types and so is not a tree structure.

An instance of the hierarchical model shown in Figure 8.19 is given in Figure 8.21. Each record occurrence, apart from **BUSINESS**, is connected to only one record occurrence at a higher level. The record occurrences of **MARKETING** and **BUSINESS/ECONOMICS**

Figure 8.21 An occurrence of a DEPARTMENT

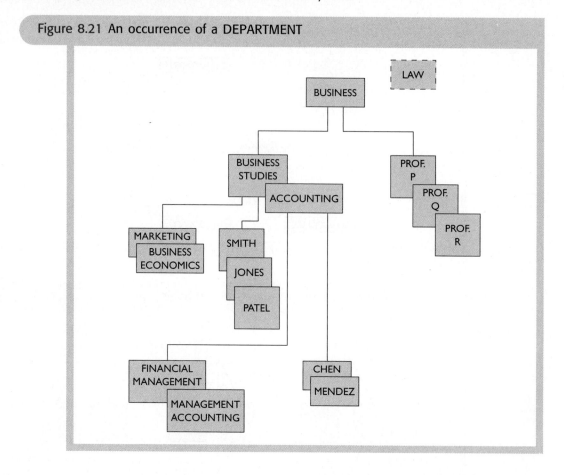

are known as **twins**. If a record is deleted, then all records connected to it at a lower level will be deleted. For instance, if the **ACCOUNTING** record is deleted (perhaps because the course is no longer offered) then the records **FINANCIAL MANAGEMENT**, **MANAGEMENT ACCOUNTING, CHEN** and **MENDEZ** are also lost from the database.

The problem of many-to-many relationships and network structures is handled by the development of independent hierarchical structures. In Figure 8.22, the project/ employee/department structure is represented by two simple hierarchies. The diagram also shows a representation of another network structure. More complex structures may require several hierarchy trees.

8.9.2 Conceptual, internal and external schemas

The conceptual schema of a hierarchical database may be taken as the set of hierarchy trees defining the structure. The conceptual schema will also specify the fields in each record type in the hierarchy. This gives a logical view of the way the database is organized.

It is difficult to equate much else in the way of external and internal schemas with hierarchical databases without consideration of specific commercial products. For instance, IMS stores each hierarchy tree as a separate single file. This file will contain record occurrences of many types. The internal schema can be thought of as a

Figure 8.22 Treatment of non-hierarchical structures in the hierarchical model

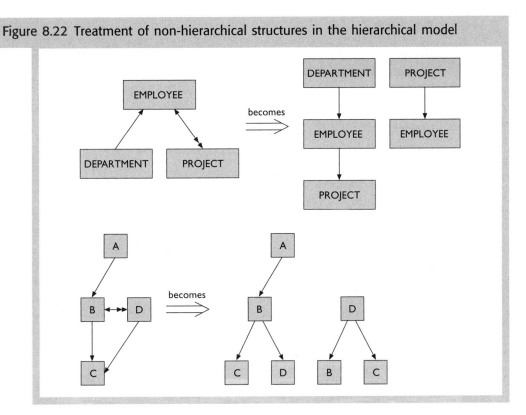

collection of specifications of the data organization of these files. The file can be stored in many ways. The occurrence in Figure 8.21 can be stored as a sequential file, with the records adjacent to one another in the following order:

BUSINESS, BUSINESS STUDIES, MARKETING, BUSINESS ECONOMICS, SMITH, JONES, PATEL, ACCOUNTING, FINANCIAL MANAGEMENT, MANAGEMENT ACCOUNTING, CHEN, MENDEZ, PROF. P, PROF. Q, PROF. R.

Processing the file sequentially is equivalent to traversing the tree in Figure 8.21 from top to bottom and left to right. This storage is known as HSAM (hierarchical sequential-access method). Other storage forms are HISAM (sequential storage but with an index for each root occurrence), HDAM (root records are stored by means of a randomizing algorithm, and pointers are used to indicate children, and from these children their children, and so on), and HIDAM (the same as HDAM except that root records are indexed).

Different users need to be presented with different views. This is achieved by linking together subsets of the hierarchy trees. In IMS, the trees are called 'physical databases' and the subsets are called 'logical databases'. The IMS external schema then is the collection of logical databases for that user.

8.9.3 Data manipulation

Records may be retrieved, stored and deleted by means of data manipulation language commands, usually embedded within a host programming language. These commands may select the required records and data items by a specified traversal of the hierarchy tree (known as 'tree traversal'). Alternatively, it is possible with some systems to select records by means of the hierarchical relationships between data items (known as 'hierarchical selection'). In Figure 8.21, if the student records contained data on each student's origin, home or overseas, a typical hierarchical selection command might be:

select all STUDENT.*name* **where** STUDENT.*origin*=overseas **from all** STUDENT **under all** COURSE **under all** DEPARTMENT **where** DEPARTMENT *name*=business studies

This would deliver the names of all overseas students in all courses run by the department of business studies.

Hierarchical database systems are most suitable where the data model for the organization falls naturally into a hierarchy, and searches of the database usually involve extracting data from subordinate records, which means moving down the tree. Although this is a limitation, it must not be forgotten that hierarchical structures are common in organizations. Examples form a wide range and include management hierarchies and hierarchies of components constituting a manufactured good.

Database management systems based on hierarchical models have now largely been superseded by systems based on relational models.

Mini case 8.2

Hierarchical databases

CrossAccess Corporation today announced that it has successfully completed testing of its eXadas(R) data integration product with IBM's new DB2 Information Integrator software. CrossAccess' eXadas offers SQL read write access to mainframe non-relational data sources that include IMS, CA-IDMS, CA-Datacom, Adabas, VSAM and DB2 Universal Database. Using the DB2 Information Integrator technology, users are able to submit SQL queries to DB2 Information Integrator and seamlessly access mainframe data sources without having to write code.

Customers today are faced with the challenge of integrating information across and beyond the enterprise in an effort to increase efficiencies and better serve customers. IBM DB2 Information Integrator software helps customers solve this pain point, enabling businesses to access, integrate and manage all types of data in real time, as if it were a single source, regardless of where the data resides. DB2 Information Integrator software also provides customers with a single, integrated view of data that is essential for business applications.

With eXadas and DB2 Information Integrator, businesses can reliably integrate and reconcile the widely dispersed customer data that resides in enterprise applications as well as unstructured document collections across channels, geographies and business units.

Industry experts estimate that 70–80% of the data residing on IBM OS/390 platforms is in a non-relational structured format. The ability to access non-relational legacy data is critical to the successful development of today's distributed applications. Organizations want to take advantage of the power of distributed computing and Web development. They must do so by effectively utilizing their legacy investment in the mainframe. DB2 Information Integrator and eXadas Data Integrator enable distributed data joins on heterogeneous non-relational and relational data platforms. End-users working with a Web or client-based application don't have to know what kind of database the information is coming from.

Adapted from: CrossAccess Corporation's eXadas extends mainframe legacy data access for IBM DB2 Information Integrator
Business Wire: 13 June 2003

Questions

1. The article refers to non-relational models. What are the two main database models other than the relational model?

2. Why are additional tools required to access data held in, say, DB2 Universal Database by using SQL?

3. Why do you think that '70–80% of the data residing on IBM OS/390 platforms is in a non-relational structured format'?

8.10 Relational models

Relational data models draw heavily on the theoretical work carried out by E.F. Codd in the 1970s. Database management systems based around the relational model (such as ORACLE, SQLServer and MySQL) offer substantial advantages over the network and hierarchical approaches.

8.10.1 The model structure

In a relational model, data is stored in a **relation** (or table) as shown in Figure 8.23(a), the table for **EMPLOYEE**. It is important to distinguish between a relation, which is a term applying to a component of a relational model, and a relationship, which is a real-world association between objects. Muddling the two terms is a mistake. They have different meanings and, as will be shown later in this section, relationships can be represented by relations, although not all relations represent relationships.

Each table consists of a number of columns or **attributes**. In the example, *employee#*, *employee_name* and *employee_salary* are all attributes. Attributes take their values from a set of values of a common type known as the **domain** of the attribute. For example,

Figure 8.23 An example of a relation: (a) the relation as a table; (b) the relational structure

(a) EMPLOYEE

employee#	employee_name	employee_salary
134	Smith	12,000
146	Harvey	15,000
139	Jones	4,600
468	Mendez	14,000
201	Patel	9,000

(b) EMPLOYEE (*employee#*, *employee_name*, *employee_salary*) *employee_salary* might have a domain consisting of integers greater than or equal to 0. Two different attributes may share the same domain.

A row of the table is also known as a **tuple**. No two rows in a table are allowed to be identical.

The number of attributes determines the degree of the relation. **EMPLOYEE** is a relation of degree 3. The number of rows or tuples is known as the **cardinality** of the relation.

An important relational concept is the **key attribute of a relation**, which is any attribute (or group of attributes) the value(s) of which uniquely identify a tuple of the relation.

A 'key attribute' is a semantic concept. This can be illustrated by considering the **EMPLOYEE** relation. A given value of *employee#* identifies exactly one row, if it identifies any at all. The same, however, appears to be true of *employee_name*. The difference is that there could be an occurrence in another row of the *employee_name* entry 'Smith' but there could not be another row with *employee#* '134'. Put another way, two employees might be named Smith, but it is not possible for two different employees to be numbered 134. Note that the key is underlined in the relational structure of Figure 8.23(b).

A formal definition of relation is:

Given a collection of domains $D_1, D_2, \ldots D_n$ (not necessarily distinct), a relation, R, on these domains is a set of ordered n-tuples $\langle d_1, d_2, \ldots d_n \rangle$, where d_1 is a member of D_1, d_2 is a member of $D_2, \ldots d_n$ is a member of D_n.

This has two important formal implications. First, the order of rows in a relation is insignificant. The row corresponding to *employee#* = 139 in **EMPLOYEE** might have been at the top of the table. It would still have been the same relation.

Second, as the set is an ordered n-tuple the column ordering *is* significant. In the *EMPLOYEE* table, if *employee_salary* occurs between *employee#* and *employee_name* then it is a different relation. In practice, both of these pure conditions may not be followed in commercial relational database management systems. Different attribute order is often allowed, as users generally do not access a value in a row by its relative position but by the column name under which it falls. Some systems also allow an ordering among rows to be expressed, for example according to ascending *employee#*. Rows can then be retrieved in order.

The theoretical system, though, allows access to a tuple only by value and there is no implied index or ordering. The physical implementation in terms of indexes and pointers is unseen by the user.

The network model and hierarchical models represent relationships by links. The relational model represents a relationship by a relation or table. This is shown in Figure 8.24. The model in 8.24(b), together with the specification of the domain of each attribute, corresponds to a conceptual schema.

Remember that each employee belongs to just one department, whereas each department may have several employees. The key to the **DEPARTMENT** relation is *dept_name* and if this is added to the **EMPLOYEE** relation we can represent the fact that an employee is a member of a department. Loosely speaking, given an *employee #*, 139, the relevant **EMPLOYEE** tuple can be identified and the fact that the employee is in the production department established. Then from the **DEPARTMENT** table the relevant **DEPARTMENT** tuple containing the information on the department of production can be identified.

Many employees are able to work on one project, and each project might have many employees assigned to it. This is shown by capturing the many-to-many relationship in a new relation, **ASSIGNMENT**. The unique key to this relation is not a single

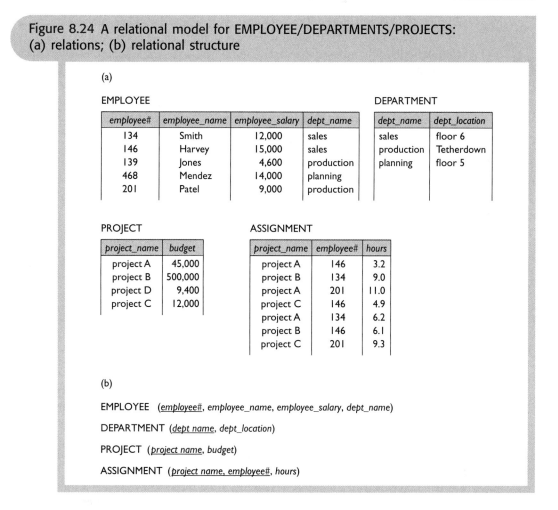

Figure 8.24 A relational model for EMPLOYEE/DEPARTMENTS/PROJECTS:
(a) relations; (b) relational structure

(a)

EMPLOYEE

employee#	employee_name	employee_salary	dept_name
134	Smith	12,000	sales
146	Harvey	15,000	sales
139	Jones	4,600	production
468	Mendez	14,000	planning
201	Patel	9,000	production

DEPARTMENT

dept_name	dept_location
sales	floor 6
production	Tetherdown
planning	floor 5

PROJECT

project_name	budget
project A	45,000
project B	500,000
project D	9,400
project C	12,000

ASSIGNMENT

project_name	employee#	hours
project A	146	3.2
project B	134	9.0
project A	201	11.0
project C	146	4.9
project A	134	6.2
project B	146	6.1
project C	201	9.3

(b)

EMPLOYEE (*employee#*, employee_name, employee_salary, dept_name)

DEPARTMENT (*dept name*, dept_location)

PROJECT (*project name*, budget)

ASSIGNMENT (*project name, employee#*, hours)

attribute but rather a combination of the key of **PROJECT**, *project_name*, and the key of **EMPLOYEE**, *employee#*. A key comprising a group of attributes in this way is termed a **combination key**. The field, *hours*, allows data on the number of hours that each employee works on each project to be stored.

In general, a 1:*n* relationship is represented in the relational model by inserting the key attribute of the entity on the *n* side of the relationship into the relation representing the entity on the 1 side of the relationship. A many-to-many relationship is represented by creating a new relation that has as its combination key the key attributes of each of the entities in the relationship.

It is important to be clear about the way the relational and network data models are data models of the world. The world can be viewed as being constructed of three types of component. There are entity types (types of objects), there are attributes of these objects, and there are relationships between the objects. The relational model represents an entity type by a relation or table and the attributes by columns of the table. An individual object with values of its attributes corresponds to a row in the table. A relationship between two objects is not modelled as a third type of component.

Rather, the key attributes of each entity type are associated in a table that acts as proxy for the relationship. Relationships are not distinguished from entity types in the relational model. We only see the distinction because the table representing a relationship has a composite key, its components being the keys of the tables representing the entities in the relationship. There are only two distinct kinds of component in the relational model – tables (or relations) and values of attributes. In contrast, the network model straightforwardly represents entity types by record types, entities themselves by occurrences of these record types, relationships by links between the record types (CODASYL sets), and values of attributes of objects by data items in record occurrences.

Some of the advantages of relational systems are:

■ Relational database models involve no non-logical concepts such as indexing, storage details or ordering, which occur in the network and hierarchical models.

■ They require no non-logical access paths (via pointers, CODASYL sets or the like) to data items. These items are retrieved purely on the basis of the rules and conditions.

■ The relational model is therefore a logical data model independent of storage considerations. It can be thought of as falling neatly into a conceptual schema level.

■ Relational database systems allow large chunks of data to be processed in a single operation.

8.10.2 Conceptual, external and internal schemas

The relational equivalent of a conceptual schema is the set of relations defined in the relational model, together with specification of the domains of each attribute. In relational database management systems, these **base tables** have an independent existence.

At the internal schema level, each base table will probably correspond to a stored file and each row in the table to a record in the file. There may be many indexes associated with a given file. The conceptual view should not reveal these indexes (or if it does, data access should not be specifiable via them).

The equivalent of an external schema for a relational model is sometimes called a **view**. A particular view consists of presenting those attributes and tables needed for the specific purpose of a user. The contents of the view will be equivalent to a set of relations generated from the relations stored in the database. These relations may be either base table or relations capable of being generated from these by the relational operations described in Section 8.10.3.

8.10.3 Data manipulation

As well as independently existing relations (known as primary or base relations), which are stored, it may be necessary to generate new and temporary relations (known as **derived** relations) to answer user enquiries. The operations that may be legitimately performed on relations can be described using either relational algebra or relational calculus. The workings of both the algebra and the calculus have been extensively investigated from a mathematical perspective, and their properties are fully understood. All data manipulation is based on these, rather than the traversal of hierarchies or networks between records.

Three relational algebra operations, **SELECT**, **PROJECT** and **JOIN**, are illustrated. Each takes a relation (or number of relations) as its argument and produces a relation as its value.

Figure 8.25 Examples of relational operators: (a) use of SELECT; (b) use of PROJECT; (c) use of JOIN; (d) use of nested operators

(a)

employee#	employee_name	employee_salary	dept_name
146	Harvey	15,000	sales
468	Mendez	14,000	planning

SELECT EMPLOYEE **WHERE** *employee_salary* > 13,000

(b)

employee_name	dept_name
Smith	sales
Harvey	sales
Jones	production
Mendez	planning
Patel	production

PROJECT EMPLOYEE **OVER** *employee_name, dept_name*

(c)

employee#	employee_name	employee_salary	dept_name	project_name	hours
134	Smith	12,000	sales	project B	9.0
134	Smith	12,000	sales	project A	6.2
146	Harvey	15,000	sales	project A	3.2
146	Harvey	15,000	sales	project C	4.9
146	Harvey	15,000	sales	project B	6.1
201	Patel	9,000	production	project A	11.0
201	Patel	9,000	production	project C	9.3

JOIN EMPLOYEE **AND** ASSIGNMENT **OVER** *employee#*

(d)

employee_name	project_name	hours
Smith	project B	9.0
Smith	project A	6.2
Harvey	project A	3.2
Harvey	project C	4.9
Harvey	project B	6.1

PROJECT (**SELECT** (**JOIN** EMPLOYEE **AND** ASSIGNMENT **OVER** *employee#*)
WHERE *dept_name = sales*) **OVER** *employee_name, project_name, hours*

1. **SELECT**: This produces a new relation consisting of a number of selected rows (tuples) from an existing relation. For example:

   SELECT EMPLOYEE **WHERE** *employee_salary* > 13,000

   gives the relation in Figure 8.25(a).

2. **PROJECT**: This produces a new relation consisting of a number of selected columns (attributes) from an existing relation. For example:

   PROJECT EMPLOYEE **OVER** employee_name, dept_name

   gives the relation in Figure 8.25(b).

3. **JOIN**: This produces a new relation from two existing relations joined over a common domain. It is best described algorithmically. First, take the first row from the first relation and compare the attribute value from the common domain with each value of the attribute from the common domain in the second relation. Wherever the two values are identical, form a row by concatenating the first row with the row from the second relation (striking out the repeat of the common attribute). Do this for each row in the first relation. For example:

   JOIN EMPLOYEE **AND** ASSIGNMENT **OVER** employee#

   gives the relation in Figure 8.25(c).

It is possible to nest the operations. Suppose that a user wishes to establish the names, projects worked on and hours worked on these projects by staff in the sales department. This could be achieved by the following nested operations:

PROJECT (**SELECT**(**JOIN** EMPLOYEE **AND** ASSIGNMENT **OVER** employee#) **WHERE** dept_name = sales) **OVER** employee_name, project_name, hours

By working from the innermost nesting outwards, the resulting relation can be constructed (see Figure 8.25(d)).

Relational algebra also uses other operations. There is a **DIVIDE** operation as well as the set theoretical operations corresponding to **UNION**, **INTERSECTION** and **DIFFERENCE**.

Relational algebra involves a procedural specification of how the final relation is to be constructed by defining intermediate relations to be produced. The relational calculus, in contrast, defines a relation in the form of a predicate. The calculus is a version of the predicate calculus applied to relational databases.

The relational algebra provides a formally precise way of extracting data. However, it is difficult to use to specify complex enquiries. It is not used itself to query a relational database or as a set of data manipulation procedures. Query languages and data manipulation languages derived from the algebra have been developed. These are straightforward to use and provide the ease and flexibility of enquiry that make relational databases powerful in the provision of information. IBM's SQL (structured query language) and QBE (query by example) are examples.

8.10.4 SQL

SQL is a relational data manipulation language developed by IBM initially for use with its relational database management system DB2. The language can be used for standalone queries or embedded in programs written in various languages. The language is simple enough that substantial parts may be employed by casual users for queries on the relational database. SQL has become the standard relational data manipulation language. Basic operations are covered below.

Projection

The project operation is implemented in SQL by the construction:

> **SELECT** ⟨attribute 1, attribute 2 . . . ⟩
> **FROM** ⟨relation⟩

The projection in Figure 8.25(b) would be framed as follows:

> **SELECT** employee_name, dept_name
> **FROM** EMPLOYEE

This produces the result in the table in Figure 8.25(b). With SQL, it is possible to specify any desired order among the columns. A different command would have produced dept_name followed by employee_name. SQL projection differs from the logical projection operation in that duplicate tuples resulting from the projection would not be removed; in other words, the result of SQL projection is not strictly a relation.

Selection

Selection is achieved by adding a qualification to the **SELECT** command. Its construction is:

> **SELECT** ⟨attribute 1 . . . ⟩
> **FROM** ⟨relation⟩
> **WHERE** ⟨qualification⟩

The qualification is a Boolean construction using **AND**, **OR** or **NOT**. Using the EMPLOYEE relation in Figure 8.24, the following selection:

> **SELECT** employee_name, employee#
> **FROM** EMPLOYEE
> **WHERE** employee_salary > 8,000
> **AND** (dept_name = Sales **OR** dept_name = Production)

would yield

> SMITH   134
> HARVEY   146
> PATEL   201

Join

Join is achieved by specifying the two attributes (with common domain) over which the join is to be made. The construction is:

> **SELECT** ⟨attribute 1 . . . ⟩
> **FROM** ⟨relation 1, relation 2, . . . ⟩
> **WHERE** ⟨attribute from relation 1 = attribute from relation 2 etc.⟩

If it is wished to select the names, project and hours worked on the projects by staff as shown in the EMPLOYEE and ASSIGNMENT relations in Figure 8.24, the join operation with the selection would be:

> **SELECT** EMPLOYEE.employee_name, ASSIGNMENT.project_name, ASSIGNMENT.hours
> **FROM** EMPLOYEE, ASSIGNMENT
> **WHERE** EMPLOYEE.employee# = ASSIGNMENT.employee#

> ## Figure 8.26 The result of the SQL **JOIN** command on **EMPLOYEE** and **ASSIGNMENT**
>
> | | | |
> |---|---|---|
> | Smith | project B | 9.0 |
> | Smith | project A | 6.2 |
> | Harvey | project A | 3.2 |
> | Harvey | project C | 4.9 |
> | Harvey | project B | 6.I |
> | Patel | project A | II.0 |
> | Patel | project C | 9.3 |
>
> **SELECT** EMPLOYEE. *employee_name*, ASSIGNMENT. *project_name*, ASSIGNMENT.*hours*
>   **FROM** EMPLOYEE, ASSIGNMENT
>   **WHERE** EMPLOYEE. *employee#* = ASSIGNMENT. *employee#*

This command gives the display in Figure 8.26. SQL commands can be nested, and several relations can be 'searched' by using join qualifications with more than two relations. The following command lists employee names, the projects on which they work and the budgets of these projects using the relations in Figure 8.24:

   SELECT EMPLOYEE.*employee_name*, ASSIGNMENT.*project_name*, PROJECT.*budget*
     FROM EMPLOYEE, ASSIGNMENT, PROJECT
     WHERE EMPLOYEE.*employee#* = ASSIGNMENT.*employee#*
       AND ASSIGNMENT.*project_name* = PROJECT.*project_name*

SQL allows nesting of the **SELECT–FROM–WHERE** construction, and it is often easier to conceptualize a query this way. For instance, the following query selects the names of employees working on a project for more than 8 hours.

   SELECT *employee_name*
     FROM EMPLOYEE
     WHERE *employee#* = **ANY** (**SELECT** *employee#* **FROM** ASSIGNMENT
                 WHERE *hours* > 8.0)

As well as searching, SQL allows deletion and insertion of rows using the **DELETE** and **INSERT** commands. These work using the same underlying principles as the constructions that apply to **SELECT**.

8.10.5 Query by example

Query by example (QBE) is a query technique for relational database systems that uses the idea of a table (relation) with which to frame the query. The language is designed to be used interactively with a VDU. The user selects the desired relation or relations and is then presented with a skeleton table. From the various fields shown the user can select the fields to be displayed in response to the query. Conditions are entered in the other fields as desired. Figure 8.27 is an example involving selection and projection from one relation. It specifies the retrieval of all employee names together with their department names where the employee earns more than £13,000 per year. More complex queries may involve several relations and complicated search conditions. QBE queries can be created that involve several relations and complex search conditions.

Figure 8.27 A QBE query on EMPLOYEE

Query

EMPLOYEE	employee#	employee_name	employee_salary	dept_name
		P. Fred	> 13,000	P. Stores

Response

employee_name	dept_name
Harvey	sales
Mendez	planning

Table 8.1 Databases compared

	Chronological development	Processing speed	Ease of physical implementation	Flexibility of representation	Flexibility of data retrieval	Ease of understanding
Network	second	2	2	2	2	3
Hierarchical	first	1	1	3	3	2
Relational	third	3	3	1	1	1

Key 1 = best, 3 = worst

The power of modern QBE facilities is approaching that of SQL; indeed, many systems allow QBE queries to be automatically converted to SQL for further editing and optimization.

8.10.6 Assessment of relational database models

The relational model, relational database management systems and relational languages have had a large impact on the development of sophisticated data resources. Their advantages over database systems based on other models are summarized below and in Table 8.1.

Advantages

- They provide a clear and conceptually straightforward representation of complex data relations.
- They allow powerful data manipulation and query languages to operate on them.
- The database is maintained in a table form, which is a 'natural' representation of data to business-oriented users.
- Query languages (such as QBE) can be developed to exploit this tabular form.
- Data is accessed by value and conditions, and the database can be accessed from any point (relation).
- Access paths are not seen (or usable) by the database users.

- The representation of the data is entirely logical, once again reinforcing the simplicity of representation from the point of view of users and application programmers.

Disadvantages

- The indexes used in implementation are often large and require heavy storage overheads.
- The operational speed of current commercial relational database systems is slower than their hierarchical or network counterparts. This makes them unsuitable for some very high-volume processing activities.

As disk storage capacities and disk access speeds rise, combined with the diminishing cost of disk storage, the flexible features of relational databases will ensure their long-term superiority in the marketplace.

8.11 Object-oriented databases

The relational database described in detail in Section 8.10 has become an industry standard for much of the database development that occurs today. The recent attention in the object-oriented model for information systems development has been reflected by interest in object-oriented databases. Whereas a relational database stores data in relations as rows of tuples, an object-oriented database stores collections of objects. This is explained further in the next section.

8.11.1 The object-oriented perspective of information systems

The relational model views the world as entities, attributes and the relationships between them. The missing component in this model is the processing carried out on that data. Proponents of the object-oriented model argue that to separate data and process in this way leads to a weakness in the design of systems. Indeed, it is using an unnecessarily artificial premise upon which to model the physical system. They would point out that real-world 'objects' are viewed and described in terms of what they do as well as what they are. Using this approach, an object such as a bank account is described using the attributes that describe its state (the account holder's name, the account number, the balance, etc.) as well as the activities that the object initiates or participates in (debiting and crediting the account, calculating interest accrued, etc). A bank account object would therefore contain both the account data and the operations that the account must carry out.

8.11.2 Object-oriented database management systems

If the world is to be modelled as objects then a database management system is required that can store these objects. Object-oriented databases fulfil this role. Each type of object is specified as a collection of data items and of functions that can be invoked. The actual instances of these objects can then be created and stored. Because the functions for every instance of a particular object type are identical, only a single copy of these functions is usually stored, with pointers to connect object instances to their functions. An example of an organization using an object-oriented database is MedStar Health, a large community-based, not-for-profit health system in the Baltimore–Washington region of the United States. The system integrates a range of functions, including financial, clinical and administrative data. It employs ORACLE database technology and object-oriented data models with online analytical processing.

Although only a small proportion of the database systems developed at present use an object-oriented database management system, a view held by many is that this will grow rapidly as object-modelling approaches gain a wider audience. Hybrid databases built on an integrated object–relational model are more likely to obtain commercial acceptance and are already gaining in popularity.

Mini case 8.3

Object-oriented databases

During the past two decades of the software industry, the database vendors ruled the roost and Larry Ellison, founder and chief executive of Oracle, was the industry's chief rooster.

But Mr Ellison has less to crow about these days. The database market is mature and global sales of new licences in 2002 dropped 6.9 per cent to $6.6bn, according to Gartner Dataquest, the IT researcher.

'This is about the third or fourth time that the database has been declared dead, but the database is more important than ever,' says Chuck Rowzat, executive vice-president of server technologies at Oracle. 'People come up with new types of data and models for how information is accessed.'

This drives innovation in database technology and creates new demand, he says. For example, in the late 1990s, the Internet created new market opportunities for storing web pages and other Internet data. Oracle responded with Oracle8, the predecessor to its current database, which was designed to support the Internet, network computing and 'richer' multimedia data types.

Oracle also included support for object-oriented development, thus answering those critics who argued that the relational database could not adapt to new types of data. In the 1990s, when object technologies were all the rage, a clutch of little-known vendors tried to create an alternative database industry around the object model. They failed to make much of an impression, although Versant, the best-known, is still around and making sales.

Manish Chandra, vice-president of marketing at Versant and a former Sybase engineer, argues that an object database is still the best choice for 'real world' data, such as GPS positioning signals or real-time data collected from the factory floor, but for mainstream commercial applications, a relational database is probably a better bet.

'There are still a few zealots who want to apply object technology to everything but we no longer try to compete with the relational database vendors,' he says.

Adapted from: **Battle to make sense of it all**
By Geoffrey Nairn
FT.com site: 6 August 2003

Questions

1. What are the arguments for adopting an object database?
2. In what ways does the object model differ from the relational model?

8.12 Personal computer (PC) databases

Many database software packages designed for PCs are currently on the market; the market leader by a considerable margin is Microsoft Access. The majority of these packages fall into the category of 'relational databases', although not all are fully relational database systems as described in this chapter. Most produce tables of records with indexes on chosen fields. The tables are held as indexed files on disk. The user can perform **PROJECT**, **SELECT** and **JOIN** operations on the tables. Most packages come with their own programming language in which the commands for these operations are embedded, and sophisticated QBE facilities. Simple applications can be developed easily and quickly by staff who have had little training. However, the user may be exposed to the physical structure of the database unless special programs have been written to provide a protected user interface. Not all packages allow different users to be presented with different views of the database or can be seen as falling easily within the ANSI/SPARC three-level model of a database system. Some of the security and monitoring features of mainframe database systems may be absent. This is not to denigrate the usefulness of PC-database packages. Such packages have been extremely effective as sophisticated record keepers and selective data retrievers – especially when used as the front end to a more sophisticated database engine. They have been instrumental in the massive rise in end-user computing described in the previous chapter. Generally, however, it would be a mistake to think, when a PC and a mainframe database system are being discussed, that each provides the same facilities.

The increasing power of business PCs allows versions of large mainframe database packages such as ORACLE to run on PCs. Much the same facilities are present on both the PC and mainframe versions of the systems (although the speed and capacity of the former are less than that of the latter). SQL has gained acceptance as a standard for a relational database query language. The future trend in medium-sized and large businesses is likely to be towards this new breed of PC database system for local databases. These will have links to mainframe databases for other enquiries. The advantage of a standard such as SQL with a package such as ORACLE is that the same SQL commands can be used to access the local database associated with the PC as can be used to access mainframe relational databases, for example – and all from the same PC. This will increase the availability of access to an extended database to PC users.

8.13 Data warehouses

A data warehouse is a massive independent business database system that is populated with data that has been extracted from a range of sources. The data can be collected on both a current and a historical basis and can come from both internal and external sources. The data is held separately from its origin and is used to help to improve the decision-making process. Any data that might be of relevance and interest to the decision makers of the business can be included in the warehouse.

8.13.1 The origin of data warehouses

To understand how a data warehouse works, it is useful to compare its operation with traditional databases. Many traditional databases are involved in recording day-today operational activities of the business. This activity is termed online transaction processing (OLTP) and is typical of information systems such as airline bookings and banking systems. Typical features of these systems are that:

- they need extensive data control and availability;
- they have high multi-user throughput;
- they require a fast response; and
- they are normally used by clerical users rather than managers.

Once an OLTP system has been established, it is possible to use the data that it generates to aid decision making. Reports and summaries can be drawn from the operational data to inform the decision-making process. This mode of working is described as online analytical processing (OLAP). The characteristics are:

- it involves trend analysis and forecasting;
- it uses summarized historical data (from operational databases);
- it entails complex queries, often building very large tables;
- it is read-intensive;
- the decisions it informs are strategic, so response is time-critical; and
- the users are managers/analysts.

A major problem with performing OLAP queries is that these compete with OLTP systems for resources, leading to poor response times. A solution is to extract and summarize the data in a data warehouse.

Mini case 8.4

Online analytical processing

It might sound like a type of Scandinavian folk dance, but Olap is an acronym for online analytical processing, a valuable type of software that helps users analyse data stored in a database.

Transforming information from raw data into a wide variety of multi-dimensional representations, Olap tools are to data what a gourmet chef is to the humble risotto.

Olap tools can do clever tricks, performing feats such as trend analysis over sequential time periods, slicing subsets of data for on-screen viewing and creating summary-level models across the different dimensions and hierarchies of a database.

Users can explore their data from a historical point of view and use 'what-if' data model scenarios to project ahead into the future.

So how do these Olap tools work?

While the souped-up data are generally accessed through a simple web interface, the brains behind the operation is the Olap server, a high-capacity, multi-user data manipulation engine specially designed to operate on multi-dimensional data structures.

Sitting between a client and a database management system, the Olap server understands how data are organized in the database and has special functions for analysing

▶

the data. This can be done in a variety of ways, which can increase or reduce response times.

Adapted from: Olap
By Chloe Veltman
FT.com site: 29 October 2003

Questions

1. Distinguish between online transaction processing (OLTP) and online analytical processing (OLAP).

2. Why is it unusual for OLTP and OLAP systems to share resources such as a common database?

3. What 'clever tricks' can be performed by the tools employed in OLAP?

8.13.2 Data warehouse architecture

A data warehouse is a collection of subject-oriented data integrated from various operational databases and other external sources. It is usually accessed by end users employing graphical analysis tools and tends to offer read-only access. A diagram showing the use of a typical data warehouse is provided in Figure 8.28.

As the data has been taken off-line and placed into the warehouse, the query functions no longer take valuable system resources from the processing of day-to-day transactions. A corollary of this is that once created, the data warehouse becomes instantly out of date. A policy of updating the warehouse at appropriate intervals must therefore be established.

In some situations, it may be appropriate to partition or copy a subset of the data warehouse into a smaller, self-contained collection of data. These smaller versions of data warehouses are often termed **data marts**. The separation of data might be carried out on a departmental or subject-related basis. A data mart can offer improvements in speed of access and search times by localizing the data, but it introduces yet more potential for inconsistencies. Data marts often provide the source data for online analytical processing and for decision support systems.

The stages in creating and maintaining a data warehouse are normally as follows:

1. **Data extraction:** Data is collected from a range of sources using gateways, e.g. the open database connectivity (ODBC) protocol, and incorporated into the warehouse.

2. **Data cleaning:** Where possible, missing fields are completed, and inconsistencies are reduced or eliminated. For example, data containing the sex of an individual might be stored as 'm/f', 'male/female', '0/1' or even 'true/false'. Data cleaning will ensure that all fields are stored in a consistent format, e.g. 'm/f'.

3. **Data loading:** The data is summarized and aggregated with the existing warehouse data.

4. **Optimization:** Indices are built to improve data access times.

8.13.3 Searching the warehouse

Data tends to have a multidimensional structure. A typical example might be information regarding sales of a particular product over different locations over a period of

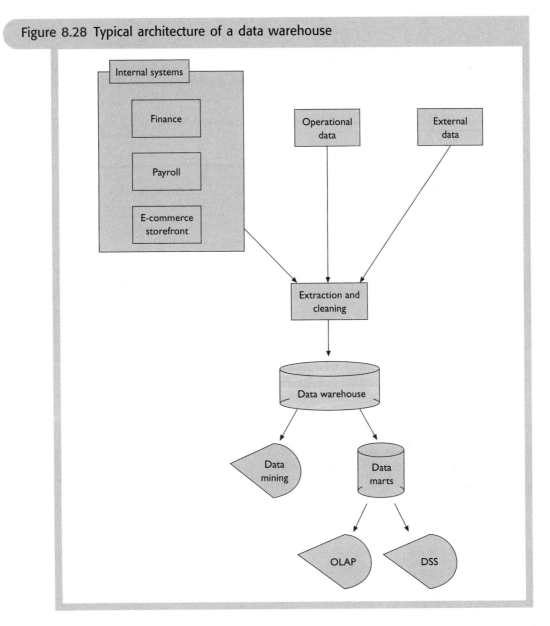

Figure 8.28 Typical architecture of a data warehouse

time sold by different sales representatives. A range of techniques exists to allow the data to be presented in different formats.

Pivoting

Different managers might want different views of this data. A sales team manager might want data summarized by sales representatives over time. A product manager might want to see summaries of production across different regions.

The ability to switch between different perspectives on the same data is known as pivoting. Figure 8.29(a) shows an extract of data illustrating sales of different

Figure 8.29 Pivoting data to provide different perspectives

(a)

	A	B	C	D	E
1	**Agent**	**Month**	**Item**	**Commission**	**Region**
2	Khan	May	Life	2200	South
3	Khan	June	Life	2300	South
4	Hanson	May	Life	1600	North
5	Khan	July	Property	300	South
6	Erikson	May	Life	3500	North
7	Peters	May	Property	2100	North
8	Erikson	June	Property	1060	South
9	Erikson	July	Property	440	South

Data / Pivot 1 / Pivot 2

(b)

	A	B	C	D	E	F	G
1	Sum of Commission		Agent				
2	Month	Region	Erikson	Hanson	Khan	Peters	Grand Total
3	May	North	3500	1600		2100	7200
4		South			2200		2200
5	May Total		3500	1600	2200	2100	9400
6	June	South	1060		2300		3360
7	June Total		1060		2300		3360
8	July	South	440		300		740
9	July Total		440		300		740
10	Grand Total		5000	1600	4800	2100	13500

Data \ **Pivot 1** / Pivot 2

insurance policies by a team of agents working in different geographical areas. Figure 8.29(b) shows chronologically how each agent has performed, subtotalled where appropriate by region. Figure 8.29(c) shows the effect of pivoting the same data again, this time summarizing the figures by agent and policy type.

Figure 8.29 (*Cont'd*)

(c)

	A	B	C	D
1	Sum of Commission	Item		
2	Agent	Life	Property	Grand Total
3	Erikson	3500	1500	5000
4	Hanson	1600		1600
5	Khan	4500	300	4800
6	Peters		2100	2100
7	Grand Total	9600	3900	13500

Roll-up and drill-down

The level of detail required from the data warehouse will vary according to context: precise figures can be obtained by drilling down into the data; a higher-level summary can be obtained by rolling up the data.

Slice and dice

The ability to partition a view of the data and work with that in isolation is known as slice and dice. Like drill-down, it allows a more focused view of a particular section of the data warehouse to be obtained.

A data warehouse is an extremely sophisticated piece of software and consequently is very expensive to create and maintain. Although the potential benefits are great, the costs can prove prohibitive for smaller organizations.

8.13.4 Data mining

Where data is held in large sets, it can be interrogated searching for trends, patterns and relationships. This process is known as data mining. Statistical techniques are applied to the contents of the data set to search for this 'hidden' information and the resulting discoveries can further inform the decision-making process.

Typical techniques employed to carry out data mining include:

- **Decision tables:** This topic was discussed in Chapter 12.
- **Nearest neighbour classification:** Where the shortest route between two items is calculated.

- **Neural networks:** Where processors often acting in parallel mimic the operation of the human brain by applying rules to local data sets.
- **Rule induction – using if–then rules:** This topic is discussed in Chapter 17.
- **K-means clustering:** This entails partitioning an aggregate set of data into logical groups.

A typical use of data mining might be as follows. A business might require sales representatives to travel across a number of geographical areas. The data concerning the details of a sale, the time of sale, location of sale, volume sold etc. for each salesperson would be stored. Mining the data might reveal that certain sales representatives are more or less productive at certain times in the year or in certain geographic regions of the country. It could also show that certain products sell particularly well independently of the person involved or that there are seasonal trends affecting the sales. These patterns might not be apparent from a cursory glance at the raw data but may be revealed using the statistical techniques outlined above. The results of data mining such as this might lead to strategic changes in the operation of the business in an attempt to gain a competitive advantage.

Often the results of data mining are presented visually to facilitate data analysis. A scatter chart, for example, plotting the age of victims of crime against the age of their alleged assailants, might reveal patterns which would assist detectives in building a profile of a typical suspect of such crime.

Data mining on the Web

Data mining is often associated with data warehousing as a data warehouse provides a large set of data, conveniently collected and aggregated, which can effectively and easily be mined. Data mining can, however, be conducted on any data set. One application that is rapidly gaining interest is the analysis of interactions between users and websites. If personal data is collected from users, along with a trace of their activity at the website, it may be possible to mine these records and detect patterns in the users' interests or in their navigation behaviour. This may reveal results such as:

- partitions of users into related groupings;
- clusters of URLs that tend to be requested together;
- ordering of activities such as the accessing of URLs.

Mini case 8.5

Data warehousing and data mining

Windber Research Institute has chosen Teradata, a division of NCR Corporation, to create the first and only central data warehouse where molecular and clinical information is being assembled and seamlessly integrated in a single data warehouse to help find the cause of breast and other forms of cancer.

Windber Research Institute is one of the world's most integrated, high-throughput biomedical research facilities specifically set up to study the relationship between genes, proteins and disease. The Institute is using the data from several sources, such as GenBank (DNA sequences for further analysis), PubMed (scientific literature), SWISS-PROT (protein information for further analysis), KEGG (metabolic pathways) and DIP (protein-protein interactions), which are then linked to WRI's own molecular (DNA, RNA, protein) and clinical data. These databases are all integrated in order to accelerate medical research to facilitate the study of gene and protein function as related to human reproductive cancers and cardiovascular disease.

The Teradata technology will enable Windber to store, retrieve, analyse and manage the massive amounts of data. In essence, Windber's approach will accelerate discovery and knowledgebase generation and will help bring individualized medicine to patients by identifying the patient-specific causes at the molecular level. They will be able to seamlessly link clinical and demographic information, DNA sequence information, protein profile, genotype, gene expression data, histopathology and radiology.

Added Nick Jacobs, president and chief executive officer of Windber Research Institute, 'We specifically referenced and sought the same data warehousing capabilities used by Wal-Mart and the top companies worldwide. We know that Teradata is the right solution for us to keep The Windber Research Institute as a leading force in medical research. It is one more powerful element that puts us beyond the leading edge, to the bleeding edge – the place we feel we need to be to cauterize and stop breast cancer and heart disease.'

The demands of Windber were to have a data warehouse that could handle 50 terabytes of information generated every nine months. With 30,000–35,000 genes present in humans, finding the subset of genes that are associated with the onset, progression and/or severity of a disease is challenging. Typically, 166 MB of information is generated from each sample. Windber also has a tissue repository with a capacity for 240,000 tissue samples. Approximately 50 terabytes of data, both images and text, is expected to be generated in nine months.

The work with Windber Research Institute is another example of Teradata's work in life sciences to help understand the root causes of disease. Teradata began working with Information Management Consultants (IMC) in 2002 to enable researchers and scientists to exponentially accelerate the pace of genetic research on mice brains that may lead to the understanding of many human conditions, including brain diseases and forms of cancer.

'Instead of taking a year to study one gene, data mining enables us to study the potential interactions of 13,000 mice genes in just one week,' said Dr. Carrolee Barlow, scientist and adjunct faculty member at Salk Institute. 'From this course of study, we hope to more quickly learn how to treat certain diseases in people.'

Adapted from: **Data warehousing used for first time to create a single database to help find the cause of breast cancer**
Business Wire: 23 September 2003

Questions

1. Why does the success of this research require more than just a traditional database storage and management system?

2. What features of the data warehouse do Windber Research hope to exploit?

3. List some of the main techniques used in data mining.

4. What benefits are likely to be gained from employing data mining techniques?

Summary

Business organizations need to keep and process data for their survival. Data is held in master files about ongoing entities of interest to the business. Examples are customer, debtor, employee and stock files. Data used to update master files is stored in transaction files. Examples are sales, payments, receipts, timesheet returns, credit notes and sales order files. The storage and access strategies for disk files go hand in hand. List structures offer the capability of sequential access while providing for fast record insertion and deletion. Inverted list structures place attribute values in indexes, and pointer fields are transferred from the records to the index. This opens the way for the retrieval of records based on properties of record fields other than the key field.

The database approach recognizes data as an important resource of the organization that is shared by many applications and so requires careful planning, management and control. Databases and database management systems have been developed to replace file-based systems of data storage. This is because, first, sophisticated file interrogation techniques have led to the need for automated data management and, second, business has demanded more flexible data retrieval and reporting facilities to meet the needs of managerial decision making.

File-based, application-led approaches to data storage often lead to problems. The duplication of data over many files, each being the responsibility of a different person or department, can lead to update difficulties and the presence of inconsistent data in the organization. The same data may also be represented in different storage formats in different files, and the files themselves may have different organization and access characteristics. The dependence of application programs on the files that serve them increases the difficulty of changing data storage structures without having to change the programs that access them.

The database approach, on the other hand, recognizes the importance of developing an integrated store of data structured in a meaningful manner for the organization. The database contains data stored with minimal redundancy and organized in a manner that is a logical reflection of the relationships between the entities on which data is held.

Database management systems are sophisticated software packages that maintain the database and present an interface to users and user programs that is independent of physical storage details. This logical presentation of the data facilitates user enquiries and applications program development – programmers need be concerned only with what data is required for an application, not with the physical aspects of how to retrieve it. The independence of the logical representation also allows physical reorganization of the database without the need for application program changes. Commercial database systems define the logical structure of the database using a data definition language (DDL) and allow data alterations through a data manipulation language (DML). Other facilities provided are data dictionaries, accounting utilities, concurrency control, backup, recovery and security features.

In understanding database systems, it is useful to identify three separate levels at which data may be represented:

1. the conceptual schema (an overall logical view of the database);
2. the external schema (a logical presentation of part of the database in the way most suitable to meet a user's requirements);
3. the internal schema (the representation of storage and access characteristics for the data).

Three data models have had significant impact on the development of commercial database management systems software. They are, chronologically, the hierarchical, network and relational models.

Both the hierarchical and network models impose restrictions on the way relationships can be represented and data accessed. The hierarchical is more limiting, restricting data to tree structures using downward-pointing $1:n$ relationships. Network structures do not allow the direct representation of $m:n$ relationships. Relational database management systems are table-based logical representations of data structures that allow simple and powerful data manipulation. The advantages of relational systems in terms of their representation and retrieval characteristics are to be set against their slow speed of operation. This makes them unsuitable for high-volume, transaction-based data processing.

The way that a data model is developed for an organization and the design of a database to incorporate this model is reserved for Chapter 13 on data analysis and modelling. The entity–relationship modelling approach will be used, and the techniques of normalization (often associated with the design of effective relational databases) will be explained there.

Recently, a great deal of interest has been expressed in the development of data warehouses. These repositories of aggregated data lie outside the day-to-day transaction-processing systems. They provide a series of time-stamped snapshots of data, which can be extracted and presented in many formats. Various techniques have evolved to search (or mine) the data. Data mining can be a valuable source of new knowledge to an organization as trends and patterns can be detected that would not otherwise be evident.

Data warehouses can prove to be a high-cost solution, but they often provide improvements in customer relationship management and can lead to significant competitive business advantage.

Review questions

1. Explain the following terms:

file	variable-length record
backup file	transaction file
record type	inverted list
file update	fully inverted file
record	master file
field	

2. Explain the difference between logical and physical files.

3. Define the following terms:

database	concurrent use of data	relational join operation
database management system	relation	database query language
data independence	attribute	data dictionary
database administrator	domain of an attribute	report generator
data redundancy	key	internal schema
data sharing	relational selection operation	conceptual schema
	relational projection operation	external schema

4. Explain the difference between a *data definition language* (DDL) and a *data manipulation language* (DML).

5. What limitations are there for the application-led, file-based approach, and how does the database approach overcome these?

6. What is the distinction between a conceptual schema and a data model?

Exercises

1. Explain the advantages and disadvantages of using a flat file as against a multidimensional file.

2. By considering a stock record, give an example of an entity, an attribute, a record, a field, a data item, a key and a repeating group.

3. Figure 8.30 shows an order form for the ABC Company.
   (a) Suggest a record structure suitable for keeping data on orders. Show any repeating fields and specify field sizes and types.
   (b) The order file is to be kept as a permanent record so that customers can make enquiries concerning the status of their order and its contents by providing the order number. The status possibilities for the order are 'received', 'awaiting stock', 'being processed', 'finished'. The file is also used in end-of-week batch processing of orders. Suggest a suitable file organization and provide a justification for your answer.

4. Using your knowledge of the way a typical business functions, suggest typical record structures for each of the following:
   (a) employee record;
   (b) stock record;

Figure 8.30 Order form for the ABC Company

```
ABC Company   _____          Delivery address _____
Order#        _____                           _____
Date          _____                           _____
Customer#     _____                           _____
Customer name _____
Invoice address _____
              _____

Item#   Item description              Quantity    Price      Total
 __      _____                     __         __         __
 __      _____                     __         __         __
 __      _____                     __         __         __
 __      _____                     __         __         __
 __      _____                     __         __         __
                                                          Subtotal __
            Discount ___%  Discount _____
                           Sales tax _____
                                                          Total __
```

(c) sales ledger customer record;

(d) salesperson commission record.

5. A road haulage company is to introduce a computer-based system to handle customer bookings for the transfer of customer freight from one town to another. Each lorry will make a special journey from one town to another if the customer's freight consignment is sufficient to count as a full lorry load. Otherwise, different consignments are accumulated and transferred from the source town to the destination town on one of the freight company's standard journeys. It has been decided to implement the system as a series of files. The following have been suggested:

(a) customer file;

(b) consignment file;

(c) journey file;

(d) special journey file;

(e) lorry file.

The application must be able to accept and record consignment bookings, assign these consignments to journeys, ensure that invoicing for completed transport of consignments occurs and answer random queries from customers on expected delivery dates. You are required to specify record layouts for the various files.

6. 'There is no reason for an accountant, financier or any other business person involved with a computerized file-based information system to know about the storage organization of data in files and access methods to that data, only about the nature of the data.' Do you agree?

7. Explain the terms *internal schema*, *external schema* and *conceptual schema*. Illustrate your answer by reference to the project/employee/department example in Section 8.5.

8. Give an example of two relations and the result of applying a **JOIN** operation without specifying the common domain over which the join is to be made.

9. Using the information in Figure 8.31:

(a) What records would be displayed in response to the following queries?

(i) **SELECT** *supplier_name*
   FROM SUPPLIER
   WHERE *supplier_city* = "London"

(ii) **SELECT** *warehouse#*
   FROM STORAGE
   WHERE *part#* = "P2" **AND** *quantity_held* > 40

(iii) **SELECT** SUPPLIER.*supplier_name*, CONTRACT.*part#*
   FROM SUPPLIER, CONTRACT
   WHERE SUPPLIER.*supplier#* = CONTRACT.*supplier#*
      AND CONTRACT.*quantity_supplied* > 30

(iv) **SELECT** *supplier_name*
   FROM SUPPLIER
   WHERE *supplier#* = **ANY (SELECT** *supplier#*
         FROM CONTRACT
         WHERE *part#* = P1)

Figure 8.31

SUPPLIER

supplier#	supplier_name	supplier_city
SI	Smith	London
S2	Jones	London
S3	Smith	Derby
S4	Patel	Kentucky
S6	Mendez	Bristol

PART

part#	part_name	price
PI	dynamo	20
P2	alternator	30
P3	carburettor	30
P7	dynamo	27

WAREHOUSE

warehouse#	w_city
WI	London
W2	London
W3	London
W4	Leeds

CONTRACT

part#	supplier#	quantity_supplied
PI	SI	43
PI	S2	49
PI	S3	58
PI	S6	14
P2	SI	5
P2	S6	134
P3	SI	19
P3	S2	19
P3	S3	14
P3	S4	21
P3	S6	31
P7	S6	34

STORAGE

part#	warehouse#	quantity_held
PI	WI	482
PI	W2	394
PI	W3	201
P2	WI	43
P2	W2	41
P2	W3	31
P2	W4	41
P3	WI	95
P3	W2	0
P3	W4	91
P7	WI	6
P7	W2	5
P7	W3	I
P7	W4	4

(v) **SELECT** supplier_name
   FROM SUPPLIER
      WHERE supplier# = **ANY (SELECT** supplier#
            FROM CONTRACT
               WHERE part# = **ANY (SELECT** part#
               FROM STORAGE
               WHERE warehouse# = "W3"))

(b) Design relational database enquiries in an SQL-like language to:

   (i) Determine the part #s of dynamos.
   (ii) Determine all supplier #s of suppliers who supply more than forty units of part # P1.
   (iii) Determine all part #s and part names stored in either warehouse 1 or warehouse 2.
   (iv) Select all suppliers located in the same city as any warehouse.
   (v) Select all supplier names who supply parts in any warehouse not located in the same city as the supplier.

10. For the relations:

   BOOK (book#, title, author, stack address)
   BORROWER (borrower#, borrower name, borrower address, borrower status)
   LOAN (loan#, borrower#, date, loan status)

specify SQL or relational algebra expressions to represent the following queries:

(a) What are the titles of all books by Tolstoy?

(b) What book titles were loaned on or before 1 April 2004?

(c) List the borrower names and book titles for staff users (*borrower status* = staff) that have been borrowed since 11 August 2004 and are still on loan (*loan status* = on loan).

Databases and XML

Databases lie at the heart of IT and 'relational' databases have dominated the way data has been organized since the late 1980s. Larry Ellison, chief executive of Oracle and one of the IT industry's best-known characters, made his fortune from them.

The relational database is much more than a way of storing and viewing data. It has been a primary influence on general IT development for over two decades.

Edgar 'Ted' Codd, the IBM researcher who invented the relational database in the late 1960s, and died earlier this year aged 79, was driven by three main goals: to improve the way computer data was organized, to devise a simple way of viewing it and to provide tools for processing 'sets' of data.

Mr Codd achieved these goals by separating the systems which store and manage data from the tools used to view and manipulate it. The same principle lies at the heart of today's distributed 'client/server' systems and the World Wide Web. He met the second goal by viewing data as a set of two-dimensional 'tables', organized in rows and columns, which could be 'related' to each other.

The PC spreadsheet program uses the same tabular view of data. And meeting the third goal led to the development of the Structured Query Language (SQL), an innovation which enabled sets of data to be processed with simple instructions.

But despite its dominance and success, the relational database is due for re-assessment. Changes in the types of data that organizations need to store have stretched the original design.

In his 1981 Turing Award Lecture, Mr Codd noted, prophetically: 'As it stands today, the relational database is best suited to data with a rather regular or homogeneous structure. Can we retain the advantages of the relational approach while handling heterogeneous data also? Such data may include images, text and miscellaneous facts. An affirmative answer is expected and some research is in progress on this subject, but more is needed.'

The relational database model has, of course, expanded to include ways to handle multimedia data. Leading suppliers IBM and Oracle have built extensions and have also embraced the eXtensible Mark-up Language (XML) which can store data formats along with the data. New approaches – some building on the relational model and others taking an innovative view – have also emerged.

But Ken Jacobs, vice-president of server technology at Oracle, dismisses any suggestion that the relational database is in decline: 'The economy has, of course, had an effect on all industries. Capital expenditure is down and IT has suffered along with the rest. But at the same time, the relational database is becoming more capable. Oracle and other database vendors have extended it to support new technologies such as object-oriented and Java.'

▶

More important, Oracle and its rivals are extending SQL to include XML. Mr Jacobs says that SQL has come a long way and Oracle, for example, can now support advanced data retrieval operations such as online analytical processing.

'SQL has become very practical with recent innovations. We support innovations such as analytical capabilities and extensions to support XML.'

Lou Agosta, a research analyst at Forrester, says that IBM and Microsoft have also been looking closely at XML: 'They all have XML extensions in their existing products and it is clear XML is very important. But it doesn't solve the problems of unstructured data.'

But new developments at Microsoft and IBM could show the way forward, he says: 'Microsoft has Xquery and IBM is working on Xsperanto – both new query languages which look at integrating different types of data such as e-mail, documents and transactions.'

Some are taking a more radical approach. Simon Williams, chief executive of Lazy Software, a UK database software company that has developed a 'post-relational' database called the 'associative' model of data, says: 'We came from a background of developing programming tools and saw that program development was more complex than it needed to be because of the relational model.'

Building on a strand of database research at IBM called Triplestore, Mr Williams claims that the Lazy database system, Sentences, reduces the complexity of writing programs around relational databases:

'Triplestore provides a data structure which does not physically change – although it is not clever enough to cope with commercial applications. We have extended the idea so we can raise programming productivity. Ted Codd aimed to free programmers from the physical structure of data – we aim to free them from the logical structure.'

It is not only technologists who are working on alternatives to the relational database, however. Some users are finding other ways to cope with special data problems. Simon Chappell, group IT director at international guide publishers Time Out, says the company struggled for 12 years with relational databases, before finding salvation with an XML-based product:

'Our big problem is we are so content-rich. We have lots of listing data – some of it structured and some unstructured. Using a conventional database was hard because defining the data was so complicated. The more we looked at databases, the more we realized it was not going to work,' he explains.

Time Out is working with Xylem's XML repository to build a flexible database which will hold its listings data and provide much greater flexibility.

'We have a lot of data locked up in publishing packages like Quark Express and we need to be able to update the data following publishing changes. We can do this with XML and it gives us a very free way of storing everything from a restaurant review to opening times,' says Mr Chappell.

There is little doubt that Ted Codd's relational model will survive – and indeed thrive. It is the best solution for dealing with structured data, but it is likely that innovative approaches will grow alongside it.

Adapted from: **Every database has its day**
By Philip Manchester
FT.com site: 6 August 2003

Questions

1. Define the three main data models that have been used in commercial database development.

2. What factors have led to the relational model becoming dominant?

3. What factors have subsequently led to the relational model being enhanced, overhauled and superseded?

4. What is XML? How has XML contributed to the development of data modelling, storage and retrieval?

5. Give examples of unstructured and semi-structured data. Why does the manipulation of unstructured and semi-structured data pose so many difficulties?

Recommended reading

Adelman S. *et al.* (2000). *Data Warehouse Project Management.* Addison-Wesley
A thorough text covering the goals and objectives and organizational and cultural issues involved in implementing a data warehouse.

Benyon-Davies P. (2004). *Database Systems*, 3rd edn. Palgrave Macmillan
This updated text gives coverage of databases, database management systems and database development. Latter chapters cover trends in database technologies, especially concerning distributed and parallel processing, and chapters on data warehouses and data mining. Although this book goes beyond the needs of many business studies programmes, its clarity would render it useful.

Connolly T. *et al.* (2001). *Database Systems: A Practical Approach to Design, Implementation and Management*, 3rd edn. Addison-Wesley
A comprehensive text covering databases, SQL, transaction management, data warehouses and data mining, and advanced concepts.

Date C.J. (1995). *Relational Database: Writings.* New York: Addison Wesley Longman

Date C.J. (2003). *An Introduction to Database Systems*, reissued 8th edn. Harlow: Longman Higher Education Division
A comprehensive classic textbook in this area. Although largely technical and written for the computer scientist, this provides a clear introduction to databases and data models.

Delmater R. and Hancock M. (2001). *Data Mining Explained: A Managers Guide to Customer Centric Business Intelligence.* Digital Press
This is a book written for managers who have a technical orientation. It explains in an easy way how data mining will determine future customer relationship strategies. The book describes how to develop a data mining strategy and shows how data mining can be applied to specific vertical markets. There are a number of case studies of key industries such as retail, financial services, health care and telecommunications.

Inmon W.H. (2002). *Building the Data Warehouse*, 3rd edn. Wiley
The book covers, at an accessible level for students or managers, data warehousing techniques for customer sales and support, including data mining, exploration warehousing, and the integration of data warehousing with ERP systems. Future trends including capturing and analysing clickstream data for e-business are covered.

McFadden F.R. (2002). *Modern Database Management*, reissued 6th edn. Benjamin Cummings
This is a standard student text covering all aspects of database design and management. Each chapter has review questions, problems and exercises.

O'Neill P. and O'Neill E. (2001). *Databases Principles, Programming and Performance*, 2nd edn. Academic Press

A detailed text taking a technical approach to SQL, the object/relation model, transactions, distributed databases and indexing techniques.

Pratt P.J. and Adamski J.J. (2002). *Database Systems Management and Design*, 4th edn. International Thomson Publishing

This is a detailed student text on databases. Also included are chapters on SQL, microcomputer database management and fourth-generation environments.

Wyzalek J. (ed.) (2000). *Enterprise Systems Integration*. Averbach

A selection of papers covering aspects of enabling technologies such as middleware, Corba and COM. Of particular interest are sections on integrating legacy, object and relational databases, and data warehouses, data mining and the Web enabling of data warehouses. Although a technical book, it is written with a business focus.

Chapter 9

Information systems: control and responsibility

Learning outcomes

On completion of this chapter, you should be able to:

- Describe the controlling effect of feedback and feedforward in an information system
- Evaluate the preventive measures necessary to effect control in an information system
- Describe controls that can be applied to data in transmission
- Evaluate a range of organizational controls that should be considered in the design and operation of an information system
- Discuss the rights and responsibilities of individuals, organizations and society in the development, implementation and use of information systems
- Apply principles of data protection legislation.

Introduction

This chapter introduces the general principles behind control and security in systems. These are then applied to computerized information systems. The increasing dependence of business on the reliable, complete and accurate processing of data by computers, often without manual checks, indicates that controls must be planned and designed. This occurs before the development of computer systems and their surrounding manual procedures. Security and control should therefore be considered prior to systems design and certainly feature in the design process itself, not as afterthoughts. The increasing use of computers in the processing and transmission of confidential data and funds has also made computer systems attractive targets for fraud. The need to take steps to guard against this possibility has been a powerful stimulus to an emphasis on security in the process of systems analysis and design.

In the early part of this chapter, the basic concepts of control systems are developed by considering the general ideas behind feedback, feedforward and preventive controls. These are explained and applied to manual business systems. Controls over computerized information systems are introduced by identifying the various goals and levels of control that are applicable. Controls over data movement into, through and out of the computer system are covered, together with controls over the transmission of data between computers or through the public telecommunications network. Some of the ways that fraud may be prevented are by restricting access to the computer system or to the data in it, or by scrambling the data prior to storage or transmission so that it is useless to any unauthorized person. The methods of achieving these ends are also explained.

Computer systems always lie within and interface with a surrounding manual system. Not only should computer aspects of this combined socio-technical system be the subject of control but also the organizational and personnel elements. To aid security, it is important that the system be structured in a way that facilitates this. The way that functions are separated as a means of control is developed in later sections of this chapter. The reliability of controls and security procedures operating over a working transaction- and information-processing system can be established by means of an audit. Although auditing is a large area in itself, the overall strategy adopted and the aid given by computer-assisted tools in the auditing of computer-based systems is outlined. The chapter also considers the relationship between information systems, organizations and individuals. Issues such as crime, privacy and acceptability of behaviour raise questions of responsibility. Who should ensure that certain practices or activities are restrained or even prevented? Is it the duty of an individual, an organization or society as a whole? There may be a collective belief amongst members of a community that there is a social responsibility in resolving a particular problem. In other situations the responsibility may rest on an organization. In this case the resolution may be in corporate governance and how the organization manages its own affairs. Also, the form of action taken may vary greatly. Checks, controls and balances take many forms. They can be imposed by legislation, they can be adopted voluntarily by individuals or organizations or they can just become custom and practice with no formal agreement. Judgments of the courses of actions taken are ethical considerations. Once a framework of policies, rules and legislation is in place, the ethics of actions taken can be considered. One example given extended treatment is that of privacy, in particular as enshrined by data protection legislation. Data on persons is the subject of data protection legislation. This has implications both for security and for the design of systems holding data on persons. The reasons for the rise of this legislation and the general principles behind the Data Protection Act in the UK are explained, together with the effects of the legislation on personal data security and access.

Finally, the need for a methodology for the identification of risk and the design of controls is stressed. Controls are an integral part of systems design, which is covered in Chapter 14 on systems design and Chapter 15 on detailed design.

9.1   Control systems

Controls, if they are to be effective, must operate in a systematic way. This section considers the general principles behind control systems before applying these to business systems. Some controls work by sensing or predicting the state of a system, comparing that state with a desired standard and then carrying out some correcting action if the state does not meet favourably with the standard. Other controls prevent (or attempt to prevent) a system moving away from a desired state. They do this by preventing abnormal but possible occurrences that would have this effect.

Feedback and feedforward are examples of the first type of control. Preventive controls are examples of the second. Feedback and feedforward controls involve the collection and processing of data and so operate within the business information system. Preventive controls prevent inaccurate and unreliable data processing, damage to data-processing equipment and unauthorized access to data, and so too are within this environment.

It is one of the responsibilities of management to ensure that adequate and effective controls are present at all levels in a business organization. There is always a cost–benefit dimension to the existence of any control – it is insufficient to consider the control outside this context. All controls have some cost associated with their installation and also a probability/possibility that they will fail in their control function. On the benefit side, there is the prevention or correction of the undesired state of affairs. It may be possible to assign a money value to this benefit, but it is important to bear in mind that this undesired state of affairs might not have happened in the absence of the control (this is particularly true with preventive controls), so probability factors also have to be taken into account here. Cost–benefit considerations surrounding a strategy for control in a business are covered in a later section of this chapter, but it should be made clear from the outset that the major question surrounding a control is not 'does it work?' but 'is it cost–benefit effective?'

9.1.1 Feedback control systems

The general nature of a feedback control system is shown in Figure 9.1. It consists of:

- A **process**, which accepts inputs and converts these into outputs.
- A **sensor**, which monitors the state of the process.
- A **controller**, which accepts data from the sensor and accepts standards given externally. The controller then generates adjustments or decisions, which are fed into and affect the process.

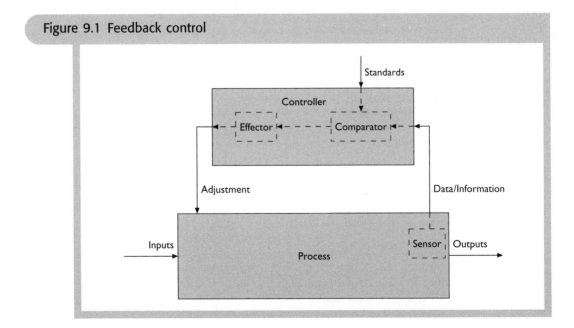

Figure 9.1 Feedback control

- A **comparator** in the controller, which compares the sensed data with the standard and passes an indication of the deviation of the standard from the monitored data to the effector.

- An **effector** in the controller, which on the basis of the output of the comparator makes an adjustment to the output from the controller.

The example often given of a controller in a feedback control system is a thermostat. It accepts data about temperature from a sensor, compares it with a standard that is set by the householder and if the temperature is below or above this standard (by a certain amount) makes an adjustment to the boiler, turning it either on or off.

Feedback control enables a dynamic self-regulating system to function. Movements of the system from equilibrium lead to a self-correcting adjustment, implying that the combination of process and controller can be left over long periods of time and will continue to produce a guaranteed output that meets standards. Automated controller–process pairs are seldom encountered in business (although they often are in production engineering). However, it is common for a person to be the controller. That is, an individual will monitor a process, compare it against given standards and take the necessary action in adjustment. This is one of the roles of management.

In an organization, it is usual for control to be applied at several levels. The controller of a process at level 1 supplies information on the process and adjustments to a higher-level controller (who also receives information from other level 1 controllers). The information supplied may be an exceptional deviation of the process from the standard (exception reporting) or perhaps a summary (summary reporting). The higher-level controller can make adjustments to the functioning and structure of the system containing the level 1 controllers with their processes. The higher-level controller will also be given standards and will supply information to an even higher-level controller. The nesting of control may be many levels deep. At the highest level, the controllers are given standards externally or they set their own. These levels of control correspond to levels of management. Above the lowest levels of control are the various layers of middle management. Top management responds to standards expected of it by external bodies, such as shareholders, as well as setting its own standards.

The study of feedback control is called **cybernetics**. Cybernetics ideas and principles have been applied to the study of management control of organizations (see for example Beer, 1994). Although real organizations are never so simple and clear-cut that they fit neatly into the feedback model, the idea of feedback provides a useful perspective on modelling management decision making and control.

In order to be useful, feedback controls, as well as satisfying the cost–benefit constraint, should also be designed in accordance with the following principles:

- Data and information fed to the controller should be simple and straightforward to understand. It must be designed to fit in with the intellectual capabilities of the controller, require no longer to digest than the time allowed for an adjustment to be made, and be directed to the task set for the controller. It is a common mistake for computerized systems that are responsible for generating this data to generate pages of reports that are quickly consigned to the rubbish bin.

    For example, a person in charge of debtor control (where the process is one of debtor-account book-keeping) may only need information on debtor accounts that have amounts outstanding over a set number of days, not information on all accounts. On these debtor accounts the controller probably initially needs only summary information, such as the amount of debt, its age profile and the average turnover with the debtor, but not the delivery address or a complete list of past invoices.

■ Data and information fed to the controller should be timely. Two possibilities are regular reports on deviations from standards or immediate reports where corrective action must be taken quickly.

■ Each controller (manager) will have a sphere of responsibility and a scope for authority (ideally these should cover much the same area). It is important that the standards set and the data provided to the controller are restricted within these limitations. The manager is in the best position in the organization to understand the workings of the process and may often be expected to take some responsibility for the setting of realistic standards.

Standard cost systems – an example of feedback control

In management accounting the term **standard cost** refers to the budgeted cost incurred in the production of a unit of output. It will be made up of various components such as material, labour and power as well as overheads such as machine maintenance. During the production process the various costs of production are monitored and the **actual cost** per unit is established. This is compared with the standard cost and variances of the actual cost from the standard are calculated. There may be some labour variances attributable to the cost of labour or the amount of labour per unit of production. There may be variances on material or overheads, or some combination of both. On the basis of the variance analysis, various adjustments to the production process may be recommended. For instance, an adverse labour variance analysis might be adjusted by speeding up a production assembly line or increasing piece-rate benefits.

9.1.2 Feedforward control system

The general nature of a feedforward control system is shown in Figure 9.2. The chief difference from a feedback control system is that the monitored data on the current performance of the system is not used to compare this performance with a standard but is used to predict the future state of the system, which is then compared with the future standard set. To do this, a further component called a **predictor** is added to the controller. The predictor takes current data and uses a predictive model of the process to estimate the future state of the system. In carrying out the prediction it is likely that future estimates of variables occurring outside the process, but affecting it, will need to be input into the predictor. The prediction is then fed into the comparator and effector, which will make any necessary adjustment to ensure that the system meets future objectives. The success of feedforward control depends on the suitability of the model and modelling information.

Cash flow planning – an example of feedforward control

Most organizations like to keep their cash balances within certain limits. To stray outside these limits leads to excess funds that could be profitably employed, or to diminished funds, making the company vulnerable to a cash crisis.

The cash inflows and outflows of a company result from a number of factors. Inflows will generally be receipts from customers, investments and sales of assets. Among outflows

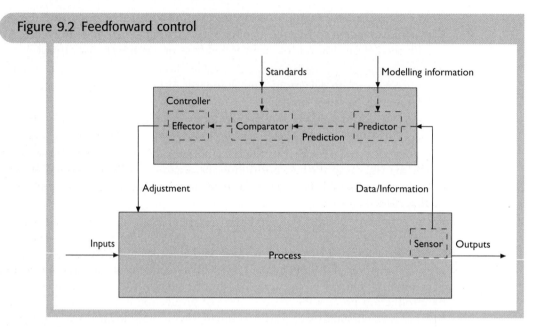

Figure 9.2 Feedforward control

will be payments to suppliers for purchases, wages and salaries, payments for overheads, payments of interest on loans, capital expenditures, tax payments and dividends. Inflows and outflows will be spread over periods of time, and the amounts and exact timing will be subject to uncertainty.

It is important that predictions (accurate within limits) are made so that adjustments can be implemented to ensure that the cash balances remain at the desired level. For instance, a predicted cash drop may be financed by a sale of securities held by the organization rather than by incurring a heavy bank overdraft with a punitive interest rate.

Feedforward systems are needed because time is required to implement the necessary adjustments, which need to be active rather than reactive. In this cash management example it is common nowadays to use computer-aided prediction either with spreadsheets or with financial logic-modelling packages. The predictions are passed to a senior manager or financial director, who takes the decision on the adjusting action.

9.1.3 Preventive control systems

Feedback and feedforward control work by a controller 'standing' outside a process and evaluating current or predicted deviations from a norm as a basis for taking adjusting action. Preventive controls, by contrast, reside within a process, their function being to prevent an undesired state of affairs occurring. Just as with the other types of control mechanism, preventive controls are an integral part of manual and computerized information systems. In business information systems, these controls are broadly aimed at protecting assets, often by ensuring that incorrect recording of assets does not occur and by preventing inaccurate processing of information. Preventive controls fall into a number of categories.

Documentation

Careful design of documentation will aid the prevention of unintentional errors in recording and processing. Several points need to be taken into account for the preparation of document formats:

- Source documentation requires enough data entry spaces on it to collect all the types of data required for the purposes for which the document is to be used.

- Transfer of data from one document to another should be minimized, as transcription errors are common. It is usual to use multipart documentation, which transfers the contents of the top copy through several layers by the pressure of the pen.

- Documents should be clearly headed with a document type and document description.

- Documents should be sequentially prenumbered. Provided that any 'waste' documents are retained, this allows a check on the completeness of document processing. It is aimed at preventing the accidental misplacing of documents and ensures that documents used for the generation of fraudulent transactions are retained for inspection.

- A document generally represents the recording of some transaction, such as an order for a set of items, and will undergo several processes in the course of carrying out the transaction requirements. It is important that wherever authorization for a step is required, the document has space for the authorization code or signature.

- The documentation needs to be stored in a manner that allows retrieval of the steps through which a transaction has passed. This may require storing copies of the document in different places accessed by different reference numbers, customer account numbers and dates. This is called an **audit trail**.

Procedures manual

As well as clearly designed forms, the accurate processing of a transaction document requires those responsible to carry out the organization's procedures correctly. These should be specified in a procedures manual. This will contain a written statement of the functions to be carried out by the various personnel in the execution of data processing. Document flowcharts (covered in Chapter 12 on process analysis and modelling) are an important aid to unambiguous specification. They indicate the path that is taken through the various departments and operations by a document and its copies until the document finally leaves the business organization or is stored.

The procedures manual, if followed, prevents inconsistent practices arising that govern the processing of transactions and other operations. Inconsistency leads to inaccurate or incomplete processing. The manual can also be used for staff training, further encouraging consistent practice in the organization.

Separation of functions

It is sound practice to separate the various functions that need to be performed in processing data. These different functions are the responsibility of different personnel in the organization. The separation is aimed at preventing fraud.

If a single member of staff were to be in charge of carrying out all the procedures connected with a transaction then it would be possible, and might be tempting, for that person to create fraudulent transactions. For instance, if a person were responsible for authorizing a cash payment, recording the payment and making the payment then it would be easy to carry out theft. When these functions are separated and placed in the hands of different individuals, fraud may still be tempting but will be less possible, as collusion between several persons is required. It is usual to separate the following functions:

- the custody of assets, such as cash, cheques and inventory;
- the recording function, such as preparing source documents, carrying out book-keeping functions and preparing reconciliations; and
- the authorization of operations and transactions, such as the authorization of cash payments, purchase orders and new customer credit limits.

These functions may also be carried out in different geographical locations (in different offices or even different sites). If documentation is passed from one department to another, the physical isolation of personnel provides further barriers to collusion.

Both functional and geographical separation are difficult to implement in a small business organization, as there may be so few staff that separation becomes impossible.

Personnel controls

A business relies on its personnel. Personnel must be selected and trained effectively to ensure that they are competent to carry out the tasks required of them.

Selection procedures should establish the qualification, experience and special talents required for the post being offered. Tests, interviews, the taking up of a reference and the checking of qualifications held will determine whether a candidate meets these requirements. The prevention of incompetent personnel being selected for tasks is an important control because once they are hired, the employment legislation in many countries makes it difficult to remove a member of staff even if that person's unsuitability for the job is subsequently discovered.

Training needs to be planned carefully to ensure that it delivers the necessary skills to staff, given their initial abilities and the tasks that they are to perform.

Supervision of staff in the workplace, as well as preventing fraud, also aids staff who are learning a new process by giving them the confidence that experience and authority are available to assist them with any difficulties that may arise.

Finally, it should never be forgotten that the personnel in an organization are people in their own right, with a wide range of interests, abilities, limitations, objectives and personality styles. If they are to work together successfully and happily, considerable ability needs to be displayed by management in preventing interpersonal differences and difficulties escalating and leading to disputes that affect the smooth running of the organization.

Physical controls

One way of avoiding illegal loss of assets such as cash is to exclude staff from unnecessary access to these assets. A range of physical controls may be used to prevent access – locks, safes, fences and stout doors are obvious methods. It may be equally important to prevent records being unnecessarily available to staff. Once again, physical controls may be used as a preventive measure. There are a range of natural hazards that affect a manual information system, hazards that can be guarded against. Fire controls, for instance, are an essential and often legally required feature of a business.

Mini case 9.1

Software piracy

German authorities on Monday arrested five men and raided 46 premises in the North Rhine-Westphalia region, in one of the country's biggest crackdowns on suspected software piracy.

The BKA, or German Federal Criminal Authority, said it had been tipped off by Microsoft some months ago that illegal copies of its software were being produced.

Following a preliminary investigation, it moved in on Monday morning to seize software and computer hardware from the 46 flats and offices. In addition to the five men arrested, three other people were detained for questioning.

The arrested men are suspected of having forged software from a number of manufacturers, including Microsoft, over a period of several years.

In addition to creating forged software on a CD pressing plant, they are suspected of illegally passing off inexpensive educational versions of software as more expensive full versions, and of selling CD-Roms and licences independently of each other.

The piracy is estimated to have caused some €16m ($18.4m) worth of damage to the software licence owners, although this sum could be found to be much higher, the BKA said, after all the seized equipment has been examined.

'Illegal copying of software doesn't often in happen in Germany. It is normally in Asia or somewhere like that. But we are very satisfied with how we have conducted this case,' the BKA said.

Adapted from: **Germany cracks down on software piracy**
By Maija Pesola
FT.com site: 10 November 2003

Questions

1. What crimes were being committed by those described in the case study above?

2. Why are software vendors like Microsoft concerned about this type of crime?

9.2   Controls over computerized information systems

If terminal operators never keyed in inaccurate data, if hardware never malfunctioned or disks never became corrupted, if there were no fires or floods, if computer operators never lost disks, if software always achieved what was intended, if people had no desire to embezzle or steal information, if employees harboured no grudges, if these or many other events never occurred, there would be no need for controls. However, they do happen and happen regularly, sometimes with devastating results.

The three types of control – feedforward, feedback and preventive – covered in Section 9.1 are applicable to manual information systems. The presence of a computer-based information system requires different controls. These fall within the same three-fold categorization, although in computer-based systems there is an emphasis on preventive controls.

Controls are present over many aspects of the computer system and its surrounding social (or non-technical) environment. They operate over data movement into, through and out of the computer to ensure correct, complete and reliable processing and storage. There are other controls present over staff, staff involvement with the computer, staff procedures, access to the computer and access to data. Further controls are effective in preventing deterioration or collapse of the entire computing function. This section starts by considering the aims and goals of control over computer systems and then covers these various areas of control.

9.2.1 Goals of control

Each control that operates over a computer system, its surrounding manual procedures and staffing has a specific goal or set of goals. These goals may be divided into categories. There are primary goals, which involve the prevention of undesired states of affairs, and there are secondary goals directed at some aspect of loss. If the primary goals are not achieved, other controls take over and provide some support. The various levels of control are:

1. **Deterrence and prevention:** At this level, the goal is to prevent erroneous data processing or to deter potential fraud. Many controls are designed to operate at this level.

2. **Detection:** If fraud or accidental error has occurred (that is, the primary goal has not been achieved), it is important that the fraud or error be detected so that matters may be corrected if possible. Indeed, the existence of detection often acts as a deterrent to fraud. Detection controls are particularly important in data communications, where noise on the communications channel can easily corrupt data.

3. **Minimization of loss:** Some controls are designed to minimize the extent of loss, financial or otherwise, occurring as a result of accident or intention. A backup file, for example, will ensure that master file failure involves a loss only from the time the backup was made.

4. **Recovery:** Recovery controls seek to establish the state of the system prior to the breach of control or mishap. For instance, a reciprocal arrangement with another company using a similar computer will ensure that the crucial data processing of a company can be carried out in the case of massive computer failure.

5. **Investigation:** Investigation is a form of control. An example is an internal audit. Nowadays, the facilitation of investigation is one of the design criteria generally applied to information systems development in business.

Controls are directed at:

1. **Malfunctions:** Hardware and software occasionally malfunction, but the most common cause is 'people malfunction'. People are always the weak link in any person–machine system as far the performance of specified tasks is concerned. They may be ill, underperform, be negligent, misread data, and so on. Unintentional errors are common unless prevented by a system of controls.

2. **Fraud:** Fraud occurs when the organization suffers an intentional financial loss as a result of illegitimate actions within the company. (Fraud might be regarded as the result of a moral malfunction!) Fraud may be of a number of types:

   (a) Intentionally inaccurate data processing and record keeping for the purpose of embezzlement is the most well-known kind of fraud. The advent of the computer means that all data processing (including fraudulent data processing) is carried out faster, more efficiently and in large volumes. Embezzlement may take the form of a 'one-off' illegitimate transfer of funds or may use the massive processing power of the computer to carry out transactions repeatedly, each involving a small sum of money.

There is a now-legendary fraud perpetrated by a bank's computer program-mer, who patched a program subroutine for calculating interest payments to customer accounts so that odd halfpenny interest payments (which are not recorded in accounts) were transferred to his own account. A halfpenny is not a fortune, except when transferred thousands of times a day, every day.

(b) The computer is used for processing transactions that are not part of the organ-ization's activities. It is not uncommon for staff to use computer facilities to word process private documents occasionally or to play adventure games when the time is available. At the other end of the scale, and more seriously, computer centre personnel have been known to run their own independent computer bureau from within the organization using large chunks of mainframe processing time, company software and their own time paid for by the organization.

(c) Illegitimate copying of data or program files for use outside the organization's activities may be considered a fraud. For instance, the transfer of company cus-tomer data to a competitor may cause financial loss.

3. **Intentional damage:** Computer centres have been the target for sabotage and vandal-ism. The angry employee who pours honey into the printer or plants a logic bomb in the software is an internal enemy. Increasingly, computer centres are aware of the possibility of external attack from pressure groups that step outside the law.

4. **Unauthorized access:** Unauthorized access is generally a prelude to fraud or inten-tional damage and therefore needs to be prevented. It occurs when persons who are not entitled to access to the computer system or its communication facilities 'break in'. Hackers generally do this for fun, but there may be more sinister motives. Many internal company personnel as well as the public at large are in the category of those not entitled to use the computer system. Alternatively, unauthorized access may occur when a person who is entitled to access does so, but at illegitimate times or to part of the computer to which he or she is not entitled. For instance, company employ-ees may access parts of the database for which they have no authorization.

5. **Natural disasters:** Included in this category are fires, earthquakes, floods, lightning and other disasters that may befall a computer installation. Each of these may be unlikely, but their effects would be serious and imply a large financial loss to the company. Power failures are rare nowadays in developed countries, but if there is a power cut and the temporary non-functioning of the computer is a serious loss then backup power supplies need to be provided. The same is true for commun-ications facilities. There are a large number of special circumstances that might need to be taken into account. For instance, a large computer installation located near a naval radar and communications base had to be rebuilt inside a Faraday cage (a large, metal mesh surround inside which it is impossible to create an electro-magnetic potential) to avoid interference.

6. **Viruses:** Computer viruses have become prevalent since the 1990s. A virus is com-puter code that has been inserted (without authorization) into a piece of software. Upon execution of the software, the virus is also executed. Its function may be innocu-ous, e.g. to flash a 'HELLO' message, or harmful, such as destroying files or cor-rupting disks. The virus may be resident in the software for a long period of time before being activated by an event, such as a specific electronic date inside the com-puter. Copying and distributing software on disks and over the Internet can spread viruses quickly. Recently, virus attacks have tended to be introduced from e-mails with infected attachments. These are often passed between unsuspecting users, who

believe they are sharing a supposedly useful or interesting piece of software. The vulnerability of e-mail address books can be a factor in particularly virulent virus attacks where e-mails are forwarded to huge numbers of users without the knowledge of the sender.

Organizations should protect themselves from these attacks by:

(a) installing and regularly updating anti-virus software;
(b) downloading the latest operating system and other software amendments (known as 'patches');
(c) briefing their staff on appropriate courses of action such as not opening e-mails from untrusted sources.

Mini case 9.2

Worms

A computer 'worm' that exploits a common flaw in the Microsoft personal computer operating system has begun to spread globally, the software company and computer security experts warned yesterday.

Although largely harmless and slow-moving by the standards of other big computer contagions, the so-called Blaster worm could turn out to be the most widespread attack on the world's PCs since the Internet made such assaults possible.

Blaster exploits a weakness in the Windows 2000 and Windows XP operating systems, which are installed on most PCs in use worldwide, Microsoft said. There are estimated to be about 500m machines running all versions of Windows.

Computer security experts have been braced for an attack on these proportions since the middle of July, when Microsoft first acknowledged the software flaw that created the vulnerability.

At the time, Microsoft produced a software 'patch' that users can download on to their machines to plug any weaknesses. However, while the information technology departments of most large companies have the procedures in place to install such software fixes, most small business and residential PC users never bother to make the repairs.

'The worst we've seen is that it would cause people's machines to crash with some regularity,' a Microsoft spokesman said.

About 127,000 computers had so far been affected by the slow-moving worm, Symantec said yesterday. By comparison, more virulent computer attacks such as Code Red and Nimda had affected virtually all vulnerable machines within 24 hours, it added.

The rogue computer code replicates itself on each computer it reaches, then immediately begins its hunt for other machines to attack. Infected PCs are also programmed to join in a co-ordinated attack on August 16 on the Microsoft web page that contains the software patch. Known as a 'denial of service' attack, this would involve every infected machine sending a request to the web page, causing it to overload.

Adapted from: **Web 'worm' attack on Microsoft software**
By Richard Waters in San Francisco
Financial Times: 13 August 2003

Questions

1. How does the Blaster worm spread?

2. What is a denial of service attack?

9.2.2 Controls over data movement through the computer system

Erroneous data processing by a computer system is likely to be the result of incorrect data input. This is the major point at which the human interfaces with the machine, and it is here where important controls are placed.

Input controls

Many of the controls over data input require some processing power to implement. They could be classed as processing controls, but given that interactive data input with real-time correction is becoming very common it is convenient to group these together as controls over input.

Accuracy controls

1. **Format checks:** On entry, the item of data is checked against an expected picture or format. For instance, a product code may always consist of three letters, followed by a forward slash, followed by two digits and then three letters. The picture is AAA/99AAA.
2. **Limit checks:** A data item may be expected to fall within set limits. An employee's work hours for the week will lie between 0 and 100 hours, for example, or account numbers of customers lie between 1000 and 3000.
3. **Reasonableness checks:** These are sophisticated forms of limit check. An example might be a check on an electricity meter reading. The check might consist of sub-tracting the last reading recorded from the current reading and comparing this with the average usage for that quarter. If the reading differs by a given percentage then it is investigated before processing.
4. **Check-digit verification:** Account reference codes consisting of large numbers of digits are prone to transcription errors. Types of error include:
   (a) **Single-digit errors:** Where a single digit is transcribed incorrectly, for example 4968214 for 4966214. These account for approximately 86% of errors.
   (b) **Transposition errors:** Where two digits are exchanged, for example 4968214 for 4986214. These account for approximately 8% of errors.
   (c) **Other errors:** Such as double-digit errors and multiple transpositions. These comprise about 6% of errors.

   In order to detect such errors, a check digit is added to the (account) code. The digit is calculated in such a way that the majority of transcription errors can be detected by comparing the check digit with the remainder of the (account) code. In principle, there is no limit to the percentage of errors that can be detected by the use of more and more check digits, but at some point the increasing cost of extra digits exceeds the diminishing marginal benefit of the error detection.

   The modulus-11 check-digit system is simple and is in common use. The principle is as follows:

   First, take the code for which a check digit is required and form the weighted total of the digits. The weight for the least significant digit is 2, the next least significant is 3. . . . If the number is 49628, then:

   $$(4 \times 6) + (9 \times 5) + (6 \times 4) + (2 \times 3) + (8 \times 2) = 115$$

   Second, subtract the total from the smallest multiple of 11 that is equal to or higher than the total. The remainder is the check digit. In the example:

$$121 - 115 = 6 \ (= \text{check digit})$$

(If the remainder is 10, it is common to use X as the check digit.) Thus the account number with the check digit is 496286.

Suppose that an error is made in transcribing this number during the course of manual data processing or on input into the computer. A quick calculation shows that the check digit does not match the rest of the (account) code. For example, the erroneous 492686 is checked as follows:

$$(4 \times 6) + (9 \times 5) + (2 \times 4) + (6 \times 3) + (8 \times 2) + (6 \times 1) = 117$$

117 should be divisible by 11. It is not, so the error has been detected.

The modulus-11 method will detect most errors. Because of its arithmetic nature, computers can carry out these checks quickly.

5. **Master-file checks:** With online real-time systems where interactive data entry is available, the master file associated with a transaction may be searched for confirming data. For example, a source document order form that is printed with both the customer code number and customer name may be handled by input of the customer number at the keyboard. The master file is searched (perhaps it is indexed on account reference number) and the name of the customer is displayed on the screen. This can be checked with the name on the source document. This type of check is very common in microcomputer-based accounting packages. Obviously, it is not possible with batch systems.

6. **Form design:** General principles of good form design were covered in Section 9.1.3. With respect to data input, the layout of source documentation from which data is taken should match the screen layout presented to the keyboard operator. This not only minimizes errors but also speeds data input. Data fields on source documents should be highlighted if they are to be input.

Completeness totals

To input data erroneously is one type of error. To leave out or lose data completely is another type of error against which controls are provided.

1. **Batch control totals:** The transactions are collected together in batches of say fifty transactions. A total of all the data values of some important field is made. For example, if a batch of invoices is to be input, a total of all the invoice amounts might be calculated manually. This control total is then compared with a computer-generated control total after input of the batch of transactions. A difference indicates either a lost transaction or the input of an incorrect invoice total. The method is not foolproof, as compensating errors are possible.

2. **Batch hash totals:** The idea is similar to control totals except that hash totals are a meaningless total prepared purely for control purposes. The total of all customer account numbers in a batch is meaningless but may be used for control by comparing it with the computer-generated hash total.

3. **Batch record totals:** A count is taken of the number of transactions and this is compared with the record count produced by the computer at the end of the batch.

4. **Sequence checks:** Documents may be pre-numbered sequentially before entry, and at a later stage the computer will perform a sequence check and display any missing numbers.

5. **Field-filling checks:** Within a transaction record, there is a computer check to verify that the necessary fields have been filled with a data value. This is of particular use with complex documentation that requires only certain fields to be entered; the required fields are often determined by the values of other fields. (If sex = *female* and marital status = *married* or *divorced* then insert married name, otherwise leave blank.)

Recording controls

These enable records to be kept of errors and transaction details that are input into the system:

1. **Error log:** This is particularly important in batch entry and batch processing systems. Many of the accuracy checks discussed previously can only be carried out during run-time processing. It is important that a detected error does not bring the run to a halt. On discovery, the erroneous transaction is written to the error log. This is a file that can be examined at the end of processing. The errors can then be corrected or investigated with the relevant department before being re-input and processed.

2. **Transaction log:** The transaction log provides a record of all transactions entered into the system. As well as storing transaction details such as the transaction reference number, the date, the account number, the type of transaction, the amount and the debit and credit account references (for a sales ledger entry), the transaction will be 'stamped' with details of input. These typically include input time, input date, input day, terminal number and user number. It is usual for multi-access mainframe systems to provide this facility, especially when dealing with accounting transactions. The transaction log can form the basis of an audit trail and may be printed out for investigation during an audit. Alternatively, audit packages now have facilities that analyse transaction logs for the purpose of identifying possible fraud. Another reason for maintaining a transaction log is to keep a record of transaction input in case there is any computer failure. The log can be used for recovery of the data position of the system prior to the failure.

Storage controls

These controls ensure the accurate and continuing reliable storage of data. Data is a vital resource for an organization, and special care must be taken to ensure the integrity of the database or file system. The controls are particularly directed at mistaken erasure of files and the provision of backup and recovery facilities.

1. **Physical protection against erasure:** Floppy disks for microcomputers have a plastic lever, which is switched for read only (3½-inch disks). Magnetic tape files have rings that may be inserted if the file is to be written to or erased. Read-only files have the ring removed.

2. **External labels:** These are attached to tape reels or disk packs to identify the contents.

3. **Magnetic labels:** These consist of magnetic machine-readable information encoded on the storage medium identifying its contents. File-header labels appear at the start of a file and identify the file by name and give the date of the last update and other information. This is checked by software prior to file updating. Trailer labels at the

ends of files often contain control totals that are checked against those calculated during file processing.

4. **File backup routines:** Copies of important files are held for security purposes. As the process of providing backup often involves a computer operation in which one file is used to produce another, a fault in this process would have disastrous results if both the master and the backup were lost. The grandparent–parent–child method provides a measure of security against this mishap in the file-updating routine.

5. **Database backup routines:** The contents of a database held on a direct-access storage device such as magnetic disk are periodically dumped on to a backup file. This backup is often a tape, which is then stored together with the transaction log tape of all transactions occurring between the last and the current dump. If a database fault, such as a disk crash, happens afterwards, the state of the database can be re-created using the dumped database tape, the stored transaction (if a tape batch update is used) and the current log of transactions occurring between the dump and the crash point.

6. **Database concurrency controls:** In multi-access, multiprogramming systems using an online database environment, it is possible for two users/user programs to attempt to access the same part (record) of the database more or less simultaneously. Provided that both of these are read requests no problem arises. If one is a write request though, the database management system prevents access to the record by other users until the write action has been carried out. This not only ensures that two users do not, for instance, book the last remaining seat on a flight but also that all users of the database are presented with one consistent view of its contents.

7. **Cryptographic storage:** Data is commonly written to files in a way that uses standard coding (such as ASCII or EBCDIC). It can be interpreted easily by unauthorized readers gaining access to the file. If the data is confidential or sensitive then it may be scrambled prior to storage and descrambled on reading. This is particularly important where data files are sent by telecommunications. Then the hacker (unauthorized entrant) not only has to gain access to the link but also has to unscramble the code.

Processing controls

It was stated in Section 9.2.2 that many of the controls over input, and incidentally over storage, involve some element of processing. This is clear from the fact that all computer operations involve processing. However, some controls are processing-specific:

1. **Run-to-run controls:** The processing of a transaction file may involve several runs. For instance, an order-processing system might have a transaction file that is used to update first a stock master file, then a sales ledger, followed by a general ledger. Various control totals may be passed from one run to the next as a check on completeness of processing.

2. **Hardware controls:** Some run-time errors are checked by circuitry. For instance, the value of a variable may be changed to zero during the execution of (part of) a program. An attempt to use this variable as a divisor (division by zero) may be detected by hardware. Other checks may involve data overflow, lost signs and checks on components. Dual circuits in the central processing unit (CPU) may duplicate computations. The outputs of each set of circuits are compared for discrepancy. This reduces the probability of processing errors.

Hardware should be designed to incorporate fault detection, avoidance and tolerance features. Duplicating central processing units, input/output channels and disk drives for comparing the results of data processing is one option. Another is to maintain redundant components, which are brought in when hardware failure occurs or during maintenance. A third option is to increase the tolerance of the system to hardware failure by having a common pool of resources such as CPUs and disk drives that meet the needs of tasks as required. If one of these fails operations can still continue, albeit somewhat degraded in performance, in the remainder.

Output controls

Output controls ensure that the results of data processing are accurate and complete and are directed to authorized recipients:

1. **Control totals:** As in input and processing control, totals are used to detect data loss or addition.

2. **Prenumbering:** Cheques, passbooks, stock certificates and other documentation of value on which output is produced should be prenumbered and accounted for.

3. **Authorization:** Negotiable documents will require authorization, and steps must be taken to ensure their safe transport from the computer centre to the relevant user department.

4. **Sensitive output:** Output that is regarded as confidential should be directed automatically to secure output devices in a location that is protected from personnel not entitled to view the output.

Data transmission controls

Data transmission occurs between the various local peripheral components of a computer system and the CPU and may, on a wider scale, also involve telecommunications links between a number of computers or peripherals and the central computing resource. These latter links are vulnerable to unauthorized access, giving rise to data loss, data alteration and eavesdropping. All communication is subject to data transmission errors resulting from electronic 'noise' interfering with the reliable transmission of 1s and 0s.

1. **Parity bit control:** Characters will be encoded as strings of bits according to some standard or other such as ASCII. A parity bit is added to the end of the bits representing a character. A protocol of **odd parity** means that the coded character, including the parity bit, must consist of an odd number of 1s. The set of bits is tested by hardware, and any failure to meet the control standard requires retransmission. For its success as a detection control it relies on the corruption of data affecting an odd number of bits, otherwise the errors may be compensating. The vast majority of errors, however, entail corruption of a single data bit.

2. **Echo checks:** The message transmitted by the sender to the receiver is retransmitted by the receiver back to the sender. The echoed transmission is then compared with the first transmission. Any discrepancy indicates a data transmission error somewhere. Echo checks are common between the CPU and VDUs or printers.

3. **Control total:** At the end of a transmitted message, a set of control totals is placed that give information such as the total number of blocks or records sent. This is checked on receipt of the message.

Internet communications controls

In response to concerns about the security of messages passed over the Internet, an enhanced version of the hypertext transfer protocol (HTTP) called **Secure-HTTP** (**S-HTTP**) has been developed. It uses encryption techniques to encode the data being transmitted and produces digital signatures. The technique is often used in conjunction with the **secure sockets layer** (SSL). Rather than focusing on the individual message, SSL encrypts the entire communications channel. The joint use of these two protocols gives combined benefits in achieving security in data transfer.

9.2.3 Access controls

Access controls are usually aimed at preventing unauthorized (as distinct from accidental) access. The controls may seek to prevent persons who are authorized for access having unauthorized access to restricted data and programs, as well as preventing unauthorized persons gaining access to the system as a whole.

Controls over access to the computer system

Before a user is granted access to the system, that user needs to be identified and that identification authenticated in order to establish authorization. It is common for users to be given login codes or user identification codes. These are not regarded as particularly secret. The authentication of the identity is established by:

- a unique characteristic of the person, such as a voice print, fingerprint or retinal image;
- a security device unique to that person, such as an identity card; or
- a password.

Unique personal characteristics are currently infrequently used but will be employed with greater frequency in the future. Developments await technological advances, particularly in voice recognition and retinal imaging.

Security devices are commonly used where physical access control is important, such as entry into the various rooms of a computer centre.

Passwords are the most common form of authentication or identification. A password scheme requires the user to enter a string of characters, which the computer checks against its internal record of passwords associated with user identification. Generally, there is a facility for the user to change his or her password once logged into the system. The use of passwords appears to be a simple and effective access control, but there are limitations.

User-selected passwords are often easy to guess. The number of people who choose 'PASSWORD', 'ABC', the name of their husband, wife, child or dog is notorious. A recent report on computer security indicated that for a number of years the chairman of a large organization used 'CHAIRMAN' as his password. It is easy to see why these passwords are selected. Users are not interested in computer security but in the easiest legitimate access to the system in order to perform the tasks for which they require the computer. They may view passwords as a hindrance, albeit a necessary one, to carrying out their tasks rather than an essential component of the organization's security system.

System-generated passwords appear to be a possible solution, but these are difficult to remember and therefore likely to be written down, which provides further security problems. An alternative is to require individuals to change their passwords regularly and to prevent selection of a previously used password. This makes them less vulnerable (whether user-selected or system-generated) but more difficult to remember.

It is generally recognized that good password security depends on better education of users in the need for security rather than on more technologically sophisticated techniques.

Password details are encrypted in the computer and are never displayed on the screen. They should not be accessible even to senior computer centre personnel. Loss of a password should require a new user identification code to be issued, as well as a new password.

Although password controls are common they are not infallible, even with the most conscientious user. Short programs have been written that repeatedly attempt to log into a computer system. The program may be set to increment the tried password in a methodical fashion until a password fitting the login code is achieved. It is easy to prevent such clumsy attempts by automatic testing of the number of password trials associated with the login code. When a given number of unsuccessful attempts have been made in a period of time, no further login is possible under that code.

It is harder to prevent other equally simple but more elegant methods of password evasion. A simple terminal emulation program may be written and run. To the user sitting in front of the screen it appears that a perfectly normal request for a login code and password is being presented. On entering these details, they are recorded on a file for future consideration by the person attempting to gain unauthorized access. The user will not realize that this has been done, as the terminal emulation program will then display a simple error message or abort and pass the login code and password to the control of the legitimate procedure for handling login access. To prevent this deception, a system should always be shut down and restarted before use.

Control over access to data

Once legitimate (or unauthorized) access has been gained to the computer system the user should then be faced with other restrictions. Obviously, any system of control should not allow all users access to all files and programs. Generally, users are restricted to:

- the execution of a limited number of programs;
- access to a limited set of files or part of the corporate database;
- access to only certain items in these files or database;
- performing only limited operations on these areas of access. For instance, one user may be entitled to read and write to various records, another may be restricted to read only, and a third to read and copy.

In deciding on data access, two issues arise:

1. the policy to be adopted;
2. the mechanisms by which the policy is implemented.

Under 1, certain principles should be followed for a sound policy on security.

- Each user should be entitled to access data and perform operations in the computer system only to the extent needed to carry out that user's legitimate tasks. Put another way, access is restricted to the minimum compatible with the user's needs. For instance, a management accountant might be entitled to read stock records but not to write to them and neither to read nor write to employee records. Once again, a member of the department dealing with weekly wages may be entitled to read the

Figure 9.3 Examples of access matrices: (a) operating system access matrix; (b) database access matrix

(a) **Subject/user** — **Object**

	File 1	File 2	File 3	File 4	Device 1	Device 2
A43801	Read		Execute			
A43802		Read/Write		Execute	Use	
A43803	Read	Read			Use	Use
A43804	Read		Execute		Use	

(b) **Subject/user** — **Stock details**

	Stock ID	Description	Quantity held	Cost price	Sale price	Reorder level	Reorder placed
Management accountant	Read	Read	Read	Read	Read	Read	Read
Inventory control	Read	Read	Read/Write		Read	Read	Read
Purchasing	Read	Read		Read	Read	Write	Write

employee records of only those who are waged (not salaried). For this policy to be carried out it is necessary to spend considerable time and effort determining for each user the nature of tasks that they perform and the range of data needed for these. As well as restricting authorized users, limitation also minimizes the damage that can be achieved through unauthorized access via the route taken by an authorized user.

■ The simpler the control mechanism the more effective it is likely to be. Complex mechanisms are more difficult to maintain and less easily understood.

■ It is often claimed that the design of the security mechanisms (although not their specific content) should not rely on secrecy for part of their effectiveness.

■ Every data access request should be checked for authorization.

Under 2, the mechanisms by which the policy is implemented are known as **access-control mechanisms**. They come into force both at the level of the operating system and independently through the database management system. They may be represented in an access matrix, where the rows of the matrix are users or user groups and the columns are the objects over which access is controlled. The cell entries indicate the type of access allowed for the user–object combination. Figure 9.3 is an illustration of the ideas behind an access matrix for operating system controls and database control over records.

Operating system access controls

These may be organized in the form of hierarchies, where superior users have all the access of inferior users plus extra rights. Another approach is to associate with each object, such as a file, a list of users that are authorized to use it and the type of operation they may perform. The access control list for a file then corresponds to the non-emptying cell entries for a column in the matrix in Figure 9.3(a). Operating systems may store files in tree structures, where a user 'owns' a tree or part of a tree as their file space. It is common for that owner to have maximum rights over the tree or sub-tree, whereas non-owners have restricted rights as specified by the owner. A facility may also be available to set passwords over trees or subtrees, so further enhancing security.

Database management system access controls

These are more fine-grained in their selectivity than operating system access controls. They will restrict access not only to records but also to specified logical relationships between these records and individual fields within the records. The nature of the allowed operations will also be defined. Read, update, insert and delete are common. Unlike operating system access controls, database management system access controls may be data-dependent as well as data-independent. In some database environments, data items are selected by value; access can therefore be allowed on the basis of the values satisfying some condition. For example, a user may only be allowed to read an employee salary field if that employee salary is less than a specified amount. Database controls are selective, so they require a detailed study of each user's data requirements if the access is not to be too slack (ineffective controls) or too tight (impeding user tasks).

Cryptographic controls

Preventing unauthorized access to the computer system and then restricting the access of legitimate users to subsets of the file base or database may be regarded as insufficient control in the case of very confidential data. If a breach of security leads to data access, then it is a further control to store the data in an encoded form so that it will be meaningless and worthless to the intruder. Cryptography is the science of coding and decoding for security purposes.

Encoding data, or encrypting it, is not only used as a secure storage form but is also particularly important in data transmission where communications channels are vulnerable to eavesdropping. Cryptography has always been important for military communications but has only recently been of commercial significance. This is a result of electronic funds transfer and the increasing use of networked computers in the transference of confidential business data.

The security process involves the conversion of the plain text message or data into cipher text by the use of an encryption algorithm and an encryption key. The opposite process, decryption, involves deciphering the cipher text by the use of an algorithm and decryption key to reproduce the plain text data or message. If the encryption and decryption keys are identical, the entire procedure is known as a **symmetric cryptoprocess**. Otherwise, it is said to be **asymmetric**.

A simple cryptotransformation of the kind used in junior school secret messages is shown in Figure 9.4. This is called a **substitute transformation**. In the case of encryption used for communication the key is transmitted over a highly secure data link from the message sender to the receiver. The cipher text can then be sent through a less secure channel, often at a much faster speed. If encrypted data is stored then the key is kept separate from the cipher text. The application of the key with the decryption algorithm (which can be public) enables decryption to produce the original plain text. Simple encryption algorithms and keys, such as those shown in Figure 9.4, which associate a unique character on a one-to-one basis with each character of the alphabet, are easy to

Figure 9.4 A simple cryptotransformation – substitute transformation

Plaintext alphabet	a b c d e f g h i j k l m n o p q r s t u v w x y z
Ciphertext alphabet	x y z a b c d e f g h i j k l m n o p q r s t u v w

KEY = 3

Plaintext message	atlantic gales
Ciphertext message	xqixkqfz dxibp

'crack'. A common method is to take the most commonly occurring cipher text character and associate it with 'e', which is the most commonly used letter in the alphabet in English prose. The next most common are then paired, and so on. More complex algorithms and keys ensure that plain text characters are coded differently depending on their position in the plain text.

The data encryption standard

The data encryption standard (DES) is a standard for non-military data. It requires splitting the plain text into 64-bit blocks. The encrypting algorithm requires the iteration of a certain transformation sixteen times to produce a 64-bit cipher text block. This is performed on each 64-bit plain text block. The key used in the algorithm for both encryption and decryption consists of 64 bits (eight of which are parity bits). Once the key is possessed, both encryption and decryption are straightforward algorithmic processes, which may be carried out effectively and quickly by a computer.

The security of the system (data stored or message transmitted) now relies on the security of storage or the security of transmission of the key. This is an improvement, as security control now has to be maintained over a piece of data of 64 bits (the key) rather than several megabytes of stored or transmitted data. Obviously, the key itself should be made unpredictable, say by generating the 64 bits randomly.

Doubt has recently been cast on the DES. Using very fast computers, a large enough piece of cipher text and its corresponding plain text, all 2^{56} possible keys can be used to decrypt the cipher text. The result of each decryption can be compared with the given plain text and the correct key established. The time taken to carry out the exhaustive search would be a matter of hours rather than weeks, and if computing power continues to increase both the cost and time taken for such an analysis will drop considerably. It has been argued, though, that the principle behind the DES is sound and can be guaranteed against plausible advances in computing power by increasing the key to 128 bits (sixteen of which are parity bits). This would require an exhaustive search of 2^{112} keys and is becoming increasingly used as an encryption standard.

Public key cryptography

While the DES uses an asymmetric crypto-process, public key cryptography is an asymmetric crypto-system. It works as follows:

- The encryption and decryption algorithms are straightforward and public.
- A receiver has a code number, which may be public. This number is the product of two very large prime numbers (each in excess of 100 digits), which are known to

the receiver but to no one else. It is impossible, because of the computational power needed, to determine these prime numbers from the public code. (The standard method of dividing the code by successively large prime numbers until a perfect divisor is found is too lengthy even with a high-powered computer.)

- The transmitter of a message selects an encryption key determined by the public receiver code number satisfying certain conditions, which are publicly known.
- As well as the cipher message, the receiver code and the encryption key are transmitted.
- It is impossible to 'back encrypt' the cipher text to reach the plain text using the encryption key.
- The decryption key can only be found by calculation using the encryption key together with the prime numbers whose product is the public code of the receiver. The system relies on the impossibility of discovering these primes from the public receiver code.

The system is very attractive, as different receivers can have different public codes, and transmitters can change encryption keys as often as is liked for security. The cipher text, the encryption keys and the receiver keys can be transmitted without jeopardizing public security. The strength of the system lies in the impossibility of determining the decryption key without the two large prime numbers. Recent research by mathematicians has come up with more efficient algorithms for determining whether a number is prime than the traditional sieve of Eratosthenes (to determine if a number is prime, divide it by each whole number less than or equal to its square root). It remains to be seen whether this will affect the security of the product of primes method of cryptography.

As data communication traffic increases in volume and the need to maintain secure data storage and transmission becomes more important it is likely that crypto-systems will become an integral part of data handling. Trends in data protection legislation, where data holders are legally obliged to take reasonable steps to ensure the privacy of personal data against unauthorized access, can only increase this movement.

Physical access controls

The access controls considered earlier in this section all assume that physical access to some aspect of the computer system, such as a terminal or data transmission channel, has been achieved and the task is to prevent the unauthorized intruder gaining further access. Physical access controls aim to prevent this initial state arising. They are particularly effective when the computer system is geographically centralized. The greater the dispersion of equipment and distribution of connected computing power the less effective they become. (It is easier to maintain control over equipment that is located in one big box (the computer centre) than when it is geographically dispersed in smaller boxes all connected by communication lines.) Currently, the trend is towards networks and decentralized computing; therefore, physical access controls play a less important role than previously in the prevention of unauthorized access. The following are some of the most common types of these controls:

- **Magnetic cards:** Plastic cards with user identification encoded on magnetic strips on the card are a popular form of access control to equipment and to the rooms containing the equipment. The user runs the card through a magnetic strip reader, and the details are checked for authenticity. In some systems, the user is also required to input a personal identification number. These systems are popular because they are cheap and also provide computer-based monitoring of access if the magnetic strip-reading equipment is connected to a computer. For instance, a computer centre may have a magnetic card reader on each door in the building. At any moment, the computer has a record of who is where in the building and how long they have been there. Moreover, the records of personnel movement may be retained on a file for future analysis if required.

■ **Smart cards:** Smart cards are the same size as magnetic cards (that is, credit card size) but contain information encoded on microchips built into the cards. They store more information and are harder to counterfeit than magnetic cards, but their cost of production is higher. They are used in a similar way to magnetic cards in access control.

■ **Closed-circuit video monitoring:** As for many other installations that require security controls, closed-circuit video can be used. It is expensive if manned operation is required but may be used as an unattended video record of computer centre occupants.

■ **Signature access:** Traditional sign-in/sign-out procedures can now be made more secure as computer-based signature checking is possible. As well as determining the authenticity of the shape of the signature (which is fairly easy to forge) checks can now be made of pressure and the way that the pen moves in forming a signature when it is not directly in contact with the paper. These latter two properties are difficult to copy.

■ **Guards and escorts:** Guards may be placed at entry points to the computer facility and act as administrators over other entry procedures and escorts for unfamiliar personnel or sensitive material.

■ **Data transmission controls:** Data transmission lines throughout the computer centre should be securely embedded. It is particularly important if the lines pass out of the building, as they may with a local area network, that attention should be paid to preventing unauthorized tapping.

9.2.4 Organizational control

Up to now in this chapter, controls over data movement through the computer system and access to the system and the data in it have been considered. Many of these controls are technical and clear-cut in the sense that they require some kind of physical or electronic mechanism (for instance a computer) to implement, or they are straightforward procedures connected with these (such as the batching of transactions and calculation of a control total prior to data input). Other controls are more general and are best thought of as principles rather than clearly defined procedures or mechanisms. In particular, the way the information systems function is organized and managed and the way the work is allocated between different personnel will affect the overall accuracy and reliability of information processing. Also, if certain principles are followed in systems project development then the resulting information systems are less prone to failure – however failure may be interpreted. These areas are outlined in this section.

Organization of the information systems function

Over recent years, the emphasis in business computer systems has shifted from the processing of data on a batch basis to the provision of information, often interactively within an integrated total information system consisting of the computer, computer centre personnel, users and tasks for which the information is provided. This move towards the information-based approach has, in some organizations, been accompanied

Figure 9.5 The organization of a generic information systems department

by the partial decentralization of equipment and application processing as a result of the proliferation of microcomputers and microcomputer-based networks. This is particularly evident in the increasing use of the Internet. It is difficult to maintain the same degree of control over microcomputer-based systems. Their easy access, their simple-to-use operating systems, and their removable CDs and floppy disks are both an attraction to users and a problem for the exercise of control. This section concentrates only on those information system functions carried out centrally in what was, and still often is, called the computer centre.

Figure 9.5 is a hierarchy chart of the typical divisions of responsibility in a generic information systems department. The functions are divided into the day-to-day data entry and processing and other activities such as the administration of the database and systems project development. The chart illustrates a project-centred approach, where programmers and analysts are assigned to development projects as they become current.

- **Director of information systems:** This person fulfils two roles. Externally to the computer centre, but within the organization, the director represents the information system at a senior managerial level (vice-president or director). He or she will be expected to play a part in deciding the overall goals and plans of the organization and in ensuring that the information system contributes to them. Internally, the director is responsible for the establishment of a structure and personnel base that will lead to a reliable and cost-efficient provision of information, not only currently

363

but throughout the changing future of the organization. As well as a thorough understanding of technical issues concerning information systems, the director needs considerable managerial and administrative skills.

- **Operations manager:** This person is responsible for the day-to-day execution of the organization's data and information processing. The operations manager reports directly to the director and administers the subordinate functions, as shown in Figure 9.5.

- **Data entry:** Personnel in this role prepare and verify source data for entry and processing. They are also responsible for input of prepared data via input devices such as keyboards and optical character readers.

- **Data control:** Data control staff record and chart the progress of data-processing jobs. They also ensure that input control procedures are followed and are responsible for the preparation and checking of control totals for establishing the completeness of input and processing.

- **Computer operators:** The computer operators load disks and tapes, monitor and respond to console messages during processing, load printers with paper and remove the output hard copy, and generally service the day-to-day processing activities.

- **File librarian:** The librarian is responsible for storing off line files held on tape and disk. It is important that the librarian maintains a record of files and programs checked out to other personnel for use.

- **Systems manager:** This management responsibility is for the development of new projects and the maintenance of existing software and the database. Within project development, the systems manager is responsible for setting standards for systems design, programming and documentation, for overall planning and coordinating new applications, and for the allocation of staff resources (analysts and programmers) to projects.

- **Database administrator:** The database administrator ensures that the database is maintained in a secure manner and functions efficiently to the satisfaction of data requests from users and applications programs. He or she will be involved in amending the database conceptual schema and defining external schema in the course of new project developments. The role of the database administrator was covered more extensively in the chapter on databases.

- **Systems programmers:** This group ensures the effective functioning of the operating system and its associated utilities, compilers, database management system and software. They will give technical support to applications programmers on programs that require special interfacing with the operating system. The system programmers will carry out operating system enhancements as supplied by the computer manufacturers.

- **Project managers:** Each project will have a manager whose task it is to ensure that adequate detailed planning and administration of the project is carried out. This will involve setting points at which various 'deliverables' such as documentation (according to standards) or programs will be completed. The manager is also responsible for ensuring that development standards are adhered to, especially in program development and testing.

- **Systems analysts:** The analyst determines the information needs of the users and produces a system design in accordance with these. The process of systems analysis and design and the role of the analyst are considered extensively in the following chapters.

- **Programmers:** The programmers convert the process design by the analyst into programming code in a specified language.

- **External information provision:** Although much documentation in a computer centre is for internal consumption there are requirements externally within the organization for details on aspects of information provision. These may take the form of newsletters, user manuals for applications programs and presentations to other department of services offered by the centre.

Separation of functions and control of personnel

The separation of functions and control of personnel was considered from a general standpoint in the coverage of preventive controls presented in Section 9.1.3. Applied to the computer centre, functional separation is accomplished between four separate areas: computer operations, project development, the file and program library, and data entry and control.

The separation of analyst/programmer functions from those of day-to-day computer operations prevents programmers who make unauthorized changes to programs having the power to put those programs into operation. Conversely, access to programs and program documentation is restricted for operations staff to prevent a computer operator making unauthorized program changes then activating that program.

Programmers should have written instructions specifying program changes, and these changes should be fully documented. During systems development the program specifications supplied by analysts provide such documentation. At all times, it is inadvisable to allow programmers access to live data or current master files.

Computer operations staff should be closely supervised. Rotation of personnel in shifts and ensuring that at least two members of staff are always present in the computer room are steps that can be taken in centres with large numbers of staff.

A separate file library in which all access to program and data files requires authorization is a further control. Details of loans should be kept.

The separation of data entry from the function of data control provides a measure of security against fraudulent transactions generated on data input. There should, anyway, be independent controls (such as batch totals) created by departments originating transactions. These should be administered by data-control personnel as well as those controls emanating from within the computer centre. In data entry, it is common to separate the functions of master file amendments (such as insertion of a new customer) from transaction entry to prevent the creation of a fictitious customer and subsequent processing of fraudulent transactions.

Systems programmers are in a particularly powerful position, and it is important that they do not have unrestricted access to live data files and are not able to execute applications programs. One further safeguard is to ensure that applications programs documentation is not made available to them.

These separations of duties are more difficult to maintain in a small organization, where it is common for one member of staff to fulfil several functions. Microcomputer-based systems are perhaps the extreme case where integration of functions is commonplace.

Mini case 9.3

Electronic patient records

One of the more compelling reasons for using Electronic Patient Records (EPR) is that it can reduce unnecessary patient deaths. A landmark 1999 study by the Institute of Medicine showed that up to 98,000 Americans die each year because of medical errors.

Illegible writing in medical records is one cause of such errors, yet it is one of the easiest to avoid. The institute has thus called for the elimination of nearly all hand-written clinical records by 2010.

In the US, legislation has driven this interest in EPR. Healthcare providers have belatedly woken up to the implications of the 1996 Health Insurance Portability and Accountability Act (Hipaa), which comes into full effect in October. 'Hipaa has done a lot to stimulate interest in EPR,' says Dr Fickenscher of CSC.

The legislation aims to eliminate inefficiencies in US healthcare by standardizing the electronic exchange of administrative and financial data. It requires healthcare organizations to protect privacy by controlling and documenting access to patient data, which is difficult to do unless you have computerized patient records.

'The reality of Hipaa's security and privacy rules demand automation,' says Eric Brown, analyst at Forrester Research.

Many other countries such as Canada, Slovenia and South Korea are also showing a keen interest in nationwide use of EPR technology. Some are going further and combining EPR technology with smart cards to simplify access to patient data and emergency health information.

Adapted from: **Better prognosis after slow start**
By Geoffrey Nairn
FT.com site: 21 May 2003

Questions

1. What problems are being addressed by the introduction of the Electronic Patient Record system?

2. Often the introduction of a computer-based record keeping system provides more concerns over privacy and confidentiality. Why might the Electronic Patient Record actually protect privacy even more?

9.2.5 Contingency planning

In spite of all the controls that may be devised to support the reliable workings of the computer centre, hazards may arise that lead to breakdowns. Some, such as a lengthy power cut, can be safeguarded against and overcome by a backup power generator. Others, such as fires, floods, riots, earthquakes or sabotage, are more devastating. Many organizations have moved away from a decentralized manual approach to data processing with pieces of paper to using a centralized electronic computer. Although their activities now depend on computer support, the organization cannot afford to come to an immediate standstill in the face of computer failure.

The recent increase in distributed systems has diminished the consequences of failure. Even if one computer site suffers a disaster the others may take over much of its important activities in the short term. This assumes that network links have not been severed and that copies of the files and database at the breakdown site are maintained elsewhere so that they may be loaded into the network. It is uncommon to opt for distributed systems purely on the basis of this graceful degradation in their function (except perhaps for military systems operating in hostile environments). Rather, it should be seen as a useful feature of distributed data storage and processing.

Some form of contingency planning is needed in order to take care of the unexpected computer failure (even in the case of distributed systems). These plans should involve several areas:

- Copies of files and databases should be made regularly and stored at a distant location so that when computer operations are restored the original position of the organization can be recovered.

- Personnel need to be appointed (beforehand) to take managerial responsibility in the event of a disaster. They will need to be acquainted with procedures to be followed and with activities that are judged to be essential to the organization (as distinct from those that can be suspended). It is impossible to plan completely for all the unlikely disruptions that may arise, and the success of the contingency plan will depend on how these personnel adapt to the changed working conditions.

- Standby procedures and operations for the period of disruption will need to be arranged.

With respect to the standby plans, a number of approaches can be taken. Generally, those that cost more give a faster and higher level of support in the case of failure. They can be broken down into the following categories:

1. **Manual backup:** This is a short-term stopgap, which may be used before other standby assistance is brought in. If stock lists and accounts (particularly sales ledger) are printed at regular intervals then the trading of the organization may be maintained for several days. There will need to be special stationery for data entry that will enable input of transactions occurring during the disrupted period after computer support has been re-established.

2. **Hot-line support:** A company may offer hot-line support as a service on the basis of an annual fee. It usually works in the following manner. The company has a set of popular minicomputers or a mainframe and also has contracts with user organizations having similar equipment to take over their data-processing activities in the event of disaster. Generally, the servicing company will guarantee immediate support in the case of computer failure in the serviced organization, and the level of support will depend on prior arrangement (and the fee). In some cases, almost total support can be guaranteed and the computer users in the serviced organization will hardly notice the switch-over to operations at another site. Problems may arise in the unlikely event of a computer failure simultaneously occurring in more than one serviced organization. There may also be reservations about processing confidential data off site.

3. **Company-owned backup facility:** This is a low-risk, high-cost way of meeting a computer failure. The entire system is duplicated at another site.

4. **Reciprocal agreement:** Two companies with the same equipment may agree to carry out each other's essential data processing in the case of failure. As well as possible security problems arising, it is unlikely that each of the organizations will have much spare computer capacity.

Survey reports have indicated that major accounting firms are concerned about the lack of computer contingency planning in British companies. Of computer disasters occurring over the five-year period surveyed, two-thirds were judged by the accountants to have been preventable, and of these, an inadequate backup facility was given as the major reason in over half the cases. Half of the accountants surveyed carried out checks and reported on disaster recovery procedures during the audit, but little interest was shown by clients. Of companies surveyed, four-fifths were inadequately protected against fire, and nearly all had no flood precautions and little or no protection against sabotage. All the current evidence points to little change having occurred since the 1990s. The combination of inadequate protection against unlikely computer failures together with poor or absent backup and recovery procedures is likely to turn a crisis into a disaster for most UK companies and underlines the need for adequate contingency planning.

9.2.6 Audits

The primary objectives of an **external audit** are to express an expert and independent opinion on the truth and fairness of the information contained in financial statements, and to ascertain and evaluate the reliability of the systems that produced this information. Secondary objectives include the investigation of fraud, errors and irregularities and the provision of advice on these and other matters to clients.

The primary objective of the **internal audit** is to evaluate controls against fraud and to maintain surveillance over the organization in order to detect fraudulent activity.

Both internal and external audits are a form of control. As well as improving preventive controls against unreliable processing, they also serve to deter fraud and detect errors once they have occurred.

An extensive coverage of auditing is beyond the scope of this book – only the basic strategies are covered and then applied to a computer-based system.

The approach to an internal audit

1. The auditor first needs to establish an understanding of the way the system functions. This will be achieved by consulting document flowcharts, procedures manuals and examples of documentation, by interviewing personnel and by observing the way that transactions are processed.

2. The next step is to document and evaluate the internal control that operates over the procedures and functioning of the system. Controls are divided into two categories. First, there are actual controls such as the provision of a check digit associated with an account code number or the preparation of a control total. The purpose of an actual control is to ensure that data is recorded and processed accurately. Second, there are higher-level controls designed to ensure that the actual controls work properly. These higher-level controls tend to conform to principles covered in Section 9.1. Examples are the separation of the custody of an asset from its recording, the supervision of personnel and the authorization of a transaction by a second person.

   The controls are evaluated to decide whether 'in theory' they are adequate to meet the standards required of the system. The auditor may have a checklist against which the controls will be evaluated. For instance, the evaluation checklist dealing with company purchase orders might have the following questions:

   (a) Can goods be purchased without authority?
   (b) Can liabilities be incurred even though goods have not been received?
   (c) Can invoices be wrongly allocated?

Each of these would be subdivided. For example:

(a)(i)   What are the limits to a buyer's authority?
(a)(ii)   Are unissued orders safeguarded against loss?
(a)(iii)   Are purchase requisitions tied to their associated orders?
(a)(iv)   Is purchasing segregated from receipt of goods, stock records and accounts payable?

3. The next stage is compliance testing. The performance of compliance tests is designed to provide the auditor with reasonable assurance that the controls established under 2 were functioning effectively throughout the period to which the audit is applied. For example, the auditor may check on compliance with the control over purchasing by:

(a) testing for evidence of a sequence check on purchase orders;
(b) testing for evidence of purchase order approval;
(c) testing for evidence of a sequence check on goods received documentation;
(d) testing for evidence of authorization of changes to purchase ledger balances.

The evidence may be provided by examination of existing documentation and records, or re-performance of the way a transaction is handled, or again by interview and enquiry as to whether and how the controls are operated. The auditor may use statistical sampling techniques in research, and these lead to statistical confidence factors.

   The auditor attempts, at this stage, to identify those areas of weakness in the system over which controls are ineffective or are not properly administered throughout the period.

4. The fourth stage is substantive testing. If empirical evidence established under 3 indicates that the controls may be relied on, little substantive testing is required. However, where the controls are weak it is necessary independently to verify that transactions have been processed properly and that account balances are correct. This is a lengthy and expensive process, and as the cost of the auditors is borne by the company it is in its interests to ensure that internal controls can be relied upon.

5. Finally, the auditor will produce an audit report, which may be qualified if material weaknesses have been discovered in the organization's system of control.

Auditing computer-based systems

The advent of the computer has meant that transaction recording and processing happen in part within the confines of a computer system. In order to testify to the satisfactory treatment of transactions, the auditor needs to take account of this new development. There are two approaches:

1. **Auditing around the computer:** The computer is treated as a 'black box'. The auditor examines the inputs and outputs and verifies that the outputs correspond to correct procedures operating on the inputs. However, the auditor does not attempt to check the processes carried out on the data within the computer. This approach can only be adopted when relatively simple computer processing occurs. The greater the complexity of the system the more serious is the omission of being able to examine the intermediate steps in the processing of transactions.

2. **Auditing through the computer:** Not only are the processes and controls surrounding the computer subject to the audit but also the computer processing controls operating

over this processing are investigated. In order to gain access to these, computer audit software will aid the task of the auditor. These packages typically contain:

- interactive enquiry facilities to interrogate files;
- facilities to analyse computer security logs for 'unusual' use of the computer system;
- the ability to compare source and object (compiled) program codes in order to detect dissimilarities;
- the facility to execute and observe the computer treatment of 'live transactions' by stepping through the processing as it occurs;
- the generation of test data;
- the generation of aids showing the logic of applications programs.

The general strategy adopted in a computer-based audit will be similar to that outlined earlier in this section. The actual controls and the higher-level controls will be evaluated and then subjected to compliance testing and, if necessary, substantive testing before an audit report is produced.

The area covered in an audit will concentrate exactly on those controls covered in Section 9.2. Specifically, the auditor will need to establish the completeness and accuracy of transaction processing by considering:

- input control
- storage control
- processing controls
- output controls
- data transmission controls.

The auditor will also need to be satisfied that there are adequate controls over the prevention of unauthorized access to the computer and the data in it. The auditor's task will further involve a consideration of the separation of functions between staff involved in transaction processing and the computer system and that adequate supervision of personnel is maintained.

As more and more firms become computerized, the importance of computer-based audits and the pressure to audit through the computer grow. Auditing is not a straightforward task that can be completed by satisfying a checklist of questions. Rather, it involves experience and the ability to apply that knowledge to differing circumstances. No two information systems are the same. From the point of view of analysis and design of computer systems, audit considerations are becoming increasingly important. Nowadays, the design of an information system needs to take not only the information provision requirements and computer security into account but also the need to design the system so that auditing is facilitated.

9.3 Ethics, social responsibility and corporate governance

Information systems have affected many aspects of our society and of our everyday lives. Any new technology brings with it changes. Changes can be good or bad. Is the impact of computerized information systems good or bad? Such a question could be the topic of a book in itself. However, with respect to information technology and information systems, where there are choices and resulting changes, decisions have to be made and there will be ethical considerations involved. In particular:

- An individual's actions can be viewed as right or wrong.
- An organization can be regarded as acting ethically or unethically.
- A society will adopt policies and legislation which can be judged ethically in terms of their social impact and the impact on the individual.

A major determinant of the actions of individuals, and of the approach taken by an organization to ethical aspects of information systems, is delimited by state policies and legislation. Within this framework, though, there remains a range of actions over which the state remains silent but where ethical decisions remain.

9.3.1 Individual's actions

There are many theories of ethics governing what actions are right and wrong for an individual. Some of these are **prescriptive** and state how we should act – examples are below:

- *Act always according to some accepted moral principle or rule* (often used by religions with reference to absolutes on right and wrong given by a god or prophet or written in a Holy Book).
- *Act towards another person in such a manner that you would find it acceptable if they acted towards you in a similar manner in similar circumstances* (often associated with Christianity or theories which seek to gain objective support for a principle by abstracting away from the self-interest of the agent).
- *Act in such a manner that the consequences of your actions maximize general welfare or happiness* (utilitarianism – attributed to a range of philosophers and influential in bringing about social reform over the past two centuries).

Other theories of ethics are **descriptive** and seek to explain why societies believe certain courses of action are right or wrong.

For information systems (IS) professionals, working either as consultants or employed within an organization, the actions they perform can be regarded by themselves and others as right or wrong. The pressures on the individual from the organization, legislation, the need to serve society as a whole and his/her own personal goals can work in harmony reinforcing a course of action. (See Figure 9.6.)

However, sometimes these pressures can come into conflict. It is at this stage that a way of choosing the right way forward is needed. For instance, the need to achieve the

Figure 9.6 Pressures on the IS professional

corporate goal of keeping within budget for a project can clash with the IS professional's personal goal of ensuring a high standard of software through extensive testing. Or again, the requirements of keeping within data protection legislation may prohibit the use of personal data needed to assure some greater public good (e.g. the use of personal held data to prevent terrorism). These dilemmas can be resolved by the individual themselves following their own code of conduct and choosing what is morally right. The IS professional though is also a member of a profession and as such the profession will have its own code of conduct to inform practice.

In the UK the major professional body concerned with information systems is the **British Computer Society (BCS)**. A professional body typically restricts membership by ensuring that those eligible have attained a high standard of competence in the area of the profession. This is achieved by the body stipulating minimum entry qualifications which the proposed member must satisfy (often in the form of passing examinations set by the professional body itself). As a member (which also involves payment of a fee) the professional status of the member is enhanced. The professional body also provides various services such as representation and staff development. In return for membership the member agrees to follow a code which governs their professional practice. Figure 9.7 contains summary extracts from the BCS code of conduct. All professions have codes of conduct. Similarly, the same profession will have a code of conduct in another country. In the USA the lead professional body for the IT professional is the **Association of Computing Machinery (ACM)**. There is much similarity between the codes of various professions and different countries.

9.3.2 Organizations and ethical policy

The managers and owners of businesses and other organizations are responsible for determining how the organization's affairs are managed; in effect determining how they behave. This is often referred to as **corporate governance**. Increasingly organizations are developing their own ethical policies. These go beyond information systems to, for example, the organization's responsibilities to its employees or its environment. With respect to information systems, areas which may be involved are the following.

Accountability

Both the quality of the information system developed and its operation can affect employees, customers and the public at large (as well as the profits of the corporation). The corporation itself may incur legal or moral liability for the effects of its system. It is good practice to put in place clear lines of responsibility for the development and operation of the information system. In this way the effects of actions can be attributed to identified individuals.

Quality of systems development and operation

This is related to the above and is of importance not only for commercial reasons but also because of the impact of information systems on individuals. The impact in moral terms of a customer who receives a late delivery is relatively small. However, when the impact is in a safety-critical system, such as an air traffic control system or a hospital records system, that impact could be large. It is generally accepted that organizations have an obligation in these areas over and above that 'forced' on them by legal liability. The organization should have in place systems and procedures for ensuring quality to complement accountability.

Figure 9.7 Summary extracts from the BCS Code of Conduct

BCS Code of Conduct

The Public Interest
1. You shall carry out work or study with due care and diligence in accordance with the employer or client's requirements, and the interests of system users. If your professional judgement is overruled, you shall indicate the likely risks and consequences.
2. In your professional role you shall have regard for the public health, safety and environment.
3. You shall have regard to the legitimate rights of third parties.
4. You shall ensure that within your professional field/s you have knowledge and understanding of relevant legislation, regulations and standards, and that you comply with such requirements.
5. You shall conduct your professional activities without discrimination against clients or colleagues.
6. You shall reject any offer of bribery or inducement.

Duty to Employer or Client
7. You shall avoid any situation that may give rise to a conflict of interest between you and your employer or client. You shall make full and immediate disclosure to them if any conflict is likely to occur or be seen by a third party as likely to occur.
8. You shall not disclose or authorise to be disclosed, or use for personal gain or to benefit a third party, confidential information except with the permission of your employer or client, or at the direction of a court of law.
9. You shall not misrepresent or withhold information on the performance of products, systems or services, or take advantage of the lack of relevant knowledge or inexperience of others.

Duty to the Profession
10. You shall uphold the reputation and good standing of the BCS in particular, and the profession in general, and shall seek to improve professional standards through participation in their development, use and enforcement.
11. You shall act with integrity in your relationships with all members of the BCS and with members of other professions with whom you work in a professional capacity.
12. You shall have due regard for the possible consequences of your statements on others. You shall not make any public statement in your professional capacity unless you are properly qualified and, where appropriate, authorised to do so. You shall not purport to represent the BCS unless authorised to do so.
13. You shall notify the Society if convicted of a criminal offence or upon becoming bankrupt or disqualified as Company Director.

Professional Competence and Integrity
14. You shall seek to upgrade your professional knowledge and skill, and shall maintain awareness of technological developments, procedures and standards which are relevant to your field, and encourage your subordinates to do likewise.
15. You shall not claim any level of competence that you do not possess. You shall only offer to do work or provide a service that is within your professional competence.
16. You shall observe the relevant BCS Codes of Practice and all other standards which, in your judgement, are relevant, and you shall encourage your colleagues to do likewise.
17. You shall accept professional responsibility for your work and for the work of colleagues who are defined in a given context as working under your supervision.

Privacy

Data protection acts (see later) outline the framework within which organizations should operate with respect to data on persons. Over and above this, the organization may wish to make explicit the way that data on individuals is going to be used. A good example involves the transmission of customer data to third parties for marketing purposes. Many organizations now are completely transparent on this and give each customer the right to state their wish to allow their personal details to be transmitted for marketing purposes – an **opt-in policy** (failure to act by the customer results in their data not being transmitted). Alternatively an **opt-out policy** may be adopted (failure to act by the customer results in their data being transmitted).

Staff development and retraining

The impact of information technology has reshaped the types of work involved within organizations. Frequently those with skills for previous jobs do not have the skills appropriate for the new technology. Many organizations have developed policies to provide the retraining necessary to enable employees to move internally. The drive to develop policies is not just the commercial consideration of 'fire and hire' as against the costs of retraining. Rather it reflects the fact that organizations regard themselves increasingly as having a moral obligation towards their workforce.

Use of IT and time

Organizations are making policy decisions on the use of their IT facilities by employees for non-work-related activities. The policy may cover, for example, the right of the employee to use e-mail for personal purposes, during or outside of work time. The content of the e-mail may also be subject to the policy (e.g. pornography) or whether the e-mail is being used for personal consultancy purposes. Issues concerning the owning of copyright on software produced by the employee either in or outside of work time but using the employer's technology will need to be clarified (often in their contract of employment).

Mini case 9.4

Corporate governance

The ever-increasing forest of regulations enforcing corporate governance standards is enough to make any chief executive feel lost.

Technology would seem the obvious solution to the corporate governance and compliance problem. Much of governance is a matter of putting rules in place and ensuring that they are followed.

Debra Logan, research director at Gartner Group, the IT advisory company, summarizes compliance issues thus: 'The main problem for companies is documentation, including internal controls and the retention of documents.'

Even e-mail has fallen under scrutiny. New accounting standards mean that audit trails must be established showing exactly how executives arrived at conclusions such as the valuation of assets.

Compliance with corporate governance standards is likely to be costly. Gartner Group estimates that Fortune 1000 companies have each spent about $2m on bringing themselves into line with the Sarbanes–Oxley Act.

Brian Gregory is the director of enterprise resource planning marketing at Oracle. In his view, 'The most important issue, [with corporate governance] is trying to make the accounts that companies present as meaningful and accurate as possible.'

The sheer volume of data presents further problems. Companies should try to simplify their systems, bringing more of their databases within a single overarching structure and reducing the number of points at which data enters the system.

Mr Gregory points out that, to a large degree, successful corporate governance depends on people: 'This is a management issue. People need training around governance, they need to be given the skills. People are central.'

Adapted from: **Software lends a helping hand to compliance**
FT.com site: 5 September 2003

Questions

1. As an auditor, what would your main objectives be in conducting an audit of a computer-based information system?

2. What strategy would you adopt to establish the validity of financial statements and the systems used to produce them?

3. Why has corporate governance increasingly become a matter for concern in the boardrooms of larger organizations?

9.3.3 Society issues and legislation

Many of the issues resulting from the impact of information technology have been experienced before with new technologies. What distinguishes the impact of information technology from previous technologies is the penetration of information technology into most aspects of our work and leisure and the power which it brings for processing information. When these impacts are regarded as undesirable existing legislation may be able to control this. Increasingly though, extant legislation cannot be applied successfully to the characteristics of information technology and new laws need to be passed. This is an example of **social responsibility**; members of a community sharing a collective belief and deciding on the most appropriate actions for the benefit of the majority while protecting minorities and the disenfranchised.

Computer crime and abuse

The rise of IT and the Internet has led to different activities which, at best, are considered to be abuse and at worst so counter to individuals and society that legislation has been passed to make these activities illegal.

1. **Theft** through the use of computers was an early activity. It often centred on the movement of money or on false accounting. Now it has extended to data theft and software theft through copying.

2. **Hackers** are individuals who attempt to electronically enter a computer system, usually remotely via the Internet, when they have no authorization to do so. Such individuals may do this for 'fun' or the 'challenge', to damage the system's functionality in some way (e.g. destroying data, or transmitting a virus), or to perpetrate theft.

3. **Pornography** is now commonly distributed across the Internet. The ability to disguise the source of the receiving address for pornography has limited police activity in enforcement of legislation on obscene materials. Further legislation has been necessary to define what constitutes the transmission and holding of pornography since the medium is electronic signals.

4. **Spamming** is the automated sending of large quantities of unsolicited e-mails. This may be for marketing purposes (largely regarded as a nuisance by the recipients) or to jam or disrupt computer facilities as these become increasingly devoted to the transmission and delivery of e-mails removing them from their legitimate processing purposes.

5. **Sniffing** is the electronic eavesdropping on electronic data transmissions. This may be of e-mails or of data which might be used for pecuniary gain, e.g. credit card details. Encryption of this data is increasingly used to ensure its security.

Countries are responding to these challenges with legislation. For example:

■ Governments, whilst clamping down on sniffing, are enshrining their rights to eavesdrop in the national interest through legislation. The **Regulation of Investigatory Powers Act (2000)** in the UK allows the government mass surveillance of electronic communication and access to Internet activity through Internet service providers (ISPs). A bill was rapidly passed in the United States after the September 11 terrorist attacks allowing the FBI to make widespread usage of its e-mail sniffing software product, Carnivore.

■ The **Computer Misuse Act (1990)** in the UK was passed to make illegal the unauthorized access to, or modification of, computer material. This has now been supplemented by the **Computer Misuse Amendment Bill (2002)** designed to prohibit denial of service attacks ('degradation, failure or other impairment of a computerized system').

However, it is often proving difficult to frame such legislation as the activity often spans several countries through web hosting and data transmission.

Mini case 9.5

Passports and fraud

The UK Passport Service (UKPS) will be using facial biometrics in the applications process by the end of next year, as a prelude to the inclusion of computer chips in passports by 2005.

Using a photograph, the technology creates a mathematical comparison of measurements between points on the face.

From the end of 2004, biometrics created from photographs submitted with new passport applications will be compared against a database of known fraudsters.

'It is the same technology that will be used to put chips into passports the following year,' said UK Passport Service chief executive Bernard Herdan. 'Once established there will be a three-way integrity check – someone at the border will be able to compare the person in front of them with the information on the chip as well as the photo.'

The scheme is part of a range of plans to use technology to combat fraud, says Herdan.

A key element is the Lost, Stolen and Recovered (LSR) database, which is due to go live on 8 December.

'Data from the LSR system will be shared not only around our own organization but also with other nations' border controls, so anyone trying to travel on a stolen passport could get stopped when they try to use it,' said Herdan.

The information will be distributed using the Omnibase network being rolled out to embassies and high commissions across the world. So far 90 of the 130 establishments have the service, says Herdan.

'All the big embassies now have access so they can see the date of issue and, for recently issued passports, the picture and signature,' he said.

Adapted from: **Passport Service poised to introduce biometrics**
Computing – United Kingdom; 27 November 2003

Questions

1. In what ways does the proposed new passport system offer greater security?

2. What additional steps need to be taken in terms of cooperation between governments for this system to be effective?

Intellectual property

Intellectual property is intangible property created by an individual or organization. Examples might be books, music or art, or ideas behind inventions. The intellectual property is often produced to make profit and considerable time, effort and funding can go into its production. In order to reward this investment the producer of intellectual property must be assured that others will not immediately take it over and reap profit from it, thereby denying the producer the reward. The two main ways of achieving this are via **copyright** and **patent**.

Copyright protects the expression or manifestation of an idea – not the idea itself. Copyright applies to a work automatically when it comes into existence. For example, when a book is written or software code is produced it becomes the copyright of the author. The author may license others to produce copies of the work or, indeed, may be required to transfer the copyright to an employer (if produced in the employer's employment and this is covered by the employment contract). Copyright prevents the copying of all or some of a work by others during the author's lifetime and beyond (different countries have different time periods). There are also international agreements protecting copyright. Software when produced is automatically copyright. However, this copyright will not prevent another from understanding the ideas behind the software and producing code to manifest the same idea.

Patent protects the idea behind an invention and the way it functions. It therefore powerfully protects the intellectual property of the author. However, it is not automatic – the patent right must be applied for. This can be a long process and to gain a patent the intellectual property must be considered to be original and non-obvious. Further, a patent granted in one country may not be acceptable in another. Therefore patents may be needed from many countries. Software is not usually patented.

Although covered by legislation (for example, **Copyright, Designs and Patents Act 1988**, UK, and **Computer Software Copyright Act 1980**, US), illegal copying of software is common and technologically usually simple. Organizations such as the global **Business Software Alliance**, with major software companies as members, bring group pressure to identify and act against illegal use of software through copyright fraud.

Liability and accountability

The new technology also throws up questions on liability and accountability for which older concepts may not be applicable. The following examples illustrate the ways in which old concepts are being challenged.

(a) It is usually accepted that public carriers are not liable for the content of what they carry. The postal service is not responsible for the fact that a package contains a faulty item or even a bomb. The telephone company is not responsible for the content of the conversation held using its services. However, difficulties in dealing with illegal pornography are leading governments to consider holding Internet service providers responsible in some ways for the services they provide – particularly for the content of websites the ISP provides.

(b) Similarly, copyright laws are being pressed by Napster and Gnutella-type network protocols which distribute copyright music, not by storing it or transmitting it, but rather by facilitating individuals who hold (illegally) the copyright material on their hard disks to distribute it freely across the network to those that demand it.

(c) Liability for the effects of the use of a computerized system is not always clear. For instance, an independent expert provides information to a software company to build an expert system which is sold to a client. In using the expert system incorrect advice is given which damages a customer. In such cases it is not always clear where liability lies.

Privacy

Information technology has significantly increased our capacity to store, transmit and analyse data held on individuals. In particular:

■ Decrease in data storage costs together with improved data access times has enabled organizations to maintain detailed databases on individuals.

■ The sophistication of data analysis techniques has enabled this data to be put to very different purposes from that for which it was originally collected.

■ The massive increase in computing power together with declining costs has enabled these analysis techniques to be applied to large amalgamated databases.

■ The increased used of networking (in particular the World Wide Web) has enabled the remote interrogation of data, the amalgamation of large databases and the near-instant recovery of the output.

These developments have enabled the bringing together of data on individuals from various sources. This is particularly useful in building **profiles** of individuals which can be sold to organizations with products to market. These profiles allow targeted marketing to occur. The data collected may be from credit card transactions (giving patterns of expenditure), point of sales systems in supermarkets (also giving more detailed expenditure patterns), to travel locations such as petrol stations or airports (giving geographical detail) as well as banking records, Internet transactions, telephone records and many more. Sophisticated technology such as **non-obvious relational awareness** software provides powerful data analysis techniques enabling the data to be prepared for marketing purposes.

All of these developments have enabled benefits but also allow for the possibility of practices which affect the privacy of the individual beyond their consent. In particular:

■ Data on a person can be used for purposes different from that for which it was originally collected or agreed to by the supplier.

■ Data from different sources can be combined and analysed to build a profile of a person not previously envisaged.

- Inaccurate data held on individuals can be erroneously copied, transmitted and combined with other data and interrogated remotely across the globe in a swift and non-recoverable way.

For these reasons many countries have adopted data protection legislation. This puts restrictions on organizations as to how data on persons is collected, what this data can be used for, how long and securely personal data is to be maintained and procedures for ensuring accuracy of data. All involve the right of the person on whom the data is held (the data subject) to have access to the data held on them and to know for what purposes it will be used. The **Data Protection Acts (1984, 1998)** of the UK are an example and are covered in detail in the next section.

Mini case 9.6

Crime and ethics

Twenty of the world's biggest financial institutions are assembling a far-reaching private database of regulatory and criminal information that will enable them to conduct global background checks on customers.

The ambitious project to combine data from more than 250 jurisdictions is partly a response to rules introduced after the September 11 attacks. But the banks' plans could fuel concerns that individual privacy is being sacrificed in the war on terror.

Regulatory DataCorp International, which is compiling the information, is funded by many of the world's leading international banks and investment houses, including Citigroup, Goldman Sachs, CSFB, Bank of America, JP Morgan Chase, Lehman Brothers, Merrill Lynch, Morgan Stanley and UBS.

RDC has been quietly operating since last July. The company said yesterday it had joined forces with an investigative firm to greatly expand the amount of international information entering the system. The New York-based James Mintz Group had gathered records from more than 100 regulatory agencies in more than 50 countries, RDC said.

The new system – the Global Regulatory Information Database, or Grid – draws on more than 20,000 sources and databases worldwide. These include disciplinary actions in the past 30 years by US regulators and their counterparts around the globe.

The database also draws on lists of terrorists, organized crime figures, fugitives and drugs barons.

It will also assemble lists of senior politicians and their associates from 'virtually every country in the world' to stop stolen funds being laundered through financial institutions.

Adapted from: **Banks set up database to check customers**
By Thomas Catýn
Financial Times: 27 November 2003

Questions

1. What ethical questions are raised by this new approach to data collection and aggregation?

2. How should information systems professions react when involved in a project such as this?

9.4   Data protection legislation

Data protection legislation has been enacted in many countries in the past 20 years in the wake of increased concern over data held on persons using powerful computer-based storage and processing technology. It is a generally recognized right that on the one hand individuals should have some protection surrounding the holding and use of data on them but on the other that individuals and organizations, including the state, also have rights to possess and use personal data to serve their purposes. Data protection legislation attempts to define this balance and to reconcile competing needs. The essence of the problem is to ensure privacy for individuals yet not restrict the legitimate workings of the state and other aspects of society.

Concern over data protection has increased as a result of the power of modern computers to process, store and transmit vast amounts of data cheaply and quickly. This sets them apart from their manual predecessors. Specifically:

- Large files of personal data can be interrogated easily, often using indexes on names, addresses, account numbers, and so on. Manual file access is more difficult.

- The speed of response to an interrogation is extremely fast in computer-based systems compared with their manual counterparts.

- Computer-based files can be interrogated from any part of the world (if telecommunications and outside access are provided).

- The presence of networking facilities means that entire files can be transmitted and duplicated anywhere in the world in a matter of seconds or at the most in minutes.

- It is technically possible to cross-reference and link disparate files to obtain 'personal profiles' on individuals.

- Individual records can be selected easily on the basis of sophisticated searches: for example, find all names and addresses of individuals owning a black Ford, living in the Greater Manchester area and with a criminal record.

In themselves, these characteristics of modern data storage and processing are not undesirable. However, they have certain implications. First, inaccurate (as well as accurate) data can be transmitted and duplicated quickly and efficiently. Second, remote data access, targeted data retrieval and the linking of files mean that data access ability in the wrong hands can lead to a severe misuse of power. Finally, there is a danger that data on private aspects of a person's life held for legitimate purposes may be spread and become widely accessible, intruding on that person's right to privacy.

These concerns have led to data protection legislation in many countries – Sweden (1973), USA (1974), West Germany (1977), Canada (1977), France (1978) and Norway (1978). However, it was not until 1984 that data protection laws were first enacted in the UK.

9.4.1 The Data Protection Act 1998

In the UK, personal data has been offered a degree of protection since the first Data Protection Act in 1984. The 1998 Act implements the EC Data Protection Directive (95/46/EC) and came into force on 1 March 2000. It increases the level of protection significantly. Importantly, it can apply to data that is:

- held on computers, or in computer-readable format;
- held manually (if held in a structured form);
- held as medical and educational records.

Many of the provisions of the Act refer only to personal data i.e. that relating to an identifiable living person. There are further restrictions on sensitive data such as medical, sexual and criminal history, religious and political beliefs, racial origin, and trade union membership.

The 1998 Act introduces some new terminology into data protection legislation.

- **The Data Protection Commissioner:** The Data Protection Commissioner supervises the implementation of the Act, considers complaints concerning breaches of the data protection principles and has powers to act against offenders.
- **Data controller:** This is normally the company or business.
- **Data processor:** Any person (other than an employee of the data controller) who processes the data on behalf of the data controller.
- **Data subject:** A data subject is 'an individual who is the subject of personal data'. This could be a customer or client.

The eight data protection principles

The 1998 Act provides eight fundamental data protection principles. These go further than those under the 1984 Act and include the activities of obtaining and disclosing data, not just the activities related to data processing. The eight principles are:

1. Personal data shall be processed fairly and lawfully and, in particular, shall not be processed unless certain listed conditions are met. These conditions deal with how essential the processing of data is and emphasize that a data subject must consent to the data collection, or, in the case of sensitive personal data, must have given explicit consent.
2. Personal data shall be obtained only for specified lawful purposes and shall not be further processed.
3. Personal data shall be adequate, relevant and not excessive in relation to the purpose for which it is processed.
4. Personal data shall be accurate and, where necessary, kept up to date.
5. Personal data shall not be kept for longer than is necessary.
6. Personal data shall be processed in accordance with the rights of data subjects under the 1998 Act.
7. Appropriate measures shall be taken against unauthorized or unlawful processing of personal data and against accidental loss of or damage to personal data.
8. Personal data shall not be transferred to a country or territory outside the European Economic Area (EEA) unless that country or territory ensures an adequate level of protection for the rights and freedom of data subjects in relation to the processing of personal data.

The new rights of data subjects

Under the 1984 Act, data subjects had the right to know what data was held about them once the data had been collected. Under the 1998 Act, data subjects have the right to know not only what data and information about them has been collected but also

- to know the nature of the data being held;
- to know why and how it is to be processed;
- to know to whom it may be disclosed;
- to have copies of the data, subject to payment of a nominal fee (currently £10);
- to object to and prevent processing of the data if damage or distress would be caused;
- to claim compensation for damage caused by any breach of the Act.

Exemptions

The Data Protection Act 1998 provides a number of exemptions that apply to various sections in the Act. For example, in the interests of the state, such issues of national security or the investigation of a crime, exceptions to the Act are possible. These exemptions are intended not to pose a threat to the privacy of the data subject.

Criticisms of the Act

In the early stages of its implementation, a number of concerns have been voiced:

- A data subject might not be aware of archived records relating to them that describe painful historical events. If these records are stored in a structured or computerized way they would need to be disclosed, causing possible distress to the data subject.
- Similarly, some archived records are known to contain some inaccuracies but are stored for reasons of historical importance. Archivists are concerned that data subjects might object to and block the storage of these inaccurate records, thereby destroying their value as a historical record.
- Data about a limited or public company is not caught by the 1998 Act. The Act applies only when an officer or employee of a company discloses data about him or herself, such as their name, e-mail address or other personal details.

Mini case 9.7

Privacy

New rules for a passenger data collection scheme operated by US authorities may carry a nasty sting for travellers. The scheme, the Advance Passenger Information System (Apis – Latin for 'bee'), threatens to cause big delays at check-in and raises ethical questions about a passenger's right to privacy of information.

Originally Apis allowed airlines to collate and forward information to US customs and immigrations services about each passenger's name, date of birth, gender and nationality. All these details are relatively easy to gather by swiping the passenger's passport through a machine-reader. Now the US wants to extend the information airlines supply to include data such as where the passenger will stay on arrival, country of residence and visa particulars. These details cannot be gleaned from a passport. Airline staff will have to add this information to the traveller's electronic reservation, known as the Passenger Name Record, the vehicle that airlines will now have to use to transmit data to the US authorities. The PNR includes many more personal details about travellers, such as address, e-mail address, telephone number, credit card numbers and even dietary preferences.

This has put European airlines in the invidious position of being punished by the US if they fail to provide access to the PNR but facing potential prosecution in the European Union if they surrender information that breaches EU data protection rules.

Then there are those ethical questions over Apis and over PNR data, even if the European Commission is content for passengers to sign away their privacy. Will the information be given to other parties? Will it be deleted at the end of the journey? It is the 'Big Brother is watching you' syndrome.

Adapted from: Security sting at the check-in
By Amon Cohen
Financial Times: 25 February 2003

Questions

1. A national government can enact privacy laws to protect its citizens. In what ways can those citizens still have concerns about maintaining their privacy?

2. The Apis system was set up in response to security threats concerning air travel. Why should air passengers therefore have concerns about complying with its requirements?

9.5 Risk identification and controls

In Section 9.2, it was stressed that controls cannot be viewed in isolation from cost–benefit considerations. The decision to implement a certain control will have initial and operating costs, and these have to be set against the likely benefit. These benefits will include the expected saving resulting from prevention of the loss that would have occurred in the absence of the control. The possibility that the control, on occasion, may be insufficient to prevent the loss occurring must also be taken into account.

Two approaches to risk analysis can be identified. These are quantitative approaches, many of which use sophisticated modelling techniques to arrive at cost–benefit optimal mixes of controls, and **heuristic approaches**, which are more concerned with situations in which controls and failures of control are not easily structured or quantifiable.

9.5.1 A quantified approach to risk and controls

The method explained in this section (covered in Burch and Grudnitski, 1986) involves deriving a matrix in which the columns are types of hazard and the rows are types of control. A type of control might be effective against several different types of hazard. For instance, input controls are effective against inaccurate data input, incomplete data input (loss of documents) and fraud. Similarly, a type of hazard such as fraud may be prevented by different types of control – personnel controls, computer access controls, data access controls and the separation of organizational functions. Part of a hazard–control matrix is shown in Figure 9.8.

Having established the type of hazard that each type of control is effective against, it is necessary to assign numerical values to the following:

Figure 9.8 Part of a hazard–control matrix

	Errors and omissions	Lost data and documents	Computer failure	Unauthorized access	Fire	Fraud
Input controls	✓	✓		✓		✓
Processing controls	✓					✓
Output controls	✓	✓		✓		✓
Storage controls		✓				✓
Operating system controls				✓		✓
Records management	✓	✓			✓	
Accounting controls	✓	✓				✓
Contingency plan			✓		✓	
Physical security			✓	✓	✓	

- the loss value associated with each type of hazard; and
- the probability over a given period of time that the hazard will occur.

The expected loss associated with the hazard can be computed by multiplying the loss value by the probability that the hazard will occur. For instance, if fire has an expected loss of £1,000,000 and the probability of its occurrence is 0.01 per year, then the expected loss is £10,000 per year. This calculation is repeated for each type of hazard and the total expected losses found. Suppose that they are equal to £55,000 in each year. This figure may then be used to justify the expenditure of £55,000 per annum on controls.

Of course, it will be pointed out that there are different types of fire, which are associated with different loss values and different probabilities. In essence, this does not affect the calculation as the expected losses for each type of fire may be calculated and the sum total for fire found. The further criticism that there may be a range of loss values occurring with differing probabilities associated with each type of fire can also be accommodated. However, there is a great danger that too much emphasis is placed on the numerical sophistication of the model when in reality accuracy is swamped by the guesswork accompanying estimation of the loss values and probabilities. It is often better to restrict the calculation to the average loss and the probability that this will occur. Even this may involve very rough estimations.

It is now necessary to establish the effect of the controls. For each control, numerical values are assigned to:

- the installation cost of the control;
- the operating cost of the control; and
- the probability over a given period of time that the control will fail.

Each control will be effective against a number of hazards, and the total cost of control per annum is equal to the sum of the following three costs:

1. the installation cost (divided by the number of years over which this is to be spread);
2. the operating cost per annum;
3. the total of all expected losses associated with each hazard over which the control is applied, multiplied by the probability that the control will fail to prevent the respective hazard occurring.

This gives some measure of the net cost of the control, and as a rule of thumb if this is less than the expected loss associated with the hazards to which the control is applied, then the control is justified.

The total impact of a range of controls can be found by summing the net costs of each control, together with the expected losses associated with hazards over which the set of controls is not applied. This assumes that the controls are mutually exclusive in the sense that no two controls apply to one type of hazard. The range of controls with the smallest cost value is the one that is most cost–benefit efficient, and this value gives a financial measure of the advantage of the range over the 'no control' situation, where the cost is £55,000.

Where the controls are not mutually exclusive, this needs to be taken into account as the loss associated with a failure of one control may be prevented by the action of another. The techniques are standard but the computation can become quite lengthy, and it is often possible to profit from computer-aided support.

Having determined and implemented the optimum mix of controls, these should be reviewed periodically as costs and probabilities change. In determining expenditure on these controls, management would also take into account the time–cost of money (by discounting or payback techniques) and also weigh the implementation of controls against alternative projects that are competing for the scarce resources of the organization.

Criticisms of the quantified approach

The method illustrated is an example of just one type of quantified approach to risk analysis. Others differ, but all concentrate on a mathematical modelling of losses, costs and probabilities. Some common criticisms are directed at all these types of approach.

First, it is agreed that the approaches do not help to determine which types of threat exist for an organization and which types of control would be effective. The quantified methods are useful only once this initial investigation has been carried out.

Second, quantitative approaches assume that figures can be assigned to expected losses and probabilities, whereas in practice this is not possible.

Both of these points have merit but should not be seen as invalidating quantitative approaches; rather, they indicate that they should be limited in scope. The first criticism shows that they are incomplete and are best regarded as part of a total approach.

The second criticism varies in strength depending on which hazards and which controls are considered straightforwardly quantifiable. For instance, research can determine the average number of errors and the resulting loss occurring in every 1000 account numbers entered via a computer keyboard. This can be used in the cost–benefit analysis. Other hazards such as fire may be estimated by consulting actuarial records (after all, insurance companies have to base their premiums on some cost–benefit analysis) or the local fire station may be able to identify particular fire hazards in a computer installation, enabling figures to be put on losses.

However, figures for some hazards, such as fraud, are notoriously difficult to estimate because they are specific to industry/company computer systems. Once important hazards and controls become impossible to quantify, the chance of a cost–benefit analysis applied to an overall system of controls vanishes and controls are justified on a piecemeal basis.

It is perhaps best to view quantitative risk analysis modelling as providing one channel of information among others relevant to managerial decisions on the nature and extent of controls.

9.5.2 Heuristic approaches

Strategies that attempt to assess risk based on experience and partial information using rules of thumb are known as 'heuristic'.

Perhaps the simplest heuristic technique is the checklist of areas that should be considered in reviewing a system of controls. This may be compiled from the experience of many practitioners and will incorporate what might be described as 'group knowledge'. The checklist may serve no more than to direct attention to the areas of possible weakness and indicate types of control that are effective.

Other approaches recognize that major computer-associated losses are caused by the accidental or deliberate actions of persons. It is important to clarify and assess the strengths and weaknesses of personnel at all levels of the organization associated with computer use. For instance, employees are known to work with greater accuracy and effectiveness in some working conditions rather than others; motivation and career prospects have effects on the likelihood of an employee perpetrating damage and fraud.

Previous incidents may also be a guide to future losses. Various scenarios can be sketched and discussed with computer personnel to assess the impact of these. Controls can then be identified and added to the scenarios, which are then reconsidered. This iterative process may be repeated many times. This type of approach can be extremely valuable in promoting communication and cooperation between those involved in considering the scenarios and so is regarded as part of an education process in the importance of controls.

Heuristic approaches are of assistance in those areas where quantitative techniques are weakest. It is becoming clear that risk identification and analysis, together with taking appropriate measures in control, are an increasingly important feature both in the operation of computerized information systems and in their design. As a result, methodologies are gradually evolving to aid this process.

Summary

The design, application and administration of controls is an integral part of the analysis and design of any information system. There are three main systems of control that can be applied to both manual and computerized information systems.

First, feedback control mechanisms monitor the state of a system and its output, compare these with a desired standard and make appropriate adjustments in the case of deviation. Feedforward control mechanisms use the current state of a system together with a model of the system to predict future states. If these do not meet systems objectives then appropriate action is taken to alter the state of the current system. Finally, preventive controls operate continuously, preventing an undesirable state of affairs arising.

Controls operate at various levels. They may deter or prevent errors occurring, detect errors that have occurred, minimize the loss associated with a failure, enable recovery or facilitate investigation. In a computerized system, they are directed at malfunctions in hardware and software, poor performance by personnel, fraud and various types of physical hazard.

Controls over data movement through the computer are particularly important in respect of transaction areas. The controls operate at key points over input, storage, processing, output and transmission of data.

Other controls, mainly aimed at fraud, prevent unauthorized access to the computer system and restrict access to files and parts of the database in it. Encryption is a way of encoding data so that in the case of a breach of security the data is meaningless.

The organizational structure of staff functions supporting the information system ensures not only that proper administration occurs but also that the separation and compartmentalization of functions lead to added security.

An important aspect of information systems development is to develop a contingency plan that is put into operation during massive computer failure. This will make provision for new staff functions to deal with the emergency, the arrangement of standby or backup facilities and the eventual recovery of the information system.

Legal requirements to audit the financial accounting aspects of a computer system, as well as ongoing audits, act as a further control. They will not only identify the effectiveness of existing controls but may have a deterrent effect on fraud. Modern computer-based audits use software tools to aid the audit process. These enable auditing through the computer rather than limiting the audit to events around it and allow the examination of input and output documentation.

Issues of rights, responsibilities and behaviour are the subject of ethics. Individuals, organizations and society as a whole form views about the way that issues should be tackled. The outcome may vary greatly. In some cases legislation may be enacted, in others voluntary codes of conduct may be adopted. Where there is no clear 'right' or 'wrong' way to act, an ethical consideration and evaluation by those concerned can lead to the 'best' or 'most appropriate' course of action. As a professional working in the information systems domain, a number of ethical dilemmas arise and it is essential that proper consideration is given to these issues.

Recent data protection legislation implies that steps must be taken to ensure that the design of an information system enables it to function in accordance with data protection principles. These include the need to take reasonable precautions over the security and accuracy of personal data as well as the facility to allow individuals to obtain personal data held on them by the system.

Managerial strategy on the implementation of a system of controls will always take into account cost–benefit considerations – the cost and effectiveness of controls versus the expected loss in their absence. Quantitative models may aid the process of risk analysis but are complementary to other approaches.

Review questions

1. Explain the ideas behind feedback control.

2. Explain the ideas behind feedforward control.

3. How do feedback and feedforward control differ?

4. How is functional separation used as a control in accounting systems? Illustrate your answer with several examples.

5. Explain the following checks and controls:

control total	master file check	transaction log
hash total	format check	concurrency control
sequence check	reasonableness check	run-to-run control
field filling check	limit check	parity bit
check digit	error log	echo check

6. Explain the difference between *fault detection*, *fault avoidance* and *fault tolerance*.

7. Explain the difference between a *symmetric* and an *asymmetric* crypto-process.

8. Describe the responsibilities of the various members of staff supporting a large computerized information system. What aspects of the functions performed by each are control functions?

9. List *five* physical hazards that may affect a computer system and state physical controls that would prevent these or aid recovery in the event that they occur.

10. What questions should an auditor be asking in order to evaluate controls over a sales ledger system?

Exercises

1. Give an illustration of feedforward control in:
   (a) inventory planning
   (b) budgeting.

   What features of your example correspond to each of the components in the general feedforward model?

2. Give an illustration of feedback control in:
   (a) production
   (b) internal auditing
   (c) credit control.

What features of your example correspond to each of the components in the general feedback model?

3. What is preventive control, and how does it differ from feedback and feedforward control?

4. (a) What categories of preventive control are there?
   (b) Give an illustration of each of these categories in the following areas of a business:

   - payroll
   - cash receipts
   - stores.

5. List and explain *five* levels of control.

6. Is there a clear distinction between input controls and processing controls?

7. Which of the following account codes (containing a check digit modulus-11 in the least significant position) is a legitimate account code?

   (a) 459364   (b) 36821   (c) 27   (d) 19843.

8. Why is it necessary for computer users to use both a login code and a secret password rather than just a secret password, which could serve as both identification and, because it is secret, authentication of identification as well?

9. Give *four* conditions that password authentication of identification should satisfy in order to ensure maximum security.

10. What characteristics should a secure access control policy exhibit?

11. Explain the difference between *substantive* and *compliance testing*.

12. 'It is insufficient to consider whether a control is justified purely on monetary cost–benefit grounds; it is equally important that it works.' What confusion is involved here?

13. 'We ensure that personal data held on the database is accessible only to authorized personnel by preventing other database users accessing personal data records by their key fields or other identifying fields such as name or address and preventing display of these fields.' Is this a secure personal data protection policy in the light of powerful query languages?

14. A bank has a centralized computer system with online terminal connections at each of its 300 branches. These terminals are operated by counter tellers. Each branch also has an automated online 'card point', which can be used by customers to withdraw cash, make deposits, request statements and pay bills to accounts directly. The bill account details must be notified in writing to the bank in advance. There is a personal identification number (PIN) code associated with each customer's card. For security purposes, this is known to the customer and no one else. The PIN needs to be entered for each 'card point' transaction. The card may also be used over the counter at branch offices to carry out the same transactions as offered by the 'card point' machine, although the teller keys in all the details.

Identify preventive controls that should be present in such a system and specify the purpose of each control.

15. The computer-based audit cannot be regarded as independent, as:

    (a) the auditor is paid by the client,
    (b) the auditor relies on the client to supply information on the workings of the computer system.

    What steps can be taken to ensure auditor independence?

16. You have been appointed data protection officer for your company. It has a large number of microcomputers holding personal data used by many users. At present, no attempt has been made to satisfy the requirements of data protection legislation. Outline the steps that you would take in order to ensure that your organization complies with legislation.

17. 'The Data Protection Act 1998 poses a severe threat to the work of historical archivists.' Do you agree?

CASE STUDY 9

Computer crime

The latest wave of attacks on online gambling sites, web retailers and Internet payment systems follow similar bombardments of companies worldwide.

Distributed denial of service attacks, once the preserve of mischievous hackers, have become the weapon of choice for organized criminals seeking to extort money from unprotected corporations. It is no less than a high-tech protection racket.

In September, more than a dozen offshore betting sites serving the US market were brought down by DDoS attacks. E-mails were then reportedly sent demanding payments of up to $40,000 (£24,000) or the attacks would be resumed. The Russian Mafia, with assaults traced back to St Petersburg, was thought to be behind the extortion attempts.

'We have seen these peaks being hit around the world,' said Paul Lawrence, Europe and Asia manager for Top Layer, a US company that provides protection against DDoS attacks. 'It does seem to be a trend, where they find a specific type of company – like online gambling – and geography is no barrier to them. They seem to be working their way around the world, picking people off quite happily.'

Law enforcement agencies say these are not groups of amateur hackers. 'While we still see offences that are done purely for mischievousness, here we are seeing great deals of money changing hands,' said Mick Deats, detective superintendent in charge of operations at the National Hi-Tech Crime Unit. 'These are for-profit crimes and all intelligence suggests that organized crime is involved.'

The classic DDoS attack begins with a break-in at a computer which then becomes the master computer for the intended attack. Several other computers are then hacked and a command is sent through the master telling them to bombard the servers of the target with bogus requests.

Industry experts say huge numbers of computers are not needed to bring down a transactional website. A single computer can issue a rapid series of data packets that can help to tie up the target's servers. It is compared with saying 'hello' repeatedly and starting numerous unfinished conversations.

'It's a relatively simplistic brute-force tool,' said Mr Lawrence. '[Hackers] will monitor the success of the attack and they will then try something slightly different if the site is not brought down.'

The data of users of the site are generally not compromised. The culprits are not interested in confidential details, they are concentrating on bringing the target network to its knees.

Tracking down the criminals can be difficult. The computers used are not their own, so tracing their Internet protocol addresses can prove fruitless. The bogus requests are also bounced off other servers around the world. If the blackmail request is made by e-mail, investigators have some opportunity, but anonymous addresses are always used and finding the source proves impossible. Law enforcement agencies are enjoying more success through following the money trail back to the blackmailers if the payments are made.

Other big DDoS attacks have included one on the root servers of the Internet last year and two on the website of Microsoft in August. Before DDoS, criminals tried to blackmail companies, such as Fujitsu and Visa, after breaking into their networks and actually stealing data. Increasing the strength of firewalls has made this more difficult.

Planned European legislation on computer crimes and increased international co-operation among law enforcement agencies will boost the efforts of police to track down criminal gangs carrying out attacks on companies from outside their jurisdiction, writes Chris Nuttall. Under existing laws a server in the UK falling victim to a distributed denial of service attack qualifies as an offence under the Computer Misuse Act, with penalties of up to five years in jail. If the attack is accompanied by a 'demand with menaces' the penalty can be as much as 14 years for that offence. Police helping other forces abroad to make arrests in countries where the attacks originate can pass their evidence on to the Crown Prosecution Service, which can seek extradition proceedings. A G8 agreement covering 32 countries is helping law enforcement agencies to gather digital evidence very quickly. Data can be frozen and preserved even before legal documentation arrives, preventing hard discs from being wiped and e-mails deleted. 'There is a lot of co-operation. Internet crime does not fit neatly into force divisions and geographic boundaries, so we have got to be joined-up about this,' said Detective Superintendent Mick Deats of the National Hi-Tech Crime Unit. The European Union is also proposing legislation to deal with newer computer crimes such as DDoS attacks. A framework decision in April with regard to protecting information systems details two new offences of illegal access to computer systems and illegal interference in them. 'The catalyst for all this is high-tech crime, there's pressure on everybody to take this seriously,' said David Porter, a security consultant at Detica, an IT services company. 'The penalties being suggested were at least four years for any attacks causing large losses or where an organized crime network is involved.'

Adapted from: **High-tech gangsters who shoot on site**
By Chris Nuttall
Financial Times: 12 November 2003

Questions

1. Define what is meant by a denial of service attack. What forms do these attacks take?

2. What strategies can be adopted to prevent these attacks by
   (a) businesses?
   (b) governments?

3. What role can professional bodies play in framing codes of conduct for their members?

References and recommended reading

Beer S. (1994). *Brain of the Firm*, 2nd edn. Wiley
This is an interesting, highly readable text, which applies cybernetic principles and control mechanisms as evolved in the human being, by analogy, to the management of an organization.

Clark L.D. (2003). *Enterprise Security: The Manager's Defense Guide*. Addison-Wesley, Pearson Education
This easy-to-read book provides a comprehensive state-of-the-art coverage of e-business security. It considers recent attack strategies and offers techniques for combating attempts at data infiltration, data destruction and denial of service attacks. As well as explaining traditional security technologies, such as firewalls and virtual private networks, it shows how these can be integrated with risk management, vulnerability assessment, and intrusion detection to build a comprehensive security plan.

David W.S. and Benamati J. (2003). *E-Commerce Basics: Technology Foundations and E-Business Applications*. Addison-Wesley, Pearson
This is a comprehensive introduction to all aspects of e-commerce. Later chapters also cover cybercrime, cyberterrorism, security and ethical issues. Chapters contain summaries, review questions and exercises.

Furnell S. (2002). *Cybercrime: Vandalising the Information Society*. Addison-Wesley, Pearson
This is an entertaining and well-researched text in which an accessible analysis of cybercrime, including hacking, viruses and other forms of malicious software, is provided. The effects of these crimes on the wider society and organizations in which they take place is considered. Areas covered include the commercial and political evolution of the computer hacker, the likely future development of cybercrime and implications for responses to this from the legal system.

James A. (2000). *Information Systems Auditing and Assurance*. South Western Publishing
A good coverage of the topics of auditing, assurance and internal control. The book considers computer operations, data management, electronic commerce systems, auditing revenue and expenditure, and it has an interesting section devoted to fraud and fraud detection.

Maiwald E. (2004). *Fundamentals of Network Security*. McGraw-Hill
This is a comprehensive textbook introduction to computers and network security. It contains chapter-end quizzes, questions and lab projects. The text provides a basic understanding of best practice for security laws and standards that are necessary to build complete security systems.

Moynihan T. (2002). *Coping with IS/IT Risk Management*. Springer Verlag
The book looks at how experienced project managers deal with the development of IT systems. Several experienced managers are interviewed as to the way they handle projects. These are then analysed by other professionals. The book is aimed at software professionals but is useful to students to give a 'real life' approach to problems.

Romney M.E., Steinbart P. and Cushing B.E. (2002). *Accounting Information Systems and Business Organizations*, 8th edn. New York: Addison Wesley Longman
This book gives extensive coverage of control as applied to accounting systems for the non-technical reader.

Singleton S. (1998). *Data Protection: The New Law*. Bristol: Jordan Publishing
This book provides an excellent, highly summarized introduction to the principles behind data protection legislation and its implications for systems analysis and design.

Chapter 10

Information systems development: an overview

Learning outcomes

On completion of this chapter, you should be able to:

- Explain the need for systems analysis and design
- Explore the origin of new information systems projects and consider the participants involved
- Define the systems life cycle and describe the structured approach to information systems development.

Introduction

The purpose of this chapter is to introduce and give an overview of the process of systems analysis and design. The first section identifies the need for analysis and design. It is recognized that systems developments do not occur in isolation, and an overall systems strategy for the organization is required. The way that steering committees provide for this is explained. Various participants are involved in the process of analysis and design. The role of the analyst is highlighted in the earlier part of this chapter. The remainder of the chapter is given over to justifying the need for a methodology – in this case a structured approach – and explaining in general terms how this is applied to the life cycle. Details of the stages involved are explained in Chapters 11–15. Chapter 16 deals with approaches to systems understanding, analysis and design that are alternatives to the structured approach.

10.1 The need for systems analysis and design

At first, the following might seem a plausible course of action by an organization when purchasing and installing a computer system. The first step is to identify the application areas. For instance, these might be accounting, budgeting and word processing. A search is then made of the computer literature in order to establish the names and reviews of accounting, spreadsheet and word-processing packages. A small group of likely candidates for each application is selected. These are then demonstrated by the dealers selling them and the package that best meets the needs of the users for each application is chosen. Compatible hardware is then purchased, often recommended by the dealer, and the equipment is installed. The software and the existing business data are loaded up and, hey presto! the organization has a working information system that meets the requirements of the users and delivers all the benefits associated with computerization.

This approach may work when a small business is in need of computer-assisted support for its standard procedures and when those needs are clearly identified. It is unlikely that it will be satisfactory for the development of a more complex system for a medium-sized or large organization. As a rule, the larger the organization the more complex and individual are the data-processing and information needs of that organization and the greater is the potential amount of funding available for a computer project. These organizations are most likely to develop their own system or pay specialist firms to do this for them. Their needs are individual and often initially unidentified. Custom designed systems are required.

For larger systems, the requirements of users must be identified and a suitable system designed and specified meeting those needs. This must take account of the hardware, the software and the data storage structure. The design must incorporate control and security features. It must also take account of predictable future needs. The hardware will be purchased and installed, the programs written and tested and existing data loaded into the data structure. Networking infrastructure may need to be installed and adequate security arrangements with external networks established. The system will be tested and necessary amendments made. Staff training will be organized. Finally, after the system is up and running, continued maintenance will be necessary. All of this requires many people with differing areas of expertise. The sums of money involved may be large, the time taken for completion many months or even years. It is essential that the project is planned and coordinated properly.

10.1.1 The need for an information systems strategy

During the past 40 years, computerized data processing and information provision have changed vastly. Developments in technology have included the microprocessor, sophisticated telecommunications systems, networking, new office automation equipment and the development of cheap, user-friendly packaged software. These changes have allowed cheap and powerful processing facilities to be open to all parts of an organization. Within the organization, the needs of users have evolved rapidly. In order to prevent anarchic chaos through the development of many independent internal information systems, it is necessary to provide some kind of control by way of a well-worked-out information systems strategy.

This strategy will aim to identify those business activities within the organization that are appropriate to computerized systems development. It will map out, in broad terms, a plan for the development of projects. The strategy will look closely at the size of the investment and consider which of the returns are appropriate and where they will come from. It will incorporate new developments in technology and future needs wherever possible. This strategy will also decide between a policy of centrally controlled development of projects and a strategy of local developments to meet local needs. This latter approach is likely to be applicable to large organizations that already have a philosophy of dispersed management control. A policy on internal charging for computer services needs to be established. For instance, is the running of the computer centre (or information centre) to be an organizational overhead or is it to be charged to user

Figure 10.1 Several projects running concurrently in an organization

departments? If charging is agreed then on what basis? Can the service be contracted out to a third party? All these issues need to be incorporated in a systems strategy if the information systems development is to have any coherence.

A large organization will not have just one computer systems project running at any one time. Rather, several projects will be under way simultaneously. Each will have a different starting point in time and a different projected completion date and will probably be in a different area. These areas will not be completely independent – there will be some overlap and interaction. For instance, a project to develop an automated stock control system may be tied into a separate project dealing with e-commerce and secure payments. These projects need to be coordinated with one another as well as ensuring that each is internally well organized. Moreover, as a project may take a number of years before it comes online and its lifetime may be short, it is often necessary to start planning and designing its replacement before it finally becomes outdated or fails to meet the changing requirements made of it (see Figure 10.1). All of this indicates some need for overall project control and coordination as well as an information systems strategy.

10.1.2 Information systems steering committees

The responsibility for overall strategic planning and control of computer systems development will usually reside with a standing steering committee. This will not be a committee required to take detailed technical decisions. In fact, many of its members will have little technical knowledge or experience. It will be required to frame overall development strategies and allocate resources. Its aim is to ensure that the information systems in the organization deliver an effective service compatible with cost efficiency. The purposes of the committee may lie within the following areas:

■ *To recommend an overall policy for information and data-processing systems development*: This will include such issues as whether or not to standardize on the computer equipment of one company, whether to go for a centralized or decentralized system, the method of charging for development and use of computer systems within the company, the policy on data protection legislation, and the resources available for information systems projects.

■ *To ensure that individual user department needs are being satisfied*: The information system should service the needs of the organization. The presence of individual user department managers or representatives ensures that user views are articulated.

■ *To initiate and monitor individual projects*: This will include specification of budgets, the scope and objectives of each project; setting up a project team for each project and determining its terms of reference; receiving progress reports and taking major decisions, for example stop/go on a project (see Figure 10.2).

■ *To coordinate individual projects*: Individual projects that will affect one another must be made aware of this in order to ensure harmonious development. It is also important that projects are not viewed independently but taken together as a strategy.

■ *To report 'upwards' to top management*: Management will need summary reports on project development and present and future costs.

■ *To be responsible for the appointment of senior personnel in the computer centre*: Job specifications and appointments will be decided at this managerial level.

Typically, the steering committee will meet regularly. It will be composed of managers of the departments that use the information systems, the head of the computer centre or its equivalent and other senior members of the computer centre, such as the chief analyst, and any other person that senior management judges necessary. One of the

Figure 10.2 The relationship between the steering committee and project groups

most important functions of the steering committee is to initiate and set the terms of reference for new projects.

10.1.3 Reasons for project initiation

Projects are initiated by the steering committee, but where does the idea for a new development come from? What causes a recognition of the need for computer systems development? There are a number of reasons, many of which can be related to Porter's models of competitive advantage introduced in Chapter 2. The following are among the most common:

1. *The current system cannot cope*: Many systems projects replace old systems. The previous system may have been a manual system or be based on a computer. Either way it may not have been able to cope with the demands on it. For instance, increases in the volume of transactions processed may have made the system so slow that it ceases to be efficient. Backlogs in orders may build up. Staff may be bogged down with excessive paperwork of a routine nature. Or a merger may lead to a change in organizational structure that renders the current system inappropriate.

2. *Cost savings*: One of the most common reasons for the earliest computerization projects was the replacement of time-consuming, and therefore expensive, manual, rule-governed, repetitive procedures by quick, cheap computer substitutes. This was most notable in the area of payroll and mass billing for the nationalized industries, where computer systems quickly and cheaply carried out the tasks of entire rooms of clerical workers. Nowadays, most savings in these areas have been made and this is rarely a reason for computerization.

3. *The provision of better internal information for decision making*: Management has recognized the ability of computers to supply fast, accurate, targeted information. If management decisions are analysed for their information requirements, information systems can be designed to enable more effective decisions to be taken.

4. *The provision of competitive customer services*: This may range from fast enquiry services and clear, itemized bills to customer-operated input/output equipment. Automatic cashpoint systems are in the latter category. Once one bank supplies this service they all must or else lose their customers.

5. *The opportunities provided by new technology*: Unlike cars, old computer systems are rarely scrapped because they wear out. It is possible though that outdated technology does not offer the same range of facilities as that currently being produced. Networks, improvements in storage devices and processing power, the development of micros with their cheap and end-user-oriented packages and the widespread adoption and application of the Internet have in themselves opened new doors for the exploitation of the benefits of computerization.

6. *High-technology image*: Some companies feel that their image suffers unless they are seen to be using computers in their operations. These companies always display the technology in prominent areas, such as reception.

7. *Changes in legislation*: Changes in legislation such as data protection legislation may act as the trigger for new systems development. Other examples include significant alterations to taxation or changes to National Insurance legislation in the UK, or the basis for the preparation of company accounts.

8. *Balancing the portfolio of projects*: An organization may have a policy of spreading the risk inherent in new project developments. This may lead to a range of projects being undertaken, from those with low risk (and possibly low business impact) through to those with high risk (but potentially with business impact).

10.1.4 The participants in analysis and design

It is common for a computer systems project to be initiated because someone has recognized that a problem exists with the way that things are currently done. Alternatively, an opportunity is perceived that will lead to an improvement on the present system. In either case, the **users** of the existing system will play an important role. They can provide information on the current system. They will also be able to specify, in their own terms, the requirements of the new system.

Systems developers or **programmers** are responsible for turning those requirements into programs. They may either be writing code from scratch, using program generators, or applying system development tools such as CASE (defined and described in more detail later) or database management systems. When executed, these will control the operation of the computer, making it perform to serve the needs of users. However, the programmer will be a computer specialist and will see the problem in computer terms. He or she will be talking a different language from the users. There is a communication gap.

This gap is filled by the **systems analyst** or **business analyst**. This person is able to understand and communicate with users to establish their requirements. The analyst will also have an expert knowledge of computers. He or she will reframe those requirements in terms that programmers can understand. Code can then be written. It is important that the analyst be a good communicator who can think in terms of the user's point of view as well as that of the programmer (see Figure 10.3).

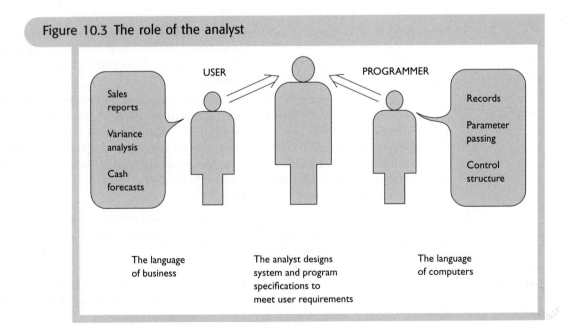

Figure 10.3 The role of the analyst

This translation of requirements is not a straightforward process. It is not, for instance, like translation from German into English. It is more helpful to think of it along the lines of architecture and building. The client (user) states his or her understanding of what the building should look like and what functions it should perform (user statement of the requirements of the system). The architect (analyst) then takes these intentions and provides a general sketch of the building that will satisfy them (logical model of the intended system). Having agreed this with the client (user) the architect (analyst) then draws up a detailed blueprint of the design (detailed program specification) from which the builders (programmers) can work. Just as the architect's task is a skilled one requiring a knowledge of building materials, so the analyst needs a knowledge of computers.

The analyst's task is not restricted to providing specifications for the programmers. The analyst has a range of responsibilities:

1. The analyst is responsible for investigating and analysing the existing system as to its information use and requirements.

2. The analyst judges whether it is feasible to develop a computer system for the area.

3. The analyst designs the new system, specifying programs, hardware, data, structures and control and other procedures.

4. The analyst will be responsible for testing and overseeing the installation of the new system, generating documentation governing its functioning and evaluating its performance.

The analyst is likely to come from either a computer science or a business background. He or she will usually possess a degree and/or be professionally qualified. Sometimes an analyst may have risen 'through the ranks' from programmer to programmer/analyst to a full systems analyst.

As well as possessing significant technical skills in computing, the analyst must fully appreciate the environment and work practices of the area in which the computer system will be used. Knowledge and experience are necessary but not sufficient. The analyst must, above all, be a good communicator with business personnel as well as with technical staff. He or she must be able diplomatically to handle the conflicts of interest that inevitably arise in the course of a project. Managerial, particularly project management, skills are another essential asset as a project involves a complex interaction of many people from different backgrounds working on tasks that all have to be coordinated to produce an end product. The design process is not mechanical, and the analyst must demonstrate both considerable creativity and the ability to think laterally. Finally, analysts need to exude confidence and controlled enthusiasm. When things go wrong, it will be the analyst to whom people look as the person to sort out the problems and smooth the way forward.

10.2 The need for a structured approach to analysis and design

Suppose for a moment that information has been collected on the workings of an existing manual system, for example a payroll system (Figure 10.4). This is a simple system that accepts as inputs:

Figure 10.4 A simple input/process/output diagram of a payroll system

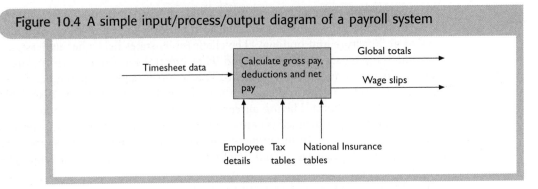

- transaction timesheet data (such as *employee #, number of hours worked, date*);
- standing data on each employee (such as *employee #, hourly wage rate, tax code*);
- standard tax and National Insurance tables that give deductions for various levels of gross pay.

The timesheet data is compiled on each employee by the manager of the department in which that employee works. The employee data is supplied by the personnel department and is held in the wages department on an employee master file.

Each week, the wages clerk works out the gross wages and deductions applicable to each employee by using the timesheet details and performing calculations after consulting the employee master file and the tax and National Insurance tables. Some global totals for management, the Inland Revenue and others are also calculated.

The systems analyst has a relatively straightforward task in analysing and designing a computer system that entirely mimics the workings of this manual system in terms of the data accepted, the processes occurring and the output produced. The computer system will have certain advantages over the manual system in terms of speed, reliability and operating costs, but the data processes, data inputs and outputs will all be similar. The analyst designs a computer master file for the employee record. This contains fields for storing exactly the same data as the manual master file. The analyst designs a data entry screen to look like the old timesheet. A program is specified that accepts timesheet data as input at the keyboard, reads the master file details on the employee, reads the two tables (now stored as files), computes the gross wage and the various deductions, writes this to a file for later printing of the wage slip and, if required, updates the employee master file with new information such as the gross pay to date.

Of course, things will not be quite this simple as the program will need to handle enquiries, produce end-of-year summaries of employees' pay and carry out a range of other tasks. However, given estimates of the average numbers of transactions processed and records maintained, standard documentation forms to record the manual system (document description forms would be an example), and standard forms to define the computer system (so that programmers have a clear specification of requirements to work from), analysis and design becomes a straightforward task. The technical expertise will lie in the selection and sizing of hardware.

The following points emerge from the example as described:

1. The computer system was expected to be a copy of the existing manual system. No evaluation or redesign of the system was expected. This enabled the analyst to

proceed immediately from a *physical* description of the existing system to a *physical* design of the computer system. The physical description of the existing system involved the description of input and output documents used and their contents, together with the records held on employees and the types of data held in those records, and a description of the manual processes undertaken to prepare a payroll. The physical design included a specification of the computer file and record structure, the data entry screen format and the program specifications.

2. The system was not expected to change much over time. The data needed for payroll does not change in form and the procedures for calculation are constant.

3. The existing system was clearly understood by those working with it. It was easily defined as data needed for calculation and the calculations themselves are precise.

4. The processes did not need to have data made available to them from outside the payroll subsystem, and data within the subsystem was not used by processes elsewhere. In other words, the system is not a small part of a larger integrated system involving shared data.

5. Although simplicity is a relative term, as can be seen from the example, producing a payroll is not a complex process. One would not expect to have large teams of analysts and programmers devising the new system.

It is easy to understand how things can be more complicated by dropping some of the assumptions implicit in the example.

1. If it is assumed that a subsystem is to be designed that is an integrated part of a much larger system with which it shares data and processes, a straightforward piecemeal *physical* description of the existing system will not lead to an integrated new system. This is because the existing geographical and departmental boundaries between subsystems will be translated into the new system. No attempt is made to 'step back' and view the system as a whole. Although individual subsystems will be designed optimally, the system as a whole may function suboptimally (see Figure 10.5).

2. The existing area may be a part of a much larger intended system, which does not currently exist in its entirety. Redesign may be required because of new features that are added with computerization or simply because a new system provides the chance to evaluate and change an existing manual system that is not running efficiently.

3. The requirements made on the system may also change over time, and the structure of the data and processes may need amending. This adds further difficulty, as in designing the system not only do current practices need to be catered for but the design must also allow for change.

4. The added complexity may mean that large teams of analysts and programmers will be involved. This in itself brings problems, as these teams need organizing, monitoring and coordinating. Communication can easily break down between and within teams.

5. Users and management need to understand what the new system is offering before major investment in hardware and software is undertaken. It is important that communication tools are developed that aid this understanding. A physical specification of a system in terms of file structures and access methods, computing processing power in instructions per second, RAM size and so on will not be appropriate.

Figure 10.5 Traditional analysis and design by way of a logical model:
(a) traditional physical design process preserving subsystems relations;
(b) design of an integrated system by means of a logical model

These considerations have led to different approaches to the analysis and design of information systems. Some focus on business processes, some focus on the management of information systems development projects, and others attempt to match social and technical aspects. A comparison of different approaches can be found in Chapter 16. Before that, the structured approach to the analysis and design of information systems is presented in detail.

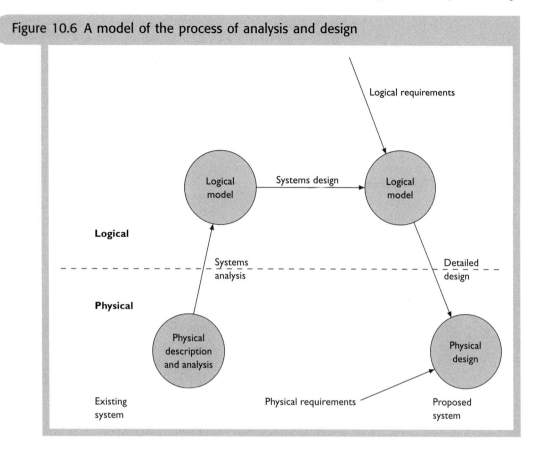

Figure 10.6 A model of the process of analysis and design

10.2.1 A structured approach

The main features (see Figure 10.6) of this approach are:

1. **(a)** Once a physical description of the existing system has been obtained, the analyst's attention is turned to building a logical model of that system. This involves abstracting away from physical details to leave the bare-bones logic of the system. For instance:

– The media on which data is stored are ignored. It is irrelevant to the logical model whether data is stored on manual record cards, scraps of paper, magnetic tape or anything else. Only the type of data is recorded in the logical model.

– The organization of the data stores is ignored. For instance, it is irrelevant that the data stored on the manual record cards is stored in employee order with a side index based on name. Only the type of data held is found in the model.

– Who or what carries out the data processes, or where they are carried out, is not relevant to the logical model. The fact that employee John Smith consults a price catalogue before pricing a customer order in the sales department is translated in the logical model as a process for pricing order details using price data from a data store. Geographical and physical boundaries are not shown in the logical model. Document flows between operations in departments become data flows between the processes that use the data.

   (b) Once this has been done, extra logical constraints and requirements are added as needed. A new system may now be designed at the logical level. The logical model of the designed system will aid in the physical design.

   (c) The new physical system is now defined and incorporates any further physical constraints. It is only at this stage that the analyst is concerned with file sizes, storage media, processor types, allocation of disk space, construction of program code, and so on.

2. (a) Complex problems and functions are partitioned and then decomposed into their parts, which themselves are further partitioned and decomposed (process analysis). For instance, a complex process such as 'establish future product availability' can be broken down into the three subprocesses: 'establish current stock', 'establish future production' and 'establish existing commitment to allocate future product'.

   (b) The basic entities in an organization are ascertained and the relations between them charted before looking in detail at the fine-grained level of what information is to be held on each (data analysis).

   (c) This is a 'top-down' approach. In contrast, a 'bottom-up' approach starts by considering in detail the individual tasks and the data items needed for these. The system is then built up from this basis. The latter approach is only effective in the case of relatively simple systems in which little redesign or alteration is needed.

3. Emphasis is placed on rigorous documentation and charting. This mirrors the *physical* → *logical* → *logical* → *physical* development discussed in this section. The documentation:

   (a) aids communication between analysts and users by concentrating on the logical aspects of a system rather than technical, physical features which may confuse the user;

   (b) encourages the design of (structured) programs that are straightforward to code, easy to test and (through their modular make-up) amenable to future alteration;

   (c) aids the organization and scheduling of teams of analysts and programmers for large projects;

   (d) enables effective design and representation of the database;

   (e) acts as permanent documentation of the system.

The need for a structured approach is most easily understood when describing the replacement of a manual system by a computerized system. The points made, however, also apply to the replacement or enhancement of an existing computerized system. This section provides a rationale for adopting a structured approach and outlines some of its main features. Section 10.3 traces an overview of the development process. Chapters 11–15 apply the structured approach in detail to these stages.

10.3 The life cycle of a system

In order to develop a computerized information system, it is necessary for the process of development to pass through a number of distinct stages. The various stages in the systems life cycle are shown in Figure 10.7. These stages are completed in sequence. The project cannot progress from one stage to the next until it has completed all the

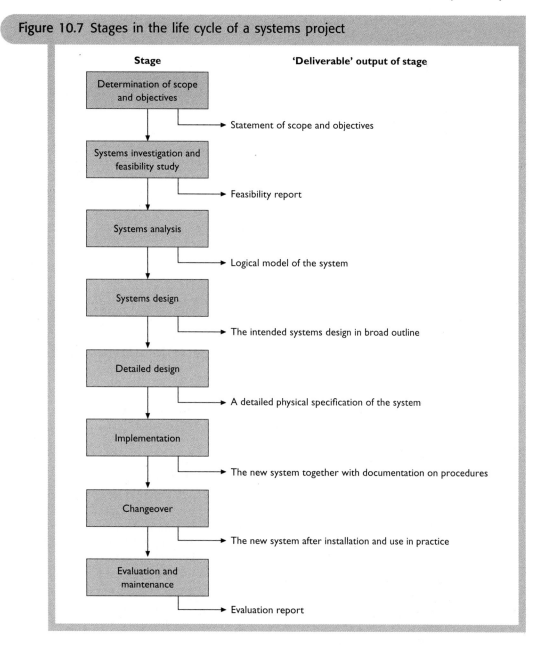

Figure 10.7 Stages in the life cycle of a systems project

Stage	'Deliverable' output of stage
Determination of scope and objectives	Statement of scope and objectives
Systems investigation and feasibility study	Feasibility report
Systems analysis	Logical model of the system
Systems design	The intended systems design in broad outline
Detailed design	A detailed physical specification of the system
Implementation	The new system together with documentation on procedures
Changeover	The new system after installation and use in practice
Evaluation and maintenance	Evaluation report

required work of that stage. In order to ensure that a stage is completed satisfactorily, some 'deliverable' is produced at the stage end. Generally, this is a piece of document-ary evidence on the work carried out. Successful completion of the stage is judged by the documentation. This is known as the 'exit criterion' for the stage.

It is common for some of the tasks carried out during a stage of the process to be initially unsatisfactory. This should come to light when the exit criteria are considered. The relevant tasks will need to be redone before exit from the stage can be made. Although 'looping' within a stage is commonplace, once a stage has been left it should not be necessary to return to it from a later stage. This structure – a linear development by stages, with deliverables and exit criteria – enables the project to be controlled and managed. The benefits of this staged approach are:

■ Subdivision of a complex, lengthy project into discrete chunks of time makes the project more manageable and thereby promotes better project control.

■ Although different parts of a project may develop independently during a stage, the parts of the project are forced to reach the same point of development at the end of the stage. This promotes coordination between the various components of large projects.

■ The deliverables, being documentation, provide a historical trace of the development of the project. At the end of each stage, the output documentation provides an initial input into the subsequent stage.

■ The document deliverables are designed to be communication tools between analysts, programmers, users and management. This promotes easy assessment of the nature of the work completed during the stage.

■ The stages are designed to be 'natural' division points in the development of the project.

■ The stages allow a creeping commitment to expenditure during the project. There is no need to spend large sums of money until the previous stages have been completed satisfactorily (see Figure 10.8).

The approach progresses from the physical aspects of the existing system (systems investigation) through logical analysis (systems analysis) and logical design (systems design) on to the physical aspects of the new system (detailed design, implementation and evaluation).

Stage 1 Determination of scope and objectives

Before an analyst can attempt to undertake a reasonable systems investigation, analysis and design, some indication must be given of the agreed overall scope of the project. The documentation provided on this acts as the analyst's initial terms of reference. This may be provided by the steering committee or written by the analyst and agreed by the committee. Either way, it delimits the analyst's task.

The statement of scope and objectives will indicate an area to be investigated, such as sales order processing. It will also specify a problem or opportunity that the analyst should have in mind when investigating this area. For instance, sales order processing might be perceived to be too slow and the company fears that it is losing customers. The document should also specify a date by which the feasibility report (see stage 2) is to be produced and the budgeted cost allowable for this.

Stage 2 Systems investigation and feasibility study

The output of this stage is a report on the feasibility of a technical solution to the problems or opportunities mentioned in the statement of scope and objectives in stage 1. More than one solution may be suggested. The solution(s) will be presented in broad outline. An estimate of the costs, benefits and feasibility associated with each will be included. The purpose of the report is to provide evidence for the steering committee to decide whether it is worth going ahead with any of the suggestions. If the whole

Figure 10.8 Cost profile of a typical systems project

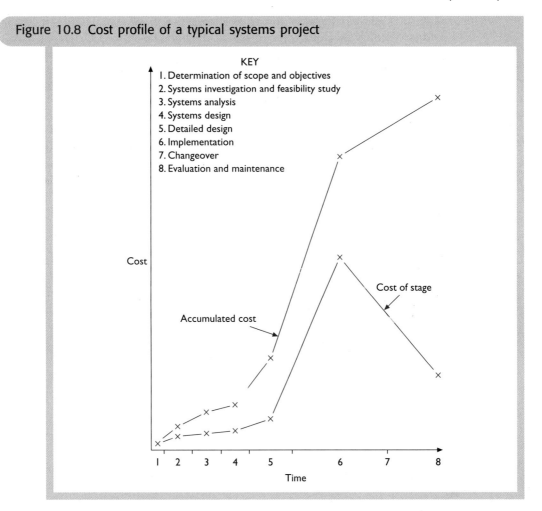

KEY
1. Determination of scope and objectives
2. Systems investigation and feasibility study
3. Systems analysis
4. Systems design
5. Detailed design
6. Implementation
7. Changeover
8. Evaluation and maintenance

Cost of stage

Accumulated cost

Cost

Time

project is dropped at this stage, there will have been very little cost to date (sunk cost) (see Figure 10.8).

In order to establish the feasibility of a future technical system, it will be necessary for the analyst to investigate the current system and its work practices. This will provide evidence for the functions that the new system must perform even in the case of substantial redesign. The analyst will need to interview users and view existing documentation. The information collected during this stage will be useful for the next stage of the life cycle as well.

Stage 3 Systems analysis

Provided that the project has been given the 'go ahead' as a result of the feasibility study, the next task for the analyst is to build a logical model of the existing system. This will be based partly on information collected during the stage of systems investigation and partly on new information gathered from the existing system.

The purpose of this stage is to establish what has to be done in order to carry out the functioning of the existing system. This 'what has to be done' is not to be confused with what actually happens in the existing physical system. That is, it is not to be confused with who does what to which document before transferring it from one department to another, or who provides what information for whom on whose authorization. Rather, the central question to be asked is 'what, logically speaking, must be done in order to satisfy the objectives and functions of the system under investigation?' This will involve a decomposition of the functions of the system into their logical constituents and the production of a logical model of the processes and data flows necessary to perform these. This is called **process analysis**. The logical model will be illustrated by data flow diagrams and structured techniques for specifying algorithms. Incorporated into this model will be any additional logical requirements to be made of the new system. No decisions on the way the system will be physically realized should be apparent from this model.

The processes will be fed by data. This data will relate to entities of interest to the organization. These entities will stand in relation to one another. For instance, data will be held on employees and the departments in which they work. Thus work is a relationship between employees and departments. These entities and relationships are combined in a data model of the organization. This procedure is called **data analysis**.

The output of this stage will be a logical process model as revealed by data flow diagrams, together with the specification of the process algorithms, data dictionary and a data model. This output is reviewed by management and users. Agreement needs to be established as to whether the model is a reflection of the logic of the problem area.

Stage 4 Systems design

Once the analysis is complete, the analyst has a good idea of what is logically required of the new system. There will be a number of ways that this logical model can be incorporated into a physical design. For instance, are the data stores to be implemented as a series of files, or is there to be a database? If a database is the chosen route, should this be centralized or distributed? The data flow diagrams will reveal the processes and the data flows between them. How many of the processes are to be incorporated into a computer system, and how many are to remain manual? Of those to be computerized, which are to be run under batch processes and which interactively online? Is the computerized system to be centralized or distributed?

There will not be one correct answer to these questions. Rather, there will be a range of alternative designs. Each of these will have different implications for cost, security, ease of use, maintainability and efficiency. Some will yield more computerized facilities than others. Structured tools, such as data flow diagrams, enable these design alternatives to be clearly identified. They also allow the various options to be presented in a manner that requires little technical expertise in order to understand them.

The analyst will suggest two or three design alternatives to management, together with their implications. Management will then decide between them. Often these alternatives will reflect a low-, a medium- and a high-cost solution to the problem. The first will provide a system that is very basic. The second alternative will incorporate more facilities, while the third may go beyond this to illustrate the full potential of extensive computerization.

By the end of this stage, the attention of the analyst is turning away from purely logical considerations to the various ways, in general terms, that the logical model can be physically implemented. This stage ends with a choice between the alternatives presented to management.

Stage 5 Detailed design

The stage has passed beyond that when the analyst can look only at the logical requirements of a system or at broad-outline design solutions. Detailed physical specifications need to be made so that the system can be purchased/built and installed. A number of distinct areas must be considered:

1. Programs will need to be developed so that the computer can perform the various functions required of it. These programs will be coded by programmers, who need a clear statement of the task to be programmed, or created using application or code generators. Structured tools make possible clear specifications from which the program is written. They also enable the programs to be easily testable and amendable if necessary.
2. Hardware requirements must be specified that, together with the programs, will allow the computer system to perform its tasks efficiently. These requirements for computers, monitors, printers, network infrastructure and so on must be detailed enough to allow the purchasing department to obtain the items.
3. The structure of the database or system of files will also be specified.
4. A schedule for the implementation of the system will be derived at this stage. This will ensure that during implementation all the various activities are coordinated and come together at the right time.

These areas can be summarized as software, hardware, data storage and the schedule for implementation. Two other threads will run through consideration of these areas. The first is security. The system must be designed to ensure maximum reliability in secure, complete, accurate and continuous processing. The second is the user–machine interface. Unless this is designed with the characteristics of the tasks and the users in mind, it is unlikely that the system will be fully effective in meeting its objectives.

The systems specification is a highly detailed set of documents covering every aspect of the system. From this it is possible to estimate costs accurately. The specification is finally ratified by senior management or the steering committee. Once it is agreed, large sums of the project budget can be spent on major purchases and programmers' time.

Stage 6 Implementation

During implementation, the system as specified is physically created. The hardware is purchased and installed. The programs are written and tested individually. As programs often interact, they will also be tested together.

The database or file structure is created and historical data from the old system (manual or computer) is loaded. Staff are trained to use the new system. The procedures that will govern the operation of the new system are designed and documentation detailing these is then drafted. Particular attention will be paid to security features surrounding the conversion of existing files, whether manual or computer-based, to the new system.

The system is formally tested and accepted before changeover.

Stage 7 Changeover

Changeover is that time during which the old system is replaced by the newly designed computer system. This period may be short if, at the time the new system starts running, the old system is discarded immediately.

Alternative methods of changeover exist. The old system can be run in parallel with the new. Although expensive in labour costs, this method does have the advantage that if the new system fails there is a backup system to rely on. The old and the new systems can also be compared with one another for discrepancies in their performance and output. Another approach is to run a pilot scheme. This involves running a small version of the system before the full systems implementation is carried out. The way that the pilot system functions allows identification of any errors and shortcomings that will be encountered in the full system. These will be involved in the life cycle of a project. No matter how extensive the planning has been, no matter how rigorous the systems testing, there are always unexpected problems during the first few days or weeks of use of a new system. The problems should be minor if the preceding stages of the project have been carried out according to correct standards. These teething troubles may be technical, or they may result from the use of the system for the first time by inexperienced (although trained) company personnel.

A further approach is to 'phase in' the new system, allowing different functionality to be introduced in a staged fashion. This is usually a less risky and sometimes less costly method of changeover and can be viewed as being more tangible than a pilot scheme. The disadvantage is that a piecemeal approach might not lead to such a robust and coherent final product. There is inevitably a complex proliferation of legacy and new systems with which to contend.

After the system has 'settled down', the next phase of the life cycle is entered.

Stage 8 Evaluation and maintenance

By now, the system is running and in continuous use. It should be delivering the benefits for which it was designed and installed. Any initial problems in running will have been rectified. Throughout the remainder of the useful life of the system, it will have to be maintained if it is to provide a proper service.

The maintenance will involve hardware and software. It is customary to transfer the maintenance of the hardware to the manufacturer of the equipment or some specialist third-party organization. A maintenance contract stipulating conditions and charges for maintenance is usual. The software will need to be maintained as well. This will involve correcting errors in programs that become apparent after an extended period of use. Programs may also be altered to enable the machine to run with greater technical efficiency, but by far the greatest demand on programmers' time will be to amend and develop existing programs in the light of changes in the requirements of users. Structured techniques of design and programming allow these changes to be made easily.

It is customary to produce an evaluation report on the system after it has been functioning for some time. This will be drawn up after the system has settled into its normal daily functioning. The report will compare the actual system with the aims and objectives that it was designed to meet. Shortcomings will be identified. If these are easily rectified, then changes will be made during normal maintenance. More major changes may require more drastic surgery. Substantial redesign of parts of the system may be necessary. Alternatively, the changes can be incorporated into a future system.

Systems failure

The Bank of England has been forced to apologize and offer compensation after the failure of a new IT system caused delays on large payments to financial institutions, government departments and foreign central banks.

The technological snarl-up is an embarrassment for the Bank, which needs to provide fail-safe operations to guarantee the smooth running of the financial system. The Bank has offered compensation to institutions that have lost interest payments because of the system failure, although it is still too early to estimate the size of payments.

The problems arose after the introduction of a new £10m IT system called Globus. The system, which has taken three years to develop, processes payments between institutions.

The Bank has written to about 1,000 institutions using the system to acknowledge that there have been 'serious problems at the launch and since'. It has also admitted 'it is now clear that the new system was launched too early', and said it 'very much regrets' the fault.

The delays in payment transfer and reporting have left some clients with out-of-date balances.

Payments to the public have not been affected, and the Bank has stressed that the operation of the wholesale payment system and money markets has not been damaged. But institutions such as building societies, banks and – most embarrassing of all – other central banks, have been hit.

Adapted from: **Bank of England apology for IT hitch**
By Christopher Swann
Financial Times: 21 August 2003

Questions

1. What do you think the Bank meant by saying the system 'was launched too early'?

2. At what stage in the systems development might problems have occurred? How could they be foreseen or rectified?

10.4 The structured approach and the life cycle

Structured systems analysis and design both define various stages that should be undertaken in the development of a systems project. In the life cycle, the structured techniques and tools are used in analysis and design. Their benefits are realized throughout the project in terms of better project control and communication, and during the working life of the system in terms of its meeting user requirements and the ease with which it can be modified to take into account changes in these requirements.

The philosophy of the approach distinguishes it from other methods used in analysis and design. Central to this is the idea that a logical model of the system needs to be derived in order to be able to redesign and integrate complex systems. This is evident in the stages of systems analysis and design. The detailed tools are explained in Chapters 11–15, but they all follow from and through this central idea. Table 10.1 summarizes these as applied to the stages of the life cycle.

Table 10.1 Stages of the life cycle

Stages	Purpose	Comments
Determination of scope and objectives	To establish the nature of the problem, estimate its scope and plan feasibility study	
Systems investigation and feasibility study	To provide a report for management on the feasibility of a technical solution	Involves the analyst in investigation of the existing system and its documentation. Interviews used
Systems analysis	To provide a logical model of the data and processes of the system	Use of data flow diagrams, entity relationship models, structured English, logic flowcharts, data dictionaries
System design	To provide outline solutions to the problem	Automation boundaries indicated on data flow diagrams, suggestions offered on type of systems: for example, centralized *v.* distributed, file *v.* database. Cost estimates provided
Detailed design	To provide a detailed specification of the system from which it can be built	Programs specified using hierarchical input process output (HIPO) and pseudo-code, hardware and file/database structures defined, cost estimates, systems test plan and implementation schedule designed
Implementation	To provide a system built and tested according to specification	Code programs, obtain and install hardware, design operating procedures and documentation, security/audit considerations, test system, train staff, load existing data
Changeover	To provide a working system that has adequately replaced the old system	Direct, parallel, pilot or phased changeover
Evaluation and maintenance	To provide an evaluation of the extent to which the system meets its objectives. Provide continuing support	Report provided. Ongoing adaptation of software/hardware to rectify errors and meet changing user requirements

10.5 Alternative approaches to information systems development

Although the structured approach is the most widely understood and practised method of systems development, many alternative viewpoints exist. These range from differing perceptions of how progress is made through the stages of the life cycle through to fundamental differences in how systems should be modelled. These alternative models are described in more detail in Chapter 16.

Summary

Organizations can best utilize the benefits from changing and improving modern information technology by designing a corporate information systems strategy. This will outline the areas and approach taken towards information systems in the organization. It will decide on the overall development plan, the resources available and the likely benefits. The information systems steering committee initiates and takes major decisions on individual projects. This committee is also responsible for coordinating project developments and monitoring their progress.

All but the smallest and simplest projects require a series of stages to be undertaken to develop them successfully. This set of stages is known as the systems project life cycle. It consists of defining the scope of the area of the project and arriving at a decision on its feasibility. A logical model of the existing system is developed taking into account the extra requirements of the new system. Various physical solutions to the task of computerization are outlined in broad detail, together with their costs and implications, during systems design. The design of the chosen solution is then developed and specified in greater physical detail. This specification acts as a blueprint from which the system is implemented. After implementation and changeover, benefits accrue to the organization during the system's working life. A post-implementation review of the success of the system in meeting its objectives provides useful information for maintenance and design of its eventual replacement.

In order to ensure that a successful development takes place, a structured approach to analysis and design is recommended. This involves the use of techniques and tools that reinforce the central idea of taking account of the logical requirements of a system before attending to the physical design. This avoids premature physical commitment to systems that would not satisfy user needs. Structured methods also facilitate the management of the project and the coordination of programmer teams and others involved in the development. Documentation ensures that communications between analyst, users and programmers are clear. The final system is likely to be one that is easily adaptable to the changing user requirements associated with any modern, evolving organization.

Review questions

1. Why is systems analysis and design essential for large systems whereas it may not be appropriate for a small system for a small organization?

2. Why is a systems or business analyst needed?

3. Outline the stages involved in a systems project. What is the purpose of each stage?

4. What is the purpose of a feasibility study?

5. Why is it important that the life cycle be divided into stages with deliverables to mark the exit from each stage?

6. What role does the information systems steering committee fulfil?

7. Why have an information systems strategy rather than developing new systems as and when they become needed?

Exercises

1. Under what circumstances is a piecemeal approach to developing a computer system appropriate and under what circumstances is it inappropriate?

2. What benefits are expected from adopting a structured approach to analysis and design?

3. What is wrong with taking early physical design decisions? Surely this would aid in an accurate early estimation of cost?

4. Outline a profile of a suitable person to appoint as a systems analyst.

5. 'It is important that a systems analyst have a strong technical background in computers rather than a background in general business practices.' What is to be said for and against this view?

6. 'User needs are often hard to identify prior to gaining experience from the running of a system. It is therefore a mistake to adopt the philosophy of designing the system to meet user needs. It is better to design and implement a "rough and ready" version of a system to see how users take to it. This can then be systematically amended to remove its shortcomings. The process of design becomes iterative rather than linear.' What is to be said for and against this view?

7. 'If the people who were going to use the computerized information systems were involved in decisions as to what kind of system was needed and how to design it then better information systems would be produced.' Do you think this is a desirable and realistic policy?

CASE STUDY 10

Enterprise resource planning and project failure

Will we never learn? For some ten years or more now, the enterprise resource planning (ERP) industry has been executing the same sales and marketing strategy: promise your customer the world, regardless of your ability to deliver and get as much money as you can out of them.

When is this 'panacea-oriented marketing' going to stop? It is an insult to marketers and salespeople everywhere and on top of that it makes our jobs much harder.

ERP software was supposed to connect many of a large organization's departments and automate their productivity. Human resources, accounting, finance, administration and others were supposed to operate much smoother, faster and efficiently. Large software companies made billions off these 'implementations'. SAP, Baan, J.D. Edwards, Oracle and PeopleSoft laughed all the way to the bank.

Then the bottom fell out of the market. According to one expert industry insider, who preferred to remain nameless due to fear of industry retribution, 'implementations were long and drawn out, often by people with little experience. Budgets were exceeded on every project I've worked on, by massive factors.'

This ERP industry whistle-blower went on to support some of the good things these enormous IT projects can accomplish while also offering keen insight into the ways in which the consultants and software companies let down their clients and then resort to mutual finger-pointing.

'In the mid-1990s,' the ERP expert added, 'when ERP became the thing to have, every consultant was demanding between £600 and £2000 per day for these projects. You can imagine what that did to IT budgets.'

Perhaps a brief history lesson is in order. Here are just a few of the past scenarios: In 1992, a group of travel industry titans, including American Airlines' parent AMR, Hilton Hotels, Marriott International and Budget Rent-a-Car, got together and wanted to create a central reservation system for air, hotel and rental car bookings.

Good idea, right? Wrong. This required an advanced ERP system that never material-ized as promised. After four years, more than $125m in investment and expected to take yet another two years minimum, the initiative crashed in flames with the partners suing each other. W.W. Grainger implemented an SAP system in 1998 that cost it more than $9m and proceeded to crash repeatedly while over-counting inventory and leading to losses during one six-month period of $19m in sales and $23m in profits.

An Oracle implementation for highly profitable and expanding Oxford Health Plans went horribly awry when the system under-estimated medical costs and over-estimated income. Thousands of HMOs (health maintenance organizations), doctors and patients were livid. Shortly thereafter, Oxford announced its first quarterly loss of $78m, while revenues were over-estimated by $173.5m in 1997 and $218.2m in the following annual period.

But perhaps the messiest and most damaging ERP implementation 'war story' involves that undertaken by Hershey, the chocolate company. In a 1990s initiative, Hershey brought in IBM to lead the integration of an SAP, Manugistics and Siebel Systems ERP project. Complicated to be sure, but Hershey had no idea how complicated, nor did IBM.

The $112m system quickly produced results in the form of an inventory and shipping nightmare for Hershey right as their biggest sales cycle of the year, Halloween, was get-ting started. Losses exceeded $150m over previous years' levels and in the first quarter the new system was running, Hershey sales dropped 12 per cent.

These are the kinds of failures that clutter the highway of ERP software schemes.

Shortly after the botched program the finger-pointing starts. First, the consultancy tries to blame the client. It does this by saying that the client's specification for the software of its installation was faulty or off-the-mark.

Then, the consultancy or systems integrator blames the ERP software company and can usually make that stick. Remember, the consultants are closer to the ultimate client and want to ensure the long-term nature of their revenue flow. 'It happens all the time,' said our industry insider, 'it's a whitewash, really. Usually, the consultancy didn't have the skill. The result is rewriting of the software.' As expensive as this kind of software is it should not have to be rewritten and this can be a harbinger of disaster.

If consultants were to excuse themselves from the entire ERP process (except where their skills add demonstrable value) maybe these types of software projects might be more direct and straightforward.

Corporations that bought into the hollow promises of ERP salespeople and paid in some case hundreds of millions (Chevron's $140m implementation, for example) to the soft-ware vendor, integrator and consulting companies discovered, as many others did, that the reality failed to live up to the promises. A Meta Group report stated that at one point 60 per cent of respondents undergoing an implementation experience a 'negative return on investment'. As if that euphemism isn't bad enough, this figure rose as high as 80 per cent depending on the particular software used in the implementation.

►

'I can't think of one implementation I've worked on that hasn't been extremely painful,' the insider added. And this is from an implementer, not even the client.

According to industry data, the average ERP implementation costs $15m takes between one and three years (21 months average) and can soak up 2 to 3 per cent of the client revenue. Then, client benefit does not even begin to accrue until an average of 31 months after completion – by which time obsolescence is undoubtedly upon them. This is an unacceptable risk to take particularly given the timelines and costs involved.

Shipping delays during crucial sales cycles, deadly inventory build-ups, accounting nightmares and worse have paralysed entire multinational corporations while costing shareholders and consumers billions after the fact. Caveat emptor indeed. Deciding which ERP software and consultancy was finally chosen has not advanced careers but ruined many as a result of time and cost overruns, for which this industry is absolutely notorious.

Despite all these career-ending results and wasted money, the expert has his hopes. The cost of implementation is coming down for two reasons, he says. First the customization process is now much easier and also the software development costs have come down by more than 50 per cent with programming occurring more and more offshore. 'With this kind of software, one action should trigger activities throughout the organization which is a beautiful thing.' One can only hope more future ERP installations result in these types of 'beautiful things'. With the amount of investment the client puts into them they should certainly achieve something approaching organizational beauty.

Adapted from: **Will ERP software ever live up to its billing?**
By Bill Robinson
FT.com site: 1 October 2003

Questions

1. Traditionally a new systems development sprang from a novel idea to automate a process and began with a 'blank sheet of paper'. How does ERP software differ from this approach?

2. Why is there such scepticism about ERP software?

3. What could have been done to ensure greater success in the projects mentioned in the case study?

Recommended reading

Benyon-Davies P. (1999). *Information Systems Development*, 3rd edn. Macmillan Computer Science Series

A non-deterministic book covering a number of frameworks, tools, techniques and methodologies for the analysis and design of systems. The book includes an interesting chapter on project management for information systems.

Brooks F.P. Jr (1995). *The Mythical Man-Month: Essays on Software Engineering – Anniversary Issue*. Harlow: Addison-Wesley

This is a twentieth anniversary publication of the important text published in 1975 – *The Mythical Man-Month*. This is a highly readable essay on software project management and how it can go wrong. The essays are based on the author's experience of project management for the IBM series 360 and the development of the massive operating system OS/360 for this. From it the author draws many morals on pitfalls to be avoided. Historically, the author was writing at a time when structured approaches to systems analysis and design were being developed to overcome such problems.

Schwalbe C. (2003). *Information Technology Project Management*. Thomson Learning

A very readable text that provides a clear introduction to project management in the context of IT developments. The book takes the reader through such issues as project scope, time, cost and risk. It also contains a guide to using Microsoft Project.

Shelley G., Cashman T. and Adamski J. (1997). *Systems Analysis and Design*, 3rd edn. Boyd and Frazer

This is a clear and comprehensive standard text on systems analysis and design. It includes case studies, discussion and review questions. The book does not promote any specific methodology but gives a good explanation of basic concepts.

Wood-Harper T. (1998). *Rapid Information Systems Development*. London: McGraw-Hill

This is a practical guide to non-experts who intend to develop and plan their own information systems. No one methodology is advocated, although the book borrows techniques from several. It includes an explanation of soft systems methods (especially problem identification), information modelling and socio-technical modelling. There is a short summary of major methodologies. This could be read in conjunction with this chapter or the one on alternative methodologies.

Chapter 11

The systems project: early stages

Learning outcomes

On completion of this chapter, you should be able to:

- Explain the need for an initial statement of the scope and objectives of an information systems project
- Describe the techniques for gaining familiarity with an existing system or a new information system and documenting the findings
- Explain the steps taken in developing a feasibility report and describe its likely contents
- Compare different perspectives on project feasibility.

Introduction

This chapter deals with the early stages in the development of a computerized information system. The main channels of information open to the analyst for information gathering during systems investigation are explained, together with their weaknesses in the accurate provision of information. It is important that the analyst has a frame of reference through which to conduct the systems investigation. Here the systems model is used. During investigation the feasibility of a proposed system is assessed. The central ideas behind the economic, technical and operational feasibility of a system are explained, together with the difficulties encountered in arriving at an overall economic assessment of the project. The feasibility report and its role in project control and decision making are covered. During this chapter, a case study is introduced that is developed in Chapters 12–15 as the life cycle of the system unfolds.

11.1 Initial stages

The impetus to develop a computerized information system arises because someone somewhere has perceived a need or opportunity that can be satisfied by the introduction of modern information technology. Ideas for developments and enhancements to information systems might originate from many sources, but in a large organization with an information systems strategy and existing technology the focus is through the information systems steering committee. In a smaller organization, the idea will be introduced by, or at least channelled through, a senior member of management.

The reason for initiation of a computer systems project, as explained in the previous chapter, is likely to be a combination of a number of the following reasons:

- The current information system, whether manual or computer-based, cannot cope with the demands placed upon it.

- Significant cost savings are realizable by the cheap processing power of a computer.

- Management perceive a need for better internal information for decision making.

- Computerization will provide better services for the organization's customers.

- The advent of new types of technology opens up a range of available facilities that the organization wishes to exploit.

- The organization wishes to promote a high-technology image, possibly as part of a much wider-ranging marketing strategy or a venture into e-commerce.

- Changes in legislation require systems redesign.

11.1.1 The case study

Throughout this and subsequent chapters on the systems life cycle (Chapters 12–15), it is helpful in understanding the stages, tools and techniques if they are explained by way of a case study. Unlike previous case studies in the book, this one is presented as part of the text rather than at the end of the chapter. The case study used here concerns a company called Kismet Ltd. Kismet purchases electrical goods from a range of suppliers and manufacturers and distributes these goods to retail trade outlets.

Case studies are a useful vehicle for understanding the process of systems analysis and design, but they will never be a substitute for learning through the actual *practice* of analysis and design. The most important respect in which any case study is limited is that it preselects information to be presented to the reader and presents this in a neatly summarized and organized way. In reality, the analyst would be subject to a large amount of (often unconnected) information collected from various interviews, existing works standards manuals, samples of transaction documents, auditors' reports, and so on.

Only a part of the Kismet organization is covered here. In Chapter 1, it was seen that it is often convenient to view a business as being made up of several subsystems, each of which is determined by the function it fulfils. Examples are the sales, manufacturing, storage, purchasing, accounting, planning and control subsystems. This study provides a slice through three of these. It deals with the basic processing of orders from customers, the generation of invoices and the provision of some management information.

Kismet case study 11.1

Kismet supplies a range of hi-fi, TV, radio and video goods to retail outlets through-out the country. The goods are supplied by manufacturers, who each supply a variety of types of equipment. Currently, Kismet has over forty suppliers, who supply a total of over 500 different item types. The number of suppliers is expected to remain fairly constant during the foreseeable future, although the range of types of equipment may alter considerably. Kismet has approximately 1200 live customers and receives on aver-age about 300 orders per day, each one averaging ten items requested.

Kismet employs about 150 people in a number of departments:

- *Sales order department*: Accepts and processes customer orders.
- *Credit control department*: Responsible for customer credit checks.
- *Stores department*: Responsible for stock control.
- *Invoicing department*: Responsible for customer invoicing.
- *Accounts department*: Handles general accounting requirements and the provision of reports.
- *Packing and dispatch department*: Responsible for goods inward and goods outward.
- *Purchasing department*: Responsible for placing orders with suppliers.
- *Sales and marketing department*: Deals with advertising and establishing new outlets.
- *Payroll department*: Prepares Kismet's payroll.
- *Maintenance department*: Responsible for general maintenance and also for main-tenance of Kismet's fleet of vans.
- *General administration*: Handles administration not specifically covered elsewhere.

Kismet was started 30 years ago by Harold Kismet and has grown rapidly in the last five years with the increased consumer use of video recorders, compact disc players and the whole range of modern electronic leisure equipment. Josephine Kismet (Harold's daughter) has pioneered this development, with a subsequent 300% increase in trade in the last three years. However, problems are beginning to emerge. Kismet's domina-tion of the north-east of the country and its expansion into the north-west is being threat-ened by a serious rival, Hardy Ltd. This company was set up nine months previously with a large injection of capital. Hardy provides a website offering customers a range of electronic leisure equipment and the opportunity to place a credit card order. Also, and this is most serious for Kismet, Hardy is now moving into the area of supplying retail outlets, in direct competition with Kismet.

The management of Kismet has been conscious for some time of slowness in satis-fying the orders received from retail outlets. These orders are taking an increasing time to process. This has been further exacerbated by the expansion of Kismet over the last three years. The entirely manual system that Kismet uses has not been able to cope adequately with the increase of trade, even though more staff have been employed. Hardy is able to offer a superior service because of its modern computerized data-processing and information systems, which give it a significant edge over Kismet.

Harold Kismet has long resisted his daughter's representations to computerize the business. This is partly because of loyalty to his older employees, who have been with Kismet since its foundation. He fears that they, like him, would be unable to make the transition to computerization. Also, he is conscious of the demise of his best friend's business, which rapidly moved from being a flourishing enterprise to bankruptcy as the result of a completely mismanaged and inappropriate introduction of a computer system.

The recent rise of Hardy and his own impending retirement have forced Harold Kismet to reconsider the possibility of computerization. He has subsequently given responsibility for the project to his daughter. Although knowing little about computers, the daughter realizes the potential and sees this as a necessary requirement if Kismet is to stave off the threat from Hardy and to expand further (possibly into satellite TV and personal computers).

Harold Kismet has called in a systems analyst with whom he wishes to discuss the problems and opportunities.

11.2   Statement of scope and objectives

It is important to 'get the project off the ground' in the right way. It would be a mistake to call in the systems analyst, provide a verbal indication of what is needed and let the analyst 'get on with it'. Very often it is not clear at the outset what the task of the analyst is to be – it is clear neither to the analyst nor to the steering committee nor to management.

A common approach that avoids this pitfall is that the analyst is required to provide a written statement of the scope and objectives of the project. It works like this. The analyst is given a rough indication, often verbally, of the problem or opportunity as perceived by the project initiator. The analyst then looks into the problem and the system within which it is located. The purpose is to come up with a written statement of what the analyst perceives to be the problems to which the systems project is addressed, its scope and objectives and some very rough estimate of the costs. This document will act as a starting point from which the analyst will investigate further and eventually produce a feasibility report.

The statement will not be the result of much investigation on the part of the analyst. Indeed, it is important that only a small amount of time, and therefore cost, is incurred before the analyst and management have an agreed understanding, however broadly specified, of the project. The investigation may take only a day or two.

Kismet case study 11.2

With respect to Kismet, the analyst spends some time with the new managing director Josephine Kismet and then tours the company for the remainder of the day, where he talks to a number of personnel.

After this, the analyst produces the statement of scope and objectives (see Figure 11.1). This is to be taken as the initially agreed scope of the project. At this stage, the analyst will not feel tied to any of the figures except the requirement to provide a feasibility report within two weeks at a cost of a couple of thousand pounds or less.

421

Figure 11.1 A statement of scope and objectives

Statement of scope and objectives

Project name: Sales order processing – Kismet Ltd date: dd/mm/yy

Current problems:

The following problems have been identified:

1. The sales catalogue of prices and products used to price customer orders is often out of date. In particular, new items are not catalogued immediately and items that are now no longer stocked still appear. The problem is located in the time-consuming nature of the manual preparation of the catalogue from the inventory records.

2. Customer enquiries are sometimes difficult to deal with as records of orders are not stored in a form that is easily accessible.

3. Orders that cannot be immediately satisfied from current stock – that is, back orders – are not processed consistently.

4. Owing to the large number of documents flowing through the system, the time taken to process an order may be days, even if all the goods are held in the warehouse.

5. Data in the system is generally stored in a way that makes it difficult for management to retrieve useful information. For instance, regular reports are time-consuming to produce and are often late, rendering them ineffective for control purposes or to aid medium-term strategies.

Objectives:

To investigate initially the feasibility for computerization of the sales order processing, invoicing and stock systems.

Constraints:

The entire project is to be budgeted for completion within six months at a cost of approximately £100,000.

Plan of action:

Investigate fully the existing sales order processing, stock and invoicing systems. Investigate the feasibility of a computerized system as a solution to the current problems.
Outline in general terms the recommended system(s) with costs.
Produce a report on this feasibility within two weeks with a budget of £1,500.

11.3 Systems investigation

The analyst must now become thoroughly familiar with the existing system. In particular, the analyst has to determine:

- the objectives of the existing system;
- how the existing system works;
- any legal, government or other regulations that might affect the operation of the system – for example, the Data Protection Act in the UK;
- the economic and organizational environment within which the system lies and in particular any changes that are likely to occur.

Why should the analyst pay much attention to the workings of the existing system, because, after all, is this system not deficient? Or else why would there be a need to replace it? There are a number of observations to make. First, although it is assumed that the problem is one that is amenable to a computerized solution, this has not yet been established. It may turn out that a change in existing manual procedures or organizational structure is the best way of solving the problem. This will only come to light after investigation of the existing system. Of course, analysts may be blind to such alternatives. Analysts are trained to look for technical solutions. They may also have a vested commercial interest in a computerized solution, so it is easy for them to miss alternative solutions. There is, though, a second reason for extensively studying the existing system. This will give the analyst a thorough understanding of the nature of the activities to be incorporated into the final computerized system. No matter how weak the existing system is, it must function at some level of effectiveness. This will provide a rich source of information from which the analyst can work.

11.3.1 The analyst's channels of information

The analyst needs to obtain information about the existing system and its environment. There are five main sources that the analyst can use:

1. interviews
2. documentation
3. observation
4. questionnaires
5. measuring.

Interviews

This is the most important way in which an analyst will obtain information. Setting up interviews with key personnel at all levels in the organization ensures a rich and complete view of what is happening. Interviewing is more of an art than a mechanical technique. It improves with experience. There are, however, several guidelines that are recognized as being essential to successful interviewing.

First, the analyst must have a clear purpose for each interview undertaken. This should be specified by the analyst as part of the preparation for the interview. It is not enough to define the purpose as 'attempting to find out more about such-and-such an area'. This will lead to a rambling interview. Rather, the analyst should establish the missing information that the interview is meant to supply. The analyst should prepare thoroughly for the interview by becoming familiar with technical terms that are likely to be used by the interviewees and with their positions and general responsibilities. The analyst should also outline a list of questions to be asked during the interview.

During the interview, the analyst should:

- Explain at the beginning the purpose of the interview. This gives the interviewee a framework of reference for answering questions.
- Attempt to put the interviewee at ease.
- Go through the questions that were prepared. General questions should be asked first, followed by more specific questions on each topic area. The analyst should always

listen carefully to replies and be able to follow up answers with questions that were not in the original list. The analyst must always bear in mind the purpose of the interview and discourage time-wasting digressions.

■ Never criticize the interviewee. The analyst is merely seeking information.

■ Not enter into a discussion of the various merits or weaknesses of other personnel in the organization.

■ Summarize points made by the interviewee at suitable stages in the interview.

■ Explain the purpose of note taking or a tape recorder if used.

■ Keep the interview short; generally 20 minutes or half an hour is sufficient.

■ Summarize the main points of the interview at the end.

■ Book a following interview, if required, with the interviewee at the end of the interview.

No checklist of guidelines is adequate to become a good interviewer, but the list given should enable any serious pitfalls to be avoided.

Problems with the interview as a channel of information

The interview, although the most valuable tool for information gathering for the analyst, is limited in that:

■ The interviewee may refuse to cooperate with the interviewer through fear of job deskilling, redundancy or the inability to cope with the new technology as a result of computerization. This may take the form of a direct refusal to take part (unlikely), being vague in replies, or, by omission, continuing to let the analyst believe what the interviewee knows to be false.

■ The interviewee may feel that they should tell the analyst how the tasks that they carry out *should* be performed rather than how they actually *are* performed. It is common for people to cut corners, not follow works procedures, adopt alternative practices. All of these may be more efficient than the officially recommended practice, but it is difficult for the interviewee to be honest in this area.

■ Clerical workers do tasks. They generally do not have to describe them and may not be articulate in doing so. Indeed, many managers might have some difficulty in articulating their decision-making processes.

■ The analyst cannot avoid filtering all that the interviewee says through the analyst's model of the world. The analyst's background and preconceptions may interfere with the process of communication. One of the distinguishing marks of good interviewers is the ability to think themselves quickly into the interviewee's frame of mind. This almost therapeutic skill is not one that is usually developed through training in computing.

Documentation

Most business organizations, particularly large ones, have documentation that is of help to the analyst in understanding the way they work:

■ Instruction manuals and procedures manuals provide a statement of the way that tasks are to be performed.

- Document blanks that are filled in by personnel in the organization and then passed between departments or stored for reference give the analyst an indication of the formal data flows and data stores.

- Job descriptions define the responsibilities of personnel.

- Statements of company policy provide information on overall objectives and likely changes.

- Publicity and information booklets for external bodies provide a useful overview of the way that a company works.

The problem with using documentation is that there is often a great deal of it, particularly in large organizations. The analyst has to read extensively in order to gather a small amount of useful information. Unlike interviews, where the analyst can direct the information that is provided by targeted questions, documents cannot be so easily probed. Finally, documentation may be out of date, and the analyst has little way of knowing this. The last thing to be changed when a clerical procedure is altered is usually the documentation governing it. Despite these weaknesses, documentation is a useful channel for information gathering.

Observation

Observation of employees performing activities in the area of investigation is another source of information for the analyst. Observation has the edge over the other methods of information gathering in that it is direct. The analyst wishes to understand the way that the existing system functions. Interviews provide reports from people of what they do, subject to all the distorting influences stated. Documents are an indication of what employees should be doing, which is not necessarily what they are doing. Only by observation does the analyst see directly how activities are performed.

However there are some notable drawbacks:

- It is extremely time-consuming for the analyst.

- When observed, people tend to behave differently from when their behaviour is unobserved – the 'Hawthorn effect' – thus devaluing the information obtained.

- Observation, unlike interviewing, does not reveal the beliefs and attitudes of the people involved.

However, observation is an important source for the analyst on informal information flows between individuals. These are often essential for the efficient execution of activities. They may not be obvious from interviews and would not appear in documentation.

Questionnaires

Questionnaires are of only limited use in obtaining information for the purposes of investigating an existing system (as opposed to market research, where they are essential). This is because:

- It is difficult to avoid misunderstandings on the part of respondents as they cannot gain clarification of a question on the questionnaire if it is judged to be vague or confusing.

- Questionnaires that are simple provide little information; questionnaires that are more ambitious are likely to be misunderstood.

- Response rates to questionnaires are often low.
- To set a good questionnaire, the analyst often has to have more information about the system under investigation than the questionnaire could hope to provide in the first place.

Certain limited situations may make a questionnaire suitable. These usually occur when the number of people involved makes interviewing prohibitively expensive, the questions are generally simple, a low response rate is satisfactory, and the questionnaire is used to confirm evidence collected elsewhere.

In designing questionnaires, it is important to:

- Keep questions simple, unambiguous and unbiased.
- Use multiple-choice questions rather than ask for comments. This makes the questionnaire both easier to answer and easier to analyse.
- Have a clear idea of the information that is required from the questionnaire.
- Make sure that the questions are aimed at the level of intellect and particular interests of the respondents.
- Avoid branching: for example, 'if your answer to question 8 was "yes" then go to question 23 otherwise go to question 19'.
- Make clear the deadline date by which the questionnaire is to be returned and enclose an addressed and prepaid envelope.

Measuring

Sometimes it is important to have statistical information about the workings of the existing system. The total number of sales ledger accounts and the activity of each will be of interest to the analyst who is looking at the possible computerization of an accounting system. The statistical spread as well as the gross figures may be relevant. For instance, with a sales order-processing system not only may the average number of sales orders processed in a day be of use to the analyst but the pattern of these orders throughout the day and throughout the week may also be of significance. Are there peaks and troughs, or is it a constant flow?

11.3.2 Approaching the investigation

Although the foregoing channels provide the analyst with information, it is necessary to have some plan or some framework within which to study the existing system.

Flow block diagrams

A flow block diagram may be developed at an early stage in the investigation to represent the system. Flow block diagrams show the important subsystems in an organization and the flows between them. They provide a good overview of a system, within which more detailed investigation can occur. It is common for flow block diagrams to be based around the traditional functions of a business – sales, purchasing, manufacturing, stores, accounting, planning, control, and so on. These diagrams were treated in detail in Chapter 1.

Kismet case study 11.3

A flow block diagram of Kismet is given in Figure 11.2.

Figure 11.2 A flow block diagram of Kismet

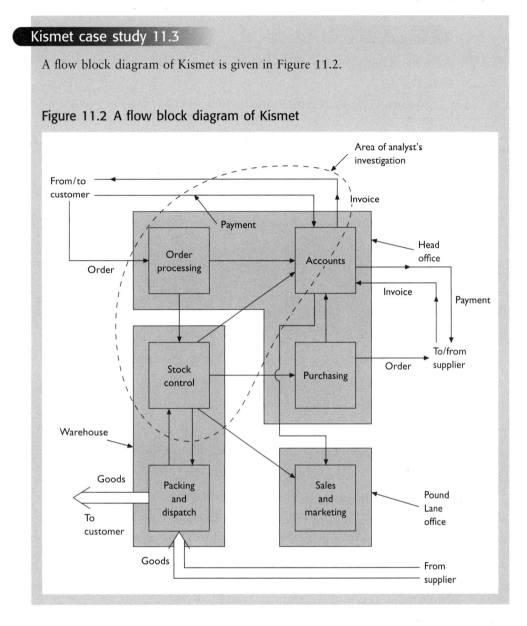

Organization charts

Organization charts show the various roles and their relationships within an organization. They are usually hierarchical in nature, reflecting relationships of control, decision flow and levels of managerial activity between the various elements of the hierarchy. The chart enables the analyst to establish key personnel for interview.

Kismet case study 11.4

An organization chart for Kismet is given in Figure 11.3.

Figure 11.3 An organization chart for Kismet

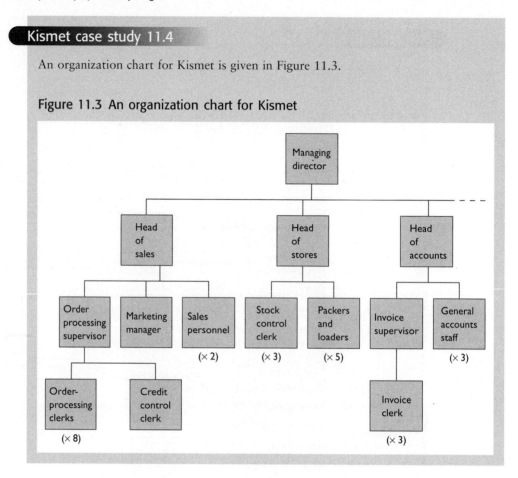

Task identification

The analyst will identify key tasks within each subsystem. A useful model to adopt is the system model (see Figure 11.4), where the task is regarded as a process for converting an input into an output. There may be intermediate storage requirements, and there will be some control over the operation of the task. This gives the analyst a template by which a task can be investigated. Key questions that should be satisfied are:

- What different types of input are there into the task?
- And for each input:
  - What is the structure of the input?
  - Where does it come from?
  - What is the rate of input (how many per hour)?
  - Is it regular, or are there peaks and troughs?
- What different types of output are there to the task?
- And for each output:
  - What is the structure of the output?
  - Where does it go to?
  - What is the rate of output (how many per hour) required?

Figure 11.4 A systems model of a task (task template)

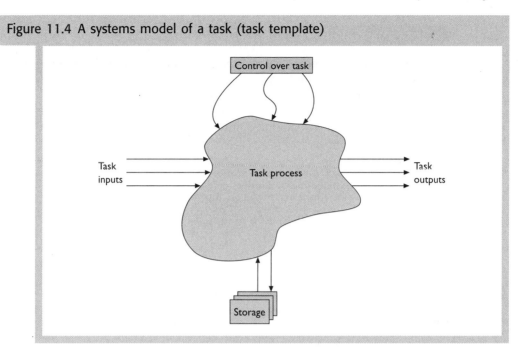

– Is it regular, or are there peaks and troughs?
– What is the purpose of the output?

■ What is the logic of the process?

■ Does it require discretion, or is it rule-governed?

■ What is the purpose of the process?

■ What experience or training is necessary to become competent at it?

■ What level of accuracy is required?

■ What stores, files or records are consulted in performing the task?

■ How often are these consulted?

■ What indexes or keys are used for selecting the correct record?

■ How many records are in the available record store?

■ What types of control are exerted over the task?

■ Who is responsible for each control?

After investigation, the analyst should have a good understanding of:

■ Who does what.

■ Where it is done.

■ Why it is done.

■ When it is done.

■ How it is done.

This framework provides a useful outline on which the analyst can base questions during an interview.

Kismet case study 11.5

Figure 11.5 gives an example of some of the questions to be asked of the sales order processing supervisor at Kismet. These are based on the framework outlined above.

Figure 11.5 Examples of questions to be asked of the Kismet sales order processing supervisor during a systems investigation

Inputs

What is the content of a customer sales order?
Does the company transcribe customer orders to company documentation?
How many sales orders are received per day?
Are there heavy/light times of the week/year?
What do you do if a sales order is incomplete in its specification?

Process

What is done with the sales orders?
How are they divided among the sales order processing personnel?
At what stage is it established that stock exists?
What is done if stock is not currently held?
How are the orders priced?
What happens to an order for an item of stock not held by the company?

Outputs

What is produced by the process?
Where does it go?
Are reports, summaries or totals provided?
How quickly are the priced sales orders produced from the customer orders?

Control

What accuracy controls operate over the transcription of the orders to company documentation?
What controls operate to ensure that all customer orders received are processed?
How is it established that customers have not exceeded credit limits?

Storage

What catalogues, records, files are consulted?
What information is obtained from them?
Whose responsibility is it for ensuring the accuracy of the information?

Staffing

How many staff are involved?
What are their roles?
How do the controls operate over staff?

Costs

What is the budgeted cost for processing an order?
What is the actual cost of processing an order?
How are costs split between variable and fixed costs?

Growth

Is it envisaged that there will be growth in demand for sales order processing?

11.4 The feasibility study and report

One of the purposes of carrying out a systems investigation, perhaps *the* main purpose, is to establish the feasibility of introducing a computer system. Among other things, this will provide some estimate of the likely costs and benefits of a proposed system.

The reason for the study is to establish at as early a stage as possible whether the project is realistic. This must be determined with the minimum of expenditure. If the project turns out not to be feasible then all the time and money spent on the systems investigation will be 'down the drain'.

There is a conflict here. On the one hand, the earlier the feasibility study the less the money that will have been sunk, but the less likely it will be that the feasibility study gives an accurate estimate of costs and benefits. On the other hand, a more accurate assessment can only be made if more money is spent on the feasibility survey.

There is no completely satisfactory way of resolving this dilemma. In practice, the analyst is more likely to recommend an extensive feasibility study in more unusual and innovative projects. This is because the degree of uncertainty in success, costs and benefits is greater. However, many analysts become familiar with certain types of project, such as the computerization of a standard accounting system. In these cases, it will be possible to make reasonably accurate feasibility assessments quickly.

There is inevitably an element of guesswork at the feasibility stage (despite what some analysts might claim). The long history of notable failures of computerization is testimony to this fact, as they can, in part, be put down to unrealistic feasibility studies. The more effort put into the study, the less the guesswork. Sometimes, parts of the stages of systems analysis and systems (high-level) design may be undertaken using the structured tools such as data flow diagrams and entity relationship models explained in Chapters 12 and 13, prior to producing a feasibility report.

Kismet case study 11.6

It is assumed here, in the case of Kismet, that the analyst has established enough information after investigation and initial interviews to have a thorough understanding of the present physical system and is able to recommend the feasibility of a computer system. The suggestion will be based on an understanding of the tasks to be performed, the volume of transactions processed and the types of information to be produced.

In looking at feasibility, the analyst considers three main areas – economic, technical and organizational feasibility.

11.4.1 Economic feasibility

As with any project that an organization undertakes, there will be economic costs and economic benefits. These have to be compared and a view taken as to whether the benefits justify the costs. If not, then the project is unlikely to be undertaken.

Economic costs

There are a number of different types of cost associated with a computer project. These are:

1. **Systems analysis and design:** The cost of the analyst must be taken into the calculation of the total cost of the project. Of course, the analyst's costs in carrying out the stages up to and including the feasibility study will not be included in this calculation. These are already a sunk cost of the project.

2. **Purchase of hardware**: Alternatives to purchase, such as leasing or renting, may be considered here.

3. **Software costs**: These are often the hardest to estimate. Software may be written from scratch, developed using fourth-generation tools or purchased, in the form of an applications package.

4. **Training costs**: Staff need to be trained to use the new system.

5. **Installation costs**: This may be a significant cost if new rooms have to be built, cables laid and work environments altered.

6. **Conversion and changeover costs**: These concern the loading of data from the existing system into the new system in a secure manner. There are also costs associated with the resulting changeover from the old to the new system.

7. **Redundancy costs**: If the purpose of computerization is to replace people with machines then redundancy money may have to be paid.

8. **Operating costs**:

   (a) maintenance costs for hardware and software;
   (b) costs of power, paper, and so on;
   (c) costs associated with personnel to operate the new system – for example, computer centre staff, data input clerks, and so on.

Economic benefits

These are often very varied. Some may be estimable with a high degree of accuracy, others may be uncertain. Many benefits will be completely non-measurable. Examples of benefits are:

1. **Savings in labour costs**: These may be predictable, allowing for uncertainties in future wage rates, and so on.

2. **Benefits due to faster processing**: Examples of these might be a reduced debtor period as a result of speedier debtor processing, or reduced buffer stock due to better stock control. These may be estimable.

3. **Better decision making**: Computerized information systems provide more targeted and accurate information more quickly and cheaply than manual systems. This leads to better managerial decisions. It is generally not possible to put a figure on the value of better managerial decisions. Even if it were, it would be impossible to assign what percentage of this improvement was the result of better information and what was the result of other factors.

4. **Better customer service**: Once again, it will generally not be possible to estimate the economic benefits of either better customer service or more competitive services. This will be only one factor affecting customer choice.

5. **Error reduction**: The benefits of this may be estimable if current losses associated with erroneous processing are known.

Comparison of costs and benefits

Both costs and benefits occur in the future, although not usually in the same future periods (see Figure 11.6). The costs occur largely during the initial stages of the systems

Figure 11.6 The time profile of costs and benefits for a typical systems life cycle

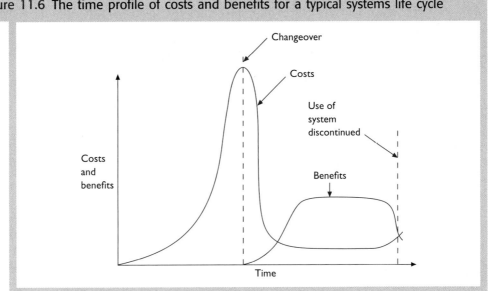

development, whereas the benefits occur later in the useful life of the system. These must be compared.

One method is to discount the future streams of costs and benefits back to the present by means of an assumed rate. This will be near to the prevailing rate of interest in the financial markets, although its exact determination will depend on the project, the company undertaking the project and the sector within which the company functions. This discount rate is arbitrary within certain limits.

All of the following factors:

- the non-measurable nature of some of the costs and benefits;
- the fact that many of the benefits occur far into the uncertain future;
- the degree of arbitrariness associated with the choice of the cost/benefit comparison calculation;

mean that the estimation of economic feasibility must be made with much reservation. It is tempting to regard the figure in the net present value calculation of the economic feasibility of the project as the 'hard' piece of data on which a decision to continue the project can be made. This would be a mistake. It ignores not only the non-measurable nature of certain costs and benefits but also other aspects of feasibility covered in the following sections.

11.4.2 Technical feasibility

This is concerned with the technical possibility and desirability of a computer solution in the problem area. Some of the issues will overlap with points brought out in the discussion on costs and benefits in the previous section. Many suggestions are not technically impossible *per se*. Rather, it is a question of how much money an organization is prepared to invest in order to achieve a technical solution. The following categories are important in determining the technical feasibility of a project.

1. **Rule-governed tasks:** If the tasks undertaken in the area of investigation are not governed by rules but require discretion and judgement, it is unlikely that computerization will be feasible. For example, the processing of a sales order, the production of a summary of aged debtors report or the calculation of creditworthiness on a points basis are all rule-governed. The selection of candidates for jobs is not. This could not be incorporated into a computer system (although new developments in expert systems raise the possibility that this might not always be so).

2. **Repetitive tasks:** If a task is performed only rarely then it may not be feasible to invest the time, effort and money in developing a program to carry it out. The tasks that are most suitable for computerization are those that are repetitive.

3. **Complex tasks:** If a complex task can be broken down into simple constituent tasks then it is generally easy and desirable to computerize.

4. **High degree of accuracy:** Humans are quite good at making quick estimates based on 'rule of thumb' assumptions in flexible circumstances. Computers are not. However, if a high degree of numerical accuracy is required then computers outstrip humans by both speed and low error rates.

5. **Speed of response:** Computer systems give fast responses if required and are designed to do so.

6. **Data used for many tasks:** Once data is inside a computer it is generally easy and cheap to use it repeatedly for different tasks.

11.4.3 Organizational feasibility

Organizational feasibility, or as it is sometimes called, 'operational feasibility', concerns the viability of the proposed system within the operational and organizational environment. The issues to consider vary from organization to organization, but the analyst is wise to address at least the following questions:

1. Does the organization for which the information system is to be supplied have a history of acceptance of information technology, or has past introduction led to conflict? Some sectors are notorious for their opposition to computerization. For instance, in the UK the print industry unions fought an extended battle opposing the introduction of computer technology. Other sectors, such as banking, have a history of acceptance of and adaptation to information technology. A previous history of opposition to the introduction of computer systems may have taken the form of a formalized union opposition, or it may have been revealed in the attitude of users. High levels of absenteeism and high turnover rates subsequent to a previous introduction of new technology are good indicators of future poor acceptance.

2. Will the personnel in the organization be able to cope with operating the new technology? It is unrealistic, for instance, to expect staff with long-established working practices to adapt readily to new technology no matter how much training is given.

3. Is the organizational structure compatible with the proposed information system? For example, a highly centralized autocratic management structure is generally not compatible with a distributed computer system. Decentralized systems inevitably lead to local autonomy and local management of computer resources. Similarly, if departments or divisions in an organization have a history of competing with one another rather than cooperating, it is unlikely that it will be easy to develop a successful integrated system.

These are all issues in the area of organizational behaviour and 'people problems'. Analysts often have a training in programming or other technical areas, and it is easy for them to ignore this vital component of feasibility.

11.4.4 Feasibility report

A feasibility report will be written by the analyst and considered by management prior to allowing the project to continue further. It will go to the steering committee in the case of a large organization. In a smaller organization without a steering committee structure, the report will be assessed by senior managers as part of their normal activities.

As well as providing information on the feasibility of the project, the systems investigation will have provided much information that will also be incorporated into the feasibility report. In particular:

- The principal work areas for the project will have been identified.

- Any needs for specialist staff to be involved in the later stages of the project will have been noted.

- Possible improvement or potential for savings may have become apparent during the investigation.

Outline headings for a typical feasibility report are given in Figure 11.7. Once the feasibility report has been accepted, the project can proceed to the next stage. This is to provide an analysis from which a new system can be designed and implemented.

Figure 11.7 The contents of a typical feasibility report

Title page: Name of project, report name, version number, author, date.

Terms of reference: These will be taken from the statement of scope and objectives.

Summary: This gives a clear, concise statement of the feasibility study and its recommendations.

Background: Statement of the reasons for initiation of the project, the background of the current system, how it features in the organization, how it figures in the organization's development plans, what problems it encounters.

Method of study: Detailed description of the systems investigation including personnel interviewed and documents searched, together with any other channels of information. Assumptions made and limitations imposed.

Present system: Statement of the main features of the current system, including its major tasks, its staffing, its storage, its equipment, its control procedures, and the way it relates to other systems in the organization.

Proposed system(s): Each proposed system, if there is more than one, is outlined. This will include a statement of the facilities provided. (Data flow diagrams, explained in Chapter 12, and other charting techniques may be used as a pictorial representation of the proposal.) For each proposal, its economic, technical and organizational feasibility will be assessed. Major control features will be included.

Recommendation: The recommended system will be clearly indicated with reasons why it is preferred.

Development plan: A development plan for the recommended system is given in some detail; this will include projected costs for future stages in the life cycle with estimates of the time schedule for each.

Appendix: This will provide supporting material to the main report. It will include references to documents, summaries of interviews, charts and graphs showing details of transaction processing, estimates of hardware costs and so on. In fact, anything that is likely to be of use to those reading the report that will enable them to make a more informed decision will be included.

Chapters 12 and 13 cover the two main aspects of analysis – analysis of processes and analysis of data. Various tools and techniques will be explained; although these are normally used in analysis, there is nothing to stop the analyst using them in the stages of systems investigation. The various charts and diagrams can then be included in the feasibility report. This is tantamount to carrying out broad aspects of *systems* analysis and *systems* design (as opposed to *detailed* design) prior to the provision of the feasibility report. This makes possible a more comprehensive development of a proposal or range of proposals. It also allows better communication of these proposals within the feasibility report as the techniques used are designed to facilitate communication.

Summary

After senior management or the steering committee has recognized the need for the development of an information system, it is necessary to carry out a formal feasibility study. This will involve an analyst. The analyst will need to have an understanding of the scope and objectives of the proposed systems project. It is customary for a written statement in this area to be agreed between the analyst and those who are commissioning the project. Although this will only give the broadest indication of the scope of the intended system, it will provide the analyst with a direction in which to proceed in systems investigation. Also, importantly, it will give the analyst a budget and schedule within which to provide a feasibility report.

During systems investigation, the analyst will obtain information by interviewing key personnel, searching current documentation and reports, observing the existing system, measuring various key variables such as the number of transactions processed and the time taken for each transaction, and possibly using questionnaires for response from large groups. All of these channels of information suffer from distorting influences that devalue the accuracy and use of the information gathered through them.

In order to organize the way that the information is obtained, it is helpful for the analyst to have a framework of reference. This is provided by the systems model. At the highest level, flow block diagrams will aid the analyst in representing the major components within the organization and the flows between them. At the more detailed level, when key tasks are considered, it is appropriate to view them as processes for converting inputs into outputs using storage while being subject to control. Organization charts give the relationships between the various roles in the organization.

A feasibility report is provided by the analyst for the systems project. As well as giving a description of the present and proposed systems it contains an assessment of the feasibility of the proposal(s). This will not only take account of the economic feasibility – the economic costs and benefits – but will also look at the technical and organizational feasibility. The feasibility study and report is essential for proper project control. It enables senior management, which is responsible for major resource decisions, to take a decision on the continuation of the project with a minimum of sunk cost. The more unusual the requirements of the proposed system or the greater the sums involved in its development, the more extensive will be the systems investigation prior to the feasibility report. Various charting and diagrammatically based techniques such as data flow diagrams and entity–relationship models, explained in Chapters 12 and 13, may also be used. After acceptance of the feasibility study the analyst, together with a project group in the case of larger systems, will proceed to full scale analysis and design.

Review questions

1. What is the purpose of a statement of scope and objectives?

2. During systems investigation, what channels are open to the analyst in gathering information about a system? What are the strengths and weaknesses of each?

3. What is the purpose of a feasibility study?

4. Explain the terms *economic feasibility*, *technical feasibility* and *organizational feasibility*.

Exercises

1. Why is it difficult to undertake an economic assessment of a project at an early stage in its development?

2. What features of a task (or group of tasks) are likely to make it technically non-feasible?

3. 'In the feasibility report, it is common for the analyst to outline more than one proposal and recommend just one of these.' Surely the analyst should either give only the recommended option or, alternatively, outline several proposals with their implications and let management decide the most suitable?

4. What benefits are likely to result from:
   (a) computerizing the records system in a library?
   (b) computerizing a sales order and invoicing system (as in Kismet)?
   (c) providing a computerized point of sales system in a supermarket?

Recommended reading

Davis W.S. (1994). *Systems Analysis and Design*: New York: Thomson Learning
   This book provides a good, straightforward coverage of feasibility studies, the content of a feasibility report and interviewing. The case studies are used to illustrate the general points.

Harris D. (2003). *Systems Analysis and Design for the Small Enterprise*, 3rd edn. Dryden Press
   This is a business-focused book that uses mini case studies and running case studies throughout. It is very readable and well illustrated.

Wiley W. (2000). *Essential Business Requirements*: Addison-Wesley
   This well-illustrated and easy-to-read book covers business events and system developments, looking at system data processes and behaviour. The book considers the estimation of project costs and has a business focus.

Chapter 12

Process analysis and modelling

Learning outcomes

On completion of this chapter, you should be able to:

- Explain the need for systems analysis and describe the techniques typically employed
- Create a logical model of a system comprising levelled data flow diagrams
- Explain the need for a data dictionary
- Create process specifications comprising decision tables, logic flow charts and structured English.

Introduction

In Chapter 11, the first stages of the life cycle for a systems project were described, namely the feasibility study and the collection of information. The analyst now has a large amount of documentation on the existing system. However, to be of use this information must be organized and analysed before a new design, probably involving computerization, can be developed.

The purpose of this chapter is to illustrate the method to be adopted by the analyst in analysing and modelling the processes that handle the data and information within the organization. The approach taken is to move from a description and analysis of the existing physical system and to derive a logical model of the processes involved. Physical analysis is illustrated using manual systems flowcharts, which picture the formal document flows within departments and processes in an organization. The logical model is derived in the first instance using data flow diagrams, which show the relationships between logical data flows and processes. The content of each data flow together with other useful information on it is contained in a data dictionary. The logical content of the processes can be described using structured English, decision tables and logic flowcharts. These are all covered in this chapter. In order to be of use in systems design, the process model of the system must be supplemented with a data model. The production of this is considered in Chapter 13 on data analysis and modelling.

12.1 Systems analysis

The purpose of systems analysis is to ascertain what must be done in order to carry out the functions of the system. This will involve a decomposition of the functions of

Figure 12.1 Tools used during the stage of systems analysis

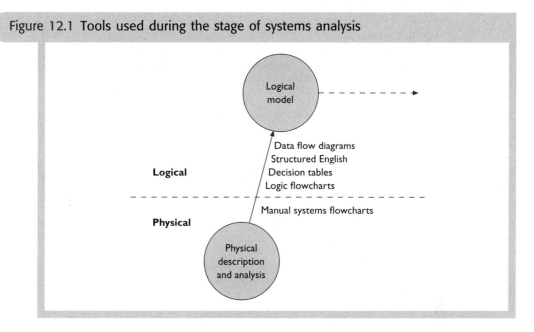

the system into their logical constituents and the production of a logical model of the processes and of the data flows necessary to perform these. The logical model will be illustrated by data flow diagrams at the various levels of process decomposition. The algorithms will be revealed by structured process specification techniques such as structured English, decision tables and logic flowcharts. The importance of concentration on the logical features of a system (what logically needs to be done in order to carry out the functions) as distinct from the physical features (who does what, where, with which file, and so on) is to avoid making premature commitments to physical design. The rationale for adopting this approach was covered in Chapter 10, which outlined the need for an information systems development methodology.

Prior to production of the logical analysis, it is often helpful to carry out a physical analysis of the document flows between processes and departments within the existing system. As well as enabling the analyst to identify key tasks, these charts can be used to evaluate control and efficiency aspects of the current system.

The output of the stage of systems analysis will be a logical model of the functioning of the system. This will consist of diagrams, charts and dictionaries, which are the product of the techniques used in the analysis. An important feature of a structured approach to systems analysis and design is the generation of clear and helpful documentation that can assist communication not only between the programmer and analyst but also between management and users and the analyst. The fact that a logical model is produced in systems analysis removes complicating and distracting physical elements that would hamper communication. The movement from the physical to the logical model and the techniques used are illustrated in Figure 12.1.

12.2 Manual systems flowcharts

After investigation, the analyst may have collected an unwieldy batch of interview notes, details of observations, questionnaire responses and sundry documents. In the initial stages of analysis, it is important to arrive at a methodical description of the existing manual system and to carry out some analysis at a physical level prior to developing a logical model of the system. The flow of *formal* information within a system often occurs through documents that pass from one department to another. A traditional tool of systems analysis is the manual systems (document) flowchart.

The basic idea is that certain tasks performed on documents are common to many applications – filing, preparing multiple copies, collating, sorting. These are given

Figure 12.2 Basic symbols used in the preparation of manual systems flowcharts

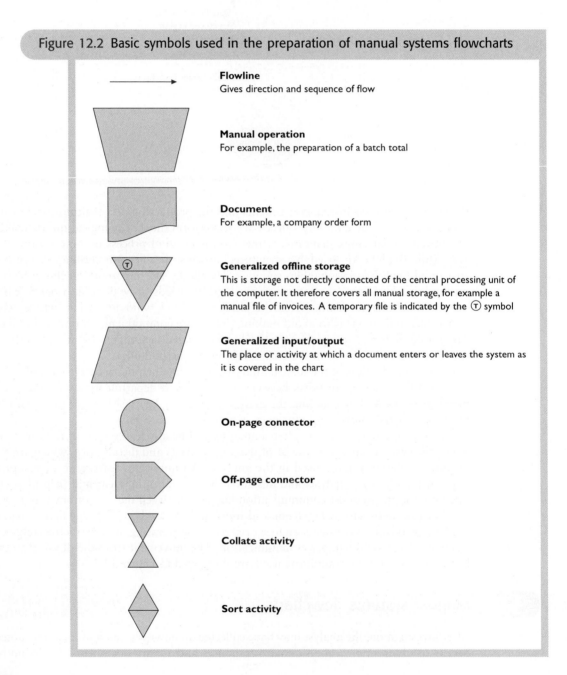

Flowline
Gives direction and sequence of flow

Manual operation
For example, the preparation of a batch total

Document
For example, a company order form

Generalized offline storage
This is storage not directly connected of the central processing unit of the computer. It therefore covers all manual storage, for example a manual file of invoices. A temporary file is indicated by the Ⓣ symbol

Generalized input/output
The place or activity at which a document enters or leaves the system as it is covered in the chart

On-page connector

Off-page connector

Collate activity

Sort activity

specially agreed symbols (Figure 12.2). The life history of a document from origination (entry from outside the system or preparation within) to destination (exit from the system or filing) is recorded on the flowchart. The passage of the document from department to department is also shown.

Kismet case study 12.1

The best way to understand a manual systems flowchart, sometimes called a document flowchart, is to study one. Here the Kismet case study is developed giving a detailed description of the processes occurring during order processing. A manual systems flowchart covering these is shown in Figure 12.3.

Order processing

Customers mail their orders to Kismet HQ. On receipt of an order in the sales order department, a five-part company order form is filled in giving (among other information) the *order#, order date, customer#, customer name, item 1 code#, item 1 quantity, item 2 code#, item 2 quantity*, and so on. The top copy of this form is filed temporarily in *customer#* sequence for customer enquiry purposes (rather than *order#* sequence, as when customers enquire about a recently placed order they will not be in possession of the *order#*). Each item is provisionally priced on the remaining copies of the form from a sales catalogue held in the order department. The priced copies are sent to the credit control section.

The credit control section provisionally calculates the order value. Brief details of the customer account are then consulted to establish that the customer exists and is correctly named and that the total value of the order, when added to the current balance, does not exceed the credit limit of the customer. If all these conditions are met then the order copies are stamped 'approved', signed and returned to the sales order department, one copy of the order being retained in the credit control department filed by *customer#*. If the above conditions are not met, the order copies are filed temporarily to be dealt with later by the credit control manager.

On receipt of the approved order copies in the sales order department, the top copy is extracted from the temporary file and sent to the customer as an acknowledgment. One of the 'approved' copies is filed in the order department in the 'approved order' file under *order#* to enable staff to retrieve details of the order in the event of further customer queries. The remaining two copies are sent to the stores department and the invoicing department. The invoicing department files the copy under *order#*.

The stores department selects the goods as ordered and enters the quantities supplied on the order form. A two-part dispatch note is made out giving the goods supplied together with their quantities. One copy of this is sent to the invoicing department, and the other is sent with the goods to packing and dispatch. If the entire order is supplied then the order form is filed in the stores department under *order#*, otherwise the goods supplied are noted on the form and it is filed in *date* sequence. Periodically, the stores department goes through the unsatisfied back orders and attempts to supply the goods ordered. The stores department also updates the inventory records.

On receipt of the dispatch note, the invoicing department prepares a three-part invoice using the sales price of the goods from the catalogue. The discount applicable to a customer is calculated. This is based on the customer's geographical location, total purchases during the last 12 months and the total value of the order. Sales tax is added and totals formed. One copy of the invoice is sent to the customer, and one is sent to accounts to update the customer accounts and other ledgers. The remaining copy is filed in the invoicing department with the order copy and dispatch note under *order#*.

The flowchart for order processing and dispatch in Kismet is given in Figure 12.3. Note that the flow lines indicate flows of *documents*.

Figure 12.3 The manual system flowchart for order processing/dispatch in Kismet

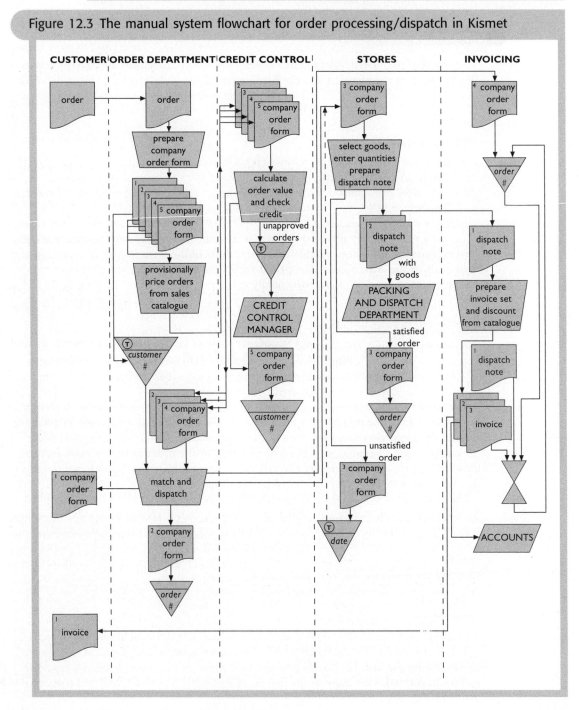

The following practical points will assist in the drawing of flowcharts:

- The chart is divided into vertical sections representing different locations for operations.
- Although not shown, a far-left section may be used for additional (brief) narrative.
- The chart proceeds as far as possible from left to right and top to bottom.
- Documents are shown at origination, on entry into a section and then again only as required to avoid confusion with other documents.
- Ensure that all documents are accounted for by being permanently filed, being destroyed, leaving the system as charted (for example to the credit control manager in Kismet) or transferring to another flowchart.

There are a number of advantages and disadvantages in the use of manual systems flowcharts.

Advantages

- Flowcharts are easier to understand and assimilate than narrative. This becomes more pronounced with increasing complexity of the system.
- The preparation of a chart necessitates the full understanding by the analyst of the procedures and sequences of operations on documents.
- Incompleteness in tracing the destination of a document is easily discovered, indicating the need for further investigation on the part of the analyst (in Kismet, where does the customer's original order go?).
- Little technical knowledge is required to appreciate the document, so it can be used as a communication tool between the user of the system and the analyst in order to check and correct the latter's understanding.
- Weaknesses in the system, such as preparation of unnecessary documents, lack of control, unnecessary duplication of work and bottlenecks, are easily located.

Disadvantages

- With heavily integrated systems, flowcharts may become difficult to manage (large sheets of paper!). The use of off-page connectors and continuation is sometimes necessary but tends to reduce the visual impact and clarity of the chart.
- They are difficult to amend.
- It must be realized that when analysing an existing system informal information is an important part. The flowchart does not incorporate any recognition of this.

The systems flowchart is not only of use to the analyst when carrying out the stages of analysis and design of a computerized information system. Management may also use the flowchart to impose uniformity on groups of systems as the structure of the processes surrounding document handling are revealed. This may be necessary to ensure that, say, one branch of an organization handles order processing in the same way as another. The flowchart may be used as an aid in the preparation of internal audit and procedures manuals. In the former case, it is possible to ensure that essential information is provided to management at the correct stage. Auditors may use the flowchart in a review of internal control as a guide to determining auditing procedures in the annual audit.

The task of evaluation of the system is often considered as part of analysis. As has been pointed out, flowcharts assist in this task.

Kismet case study 12.2

A typical approach to evaluation of the order and dispatch system of Kismet would use the chart to answer a number of questions. Note how easy it is to answer the following typical list of questions by using the flowchart:

1. Can goods be dispatched but not invoiced?
2. Can orders be received and not (completely) dealt with?
3. Can customers be invoiced for goods that are not dispatched because of low stocks?
4. Can goods be dispatched to customers who are not creditworthy?
5. Can invoicing errors occur?
6. Can sales be invoiced but not recorded?

12.3 Data flow diagrams

Although systems flowcharts provide a useful tool for analysing a physical description, they may impede the design process. This is because they draw attention to physical detail. It is important to realize that the systems analyst will be designing a system to *do* something. This 'something' can be specified by describing its logic and the actions on data. To concentrate on existing physical detail will obscure the functions of the system, restrict the designer's creativity and cause premature commitments to physical design in the early stages of the project.

Kismet case study 12.3

An example of the concentration on physical detail described above is given here. It is of little importance to a computer design that one copy of a Kismet company order form is filed temporarily in the order department while four copies go to credit control, where, after approval, one is filed, the remaining copies being returned to the order department, after which the first copy is sent to the customer.

If the whole procedure is to be computerized, including the order approval, the process will occur within the computer as an exchange of data between files or a database and programs. But again, to assume total computerization is to make a possibly premature physical design decision. It may be more effective to retain parts of the old manual system or design new manual procedures.

The point to realize is that the processes, the exchanges of data and the stores of data are important, not their particular physical representation, whether it be, for instance, a sequential file on tape, an indexed file on disk or a composition of two manual files in two separate locations.

Figure 12.4 Symbols used in data flow diagrams

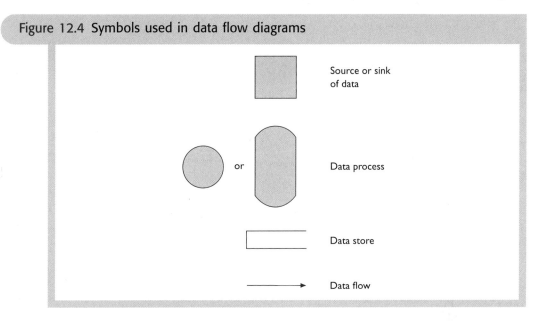

Source or sink of data

or   Data process

Data store

Data flow

Data flow diagrams assist in building a logical model of the system independent of physical commitments. They show the various flows of data between the processes that transform it. Data stores and the points at which data enters and leaves a system are also shown. The basic symbols used in drawing data flow diagrams are shown in Figure 12.4.

- **Data source** or **data sink**: The square indicates a source or sink for data and is a reflection of the ignorance as to what happens to the data prior to its emergence from the source or after its disappearance into the sink.

- **Data process**: The circle or rounded rectangle indicates a data process. In this, a brief but meaningful identifier of the process is written. It is important to realize that only *data* processes occur in a data flow diagram. Physical processes are not mentioned. For instance, the fact that goods are selected from their stock locations to satisfy an order is not a data process but a material task. A data process is one that transforms only data. It may be that this process will be carried out by a computer program, a part of a computer program, a set of computer programs or manually. The data flow diagram is neutral on this point.

   The identifier used in the data process symbol should, ideally, be both meaningful and succinct. It is good practice to restrict identifiers to a concatenation of imperative verb and object. For example *process stock transaction* or *check credit status* are both acceptable. It is bad practice to try to describe the process. For example, it is a great temptation for the novice to 'name' a data process as *check the application for the account against the credit point list to establish the creditworthiness and the credit limit of the customer*. This is not acceptable.

- **Data store**: A data store is represented by an open-ended rectangle with a suitable identifier. This is distinguished from a data sink by the fact that the data is stored and it (or some part of it) will be retrieved. A sink indicates ignorance, as far as the

Figure 12.5 Part of an erroneous data flow diagram

diagram is concerned, of the fate of the data. No particular storage medium is implied by the data store symbol. It could be a magnetic tape or disk, a document or even some person's memory. Once again, it is a great temptation for the newcomer to represent material stores. This is a mistake.

- **Data flow**: The line represents a data flow. The nature of the data is indicated by a name (or names). Wherever that piece of data flows within the diagram it should be tagged with the same name. Once again, it is important to realize that these are flows of *data* and not material flows. If a data flow diagram is drawn representing part of a system in which goods accompanied by a dispatch note are moved, it is the dispatch note, or to be more exact the dispatch note details, that appear on the data flow diagram. There is no mention of the goods.

It is also a common error to confuse data flows with flows of control. This is illustrated in Figure 12.5. Obviously, what the designer of the diagram intended is that the exit data flow travels one way if there is sufficient stock and the other way if there is insufficient. It is not usual to indicate the conditions under which data flows on a data flow diagram. This would tempt the analyst into thinking of the system from the point of view of control rather than data flows.

The difference between a data store and a data flow often confuses the beginner. It is helpful to think of an analogy with water. Water flowing down a pipe is analogous to a data flow, whereas water in a reservoir is the analogy for a data store.

12.3.1 Data flow diagrams in detail

In systems investigation, the analyst will have collected a great deal of information on tasks performed on document flows within the system. These tasks will be involved in the processing of business transactions and the generation of management information. The document processing will probably have been charted in a manual systems flowchart. In drawing data flow diagrams a logical approach is taken. It is important to ignore the location of processes in the manual system, the documents involved and who is responsible for the tasks. The designer should concentrate on the functions that are carried out.

If Kismet is considered, as described in Section 12.2, it can be seen that one very general course of action is taken. Orders from customers are processed to generate dispatch notes (which eventually accompany goods sent to the customer) and to make up invoices (sent to the customer and to the accounts department). In doing this, a price catalogue and customer account details are consulted and inventory records are updated.

This is indicated in Figure 12.6. In itself it is not very informative, although, even at this level, in a more comprehensive analysis of all Kismet's functions there would be other interfacing subsystems, such as purchasing, payroll and accounting. If the analyst had seriously misunderstood the structure of the system, this would be obvious at a glance.

Further progress can be made by decomposing this order-processing function into its component parts. Three different types of task occur when Kismet processes a customer order. First, the company order is generated and approved. Second, stock is selected, inventory updated and a dispatch note prepared. Finally, invoices are made up and sent to the customer and to accounts. Involved in this are various data flows, stores, processes, sources and sinks.

Read the case study and note where the sources, sinks, processes, stores and flows occur. These are:

Figure 12.6 A high-level view of order processing for Kismet

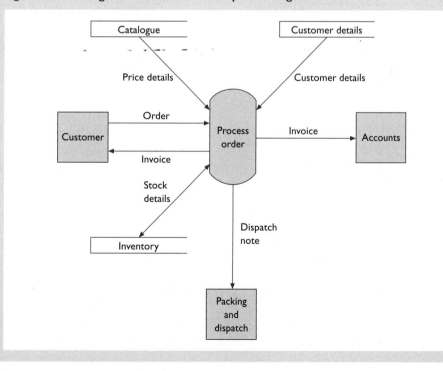

447

Figure 12.7 A level 1 data flow diagram of the Kismet order-processing system

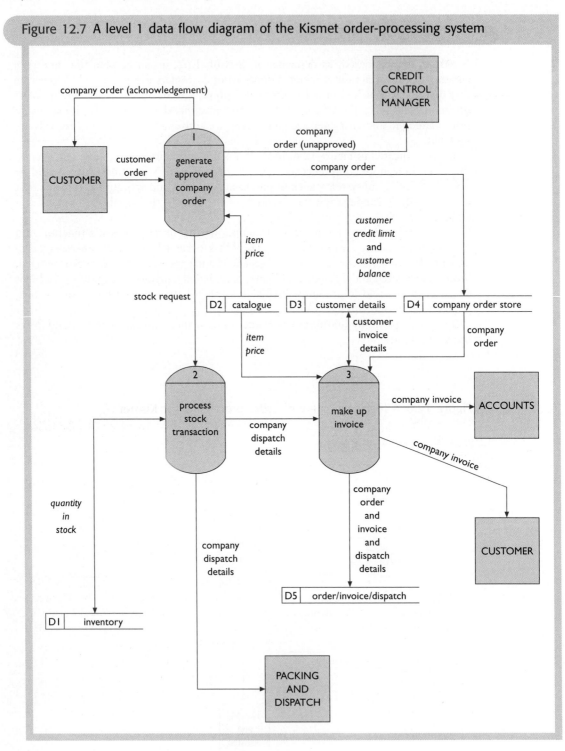

1. **Sources/sinks:**

   (a) customer
   (b) credit control manager
   (c) packing and dispatch department
   (d) accounting.

2. **Processes:**

   (a) generate approved company order
   (b) process stock transaction
   (c) make up invoice.

3. **Data stores:**

   (a) inventory
   (b) catalogue
   (c) customer details
   (d) company order store
   (e) company order/invoice/dispatch note.

4. **Data flows:**

   (a) customer order
   (b) company order
   (c) price details
   (d) stock details
   (e) customer credit details
   (f) invoice
   (g) customer invoice details
   (h) dispatch note.

The data flow diagram at the first level can now be drawn (Figure 12.7). The following points should be noted:

1. The diagram can be thought of as starting at the top left and moving downwards and to the right. This gives some idea of the sequence of tasks performed, although it is not a rigid rule.

2. Each data flow, source/sink, process and store is labelled. It is a convention that where source/sinks or stores are repeated they are given a diagonal line at the corner of the symbol (see the CUSTOMER source/sink). A data flow that is repeated is given the same name.

3. Certain tasks are left out of a data flow diagram. Any error-handling routine is usually omitted. For instance, although not stated, there would be a procedure for handling an incorrectly prepared company order form when the *customer name* and *customer#* were found not to correspond.

4. Departments and physical locations are ignored in the data flow diagram, except where they appear as sources or sinks. For instance, although the processing of the stock transaction occurs in the stores and the generation of the approved company order occurs in the order department, this information does not appear in the diagram.

5. Although the goods would accompany the dispatch note to PACKING AND DISPATCH, this is not shown on the data flow diagram as it is not a data flow.

The data flow diagram shows a great deal about the flows of data between processes. However, it is important that the contents of data flows and the data stores also be specified precisely. This will be of use when designing files or a database and when writing programs. A tabular representation of the contents of the various data elements appearing in the data flow diagram is shown in Figure 12.8.

Figure 12.8 Table of descriptions of the data flow diagram elements for Kismet

Source/sink
Customer
Credit control manager
Packing and despatch
Accounting

Process
(1) Generate approved company order
(2) Process stock transaction
(3) Make up invoice

Data flow

Customer order
  customer#
  customer name
  [item#
  item quantity]*
  delivery address

Company order
  order#
  order date
  customer#
  customer name
  customer address
  delivery address
  [item#
  item quantity
  item price]*
  total

Company dispatch details
  dispatch#
  order#
  customer#
  customer name
  delivery address
  despatch date
  [item#
  item quantity]*

Company invoice
  invoice#
  invoice date
  customer#
  customer name
  customer address
  order#
  [item#
  item price
  item quantity]*
  subtotal
  sales tax
  discount%
  total payable

Stock request
  order#
  customer#
  customer name
  delivery address
  [item#
  item quantity]*

Customer invoice details
  customer#
  customer name
  customer address
  turnover year to date

Data store

D1 Inventory
  item#
  quantity in stock
  .
  .
  .
  .
  .

D2 Catalogue
  item#
  item price
  .
  .
  .
  .
  .

D3 Customer details
  customer#
  customer name
  customer address
  [delivery address]
  customer balance
  customer credit limit
  turnover year to date
  registration date
  .
  .
  .

D4 Company order store
  see Company order

D5 Order/invoice/dispatch
  see Company order
  and invoice
  and dispatch details

The following points arising from this diagram should be noted:

- The description in the case study does not go into much detail on the contents of each document or file (except in the case of the company order form). These contents are either implied by the nature of the task (*customer address* must be present to dispatch the invoice) or should be found on the 'document description form' prepared by the analyst during investigation.

- Extra detail will be stored for other tasks that are not part of the case as documented. For instance, under inventory there would be reorder levels. This omission does not matter as it would be remedied when the procedures for purchase and reorder of goods were incorporated into a data flow diagram.

- The exact content of the data stores and flows will be recorded in a **data dictionary**. This is often described as a store of data about data. The dictionary is of considerable importance in analysis and design and is covered in Section 12.4.

- The meaning of [. . . .]* is that the contents of the brackets may be repeated an indeterminate number of times.

Data flow diagrams for simple systems are relatively straightforward to design. However, for larger systems it is useful to follow a set of guidelines. These are:

1. Identify the major processes.
2. Identify the major data sources, sinks and stores.
3. Identify the major data flows.
4. Name the data flows, processes, sources, sinks and stores.
5. Draw the diagram.
6. Review the diagram, particularly checking that similar data flows, stores, sources and sinks have the same name and that different data flows and so on have different names.

12.3.2 Data flow diagrams at various levels

Two interconnected questions arise concerning data flow diagrams. These are:

1. What level of discrimination of processes should be shown on the data flow diagram? For instance, in Figure 12.7 the data process *generate approved company order* could be regarded as consisting of a number of subprocesses, such as *accept order*, *check credit limit* and *price order*. Should these be shown as processes?
2. What is the maximum number of processes that should be shown on a data flow diagram?

A major objective of a data flow diagram is its use in communication of the logical process model of the organization. It is difficult to understand a data flow diagram when it has more than seven to nine processes. This is the practical upper limit. If there is a tendency to overstep this then the data flow diagram should be redrawn, with processes that are logically grouped together being replaced by a single process that encompasses them all. The processes are not 'lost' from the model. They should appear on another data flow diagram that shows how this combined process can be exploded into its constituents. These constituents themselves may be complex and can

Figure 12.9 Data flow diagrams at various levels

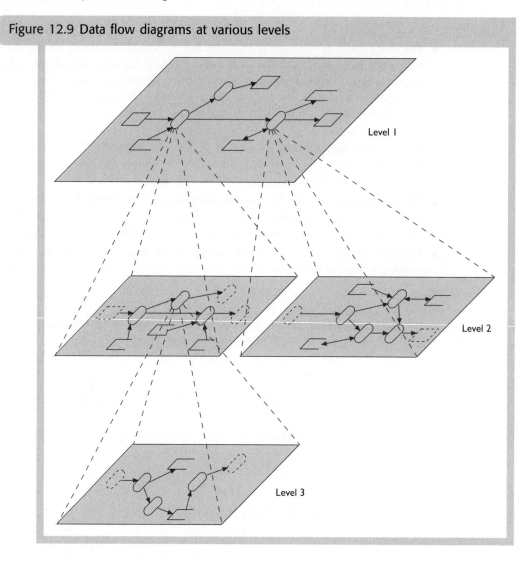

be broken down into linked data processes shown on a data flow diagram at a lower level. This should be repeated until the processes are logically simple: that is, until they cannot be broken down any further. This is illustrated in Figure 12.9.

The generation of levels in data flow diagrams has two other advantages. First, it naturally falls into line with the analyst's approach to top-down decomposition. That is, the analyst considers the major functions and processes first. These are then decomposed into their constituents. The analyst can therefore concentrate on the higher-level data flow diagrams before designing the others. Second, the various levels correspond to the various degrees of detail by which the system is represented. This is useful for the analyst when discussing the results of the analysis with members of the organization. Senior managers are more likely to be interested in a global view as given in a high-level data flow diagram. Other personnel will be concerned with more localized areas but in greater detail.

Kismet case study 12.5

The person responsible for supervising the generation of approved company orders in Kismet will be interested in a lower-level, more detailed explosion of the *generate approved company order* process.

The processes in the data flow diagram for Kismet (Figure 12.7) can be further decomposed. The generation of an approved company order is really a number of tasks:

1. Accept the order.
2. Prepare the company order form.
3. Price the goods.
4. Provisionally calculate the value of the order.
5. Check the creditworthiness of the customer.

This is shown on a level 2 data flow diagram (Figure 12.10). The number 1 task in level 1 is exploded into seven tasks, 1.1–1.7. The inputs and outputs of this exploded chart must match those of the *parent* for which it is the functional decomposition. ▶

Figure 12.10 A level 2 data flow diagram of the Kismet *generate approved company order* process

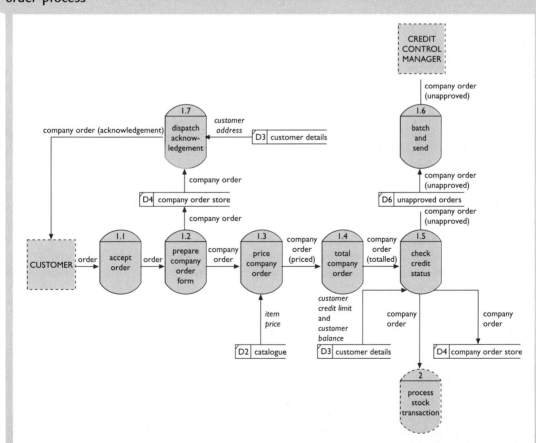

There are two exceptions to this. First, certain local files need not be shown on the parent. In Figure 12.10, the *unapproved orders* store is such a file. It is only used as a temporary repository for the unapproved orders and does not feature in the rest of the system. Second, for the sake of clarity it may be necessary to amalgamate a number of data flows at the parent level. If functional analysis were to be carried out on function number 2, *process stock transaction*, the input/output data flow would be composed of an input flow with *item#* and *quantity in stock* as the data elements and an output with *item#*, *transaction type* and *item quantity* as elements.

If necessary, further analysis of the level 2 diagram could be undertaken by exploding chosen processes to a level 3 diagram.

12.3.3 Design commitments of the data flow diagram approach

It is important to separate the process of analysis from that of design. This may be difficult. The process of analysis goes beyond description, as every case of model building is partly a process of design. Another aspect of design is that the choice of data flows, stores, processes, sources and sinks is just one way of characterizing what is important in an organization's information system. To use these to build a model already commits the analyst to a certain design strategy: that of top-down, reductionist design.

However, within the design implications inherited through the use of structured techniques such as data flow diagrams, there is some separation of analysis from design.

Kismet case study 12.6

In the case of Kismet, the generation of an approved company order follows a certain (unnecessarily repetitive) procedure, which is illustrated in the data flow diagram (Figure 12.10). In an ideal design, it is unlikely that the company order emanating from task 1.2 would be stored in the company order file awaiting the trigger from the successful order vetting (task 1.5) before dispatch of the acknowledgement. Rather, a copy of the approved company order form would be sent to the customer as part of the output of task 1.5.

In analysis, the analyst considers what, logically, *is* done in order to carry out the functions of the organization. In design, the analyst states what, logically, *should* be done for the organization to carry out its functions efficiently and effectively. The data flow diagram, by stripping away the physical aspects of a system and revealing its logic at the appropriate level of detail, makes it easy to see improvements that can be made.

12.3.4 Summary so far

The data flow diagram is an important tool of structured analysis and design. It ensures that a top-down approach is taken. This promotes a logical, as opposed to physical, view of data stores, flows and processes. In this way, no premature commitment to physical aspects of design is made. Eventually, the data stores *may* form part of the file structure or database of the system, and the data processes *may* become the programs or subroutines. The flows will then correspond to the data passed in and out of programs and to and from the file structure or database. However, this can be decided at a later stage.

The levels of data flow diagram correspond to the levels of top-down decomposition and the various levels of detail that management and users will need in order to discuss sensibly the analyst's understanding of processes.

The diagram may also be part of the agreed document provided at the end of analysis. Its non-technical nature means that it can be easily understood by users and agreed upon as a correct analysis of the system. This makes it a powerful communication tool, bridging the gap between analysts and users.

Finally, it makes it easy to sketch out different design alternatives for a future computerized system. How this is done will be covered in Chapter 14 on systems design.

12.4 Data dictionaries

A data dictionary is a store of data about data. It provides information on the structure and use of data in an organization. It is therefore closely connected to the data flow diagram and, as covered in Chapter 13, to the data model. The contents of a typical entry in a data dictionary are given in Figure 12.11.

Figure 12.11 Typical contents of a data dictionary entry

Name:
Included here are all the names by which this data element is known. If there is more than one then these are termed 'aliases'.

Type of data
For example: data flow, data store, data item.

Structure
In the case of a data flow or data store this gives the list of data items, including repeats. If the type of data is a data item its 'picture' may be given – for example. 'AA9999' – together with the range of permissible values.

Usage characteristics:
This details the list of processes that the data flows/data stores interact with. In the case of a data item this list will give the data aggregates which use the item. Information on the data such as the frequency, volume and security issues surrounding the data is often given, as this will aid the designer in deciding on the physical characteristics of the proposed system.

Name: **Type:**
   Invoice   Data flow

   aliases:
      customer invoice
      client invoice

Structure:
   Aggregate: (*invoice#, invoice date, customer#, customer name, order#, [item#, item price,
              item quantity]*, subtotal, sales tax, discount%, total payable*)

Usage characteristics:
   Output process *3 – make up invoice*
   input to sink – *accounts*
   input to sink – *customer*

The data dictionary provides a precise and unambiguous specification of the data elements within the system. It is normally stored on a computer to facilitate cross-referencing between data elements. The data element *order#* referred to in the entry under invoice can easily be cross-referenced to discover that its structure is, for instance, followed by five digits.

It is important that data descriptions held in a data dictionary not be duplicated in several places. This is done so that if a change is made to some aspect of a data element the alteration is made in only one place in the dictionary, thus ensuring the maintenance of consistency.

The data dictionary is used right through the process of analysis to detailed design and into programming as the reference point to which any questions on the structure of data can be directed. Nowadays, computerized data dictionaries, sometimes called **data encyclopedias,** enable a considerable amount of extra information to be held on data, thus increasing the reliance of analysis and design on an adequate data dictionary.

If a table is made out when a data flow diagram is first drawn (as in Figure 12.8), this will provide much of the information for the data dictionary. Along with the data flow diagrams and process specifications (covered in Sections 12.5–12.7) the data dictionary constitutes the logical model of the system.

12.5 Decision tables

The data flow diagram demonstrates the decomposition of the functions performed in an organization into simpler data processes and flows. Some of these processes may be complex in themselves but are not suitable for further decomposition in the data flow diagram.

Kismet case study 12.7

An example of the use of decision tables might be Kismet's procedure for calculating discounts. Although not given previously in the case study, the firm's policy was summarized by the invoice manager to the systems analyst as follows:

Three factors determine the percentage of discount. The first is the total value of the order (we like to encourage our customers to place large single orders rather than smaller multiple orders as it makes delivery and van scheduling easier). The discount is 3% for orders over £4000. If the delivery is within 50 miles of the warehouse, delivery costs are lower and a 2% discount is given, except if the 3% discount for large orders has been granted. In this latter case, only a 1% discount is given if the delivery is within 50 miles. Customers who have made purchases of more than £100,000 over the past 12 months are granted a further 2% discount. These measures are designed to encourage large purchases from local high-turnover retailers. We would like to offer a more targeted discount policy, although this would be more difficult to administer. We hope that one aspect of computerization is that automated discount calculation will help us to give more personalized encouragement to our customers.

The decision table for this policy is shown in Figure 12.12. The conditions that are important for determining the discount are shown in the top left-hand quadrant. In the top right-hand quadrant are the range of entries for these conditions. In this case, a condition applies (Y = yes) or does not (N = no). Note the pattern of the entries.

Figure 12.12 A decision table for Kismet's discount policy

Order > £4,000	Y	Y	Y	Y	N	N	N	N
Delivery < 50 miles	Y	Y	N	N	Y	Y	N	N
Turnover > £100,000	Y	N	Y	N	Y	N	Y	N

Discount									
	0%								X
	1%								
	2%						X	X	
	3%				X				
	4%		X			X			
	5%			X					
	6%	X							

Figure 12.13 The format of a decision table

Conditions being tested	Condition stub	Condition entries
Range of possible actions to be taken	Action stub	Action entries

It makes it easy to see that all eight entries have been included. Each column can be thought of as representing a type of order. For instance, column 3 represents a large order (> £4000), not delivered within 50 miles, from a customer with a turnover of more than £100,000. The action to be taken can be found by following the column down to discover that a discount of 5% (X = action) is to be allowed. This is an example of the general format for decision tables. This format is given in Figure 12.13.

Figure 12.12 is a simple decision table. There are only two possible entries for each condition, Y or N. This is called a **limited-entry decision table**. With three conditions there are $2^3 = 8$ columns; with four conditions there are $2^4 = 16$ columns. If there are n conditions there will be 2^n columns. With a large number of conditions, the decision table becomes very wide: for example, seven conditions leads to $2^7 = 128$ columns. Fortunately, it is often possible to collapse the columns. Wherever two columns differ only to the extent of one entry and the action(s) associated with each column are identical, the effect of the Y or N entry is nil. The two columns can be replaced by one column, which has the Y and the N replaced by a single '–' but is otherwise identical to the columns it replaces. The decision table can be collapsed until no two columns satisfy the pairwise condition stated.

As well as limited-entry tables there are **mixed** or **extended-entry tables**. These are used when there is not a simple value yes or no (true or false) associated with a condition. For instance, there might have been three possible ways of differentiating the size of the order as far as discounting was concerned: < £2000, ≥ £2000 but > £5000 and

$\geq £5000$. These three entries would appear in the condition entry, and the condition 'order size' would appear in the condition stub.

Finally, there are a range of special actions that may be present in the decision table. These concern the way that the user of the decision table moves around the table or to another table. Perhaps the most useful is the **GOTO** action, which causes the execution of another decision table. This is used when the types of action and conditions applicable to a case divide neatly into exclusive classes depending on the value of some condition. Care should be taken when using this action, as a number of tables interconnected by **GOTO**s can give the appearance of logical spaghetti.

Kismet case study 12.8

The variations on the basic table are illustrated in Figure 12.14. This is the revealed discount policy of Kismet's competitor, Hardy Ltd.

Figure 12.14 Decision tables illustrating Hardy's discount policy

Table A

Retail store chain	Y	Y	Y	Y	Y	Y	Y	Y	N
Order size	<£2,000	<£2,000	£2,000 to less than £5,000	£2,000 to less than £5,000	£5,000 to less than £10,000	£5,000 to less than £10,000	>£10,000	>£10,000	–
One delivery	Y	N	Y	N	Y	N	Y	N	–
Discount 4%		X							
6%				X					
9%	X								
10%						X		X	
11%			X						
15%					X		X		
Note to manager							X	X	
GO TO table B									X

Table B

Order > £3,000	Y	Y	Y	Y	N	N	N
Order > £5,000	Y	Y	N	N	N	N	N
Delivery < 50 miles	Y	N	Y	N	Y	N	N
Turnover > £100,000	–	–	–	–	–	Y	N
Discount 0%							X
3%						X	
4%					X		
5%		X		X			
9%	X		X				
Send note to manager	X	X					

In the case of an order from a retail electrical store chain a discount of 4% is allowed if the order is less than £2000, 6% if the order is between £2000 and £5000 and 10% if the order is £5000 or more. There is a further discount of 5% if there is only one delivery address. A note of the invoice is sent to the manager if the total amount invoiced is greater than £10,000. With all other types of customer, a 4% discount is given if the order is more than £3000. A 5% discount is also allowed if the delivery is within 50 miles. 3% is allowed if no other discounts have been made and the customer has an annual turnover with Hardy of more than £100,000. A note of any invoice in excess of £5000 is sent to the manager.

Decision tables are a valuable tool in analysis. Within the general format of the table, conditions are specified unambiguously and separated from actions, which are clearly stated. The declarative style of the table accords well with the way that certain processes are considered as the implementation of a set of conditions.

The straightforward, non-technical character of the tables makes them a valuable communication tool between analysts and users in checking the analyst's understanding of a process. In design, the tables can be used to specify the requirements of a program. They facilitate analyst–programmer communication.

Although it takes intelligence to construct a decision table, it requires a very limited repertoire of mental abilities to use one. They are therefore in a form suitable for incorporation into a computer program. There are programs that accept a decision table as input and produce program code to implement the table as output. The program runs interactively with users by requiring answers to basic questions. These questions correspond to the conditions.

Finally, decision tables cover in a methodical way the totality of possible combinations of conditions that might apply in a particular case and so can be used to check on the completeness and consistency of a policy that involves the taking of different actions when different conditions are satisfied.

Kismet case study 12.9

In order to appreciate the completeness and consistency of a policy, consider the following example:

Kismet's management has decided that computerization offers it the opportunity to offer a more complex and targeted discount policy. It has decided to offer its customers a differential discount depending on whether the order is large (over £5000), whether the year-to-date turnover of the customer is large (over £100,000), whether the order is to be delivered to one address only and whether the delivery, or deliveries, is within 50 miles. After many hours of discussion, the management has arrived at the following policy:

1. A high-priority order is defined to be one from a high-turnover customer who requires a large order or who is using only one delivery address.

2. A low-priority order is defined to be one that is neither large nor from a customer with a high turnover.

3. If the order is large and to be delivered to only one address a discount of 10% is allowed, with an additional discount of 5% if that address is within 50 miles.

459

Figure 12.15 The use of a decision table to illustrate inconsistency

		H	H	H	H					H	H			L	L	L	L
Large order		Y	Y	Y	Y	Y	Y	Y	Y	N	N	N	N	N	N	N	N
Large turnover		Y	Y	Y	Y	N	N	N	N	Y	Y	Y	Y	N	N	N	N
One address		Y	Y	N	N	Y	Y	N	N	Y	Y	N	N	Y	Y	N	N
Within 50 miles		Y	N	Y	N	Y	N	Y	N	Y	N	Y	N	Y	N	Y	N
Actions																	
Give	Rule 3	15	10			15	10										
	Rule 4			≤5	≤5			≤5	≤5			≤5	≤5			≤5	≤5
	Rule 5									10	10	5	5				
percent	Rule 6	≥5	≥5	≥5	≥5					≥5	≥5						
	Rule 7													3	3		
discount	Rule 8							5	5								
	Rule 9	≥10		≥10		≥10		≥10									
TOTAL		15	10	(a)	5	15	10	(b)	5	10	10	5	5	3	3	(c)	(c)

Notes

H = High-priority order (Rule 1)

L = Low-priority order (Rule 2)

(a) Rules 4, 6 and 9 are inconsistent

(b) Rules 4, 8 and 9 are inconsistent

(c) There is insufficient information to assign a discount.

4. No order that is to be delivered to multiple addresses may receive more than 5% discount.

5. However, an order that is not large from a customer with a turnover of more than £100,000 should receive a 10% discount except in as far as this conflicts with rule 4, in which case they will obtain the maximum discount applicable under that rule.

6. High-priority orders are to be given at least 5% discount.

7. Low-priority orders are to be given a 3% discount if there is only one delivery address.

8. Orders from customers with a turnover of less than £100,000 to be delivered to multiple addresses shall receive a discount of 5% if the order is large, irrespective of whether the delivery is within 50 miles or not.

9. All large orders that are to be delivered within a 50-mile radius are to receive at least 10% discount.

10. All applicable discounts are to be totalled.

This policy has been analysed in Figure 12.15. Although this does not exactly follow the format of Figure 12.13, it is, in principle, a decision table separating conditions and actions. The effects of each of the rules on each of the types of order (each type of order corresponds to one column in the condition entry quadrant) are shown in the action entry quadrant. The total effect of all rules on a type of order is shown, where possible, in the TOTAL row. For example, column 2 corresponds to a large order from a customer with a turnover in excess of £100,000. The order has one delivery address, which is not within the 50-mile zone surrounding the Kismet warehouse. It is judged to be a high-priority order (rule 1) and so is to be accorded at least 5% discount (rule 6). The order satisfies rule 2 and so is given a 10% discount.

It is clear that the policy is inconsistent. Notes (a) and (b) of Figure 12.15 indicate where the inconsistency arises. This could be eliminated by removing rule 9. It would be the analyst's responsibility to point out to management the inconsistency and advise on possible ways of eliminating it. An inconsistent policy cannot be incorporated into a program. It is ultimately the responsibility of Kismet to decide on the policy. It is a business decision. Normally, all the analyst would do is to comment on the formal properties of the policy.

In summary, there are a number of advantages and disadvantages in the use of decision tables to represent the links between conditions and actions.

Advantages

- They provide a clear tabular representation linking conditions with actions and so act as a communication tool.
- The declarative style corresponds to the way that many processes are understood as conditions that determine actions.
- They ensure an exhaustive coverage of all possible cases.
- They can be used to investigate inconsistency and redundancy in a set of rules.
- They are easy to follow in operation.
- They can be incorporated into program specifications.

Disadvantages

- They can become very large and unwieldy with large numbers of conditions.
- They are only suitable for representing processes where there is little interleaving between the evaluation of conditions and the execution of actions.

12.6 Logic flowcharts

Decision tables are one way of clearly representing the logic of a process and are most suitable when only few actions need to be undertaken as a result of the evaluation of a (possibly complex) set of conditions. If, though, the process is one that involves intermingling the evaluation of conditions with the execution of various actions, then the proliferation of **GOTO** statements to subsidiary decision tables makes it difficult to follow the logic of the process. Logic flowcharts overcome this difficulty. The symbols used in logic flowcharts are shown in Figure 12.16.

Figure 12.16 Basic symbols used in the preparation of logic flowcharts

Flowline
Used to indicate the direction of movement between other symbols: that is, control

Terminator
Used to indicate the start and finish of the flowchart

Process or **Action**
Used to illustrate the occurrence of any process: for example, add I to the running total

Decision or **Question**
Used to distinguish between two states of affairs: as a consequence the flow of control is directed one way or another. There are only two possible exits to a decision box, YES and NO

Kismet case study 12.10

The use of logic flowcharts can be illustrated by the representation of the following example. It concerns the approval of orders in the credit control section of Kismet. The procedure, stated here, can be regarded as a fuller version of the summary that appeared previously in the Case Study 12.1. The additions mainly concern the procedure to be followed in the case of error discovery and the maintenance of a running total of the value of approved orders. The order set has been priced and valued. Now is the time for credit approval.

> The credit control clerk processes a stack of order sets for which provisional values have been calculated and inserted. The presence of the *customer#* and *customer name* are first checked. If either is absent then the customer file is consulted and the missing entry inserted. If there is no reference to the customer in the file the order set is sent to the credit control manager. If the number and name are found not to match then the order 4 set is sent back to the order-processing section together with an internal company P22 form for investigation. In all other cases, the *order value* is added to the *current balance* and compared with the *credit limit*. If this has been exceeded, the order set is sent to the credit control manager along with the customer records. If the order has passed these tests, the order set is stamped 'OK approved' and put in the out tray. At the end of the stack, the contents of the out tray are returned to the order-processing section, and the total value of all approved orders is entered on the daily totals sheet.

The flowchart is shown in Figure 12.17. The flow lines indicate flows of control, *not* flows of data or documents. When it is said that there is a flow of control between points A and B, all this means is that after the operation at A has been carried out the operation at B is carried out. Nothing passes between points A and B.

Figure 12.17 The logic flowchart for credit approval in Kismet

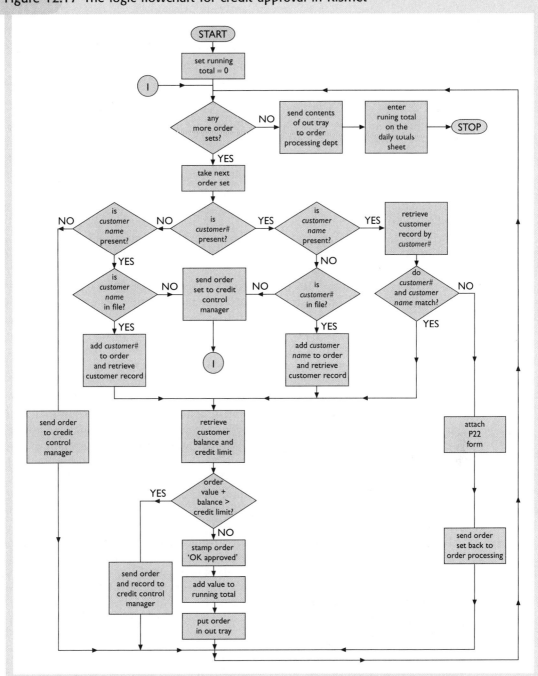

The following conditions apply to flowcharts:

- Each question or decision box has exactly two exits: one corresponding to 'yes' or 'true' and the other to 'no' or 'false'.

- All flows of control must end in a decision box, action box or terminator and must always ensure that the process eventually stops.

- Generally, the flowchart is designed so that the flow of control goes from the top of the page downwards.

The flowchart in Figure 12.17 follows these principles. The repetitious nature of the processing of one order after another is accomplished by directing the flow of control from the end of the approval process, as applied to one order, back to the top of the chart. There, a test is performed to establish whether there are any more orders in the stack before proceeding. A running total is maintained.

Flowcharts have several advantages. Their pictorial representation makes them easy to follow and understand – the different paths through the process are obvious at a glance. They can therefore be used as a basis for agreement between the analyst and the user on the correctness of the analyst's understanding. They may also form part of the firm's procedures manual.

Flowcharts can be given for high or low levels of analysis. For instance, to answer the simple question 'is the customer name in the file?' requires the execution of a number of actions and the consideration of further questions. If the records in the file are ordered by *customer#*, it implies the following type of procedure for the clerk. Go to the filing cabinet, start at the first record, compare the *customer name* with the target *name*, if identical, stop – the *customer name* is in the file, otherwise carry out the procedure on the next record, and so on. The level of the chart is generally high at the analysis stage, and such low-level specifications are ignored.

Logic flowcharts can also be used in the design stage as a way of specifying a procedure precisely. If it is intended that a program be written from this specification, it is called a **program logic flowchart**. The flowchart will be presented generally at a much more detailed level. Variable names will be included, procedures for establishing counts will be outlined, and so on. The presence of the decision box encourages the use of the **GOTO** programming structure, so program flowcharts may lead to programming techniques that result in non-structured programs. This may be a reason to discourage their use at the design stage.

In summary, the main advantages and disadvantages in the use of logic flowcharts are:

Advantages

- They provide a pictorial representation of a series of actions and are therefore easy to understand and natural to follow.

- They are used in procedures manuals to indicate the sequences of actions that are to be followed in carrying out a task – for example, an audit.

- They are very good at representing cases where there is an interleaving of actions and the evaluation of conditions (compare this with decision tables).

- They may be used to specify programs to programmers.

Disadvantages

- They encourage the use of **GOTO** statements if used in program specifications in design. This may lead to programs that have a logic that is difficult to unravel.

- They force the developer to work at a very low level of detail at an early stage of the project, therefore losing the benefit of the top-down approach previously advocated.

- They are difficult and time-consuming to alter once drawn.

12.7 Structured English

As well as using decision tables or logic flowcharts, procedures can be represented through the use of structured English. This also has the effect of imposing a structure on the specification, which encourages the use of structured programming. Structured English is a precise, highly restricted subset of the natural English language. There is no accepted standard for structured English, but all usages have a number of features in common. The vocabulary of the language is restricted to:

- Precise verbs phrased in the imperative mood. All adjectives, adverbs and words with vague or ambiguous meanings are avoided. Complex sentence structures involving subordinate clauses are broken down into their atomic constituents. Irrelevant phrases are dropped. For instance, the sentence 'The large document containing the particular details on the customer should now be edited carefully by the clerk making sure that all entries are made clearly with an indelible pen' would probably be reduced to 'edit document containing customer details'.

- References to items of data should use the same terms as applied in the data flow diagram and the data dictionary.

- Certain reserved words are used for revealing the logical structure of processes.

The logic of any process can be described by using three structures (Figure 12.18):

1. **A sequential block of statements:** The statements should be concise and contain a verb and object. For example:

    (a) Compute total
    (b) Set sales tax equal to total multiplied by sales tax rate
    (c) Set total equal to total plus sales tax
    (d) Compute discount
    (e) Set net total equal to total minus discount
    (f) Write net total on invoice.

2. **Decision structures:** These are used when it is required that one sequence of operations be carried out if a condition is satisfied and another set if it is not satisfied. The structure takes two forms:

    (a) The two-way decision:

    > **IF** ⟨condition⟩
    >   **THEN** ⟨block-1⟩
    >   **ELSE** ⟨block-2⟩

    where the **ELSE** is not compulsory. For example:

    > **IF** total > credit limit **THEN** refer to credit control manager
    >   **ELSE** stamp 'OK approved'

Figure 12.18 The logical form of structured English

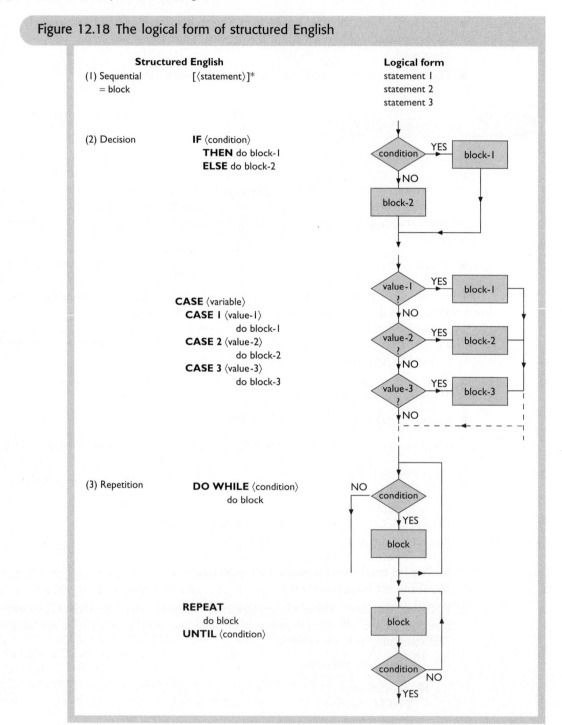

(b) The multi-way decision:

CASE ⟨variable⟩
CASE 1 ⟨value-1⟩
    do block-1
CASE 2 ⟨value-2⟩
    do block-2
CASE 3 ⟨value-3⟩
    do block-3

For example:

CASE invoice value
  CASE 1 invoice value < £2000
      add 1% to discount percent
  CASE 2 £2000 ≤ invoice value < £5000
      add 3% to discount percent
  CASE 3 invoice value ≥ £5000
      add 6% to discount percent

3. **Repetition structures**: These are used where a process is repeated until some condition is met. There are two forms of repetition statement:

DO WHILE ⟨condition⟩
  do block

and

REPEAT
  do block
UNTIL ⟨condition⟩

In the former, the test as to whether the condition is satisfied occurs before the loop is entered (so the loop will not be traversed at all if the condition fails first time). In the latter, the test occurs after the loop has been traversed, implying that the loop is traversed at least once. For example:

DO WHILE stack of invoices is not empty
  get next invoice
  add invoice total to running total

Structured English representations of processes may be a little difficult to follow for the uninitiated, particularly if there is a high degree of internal nesting. However, as mentioned at the beginning of this section they do have the attraction of encouraging structured coding of programs.

Whether decision tables, a logic flowchart or structured English is chosen as the representation of a process depends on its nature. Complex sets of conditions determining few actions with little iteration suggest a decision table representation. Otherwise a logic flowchart or structured English representation will be suitable, the choice being the result of the trade-off between diagrammatic clarity and the wish to encourage structured code in the design stage.

Kismet case study 12.11

The example now discussed illustrates the use of structured English to specify a process. It concerns the task of pricing the Kismet company order sets and is taken from a statement supplied by the clerk responsible for pricing the orders. It covers error cases not given in the case study.

I get the stack of orders to price from the supervisor. I first of all tidy the pile and then go through the orders one by one until I have finished. After this I put the stack of priced orders in the credit control section's in tray. I carefully price each item in turn by consulting the sales catalogue. Sometimes I cannot find the item because it is a new product and I then have to look at the supplement. If I have no luck there I just put a big query mark by it on the form. After I have finished I put the order in the out tray.

The structured English version is given in Figure 12.19(a). Note how the rambling description of the process, as given by the order pricing clerk, is transformed into a set of precise statements.

The indenting is important as it gives a clear indication of the structure of the logic governing the process. Statements may also be nested, as shown in the example.

Figure 12.19 The structured English representation of the pricing process for Kismet: (a) structured English without ENDIF and ENDDO; (b) structured English with ENDIF and ENDDO

468

To illustrate the scope of an **IF** statement or a **DO** statement it is sometimes clearer to use **ENDDO, ENDIF** and **ENDCASE** statements. These fill a role analogous to brackets in elementary arithmetic. The expression $6 - 3 \times 7 + 3$ can be made much clearer by the insertion of brackets: $(6 - (3 \times (7 + 3)))$. In fact, in many cases the brackets are necessary to indicate the precise meaning of the formula. Similarly, **ENDDO, ENDIF** and **ENDCASE** fulfil the role analogous to the right-hand bracket.

The structured English version of the Kismet pricing clerk's routine using **ENDDO** and **ENDIF** statements is shown in Figure 12.19(b).

Summary

The purpose of systems analysis is to arrive at an understanding of a system that is sufficient to design a computerized replacement. This replacement may involve substantial redesign and the integration of physically disparate manual systems. In order to achieve this, a structured approach is taken to systems analysis. This chapter was concerned with structured process analysis and modelling. Its main features are:

■ a commitment to a 'top-down' decomposition in which data and processes are analysed into their constituent parts;

■ an emphasis on the development of a model of the system as a prerequisite for successful design; and

■ an assumption that developing an information system is largely a technical exercise.

The main tool used is the data flow diagram, which models the data flows between data processes, stores and sinks. This diagram reveals the logical model at various levels of detail, depending on the degree of decomposition and the intended recipient of the diagram. The nature of the processes is specified via decision tables, logic flowcharts or structured English, all of which have their relative strengths and limitations. The data dictionary maintains information on the nature of the data itself. The entire repertoire of techniques is aimed at deriving a logical model, independent of physical commitments, and at producing documentation that is precise, thus facilitating communication between users, management, programmers and the analyst.

Much attention has been given to the analysis of the organization into its functional components, the further breakdown of these into individual processes, the charting of the data flows between them and their representation by various tools. What has been missing from the analysis is the treatment of the data stores and the nature of the data itself. Some would regard this as perhaps the most important feature of analysis, and it is to this that the next chapter is devoted.

Review questions

1. What are the scope and objectives of systems analysis?

2. When considering a complex integrated system, why is it important to use a methodical approach to systems analysis and design?

3. What benefits are to be obtained in analysis by initially focusing on processes and functions at a general rather than a detailed level?

4. What are the advantages and limitations of:
   (a) decision tables
   (b) logic flowcharts
   (c) structured English
   as representation tools for processes?

5. What are the advantages and limitations of manual systems flowcharts?

6. Explain the purpose of a data dictionary.

Exercises

1. Can a situation represented by a logic flowchart, decision table or structured English always be represented without loss of information by all three? What determines the choice of method of process specification?

2. 'There is little difference between data flow diagrams and document flowcharts – they both represent the flow of data between processes.' Do you agree?

3. 'At the stage of analysis an understanding of the existing system is more important than technical computer expertise, and as the tools of analysis are relatively easy to understand, it is more effective if existing users carry out the analysis and computer experts are brought in only at the design stage.' Do you agree?

4. 'By concentrating on formal data and processes, the analyst ignores the fact that much useful information in an organization is of an informal nature – opinions, hunches and qualitative approximations. The analyst is therefore bound to produce an inadequate analysis and design of a computerized information system.' What is to be said for and against this view?

5. A large lending library handles book issues, returns and enquiries and sends out notices regarding overdue books to borrowers. All procedures are currently manual. The library deals with a large number of postal and telephone transactions. The majority of its books are stored in underground stacks. The library thus needs a fast response information system and to this end has purchased a database management system.

   Initial analysis indicates that the following information has been stored on books, borrowers and loans in the current manual system:
   - For each book: book number, author, title.
   - For each borrower: ID number, name, address.
   - For each loan of a book to a borrower: date due for return.
   - A record of books reserved for potential borrowers is also maintained.

   The database is to be designed to support the following functions currently carried out manually:
   - *Book issue processing*: On receipt of a request for a loan the librarian makes an enquiry to establish whether the book is held by the library and is available (that is, not on loan). If the book is not held, then that information is given to the potential borrower by a note.

      If the book is held but is on loan the potential borrower is also informed, a note that the book is to be reserved on return is made, and it is established by enquiry whether the book is overdue or not. If it is overdue, a note is sent to the current borrower pointing out the overdue status of the loan and that a request for the book has been made. If the book is directly available then it is issued to the potential borrower and details of this loan, including the date due for return, are stored.

- *Book return processing*: On receipt of a returned book, the librarian cancels the loan and makes an enquiry to establish whether the book is reserved. If it is reserved, then it is issued to the reserver and the reserve note is cancelled. Otherwise, the book is returned to the stack.

- *Enquiry processing*: There are two types of enquiry:
  (a) Given the name of the borrower, establish what books he/she has on loan and when they are due for return.
  (b) Given the name of the book, establish which borrower, if any, has the book and the date due for return.

- *Overdue processing*: When books become two weeks overdue, a notice is sent out requesting their return. A similar note is sent every two weeks until return.

  (a) Draw a high-level combined data flow diagram for the processes.
  (b) Draw an exploded data flow diagram for each of the processes.

6. The daily invoicing routine for an invoice clerk is as follows. At the beginning of the day the stack of sales orders with their associated dispatch notes is taken from the in tray and processed. The details of each order are checked against the details of the relevant customer account and a discount is calculated. A customer in the trade is allowed 15% off the list price. There is also a special 5% discount for any customer who has been ordering regularly for 2 years, provided that the customer has not received the trade discount. Any order over £1000 is allowed a bulk discount of 10% off the list price in addition to any other discounts. If the total to be invoiced exceeds the customer's credit limit, a note is sent to the manager prior to dispatch of the invoice. When all invoices have been dispatched, a note of the total invoiced is sent to the manager.

   (a) Draw a logic flowchart illustrating the day's procedure.
   (b) Represent the above by using structured English.

7. Design a manual systems flowchart to illustrate a procedure that Kismet might use to handle return of goods. This flowchart should be compatible with Figure 12.3.

8. The following is an account of the manual operations that occur at the head office of a chain of supermarkets:

   Each supermarket submits a daily cash report plus supporting documentation to the head office by post. This is passed from the mail room to the area manager. The area manager's staff carry out checks on the arithmetic of the cash reports and on submitted bank deposit slips and petty cash vouchers. All of these documents are then passed to the cashier's department after any queries have been reconciled.

   Each day's cash report is summarized and entered into a cash analysis book in the cashier's department. This cash analysis book forms part of the main cash book into which weekly totals are entered. At the end of each week, the cashier's department reconciles the cash book with the bank pass sheets. The cash reports are then sent to the accounts department.

   Every week, each supermarket also submits, by post, records of deliveries made by suppliers together with other stock movement details. These are sent to the area manager's office, where the unit costs and sales prices are entered on the document and delivery records. The complete set of documents is then passed to the accounts department. The area manager's office also receives delivery sheets sent from the company's own warehouses. These are for goods supplied to the supermarkets. These sheets are priced at cost and at selling prices before being submitted to the accounts department.

The accounts department receives the stock movement forms, the direct and internal delivery sheets and the cash reports. The department then prepares a monthly report for each supermarket at cost and selling prices.

Draw a document systems flowchart with any necessary narrative showing the various document flows. (Note that many temporary and permanent files are implied in the description without being explicitly stated.)

9. When a library first receives a book from a publisher it is sent, together with the accompanying delivery note, to the library desk. Here the delivery note is checked against a file of books ordered. If no order can be found to match the note, a letter of enquiry is sent to the publishers. If a matching order is found, a catalogue note is prepared from the details on the validated delivery note. The catalogue note, together with the book, is sent to the registration department. The validated delivery note is sent to the accounts department, where it is stored. On receipt of an invoice from the publisher, the accounts department checks its store of delivery notes. If the corresponding delivery note is found then an instruction to pay the publisher is made, and subsequently a cheque is sent. If no corresponding delivery note is found, the invoice is stored in a pending file.

Draw a data flow diagram for this information.

10. As a systems analyst, you have been commissioned by the ABC Company to computerize its sales order processing. It is believed by the board of ABC that the attractiveness of its product to customers can be increased by ensuring that all customers receive a discount off the list price of ABC's products. It is further intended that a maximum discount of 25% on any transaction should not be exceeded. To this end, it has isolated the following customer/transaction features:

- regular customers
- cash transactions
- bulk order
- trade customers.

The board suggests the following policy, where (all discounts are off the list price and are to be added together):

(a) Those customers who are trade receive 15% discount, provided that the transaction is a bulk order; otherwise, the discount is 12%.
(b) Non-trade customers are allowed 5% discount, provided that the order is bulk.
(c) Cash transactions receive 13% discount if trade; if not a 10% discount.
(d) All regular customers are allowed 10% discount unless the total discount allowable under rules (a), (b) and (c) is greater than 10%, in which case the greater discount will apply.

By means of a decision table, advise the board as to the suitability of its discount policy in the light of its stated aims.

11. A stack of student records, ordered by *student#*, contains up to five records on each student covering the student's exam results in one or more of the following – accounting, economics, law, maths, systems analysis. A clerk is required to process these records and must produce an average for each student, which is then entered on a summary

sheet. Not all students take all five subjects. The clerk also computes an average mark for each exam for each of the five subjects and enters it on the summary sheet.

(a) Produce a structured English specification of a suitable process to achieve these aims.

(b) Represent this process by a logic flowchart.

12. A firm pursues the following discount policy on its products (all discount being offered as a percentage of advertised price).

(a) Those customers ordering more than ten items receive at least a 1% discount.

(b) Those customers who are not regular customers receive at most a 2% discount.

(c) All those regular customers who order more than ten items receive a 2% discount plus an additional 1% discount if they pay cash.

(d) Any person paying cash and who is either a regular customer or orders more than ten items (but not both) is to receive a 2% discount.

(e) All customers who satisfy just one of the following conditions – ordering more than ten items, paying cash or being a regular customer – receive a 1% discount in as far as this does not conflict with rules (a)–(d).

(f) Any customer not covered by the preceding rules receives no discount.

Using decision tables, evaluate the above rules as to their consistency, comprehensiveness and redundancy. Can the rules be replaced by a simpler set?

CASE STUDY 12

Kemswell Theatre

The Kemswell Theatre is a small regionally based theatre in south-east England. For most of the year the theatre stages plays, but it also screens cinema films, hosts visiting speakers and stages musical events. The theatre accepts postal and telephone bookings for its forthcoming performances up to six months in advance. About half of the bookings are directly from the public, the remainder being from agencies. The theatre employs twenty-five people, whose functions range from set design and special effects through to marketing, box office and accounting functions.

When a member of the public makes a booking by telephone either a credit card number is taken and the booking is firmly made, or a reservation for the seat is taken. In the latter case, the member of the public must collect and pay for the ticket at least half an hour before the performance.

In the case of agencies, on receipt of a block booking request by phone or mail, the theatre runs a credit check on the agency account and makes out a confirmation note for those requested seats that are still available.

This is sent to the agency as both a confirmation of booking and an invoice. At the end of each month, the theatre sends a statement of account to each agency.

Half an hour before the performance starts, all those seats that have been reserved by the public but have not been collected are released for general sale. The theatre also receives enquiries on seat availability from both agencies and the public.

1. Draw a data flow diagram illustrating the data flows, processes and stores necessary to carry out the invoicing, enquiry and booking facilities of the theatre.

2. For each data flow and data store, illustrate the structure of the data concerned.

Recommended reading

Avison D., Wood-Harper A.T., Vidgen R. and Wood R. (1997). *Multiview*, reissued 2nd edn. Oxford: McGraw-Hill

This book applies the structured techniques covered in this chapter to a case study. The approach is integrated with other approaches, particularly data analysis as covered in Chapter 13.

Bowman K. (2003). *Systems Analysis: A Beginner's Guide*. Palgrave Macmillan

This provides a helpful introduction to the topic of systems analysis. Concepts are illustrated by case studies that run through the book.

Cutts J. (1997). *Structured Systems Analysis and Design Methodology*, 3rd edn. Oxford: Blackwell Scientific Publications

This is a standard text on structured systems analysis and design. It is comprehensive, clear and suitable for a detailed understanding of structured methods.

De Marco T. (1980). *Structured Analysis: Systems Specifications*. (Yourdon) Prentice Hall

Deeks D. (2002). *An Introduction to System Analysis Techniques*, 2nd edn. Addison-Wesley

A good all-round introduction to the analysis of data and processes in both structured and object-oriented paradigms.

Gane C. and Sarson T. (1979). *Structured Systems Analysis: Tools and Techniques*. Prentice Hall

The books by both De Marco and Gane and Sarson are classics in the application of structured techniques to systems analysis and design. Both are designed for the professional analyst yet are readable by those without an extensive computer science background.

Kendall K. and Kendall J. (2002). *Systems Analysis and Design*, 5th edn. Prentice Hall

An accessible and well-illustrated book that covers the topics of data flow diagrams and data dictionaries particularly well.

Chapter 13

Data analysis and modelling

Learning outcomes

On completion of this chapter, you should be able to:

- Compare different approaches to data modelling
- Carry out entity–relationship modelling
- Explain the process of normalization of data
- Identify the linkages between process modelling and data modelling.

Introduction

The data flow diagram shows the data processes and the flows of data between them but does little to represent the contents of the data store. The trend towards the use of integrated databases in business information systems means that the analysis and design of the database is an important stage in the systems life cycle. In this chapter, entity–relationship modelling is introduced to derive a data model of the organization. The resulting data model is 'fine-tuned' through normalization. Finally, the adequacy of this model is tested against the functions that it will be required to service. The aim is to provide a data model that leads to an effective database design, which is sufficient to satisfy the organization's data processing and information needs. The latter part of the chapter deals with the interrelationship between data modelling and process modelling.

13.1 Top-down versus bottom-up approaches to data modelling

A bottom-up approach to designing the data store involves extracting data fields as indicated on the document description forms. These are the forms that the analyst uses to specify the data content of existing documents in the system. Any extra data elements that might be required as inputs to processes that are new to the system are then added. These data elements are then grouped into records. It is quite likely that each of the original documents in the manual system gives rise to a record. For instance, a company order form might give rise to a record, the fields of which are *order#, order date, customer#, customer name, [item1#*, [item1 quantity]*. . . .* (Note: we continue the previous practice of abbreviating *order number* to *order#*, etc.) These records form the basis of files. There is a record for each order, and the collection of these is the order file.

Decisions are then made on the medium for each file, on the way the file is to be organized and on the indexes needed to retrieve the information for an application. This approach to analysis and design is called **bottom-up** because the system is developed from the basic building blocks – the data fields – upwards through the records and files.

This approach is adequate if small systems that require little or no internal integration are to be designed. However, if there are a large number of fields, which are shared between many applications, it becomes increasingly difficult to design the system without repeating the same data fields unnecessarily.

Kismet case study 13.1

This issue of repeating data fields can be made by using an example from Kismet. A bottom-up approach leads to the design of a stock file that contains stock records having as fields *item#*, *item description*, *quantity held*, etc. This is the responsibility of the stores department. There is also a catalogue file of records containing fields such as *item#*, *item description*, *price*, etc. This is the responsibility of the sales department. Each time a new item is entered on the stock file it needs to be entered on the catalogue file, and each time a description is altered on one it needs to be altered on the other.

One solution to the problem of repeating data fields is to design a program that will take the contents of one file and reconcile them with the other. However, this is a piecemeal solution to a problem that has been created by designing the data store in a piecemeal fashion to satisfy each of the applications separately.

A deeper problem with this approach occurs if substantial redesign of the system is required. Here, the existing documentation is not a good guide to the final data store contents. It is difficult to decide on the fields required at the outset and the extent to which they are to be shared between applications.

What is needed is a way of developing the data store for the organization so that it does not suffer from the limitations of the bottom-up approach. Data analysis using **top-down** data modelling achieves this. This approach leaves physical design considerations until the last available opportunity in the analysis and design cycle. If the logical rather than physical structure of the data is considered, the analyst is not likely to be sidetracked by details on sequencing of records or indexes on files. In the spirit of decomposition associated with structured techniques, a top-down approach to data analysis first considers the types of object on which the organization would wish to keep data and the relationships between them. This is followed by a consideration of the kinds of data to be kept on these objects and only at a later stage how this is to be physically stored in the computer system.

There are other reasons for taking this approach to data analysis. The functions for which data is used in an organization are likely to change over time, although the structure of the data itself may remain constant. For instance, different types of report may need to be drawn from the data from one year to the next. The data structure can be seen to be the fixed element and the functions as dependent on it. If this is assumed then it becomes clear that to design a data store that satisfies the temporary functional contingencies of the time will be unsatisfactory when these change. It seems more sensible to design the data store in such a way that it mirrors or models the structure of the objects and relationships within the organization and also the data held on these.

Integrated databases and the programs that interact with them (database management systems) have been explained fully in Chapter 8 on databases. It is important to realize that many commercial database systems allow the database to be defined by providing a high-level logical model of the data structure. The storage structure details are (largely) controlled by the database management system. The outcome of top-down entity–relationship data modelling provides such a suitable model.

13.2 Entity–relationship modelling

The fundamental assumption behind entity–relationship modelling is that an organization's data structure can be modelled with the use of just three distinct sorts of object. These are as follows.

13.2.1 Entity type

An entity type is a type of thing that is capable of an independent existence and on which the organization may wish to hold data. This is the key characteristic of an entity type. For instance, the entity type **EMPLOYEE** is the type of thing on which a payroll department may wish to keep data such as *employee#* and *date of birth*. The entity type is an abstract concept of which there are particular entity occurrences. It is on these occurrences, strictly, that data is held. An example of the entity type **EMPLOYEE** is the man called 'Tom Yorke' by his work colleagues and 'father' by his daughter. Entity types may also have as their occurrences documents, such as the entity type **ORDER**, or more abstract occurrences, such as the entity type **ACADEMIC COURSE** (it is not possible to see, touch or feel a BA in business studies). To reiterate, if an organization wishes to keep data on a type of thing that has an independent existence, then it should be regarded as an entity type.

13.2.2 Relationship

The entity types applicable to an organization may bear some relationship to one another. For example, the entity type **EMPLOYEE** will bear some relationship to the entity type **DEPARTMENT** because the structure of the organization requires each employee to be a member of a department. Not all entity types will bear relationships to other entity types – the entity type **ORDER** will not have any special relationship with **EMPLOYEE**, for instance. The relationship between an employee and the department of which he/she is a member will be called the 'membership' relationship – any other meaningful name could have been used. Such relationships exist (in reality), and therefore questions are often asked concerning them, such as 'Which department does Tom Yorke belong to?' or 'Who belongs to the stores department?' This suggests that relationships between entity types form an important feature of an organization, one that is worth modelling.

13.2.3 Attribute

The entity types that are deemed applicable to an organization also have attributes. These can be thought of as properties. The entity type **EMPLOYEE** has the attributes *name*, *employee#*, *date of birth*, *sex*, and so on. For a particular occurrence of the type **EMPLOYEE**, say the man Tom Yorke, these attributes have the values *Thomas Edward*

Yorke, 3123, 7 October 1968, male. The man, Tom Yorke, will have other properties, such as inside leg measurement, colour of eyes and passport number, but only some of these will be relevant to the entity type **EMPLOYEE** and so be attributes of that entity type. Each entity occurrence of an entity type must be separately identifiable by some attribute. This attribute is called the **key attribute**. The key attribute of **EMPLOYEE** would be *employee#*. This is because each *employee#* will identify one and only one employee. Two employees could not have the same *employee#*. If they could, then *employee#* would not be a key attribute.

The use of the categories entity, relationship and attribute is one way of viewing the world, or in this case the organization. Although these terms carry no physical implications about the way that data will be physically represented in the computer, it is often the case that a direct correspondence will eventually be set up. The entity type will be represented by a record type. The attributes will be represented by fields of the record type. An individual occurrence of an entity will then correspond to a particular record with certain values for the fields. So the entity type, **EMPLOYEE**, and the entity occurrence, Tom Yorke, can be represented by the record type and record:

record structure:
name employee# date of birth sex

record occurrence:
Thomas Edward Yorke 3123 07/10/1968 male

The relationships between the entity types can be represented in different ways. One way is by the use of a pointer from one record standing for one entity to another record corresponding to the second entity involved.

13.2.4 Types of relationship

There are a number of useful distinctions between various types of relationship. These distinctions are determined by the number of occurrences of the respective entity types that play a part in the relationship.

1:n relationships

Figure 13.1(a) shows a 1:n relationship. This can be understood as stating that each department has n employees as members and each employee is a member of one department. A representation of occurrences exhibiting this is shown in Figure 13.1(b). Note that the relationship is still 1:n even though Stores has only one member, Salvador Mendez. The restriction on the relationship is that each employee can be a member of *at most* one department. If departments can exist without having any employees as members (a possible though unlikely occurrence) then this may be as shown in Figure 13.1(c). The dotted line indicates that an occurrence of a department need not be attached to any employee. Similarly, Figure 13.1(d) indicates that it is possible for an employee to exist who is not a member of any department.

m:n relationships

Suppose that each item that exists in the stores department may be supplied by many suppliers, and each supplier may supply many items. This is said to be an *m:n* relationship. Figure 13.1(e) and (f) indicate *m:n* relationships.

Figure 13.1 Examples of relationship types

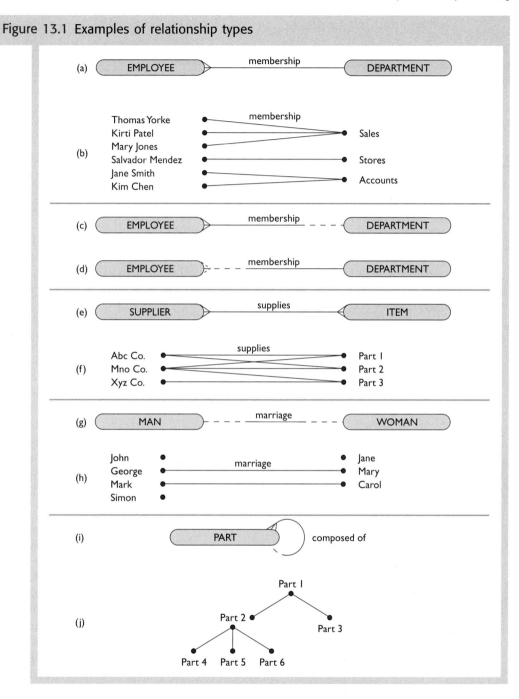

1:1 relationships

There are also 1:1 relationships. In most societies, each man is allowed to be married to at most one woman, and each woman may be married to at most one man. This is shown in Figure 13.1(g) and (h).

Involuted relationships

Relationships may occasionally be involuted. This means that an example of an entity type is related to another example of the same entity type. For instance, it is common for a part used in a later stage in a production process to be composed of parts that are manufactured at an earlier stage. Thus components are made up of components, which are themselves made up of components, and so on. This is shown in Figure 13.1(i), which implies that the parts and composition follow the tree-like structure in Figure 13.1(j). The dotted line is necessary because there must be some parts that will be basic: that is, not composed themselves of parts.

13.3   Data analysis and modelling – an overview of the method

In top-down data analysis using entity–relationship modelling the analyst follows the steps outlined in Figure 13.2. As an example, this method is later applied in Section 13.3 to the Kismet case study. First, an overview of the method is given:

1. *The analyst defines the major data areas to be covered by the model.* These major data areas will usually be determined by the major functions of the organization. Sales order processing, marketing, accounts, purchasing, manufacturing, inventory and administration are all examples of major functional areas. The analyst will then concentrate on each of these areas in turn and develop a data model for each. Later, the models will be amalgamated. This division into functional areas is only carried out if the organization is complex. With a simpler organization, the development of a data model will be attempted without division.

2. *The analyst selects all the important entity types for the chosen data area in the organization.* There is no mechanical rule that can be applied to determining the selection of entity types. However, a good rule of thumb to determine whether something is an entity type is to ask the question 'Is this the sort of thing that the organization is going to wish to keep information on for any reason?' The analyst will obviously be guided by the results of the systems investigation phase. It is clear that an organization like Kismet holds information on orders, items, invoices, and so on. The analyst lists these entity types. At this stage, the analyst should specify the key attribute for each entity.

3. *The analyst determines what relationships exist between the entity types.* At this stage, the analyst determines what relationships within the organization hold between the entity types previously identified. In deciding what relationships exist, the analyst must look not merely at what actually is the case but also at what could be the case. Suppose that **PART** and **SUPPLIER** have been isolated as entity types and that they stand to one another in the relationship 'supplies' – suppliers supply parts. Suppose further that *as a matter of fact* each supplier supplies many parts, and each part is supplied by only one supplier. The relationship would not be regarded as $1:n$ if it *might be* the case that a part could be supplied to the organization by more than one supplier. It would properly be regarded as $m:n$. The analyst has to determine not just the factual position concerning entity occurrences but also the semantics of the relationships themselves, for example the business policy or business rules concerned.

4. *The analyst builds the entity model and draws an entity diagram.* The entity model is the aggregation of all entities and the relationships that exist between them. The

Figure 13.2 The method of data analysis

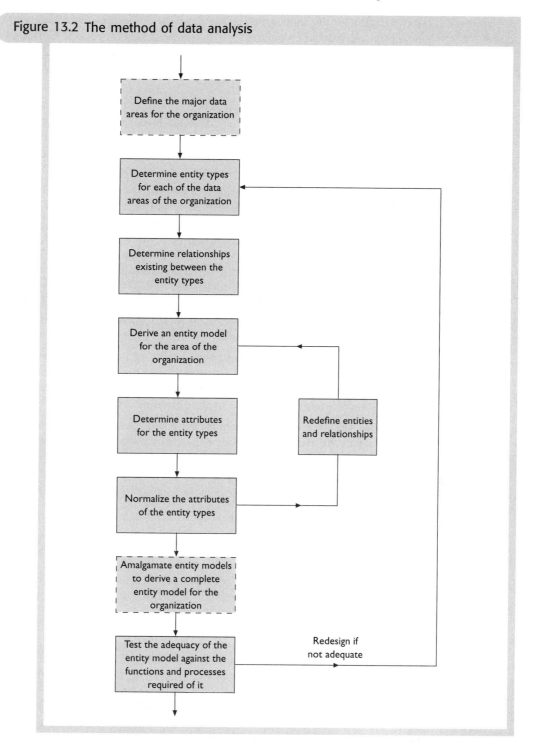

entity diagram is the representation on paper of the model, using the symbols and conventions displayed in Figure 13.1. It has been developed as a high-level logical model of the organization. As yet, no thought has been given either to the detailed data to be stored or to the physical details of that storage.

5. *The analyst determines the attributes of each entity.* Having decided on the overall structure of the model, the analyst will begin to fill in the detail by listing attributes of each of the entities. These will correspond to data that will be stored on each entity. Although it is a good idea to make these attributes as comprehensive as possible – it assists later stages – it is likely that there will be additions and deletions to the attribute list attaching to each entity as the design continues.

6. *The attributes on the entity model are normalized.* Normalization ensures that the entity model consists of entity types in their simplest form. This is important for the design of a data model that will lead to an efficient database as an end product of design. The effect of normalization will be to decompose entity types into their simpler constituent parts. These parts are themselves entity types. The process of normalization continues until certain formal constraints have been met. Normalization is explained in its application to Kismet in case study 13.2. Normalization is also used at the later stage of detailed design to ensure that the final database exemplifies a structure that minimizes duplication of data and so avoids inconsistencies and other anomalies in the database.

7. *The separate entity models are amalgamated into an entity model for the organization as a whole.* This step is relevant only if separate data areas were previously defined for the functions within the organization. In a simple organization, the entity model initially developed is for the organization as a whole.

8. *The adequacy of the entity model is tested against the functions and processes required of it.* How can the analyst be sure that the entity model that has been developed is adequate? There are two questions to be answered:

(a) Will the required data be present?
(b) Can the data be accessed?

A clear idea of the data that is required for the functions and processes of the organization has been established during process analysis and modelling (Chapter 12). The data flow diagrams and the specification via structured English, logic flowcharts and decision tables give a clear picture of what data is required. The analyst should check that all the data required is present in the data model. This will mean establishing that data required for processes is contained as attributes. It will also mean that paths through the model to extract the data are present.

To see this, consider the following example. Suppose that a process for automatic reordering of an item in stock is triggered every time that the quantity held falls below its reorder level. In order to carry out the application, a list of suppliers that supply the item must be available to the process. In other words, given an item it needs to be ascertained that the set of suppliers for the item can be retrieved. The most obvious way for this to happen is if the entity type ITEM is connected to the entity type SUPPLIER through the relationship 'supplies'. Given the value for the identifying attribute of ITEM, in this case *item#*, it is possible to retrieve all suppliers connected through the relation (see Figure 13.3). The top part of the diagram is the relevant part of the entity model showing that the ITEM entity is accessed (illustrated by the double-ruled arrow) and retrieved. Then the SUPPLIER entity is accessed through

Figure 13.3 An example of a functional entity model

Entity accessed	Relationship used	Criterion for selection	Action
ITEM		item# = ?	retrieve
SUPPLIER	supplies	all	retrieve

Figure 13.4 Marriage as (a) a relationship, (b) an attribute and (c) an entity type

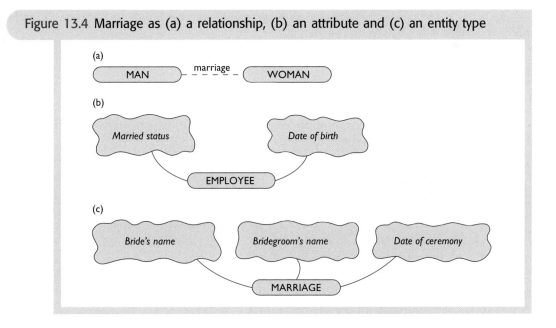

the relationship 'supplies' (illustrated by the single-ruled arrow). All occurrences of the entity type attached to the selected **ITEM** entity are then also retrieved.

Once all these steps have been carried out, the analyst will have produced a data model of the organization sufficient for the provision of data for the various functions and processes that the information system will need to fulfil.

The foregoing is portrayed as a clear-cut, straightforward process, but in practice development of the entity and functional entity models may be messy. One problem is that it is not always clear whether something should be treated as an attribute, an entity or a relationship. To see this for a simple example, consider the treatment of marriage:

1. **Relationship:** 'Marriage' can be regarded as a relationship between two entity types – **MAN** and **WOMAN**. This is a one-to-one relationship, as shown in Figure 13.4(a).

2. **Attribute:** Marriage, or rather *married status*, can be regarded as an attribute of a man, woman or employee. Married status is shown in Figure 13.4(b) as an attribute.

3. **Entity type:** MARRIAGE can also be regarded as an entity type. After all, marriage is an event and data on it can be stored – its date, the church or registry office where officiated, the name of the bride, and so on. The entity type MARRIAGE is illustrated in Figure 13.4(c).

There is no single answer as to the correct way to treat marriage. It all depends on the circumstances. If the marital status of an employee is to be recorded for tax calculation purposes then marriage, or more accurately *married status*, will be an attribute. If, when given details of a person, details of the spouse need to be established then marriage will be represented as a relationship between entity types. However, the public records office will wish to keep information on marriages, and for it marriage is appropriately modelled as an entity type.

Part of the skill in conceptual data modelling is deciding on these categories. It is not uncommon for an analyst to revise a decision and redesign an entity model treating a former attribute as a relationship.

The remainder of this section uses the Kismet case study to illustrate the techniques of data analysis and modelling.

Kismet case study 13.2

1 The analyst defines the major data areas to be covered by the model

In Kismet, the case study is restricted to the sales order processing subsystem. In a complete system to Kismet, other areas would also be involved. The major data areas correspond to the major functional areas of the system. Examples of these would be purchase order processing, stock control and dispatch scheduling.

2 The analyst selects all the important entity types for the chosen data area in the organization

If the Kismet case study given in Section 12.2 is consulted, it is seen that the following are good candidates for entity types for the order-processing function area. It is important to remember that the crucial question to ask is 'Is this the type of thing that the organization would want to keep information on?'

CUSTOMER	MAIL ORDER	COMPANY ORDER	ITEM
SALES CATALOGUE	GOODS	DISPATCH NOTE	INVOICE

On further consideration, it is clear that some deletions can probably be made from this list.

The mail order from the customer is probably a document that is filed for future reference. All of the information on the order is transferred to the company order form. The company order is therefore the obvious entity type, and the mail order can be removed. The company order entity type will be referred to now as the ORDER. This could only be realistically checked by the analyst by asking such questions as 'Is all the information on the mail order transferred to the company order form?'

The terms 'item' and 'goods' refer to the same type of thing. So this would be one entity type – ITEM.

The sales catalogue might be an entity type in itself, with such attributes as *date of preparation* and *person responsible for preparation*. Conversely, it may be no more than a selection from the set of data that is already held on the items, such as *item#*, *item description*, *selling price*. If the latter is true, then it should be removed from the list of entity types and viewed as the output of a process that selects certain attributes of ITEM.

No reference has been made to an entity type DEPARTMENT. This would obviously be an entity type in a complete data analysis of Kismet but has been left out here for simplicity.

The list of entity types is CUSTOMER, ORDER, ITEM, DISPATCH NOTE, INVOICE.

The analyst determines that the key attributes, that is the attributes by which the entities are to be identified, are:

customer#, order#, item#, dispatch#, invoice#

3 The analyst determines what relationships exist between the entity types

The various relationships in which the entity types are involved can be obtained by consulting the case study in Chapter 12. The analyst may be tempted here to use his/her general knowledge of the semantics of business entity types, but it can be dangerous to assume that what is true in most business organizations is true in all. The analyst should be relying heavily on interviews. For the purposes of Kismet, it is assumed that the details of relationships have been established or checked by the analyst. Most will be obvious. Here, two examples are considered:

Each customer may place many orders, but each order can be placed by only one customer. The relationship is therefore $1:n$.

Each order requests many items, and each item can appear in many orders. The relationship is therefore $m:n$.

In the latter case, it is important to be clear that an occurrence of the entity type ITEM is itself an abstract object. An example of an occurrence is the Glauckman 20-watt hi-fi speaker (of which there may be many physical examples in stock). An attribute of the Glauckman 20-watt hi-fi speaker is *quantity held*, the value of which might be six. Individual examples of the Glauckman 20-watt hi-fi speaker have not been referred to. (This is very different from the example EMPLOYEE used in Section 13.2, which has as an occurrence, the physical object Tom Yorke.)

The relationships between the entities are listed in Table 13.1.

Table 13.1 Relationships between entity types for sales order processing in Kismet

Entity	Entity	Relationship name	Degree
CUSTOMER	ORDER	places	$1:n$
ORDER	ITEM	requests	$m:n$
DISPATCH NOTE	ITEM	comprises	$m:n$
DISPATCH NOTE	ORDER	relates	$n:1$
INVOICE	ITEM	bills	$m:n$
DISPATCH NOTE	INVOICE	relates to	$1:1$
DISPATCH NOTE	CUSTOMER	sent to	$n:1$

Wherever possible, each relationship is given a name that is meaningful. Customers place orders. An obvious name for the relationship between **CUSTOMER** and **ORDER** is 'places'. Other names are more artificial. Difficulties arise when the relationships do not have natural names or where the same name would normally be used for different relationships. Apart from clarity, the reason for naming is that there may be more than one relationship between two entity types, and it is necessary to distinguish them.

4 The analyst builds the entity model and draws an entity diagram

The entity diagram is shown in Figure 13.5. This is a representation of the listing of entity types, relationships and their degrees as established in Table 13.1. The purpose of the diagram is to reveal clearly the structure of the relationships between entities. It is much easier to see the nature of the data model from the diagram than from the table.

The dotted connections exist on the relationships 'requests', 'comprises' and 'contains' as it is possible that there are items that have not been ordered and therefore not invoiced and dispatched. The dotted connection on 'relates' is a recognition that time delays can occur between the placing of an order and its dispatch, so the former may exist without the latter.

It is sometimes possible to collapse the entity types involved in a 1:1 relationship and form an amalgamated entity type. This has not been done here with **DISPATCH NOTE/INVOICE** as they are independent and take part in separate and different relationships.

5 The analyst determines the attributes of each entity

It is necessary to establish what data is to be kept on each entity: that is, the attributes of the entity that are of interest to the organization. The existing documentation and interviews provide the analyst with key information. For Kismet, the attributes of the various entity types are shown in Table 13.2. Notice that some of these are repeated sets of attributes – those indicated with a *. At this stage, it may be discovered that new entities need to be defined. The attributes of each entity should be defined within the data dictionary. Remember that a data dictionary is a store of data about data. This enables a consistent development of the data model and also ensures that data flows to and from data stores, as indicated in the data flow diagram, can be serviced.

Figure 13.5 Entity diagram for order processing at Kismet

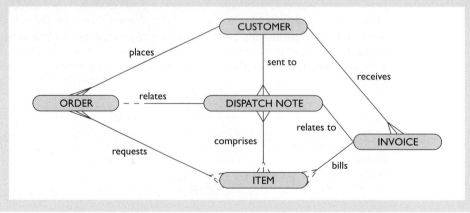

Table 13.2 Attributes associated with the entity types in Kismet's processing

Entity	Attributes
ORDER	order#, order date, customer#, customer name, [item#, item quantity, item price]*
CUSTOMER	customer#, customer name, customer address, [delivery address]*, contact name, contact telephone number, customer analysis code, credit limit, credit terms, standard discount, turnover year to date, current balance
DISPATCH NOTE	dispatch#, dispatch date, order#, customer#, customer name, customer address, [item#, quantity]*
INVOICE	invoice#, invoice date, order#, customer#, customer name, customer address, [item#, item description, item price, item quantity]*, subtotal, discount, sales tax, total payable
ITEM	item#, item description, quantity in stock, average item cost, item price, reorder level, stock analysis code

6 The attributes on the entity model are normalized

Normalization results in a fine-tuning of the entity model. It may lead to more entities and relationships being defined if the entity model does not contain entities in their simplest form. The analyst is moving away from considering a high-level logical model of the organization to the detailed analysis of data and its impact on that model. Looking ahead to the design stage of the data store, a normalized entity model will lead to a normalized data model. This ensures that data is organized in such a way that (1) updating a piece of data generally requires its update in only one place, and (2) deletion of a specified piece of data does not lead to the unintended loss of other data.

Normalization is a formal technique. It is not described here with formal rigour but, rather, it is sketched in order to provide an overview of the process. Normalization applied to entities is aimed at ending up with a set of entity types, attributes and relationships that are normalized. An entity type with a key attribute, or key set of attributes, is normalized if

> each non-key attribute is a 'fact' about the key attribute, the whole key attribute and nothing but the key attribute.

This normalization is called **third normal form** (3NF). To obtain normalization of the entity types to third normal form, the entity types and attributes are analysed into their constituents. Initially, first normal form (1NF) is achieved, then second normal form (2NF) and finally third normal form (3NF). Normalization for the entity type **ORDER** is carried out as an example. This is illustrated in Figures 13.6–13.9.

Figure 13.6 shows the entity type **ORDER**, the attributes of **ORDER** with the key attribute underlined, and a set of example data on three orders.

First normal form

An entity is in first normal form if there are no repeating groups of attributes.

It is clear that for each **ORDER**, *item#, item quantity, item price* are repeated for each item ordered. These repeating groups can be removed by recognizing that each order contains a number of order details. Thus **ORDER DETAIL** is an entity type. Each order is made up of many order details. So the relationship is 1:*n*. This is shown in Figure 13.7. Note that the entity type **ORDER DETAIL** contains the *order#* of the **ORDER** to which it relates. This ensures that the order details are always linked to the relevant

Figure 13.6 Entity type ORDER showing repeating groups of attributes

ORDER

ORDER (<u>order#</u>, order date, customer#, customer name, [item#, item quantity, item price]*)

ORDER

order#	order date	customer#	customer name	item#	item quantity	item price
123	11/09/2004	101	Smith's	12	19	23.78
				14	2	145.99
				15	5	200.00
				23	1	96.00
126	11/09/2004	102	HI-FI Ltd	11	2	67.89
				14	3	145.99
127	12/09/2004	101	Smith's	13	1	99.99
				14	2	145.99

Figure 13.7 Entities in first normal form

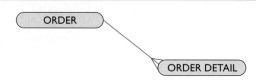

ORDER (order#, order date, customer#, customer name)
ORDER DETAIL (order#, item#, item quantity, item price)

ORDER

order#	order date	customer#	customer name
123	11/09/2004	101	Smith's
126	11/09/2004	102	HI-FI Ltd
127	12/09/2004	101	Smith's

ORDER DETAIL

order#	item#	item quantity	item price
123	12	19	23.78
123	14	2	145.99
123	15	5	200.00
123	23	1	96.00
126	11	2	67.89
126	14	3	145.99
127	13	1	99.99
127	14	2	145.99

order where the non-repeating attributes, such as *order date* and *customer#*, appear. The key for **ORDER DETAIL** is the set of attributes consisting of *order#, item#*. Each on its own will not identify a unique occurrence of **ORDER DETAIL**, but together they guarantee this.

Second normal form

An entity is in second normal form if it is in 1NF and every attribute that is not part of the key depends on the whole key.

In Figure 13.7, the entity type **ORDER** has only one attribute as its key, so all the other attributes depend on this attribute. Considering **ORDER DETAIL**, *item quantity* depends on the whole key. This is because the quantity of an item in an order does not depend only on the item (the item is ordered in other orders) or only on the order (there are other items ordered in the order). However, the combination of *order#* and *item#* fixes *item quantity*. The same is not true of *item price*. This depends only on *item#*. When it is realized that order details are about items ordered, it becomes clear that **ITEM** is an entity type.

This is shown in Figure 13.8. Each order detail is about only one item, but each item may be referred to by many examples of order detail from different orders. The relationship is 1:*n* as shown. The advantage of second normal form is that data on an

Figure 13.8 Entities in second normal form

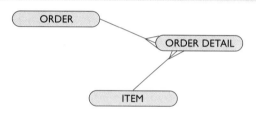

ORDER (*order#, order date, customer#, customer name*)
ORDER DETAIL (*order#, item#, item quantity*)
ITEM (*item#, item price*)

ORDER

order#	order date	customer#	customer name
123	11/09/2004	101	Smith's
126	11/09/2004	102	HI-FI Ltd
127	12/09/2004	101	Smith's

ORDER DETAIL

order#	item#	item quantity
123	12	19
123	14	2
123	15	5
123	23	1
126	11	2
126	14	3
127	13	1
127	14	2

ITEM

item#	item price
11	67.89
12	23.78
13	99.99
14	145.99
15	200.00
23	96.00

item such as its price occurs only once. This contrasts with the repeated prices for items with *item#* 1 and 2 in Figure 13.7. The data model will be used to design an effective database. A good database design minimizes the duplication of data.

Third normal form

An entity is in third normal form if it is in 2NF and each attribute (or set of attributes) that is not part of the key depends on nothing but the key.

In Figure 13.8, both ORDER DETAIL and ITEM contain only one non-key attribute each. So each of these attributes can depend, by definition, only on the key. However, the entity type ORDER has an attribute *customer name* that depends on the *customer #*. Customer name is a fact about the customer. Customers place orders.

This is shown in Figure 13.9. A new entity type CUSTOMER is introduced. This has a key, *customer#*, and one non-key attribute, *customer name*. Each customer may place

Figure 13.9 Entities in third normal form

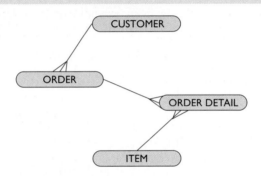

ORDER (*order#*, order date, customer#)
ORDER DETAIL (*order#*, *item#*, item quantity)
ITEM (*item#*, item price)
CUSTOMER (*customer#*, customer name)

ORDER

order#	order date	customer#
123	11/09/2004	101
126	11/09/2004	102
127	12/09/2004	101

CUSTOMER

customer#	customer name
101	Smith's
102	HI-FI Ltd

ORDER DETAIL

order#	item#	item quantity
123	12	19
123	14	2
123	15	5
123	23	1
126	11	2
126	14	3
127	13	1
127	14	2

ITEM

item#	item price
11	67.89
12	23.78
13	99.99
14	145.99
15	200.00
23	96.00

many orders, but each order is placed by only one customer. The relationship is 1:*n*. Note once again that the new model avoids repeating data. The customer name, Smith, appears only once.

Another important feature of normalization is that a fully normalized set of entities and attributes ensures that data on entities is not dependent on the existence of other entities. Returning to Figure 13.6, it is clear that if there had been no order with *order#* = 126 then data on customer 102, such as the customer's name, HI-FI Ltd, and data on item 11, such as the item price, £67.89, would not appear. The normalized form of the entity–relationship model allows maintenance of this data because it is in its 'proper' place connected with the entity to which it relates.

In summary, normalization of entity types leads to a data model that will form the basis of a good database design because it:

■ decomposes entity types into their simple atomic constituents;

■ ensures that data is not unnecessarily repeated; and

■ allows data on entities to be independent of the existence of other entities.

It is also important to realize that the data that was associated with the original unnormalized entity is still recoverable. All the data in Figure 13.6 on individual orders can be reconstructed from the entities and attributes in Figure 13.9. The entities are connected at the table level by their key attributes.

Having normalized each of the entity types in the model, it is possible to amalgamate them to provide a new comprehensive entity model for the data area under analysis. This is shown in Figure 13.10. The decomposition of the entity type ORDER has given rise to only one new entity type, ORDER DETAIL. Both CUSTOMER and ITEM already appeared in the model, and their attributes were already in the attribute list.

Figure 13.10 Entity diagram after normalization for order processing at Kismet (relationship names have been omitted)

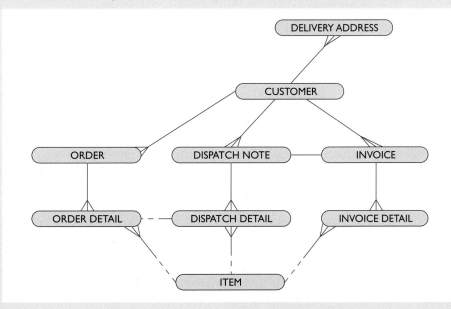

7 The separate entity models are amalgamated into an entity model for the organization as a whole

If the system for which the data model was being derived was relatively simple, then the result of stage 6 will be the entity model for the organization, or rather that part of the organization that is the subject of investigation. If, though, division into separate data areas was carried out, these must now be amalgamated to provide a comprehensive data model. In doing so, it will be discovered that entity types appearing in one area also appear in others. Obviously, the resulting attributes of the entity type will be the combined set of attributes appearing in every data area in which the entity type occurs.

A combined entity diagram for Kismet dealing with stock control and purchase order processing, as well as sales order processing, is given in Figure 13.11.

Figure 13.11 A combined entity diagram for Kismet
(relationship names have been omitted)

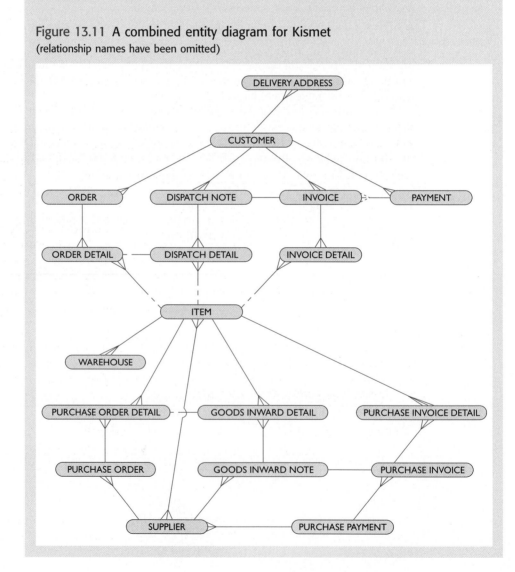

8 The adequacy of the entity model is tested against the functions and processes required of it

Top-down data analysis produces an entity model that is a representation of the entities on which the organization may wish to hold information and of the important relationships between them. The model will form the basis for design of a computerized data store and is derived independently of any analysis of the functions or processes that will require access to the data. Although the functions and processes that use the store may change over time, it is important to establish that the current needs can be met. Functional analysis is concerned with the way that functions and processes map on to the data model. It acts as a test of adequacy of the model.

The processes that are going to need data from the data store have been established in the course of process analysis and modelling, which was covered in Chapter 12. For each of these processes, functional analysis applied to the data model provides:

- a list of entity types that need to be accessed to provide the data for the process;

- the order in which the entities are accessed;

- the criteria used to select the entities – for example, an order might be selected by a given *order #*, or all orders connected via a relationship to a customer might be selected;

- the nature of the access to the entity (retrieve, update, delete and create).

A functional diagram is then drawn. This is a diagram of the relevant subset of the entity model. It shows the direction and movement around the model to access the entities needed to satisfy the function or process. A table of the criteria and resulting actions is also given. This is illustrated with two examples from Kismet.

After the investigation stage of Kismet has been performed, the analyst has established the following functions (among others):

- *Function 1*: For a given customer, a list of those items ordered is needed together with their order dates and order # (*order#, order date, item#, item description, item price, item quantity*) where the items have been ordered more than four days previously and have as yet not been dispatched. This is needed for management information purposes to ensure that good customer service and relations can be maintained.

- *Function 2*: Create an order for a customer after determining the credit status of the customer.

When checking the model to ensure that the data can be supplied for the function, it is important to realize that the purpose of the test is not to carry out the function or process, as that will be achieved by a program working with the data, but merely to establish the accessibility of the needed data.

In order to carry out Function 1, the following has to be performed:

1. Retrieve the given CUSTOMER entity, selected by *customer#*.

2. Retrieve all orders placed by that customer through the CUSTOMER/ORDER relationship where the *order date* is less than today's date minus four days.

3. Retrieve the details of all those orders through the ORDER/ORDER DETAILS relationship.

4. Establish which of those order details have not as yet been satisfied by retrieving the related dispatch details via the relationship ORDER DETAILS/DISPATCH DETAILS.

▶

Figure 13.12 Functional entity diagram for Kismet – Function 1

Entity accessed	Relationship used	Selection criterion	Action
CUSTOMER	—	*customer# = ?*	retrieve
ORDER	CUSTOMER/ORDER	*order date < today–4*	retrieve
ORDER DETAIL	ORDER/ORDER DETAIL	all	retrieve
DISPATCH DETAIL	ORDER DETAIL/DISPATCH DETAIL	all	retrieve
ITEM	ORDER DETAIL/ITEM	all	retrieve

Figure 13.13 Functional entity diagram for Kismet – Function 2

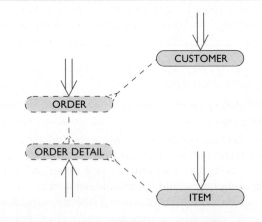

Entity accessed	Relationship used	Selection criterion	Action
CUSTOMER	—	*customer# = ?*	retrieve
ITEM	—	*item# = ?*	retrieve
ORDER	—	—	create
ORDER DETAIL	—	—	create
—	CUSTOMER/ORDER	—	create
—	ORDER/ORDER DETAIL	—	create
—	ORDER DETAIL/ITEM	—	create

5. Retrieve the required details of those items that have not been dispatched through the ORDER DETAILS/ITEM relationship.

This is shown in Figure 13.12. The diagram and the accompanying table show only the entities accessed and paths taken but do not show what is done with the retrieved data. The single arrow indicates a path through the data model, whereas a double arrow implies access from the outside. The analysis and specification of the processes are covered in process analysis and modelling in Chapter 12.

For Function 2, the CUSTOMER and ITEM entities are accessed. ORDER and ORDER DETAILS are created. The order can now be priced, as all the necessary information has been obtained. The value is compared with *credit limit* and *current balance* obtained on the CUSTOMER entity. The relationships between CUSTOMER, ORDER, ORDER DETAILS and ITEMS can now be created. This is shown in Figure 13.13. Once again, note that the path only guarantees that the data can be accessed; it does not show what use is made of this data. The dotted lines are used to show that an entity or relationship is being created rather than being used.

13.4 Process modelling and data modelling – the links

It would be wrong to think that process analysis and modelling as described in Chapter 12, and data analysis and modelling as described in this chapter, are rival approaches to systems analysis. Rather, each has evolved in response to particular problems and conditions.

Structured process analysis was developed in an attempt to overcome the difficulties of designing large integrated systems. Such systems cannot be designed by individuals by themselves. The task is too complex and time-consuming. Instead, teams of programmers and analysts are assigned to a project. A large project will require several teams, each dealing with a particular aspect or subsystem of the total system considered. In the development of an integrated system, the interests of each individual and each team overlap and it is necessary to establish effective communication. The problem is that agreements between parties on some aspect of analysis or design are likely to impact on the work of others. Multi-way communication is necessary. It is all too easy to develop a tower of Babel, where communication and project control, rather than the system under investigation, become the problem. It was common for projects to drift over budget and fail to meet time deadlines. An initial response to a project that was slipping behind its schedule was often to add more manpower in the form of extra analysts or programmers. This often aggravated, rather than alleviated, the problem by increasing communication difficulties.

One of the aims of structured process analysis and design is to respond to these software engineering problems by providing an approach that makes effective project control easier. This is achieved by concentrating initially on the logic and not the physical detail of the processes in an organization. These processes are systematically decomposed into manageable chunks or modules. At the program development stage, the individual modular specifications can be coded separately in a form that is easy to test. Various standards for documentation go with this approach, which in the early stages emphasizes features important to the eventual users.

In contrast, top-down data analysis was developed in order to take account of the fact that processes often share the same data and that the data stores need to be designed in an integrated manner that allows this. To do this, an effective data model of the organization is developed. With the realization that the data structure of the organization is unlikely to change much over time, although the processes that use the data might alter, came the emphasis on the importance of data analysis and even on the priority of data analysis over process analysis.

It is impossible for an analyst to concentrate on either process or data analysis to the exclusion of the other. The degree of attention paid to each will depend on the nature of the system under investigation. A system in which there is a high degree of integration and shared data, and for which it is intended to design a database that can service not only the present but the future needs of an organization, will require a heavy initial input of data analysis in conjunction with process analysis. By contrast, complex processes using simple data structures will require only cursory attention to data analysis.

The way that data and process analysis and design interact is shown in Figure 13.14. Here, the approach taken has been that structured process analysis and modelling is complementary to data modelling.

Figure 13.14 The interaction of data analysis and process analysis

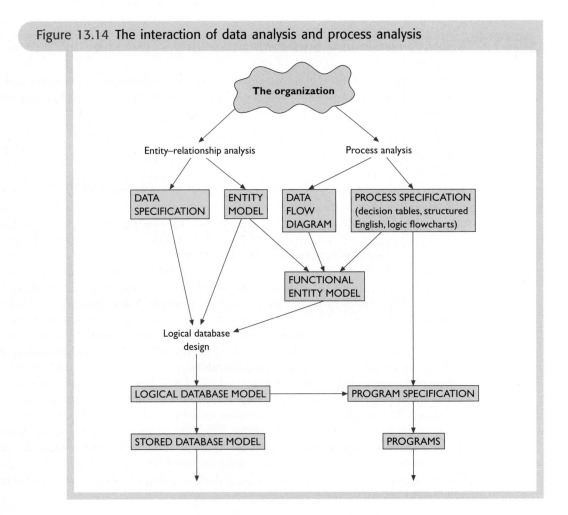

One point of contact is in the development of the functional entity model, where the entity model, as derived from a 'snapshot' picture of the entity–relationship structure of the organization, is tested against the requirements of the existing processes, as analysed and revealed through data flow diagrams, structured English descriptions, decision tables and logic flowcharts. If it is found to be lacking, then the entity model may be changed at this stage.

Another point of contact is via the data dictionary (not shown). Lists of attributes on each entity type, arrived at during data specification, are reconciled with the data needs of processes as revealed in the data flows in the data flow diagram.

The logical model of the database is designed from the entity model and data specifications. This will incorporate any constraints imposed by the limitations of the chosen model type: for example, hierarchical database model. Eventually, this gives rise to the stored database model and the database itself. Process specifications lead to the program specifications. From these, the programs are written that carry out the required data and information processing for the organization. These will require stored data and so will make calls on the database.

The approach to analysis taken in this chapter and in Chapter 12 can be considered 'scientific' in that it is based on some of the fundamental assumptions of natural science and engineering. The approach has the following characteristics:

- **Reductionist**: Progress is achieved by the decomposition and analysis of problems and processes into their constituents.

- **Importance of technical considerations**: Data and processes are the subjects of analysis and design; people are seen as important only in as far as they interface with the system.

- **Technology-oriented**: It is expected that the end result of analysis and design is to provide a computerized system that overcomes the shortcomings of the existing system.

- **Realist**: The system being analysed, its objectives, its structure and processes, are taken as having an existence and form independent of any subjectivity of the analyst.

This approach has a great deal to recommend it but, as will be seen in Chapter 16, there are limitations and alternatives.

Summary

The aim of analysis is to summarize and model key elements of a system in a way that facilitates understanding, enables evaluation and aids design. Data analysis is concerned with the development of an abstract data model of an organization appropriate for the design of an effective database.

The importance of data analysis has been increased by:

- the increase in the use of integrated databases;

- the treatment of data as a resource of an organization rather than an input/output product;

- the recognition that although processes change over time the structure of the data held by an organization is relatively stable.

Data modelling is specifically aimed at creating a structure for the store of data that meets organizational requirements. This is achieved by identifying the basic entities and relationships in an organization. Attributes are determined and a normalized set of entity types derived. The entity model is then designed. Its adequacy is established by testing it against the data requirements of the processes that it will serve. This leads to the construction of functional entity models, which indicate the order and selection criteria for data access during a process. The entity–relationship model and its associated data specification of entity attributes are the basis from which the logical database model is designed.

Data analysis and process analysis are complementary activities in the analysis of a system. Although the first concentrates on deriving a data model of the organization, while the second concentrates on modelling processes, the adequacy of the data model is dependent on its ability to serve the processes with the required data. The links are established through the functional entity model and the data dictionary.

The approach to analysis in this chapter and in Chapter 12 is often regarded as 'scientific'. It has all the hallmarks of an engineering philosophy. The approach is reductionist; it concentrates on data and processes by restricting the scope of analysis to technical rather than social aspects of a system; it views the problem solution in terms of computerization; and, finally, it assumes a realist philosophy with respect to the systems, their functioning and their objectives.

Review questions

1. Explain the difference between *bottom-up* and *top-down* data modelling. Why is top-down data modelling generally preferable? Under what circumstances is bottom-up modelling appropriate?

2. Explain the difference between an *entity type*, a *relationship* and an *attribute*. Give examples of each.

3. Give examples of 1:*n*, *m*:*n* and 1:1 relationships.

4. What is a *key attribute*?

5. What is the purpose of normalization?

6. Explain the differences between 1NF, 2NF and 3NF.

7. What is the purpose of deriving a functional entity model?

8. What reasons might an analyst give for carrying out data analysis prior to attempting process analysis?

Exercises

1. Given that Thomas Yorke is both an employee in an organization and a project leader, then he is an occurrence of both the entity types EMPLOYEE and PROJECT LEADER. If the same data (values of attributes) is kept on Thomas Yorke at two occurrences, is this a weakness of entity–relationship modelling?

2. Entities have attributes and stand in relationships to one another. However, relationships also may have attributes. For example, an employee (entity) works (relationship) on a

project (entity). Not only do both the employee and the project have attributes but so does the relationship – works. Mary Jones works on Project A from February to April. This period of work is not an attribute of Mary Jones or of Project A but of the relationship of Mary Jones to Project A. Can entity–relationship modelling handle this difficulty?

3. An object may fall under two distinct entity types. This is particularly true of people who play different roles in an organization. For instance, John Black is both a lecturer to students and a course director. Can the entity–relationship model deal with this adequately, or does it need a new category – that of role?

4. Using the data given in Exercise 6, Chapter 12:
   (a) Identify entities, attributes and relationships for the library.
   (b) Design a suitable entity model and functional entity models for the system.

5. Each department in an organization consists of a manager and several departmental staff. Each manager is in charge of only one department, and departmental staff are assigned to a single department. Attached to each department are several projects. All departmental staff are assigned to projects, with some staff being assigned to several projects, not necessarily in the same department. Each project is run by a management group consisting of the manager of the department together with a selection of staff working on the project. No departmental staff member is ever required to sit on more than one management group.
   (a) Draw an entity diagram for this information.
   (b) Draw a functional diagram for the function: determine which departmental staff working on a given project are not attached to the department responsible for that project.

6. A local hospital consists of many wards, each of which is assigned many patients. Each patient is assigned to one doctor, who has overall responsibility for the patients in his or her care. Other doctors are assigned on an advisory basis. Each patient is prescribed drugs by the doctor responsible for that patient. Each nurse is assigned to a ward and nurses all patients on the ward, although they are given special responsibility for some patients. Each patient is assigned one nurse in this position of responsibility. One of the doctors is attached to each ward as an overall medical advisor.
   (a) Draw an entity diagram representing these relationships.
   (b) Draw a functional diagram representing:
      – Function 1: Determine which nurses are responsible for those patients that are the responsibility of a given doctor.
      – Function 2: Determine the drug usage prescribed by a doctor.
      – Function 3: Determine the range of wards covered by a doctor in any of his/her roles.

CASE STUDY 13

Lift Express

Lift Express is a nationwide organization concerned with the servicing and repair of lifts supplied and installed by its parent company. Lift Express divides the UK into five regions; all service and repair operations within a region are handled by the regional headquarters. At present, all operations are based on a manual system.

◄

On discovery of a lift fault or of the need for it to be serviced, a customer telephones or writes to the regional headquarters. Details of the request for service/repairs are made on standard company documentation by clerical staff at the HQ. Service engineers are all home-based, and details of the customer's requirements are phoned (fault) or posted (service request) to a selected engineer who is based in the same region as the customer. (In the case of faults, documentation detailing the fault is posted later to the engineer.) After visiting the customer, the engineer produces a charge sheet for the job, a copy of which is sent back to the regional HQ, where it is stapled to the original request details. An invoice for the customer is generated and then posted.

Currently, Lift Express is losing work to a rival company. The reason has been located as an inadequate customer request and information-processing system. Specifically, there are significant delays in paperwork, leading to an unacceptable period occurring between a customer request and an instruction to the engineer, and between a job being completed and an invoice generated. There are difficulties in scheduling engineers' workloads – some are overworked, while others are not fully employed. Management is finding it difficult to extract decision-making information from the system, for instance given a customer – the number of calls booked not as yet completed, or an individual engineer – the amount of income generated per month by the engineer.

In order to remedy these faults, it has been decided to implement a computerized information system.

Questions

1. Explain the principles of data analysis and suggest how these can be applied in designing the information system for Lift Express.

2. Define entity types and relationships important to the functioning of the system and then design an entity model.

3. Design a functional model and data access table for the following: determine the number of calls handled by a given engineer for a given customer.

Recommended reading

Avison D., Wood-Harper A.T., Vidgen R. and Wood R. (2000). *Multiview*, reissued 2nd edn. Oxford: McGraw-Hill
This book applies data analysis to a case study. The approach is integrated with other approaches, including structured process modelling as covered in Chapter 10.

Benyon D. (1996). *Information Management and Modelling*, 2nd edn. London: McGraw-Hill
This covers in detail methods of information analysis and modelling. Aimed at students of management and business studies, this is a clear text extending the contents of the current chapter.

Benyon-Davies P. (2004). *Database Systems*, 3rd edn. Palgrave Macmillan
This updated text gives coverage of databases, database management systems and database development. Latter chapters cover trends in database technologies, especially concerning distributed and parallel processing, and chapters on data warehouses and data mining. Although this book goes beyond the needs of many business studies programmes, its clarity would render it useful.

Bowman K. (2003). *Systems Analysis: A Beginner's Guide*. Palgrave Macmillan
This provides a helpful introduction to the topic of systems analysis. Concepts are illustrated by case studies that run through the book.

Chen P. (1976). The entity–relationship model – toward a unified view of data. *ACM Transactions on Database Systems*, **1** (1), 9–36

A comprehensive coverage of the entity–relationship approach involving rigorous specification of terms.

Deeks D. (2002). *An Introduction to System Analysis Techniques*, 2nd edn. Addison-Wesley

A good all-round introduction to the analysis of data and processes in both structured and object-oriented paradigms.

Halpin T. (2001). *Information Modeling and Relational Database: From Conceptual Analysis to Logical Design*. Morgan Kaufmann

This adopts an idiosyncratic approach to arriving at the well-understood data models which can then be employed to generate a relational database.

Chapter 14

Systems design

Learning outcomes

On completion of this chapter, you should be able to:

- Explain how new system requirements and inefficiencies in the logical model are addressed in the systems design
- Suggest alternative designs for an information system
- Delimit a system in terms of automation boundaries
- Define the walk through and the formal review and explain their function as part of systems design.

Introduction

In Chapters 11, 12 and 13, it was seen how the analyst proceeds from the collection of descriptive material on the functioning of the existing physical system through to the analysis and development of a logical model of that system. Data flows between processes were represented and analysed using data flow diagrams at various levels, data processes were specified using decision tables, structured English and logic flowcharts, and a conceptual data model for the system was derived.

This chapter deals with the transition from analysis to design. This initially involves the recasting of the high-level models to eliminate any remaining physical aspects and to take account of any additional requirements that a new system must satisfy. These models can be used to design, in outline, various proposals for the new system. At this stage, the extent of computerization will be decided, together with which processes are to be carried out in batch as distinct from online mode. Decisions will also be taken on whether to centralize or distribute the system and on whether to opt for a file-based or database system. Design considerations for these alternatives are outlined in this chapter. Two or three alternative designs are submitted and assessed through a formal review. As soon as one of these outline proposals has been accepted, then detailed design work can commence. Detailed design is covered in Chapter 15.

14.1 The transition from analysis to design

The aim of analysis is to derive a logical model of the way that the existing system works. This is on the assumption that the existing system provides a good guide to *what* is required of a new system (as distinct from *how* the new system is to achieve these requirements). Certain limitations should be obvious:

1. There may be requirements of the new system that are not being satisfied by the current system – these need to be taken into account.

2. Inefficiencies in the existing system may become translated into the logical model; ideally, the model should reveal the logic of an efficient system and so should be amended.

3. It is often the case that physical aspects creep into the logical analysis – these should be removed.

These three points are now dealt with.

14.1.1 Treatment of new requirements

It is desirable to review the requirements to be made of an information system when it undergoes a major change, such as computerization of a manual system or replacement of an existing computer system by another. This review may throw up new requirements. These will be established by interviews with management and users. By definition, the logical model of the existing system cannot contain these. It is important, then, that the logical model be amended to reflect these new requirements.

These additions are likely to lead to new processes, which will be added to the higher-level data flow diagrams. They will interact via data flows with existing data stores and/or processes. Added processes are decomposed into their exploded functional constituents on lower-level data flow diagrams. If their operation is governed by sophisticated logic, then this must be specified using one of the tools of specification, such as structured English.

Often, new requirements concern the extraction of new types of management information from data stores rather than the alteration of the existing pattern of transaction processing. This can be accomplished simply at the data flow diagram level by inserting a process that accepts as input the data flows from the relevant data stores and produces as output the required data. It will also be necessary to establish that the entity model, as revealed by the entity diagram, is sufficient to provide the data for the function. In other words, the access path through the model must be checked by drawing a functional entity diagram.

Kismet case study 14.1

With the Kismet case study, one of the problems that management listed with the existing document-handling system was the difficulty of deriving useful management information. For example, management needed a regular report on the total value of goods sold, analysed by each item type within customer types. This is vital information to establish which sectors of the market are growing and which are declining with respect to sales. Examples of customer types might be specialist retail chains (chain stores dealing with electrical goods only), non-specialist retail chains, specialist single shops (the local hi-fi shop) and non-specialist single shops. Examples of item types are compact disc, turntable, mini rack system and graphic equalizer. An example of a partial report is given in Figure 14.1.

▶

Figure 14.1 Sales analysis report by customer type within item type

Start date 12/09/2004	Stop date 12/10/2004	
Stock analysis code	Customer analysis code	Value
A1	1	45,123
	2	100,876
	3	1,122
	4	0
A2	1	107,879
	2	232,112
:	:	:
:	:	:

Figure 14.2 A data flow diagram for the production of the sales analysis

customer#, invoice date,
[stock analysis code, sales price, item quantity]*

D5 | company invoice

4

Prepare sales analysis

customer analysis code

sales analysis

D3 | customer details

MANAGE-MENT

sales analysis
[start date, end date, [stock analysis code, [customer analysis code, value]*]*]*

It is a notable weakness of the existing system that such reports are difficult to extract. The documents are stored in a manner that makes it time-consuming and costly to obtain this information. One of the benefits of computerized information systems is that information for use in decision making can be extracted quickly and cheaply from the results of transaction processing.

The process for generating this report can be incorporated in a straightforward way into a data flow diagram (see Figure 14.2). In order to produce this report for any selected invoice, it is necessary to extract the invoice details (and hence the stock analysis codes of the items sold), and the customer for whom the invoice is generated. The analysis code of the customer can then be obtained.

This may be established by reference to the entity diagram developed in Chapter 13 and shown in Figure 13.10. The new functional entity diagram governing this process is shown in Figure 14.3. For any selected invoice, it is possible to retrieve the customer

Figure 14.3 Functional entity model showing the entities accessed for the sales analysis report

CUSTOMER	(customer#, customer analysis code, ...)		
INVOICE	(invoice#, invoice date, customer#, ...)		
INVOICE DETAIL	(invoice#, item#, item quantity, sales price)		
ITEM	(item#, stock analysis code, ...)		

Entity accessed	Relationship used	Selection criteria	Action
INVOICE	—	by invoice date	retrieve
CUSTOMER	INVOICE/CUSTOMER	all	retrieve
INVOICE DETAIL	INVOICE/INVOICE DETAIL	all	retrieve
ITEM	INVOICE DETAIL/ITEM	all	retrieve

receiving the invoice through the **CUSTOMER/INVOICE** relationship and hence determine the *customer analysis code*. For the invoice, it is also possible to retrieve the invoice details through the **CUSTOMER/INVOICE DETAILS** relationship. This gives the *item #*, *sale price* and *item quantity* for each item sold under the invoice. The value of that item can then be calculated. The item can then be retrieved via the **INVOICE DETAIL/ITEM** relationship and hence the *stock analysis code* obtained. There is now sufficient data to derive the analysis of all invoices between specified dates by customer analysis code within the stock analysis code and so provide the report.

14.1.2 Treatment of inefficiencies

The development of data flow diagrams has been accomplished using top-down decomposition of the major processes, such as those occurring in the Kismet order-processing system. Inevitably, the decomposition as revealed by lower-level data flow diagrams is not purely a result of a logical analysis of the nature of the major processes. Rather, the lower-level structure tends to be determined partly by what is done in the existing system to fulfil a function as well as by what needs to be done as determined by the logic of the function. If what is done is unnecessary or inefficient, this may have unfortunate repercussions on the logical model. It is at this transition stage that the model should be adjusted.

Kismet case study 14.2

An example of this adjustment of the model can be seen in the Kismet case study. From Figure 12.10, process 1.2 and the surrounding processes have been extracted and are shown in Figure 14.4. The copy of the company order is stored temporarily in the company order store D4. Another copy is priced and then a credit check is performed on the customer. If successful, the credit check triggers the dispatch of the stored company order to the customer as an acknowledgement of receipt of the order. This is clearly unnecessary. Why not send the acknowledgement company order as an output of process 1.5, the credit check? Historically, the reason for the temporary store is to maintain a record of the order in the sales department while the company order is sent to the credit control section and back. This would take time, and the sales department might need to answer a query on the customer order while it is in transit (the enquiry process is not shown). If the entire system is to be computerized (perhaps a premature judgement) then this time lag may not occur. In fact, in an online system the aim is to eliminate this time lag completely. The logical model of the system has inherited the inefficiency of the physical system on which it is based.

Figure 14.4 A partial data flow diagram illustrating the process of generating an approved order

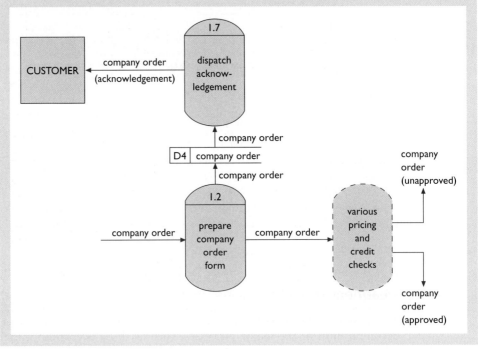

The important point to be made here is not to reach a definite answer on the peculiarities of the Kismet case but rather to reinforce the observation that there is nothing sacrosanct about a logical model derived from the study of an existing system – it can be changed as seen fit. Nor is there any clear-cut set of rules as to how to modify the model before design can start. Indeed, any modification could be considered to be part of design, although here these changes are referred to as a transition from analysis to design.

14.1.3 Treatment of physical aspects

Certain physical considerations may have crept into the logical model.

Kismet case study 14.3

Data store D5 in Figure 12.7 contains the order/invoice/dispatch note trio. These are disallowed as bedfellows in the logical model and should be indicated on the data flow diagram as separate stores. They have been thrown together purely for convenience in ▶

Figure 14.5 An amended data flow diagram of the Kismet order-processing system

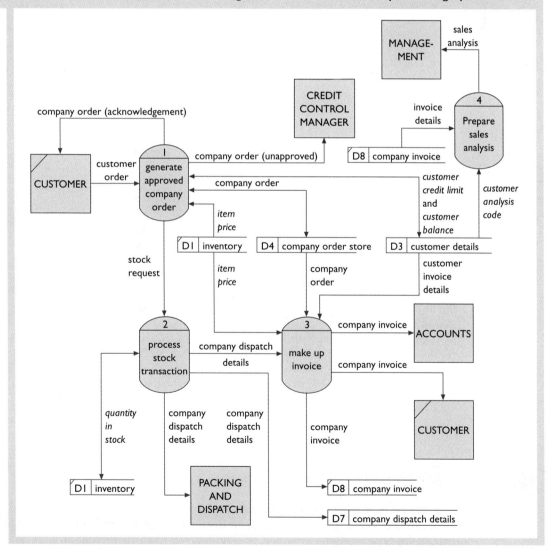

Figure 14.6 An amended level 2 data flow diagram of the generation of an approved company order

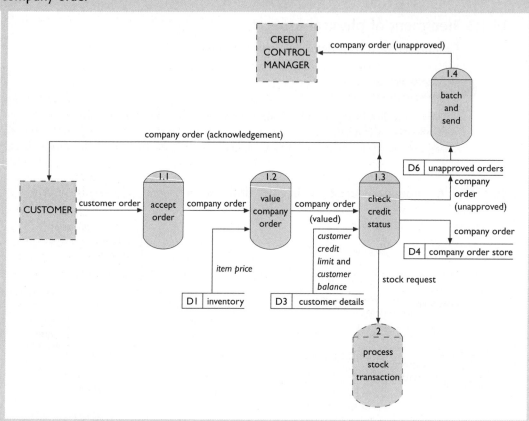

the physical manual files. There is no fear that by separating these the connection between them will be lost. The links remain at an attribute level, as each of the trio contains the attribute *order#*. Also, each order is linked to its relevant invoice(s) and dispatch note(s) through relationships in the entity model.

Amended data flow diagrams are shown in Figures 14.5 and 14.6. These incorporate the addition of the sales analysis generation process and the other comments given in this section. Notice also that the catalogue has disappeared as a separate store. The information on item sale prices is held in the inventory store (the **ITEM** entity), and this is accessed for prices during the generation of a company order and invoice.

14.2 Suggesting alternative designs

Up to this point, the analyst has concentrated on the question of *what* is to be done in order to satisfy the data-processing and information-provision requirements of the organization. The analyst's attention is now directed towards the question of *how* to do it. This is a two-step process. First, the analyst suggests, in outline, two or three alternatives. This is termed **systems design**. One of these is selected by management. Second, the detailed design of the chosen system is carried out. Detailed design is covered in Chapter 15. Is it worth emphasizing that the authors are deliberately separating the stages of systems analysis and design in this book. It is thought that by exaggerating the issues particular to each stage, a clearer understanding can be formed. In reality, the stages are often much more blurred and the transition between them less obvious.

Why should the analyst be presenting general alternative systems when there has already been a costed proposal in the feasibility study? The analyst now has a much greater understanding of the system than earlier on in the investigation. There may be new opportunities for a different extent or type of computerization from what was previously envisaged. Having developed a logical model, it is also easy to sketch and present these alternatives to management.

In preparing a design, the analyst will need to make various choices. There will be decisions on the extent of computerization – which processes in the process model will be computerized and which will be manual – and decisions on the type of system for those processes that are computerized. Although this is the stage where the decisions are made explicit, it is likely that some consideration of the type of system will already have been made throughout the process so far. This is inevitable given that the decisions represent important strategic choices for the organization. The principal choices concern:

- centralized or distributed systems
- file-based or database systems
- batch or online systems
- input methods
- applications packages or specially designed programs
- hardware.

General design considerations on each of these are summarized here and then applied to Kismet.

14.2.1 Centralized and distributed systems

A distributed computer system is one where:

- there are two or more geographically separated computers;
- these are linked by telecommunications; and
- the network of computers serves a single organization.

A centralized computer system is one with a single computer servicing the needs of the organization. There may be remote terminals connected by telecommunications.

A large organization on many different sites may decide to have a distributed system because most of the data processing and information provision is localized to each site. Local data storage and processing are then feasible. The need for distributed computing (as distinct from several stand-alone computers) comes from the requirement that data and the results of processing at one site are available to computers at other sites.

A single-site organization may also decide to have a collection of micro/minicomputers and connect these via a local area network. This is possible if no large centralized processing power is needed. It has the advantage that each node on the network can be devoted to local needs such as decision support using spreadsheet modelling or word processing, and nodes can be added to the network when needed.

Advantages of distributed computing

- Telecommunications costs between several sites are reduced, provided that most of the processing is locally based.
- There is greater flexibility, as additional computers can be added to the networks as needed.
- The organization is not reliant on a single computer, which might break down.

Disadvantages of distributed computing

- Commonly used data is often replicated at many sites – changes in this data, unless happening to all occurrences, can lead to an inconsistent organizational data store.
- With several computers at dispersed sites, lack of standardization of equipment, software and data storage is possible.
- Control is more difficult.

14.2.2 File-based and database systems

The data store serving the programs with data can be designed either as a series of independent files or as an integrated database. The choice will depend on a number of factors. The differences between file-based and database systems have been extensively covered in Chapter 8. Here, only summaries of the main points are made. The following features suggest that a database system is more appropriate:

- The same data is commonly shared by several applications.
- Data in one part of the organization is related to, and integrated with, data in other parts.
- The data structure for the organization is stable.
- The applications for which the data is to be used are likely to change over time.
- There is a need for flexible enquiry and reporting facilities.

The following features suggest that a file-based system may be suitable:

- There is little or no common data usage between different applications.
- There is a need for fast transaction processing.
- Sophisticated, flexible enquiry facilities are not required – reports are standard and unchanging.

Database systems, if appropriate, offer substantial advantages over file-based systems in the same circumstances:

- Data redundancy is minimized, and database consistency is maintained.

- Application programmer productivity is enhanced.

- Control over data is centralized, leading to better data management.

- Data can be shared easily between different applications.

- The physical details of data storage are hidden from users, who are presented with tailor-made logical views of relevant data.

Difficulties and disadvantages of database systems include:

- The need for integrated initial design (difficult) rather than piecemeal design of files to meet problems as they arise (easy).

- Processing is usually slower than with file-based systems.

- The need to purchase costly database management software and extensive disk storage.

14.2.3 Batch and online systems

Another choice to be made by the analyst is between batch and online systems. Some parts of the system can be designed in batch mode, whereas others may use online processing.

In **batch mode**, transactions are entered into the computer system and held temporarily before processing until a batch has been input. The entire set of transactions is then processed. The advantages of batch processing are:

- **Control:** Because data is not processed immediately on entry there is a further chance to detect and correct errors before processing. The following controls are possible:
  - **Control totals:** A total for, say, the value of all invoices in a batch is generated manually and then compared with a computer-generated total before processing.
  - **Hash totals:** This is the same as a control total, except that the figure is meaningless – for example, the sum of all account codes in a batch.
  - **Visual checks:** A list of all input transactions can be printed after batch input and compared with the source documents before processing.
  - **Transaction counts:** A computer-generated count of the number of input transactions is compared with a manual total.

- **Efficient processing:** Data can be held and then processed at a time when there is little demand on computer resources.

Batch-processing systems are used for processing large volumes of repetitive transactions where control considerations and the efficient utilization of computing capacity are important. Typical applications are payroll, sales and purchase ledger processing, and stock movements. The drawback of this form of processing is that it may take some time after input for a transaction to change relevant files or a database. This is only a disadvantage where up-to-date reports or enquiry results are needed.

Online processing occurs when a transaction is processed immediately on input. Batch controls over erroneous input are not possible, because each transaction is handled one by one. The requirement that immediate processing occurs implies that the computer must be available at all times to accept and process. This leads to under-utilization of resources during slack periods. Any application that requires an immediate response, as many enquiries do, must be carried out in online mode. Similarly, some applications require the effects of an updating transaction to be immediate. Airline booking systems and current stock systems are examples.

14.2.4 Input methods

At this stage, the analyst will also specify the main types of input media and methods that are to be used. The main considerations are:

- volumes of transactions to be input
- speed of input required
- initial and operating costs of the chosen method
- degree of accuracy required over input
- special characteristics of the application.

The input method will be intimately connected with the decisions on batch and online processing. Those methods associated with fast, high-volume, repetitive input are more likely candidates for batch processing. A detailed range of input devices and media was provided in Chapter 3; the main alternatives are:

- **Keyboard:** Keyboard input is cheap on initial cost but high on operating costs because it is a heavily labour-intensive form of input. Without sophisticated computer-operated checks (check digits, master-file checks, and so on) there are likely to be high error rates unless batch entry with its associated controls is chosen. The main advantage of keyboard entry is that it is very flexible on the kinds of data that can be input.

- **Preprinted character recognition:** The main examples are optical character recognition (OCR) and magnetic ink character recognition (MICR). The input equipment 'reads' the input document and converts the characters to a machine-understandable form. There is a high initial cost for the purchase of the equipment but very low operating costs, as little labour is used for input. This means that this method is suitable for high-volume input. Low error rates are also a feature. The method is limited to those applications where known identifying data can be preprinted on documents – for example the cheque and account number together with the bank sort code on a cheque, or the account code and amount on an electricity bill. The method is inflexible on the kinds of data to be input.

- **Optical mark recognition:** This is used where a preprinted document is produced that contains selection boxes. These are marked indicating choices and can be 'read' by special equipment, which is preprogrammed as to the location of the boxes. The presence or absence of a mark is converted to a machine-understandable form. Once again there are high initial costs, low operating costs and low error rates. This method is suitable for high-volume applications where selection between alternatives is required. Typical applications are market research surveys, automated marking of multiple-choice examination questions and stock selection.

- **Bar-code reading:** Bar-codes that identify items are preprinted and attached to the items. The bar-codes are read in by special readers, often using laser light. Bar-codes need to be attached to items, so the method is associated with data input over the movement of material goods. Examples are the sale of goods in supermarkets, library loans and stock movements. Input of data is simple to achieve, needs no skill and is error-free. The applications to which it is put are mainly in the handling of items of stock.

- **Voice input:** Speech input is now widely available. A number of simple applications where a limited vocabulary is employed, such as navigating the menus of a call centre, can already be controlled completely by voice. Developments in speech recognition are leading to the use of speech input for more general activities such as word processing.

- **Remote input:** If the system can be accessed remotely, for example by Internet access to a web server, input data may be transmitted directly to the system by the customers or employees themselves. The data input process may be automated, as in the case of EDI, or may entail a manual submission, as in the case of a business-to-customer e-commerce site.

14.2.5 Applications packages and specially designed programs

It may be possible to purchase an applications package rather than writing special programs for the system. Packages are written by a third party and sold to many customers, so the cost of this alternative is considerably lower than designing, coding and testing programs from scratch. Packages also have the advantage that they are quick to implement, can be demonstrated in action prior to purchase and generally have good documentation. They will also have been tried and tested by many previous purchasers. These can be consulted on the quality of the package and the support given by the software house or dealer selling it.

However, packages may not integrate easily with existing software that has been written especially for the organization. The package may also not suit precisely the data-processing and information needs. The software house selling the package will attempt to introduce as much flexibility as possible into it, thus accommodating as wide a market as possible. However, this may introduce unwanted inefficiency into the program.

More recently, the trend has been away from 'purpose-built' software and towards the use of packages that can be customized to fulfil the differing requirements of particular organizations. Some of these products are aimed at quite specific markets, such as the student record-keeping systems produced by software vendors for use in colleges and universities. The core of the system is retained for each implementation, but additional modules or different functionality can be purchased; the system can be customized to take into account the particular regulations and procedures of each institution. Other examples are more generic in function. Examples are the enterprise resource planning software produced by companies such as SAP and Oracle. These packages attempt to bring together the information systems supporting the different functional areas in an organization. These were described in detail in Chapter 2. Also, the accounting software produced by vendors such as Sage is sector-independent but can be tailored to meet specific local conditions. The business reasons for this approach provide advantages for both the purchaser and the vendor. For the purchaser, the costs of production are shared between many, thereby reducing the purchase price. Also, the ability to tailor the package to local needs is an attractive option. For the vendor, the opportunity arises to resell the core of a product that has already been developed. Also, the flexibility to adapt the product often leads to ongoing contracts with the purchaser for maintenance and enhancement.

The analyst is more likely to recommend a package if:

- Cost is a major consideration.
- The system needs to be implemented quickly.
- The data-processing and information requirements are standard ones for the type of business function to be computerized.
- The organization does not have a mature computer centre that can write and maintain software.
- Well-established packages from reputable companies exist.

Some business functions are more amenable to packages than others. For instance, all businesses have standard accounting activities – sales, general and purchase-ledger processing, and payroll. It is common to buy packages for these. Even quite large companies will purchase mainframe software in these areas.

14.2.6 Hardware

Different designs will have different hardware requirements. Some of these factors have been taken into account in the choice of input method and equipment. The analyst will need to take decisions on suitable processing, output, communications and storage hardware. This will depend largely on the amount of processing required by the system, the complexity of the software and the number of users attached to the system. Choices on whether to develop a centralized or distributed system will obviously have hardware implications. The amount of data to be stored and decisions over adopting a file-based approach as opposed to a database with a database management system will affect storage hardware needs.

The analyst suggests two or three alternative systems to management. All the factors discussed in this section will be taken into account in each design. Management will need not only an explanation of the alternative designs but also estimates of the costs and time schedules associated with each alternative. The data flow diagrams will provide a valuable tool for the analyst in developing alternative high-level designs, as they can be used to indicate which features of a system are to be computerized and how this is to be achieved. The way that data flow diagrams do this is treated in the next section.

14.3 ■ Automation boundaries

As well as revealing the logic of data flows between processes in process modelling, the data flow diagram can be the basis of design in selecting and communicating which processes are to be computerized and how this is to be achieved. Automation boundaries are used. The data flow diagram as a design aid can best be understood by a consideration of the following examples.

Kismet case study 14.4

In Figure 14.7(a), the automation boundaries suggest that the entire order-processing system for Kismet is to be computerized. Customer orders flow into the system, and company invoices, dispatch notes, and approved and unapproved company orders flow out.

In contrast, Figure 14.7(b) shows the automation boundaries as encompassing the production of the company order (approved as a customer acknowledgement or ▶

Figure 14.7(a) Automation boundaries for the Kismet system suggesting a fully computerized order/stock/invoice processing system

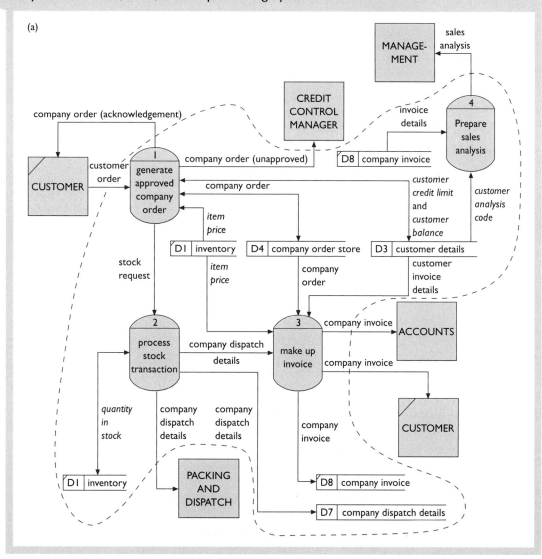

unapproved and sent to the credit control manager) together with the company invoice. Stock processing and generation of the dispatch details are carried out manually. The computer system produces a stock request, which is (presumably) sent to the warehouse, where the goods are picked and a dispatch note generated manually and sent with the goods to packing and dispatch. The dispatch note details are then input into the computer system, which retrieves a copy of the order from the company order store and generates a company invoice. These two alternative approaches can be presented clearly and discussed with the aid of the data flow diagram.

Figure 14.7(b) Automation boundaries for the Kismet system suggesting a computerized order/stock/invoice system with a manual stock control system

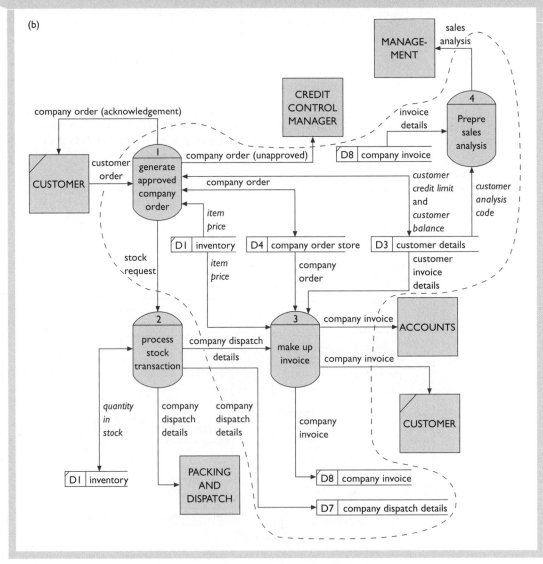

Figure 14.8 provides two alternatives for process 1 – that of generating an approved company order. The diagrams show the difference between the representation of a batch-processing system and an online real-time system.

Figure 14.8(a) illustrates an online system for the processing of approved orders. The customer order details when input are immediately subject to pricing and credit checking and if successful a stock request is output to process 2 – process stock transaction. The unapproved orders are stored temporarily in D6, where they are output in a batch for the credit control manager.

In Figure 14.8(b), the orders are input and stored temporarily prior to pricing and credit checking. The automation boundaries suggest that the input of the orders is distinct from the processes that follow. In the data flow diagram, it is also easy to see that the unapproved orders are stored and then output in a batch for consideration by the credit control manager. Likewise, the stock requests from the approved orders are stored and later used as input to the stock process.

Figure 14.8(a) Automation boundaries for the process of generating an approved company order (process 1) showing online order processing of customer orders

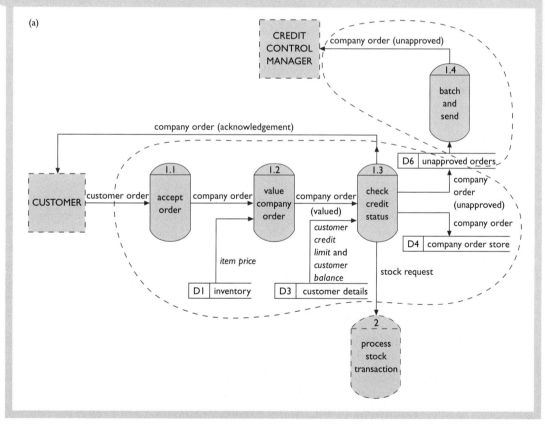

Figure 14.8(b) Automation boundaries for the process of generating an approved
company order (process 1) showing batch processing of customer orders

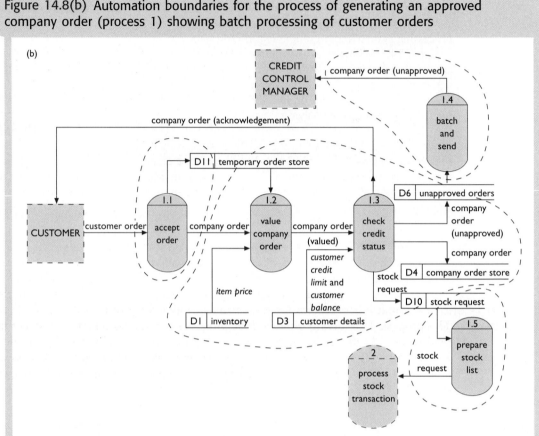

At this stage, the analyst should present several alternative designs as suggestions
for the way in which the new computer system can be developed to meet the needs of
the organization. Two or three alternatives should promote sufficiently wide-ranging
debate without losing focus on the central issues. These designs may be different ways
of physically providing much the same facilities – the choice between online and batch
processing or between centralized and distributed systems can be regarded as falling
under this heading. Or they may be different designs providing different levels of facilities. In the latter case, the suggestions might be:

- A minimal, low-cost system that meets the basic needs for which the systems project was initiated.

- A medium-cost solution that will indicate extra opportunities that can be realized
  by computerization at moderate cost.

- A grander system that illustrates how the organization can exploit the full benefits
  of computerization in the area of the system under consideration.

A basic design for Kismet would cover just the order processing and invoicing, as in Figure 14.7(b). A medium-cost solution (Figure 14.7(a)) will handle stock control as well. This can include an automatic reordering system that produces purchase orders for suppliers when stocks of an item fall below a certain level. In other words, the analyst may provide a basic design and also one that provides extra facilities (at extra cost). A more extensive computerization would involve the integration of the accounting system with the order-processing system and stock control systems, would have facilities for accepting credit card purchases direct from the public by phone or through a website, and would have programs that optimally schedule van deliveries.

In presenting the various alternative designs, the analyst will have made decisions on all the features listed in Section 14.2 – online and batch, centralized versus distributed systems, file-based versus database systems, packages and specially written programs, hardware, and input methods. For each design, the analyst will be required to submit cost estimates and a schedule for the time to be taken to complete the project. It is crucial in systems design that the analyst always maintain a clear idea of the management constraints and organizational objectives under which the project is being developed.

The suggested systems designs will be presented to management at a structured formal review. At this stage, management will select one system and will give the 'go ahead' to the analyst to start the work of deriving a detailed design for this system. Walkthroughs and formal reviews occur at several stages during a project's life cycle. Section 14.4 covers these.

14.4 Walkthroughs and formal reviews

At various stages, the analyst may wish to present aspects of his or her work to others. This is achieved through walkthroughs and reviews. The difference between them is that a walkthrough is an interactive presentation of some part of the system by the analyst. The aim is for the analyst to present ideas or problems and receive useful feedback from the participants. In contrast, the formal review is a public presentation of some aspects of analysis and design and is used as a milestone in the computer project. Formal reviews are often used as exit criteria from one stage in the analysis and design process so that progress may be made into the following stages.

14.4.1 Walkthroughs

A walkthrough consists of perhaps three or four people, including the analyst, who will present some aspect of the system in the stages of analysis or design. Data flow diagrams, entity–relationship models and flowcharts may be used to illustrate points. Each walkthrough should last no more than 20 to 30 minutes – much longer and the participants' attention will wander. The participants, other than the analyst making the presentation, may be other analysts or programmers, users or management.

The purpose of the walkthrough is to communicate some particular aspect of systems analysis or design to the group so that useful feedback may be provided for the analyst.

The walkthrough is often used when analysts run into particular problems or wish to check out their understanding of a part of a system with users. They are informal, semi-structured meetings that occur on an *ad hoc* basis throughout analysis and design. Communication is of the essence in a walkthrough, so structured tools, with their emphasis on logic rather than physical details, are indispensable aids.

14.4.2 Formal reviews

Formal reviews may occur at many points during the systems analysis and design of a project and are used as a formal recognition that some major point has been reached in the process. A successful formal review implies that the next stage may be started, an unsuccessful one that some failure in analysis or design has been noted and needs to be reworked.

At formal reviews (sometimes called **inspections**), the analyst or team of analysts make a formal presentation. This will be backed up by documentation, which will have been previously circulated to participants. It is the purpose of the review to find errors or shortcomings in the stage of analysis or design presented.

The participants in a formal review are generally as follows:

1. **The moderator or review leader:** This individual is responsible for organizing the review after being notified by the analysts that the required stage has been achieved. The review leader circulates the documentation, schedules the meeting and ensures that all relevant and interested parties are invited as inspectors.

   During the inspection, the review leader ensures that all the relevant points are covered in a proper manner. Given that the nature of the inspection process is fault finding, it is important that all participants in the project realize that finding faults at this stage is beneficial to the project as a whole. To discover these later will need redesign, which will undoubtedly be both expensive and troublesome. Equally, it is important for the inspectors to realize that an over-critical stance may be counter-productive. Either analysts will be induced to cover up or minimize the importance of errors, or they may not wish to make a presentation until everything is '110% perfect'. Political considerations may also influence the review session. Participants may have a vested interest in delaying, blocking or changing the course of development of a project. It is the responsibility of the review leader to ensure that the review is conducted in the most unbiased, constructive way possible.

2. **Inspectors:** The inspection group consists of:
   (a) technical people who may be brought into the review for their experience in the area;
   (b) representatives of those who will use and be affected by the new system;
   (c) specialists who will have an interest in the system once it is working.

   Auditors are the most important examples of this last group.

   The role of the inspectors is to assess the proposed stage with a view to locating errors or shortcomings. They will base their examination mainly on documentation provided beforehand by analysts.

3. **Systems analysts:** The systems analyst provides beforehand the documentation on which the presentation will be based. During the presentation, the analyst may provide a brief overview of the contents of the documentation. The main part of the presentation, though, will revolve around questions on the documentation raised by the inspectors and answered by the analyst.

After the formal review (at which a secretary may take notes on the major points raised), it is the responsibility of the analyst to rework areas that have been found to be lacking and to satisfy the review leader that this has been done. In the event of serious shortcomings, another review will be required.

Formal reviews may occur at a number of points during the development of a project. Major reviews will probably occur at the following:

1. **Systems design**: To consider alternative designs.

2. **Detailed design**: To consider the systems specification consisting of:
   (a) hardware specifications
   (b) database or file specifications
   (c) program specifications
   (d) input/output specifications
   (e) identification of procedures surrounding the system
   (f) implementation schedules.

3. **Implementation**: To consider the results of a formal systems test.

Reviews are one of the important controls that may be exercised over the development of the project.

Summary

The purpose of systems design is to present alternative solutions to the problem situation. High-level logical models have been developed for the system, involving no prior physical design considerations, so it is easy to illustrate and communicate different approaches in outline for new systems.

The logical model of the system needs to be amended to incorporate any new requirements. At this stage, inefficiencies in the model and any physical aspects are removed. Both of these are legacies of having used an existing physical system as the basis for analysis and design. Alternative designs are illustrated using automation boundaries on the data flow diagrams. In deriving these designs the analyst must pay attention to physical design features. The most important of these concern decisions over centralized and distributed processing, file-based and database systems, online and batch processing, packages and programs, input methods and hardware. The analyst will restrict the number of suggested designs to two or three. For each, a cost estimate and implementation schedule will be given. The presentation of these suggestions will be made during a formal review. Management will decide on which, if any, of the presented systems is to be undertaken. The analyst will carry out a detailed design of the chosen system. This work is covered in Chapter 15.

Review questions

1. What are the objectives of systems design?

2. How is *systems analysis* distinguished from *systems design*?

3. In providing alternative systems designs, what considerations should a systems analyst employ?

4. How do automation boundaries help in the design process?

5. How is the difference between online and batch processing shown with the use of data flow diagrams and automation boundaries?

6. What is the difference in purpose between a *walkthrough* and a *formal review*?

7. What roles do the participants in a formal review play?

Exercises

1. What are the specific advantages and disadvantages for Kismet in adopting a batch system as distinct from an online system for order approval as shown in Figure 14.8?

2. What are the specific advantages and disadvantages for Kismet in adopting a more highly automated system as indicated in Figure 14.7(a) as compared to that shown in Figure 14.7(b)?

3. 'A proposed system was given in the feasibility study along with its associated costs and benefits. It is a waste of time and money to present alternatives at this stage when a system has already been agreed.' How would you answer this criticism?

CASE STUDY 14

Kemswell Theatre

Go over your answers to the data flow diagram produced for Case Study 12 (the introduction to the Kemswell Theatre booking system):

1. Eliminate reference to any physical aspects that have entered the model.

2. Suggest additional processes/functions that would be useful to a theatre booking system and incorporate them into the data flow diagrams.

3. Derive two alternative designs and illustrate them by automation boundaries in the data flow diagrams.

Recommended reading

Avison D. and Fitzgerald G. (2003). *Information Systems Development: Methodologies, Techniques and Tools*, 3rd edn. McGraw-Hill

This well-established book covers a range of techniques and methodologies for systems analysis and design. The book provides a comprehensive coverage of data, process, rapid, blended, and people-oriented methodologies. This edition contains new material on ERP and the development of e-commerce applications. The book is suitable for those covering an information systems course at undergraduate level.

Bittner K. and Spence I. (2002). *Use Case Modeling*. Addison-Wesley

Use case modelling provides an interesting context to the topic of automation boundaries which are covered in this chapter.

Evans E. (2003). *Domain-driven Design: Tackling Complexity in the Heart of Software.* Addison-Wesley

This tackles the issues of systems design in the context of a particular approach called domain-driven design. The book provides examples of best practice in design and includes a number of case studies.

Farmer R., Skidmore S. and Mills G. (1998). *SSADM: Models and Methods.* NCC Blackwell

A clear, straightforward text suitable for reference on SSADM.

Flowers S. (1999). *Software Failure, Management Failure: Amazing Stories and Cautionary Tales.* Wiley

This book is a collection of case studies of systems failures such as the Performing Rights Society, the London Ambulance Service and the Taurus London Stock Exchange system. The book encourages the reader to learn lessons about good and bad systems design by analysing systems developments that have failed.

Flynn D.J. (1997). *Information Systems Requirements: Determination and Analysis*, 2nd edn. Maidenhead: McGraw-Hill

This is a comprehensive coverage of information systems analysis and design suitable for the student of computing studies who wishes to become acquainted with management and non-technical issues in analysis and design.

Yourdon Inc. (1993). *Yourdon Systems Method: Model Driven Systems Development.* Englewood Cliffs, NJ: Prentice Hall

This is useful as a statement of a systems development methodology by one of the founding father companies of structured systems analysis and design. It is suitable as an example reference of a commercial methodology.

Chapter 15

Detailed design, implementation and review

Learning outcomes

On completion of this chapter, you should be able to:

- Describe how the high-level logical model derived from analysis of a system is converted into a physical design and systems specification
- Use a range of techniques to specify the physical design of a system
- Appreciate the importance of input and output design
- Explain the advantages of adopting a modular approach in systems design
- Define the function of schema in database design
- Evaluate different approaches to and plan effectively for systems changeover
- Describe the role and importance of evaluation and maintenance in systems development.

Introduction

In Chapter 14, it was seen how the system developer (or analyst) uses the logical model of the system to suggest design alternatives for the new physical system. Broad decisions were taken over the extent of computerization and the types of system that could be developed for this. Having obtained agreement from the relevant management authority on the choice of system, the analyst must now carry out detailed design of the new system. This chapter covers this and subsequent stages in the systems life cycle.

The detailed design of the system includes specification of the hardware, software, database, user interface and schedule for implementation. The detailed specification is analogous to an architect's or engineer's blueprint – it is the document from which the system will be built. Once agreement has been obtained on the detailed design, steps will be taken to acquire and install the hardware, write or purchase and test the software, train staff, develop the database and convert and load the contents of existing files. The system is then ready to take over from the current one. Various methods of changeover are discussed. After changeover, a post-implementation review considers the effectiveness of the system and its relation to its specification and original objectives. Finally, ongoing maintenance and development will be needed during the useful life of the system.

15.1 Detailed design

Data flow diagrams were used to develop a high-level logical model of the processes and the data flows between them in the system. They were particularly helpful in sketching design alternatives using automation boundaries. The logic of the processes themselves has been captured in structured tools such as decision tables, structured English or logic flowcharts. The data model of the organization has been produced using entity–relationship modelling.

The use of this logical approach has ensured that no premature physical design decisions have been taken. The concentration has always been on the question 'What logically is required of the system and what logically must be achieved in order to do this?' not 'How are we physically going to accomplish this?' However, the time has come to move away from these logical models towards the detailed physical design of the computerized system (see Figure 15.1). The data flow diagrams and logic representations developed so far will be invaluable in producing program specifications. The entity model will be essential in designing a database model.

Figure 15.1 Tools used during the stages of systems analysis and design

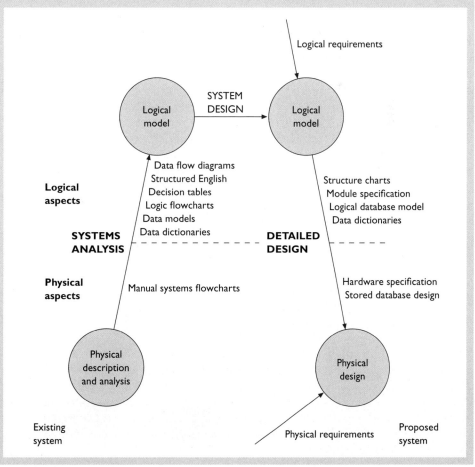

Any system can be considered as being composed of input, output, storage and processing elements. This approach is used in looking at the various tasks to be covered in detailed systems design. Control in systems has been covered extensively in Chapter 9. Control features figure prominently in the design of all the other elements.

15.1.1 Process design

Process design covers the need to design and specify the processing hardware, and to design and specify the software to run in the central processing unit.

The specification of processor hardware is a technical skill beyond the scope of this text. The analyst will need to consider the demands to be made on the processor. In particular, the volume of transactions to be processed per day and the processing requirement for each, the speed of response needed for interactive enquiries, the number of simultaneous users, the types of peripheral devices required, the amount of RAM, the complexity of programs, and the extent to which the system should be able to cope with future increases in demand are all determinants of the processing power required. Decisions taken on whether to centralize or distribute computing and the mix between batch and online processing will all affect the decision.

Figure 15.2 Part of a structure chart dealing with payslip preparation for a payroll application

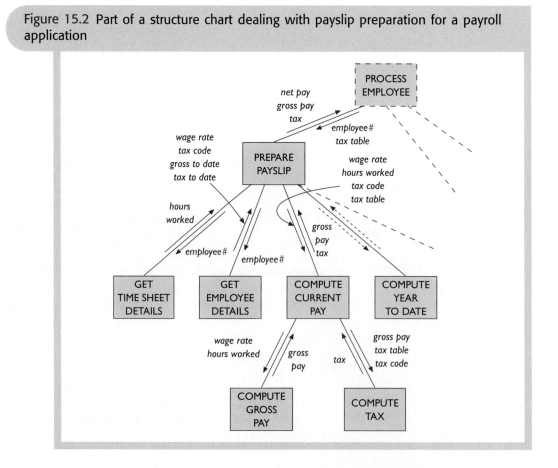

Figure 15.3 A module specification for the input/process/output for the PREPARE PAYSLIP process

SYSTEM	PAYROLL PROCESS
MODULE NAME	PREPARE PAYSLIP
AUTHOR	J. SMITH
DATE	03/07/2004
MODULE CALLS	GET TIME SHEET DETAILS
	GET EMPLOYEE DETAILS
	COMPUTE CURRENT PAY
	COMPUTE YEAR TO DATE
	: : : :
	: : : :
MODULE IS CALLED BY	PROCESS EMPLOYEE
MODULE INPUTS	*employee#*
	tax table
MODULE OUTPUTS	*gross pay*
	tax
	net pay
PROCESS	**DO** GET TIME SHEET DETAILS
	DO GET EMPLOYEE DETAILS
	DO COMPUTE CURRENT
	SET *net pay = gross pay − tax*
	DO COMPUTE YEAR TO DATE
	: : : :
	: : : :

The development of program specifications is facilitated by the structured tools used so far. Programs are regarded as being composed of various modules. These program modules should be constructed so that each performs a single independent function, is independently testable and leads to code that is easy to understand and amend at a later date if necessary. The modular design should also facilitate the addition of extra modules if needed later and so aid the flexibility of the system. Connections between **modules** can be illustrated with a **structure chart**. These terms will now be explained. An example of part of a structure chart and a module specification can be seen in Figures 15.2 and 15.3.

Modules

A module contains a set of executable instructions for performing some process. At the design stage, these instructions may be specified using structured English or decision tables. At a later stage, this specification will be converted into program instructions in the chosen programming language.

Data may be passed from one module to another. This is akin to being passed from one data process to another in a data flow diagram. In Figure 15.2, part of a set of interconnected modules handling a payroll process is shown. Each module is named, and the data flows between modules are illustrated.

The chart shows that the module PREPARE PAYSLIP requires that four other modules be executed. These are GET TIME SHEET DETAILS, GET EMPLOYEE DETAILS, COMPUTE CURRENT PAY and COMPUTE YEAR TO DATE. The module COMPUTE CURRENT PAY is said to be called by the module PREPARE PAYSLIP. COMPUTE CURRENT PAY itself calls COMPUTE GROSS PAY and COMPUTE TAX. The inputs and outputs from any module are shown entering or leaving the module box. Needless to say, all the data inputs and outputs will be in the data dictionary.

A module is independently specified in a module specification as illustrated in Figure 15.3. This is sometimes called an **input/process/output (IPO) chart**. The module specification, together with the data dictionary entries, is sufficient on its own for the programmer to write code. It is not necessary when coding a module to have any understanding of the other modules in the system or to have them fitting together.

This is very different from traditional programming methods, where monolithic code would be produced. The integration between functions then allowed programmers to produce a code that was very efficient in its use of central processor time. However, programs were difficult to understand, and bugs were frequently time-consuming to find and correct. Alteration of the code at a later stage, for example to introduce an additional function, might lead to unpredicted effects elsewhere in the program. It soon came to be the case that over 50% of the cost of a project over its life cycle was concerned with debugging, amending and generally maintaining software.

Central processing power is now cheap. It is not necessary to produce monolithic code designed to be efficient in its use of computing power. Rather, the aims have been to maximize flexibility so that programs are easy to alter, to enable programmers to produce code that is readily understandable once written and to ensure that addition of new functions is straightforward. The programming task as a consequence becomes more predictable. This is one of the advantages of the structured approach – the programming task is more easily controlled (and, incidentally, more easily costed). As will be seen in Section 15.1.2, data flow diagrams can be translated directly to produce interconnected modules.

Structure charts

The structure chart, part of an example of which is shown in Figure 15.2, is a diagrammatic representation of the way that modules are connected. For each module, it shows what data is input and output and what other modules call it or are called by it. There is no more information (in fact considerably less) in a structure chart than in the set of module specifications. However, the structure chart does give a picture of the system that is easy to understand. Frequently, the data flows between modules are omitted for the sake of clarity. The structure chart is hierarchical. The use of hierarchical charts together with input/process/output specifications is called the **HIPO (hierarchical input/process/output) technique**.

Looking at Figure 15.3, it can be seen that the module PREPARE PAYSLIP calls up the four modules GET TIME SHEET DETAILS, GET EMPLOYEE DETAILS, COMPUTE CURRENT PAY and COMPUTE YEAR TO DATE in that order. These will each be specified independently. Figure 15.2 shows these as occurring in order from left to right. This is the implied sequence of execution of modules.

Corresponding to the three basic structures of structured English:

sequential (DO A, DO B . . .)

decision (IF ⟨condition⟩
        THEN DO A
        ELSE DO B)

repetition (REPEAT A
        UNTIL ⟨condition⟩)

there are notational variants in the structure chart. These are illustrated in Figure 15.4.

Each module is normally considered to call its submodules and execute or perform them from left to right, as shown in Figure 15.4(a). Each submodule may itself call submodules and is not considered to have been executed until all its submodules have been executed. This order is shown in Figure 15.5.

Wherever a decision has to be made to execute one module rather than another, this is indicated by a diamond placed at the connection point, as in Figure 15.4(b). For instance, a part of a module dealing with processing a stock transaction will carry out

Figure 15.4 The relation between structure charts and structured English: (a) sequence; (b) decision; (c) repetition

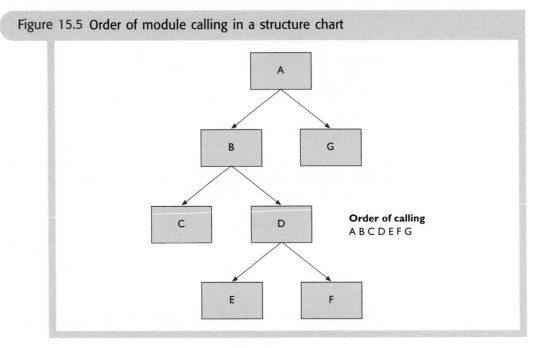

Figure 15.5 Order of module calling in a structure chart

Order of calling
A B C D E F G

different procedures if the transaction is an increment to stock (receipt of a delivery corresponding to a purchase order) than if it is a decrement (dispatch corresponding to a sales order). The parent module will test the transaction to determine its type.

A module may be executed repeatedly. This will be the case with batch transaction processing, where each one of a batch is treated in the same way. For instance, in preparing payslips the process of computing pay is repeated for each employee. This iteration is shown by means of a circular arrow, as in Figure 15.4(c).

15.1.2 Modular design

The advantages of modular design as represented using hierarchical structure charts and module specifications are:

- Easier design of programs: analysts can specify major tasks at a high level and later break these down into their detail. This complements the development of the analysis stage, in which top-down decomposition was stressed.

- The structure developed through modular design consists of manageable chunks. This means that the parts of the system and their interrelations are represented in a way that can be understood as a whole.

- Individual programmers and designers can be given different modules and can work relatively independently of one another.

- Project management, scheduling of design, costing and allocation of manpower are made easier.

- The separate modules may be tested individually so that errors can be located precisely and easily corrected.

■ The final system will be modular. Individual modules can be 'lifted out', altered or inserted easily with the confidence that their effect on other modules is specified by input and output data and the processes that occur.

In order that design may achieve these ends, it is crucial that modules are loosely coupled and cohesive.

Coupling

The idea of coupling was introduced in Chapter 1, where the degree of subsystem coupling was defined in terms of the extent to which a change in the state of one subsystem led to a change in the state of another. Modular decoupling is similar in concept. As data is what passes between modules, it is data connections that are important.

Two modules are less coupled:

■ the fewer the number of types of data item passed from one to the other;

■ the less they share the same data from a data store.

A module that is only loosely coupled to other modules has a simple interface and is therefore easy to design, code, change and test independently.

Cohesion

Modules, as well as being loosely coupled, should be cohesive. This is harder to define. A module is more cohesive if:

■ It consists of one single function, such as **COMPUTE GROSS PAY**.

■ It consists of more than one function, but each is executed in sequence: for example, **PREPARE PAYSLIP** consists of four sequentially executed modules.

■ It performs a set of independent actions that are linked by being performed at the same time. Examples of this are initialization and termination routines concerned with data structures used by a set of processes.

The advantages of modular design as stated can only be fully realized with modules that are loosely coupled to one another yet highly cohesive internally.

Kismet case study 15.1

This part of the Kismet case study introduces the development of the structure chart and module specification. The level 1 data flow diagram for the Kismet order-processing system is given again in Figure 15.6(a) and the level 2 breakdown in Figure 15.7(a). These will be used to generate a (partial) structure chart for the Kismet system.

The main part of the level 1 data flow diagram suggests that there are three separate functions. The first deals with the generation of approved orders. The second processes stock transactions to update stock records and produce dispatch notes. Finally, invoices are made up and dispatched. This can be seen in the simple structure chart of Figure 15.6(b).

The structure chart dealing with the generation of approved orders is shown in Figure 15.7(b). As is common in the production of hierarchical structure charts, the data flows between the various modules are omitted. This is usually done to simplify the chart. However, there is another reason. The structure is prepared before the individual module specification, and it is at this point that the analyst's attention is devoted to

▶

Figure 15.6 (a) A data flow diagram of Kismet's order-processing system;
(b) part of a structure chart for the Kismet order-processing system

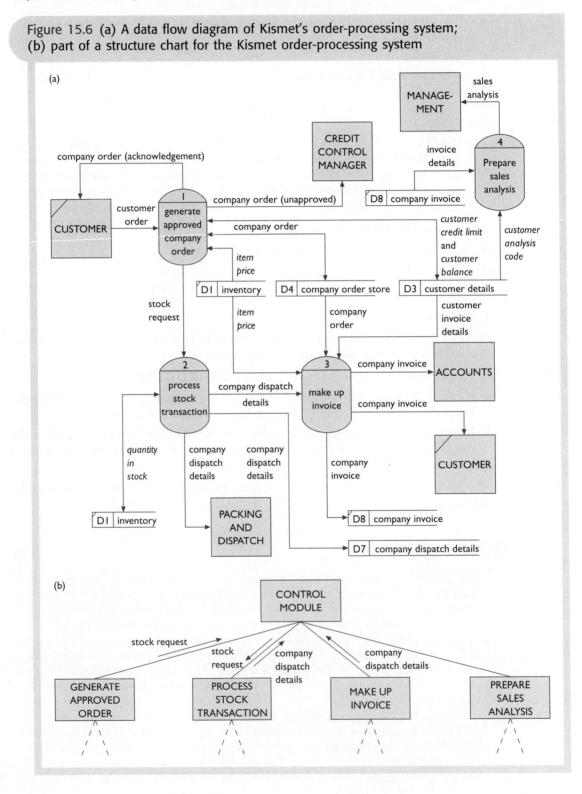

Figure 15.7 (a) The data flow diagram for the generation of an approved order;
(b) a structure chart for the generation of an approved order

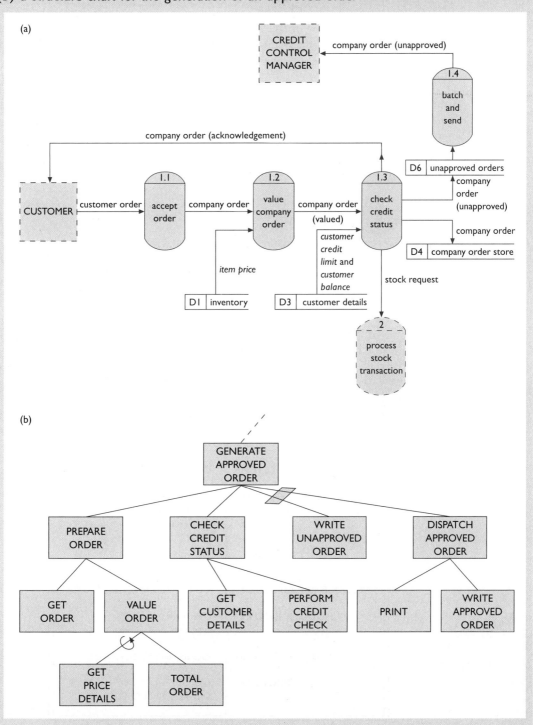

the precise description of the data flows. Structure charts are then first derived without all the data flows.

Consideration of the data flow diagram in Figure 15.7(a) indicates that the process of generating an approved order includes three important parts: preparing the priced company order, checking the credit status of the customer for the order and, depending on the result of the credit check, handling the order in one way or another. This is shown by the second-level decomposition of the tasks in the structure chart (Figure 15.7(b)).

Preparing the priced order consists of two tasks. First, the order details are obtained through keyboard entry. This is shown by the module **GET ORDER**. Second, the order details are then used to value the order (**VALUE ORDER**). This itself consists of two tasks. The first is to obtain the price details for each item ordered, and the second is to calculate the total value of the order. Note that preparing the order involves the two processes **GET ORDER** and **VALUE ORDER** in that sequence. This is just the sequence of the two corresponding data processes in the data flow diagram – process 1.1 and process 1.2 (Figure 15.7 (a)).

The next process in the chain, process 1.3, is performed by the next module to be executed – **CHECK CREDIT STATUS**.

Finally, depending on the outcome of the credit check, the order is stored (unapproved) in store D6 or printed for dispatch to the customer and stored (approved) in store D4. This corresponds to the alternatives shown on the structure chart (Figure 15.7(b)).

The approved order is also needed by the module concerned with processing the stock transaction. It is passed, minus its price details, as the output 'stock request' of the **GENERATE APPROVED ORDER** module via the control module.

A sample of a module specification is given in Figure 15.8. The data inputs and outputs will be defined in the data dictionary. Note that the position of the module **CHECK CREDIT STATUS** in the hierarchy chart is determined by identifying the module that calls it, and the modules that it calls.

Figure 15.8 A module specification for CHECK CREDIT DETAIL

SYSTEM	ORDER PROCESSING
MODULE NAME	CHECK CREDIT STATUS
AUTHOR	J. SMITH
DATE	03/07/2004
MODULE CALLS	GET CUSTOMER DETAILS
	PERFORM CREDIT CHECK
MODULE IS CALLED BY	GENERATE APPROVED ORDER
MODULE INPUTS	*order total*
	customer#
MODULE OUTPUTS	*company order approval flag*
PROCESS	**DO** GET CUSTOMER DETAILS
	DO PERFORM CREDIT CHECK

15.1.3 Summary so far

The way a data flow diagram is used for the preparation of a structure chart can be summarized as follows:

1. View the diagram to establish whether the data processes fall into groups, each associated with a type of process. View the resulting grouped collections of data processes to establish the key functions in each group. If each group has only a single data process in it, this is straightforward.

2. Decompose these functions to obtain modules that are highly cohesive and loosely coupled. Note that the sequence of data processes will indicate the left-to-right ordering of modules. Data flows that are conditional on a test performed in a data process will correspond to alternative module selections. This can be indicated using the diamond symbol. Lower-level data flow diagrams are to be used in this decomposition.

3. Now specify each module separately ensuring that named data items and data collections are entered in the data dictionary and that the data produced by major modules corresponds to the data being passed between processes in the data flow diagrams.

This gives a general idea of the development of a hierarchical structure chart and module specification. Do not form the impression that once the data flow diagrams have been developed the production of the modular structure chart is a mechanical task. It is not. The analysis of high-level diagrams can often be difficult. Most important is the realization that to discover key functions and to decompose these into their constituents, each of which performs a single logical function that is translatable into a cohesive module, requires more than an uncritical reading of a data flow diagram. It is necessary for the analyst to obtain a deep appreciation of the system and the functions it performs. Although structured methods attempt to replace the art of design by the science of engineering, there is still a place for creative understanding.

15.1.4 Data store design

During systems analysis and design, a conceptual data model of the organization was developed. This was based on modelling entities and their relationships. Later, attributes of the entities were established. A normalized entity model was then developed to third normal form. The resulting normalized entities have been checked by deriving functional entity models to ensure that the various processes can be served with the data that they need. During systems design, a decision will have been made as to whether to service the future data needs of the organization via a database approach using a database management system or via an application-led, file-based approach. The considerations involved in this choice were covered in Chapter 14. Either way, detailed design of the data store will be required, and this will be aided by the normalized data model.

File-based systems

In general, a file-based approach will have been chosen if there is little or no common data usage between applications and there is a need for fast transaction processing. The analyst will need to design record layouts. This involves specifying the names of the fields in each record, their type (for example, text or numeric) and their length. Records may be of fixed or variable length. In the latter case, this is either because fields are allowed to vary in length or because some fields are repeated. Record structures can become quite complicated if groups of fields are repeated within already repeating groups of fields.

As well as record design, the storage organization and access for each file must be decided. This will determine the speed of access to individual records and the ease with which records can be added and deleted within the file. The most common types of storage organization are sequential, indexed, indexed-sequential, random storage with hashing, lists and inverted files. Different file organizations have different characteristics with respect to ease and speed of data storage and retrieval. Depending on the type of application, the most appropriate organization is chosen. The topic of files, file organization and file design was covered extensively in Chapter 7, and the reader is referred there for further information.

The analyst will need to specify suitable backing-store hardware. This is likely to be optical or magnetic disk-based unless the system is concerned with archiving data, in which case magnetic tape might prove a cheaper option. In order to select appropriate hardware, the analyst must take into account the number of files and within each file the number of records and the storage required for each, the file organization chosen, the response time required and likely future developments, especially in terms of increases in size. These characteristics will allow the analyst to calculate the total storage requirements and to specify appropriate hardware.

Database systems

It is likely that a database approach will have been selected if the same data is shared between many applications, if there is a large degree of integration of data and if flexible reporting and enquiry facilities are needed.

The analyst will use the conceptual data model as a guide to selecting the appropriate database model. Relational database systems allow great flexibility in the storage and retrieval of data. Although their relatively slow access times and high storage overheads can be a disadvantage, current developments in both hardware and relational database management systems are diminishing these drawbacks.

Relational databases have now established themselves as the most popular choice for database solutions. Relational database management software is usually accompanied by sophisticated query/fourth-generation languages, interfaces with spreadsheet models and networking facilities with other relational databases. Pre-written template software produced by fourth-generation languages for standard business functions, especially accounting, can also be purchased and tailored to the needs of the organization. An example is ORACLE, a relational database system, with SQL.

If the conceptual data model is hierarchical in nature, the applications for which it is to be used generally require hierarchical access, and if fast access to records is required, it is possible that a database management system operating with a hierarchical model will be chosen. This solution is diminishing rapidly in popularity; hierarchical databases are now largely confined to specialist applications and almost always operate on a mainframe computer platform.

Databases, database management systems and data models were covered extensively in Chapter 8 on database systems. The reader is referred to this chapter for a fuller account of the terms and concepts used in this section.

Provided that the database management system intended for purchase is known, the analyst can begin to design the **conceptual schema**. This is an overall logical view of the data model cast in terms of the data definition language of the database management system. It will contain integrity and authorization rules. In the case of a relational model, this will be a relatively straightforward translation of the normalized entity model. Each entity and each relationship will become a table. Each attribute of an entity will become a column in the table corresponding to the entity. The derivation of a conceptual model for hierarchical and network systems is less straightforward. This is partly because the notion of a genuine conceptual schema does not strictly apply.

For each user of the database an external schema is defined. This is part of the database that a user is entitled to access in order to carry out a function. The analyst will have determined the data needs of the users for their various tasks during systems analysis. This can now be accommodated in the database design. The access will correspond to certain entities, attributes of those entities and paths through the database via relationships.

The analyst must also design the internal schema. This describes how the database is physically stored. It will make reference to record ordering, pointers, indexes, block sizes and access paths. Good internal schema design will ensure an efficient database. Unlike conceptual and external schemas, an internal schema makes reference to physical aspects of the database. The way that external schemas relate to the conceptual schema, and the way this in turn relates to the storage schema, is specified in terms of external/conceptual and conceptual/internal mappings.

The design of the database must proceed in tandem with the module design as the programs specified need access to the database. There are therefore intimate relationships between the data flow diagrams, data models, structure charts, module specifications, database schemas and data dictionaries. For a large organization, there will be many data flow diagrams. The entity model may have several *hundred* entity types. It is a complicated task coordinating the interrelations between the various elements in analysis and design. **Computer-aided systems engineering** (CASE) software packages help in this. They also semi-automate the design process. See Chapter 16 for a longer discussion.

As in the case of file-based systems, the analyst will need to estimate sizes and types of hardware required.

Kismet case study 15.2

We can now consider the data store design for Kismet. The analyst has decided to develop a relational database system for Kismet. Although the organization carries out transaction processing, one of the major requirements of the new system is that it will be able to provide flexible enquiry and reporting facilities. This, together with the stable and integrated nature of the model, suggests that a relational database is appropriate.

The analyst will convert the fully normalized conceptual data model to produce the relational conceptual schema. Part of this schema is shown in Figure 15.9(a). It is defined within a typical relational data definition language (DDL). This definition should be compared with the corresponding normalized entity model for Kismet developed in Chapter 13, which covered data analysis and modelling. As can be seen, the derivation is straightforward. The fields *order#* and *item#* are character fields, each composed of six characters. The fields are not allowed to be empty for any row of the table. The *item quantity* is an integer.

Figure 15.9 Conceptual and external schema definitions for Kismet: (a) part of a relational conceptual schema for Kismet; (b) an external schema definition for a user making enquiries on the status of customer orders at Kismet

(a)

CREATE TABLE ORDER DETAIL (order# (**CHAR (6)**, **NONULL**
item# (**CHAR (6)**, **NONULL**
item quantity (**INTEGER**))

CREATE TABLE ORDER (order# (**CHAR (6)**, **NONULL**
(order date (**DATE**)
customer# (**CHAR (8)**))

(b)

DEFINE VIEW ORDER ENQUIRY

AS SELECT	ORDER.customer#, ORDER.order#, ORDER.order date, ORDER DETAIL.item#, ORDER DETAIL.item quantity, DISPATCH DETAIL.dispatch#, DISPATCH DETAIL.item#, DISPATCH DETAIL.dispatch quantity
FROM	ORDER, ORDER DETAIL, DISPATCH DETAIL
WHERE	ORDER.order# = ORDER DETAIL.order#
AND	ORDER DETAIL.order# = DISPATCH DETAIL.order#
ORDER BY	customer#

One of the functions required by Kismet is online enquiry of the status of any customer order. Given a customer *order #*, it is required that the contents of the order and the items and quantities dispatched against this order be accessible. This is defined as a view or external schema in Figure 15.9(b). The fields selected and tables accessible are specified. The relational join ensures that an *order #* is followed through the three tables. Once again, the reader should compare this with the conceptual schema and the entity model developed in Chapter 13.

15.1.5 Input/output design

There are two main aspects of input/output design. One is the specification of the hardware. The other is the design of the user–machine interface.

In the specification of hardware, many decisions will have already been determined by the data input methods broadly outlined in systems design, by the choices between batch and online systems and between centralized and distributed systems. The analyst will need to determine the number and range of input and output devices required in line with these decisions.

User interface design

The design of the user interface is a crucial aspect of program design. Most programs require data entry screens and screen or printed output. This will be controlled by software. However, design of this interface will not normally fall out of data flow diagrams but should be determined by an understanding of the types of user, their requirements and their levels of ability – in short, a model of the user.

The following factors have to be considered, along with a model of the user, in interface input design.

Screen design

The format and presentation of material on the monitor screen will affect the way that a user interacts with the system. Bad layout will result in errors of input, user fatigue and a tendency towards user rejection of the system.

Screen presentations should ensure that the material presented on screen is relevant, is provided in a logical manner and is simple and coherent. If data is to be input from documents, then the screen should mirror the layout of the document as far as possible.

Screens can be presented to the user in the form of:

- **Menus:** to allow simple selection.
- **Form filling:** where a cursor jumps from field to field on the screen waiting for data input at each field.
- **Interactive commands:** where a user keys in individual commands and data.

Controls

Users make mistakes. This occurs in transcription. Also, the source data from which they work can contain errors. Controls need to be built into the user interface to cover input. Controls were dealt with extensively in Chapter 9. The major controls over input are:

- **Batch controls:** such as sequencing, control totals, hash totals, listings for visual comparison.
- **Software controls:** such as check digits, master-file checks and echoes, range checks and layout checks.
- **Screen design:** sensible screen design prevents the errors already stated.
- **Codes:** the coding of items, accounts, and other entities can be accomplished to cut down data entry costs and at the same time ensure greater accuracy.

User guidance

Novice users will be unable to sit in front of a VDU and achieve much without considerable guidance and help from the system. In particular, users should always be capable of ascertaining where they are in a system – this is particularly important deep into a menu structure – and what the purpose is of the present facility. Even expert users may 'become lost' in a complex system and need guidance.

Help facilities should be available at all times to the user. There should be general help on the system and how to use it. Contextual help is also important. This is where pressing the 'help' button yields help based on the command that was used prior to the call for help. As well as aiding legitimate users, well-designed help systems unfortunately aid the unauthorized user in trespass.

Where a common entry is needed the system may suggest a default or at least a type of entry. For example:

DATE - - - - - - - -

is much less helpful than

DATE *DD/MM/YYYY*

or

DATE *04/07/2004*

where the current date is presented as default.

Error messages

Error messages should always be helpful in identifying the error. Messages such as 'UNIDENTIFIED COMMAND' or 'PARAMETER NOT RECOGNIZED' are unhelpful, although not as bad as 'ERROR 243 @45'. A helpful error message should not only analyse the error but also provide help to the user in recovery; for example, 'NUMERIC ACCOUNT CODE NOT EXPECTED. ALL ACCOUNT CODES BEGIN WITH A CHARACTER. PLEASE TRY AGAIN (FOR LIST OF ACCEPTABLE ACCOUNT CODES PRESS FUNCTION KEY 1)'.

Response time

Generally, response times to commands should be short. Lengthy response times, particularly for regular users, lead to irritation, errors and non-acceptance of the system. For complicated tasks and requests, though, especially with inexperienced users, rapid response times may increase errors and prevent learning.

Given all these considerations, the analyst will design the user interface with a model of the user in mind. Users can be categorized in several ways that affect the design. Three important categories are:

1. **Casual *v*. regular users:** Regular users become more knowledgeable about the system through use. They are also more likely to be provided with training if interaction with the computer system occupies much of their job. For such users, fast response times, interactive commands and defaults are important.

2. **Passive *v*. interactive users:** Interactive users are those who either develop systems or build decision support models. They are liable to have or want to have the facility to navigate around the system. Those responsible for using the system to answer online enquiries also often fall within the category of interactive user. These users rely heavily on a systematic knowledge of command structures. Passive users are best served with menus and form filling, which restrict their area of choice. Data input personnel fall into this category.

3. **Novice *v*. expert users:** This category is not the same as casual *v*. regular users. For instance, it is possible for both a novice and an expert to be a casual user of the system. Expert casual users are likely to require targeted but unobtrusive help facilities, whereas novices will need a complete step-by-step set of screen instructions.

The design of the user interface is one aspect of the design of the total system involving the user. **Human–computer interaction**, covered in a previous chapter, locates issues in user interface design within the much broader framework of the function of the system and the place of technology and people within this.

Reports and input documents

The analyst will also be responsible for designing documents that are used for input and for reports produced as output by the system. Many of the same considerations apply as for user interface design. Input documents should match screens as far as possible. Printed reports should always be designed with the aim of logical presentation and clarity in mind.

Kismet case study 15.3

Kismet users fall into a number of categories. There are data input personnel such as those concerned with order entry, payments received, purchase orders, and so on. These will be regular users passively responding to forms as presented on the screen. There will also be staff dealing with and tracing particular orders, dealing with customer enquiries and the like. These may be the same people as the order entry staff, although they need different and more flexible skills.

Middle management will use the system for monitoring and predicting the performance of the company. For example, the sales manager will wish to draw off reports of sales by customer type, by geographical area, by type of item, by date and by other parameters. This user is not likely to be a regular user of the computer system. Other members of the sales and accounts departments involved with sales and profit forecasting will interactively use and develop spreadsheet models fed by actual data. These will become expert interactive users.

An example of a specification of a form to appear on a screen is given in Figure 15.10. The customer order entry is carried out by a regular user of the system. A number of points should be noted and would be included along with the specification. The system generates the date, time and order number. This not only saves time but is done for reasons of security and control. The data entry clerk is presented with a customer number data entry field. The customer name is then displayed as an error control. The delivery address is extracted from the customer account details and displayed on screen, but the operator has the ability to overwrite this. The items ordered are entered by item number with a flashback description check. This screen is one of two. The

Figure 15.10 A screen layout design for customer order entry

second screen would allow more items to be ordered. The data entry clerk has the option to accept or reject the entered data as displayed on the screen. Various other checks would be performed. For example, the data would be validated as being possible: for example, not 31 June. The user is a regular user, so no on-screen help is given. If help is required, particularly as a result of error messages, this can be called up as described using keyboard function F1.

There will be a large number of such layout designs specifying the complete user interface. The analyst will have designed these with the different types of user in mind.

15.2 Systems specification

Detailed design results in a **systems specification**. This is a comprehensive document describing the system as it is to be produced. There is no agreed format for this specification, but it is likely to include the following:

- An executive summary: this provides a quick summary of the major points in the specification.
- A description of the proposed system and especially its objectives. Flow block diagrams and data flow diagrams can be used. The work to be carried out by the system and the various user functions should be covered.
- A complete specification of:
  - Programs: these will include module specifications and structure charts, together with test data.
  - Input: this will include specimen source documents, screen layouts, menu structures and control procedures.
  - Output: this will include specimen output reports, contents of listings, and so on.
  - Data storage: this is the specification of file and database structure.
- A detailed specification of controls operating over procedures within the system.
- A specification of all hardware requirements and performance characteristics to be satisfied.
- A specification of clerical procedures and responsibilities surrounding the system.
- A detailed schedule for the implementation of the system.
- Cost estimates and constraints.

The systems specification fulfils a number of roles. First, it is used as the exit criterion from the stage of detailed design prior to the stage of implementation. The systems specification is agreed by senior management, often the steering committee. Once accepted, large amounts of money are allocated to the project. This is necessary to purchase hardware, to code software and to carry out physical installation. Second, the specification acts as source documentation from which programs are written and hardware tenders are arranged. Third, the document acts as a historical record of the system for future users and developers. Finally, it is used in the assessment of the system once the system is being used. Does the system meet its response times? Is it built according to design? These are examples of questions that can only be answered in consultation with the systems specification.

15.3   Implementation

Once the systems specification has been agreed, its implementation can begin. This is the stage when things are done rather than analysed or designed. There are various separate but related tasks to be accomplished. Programs are written and tested, hardware is acquired and installed, staff are trained, the system is tested, and historic data from the old manual system or computer system is loaded into the files or database. Many of these tasks are carried out simultaneously. It is important that they are all completed before changeover to the new system is effected.

15.3.1   Program development and testing

One of the outputs of the detailed physical design stage was a set of program specifications. These are used by programmers as the blueprint from which to write the software. Program development and testing is one of the most costly phases in the systems life cycle. Historically, it was also the phase most likely to be over budget and completed late. Early programming techniques compounded these difficulties. The software produced was often unreliable and costly to debug and maintain.

Structured techniques, though, have produced a set of specifications for cohesive decoupled modules. These reduce programming complexity and ensure reliability and easy maintenance of software. Each module can be coded and tested separately. Structured analysis and design facilitates structured programming.

Structured programming allows only a small number of logical coding structures. In particular, the **GOTO** command, so popular with novice programmers, is disallowed. The use of **GOTO** commands, which direct a change in the order of program statement execution, leads to logical spaghetti in program execution. It becomes extremely difficult to understand and debug programs once written. The coding structures allowed correspond to those in structured English. It is common for programming languages to use instructions such as **REPEAT . . . UNTIL** and **IF . . . THEN . . . ELSE** . . . statements. Blocks of code are nested within these logical structures in the program. Internally, the blocks themselves will exhibit the same allowable logical structure (see Figure 15.11). The other main feature of structured program code is that although variables (containing data) are passed in and out of a module, all variables used only within that module have no meaning outside it. In structured programming, the variables are declared in the code. This corresponds to structured module specifications and structure charts, where data flows are stated explicitly.

Program testing is of critical importance in the development of software. It is one of the tasks of the analyst to specify test plans for the software. Individual modules are tested as they are written. This ensures that separately they perform to specification. Modules are then tested grouped together. This enables an assessment of their successful integration to be made. Finally, the entire set of programs is tested.

It is difficult to state what constitutes an adequately tested program. For instance, a program may perform perfectly well with standard data input, but how does it perform with erroneous data – a negative-value sale for instance? How will the program react to an unusual set of input data? Much program code is devised to deal with these situations. It has been estimated that from 50 to 80% of program code is devoted to error handling of one sort or another. There are a number of types of testing:

Figure 15.11 Allowable coding structures and their relation to structured English

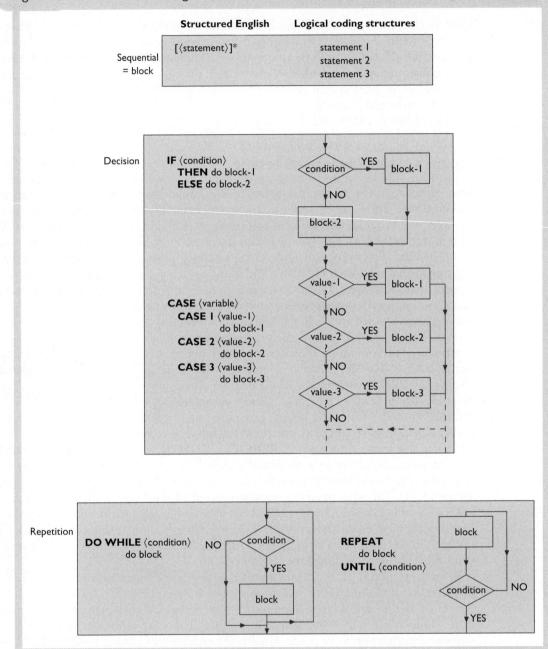

- **Random test data** can be generated, processed and the accuracy of processing checked.
- **Logical test data** may be developed using the logical limits for acceptable and unacceptable data.
- **Typical test data** assesses the performance of the software using actual past data.

It has been assumed that programs are to be developed especially for the system using conventional high-level languages and structured techniques. There are other approaches. For example, it may have been decided at the systems design stage to opt for applications packages for some or all of the data-processing and information provision. The benefits and limitations of this approach were covered in Chapter 3. A decision to adopt a package will have been taken on the basis of an analysis of the organization's requirements and the existence of the appropriate software package. It is unlikely that this software can be just loaded into the system and run. It is usual for the package to require tailoring to meet the needs of the organization. This is not to say that programs must be written. Rather, the package will have routines already available for customization. Examples are the design of reports, the determination of an account-coding structure and the setting of password controls. Alternatively, it may have been decided at an earlier stage to adopt a prototyping approach to software and systems development using a fourth-generation language. Prototyping and the use of fourth-generation languages were covered in Chapters 3 and 7.

Extreme programming

Extreme programming, sometimes called **XP** (not to be confused with Windows XP), is a methodology for software design and development initiated in the late 1990s. It stresses customer involvement and emphasizes success through customer satisfaction. Extreme programming is most applicable for projects where

- systems requirements are expected to change regularly;
- systems requirements are often difficult to specify completely in advance;
- systems need to be developed quickly;
- systems are relatively small.

Extreme programming projects involve small groups of developers (at least two and typically no more than 12) together with selected managers (customers). The smallness of the development group is the key to its success as it facilitates communication and feedback. Use of the methodology, though iterative, can be classified in four stages:

Planning

During this phase short **user stories** (often each a few lines of text) are developed for each of the requirements of the system. These are produced by the customers and are accompanied by a specification of an acceptance test – a test which will determine whether the code when produced performs what is required of it. These user stories are different from the large formal systems specifications developed in some methodologies, e.g. structured systems analysis and design. A group of user stories (e.g. containing 70 stories) forms a release plan which is used to schedule the rest of the project. This release plan may go through several iterations.

Design

During systems design great emphasis is placed on simplicity. Functionality is not added until and unless it is scheduled. Care is taken to name classes of objects and methods consistently. Generally, object approaches are used in design. These may be facilitated by techniques such as the use of Class, Responsibility and Collaboration (CRC) cards each of which captures for each class of objects the responsibility it fulfils and the classes with which it interacts. Design sessions involve verbal simulations of message passing between objects and investigating processes. There is not generally a formal document design coming out of this phase but rather a deeper understanding, amongst the small team of developers, of the ways to implement the user stories in code.

Coding

During the coding process the customer is always available to clarify any questions on functionality required. The test code is developed first, before producing the main code, thus emphasizing the focus of the development. All code is produced to agreed formal standards. A key feature of the programming is the use of **pair programming**. All code is produced by programmers working in pairs, each programmer side by side on the same computer. One of the pair concentrates only on the detailed implementation of the code and has control of the keyboard and mouse. The other programmer, the observer, concentrates only on tactical issues (e.g. syntax checking, defects) and, importantly, on strategic issues about how the code fits together in the larger picture of the system being developed. The programmers frequently switch roles. Pair programming yields results almost as quickly as two programmers working separately. The main advantages are in terms of the reliability and customer satisfaction of the software produced, together with the sense of common ownership and a lack of programmer alienation. Code when produced is held in a central repository and can and should be accessed and amended by the pair to ensure integration with code produced by other pairs.

Testing

Unlike traditional methods where testing is a function that is performed *after* code has been produced, within extreme programming the development of unit test code occurs *before* the program code is developed. This is viewed as essential to the development process. The process of extreme programming also allows for changes to be implemented as the system is developed. This requires reconsideration of unit tests and frequent reintegration using the central repository of code reflecting the sum total state of development. A system is regarded as acceptable when it passes all acceptance tests to the customer's satisfaction.

Extreme programming, as a methodology, is gaining importance where fast development of (relatively) small systems in a dynamic environment is required. It is often linked with the systems development approach called Rapid Applications Development (RAD) which is discussed in more detail in Chapter 16.

15.3.2 Hardware acquisition and installation

The characteristics of the hardware required were included in the systems specification. The analyst may have had certain manufacturers of hardware in mind. This is likely to be true if the organization already has a commitment to an existing manufacturer in its current and ongoing systems. In other cases, the hardware specification can be put out to tender and it is up to different suppliers to make contract offers.

Hardware is usually purchased new, although an alternative to purchasing is leasing. This is recommended in circumstances where there are tax concessions to be gained. Computer rental is sometimes used when extra hardware is needed for peak periods or where the system has a short designated lifespan.

Installation of hardware is costly. It may require building new rooms that are air-conditioned and dust-free. It will almost certainly involve laying data communication and power cables. Physical security such as fire alarms, video monitoring and secure rooms for data file libraries will also be installed.

15.3.3 Training and staff development

Users are the key element in any successful computer system. Their knowledge and understanding will have been tapped during systems investigation and analysis. Models of users will have influenced the user–machine interface design, but unless staff are adequately prepared for the new system it will have little chance of being used effectively. This requires staff training and education.

Education is to be distinguished from training in that the former involves providing staff with a general understanding of the system, the way it functions, its scope and its limitations. They will be informed of how the system can be used to provide information for their needs or carry out processing tasks for them. Training, in contrast, involves the familiarization of staff with the skills necessary to operate the computer system to perform tasks. In either case, there are several approaches:

- Lectures and seminars can be used for instructive overviews. Their advantage is that a large number of staff are reached using one instructor.

- Simulation of the work environment is used for training. This is a costly, though effective, training technique.

- On-the-job training involves supervision of personnel as skills that are progressively more complex are gradually mastered. This is a popular way of training new staff on an existing system.

- Software packages are used for training personnel in applications software. For example, there are tutorial programs for most of the major word-processing packages.

- The information centre should devise training courses for staff involving some, if not all, of these techniques.

Staff training and education need to take account of the abilities of the trainees as well as the tasks for which training is provided. Staff will have different requirements and expectations of training. Insufficient attention to staff development is one certain way of ensuring that an information system will fail.

15.3.4 Data store conversion

The file or database structure will have already been designed. In the case of a database, the conceptual, internal and external schemas were defined using the data definition language of the database management system. An organization will have historic data that must be entered into the files or database of the new computer system before it can be used for the organization's needs.

In the case of computer-held data, this generally involves writing programs that accept data from the old files or database and convert it to the format required for the new system. This data is then written to the new system.

With manual files, the task is more time-consuming. Decisions are made as to what data to transfer. This data is unlikely to be in the format required for input into the new system. It is common for data to be transcribed on to intermediate documentation prior to data entry. Although costly, this minimizes errors in transcription. Careful attention must be paid to control during this conversion. Batch and hash totals can be used in the transfer of accounting data. Balances should be agreed with clients of the system, whether such clients are internal or external to the organization. Listings of input are produced and maintained for later queries and visual inspection.

During data store conversion, the organization is continuing to function as nearly normal as possible. The old data store itself will be changing rather than remaining static. This adds further problems.

15.4 Systems changeover

At some stage, the new computerized system will be brought into operation. How and when this is done will depend on the confidence that management has in its reliability. All systems will have undergone a **systems test** involving the use of the installed software and hardware. However, this is very different from the situation that the system is likely to encounter in practice – peak loading, many users and many users committing errors in interacting with the system.

Four changeover strategies are considered here (see Figure 15.12). They are not mutually exclusive. Each has its benefits and limitations. They have varying degrees of safeguards against the effects of system malfunctions on the organization.

15.4.1 Direct changeover

With direct changeover, the new system is brought into operation in its entirety on a designated date. This has the advantage of being quick but relies heavily on the reliability of the systems design, implementation and testing, and on how the staff were trained. It is not generally recommended, although it may be unavoidable in cases where the system does not replace an existing one.

15.4.2 Parallel approach

The parallel approach, or some version of it, is very common in practice. It can be used when there is a great deal of similarity between the old and the new systems. This similarity needs to exist between inputs and outputs. Both systems are run in parallel until there is enough confidence in the new system to dispense with the old.

Figure 15.12 Systems changeover strategies: (a) direct changeover; (b) parallel changeover; (c) pilot or modular approach (direct); (d) phased changeover (direct)

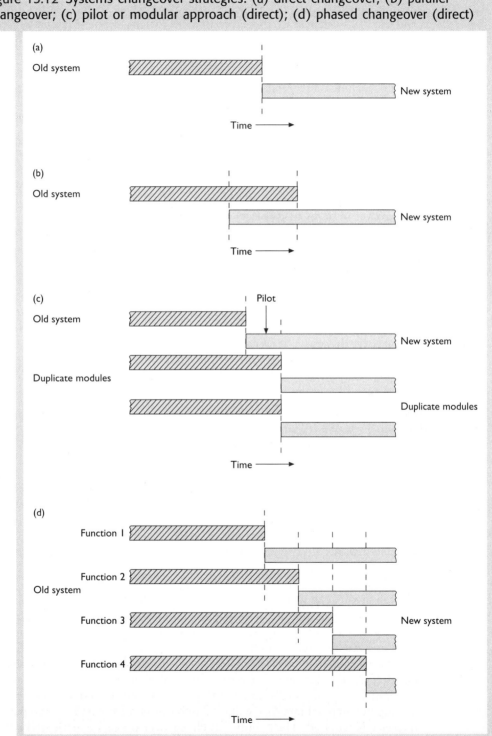

Parallel running can take weeks or months. An advantage is that if the new system malfunctions then there is a backup system on which to rely. The output of the old and the new systems can also be compared. If there is any discrepancy, then this can be investigated.

It is easy to stress the advantages of the parallel approach while ignoring its limitations. Staff will be put under enormous pressure if they not only have to use the old system but must also repeat the same operations with an unfamiliar new system. If staff were working near to capacity prior to the introduction of the new system, it is doubtful whether they will be able to handle the extra load. Overtime working and temporary staff are possible solutions, although each carries dangers. In the former case, staff will not be performing at peak efficiency – not a desirable situation in which to run a new system. In the latter, the temporary staff will need to be trained. Should they be trained to use the old or the new system, or both? These difficulties cannot be brushed away glibly, particularly if it is desired to reap the benefits of parallel changeover in terms of its safety and reliability.

15.4.3 Pilot or modular approach

Some systems can be broken down into several identical and duplicate modules. For instance, an automated point-of-sale and stock-updating system for a supermarket chain will be repeated in many branches. A stock control system for handling 10,000 types of item performs identical functions on each type of item, independent of its type. Changeover to these systems can be effected by first changing over to one module either in parallel or directly. If this proves satisfactory, then changeover to the entire system can be made. This is a way of minimizing the risks. The pilot system can also be used for on-the-job training of staff.

15.4.4 Phased changeover

Where a system is composed of different self-contained modules performing different functions, it may be possible to phase in the new system while gradually phasing out the old. For example, a system involving nominal, sales and purchase ledger accounts, stock control, financial planning, sales forecasting and payroll can be phased in gradually, one function at a time. Although in the final integrated system there will be data flows between these various modules, each is sufficiently self-contained and directed towards a recognized business function that it is possible to phase in modules gradually.

This creeping commitment to computerization need not be restricted to changeover but can involve the whole development process. Its advantage is that cash flow outlay can be spread over time, analysts and programmers are employed consistently, resources are generally distributed more evenly over time, and the gradual commitment to the computerized system ensures that any difficulties in changeover are more easily handled. The drawback is that interfacing modules will need to have continuously changing modes of interface. For example, between a financial planning and sales ledger system there will initially be a manual–manual interface. If the ledger system is computerized, then a computer–manual interface will need to be developed. Finally, a computer–computer interface is required. The continuous changeover process experienced by users, while distributing resources over time, can also give the feeling that computerization is a never-ending process. This can be bad for morale.

The central purposes in developing a computerized information system for Kismet were to:

- process customer orders quickly;
- be able to satisfy customer enquiries in such areas as the status of orders, prices of goods and delivery availability;
- provide management with a greater variety of relevant, up-to-date information on company performance.

Kismet is a firm that is beginning to embark on computerized systems. It does not currently have the experience or confidence gained by organizations that have a continuing systems development policy, possibly over 20 years or more. Kismet therefore wishes to embark on a changeover strategy as risk-free as possible. Much of the new system, such as the part dealing with transaction processing, is very similar to the old system. A parallel changeover will allow the necessary processing checks to be carried out and at the same time will allow a manual system to be provided as backup. There will be difficulties performing these checks, as the computerized system works almost instantaneously, whereas the manual system took many days to process orders – that was one of its faults. With respect to order enquiry, it has been decided to rely entirely on the new system, although sample checks are to be recorded and verified later. Similarly, the management reports as generated by the new system will be used. Sample checks against reports from the old system are to be made, but given the limited number of types of report that were generated, this part of the system will rely heavily on the adequacy of systems testing prior to changeover.

The parallel run is to be initially for a period of one month. There will then be a formal review of the system prior to its final acceptance and the discarding of the old manual system.

15.5   Evaluation and maintenance

No computerized system once implemented remains unaltered through the rest of its working life. Changes are made, and maintenance is undertaken. Hardware maintenance is usually carried out under a maintenance contract with the equipment suppliers. Hardware maintenance involves technical tasks often requiring circuitry and other specialized parts.

Software maintenance is also carried out. In time, bugs may be discovered in the programs. It is necessary to correct these. Modular program design, structured code and the documentation techniques of structured systems analysis and design ensure that this task can be effected efficiently.

Software maintenance continues to be a complex and costly contributor to the entire systems project. Many project managers are now recognizing the **total cost of ownership** of information systems. This incorporates the entire cost of software, from initial feasibility studies through analysis and design to post-implementation maintenance. Eventually, the new development will become outdated, and for completeness the cost of creating and dealing with that legacy system must also be included. The importance of good documentation and design, and the reusability and maintainability of the code generated, are all important factors in calculating the total cost of ownership.

User needs also evolve over time to respond to the changing business environment. Software is amended to serve these. New applications programs must be written. It is the responsibility of the computer centre or information centre to ensure that the system is kept up to date.

Some time after the system has settled down, it is customary to carry out a **post-implementation audit**. The purpose of this audit is to compare the new system as it actually is with what was intended in its specification. To ensure independence, this audit will be carried out by an analyst or team not involved in the original systems project.

The audit will consider a number of areas:

- The adequacy of the systems documentation that governs manual procedures and computer programs will be checked.
- The training of personnel involved in the use of the new system will be assessed.
- Attempts will be made to establish the reliability of systems output.
- Comparison of the actual costs and benefits incurred during implementation is made against the estimated costs and benefits, and significant variances are investigated.
- Response times will be determined and compared with those specified.

The original purposes of the systems project will once again be considered. Does the system as delivered meet these objectives? The post-implementation audit will yield a report that will assess the system. Suggestions for improvements will be made. These may be minor and can be accommodated within the ongoing development of the project. If they are major, they will be shelved until a major overhaul or replacement of the system is due.

During the course of the useful life of the system, several audits will be made. Some of these will be required by external bodies. Examples are financial audits required by the accountancy profession for accounting transaction-processing systems. Other audits are internal. They will deal with such matters as efficiency, effectiveness, security and reliability. The topic of auditing of computer systems was covered in Chapter 9 on control.

Great achievements can be made using structured systems analysis and design. Information systems have been produced that:

- involve integrated redesign rather than piecemeal copying of old manual systems;
- are based on the logical information requirements of the organization rather than the physical dictates of old processing patterns;
- are more likely to be delivered on time and on budget because of the added control that modular development confers on the project;
- contain software that is reliable, well documented and easily amendable.

However, there are some who point to limitations in structured analysis and design. They comment on its lack of suitability in all cases. These reservations are founded on three implicit assumptions:

1. A technical solution to an organization's information problems is always desirable and possible.
2. The experts in systems analysis and design are the analysts and programmers. Users come in only to provide information about the existing system during investigation

and as a consideration in interface design. They themselves do not design and develop the system.

3. The correct approach to development is to progress in a linear fashion through a number of clearly definable stages with exit criteria.

Chapters 6 and 16 consider how these assumptions have been challenged by soft systems analysis and design, user participation in socio-technical analysis and design, and prototyping as an approach to systems development.

Summary

Having selected the overall systems design, detailed design of the system then commences. Programs are defined by the use of structure charts and individual module specifications. These ensure that the programming task can be carried out in a controlled and reliable way. The data store is designed. In the case of file-based systems, this involves the specification of file and record layouts. For databases, schema design is required. An important aspect of input/output design is that of the user interface. This is determined not only by the types of task for which input or output is used but also by a model of the user. There are various categories of user. In all these areas, hardware requirements must be established, given the data-processing and information-provision requirements of the organization as identified during analysis.

The systems specification is an important landmark between detailed design and implementation. This is a report covering all aspects of the systems design in detail. As well as giving cost estimates, it will also provide a schedule for the implementation stage of the project. Once the specification has been agreed with management, implementation can then commence.

During implementation, large sums of money are allocated and spent. Hardware as specified is acquired and installed. Programs are coded and tested. The structured hierarchical input/process/output design facilitates the use of structured programming. Targeted training and education are provided for staff. Historical data is loaded into the system. The systems test is a major step in the implementation stage prior to changeover to the new system.

Systems changeover can be effected in a number of ways, each of which has certain benefits, drawbacks and areas of application. After the system has been running for some time, a post-implementation audit compares the system as delivered with that as specified. Suggestions for further improvements are made. As the information needs of the organization evolve so the system is amended, programs adapted and new applications software written to take account of this.

Review questions

1. Outline the areas to be covered in the detailed design of a system.

2. What benefits accrue when software has been developed as a result of modular design?

3. Explain the terms *module decoupling* and *module cohesion*. Why are they desirable characteristics in modular software design?

4. What is the role of a systems specification?

5. Distinguish between the various types of test carried out during implementation.

6. What security features must be present in the conversion of historic accounting data for entry into a new system?

7. What are the purposes of a post-implementation audit?

Exercises

1. Using the data flow diagrams developed for the library example (Chapter 12, Exercise 5) derive a hierarchical structure chart for the system.

2. What is the difference between a *conceptual data model* and a *conceptual schema*?

3. What features of interface design affect the acceptance of computer systems by users?

4. How do structured techniques in systems analysis and design aid systems development in the later stages?

5. How could each of the following be analysed according to the categories of systems users covered in the text:
   (a) customer order data input personnel?
   (b) customer cashpoint users?
   (c) flight booking and reservation enquiry personnel?
   (d) spreadsheet model developers?
   (e) programmers?
   (f) middle-management users of summary accounting decision support information?

6. Which of the following should be incorporated into a systems test: hardware, software, data storage, manual procedures, backup facilities, computer operations staff, users, data communications, security and control?

7. Explain *four* different changeover strategies. Are they mutually exclusive? In each of the following cases, suggest a changeover strategy. Explain its merits and drawbacks. Justify your choice by giving reasons why other strategies are not appropriate.
   (a) A computerized inventory control system to replace antiquated manual methods. It is to be installed in eight warehouses and deals with 10,000 types of item.
   (b) A major high street bank has commissioned an automated cheque and cash deposit system for its branches. It is to be operated by the bank's counter personnel and will allow instant account updating for deposits.
   (c) A new company has developed a computerized lottery system to be installed in lottery ticket offices throughout the country.

8. Why is software maintenance, as distinct from software creation, traditionally regarded as an arduous, unpopular task?

9. Why is software maintenance necessary?

CASE STUDY 15

Evaluation and maintenance

1. Consider the first month of operation of the new Kismet system. A formal review will take place at the end of that period and an evaluation will be made as to whether the parallel running of old and new systems will come to an end. You have been commissioned to write this report for managers at Kismet. Draft an outline of the report making your recommendations.

2. Consider now the first year of operation. What might be the maintenance issues in hardware and software during that time? What about the issues over a five-year period?

Recommended reading

Astels D. (2003). *Test Driven Development: A Practical Guide*. Prentice Hall PTR

This book introduces an approach to software design which encourages the developer to plan test routines for code before the code is written, thereby predicting and anticipating where errors could occur and avoiding them.

Budgen D. (2003). *Software Design* 2nd edn. Addison-Wesley

This is a clear, comprehensive text suitable for final-year undergraduates in systems analysis and design. Part 1 explores the nature of the design process and the various roles played in software development. Part 2 gives a detailed examination of well-established structured approaches – JSP, SSADM and JSD.

Galitz W. (2002). *The Essential Guide to User Interface Design: An Introduction to GUI Design Principles and Techniques*. Wiley

This describes the fundamentals of good interface design. The book covers a range of GUI applications, including design for the web.

Isaacs E. (2002). *Designing from Both Sides of the Screen: A Dialogue Between a Designer and an Engineer*. Sams

This is equally relevant to software engineers and designers. It covers the principles of good interface design and provides many examples of good and bad practice. An extended case study provides the context for much of the theory.

Snyder C. (2003). *Paper Prototyping: Fast and Simple Techniques for Designing and Refining the User Interface*. Morgan Kaufmann

This provides an innovative approach to user interface design employing tools which encourage low cost and rapid development.

Somerville I. (2001). *Software Engineering*, 6th edn. Pearson Education

This classic text covers many topics, including systems design, user interface design, validation, evolution and management of software, legacy systems and configuration management.

Chapter 16

Systems development: further tools, techniques and alternative approaches

Learning outcomes

On completion of this chapter, you should be able to:

- Define CASE, explain what CASE tools are and describe the role played by CASE in systems development
- Outline the concept of rapid applications development as a framework for the development of information systems
- Describe object-oriented approaches
- Compare and contrast hard and soft approaches to systems analysis.

Introduction

This chapter introduces and examines some additional tools and techniques and approaches that have attracted significant interest and gained importance with the developers of information systems. In some cases, they are complementary to the approach described in Chapters 9–15, in others they are alternatives. First, the increasingly important use of computers themselves as tools in the process of analysis and design is described. The power of modern hardware and software has brought about an increasing reliance upon computer-aided software engineering (CASE) to address the complexity of managing large systems development projects.

Next, rapid applications development (RAD) is considered as a framework for employing the chosen systems development methodology. Like CASE, the interest in RAD also reflects concerns over the management of large projects and the failure in some cases of traditional methodologies. RAD is not necessarily an alternative to these methodologies, as it does not claim to be a complete methodology itself. However, it does provide a framework of techniques that proponents claim allows the chosen methodology to be implemented more effectively.

Up to now, a particular approach to the analysis and design of computerized information systems has been taken. This is not the only approach. Nor is it the most appropriate approach in all circumstances. Different approaches have differing strengths and weaknesses, differing areas of applicability and differing objectives. It is the purpose of this chapter to outline some alternatives and highlight their points of difference. The object-oriented approach to systems development is introduced first. Although adopting a fundamentally different approach to modelling systems, object-oriented approaches join those already introduced in the category of 'hard' approaches to systems development. By way of contrast, two 'soft' approaches will then be introduced: the first is due to Peter Checkland and generally known by his name; the second is a socio-technical approach stressing the participation of users in analysis and design. Here, both of these will be termed 'soft' approaches, compared with the 'hard' approaches, of which the structured and object-oriented methodologies considered so far are exemplars.

This chapter will also provide a general comparison between hard and soft methodologies. The underlying philosophies of each will be explained and contrasted. It is not intended to treat these additional approaches in detail but rather to give the reader a flavour of the debate that occurs between the proponents of hard and soft methodologies. This is a fruitful topic for discussion. It not only reveals deep and important divergences in attitudes to the analysis and design of information systems, particularly those in which people as social beings are heavily involved, but also sets the framework for a debate that is likely to persist for several years and may mark an important turning point in the development of attitudes to systems analysis and design.

16.1 Computer-aided software engineering

Computer-aided software engineering (CASE) provides new tools for the rapid development of reliable computer systems. The traditional cost curve for the design and development of a business information system locates most of the cost as falling within the area of implementation, particularly coding. Fourth-generation languages (4GLs) and other applications-generation tools are an attempt to cut the cost in this area by enabling speedy development of systems through the automation of the production of code.

The success of this can be measured by the fact that it is now possible to build a system and, if it fails to meet user needs, to redevelop it quickly and cheaply. This, in essence, is the philosophy behind prototyping. A problem with the approach is that it diminishes the role of formal requirements specification and systems design. This may be acceptable or even desirable for small systems, particularly for decision support, but the approach cannot cope with larger projects unless considerable design effort has been undertaken.

Structured methodologies, developed in the late 1970s and early 1980s and covered elsewhere in this book, were a significant improvement in approaches to systems analysis and design compared with previous methods. By clearly identifying stages, tools and techniques, and documentation standards, consistency and quality control were maintained for systems design projects. Design errors were significantly reduced.

However, requirements analysis, especially if linked to strategic requirements, is not readily accessible to structured techniques. This dysfunctionality is developed later in this chapter. Errors still occur as a result of inaccurate requirements analysis and specifications, and changes in requirements mean lengthy redesign. But just as the computer itself has been utilized to assist the coding process (4GLs and application generators), the next step is to use the computer in the requirements specification, analysis and design process itself. This is the place of computer-aided software engineering (CASE) (Figure 16.1).

Figure 16.1 The place of CASE tools in software development

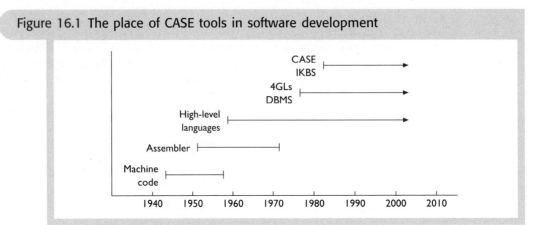

CASE automates various stages of the analysis and design process with the assistance of software tools. The CASE philosophy involves the use of these software tools working together with a methodology of systems analysis and design to:

- develop models that describe the business;
- aid in corporate planning;
- provide support for systems specification, documentation and design; and
- aid in the implementation process.

CASE tools are used by computer professionals to carry out some part of the systems analysis/design process. They are not end-user-oriented, although they may be used in conjunction with end users. The tools are normally run on high-performance development workstations.

CASE support

CASE tools provide assistance in the following ways (see Figure 16.2):

1. **Corporate planning of information systems:** Software is used to describe the organization, its goals, resources, responsibilities and structure. These descriptions may be used to create strategic plans. The software will be used to indicate and track relationships between the various components of the plan. The planning specifications will identify activities for incorporation into information systems developments. Many CASE tools also include facilities for cost estimation calculations. Outline design parameters are fed in, and an indication of the expected cost and duration of the project is generated.

2. **Creating specifications of requirements:** This corresponds to the non-strategic stages of systems analysis. At this stage, an information system is analysed into its component activities and data requirements. Many diagrammatic tools familiar to the reader from the stages of structured process and data analysis are used – for example, data flow diagrams and entity models.

3. **Creating design specifications:** CASE tools can be used to specify a design for a new system. These tools include software for producing HIPO charts, structured module specifications and decision tables.

Figure 16.2 CASE assistance in the systems development process

4. **Code-generation tools:** CASE support in this area will accept the outputs of the design specification and produce computer-generated code for direct execution.

5. **An information repository:** Central to any CASE assistance in systems analysis, design and implementation is the information repository. This stores information on entities, processes, data structures, business rules, source code and project management data. It is important, as at any one stage of development consistency and completeness must be maintained in descriptions of data, processes, rules, and so on. Throughout the various stages of analysis and design, it is vital that as each component develops from, for example, an item in a high-level plan through to a record type in a database, it can be tracked. In short, the information repository does for the CASE process what the data dictionary, in a more limited way, does for structured process analysis and design.

6. **A development methodology:** Underlying any CASE approach is a development methodology. The CASE tool provides the developer with support for the various development stages identified by that methodology. Automated facilities allow for the production of the particular style of diagrams expected of the methodology. The cost estimation routines will similarly reflect the philosophy of the methodology.

CASE terminology

There are no agreed international or *de facto* standards on CASE. This is a problem not least because the terminology can be used in widely varying ways. However, the following are in common use.

Front-end CASE/upper CASE/analyst workbench

This refers to a set of tools that aid productivity in the analysis, design and documentation of systems. These tools are used to define the systems requirements and the systems properties. Typically, the outputs of front-end CASE are:

- process and data structure specifications: data flow diagrams, state transition diagrams, flowcharts, entity–relationship diagrams, data dictionaries, pseudo-code, structured English, decision tables, decision trees, structure charts, module specifications, Warnier–Orr diagrams
- screen definitions
- report definitions.

In order to achieve this, there will be a wide variety of highly interactive screen-based prototyping facilities, including:

- diagram editors
- screen painters
- dialogue prototyping aids.

Back-end CASE/lower CASE/code generator/4GL generator

This refers to tools that automate the latter stages of the implementation process. As input, back-end CASE tools may take the output specifications of front-end CASE tools. The outputs of back-end CASE might be:

- source and object program code
- database and file definitions
- job control language.

Life cycle CASE/I-CASE

This encapsulates tools covering the entire process of corporate analysis and planning, systems analysis and design, and implementation. For example, the unified modelling language (UML), proposed as a standard for object-oriented development, is incorporated into several I-CASE tools.

Reverse engineering/re-engineering

Reverse engineering is the opposite of the standard implementation process for the production of code. Reverse engineering takes existing unstructured code as input (often COBOL programs that can be found in legacy systems) and produces restructured code as output. In particular, the reverse engineering process produces output where:

- Common subroutines and modules are identified.
- Conditional branches and loops are simplified in structure.
- Blocks of code are collapsed into single-line statements for ease of reference and use.
- Subroutines are called in hierarchies.
- New source code is generated fitting the above conditions.

The need for reverse engineering is generated by the recognition that most software used in an organization needs enhancement from time to time. Unless this was produced using a rigorous methodology (and many systems still in use based on COBOL code were not), the task facing the programmer is immense. Complex spaghetti logic structures are impossible or, at best, time-consuming to disentangle and alter. If the software has undergone amendment, the side-effects of code alteration are not easily identifiable. The software tends to be bug-ridden and difficult to validate. Reverse engineering creates code that is structured and easily amendable. It thus enables existing software to be enhanced rather than abandoned when update is necessary.

CASE benefits

CASE has grown rapidly in use over the last decade and is predicted to continue to increase in importance over the next decade. Some of the benefits of CASE are as follows:

1. **Enhancement of existing applications:** This can occur in two ways. First, systems produced using CASE tools can be rejuvenated when required by altering the systems specifications, already incorporated into the previous use of CASE, to take account of new needs. These can then be fed into back-end CASE tools to produce new code. The process is considerably quicker than attempting alterations via manually held systems specifications. Second, using reverse engineering tools, existing applications can be recast in a way that makes them suitable for amendment.

2. **Complete, accurate and consistent design specifications:** Most errors in the development of a new system occur in the systems specification stage. Most of these are not picked up until acceptance testing by users has taken place. CASE, by the use of computer specification tools and a central information repository, forces certain aspects of consistency and completeness on the design process.

3. **Reducing human effort:** CASE tools reduce human effort in analysis and design by offloading development work on to computers.

   Diagramming and charting tools cut the development time, especially when it is considered that each diagram may have to undergo several versions before completion.

   By keeping track of the development process, CASE tools can relieve the human of considerable project management burdens. These tools keep note of authors, versions of models and a calendar. CASE tools also provide for consistency and completeness checking across various stages of the development process. They do this by tracking entities, processes, data definitions, diagrams and other things that would otherwise take up much human effort.

   Back-end CASE tools significantly reduce the human programming requirement by generating source and object code, and database definitions.

4. **Integration of development:** CASE tools, particularly I-CASE tools, encourage integration of the development process from the early stages of corporate analysis through information systems specification to code implementation. This is a trend that has been emerging in paper-based methodologies and is now mirrored in CASE tools and methodologies. It is based on a recognition that the design of an information system is not merely a technical issue deriving from a clear understanding of where we are now and where we want to go, but rather an activity that has to link and translate corporate information systems requirements into deliverable systems.

5. **Speed:** CASE tools speed up the development process for a project. The tools also allow considerable interactive input from systems developers during the process. This is compatible with a prototyping approach to systems development.

6. **Links to object-oriented analysis:** Object-oriented analysis and design are rapidly gaining support. Object-oriented methods are particularly suited to incorporation into CASE tools as the terminology and diagrammatical requirements are similar throughout the stages of development. The emphasis in object-oriented methodologies on team development, reuse of code and message passing between objects are all facilitated by the central repository, libraries and group support found in CASE tools.

16.2   Rapid applications development

Rapid applications development (RAD) grew out of the recognition that businesses need to respond quickly to a changing and often uncertain environment in the development of their information systems. RAD is directly opposed to the traditional life-cycle approach, which is characterized by a completely linear development of a system and a concentration on technical perspectives. In traditional approaches, the *requirements* of a project are fixed at an early stage, but the *resources* and *time* tend to vary to fulfil those requirements. In RAD, the opposite view is taken. *Time* is fixed and *resources* are fixed as much as possible, but *requirements* are allowed to change as the project develops to meet the real business objectives.

RAD borrows from other approaches and uses prototyping, participation and CASE tools as well as other formal techniques. It recognizes the importance of gaining user participation, particularly senior management involvement, in its evolutionary approach to information systems development. RAD was first separately identified and introduced by James Martin (1991). His exposition was set clearly within his information engineering approach to the development of business information systems. Now, however, the term 'rapid applications development' is used much more loosely to encompass any approach which emphasizes fast development of systems. Rather than being a methodology itself, RAD is a framework for systems development that can be applied to a range of methodologies. In the UK, a consortium of systems developers have defined a set of standards for RAD called the dynamic systems development method (DSDM).

16.2.1 RAD concepts

Central to the concept of RAD is the role of clearly defined workshops. These should:

- involve business and information systems personnel;
- be of a defined length of time (typically between one and five days);
- be in 'clean rooms' – i.e. rooms set aside for the purpose, removed from everyday operations, provided with technical support, and without interruption;
- involve a facilitator who will be independent, control the meeting, set agendas and be responsible for steering the meeting to deliverables;
- involve a scribe to record.

RAD has four phases:

1. **Requirements planning:** The role of joint requirements planning (JRP) is to establish high-level management and strategic objectives for the organization. The workshop will contain senior managers, often cooperating in a cross-functional way. They will have the authority to take decisions over the strategic direction of the business. The assumption behind RAD is that JRP will drive the process from a high-level business perspective rather than a technical one.

2. **Applications development:** Joint applications development (JAD) follows JRP and involves users in participation in the workshops. JAD follows a top-down approach and may use prototyping tools. Any techniques that can aid user design, especially data flow diagrams and entity modelling, will be employed. I-CASE (see Section 16.3)

will be used at this stage. The important feature of applications development is that the JAD workshops short-circuit the traditional life-cycle approach, which involves lengthy interviews with users and the collection of documentation, often over considerable time periods. In JAD, the momentum is not lost and several focused workshops may be called quite quickly.

3. **Systems construction:** The designs specifications output by JAD are used to develop detailed designs and generate code. In this phase, graphical user interface building tools, database management system development tools, 4GLs and back-end CASE tools are used (see Section 16.3). A series of prototypes are created, which are then assessed by end users, which may result in further iterations and modifications. The various parts of the system are developed by small teams, known as SWAT teams (*s*killed *w*ith *a*dvanced *t*ools). The central system can be built quickly using this approach. The focus of RAD is on the development of core functionality, rather than the 'bells and whistles' of the system – it is often claimed that 80% (the core) of the system can be built in 20% of the time.

4. **Cutover:** During cutover, users are trained and the system is tested comprehensively. The objective is to have the core functioning effectively. The remainder of the system can be built later. By concentration on the core and the need to develop systems rapidly within a 'time box', the development process can concentrate on the most important aspects of the information system from a business perspective. If the process looks as though it is slipping behind schedule, out of its time box, it is likely that the requirements will be reduced rather than the deadline extended.

Rapid applications developments make the assumptions that:

- Businesses face continuous change and uncertainty.
- Information requirements and therefore information systems must change to meet this challenge.
- Information systems development should be driven by business requirements.
- It is important that information systems be developed quickly.
- Prototyping and development tools are necessary to ensure quick responses.
- Users should participate in development.
- The 'final system' does not exist.

16.2.2 RAD and e-commerce

The growth in web-based technologies has led in many businesses to a review of their approaches to information systems development. With its focus on fast development, prototyping and user involvement, RAD appears to be an attractive candidate as a framework for developing e-commerce activities. Proponents of RAD, who believe that it is ideally suited to electronic business activities, give the following reasons for its adoption:

- **Time to market:** The fast-changing technology of e-commerce requires a rapid development cycle to preserve competitive advantage. Business needs must often be met within weeks rather than months.
- **Whole system solutions:** A move into electronic business requires significant changes in work practices. As a consequence, the system needs to be developed and introduced collaboratively in order to be successful.

- **Fast-changing requirements:** The constant change in the electronic economy means that it is almost impossible to establish the business requirements at the outset of the project. RAD, unlike the traditional methodologies previously discussed, does not insist on a complete understanding of the requirements at the outset of the initiative.
- **Decision taking:** Many hard decisions have to be taken as the requirements of the project change. RAD provides effective frameworks for taking and implementing these difficult decisions.

16.3 Object-oriented analysis and design

Data analysis and structured process analysis have been highly influential in generating commercial methodologies centred on one or both approaches. However, some of the difficulties experienced in analysis and design using these perspectives are rooted in the assumption that an organization can be understood separately in terms of processes that manipulate data and in terms of objects on which data is stored. This separation between processes and objects, as practitioners of object-oriented analysis and design would claim, is ill founded.

It is suggested that our understanding of the world is based on objects that have properties, stand in relationships to other objects and take part in operations. For example, we understand a motor car in terms not just of its static properties and relationships (is a Ford, has four wheels) but also in terms of the operations in which it takes part (acceleration, transportation of people). In a business context, an order is not merely an object that has an order number, a date, an item number ordered and a quantity ordered; it also takes part in operations – is placed by a customer, generates a stock requisition. This notion of object is central to an understanding of object-oriented analysis.

From the perspective of programming rather than analysis, objects and object types were a natural development out of the need to define types of things together with permissible operations performable on them. In early programming languages, there were only a few types of object (data types). Examples were integer and string. Certain operations were permissible on integers, such as addition, but not on strings. Other operations were defined for strings, such as concatenation, but not for integers. Later, the ability to define many different data types, together with their permissible operations, became incorporated into languages. This meshed with an object-oriented approach to analysis. Object-oriented approaches are playing an increasing role in end-user computing, particularly in the design of the interfaces to information systems and in the development of systems for the Internet. This development is often supported by the use of CASE tools and prototyping.

16.3.1 Essential concepts in object orientation

Object

An **object** is anything on which we store data, together with the operations that are used to alter that data. An **object type** is a category of object. For instance, an object might be Tom Yorke, which is an instance of the object type *employee*. Another object is order # 1234, which is an instance of the object type *order*.

A **method** specifies the way in which an object's data is manipulated – the way in which an **operation** is carried out. For instance, the sales tax on an invoice might be produced from a method that takes the sales amount and calculates a percentage of this. The important point is that the object consists not only of the data but also of the operations that manipulate it. This is one of the important features that distinguishes an object from an entity as used in entity–relationship modelling.

Encapsulation

The data held on an object is hidden from the user of that object. How then is data retrieved? All data operations and access to data are handled through methods. These are programming routines that act as interfaces to the data; they typically provide 'get' and 'set' functions to access or amend the data. Packaging the data so that the data is hidden from users is known as **encapsulation**. The data is also hidden from other objects.

In implementation, the methods are not considered to be packaged with the object but rather with the object type, as the same method for handling a certain type of data applies to all objects of that type. This corresponds well with object-oriented languages, which store the method as program code with the object type (or **object class** as it is known). See Figure 16.3.

Message

In order to retrieve data, or indeed carry out any operation on an object, it is necessary to send a **message** to the object. This message will contain the name of the object, the object type, the name of the operation and any other relevant parameters – for example, data values in the case of an update operation. When an operation is invoked by a message, that message may have come from another object or, more strictly, from an operation associated with that object. The first object is said to send a **request** to the second object. The request may result in a response if that is part of the purpose of the operation. This is the way that objects communicate. See Figure 16.4.

Inheritance

Object types may have subtypes and supertypes. The type *dog* has as subtypes *Alsatian* and *poodle*, and as supertypes *carnivore* and *mammal*. All Alsatians are dogs, all dogs are mammals, and all dogs are carnivores. Rover has certain properties by virtue of being an Alsatian; Fifi by virtue of being a poodle. Alsatians are said to **inherit** their dog characteristics by virtue of those properties being had by their supertype *dog*. Similarly for poodles. Dogs inherit their mammalian characteristics, such as suckling young, from their supertype *mammal*.

An object type will have some operations and methods specific to it. Others it will inherit from its supertype. This makes sense from the point of view of implementation, as it is only necessary to store a method at its highest level of applicability, avoiding unnecessary duplication. *Manager* and *clerical staff* are two object types with the common supertype *employee*. An operation for employee might be *hire*. This would be inherited by both *manager* and *clerical staff*. See Figure 16.5.

16.3.2 Object-oriented analysis

Modelling using object-oriented analysis differs from the approach adopted earlier in this book. Instead of the key components being entities and processes, the model built is composed of object types and what happens to them. The two key aspects of the analysis phase are the analysis of the structure of the object types (object structure analysis) and an analysis of their behaviour (object behaviour analysis).

Figure 16.3 Representation of an example of an object type and one of its instances

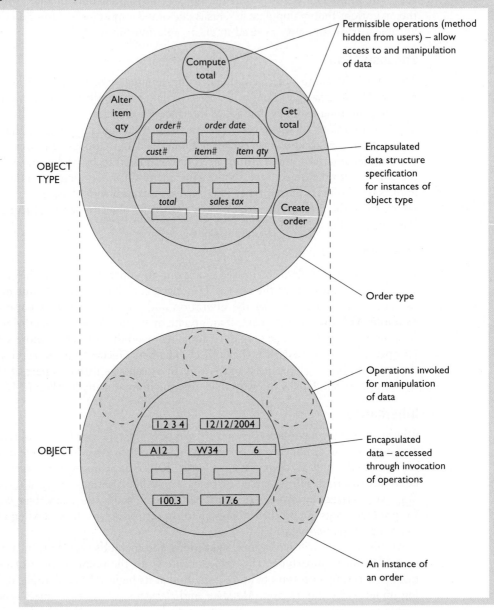

Object structure analysis

The following tasks are undertaken:

■ The object types and their relationships are identified. This is very similar to the process of establishing entities and their relationships. The diagrammatic conventions are similar. Two special types of relationship, described below, are identified separately – composition and generalization.

Figure 16.4 Objects send requests to other objects

Figure 16.5 Inheritance

Figure 16.6 Representation of the composition of objects

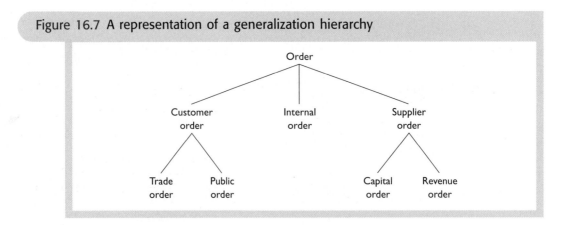

Figure 16.7 A representation of a generalization hierarchy

- Some types of object are complex as they are composed of others. These compositions are identified. Each complex object can be manipulated as a single object composed of other objects. A typical representation is shown in Figure 16.6.
- Generalization hierarchies, used to indicate inheritance, are established and represented by diagrams, as in Figure 16.7.

Object behaviour analysis

In object behaviour analysis, event schemas are designed. These show the sequence of events that occur and how they affect the states of objects. When a customer places an order, an event has occurred. This triggers off a series of events. The placing of the order leads to the creation of a company order. This is then checked. As a result, the order may be denied or it may be assembled and then dispatched. Each of these events triggers an operation on the object. This changes its state. The operations may trigger operations on other objects, such as the creation of an invoice.

The following are tasks carried out in object behaviour analysis:

- The possible states of an object type are determined and the transition between these illustrated (see Figure 16.8).

Figure 16.8 Representation of the transition between the possible states of the object type *order*

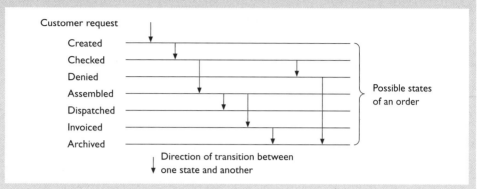

Figure 16.9 An event schema demonstrating the sequence of events triggering operations leading to transition of state of the object type *order*

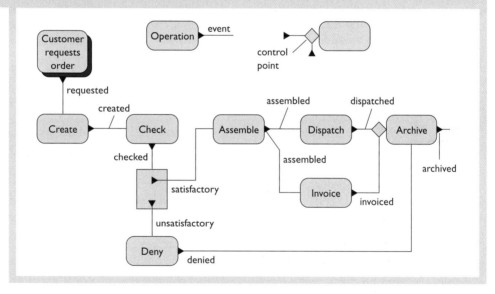

- Event schemas are designed that show the sequence of events that triggers operations leading to a transition in state of an object type (see Figure 16.9). Events themselves may be complex and if necessary can be exploded in greater detail at a lower level.
- At a higher level, where groups of events form activities that interface with each other and produce objects that themselves are passed between the activities, object interaction diagrams may be used. These are like data flow diagrams except that the flows are not restricted to data and data stores are not used.

16.3.3 Object-oriented design

Object-oriented analysis, with its concentration on the specification of object types and the behaviour they exhibit, leads to a design stage that naturally yields a specification suitable for coding in an object-oriented programming language such as C++ or Smalltalk.

At this stage, the following tasks are carried out:

- A decision on which objects are to be implemented as classes is made, and the data structure for each class is specified.
- Operations to be offered by each class are identified, and the method of carrying out these operations is specified.
- Decisions on the extent of class inheritance are made, and the way this is to be carried out is specified.

If a fully object-oriented approach is to be carried through, then an object-oriented programming language is used for implementation together with an object-oriented database. The latter has the facility for storing objects and therefore operations on these as well as data. If a hybrid approach is adopted, the object-oriented analysis and design will be the precursor to a relational database implementation. An object/relational mapping will be necessary to effect this implementation. This has the advantage of combining the semantic richness of object modelling with the benefits of existing popular relational database technology. A disadvantage is that the mismatch between paradigms leads to an additional level of complexity and may result in a loss in performance.

16.3.4 Unified Modelling Language

In recent years, a number of experts in object-oriented approaches have pooled their ideas and collaborated in order to produce a single set of development tools and techniques. Their combined efforts have resulted in the development of the Unified Modelling Language (UML). UML has rapidly become the industry standard for specifying and documenting object-oriented systems.

UML is defined as a language rather than a complete methodology. It does not prescribe how projects should be undertaken or managed. It does, however, provide a vocabulary and set of diagrammatic aids to allow developers to visualize, construct and document the development of a software system.

UML is maintained and developed by an organization called the Object Management Group (OMG). It is founded upon the philosophy of object-orientation and provides a pure OO toolset for systems development. The OMG actively dismisses any artefacts, such as data flow diagrams, which model systems under paradigms other than object-orientation.

The primary design goals of UML cited by the Object Management Group are as follows:

- To provide users with a ready-to-use, expressive visual modelling language to develop and exchange meaningful models.
- To furnish extensibility and specialization mechanisms to extend the core concepts.
- To support specifications that are independent of particular programming languages and development processes.
- To provide a formal basis for understanding the modelling language.

- To encourage the growth of the object tools market.
- To support higher-level development concepts such as components, collaborations, frameworks and patterns.
- To integrate best practices.

The language allows for a relatively seamless progression through the development of information systems. Much of the terminology employed persists throughout the process, from requirements capture through design to implementation.

At the early stages, diagrams are employed to model the static aspects of the system. Each class is represented in a **class diagram**. For each class, the diagram captures the attributes that will store the state (or data) of an object, and the methods (or functions) that allow the objects to communicate and to alter the content of the attributes (see Figure 16.10(a)). In addition, the associations and relationships between different classes can be modelled. In Figure 16.10(b) the class diagram shows an association between units and rooms: a unit is always taught in one single room, but each room may be used for many different units. The diamond shape on the association between Course and Unit shows that a course comprises a number of units. This type of association is called 'aggregation'.

Figure 16.10(a) UML student class

Figure 16.10(b) UML class diagram

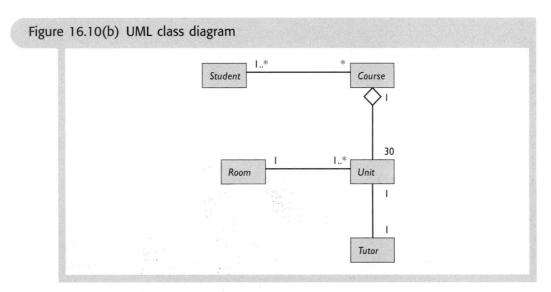

Figure 16.10(c) Sequence diagram

The system design is then further developed by modelling the dynamic aspects, such as the message passing between objects and the ordering of activities that accomplish each task. These aspects are captured in **collaboration diagrams** and **sequence diagrams**.

The sequence diagram shows the exchange of messages between an applicant applying to attend a course and the university. The objects are shown as rectangles at the top and their time lines extend vertically downwards providing a canvas for displaying interaction and message passing between them. In Figure 16.10(c) the applicant is shown making an enquiry and specifies the course required. Within the university information system, objects communicate to establish, first, whether there are any places left, and then what entry requirements apply (requests for information are shown as solid arrows; return messages are shown as dashed arrows).

One contentious feature of UML is the inclusion of **use case diagrams** (see Figure 16.10(d)). These diagrams allow the system modeller to partition the system into functional activities (shown as an ellipse) linked to the beneficiary of the activity (shown as a stick person). This process is in accordance with the widely accepted technique of top-down design where a system is broken into increasingly more detailed viewpoints. However, some critics feel it concentrates excessively on procedural aspects, which can break the object-orientation principle of encapsulating procedural detail along with data requirements at the class modelling stage.

16.3.5 Object-oriented approaches – benefits

Object-oriented approaches are still maturing, and their impact on commercial systems is far from being all-pervasive. Proponents of object-oriented approaches claim that as well as the benefits associated with structured approaches to systems analysis and design, object-oriented approaches offer the following:

■ The idea that an object type is inseparable from those operations in which it participates and which change its state is fundamental and natural to our way of viewing the world. In so far as information systems are meant to model the organizations they serve, this implies that business information systems developed with object-oriented techniques are more likely to be successful.

Figure 16.10(d) Use case diagram

- The same tools, techniques and terminology are used throughout the development cycle, making the transition between stages appear 'seamless'.

- The approach generates modules that are easily amendable. The business implications of this can be significant given the high cost of maintaining and updating software.

- A store of reusable code and a repository of defined classes is created. Again this can reduce the software costs, both in the creation of programs from libraries of building-block classes and in amending code by 'unplugging' classes and 'plugging in' newer versions.

- The approach meshes with object-oriented languages, which use the same structures and terms as those employed during object analysis and design.

The links between object analysis and object design are shown in Figure 16.11.

Recently, interest in object-oriented approaches has escalated. This is in response to many factors, including the growth in the use of the Internet, the need for more distributed applications and the expectations of users as the quality of interfaces has improved. Many of these development areas can benefit greatly from modelling the world in terms of communicating objects and by generating system features using new classes that have been derived from existing ones. Two examples are given here as illustration:

1. **Communications modules:** Many Internet-enabled applications need to establish communications links between a server and a client. Object-oriented languages usually provide a set of predefined classes, often called **sockets**, to facilitate this link. A socket-server class will be used to create the server, which accepts remote requests and

Figure 16.11 Object-oriented analysis and design

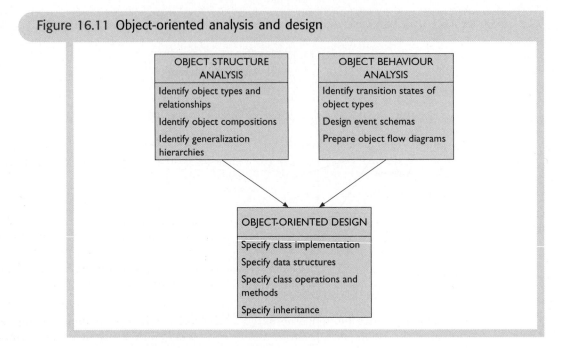

distributes data, and a client-socket class will be used to create the remote application from where the requests are issued and the results sent. This use, or rather reuse, of code is typical of object-oriented approaches.

2. **User interface design:** The graphical user interface has certain recognizable components: the menu bar, the command button, the scrolling list. Clearly, a programmer will not want to create these objects from scratch every time one is required. An object-oriented development environment will provide not only the library of reusable code to create these objects but also a common set of protocols for accessing and using them. Through the inheritance mechanism, it will follow that an object such as a list box will inherit all of the attributes and functions of a standard window class (e.g. the style of border surrounding it, click to gain focus) plus the additional functionality of a list box (e.g. a column of scrollable selectable data items, double-click on any item to select it). This greatly simplifies the task of implementing the interface design.

16.4 An evaluation of 'hard' approaches to systems analysis and design

Several approaches to the analysis and design of information systems have been termed 'hard' approaches. What do they have in common? In answering this, it is useful to take a look at three central examples of hard systems approaches as applied to the analysis and design of computerized information systems. The common features of these will then be more apparent. The three examples chosen here are structured functional/ process analysis and design, data analysis and the object-oriented approach to the development of computer systems. The first two of these have been covered extensively in

Chapters 11–13. There, though, the emphasis is on an explanation of the tools and techniques and how these are applied through the systems life cycle. The focus of the remainder of this chapter is different, in concentrating on the underlying assumptions, philosophies and typical areas of application of each approach. The aim is to compare and assess them rather than explain how to undertake practical projects.

16.4.1 Structured functional/process analysis and design

This has spawned many commercial methodologies. These are highly detailed, giving precise instructions as to the tools to be used at each stage and the documentation to be completed. Although each of these methodologies will differ, they all share most of the following characteristics:

- **Function/process-oriented:** The attention of the analyst is concentrated on analysing and designing what are seen as the most important elements in systems analysis and design. These are the functions and processes that are carried out in the existing system and are designed to be present in the new system. Once these are clearly specified, the remainder of analysis and design is seen to follow naturally.

- **Top-down:** In analysis and design, the approach taken is to concentrate on the most general processes and functions in the initial stages. Only then are these decomposed again and again until a fine-grained representation of the systems processes is obtained.

- **Logical has priority over physical:** Compatible with a top-down approach is the emphasis on a logical analysis of the functions/processes of the existing system and on the design of a logical model of the desired system. Physical aspects of design – file, program and hardware specifications – are postponed for as long as possible. This lack of early commitment to the physical aspects of design is seen as preventing premature physical decisions that would constrain design alternatives. In the early stages, physical analysis is seen as a necessary stepping stone to deriving a logical model of what the existing system does. It then plays little role in the remainder of the project.

- **Stages and exit criteria:** In common with other hard approaches to systems analysis and design, the process is seen as a linear development from the initial systems investigation and feasibility study, through analysis and design, to implementation and review. Each of these has its own exit criteria. For instance, the feasibility study is completed by the production and agreement of a feasibility report. This staged approach with objective deliverables is a characteristic of approaches that place a high emphasis on project control.

- **Tools and techniques:** Structured tools and techniques emphasize the general philosophy of the approach. Processes, top-down analysis and design, and the development of logical models are encouraged by use of the techniques. Data flow diagrams illustrate the logical flow of information and data between processes, structured English represents the logic of a process, and data dictionaries specify the logical content of data flows and data stores. The emphasis is always on the logical rather than on the physical aspects of information systems, so these paper representations are clear communication devices between users, analysts and programmers. Repeated use of these structured tools ensures a program specification suitable for structured programming techniques and the use of structured programming languages.

Hierarchical input/process/output charts ensure that complete modular specifications are developed. Different programmers can work independently on different parts of the system.

The movement to develop structured methods arose from severe problems arising in software engineering. It was not uncommon for computer projects to run considerably over budget on both time and costs. This often arose out of the difficulty of coordinating large teams of programmers. By concentrating on a top-down approach leading to modular specifications, structured approaches make possible a more accurate estimation of costs and schedules.

Another area in which structured approaches attempt to overcome difficulties is in the design of complex, highly integrated systems. Traditional methods are unsuitable for these. By concentrating on the overall logic of an information system, it is possible for the analyst to transcend the barriers imposed by physical departmental divisions.

Structured techniques in analysis and design, backed up by structured programming, ensure that the final software is modular in nature. This means that not only individual programs but also parts of programs are testable separately and can be amended easily. The modular nature of the program specifications also allows more adequate project control. The scope of the programmer for ingenuity and creativity is significantly reduced. Quality control techniques are more easily applicable to the programmer's end product. This changes the nature of the programmer's task. The 'art' of programming has been deskilled to meet the needs of 'scientific' management.

16.4.2 Data analysis

All approaches to systems analysis and design require attention to be paid at some stage to the data store aspects of the information system. What distinguishes approaches that are said to be based on data analysis is the importance and priority attached to the analysis and design of a logical *data* model of the organization in the design of an information system.

Up to now, an entity–relationship approach to data modelling has been taken. This is the most common, although there are now alternatives that attempt to overcome some of the limitations imposed by the over-simplicity of the entity–relationship structure. The various methodologies based on data analysis share the following features:

■ **Data model-oriented:** The emphasis is on deriving a data model of the entities and relationships within the organization rather than attempting to analyse or model the functions and processes. The thinking behind this is that the overall structure of an organization changes little over time. Once an accurate data model of this has been established and incorporated into a computer-based data store, it will be the foundation on which applications programs can be written. These programs will carry out the various data processes required by the organization. Applications change over time. It is therefore sensible to analyse and design around a common database rather than on the shifting sands of changing functions.

■ **Logical has priority over physical:** The emphasis is on building a logical data model of the organization prior to taking any physical decisions on how this is to be incorporated into a physical database, how many records there are, what file sizes will be, and so on. The logical model is later translated into a form suitable for implementation, using one of the commercial database systems.

- **Top-down:** Data analysis approaches stress the need to concentrate on an overall analysis prior to detail. For example, in entity–relationship modelling the important entities and their relationships are identified first. The structure of the model is then specified. Only at a later stage will attention be directed to attributes. This is to be contrasted with a bottom-up strategy, in which the concentration would be on the attributes at an earlier stage.

- **Documentation:** All approaches based on data analysis emphasize the importance of structure. The clearest way of revealing structure is pictorially. Diagrammatic representations play an important role in data analysis at the early stages.

The impetus to develop methodologies based on data analysis came from a number of areas. Modern commercial databases allow the sharing of common data by different applications and users within an organization. They also allow for considerable complexity in storage structures and retrieval. It is crucial to ensure that the best use is made of these facilities. Entity–relationship modelling and other data analysis modelling approaches assist the design of the complex models suitable for modern database management systems.

Another reason for the emphasis on data analysis is the recognition that data structures, if they are to be enduring, should mirror the real world of the organization. Organizations have complex structures. It requires more than a piecemeal approach to deal adequately with the modelling task.

16.4.3 Object-oriented approaches

The distinctive way of modelling and implementing a system using object-oriented approaches has already been described in Section 16.3. The characteristics of object-oriented approaches are:

- **Logical has priority over physical:** The emphasis is placed on building a logical object model of the organization and establishing the necessary associations and communications between the logical objects prior to taking any physical decisions on how the objects are to be implemented.

- **Top-down/bottom-up:** The modelling of the system usually starts with a top-down partitioning into related groups of classes. The terminology for these groups differs; Bertrand Meyer (1995) calls them **clusters**, whereas Coad and Yourdon (1991) describe them as **subjects**. This initial partitioning is then followed by a combination of top-down and bottom-up development activities. The top-down development can be illustrated by the inheritance mechanism, whereby abstract classes are created and then refined into more specialized classes that implement specific activities in the system. The bottom-up development is evidenced by the use of primitive (building block) classes, which are aggregated together into larger so-called container classes to implement increasingly complex levels of the solution.

- **Transition between stages:** A major attraction of object-oriented approaches is the uniformity of terminology and concepts throughout the development process. The analyst searches for candidate classes and considers the data (attributes) and functions (methods) that each class must implement. The designer puts detail into the implementation of the methods and considers the associations and the message passing between classes. The programmer implements the classes, their attributes and methods. Because of the uniformity, it is said that transition from one stage to the next is **seamless**.

■ **Documentation:** At each stage of analysis and design, detailed documentation is produced. This is often generated by a CASE tool. The seamless nature of the transition between stages described above means that the same diagrams produced at the analysis stage can be enhanced at the design stage. Many CASE tools can then generate skeleton code from those diagrams, extending the seamless feel throughout the development process. The documentation, automatically generated by a CASE tool, is particularly beneficial in recording the libraries of classes, both newly created and reused.

16.4.4 Characteristics of 'hard' approaches

The examples of 'hard' systems approaches covered in the previous sections of this chapter may seem to have little in common. Why, then, are they characterized together as 'hard' approaches?

1. They all assume that there is a clearly identifiable existing system in some state or other. To make this discovery is essential to the process of systems analysis and design. No major problem is presented by this task; it is a matter of investigation and documentation.

2. There can be a clear and agreed statement of the objective of systems analysis and design. Generally, this is established in conjunction with the 'owners' of the system. It is the role of the systems analyst/designer and programmer to provide this system on time and within cost.

3. It is assumed that the end result of the process of analysis will be a design that will incorporate a technological system. In other words, the problem – that is, the disparity between the existing system and the desired system – is seen to be soluble by technical means. In most cases, this means a computer.

4. Just as it is clearly possible to describe the existing system objectively, it is possible to determine whether the designed system, once implemented, meets the objectives set of it. Thus there is a measure of performance.

5. The process of analysis and design needs to be carried out by experts. This follows from the general assumption that the solution to the problem will be technical. The client/expert dichotomy is essential to 'hard' systems approaches.

As a summary, it can be said that 'where we are now' and 'where we want to go' can be clearly established. The problem facing the analyst is 'how to get there'. The solution is in terms of a prescribed progression from the current state to the desired state through several stages. Four distinct phases can be identified:

1. Investigating the existing system – information gathering, problem identification, feasibility study.

2. Analysis of the existing system and the provision of a solution to the problem by designing a new system on paper or using a CASE tool.

3. Implementing the solution.

4. Evaluating its effectiveness.

Although 'hard' approaches have been presented as applying to the analysis and design of information systems, their scope is much larger. They are similar to a general engineering approach to problem solving. The assumptions and overall strategy are similar whether one is designing a transport network, building a bridge, running a project to put someone on the Moon or designing a computer system.

Hard systems approaches have their antecedents in engineering and military applications. They emphasize a scientific approach towards problem solving rather than intuition or experience. A high premium is placed on logic and rationality. Philosophically, they assume a realist view – the world is 'out there' independent of us; all that has to be done is to discover it and alter it to meet our desires. In so far as people enter analysis and design considerations, they are either sources of information about the current system or operators of the new system. In the latter case, their importance is taken into account in the design of the human–computer interface.

16.4.5 Criticisms of 'hard' systems approaches

Hard systems approaches have vastly predominated in the development of computer systems. Project control failures, difficulties in designing highly integrated systems and the increasing importance of data model design for databases have led to the evolution of hard methodologies, which have superseded the more traditional approaches. Hard systems analysis and design has been hugely successful. However, there have been some notable failures. Systems that have been designed, implemented and are technically perfect but nobody uses them, systems that seem to be built to solve a problem that does not exist – these are two such examples. These failures may be located not in the poor application of systems analysis and design techniques but rather in the (mis)application of these techniques in the first place. Hard approaches make certain assumptions that limit their applicability. They do not provide fix-all methodologies that are universally applicable to all situations.

1. Hard systems approaches assume that an engineering perspective is applicable in all cases. This is unlikely to be true in situations that are unstructured. This may occur when there is no common agreement about the cause of the current problem. There may not even be a clearly identifiable problem. Once again, there may be no agreement about a desired solution. In these circumstances, hard approaches find it difficult to get off the ground. They assume that there is no difficulty in defining the existing and desired states of the system. When this assumption fails, they provide no help in further analysis.

2. Hard systems approaches are mathematically/logically based. This limits the range of problems that can be tackled. Moreover, they assume that factors and models to be used in remedying problems also have this orientation. Decision tables, entity–relationship models and logic flowcharts are all cases in point from the area of systems analysis and design. However, it goes further than this. As one might expect from their antecedents in engineering, operational research techniques play an important part in suggested aids to decision making. Linear programming, queuing theory, Monte Carlo simulation and statistical sampling theory are used. These all presuppose that a mathematical model is useful in the decision process. However, problems in an organization may not be amenable to this type of approach. For example, a failure to coordinate production schedules may not be the result of poor information flows and scheduling, which can be solved by the use of a computerized system with computer-based operational research-scheduling techniques. It may be caused by disagreement about the role of production and sales in the organization, personality conflicts, individual interests not coinciding with company objectives,

or any number of things. To use a hard approach is already to straitjacket the problem as one soluble by mathematical/logical techniques when it may not be.

3. The emphasis on mathematics and logic presupposes the importance of quantitative information as compared with qualitative or vague information, intuition and psychological models of decision making. This may be acceptable when there is clear agreement on problems and solutions and the task is seen as one of moving from the given undesirable state to a new desired state. In other cases, however, the range of useful types of information is broader. Closely connected to this is the assumption that quantitative information equals objectivity, whereas qualitative information equals subjectivity. From the scientific outlook, the latter is to be avoided. Whether subjectivity is to be avoided is a moot point. However, the proponents of a hard approach often ignore the fact that the requirement to provide quantitative information where none is accurately known often leads to unjustified assumptions being made. Claims to objectivity can then be seen to be spurious.

4. Closely allied to the previous points is the lack of recognition given to the organizational context in which a problem lies. Hard approaches tend to concentrate on data, processes, functions, tasks, decisions, data stores, flows, entities and relationships. They do not pay any attention to the social or organizational aspects of the system.

5. The emphasis is always on linear problem solving: there is a problem, it is solved, the next problem arises, it is solved, and so on. This leads to a reactive approach to management. An alternative is an ongoing developmental approach that stresses proactive attitudes.

6. The dichotomy between the client and the expert can act as a barrier to successful systems analysis and development. This may happen in a number of ways. There may be communication problems. The client is an expert in the area for which systems analysis is being carried out. The expert is probably from a technical background, so they do not share the same language. Tools used in structured approaches help to overcome this limitation. By stressing the logical aspects of the system and using diagrammatic tools that illustrate this, technicalities that may confuse the clients are removed. However, there is a more subtle effect of this dichotomy. The expert is seen to be outside the problem area. He or she observes it objectively. Not so! Once involved, the analyst interacts with the system – particularly the people operating within it. The analyst brings his or her own set of experiences, knowledge, prejudices and background to bear on the problem area.

These comments on hard approaches to systems analysis and design are not meant to be damning. Rather, they illustrate the need for caution before adopting a hard methodology. In particular, the applicability of the chosen methodology should first be established. Areas that are unstructured, with a lack of agreement on problems and what would count as a solution, are just those areas that are not suited to a technical approach to systems analysis and design.

16.5 'Soft' approaches to systems analysis and design

Hard approaches to systems analysis and design have been very successful in developing computer systems that, viewed from a technical perspective, are efficient and effective information providers. However, there have been cases when new information systems have not had user acceptance or have seemed to be misplaced as a solution to a spurious problem. These difficulties have led to developments that challenge the assumptions made by approaches deriving from a 'hard' view of systems.

Two approaches are outlined in this chapter. Each perceives different weaknesses in the approaches considered so far, so each has a different remedy. They both identify the presence of people in a system as leading to complications not acknowledged by proponents of hard approaches.

Checkland's approach recognizes that different people have different perceptions of problems and of the systems in which they lie. It is therefore a mistake to assume automatically that there is agreement on 'where we are now' or even on 'where we want to go'. Rather, problems are much less structured, much fuzzier than supporters of hard approaches would have us believe.

The socio-technical approach stresses the recognition that computerized information systems are part of interacting social and technical systems. If one part is changed, for example the technical system, by means of computerization, then the other will be affected. It is important to realize that the social and technical systems (the socio-technical system) cannot be designed independently of each other. One way to ensure that sufficient weight is given to the social aspects of the system is to involve users in the process of analysis and design. This undercuts the assumption of 'hard' approaches that the end product of design is a purely technical system. It also challenges the assumption of the necessity or desirability of the expert/user division.

16.5.1 Checkland's approach

In order to understand the rationale for Checkland's approach, it is helpful to look at some of the underlying philosophical assumptions made.

First, the assumption is that problems are not regarded as being 'out there' in a realist sense. There are no objectively given problems. Different people may see different problems in the 'same' situation.

It is, perhaps, misleading to talk of the 'situation' as though it were objectively given. A situation is a combination of the external world together with the way that it seems to the observer. This will be influenced by the background and beliefs of that observer. For example, an experienced doctor will unconsciously interpret an X-ray photograph and see shapes of importance in it. However, to the untrained observer there is very little of substance. Or again, different cultural backgrounds interpret voice inflections in different ways. So the same sentence uttered by two different people may be variously interpreted as being hostile or friendly.

Not only will different people disagree over the 'neutral' description of a situation but they will also disagree as to its problematic nature. For example, the student may regard end-of-course failure rates in professional exams as a problem – another hurdle to cross on the way to a career. However, a qualified professional may regard them as a non-problematic essential for the maintenance of small numbers of qualified professionals. This guarantees high incomes for those who are qualified. The professional institute setting the exams has a third view – the failure rates are taken as evidence that standards are being maintained.

It should be clear not only that different people may see the same situation as problematic in different ways but also that some may not see any problem at all. One man's meat is another man's poison. What determines an individual's view of a situation is the nexus of beliefs, desires and interests that the individual has. It is the combination of beliefs about 'what is' and 'what ought to be' that is so important in determining a situation as 'problematic' for an individual.

Second, just as problems are intellectual constructs, so are solutions. Two people may agree on a problem and yet disagree as to what constitutes a solution. Take an examination for example. Very high failure rates on a course may be regarded as problematic by both students and the course director. Students see the solution in terms of easier examinations and more effective teaching. The course director sees the need to raise entry qualifications.

The third assumption states that problems very rarely come singly, neatly packaged and ready for a solution. It is more likely that there are several interlocking problems. Moreover, if one problem is solved, this may generate a problem elsewhere. Problems are often messy and not amenable to simple solutions such as the installation of a computerized information system. This is another reason why the term 'problem situation' rather than 'problem' is used to describe what confronts the analyst.

Fourth, it is obvious from these points that it is important that the problem area be investigated and analysed prior to any decisions on the desirability of computer systems. The role of the systems analyst is seen, at least initially, as much more akin to a therapist than to a technical computer expert. The analyst encourages participants in the existing system to examine their own perceptions of the system and its interconnections with others, its objectives, their role in it and the role of others. This learning process is an essential prerequisite for development. It is recognized at the outset that a computer system may not be suitable for the organization, or at least not a total solution.

The final assumption implies that the analyst cannot be divorced from the system and the participants involved in it owing to the early therapeutic role of the analyst.

The methodology

Checkland's methodology (Figure 16.12) evolved out of the area of management consultancy. The analyst is not an expert in any particular area so is therefore not employed to give technical advice. Rather, the analyst should be thought of as a change agent or therapist who is able to stimulate others to new perceptions of the problem situation. The approach is particularly effective compared with other methodologies in cases where there are messy problems. The stages are now outlined. Although progression is from one stage to the next, there is not the same rigidity and control over stage exits as in the structured life-cycle approach. Stages may be re-entered once left. The process is iterative rather than linear.

Stage 1 The development of rich pictures

The first task of the analyst is to become acquainted with the problem situation, and an attempt is made to build up a **rich picture** of the problem situation. This is a cartoon of the important influences and constituents of the problem situation. The analyst collects information to incorporate into this picture. Not only is hard information collected, such as facts and other quantitative data, but soft information is also obtained. Here are included the participants in the problem situation, any worries, fears and aspirations they have that are thought by the analyst to be relevant, conflicts and alliances between departments or individuals, and hunches and guesses. In particular, the analyst is looking for structure, key processes, and the interaction between process and structure.

It is important that the analyst does not impose a systems structure on the problem situation at this stage. The analyst will be interested in determining meaningful roles

Figure 16.12 The stages in Checkland's methodology

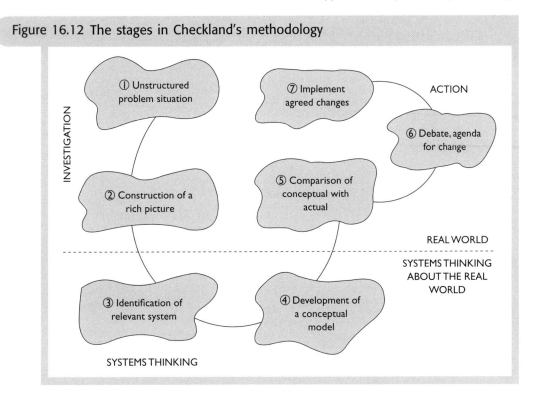

that individuals fulfil, such as boss or counsellor. In drawing the rich picture, the analyst will identify primary tasks and issues and will attempt to see varying perspectives. At this stage, the analyst should take particular care not to pigeonhole the problem, say as a marketing problem or a communications problem. This will limit the types of change that may ultimately be suggested.

Three important roles in the problem situation are identified. The **client** is the individual who is paying the analyst. The **problem owner** will be the individual who is responsible, or the area within which the problem situation arises. It may not be clear initially who the owner is. Different perceptions of the situation will assume different problem owners (we are all familiar with the conversation 'that's your problem', 'no it's yours'). The analyst may need to experiment with several individuals in order to establish a realistic problem owner. The **problem solver** is normally the analyst. These three roles may be held by three different people, or they may coincide in two individuals. It is common for the client and problem owner to be the same person.

Kismet case study 16.1

An example of a rich picture is shown in Figure 16.13. It corresponds to the Kismet case study covered in Chapter 11. A few details have been added in order to make the problem area more unstructured, and the picture therefore richer, as the original case as presented was fairly 'cut and dried'. Unlike the models produced so far, the rich picture attempts to capture the roles played by various participants. Examples are the customers who might take their business to Hardy, or the soon-to-retire head of the ▶

Figure 16.13 A rich picture of Kismet

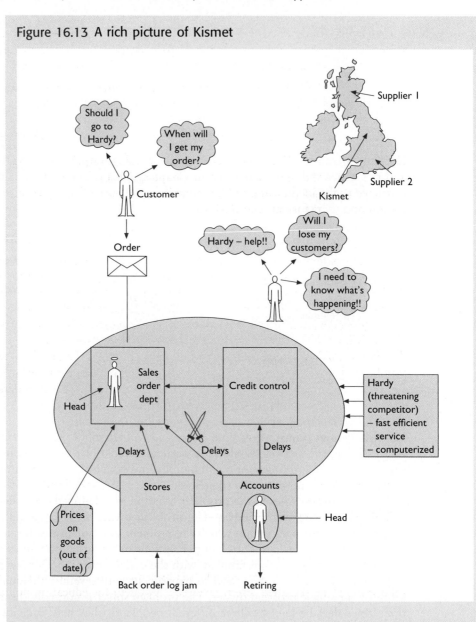

accounts department, who may be the sole source of information about key aspects of control in the current system. The diagram also acts as a prompt for further investigation, such as the log jam of back orders or the out-of-date price lists. It also poses certain questions as to the interaction between roles and events; for example, 'is the back order log jam causing customers to turn to a competitor?'

The purpose of a rich picture is:

■ To help to visualize a complex mess of interacting people, roles, threats, facts, observations, and so on. Its purpose is to facilitate understanding of the problem situation.

- To avoid imposing a rigid structure on the appreciation of the problem situation. A systems perspective is to be avoided at this early stage. It would tend to force perception of the problem through systems concepts such as inputs/outputs, systems objectives, feedback and the like. This may not be appropriate for the situation.

- To aid an investigative approach by the analyst towards the problem situation.

- To act as a communication tool between participants. This will aid a consensus perception of the problem situation. It is all too easy for the fact that different participants have importantly divergent views of the situation to go unnoticed.

It should already be clear that there is considerable divergence between this approach and the structured approach taken in Chapters 10–15. There, the initial stages were restricted to the identification of key functions and processes, key entities in the organization and their formal relationships.

Stage 2 Identification of the relevant system and the root definition

The rich picture is a pictorial representation of the problem situation. In order to progress, it is necessary to view the problem from a systemic point of view. This is where the idea of a **relevant system** comes in. This is the most appropriate way of viewing the problem situation as a system. It is not always clear what the relevant system is. The relevant system is extracted from the rich picture. There is no one correct answer to the question 'what is the relevant system?' Several suggestions may be made. The one that is accepted is agreed by negotiation, often between the problem owner and the problem solver. This relevant system should be the one that provides most insight into the problem situation and is most appropriate for stimulating understanding and change in the organization – the ultimate goal of the methodology.

Kismet case study 16.2

Discussions take place with the managers of Kismet to establish the relevant system. In the case of Kismet the task is reasonably straightforward. It is a system for processing orders effectively and efficiently.

Other cases where things are less structured may require consideration of several 'relevant' systems before one that fits becomes apparent. For instance, a local technical college might be regarded alternatively as 'a system for educating pupils in order to meet the labour need of the local area' or 'a system for removing local unemployed adolescents at their potentially most disruptive and destructive age from the streets'. Or again, the owner/manager of a small business may regard it as 'a system for maintaining a stable financial income', 'a system for maintaining a stable and interesting employment for himself and his employees' or 'a system for providing a valued community service'.

Generally, relevant systems are issue-based or primary-task-based. When agreed on, they may come as quite a revelation to some of those participating in the problem situation. Identification of the relevant system may help to cast light on the otherwise seemingly non-understandable behaviour of their colleagues.

Just to name the relevant system gives a highly generalized specification of the area associated with the problem situation. It is important to be more precise. This is done by developing a **root definition** of the relevant system. The root definition gives a precise description of the *essence* of the relevant system.

Producing a root definition is not a mechanical task. It can only be achieved through trial and error. However, there is a checklist, called by its mnemonic CATWOE, which every adequate root definition should satisfy. All the CATWOE components should be present (or at least their absence needs to be justified and acknowledged).

1. **Customers:** These are the group of people or body who are served by or who benefit from the system. In the Kismet case, it is not only the customers of Kismet but also the stores and accounts functions.

2. **Actors:** These are the people, or rather types of people, who carry out the essential activities in the relevant system.

3. **Transformation process:** This is what the system does – that is, the process that converts inputs into outputs.

4. *Weltanschauung*: The *Weltanschauung* or 'world view' that is relevant to the system is specified somewhere in the root definition. In the case of Kismet, this is indicated by the assumption of performance according to cost and time constraints.

5. **Owners:** The owners of the system are those to whom the system is answerable. They have power to change the system or make it cease to exist. In the case of Kismet, this will probably be the management of the company.

6. **Environment:** This is the environment in which the relevant system is located.

Kismet case study 16.3

The CATWOE components for Kismet are now discussed. The following summary is produced:

- Customers: For Kismet, it is not only the customers but also the stores and accounts functions that must be considered.

- Actors: The task of identifying actors can be assisted by the work done on the creation of rich pictures. For example, a number of actors are present in Figure 16.13.

- Transformation process: The processing of inputs and outputs can be summarized as transforming the orders placed by customers into requests for stock and notifications to accounts.

- The 'world view': In the case of Kismet, this is indicated by the assumption of performance according to cost and time constraints.

- The owners of the system: For Kismet, this will probably be the management of the company.

- The environment in which the relevant system is located must be established.

This leads to a root definition of the Kismet sales order processing as follows:

A business function within Kismet operated by sales and credit control staff to accept and process orders provided by customers, transforming them into validated requests to stock and notifications into accounts, within speed and cost constraints set by Kismet management.

The purpose of identifying the relevant system and deriving a root definition is to concentrate on the *essence* of the system covering the problem situation. It is then easier to proceed to develop a logical model of a system that meets this description.

Stage 3 Building a conceptual model

Given that the relevant system has been identified and a root definition has been provided, the next stage of the methodology is to develop a conceptual model. This is a logical model of the key activities or processes that must be carried out in order to satisfy the root definition of the system. It is not a model of the real world. It may bear no resemblance to what occurs in the problem situation and is not derived by observing it. Rather, it consists of what is logically required by the root definition. The distinction between what *must* be done in order to satisfy the root definition and what *is* actually done in the system is of fundamental importance. Its recognition is at the heart of the usefulness of the methodology in stimulating organizational learning and change.

The key activities are shown in the conceptual model in Figure 16.14. Each of these key activities themselves represents a subsystem that would carry the activity out – for

Figure 16.14 A conceptual model

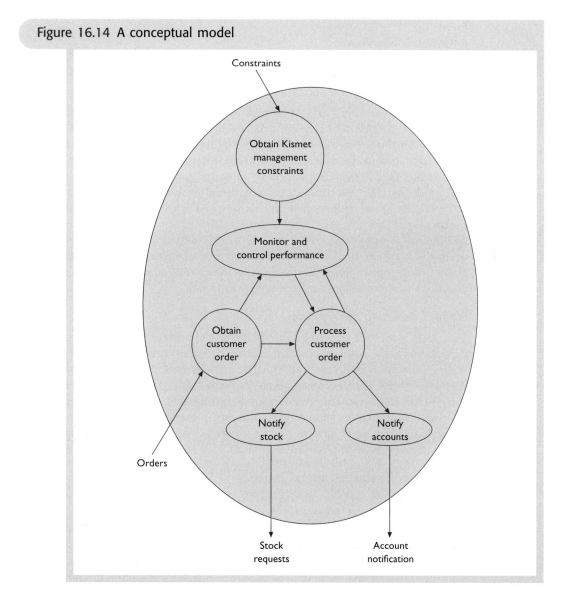

example, the subsystem to monitor and control performance. These high-level activities give rise to second-level activities that must be performed in order that the high-level activities can be executed. For instance, monitoring and control require collection of the standard, collection of the sensed data, comparison between the two and taking the necessary action. This gives rise to second-level conceptual models that can replace the relevant part of the first-level model.

When completed, the conceptual model is tested against the formal requirement of a general systems model (a systems model was covered in Chapter 1). Examples of typical questions that need to be asked are:

- Does the model illustrate an activity that has a continuous purpose?
- Is there a measure of performance?
- Is there some kind of decision-making process or role?
- Are there subsystems that are connected?
- Is there a boundary?
- Is there some guarantee of long-term stability?

Stage 4 Comparing the conceptual model with the real world

The previous two stages have attempted to build up some ideal model of what should happen in a system that carries out the essential activities required by the agreed root definition of the relevant system. Now is the time to see what actually happens.

The rich picture provides a good representation of the real situation, and it is against this that the conceptual model must be compared. Alternatively, the conceptual model may be compared directly with the problem situation. Differences should be highlighted as possible points for discussion. Typical of the questions considered by the analyst at this stage are 'Why is there a discrepancy between the conceptual model and the real world at this point?' and 'Does this activity in the conceptual model really occur?' The point of this investigation is not to criticize the way that things are actually done but rather to derive a list of topics – an **agenda for change** – that can be discussed with the actors in the problem situation.

Stage 5 Debating the agenda

This stage involves a structured discussion of the points raised on the agenda with the participants in the problem situation. It is important to realize that this is a consciousness-raising exercise as much as anything. The analyst should restrict discussion to changes that are systemically desirable and culturally feasible. That is, the changes should not run counter to the thinking that has gone into the selection of the relevant system and the root definition. Nor should they ignore the particular organizational culture within which the participants have lived and worked. The aim is to obtain agreement on a list of changes to be implemented.

Stage 6 Implementing agreed changes

Checkland is not very specific on how this stage is to be carried out. This is understandable in that a large range of changes might be agreed as feasible and desirable. It may be the case that a need for a computerized information system that will serve specific functions has been identified. In this case, it is probable that formal information modelling and structured analysis and design techniques will take over. However, the need for other types of change may be agreed. For instance, it may be thought necessary to change aspects of the organizational structure such as departmental responsibilities, the degree of centralization, or even the physical layout. Changes in overall policies, strategies or procedures may be agreed. The process of analysis may have revealed divergent attitudes concerning the problem situation. The outcome of the debate on the agenda may be an agreement to foster changed attitudes within the problem situation.

The stages in Checkland's methodology are not necessarily carried out in a linear fashion. It is often necessary to re-enter an earlier stage for revision. For instance, when comparing the conceptual model with the real world it may become apparent that the relevant system has not been identified correctly. This will require backtracking. There is another important way in which Checkland's methodology is not linear. It would be a mistake to assume that once the stages have been executed the problem in the problem situation has been resolved. It is not a problem-solving methodology but rather aims at *improvement* of situations through organizational understanding, learning and change.

16.5.2 Participation in socio-technical analysis and design

The socio-technical approach grew out of work started in the Tavistock Institute for Behavioural Research in the 1950s. This derived from the introduction of new technology in the coal mines. The approach recognized that successful introduction of new technology required the identification of social needs and goals as well as technical/economic objectives. The underlying assumption was that a system will only function effectively if human needs such as job satisfaction are acknowledged.

In the 1970s, the socio-technical approach began to be adopted in various guises for the development of computer systems in organizational environments. The common element in these approaches is the recognition of the interdependence of four factors – technology, tasks, people and the organization (Figure 16.15). If one of these is altered,

Figure 16.15 Socio-technical connections

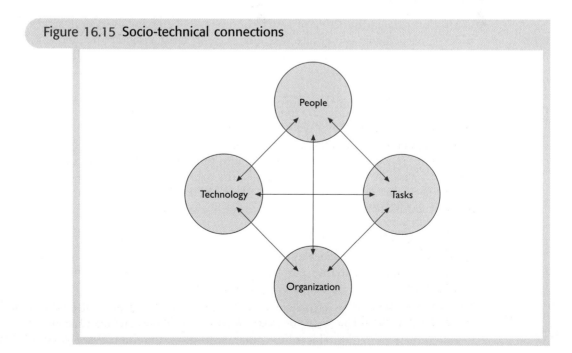

for example the introduction of new computerized technology, it will have an impact on all the others. It therefore makes sense to take account of all aspects of the socio-technical system in computerization so that harmony can be maintained.

One socio-technical approach, due to Mumford (and colleagues) (Land and Hirscheim, 1983), sees the best way of obtaining this harmony as involving users participatively in the process of analysis and design. This idea meshes neatly with the general trend towards industrial democracy experienced over the last 20 years, together with the increasing acceptance of humanistic values as applied to the workplace.

Benefits of participation

From the management point of view, participation in analysis and design enables the valuable knowledge and skills of the workforce to be incorporated into the final system. The analyst may be a technical expert in the area of computers but is unlikely to be familiar with the organization, tasks and people within which the final system must fit. Participation is seen as a more effective way of obtaining this experience than the 'classical' approaches such as the formal interview or questionnaire.

Also, from the management perspective, it is more likely that users will show commitment to and confidence in the final installed system if they have had a hand in its development. This stems from two sources. First, it is difficult for an individual to participate in the design of a system and not establish a psychological investment in and therefore commitment to it. Second, the continued presence of the participants in the process of analysis and design educates them in an appreciation of the final system and also allays their fears of its likely effects. Users may fear job deskilling, removal of job satisfaction or their ability to cope with the new system. Even if groundless, these fears lead to resistance to the implementation of the new system and ultimately to its ineffective use or failure. Participation allays these fears by providing information as the system is developed.

From a 'worker' point of view, participation can be seen as a way of maintaining control over the introduction of new technology. By being involved at all stages of the process, participants can ensure that jobs and job satisfaction are maintained. It also serves as a public recognition of the importance of participants' knowledge and skills in the workplace.

Issues involved in participation

Several issues are involved in participation:

1. What role do participants play in the design process?
2. At which stage in the life cycle are participants involved?
3. Which groups should participate in the design process?
4. How are participants to be selected?

These questions are dealt with below:

1. **What role do participants play in the design process?** Three different levels of involvement can be identified for participants. These correspond to deepening degrees of commitment to the participative approach.

   (a) **Consultative:** The participants are consulted for their views and understanding by an expert. The expert analysts note these responses and take account of them at their discretion. This is little different from the 'traditional' approach towards interview as a source of information about the system. Where this differs in a socio-technical approach is that the analyst will be interested not only in the technical aspects of analysis and design but also in a complete socio-technical design.

(b) **Representative:** Selected users from relevant interest groups join the design teams. Their views are taken into account, although it is still recognized that the analysts are the 'experts' and ultimately they are responsible for design.

(c) **Consensus:** With consensus participation, the interest groups take over responsibility for the analysis and design. Analysts are now regarded as just another interest group whose responsibility it is to provide technical knowledge and to ensure that the design is technically sound.

2. **At which stage in the life cycle are participants involved?** This may happen at any or all stages of the project. Major stages are as follows:

(a) Project initiation – it is unlikely that management will allow participation at this stage. It is traditionally regarded as the province of strategic decision making.

(b) Definition of systems objectives.

(c) Description and analysis of the existing system.

(d) Identification of problem areas within the existing system.

(e) Suggestion, design and evaluation of alternative solutions to the problems identified in (d).

(f) Detailed design of the human work (social) and computer (technical) systems.

(g) Preparation of systems specification.

(h) Implementation of the human work and computer systems.

(i) Evaluation and monitoring of the working system.

3. **Which groups should participate in the design process?** The answer to this is 'any group that will be significantly affected by the computer system'. This may include outside groups in the early stages (such as watchdog committees for the nationalized industries) as well as groups from within the organization. Examples of the latter are trade unions, clerical and shopfloor workers, middle management, and programmers and analysts.

4. **How are participants to be selected?** Interest groups may elect their own members, or participants may be chosen by management. Both approaches may be politically sensitive. With the former method, it may be the case that only those with the most strongly militant anti-technology views are put forward, whereas with the latter, management's buddies may be chosen.

The presupposition so far has been that participation is to be thought of as being limited to analysis and design. There is no reason why participants should not be involved in the decision-making process. However, this is unlikely to be agreed by management at the major decision points – when global terms of reference are being established for the project or when stop/go decisions are needed. At other points – fixing of local terms of reference or choice between alternative solutions – the decision-making process is almost invariably interwoven with analysis and design. Then participation in decision making goes hand in hand with analysis and design.

Methodology

In order to gain the benefits promised by participation, it is necessary to have an effective methodology. Without this those involved in participation will be directionless. The methodology outlined here is due to Enid Mumford. It involves various procedures such as variance analysis, job satisfaction analysis and future analysis to aid the participative approach: these procedures are briefly described. However, it does not preclude the use of other tools or techniques, such as data flow diagrams or entity–relationship modelling, particularly in the latter stages of systems design. Mumford has given her approach to IS development the acronym ETHICS (*e*ffective, *t*echnical and *h*uman *i*mplementation of *c*omputer *s*ystems). The important components in the approach advocated by Mumford are now discussed.

The diagnosis of needs and problems

Three diagnostic tools are used here, variance analysis, job satisfaction analysis and future analysis:

1. **Variance analysis:** This involves identifying weak parts of the existing system that produce operational problems. The design group will identify key operations within a department and note those areas where there is a systematic deviation of the results of those operations from the standards set. This may often occur on the boundaries of a system, where there are coordination problems. Variances may affect one another; therefore it is important to reveal connections and dependencies. A variance matrix may be of assistance here. In systems design, the aim is to control these variances where they originate rather than by control at a later stage.

2. **Job satisfaction analysis:** The amount of job satisfaction obtained in a work situation may be explained in terms of the fit between what participants expect from their jobs and what they are obtaining. Three important needs should be considered. These are connected with the personality of the individual, the personal values held by that individual and the need for competence and efficiency. If systems are designed with these in mind, job satisfaction will be improved. This is a necessary condition to ensure that the socio-technical system will function effectively.

3. **Future analysis:** Large systems take a long time to design. If a large project is undertaken, it may be three or four years or even longer from initiation to the start of the successful operation of the new system. The life of the new system will need to be more than three or four years in order to recover the costs of the project. This implies that in analysis and design the time horizon with which the project is concerned is many years. In order to achieve a system that will meet the needs of the future, then the future has to be predicted. This becomes more difficult and uncertain the greater the forecasting period. Future changes may not be just in volumes of transactions processed or types of information required of the information system. Changes in the economic climate, new technology and changes in organizational structure such as decentralization or merging of companies will all have a significant impact on the satisfaction of future needs by the system currently being designed.

   Many traditional approaches do not take the need to design for the future seriously and have consequently produced systems suffering from the 'dinosaur syndrome'. The requirement of a system to meet future demands can be achieved by:

   (a) **Predicting the future by modelling and simulation:** The predictions are then catered for in current design.
   (b) **Designing a system that is robust:** This means that the system has built-in redundancy and flexibility to deal with uncertain future requirements. The system is also designed to be modular for easy adaptation.

(c) **A structured approach to future analysis:** This involves the design team(s) drawing up a list of factors of relevance to the system that may be the subject of change. The likelihood of each of the factors changing over the lifetime of the system is then evaluated. The impact of these changes on the system is then assessed. The components of the system that are subject to these effects should be identified so that the stage of design can take account of them.

The consideration of the groups affected by the system

The groups that will be affected by the system are identified. The goals of these are then established by consultation with company policy and the diagnosis of user needs and job satisfaction analysis. An attempt is made to establish the weightings to be associated with each goal. Ideally, this would be by consensus between the various groups as a result of negotiation.

Socio-technical approach to the analysis and design of the system

The purpose of socio-technical analysis and design is to produce an end system consisting of social and technical structures that satisfies both technical and social goals. This proceeds by using a general stage, which is followed by a detailed one.

Initially, alternative systems strategies are suggested. The effects of each of these are forecasted for the period of the planning horizon. The impact of each strategy is then compared against both the goals of the system and the predicted performance of the existing socio-technical system up to the planning horizon. Optimistic and pessimistic estimations are made for each strategy by changing the values of uncertain parameters. The strategy with the best fit to the social and technical goals is selected.

Detailed design progresses through social and technical analysis. In technical analysis, logically integrated sets of tasks, called **unit operations**, are identified. These unit operations consist of tasks that are logically cohesive in transforming an input into an output in preparation for the next unit operation or stage. For example, a unit operation would be the batching, error checking and input of sales data into a day-book preparatory to updating the sales ledger. Each design group receives one or more operations within its scope. In the analysis of the social aspects of the work system, the relationships between individuals and the roles they play are investigated. The results of job satisfaction analysis would be used at this point. Each work group has the responsibility for eliminating variances that have been discovered in variance analysis. Within the work group, the existing and future users of the system are of particular importance in the development of the social system and the earlier stages of technical analysis. The impact of the computer analysts is felt most during the latter stages of technical design.

Implementation

Once designed, the system can be implemented. This may occur as a linear process or may take the form of prototyping. In prototyping, an experimental smaller version of the system is built. This will not have the full functionality of the final system and will probably not be technically efficient in a computing sense. However, it does enable an evaluation to be made of the extent to which it meets some of the social and technical goals of the design. This will provide a direction for improvement of the final system before any major expenditure has gone into its weaknesses. Indeed, several prototypes may be built before a satisfactory version on which the final design can be based is reached.

Post-implementation evaluation

After the system has been installed and running, some assessment of its performance in the light of its social and technical goals is made. This allows correction as part of normal ongoing maintenance or provides valuable knowledge that is relevant in the design of a future system.

In summary, the participative approach differs from 'hard' approaches in a number of ways:

1. There is a recognition that technical systems cannot be treated independently of the social systems with which they interact.

2. Following from point 1, in the design of computer-based information systems the social system within which the work occurs must be the subject of analysis and design as much as the technical system itself. Without this harmonious design, any result-ant technical system is subject to a high risk of failure on the grounds of its inad-equacy from a social point of view.

3. The current and future users of the system possess a knowledge of existing work practices and deficiencies that makes their experience valuable in the process of analysis and design. In order to utilize this experience, it is necessary to use a set of diagnostic procedures (job satisfaction analysis, variance analysis, and so on). The traditional role of the expert systems analyst is restricted to technical aspects of analysis and design.

4. Participation in analysis and design is a prerequisite for a successful implementa-tion of technical systems as it reduces users' fears over the introduction of new technology.

5. There is an ethical commitment to the belief that users of technology and those affected by it have a right to have some say on the design and operation of these systems.

16.5.3 Checkland's methodology and the participative approach: reservations

Both Checkland's methodology and the participative socio-technical approach offer alternatives to the 'hard' approaches covered in previous chapters. How realistic are they? Although they both have their supporters, there are serious questions that need to be addressed.

Checkland

The main criticism levelled at Checkland's methodology is its lack of comprehensive-ness, particularly in the later stages of analysis and design. This has led critics to argue that it is not a methodology that takes the analyst through the life cycle. The idea of a 'life cycle' is not one that fits well with Checkland's approach, although it is unde-niable that the methodology is strongest in the early stages of problem identification and analysis. At the very least, proponents would argue that it explores possibilities for organizational learning and progress in problem situations that are neglected by 'hard' approaches. The methodology from this viewpoint is regarded more as a front-end approach to carrying out the necessary problem analysis prior to the technical ana-lysis that would imply a computerized system.

Another comment made on the methodology is that the analyst is not only in the position of attempting to understand an existing system but is also required by the methodology, via root definitions and conceptual models, to be an originator of systems. Although this remark has some foundation, it is not clear that it does not also apply to structured methods if properly carried out. In these, during the transition from analysis to systems design, there is always an element of assessing what needs to be done logically in order to perform a function, as well as analysing what actually is done.

Although Checkland's methodology has been used commercially, it does not have the same extensive track record as is associated with the structured methods covered in Chapters 10–15. This is not to say that there have been significant failures using the methodology but rather that the number of times it has been employed provide an insufficiently large sample from which to draw conclusions. It remains to be seen whether the methodology will have a lasting impact on approaches to analysis and design.

Participative socio-technical approaches

The participative element of this has been criticized from the point of view of its heavy cost. To involve users participatively in analysis and design places a great burden on the personnel in an organization. Proponents of the approach would not argue with this but would point out that the extra cost is more than justified by the production of systems that are accepted by and meet user needs – it produces effective and not merely technically efficient systems.

The emphasis on participation and the omission of specific tools is seen as a shortcoming by critics. However, the approach should be seen as setting a framework within which successful analysis and design can be carried out. It does not preclude the use of data flow diagrams, entity modelling or any other technique that aids analysis and design. Participation is seen as a recognition of the importance of implementing a system that meets socio-technical as well as purely technical goals.

There may be resistance to the use of participation in its fullest forms. From one quarter, management can see it as a way of losing managerial control; from another, analysts can view it as diminishing the importance of their status and roles. This is not an objection to the approach, but resistance to its use will weaken its effectiveness, so it is important that a commitment to participation be obtained from all parties involved.

Finally, in common with Checkland's methodology, there are too few cases in which the approach has been applied to judge its success from an empirical standpoint.

Both Checkland and those who have developed the participative approach have undoubtedly identified weaknesses in the universal applicability of 'hard' approaches. It remains to be seen whether their solutions will fulfil the promises they intend to keep.

16.6 Contemporary usage of methodologies, tools and techniques

Establishing the actual usage of information systems methodologies is a complex process. Software vendors might appear to be a useful source of data in this respect. Many software houses do purport to adopt a particular methodology for their systems development activities. However, it does not follow that the chosen approach is consistently applied in all projects undertaken. An alternative viewpoint is to track individual projects and to investigate the methodology employed. Although the methodology may

Table 16.1 Use of development techniques in IS projects (not mutually exclusive)

Techniques employed	Analysis phase	Design phase
Entity relationship models	107 (44.0%)	91 (39.7%)
Data flow diagrams	105 (43.6%)	74 (32.3%)
Flowcharts	80 (33.1%)	65 (28.4%)
Normalization	68 (28.1%)	55 (24.0%)
Class/object models	48 (19.8%)	46 (20.1%)
None	40 (16.6%)	35 (15.4%)
Structured English	39 (16.1%)	57 (24.9%)
Use CASE models	38 (15.3%)	26 (11.4%)
Formal methods	32 (13.2%)	27 (11.8%)
Structure diagrams	13 (5.4%)	14 (6.1%)
Other	20 (8.3%)	14 (6.1%)

not be applied rigorously at every stage in the project development, the strategy of tracking projects in this way does permit questions to be asked relating to the particular usage and success of the techniques employed.

Using the project-tracking approach (Cobham *et al.*, 1999) suggests that the most popular type of methodology in current use is structured (42% of IS projects), followed by object-oriented (20%), while 24% of projects appear to use no formal methodology at all. Some 8.5% of all projects use a rapid application development approach, with DSDM accounting for one-third of these projects.

It has been suggested (O'Callaghan and Leigh, 1994) that the successful use of a methodology requires that it be applied completely throughout the project development life cycle. In reality, some projects are developed in a more piecemeal fashion using preferred techniques and omitting others at various stages. Other projects employ a hybrid approach combining techniques from more than one methodology. Attempts to evaluate the success of these piecemeal and hybrid approaches have been inconclusive, although it is generally accepted that the least successful projects tend to be those that employ no recognized techniques at all.

Table 16.1 lists the popular techniques employed in IS project development, regardless of the methodology claimed. The techniques that were presented in Chapters 10–15, namely data flow modelling and the use of structured English, and entity relationship modelling leading to a normalized data model, are clearly the most popular. The use of class/object modelling in nearly one-fifth of all projects reflects the current interest in object-oriented approaches. Given the reasons for this popularity, which were outlined earlier in this chapter, it is likely that this figure will increase.

Summary

Approaches to systems analysis and design have been divided into two categories – 'hard' and 'soft'. Although this is a useful division, it must always be remembered that there are many differences in the underlying assumptions and practices between different methodologies within each category.

'Hard' approaches seek to develop a technical solution to problems through the implementation of a computer system (Table 16.2 – structured, data analysis, object-oriented).

Table 16.2 Comparison of approaches

Approach	Reasons for development	Aim	Area	Method	Key words/concepts examples
Structured	Failures at developing large integrated systems and inability to coordinate programmer teams	To develop a technically efficient, modular, integrated system	Functions, total systems	Development of a logical model of a system emphasizing functions, data processes and data flows	Data flow diagrams, data dictionaries, structured HIPO charts
Data analysis	Development and increasing importance of database technology	To develop a database structure suitable for supporting the organization's changing applications	Organizational data structures	Development of a logical data model of an organization emphasizing entities, relationships and structures	Entity–relationships models
Object-oriented	Failures of structured methodologies to produce systems on time, within budget and future-proofed	To develop and maintain applications with greater ease and higher quality	Objects, total systems	Development of static and dynamic object models emphasizing associations, inheritance structures and message passing	Class/object model, object interaction diagram, state transition, inheritance, reuse of previous designs and code
Checkland	Failure to take account of fuzzy problems in organizational contexts	To achieve user understanding of organizational problem situations, thereby leading to learning and improvement	Fuzzy systems, problem situations	Development of a conceptual model of an ideal system through which participants can identify weaknesses and stimulate change	Rich pictures, conceptual models, root definitions, CATWOE, agenda for change
Socio-technical participation	Failures of systems as a result of user non-acceptance	To develop a fit between social and technical systems by participation, thereby ensuring systems acceptance	Socio-technical system	Involvement of the user in the process of analysis and design	Participation, consensus, job satisfaction, variance analysis, autonomous work groups
Rapid applications development	The need to develop systems quickly to respond to changing business needs	To develop an effective core system quickly to meet user needs	Functions, end-user needs	Involvement of management and users in an iterative development process, which may involve a variety of tools, including CASE	Joint requirements planning, workshops, joint applications development, prototyping

They assume the possibility of a clear and agreed statement both of the current situation and its problems and of the desired state of affairs to be achieved. The problem for systems analysis and design is then seen as designing a solution that will take us from where we are now to where we want to go. The assumptions underlying this approach are akin to those in engineering. Users of the existing system are seen as providers of useful information about it. Users of the proposed system are seen in terms of their information requirements and as devices for input of data. The role of the analyst is as *the* expert brought in on a client–consultant basis to design the system.

Traditional methodologies concentrate on the automation of existing business processes. They do this by recommending procedures and documentation to describe the current system and turn this into a set of program and file specifications. Structured process analysis and design grew out of the failure of traditional methods when designing complex integrated systems or when providing systems that involve substantial redesign of functions or procedures. The emphasis is on transcending the physical limitations of the current system by developing a logical model of data flows, functions and processes prior to design. The perspective of approaches based on data analysis acknowledges that databases are a corporate resource and consequently need careful design. This is achieved by deriving a logical data model of the organization from which a database structure can be defined.

'Soft' approaches recognize the impact of human beings in the area of systems analysis and design (Table 16.2 – Checkland, socio-technical participation). First, these methodologies deny the premise that it is easy to specify current and desired systems – problem situations are messy, and the solutions are intellectual constructs as perceived by actors within the system (Checkland). Second, the role of the analyst is not one of an expert to give definitive knowledge on systems analysis and design but rather that of a therapist (Checkland) or as just one of a design team involving users (participative approach). Third, the role of participants in the existing system is integral to successful system development. Checkland's approach concentrates on enriching the systems participants' perceptions of the current system. This is aimed at stimulation of change and improvement of the problem situation in the fuzzy system within which it occurs. The participative approach emphasizes the need to obtain a harmonious design of interacting social and technical systems by involving users in the process of analysis and design. Both deny that a computer system is the *only* solution: the former by recognizing that not all problems require computer-based solutions; the latter by asserting that designing a technical computer system independently of people's needs will lead to failure.

Approaches to development are not static. The influence of CASE tools on the process of analysis and design is becoming increasingly significant. These are likely to be centred on object-oriented approaches, which concentrate on a perspective of the world as being composed of objects, relationships between objects and operations using those objects. CASE may cover the entire spectrum of systems analysis and design from the strategic planning of information systems to the automatic generation of executable code.

The recent development of rapid applications development (RAD) has emphasized the need for fast core systems development to meet rapidly changing business needs. RAD is gaining popularity, particularly in the development of e-commerce solutions.

Review questions

1. Explain the difference in the meanings of the terms *hard* and *soft* as applied to approaches to systems analysis.

2. State *four* main features of:
   (a) structured process analysis and design
   (b) structured data analysis and design
   (c) object-oriented systems analysis and design.

3. What are the limitations of 'hard' approaches to systems analysis and design?

4. Outline the stages in Checkland's methodology.

5. What is the purpose of drawing rich pictures?

6. What is a CASE tool? What benefits can be gained from using a CASE tool? What are the drawbacks?

7. Object-oriented approaches are said to provide a seamless transition between development stages. Explain why this is more true of object-oriented than structured approaches to systems development.

Exercises

1. What is meant by 'a participative approach to socio-technical design'?

2. Explain and distinguish the different possible levels of involvement of participants in the analysis and design stages of a project.

3. What benefits are claimed for user participation in analysis and design?

4. What roles do variance analysis, job satisfaction analysis and future analysis play in socio-technical analysis and design?

5. The hard approaches to analysis and design are often criticized for assuming that by using a technical solution it is possible to solve, or at least alleviate, problems in an organization. But if a technical solution is what the organization wants, why should this be a criticism?

6. 'User participation is an advantage in analysis and design, but the real benefits for the workforce and ultimately management would occur if users also participated in the decision process involving new technology and information systems.' Do you agree?

7. What are the key features of a RAD approach? Why has RAD been described as being 'well suited' to e-commerce systems developments?

8. This chapter, in common with many texts, uses the term *methodology* frequently. Provide and justify a definition of a methodology.

CASE STUDY 16

Rapid applications development

Post Office IT (POiT) supplies technology solutions to the Post Office and its businesses and as such is one of the largest IT suppliers in the UK. POiT had investigated ways of improving productivity and understood that rapid application development (RAD) could deliver benefits such as:

- reducing time to market for new applications by cutting development times;
- getting more for less by improving productivity; and
- building greater user buy-in by including end users from the word go.

But the challenge facing POiT staff was how to put RAD into practice and realize these benefits.

POiT had an ideal opportunity to use RAD as it needed to demonstrate reduced lead times and costs for one of its main clients, SSL. SSL (Subscription Services Ltd) is a customer management and telemarketing specialist and is particularly well known as the organization that collects the TV licence fee on behalf of the BBC under the brand TV Licensing. POiT had been retained to develop a system to automate a small specialist licensing section, which it had not previously been cost-effective to automate; SSL and POiT jointly chose this as the pilot RAD project. When they had investigated RAD in the past, POiT had chosen the dynamic systems development method (DSDM) – the industry-standard, public domain methodology for RAD. POiT was already an active member of the DSDM Consortium, the body that promotes the method, and decided that DSDM would underpin the approach that it adopted for the pilot project.

When it started out on the pilot, POiT was given a rigorous set of targets. This included doubling productivity against traditional methods and developing the new system to a very tight development budget. In fact, the entire project took seven and a half months – for an application that would have taken thirteen months to develop by normal methods, thus halving the labour costs of the project. As everyone becomes more and more price-conscious, the need to deliver to fixed cost is becoming an ever more important driver, and users are beginning to expect this for IT as well as other services and products they purchase. The POiT pilot was no exception. Once the functional model had been defined, the project was supplied to a fixed price, yet it delivered almost 50% more function than was planned.

To outsource or mentor?

To implement a new way of working and deliver significant quantifiable benefits in one project is a very tall order. If POiT was to be successful, it had to get up to speed fast. It felt that, while it could have hired expertise to deliver the project in double-quick time, when the 'hired guns' left, it would have found itself back at square one. POiT wanted to retain RAD knowledge at the end of the project.

Mentoring is an excellent way of investing in in-house staff so that they retain knowledge and experience gained from the real world in real projects. To this end, POiT looked around for a partner who could not only transfer expertise and knowledge but also support it as it worked through the pilot. Like POiT, IBM is an active member of the DSDM Consortium, and as a founder member has worked with the method since its inception. This, combined with its willingness to work in true partnership with customers, made IBM the natural choice.

Shortening the learning curve

In order to get everyone 'singing from the same hymn sheet', the IBM consultants implemented an intensive programme of training and education. Equally important as education is building team spirit and motivation, which is vital to a successful RAD project. These intensive education sessions, which included users and IT staff, provided the ideal catalyst.

POiT was well aware that the best way to learn is not necessarily in the classroom. Indeed, its experience was that learning 'on the job' was often more useful, so it was delighted with IBM's approach.

IBM followed up the initial education sessions with regular health checks. These sessions reviewed the entire project, including the people, the development environment and the technology. These reviews formed the basis of a positive feedback loop, which meant that lessons learned throughout the life of the pilot were acted on as it progressed. This positive feedback loop enabled vital fine-tuning of the development process, helping to ensure that all members of the team were able get the most from the learning experience that the pilot project provided.

Building assets for the future

It is one thing to retain the knowledge and experience once the consultants have left, but what about the process? POiT was keen to build a repeatable process so that when the next project came along it would not have to 'reinvent the wheel'. With this in mind, IBM set up a DSDM workbench, comprising techniques and guidelines based on its wealth of experience in traditional and RAD projects. This meant that through the pilot, although the first using RAD and DSDM, POiT was already building work practices and an environment that could be expected to be found in companies with far more experience.

The way forward

The project was successful as a pilot and pioneered many new tools and techniques that POiT can use in the future. One of the benefits of combining IBM's mentoring with DSDM is that POiT is now in a position to pick and choose from the DSDM elements available without being tied to the entire structure. It can do this safe in the knowledge that it knows what it is doing.

Both POiT and SSL are keen to use RAD again and to continue developing and refining their processes and standards. In fact, a senior SSL manager was heard to ask 'When are we doing the next project?'

Questions

1. In what ways did the RAD approach followed in the PoiT project differ from the traditional structured analysis and design approaches introduced in earlier chapters?

2. Identify the features of the PoiT project that made it particularly successful.

3. Were there any aspects of the PoiT project that made it particularly suited to an RAD approach? Can RAD deliver better-quality solutions in all situations?

References and recommended reading

Avgerou C. and Cornford T. (1998). *Developing Information Systems*, 2nd edn: *Concepts, Issues and Practice*. Basingstoke: Palgrave (formerly Macmillan)

This provides an interesting introduction to approaches and issues in information systems development. The book adopts a conceptual and critical perspective. It is suitable as a supplementary to a detailed explanatory text.

Avison D. and Fitzgerald G. (2003). *Information Systems Development: Methodologies, Techniques and Tools*, 3rd edn. McGraw-Hill

This well-established book covers a range of techniques and methodologies for systems analysis and design. The book provides a comprehensive coverage of data, process, rapid, blended, and people-oriented methodologies. This edition contains new material on ERP and the development of e-commerce applications. The book is suitable for those covering an information systems course at undergraduate level.

Bennet S., McRobb S. and Farmer R. (2002). *Object Oriented Systems Analysis and Design using UML*. McGraw-Hill

This text for undergraduate courses presents various life cycle models and develops object-oriented approaches using UML. The book contains two extensive case studies with end of chapter summaries, questions and case reviews.

Brown D. (2002). *An Introduction to Object-Oriented Analysis: Objects in Plain English*. Wiley

This book is aimed at students doing information systems and business information systems courses on business degrees or MBAs. It presents object-oriented analysis and object-oriented concepts in a straightforward way using 'plain English' and business-related examples. Each chapter has self-test questions and other exercises, along with explanations of key concepts.

Checkland P.B. (1999). *Systems Thinking, Systems Practice*. Chichester: Wiley

This book develops the thinking behind the Checkland methodology.

Coad P. and Yourdon E. (1991). *Object-oriented Analysis*, 2nd edn. Englewood Cliffs, NJ: Prentice Hall

A straightforward introductory text covering the major tasks associated with object-oriented analysis.

Cobham D., Harston J., Kretsis M. and Kyte J. (1999). *The Uptake and Usage of Object Technology*, Proceedings of BIT Conference

Fowler M. (2004). *UML Distilled: A Brief Guide to the Standard Modelling Language*. Addison-Wesley, Pearson

This is a short practical book enabling readers to become up to speed with UML 2.0 and learn the essentials of the UML language. The book gives a clear coverage of UML diagramming tools and a useful introduction to OO techniques in software development.

Land F. and Hirscheim R. (1983). Participative systems design: rationale, tools and techniques. *Journal of Applied Systems Analysis*, 10

Martin J. (1989). *Information Engineering*. Englewood Cliffs, NJ: Prentice Hall

A clear and comprehensive statement of the main ideas behind the influential methodology of information engineering.

Martin J. (1991). *Rapid Applications Development*. Englewood Cliffs, NJ: Prentice Hall

This is an important text as the first identifiable approach with the underlying theme of rapid applications development. Other texts on RAD have diverged from Martin's original approach, and the term 'RAD' is now more loosely defined.

Meyer B. (1995). *Object Success*. Oxford: Prentice Hall

A very clear exposition of Meyer's view of object-oriented approaches, illustrated with many real case studies and some amusing anecdotes. The book contains a useful section on managing projects in an object-oriented environment.

Newman W. M. and Lamming M. J. (2004). *Interactive Systems Design*. Harlow: Addison-Wesley

This text provides a coherent framework for user-oriented design covering all stages of analysis, design, implementation and evaluation. It illustrates points with examples from air traffic control, police detective work and medical practice. Prototyping and evaluation play a major role in this approach, and this is fully explained.

Chapter 17

Expert systems and knowledge bases

Learning outcomes

On completion of this chapter, you should be able to:

- Define artificial intelligence and expert systems
- Describe the typical architecture of an expert system
- Contrast alternative ways of representing knowledge
- Explain how inferences are drawn in an expert system
- Give examples of the application of artificial intelligence in the World Wide Web.

Introduction

In Chapters 7 and 8, various ways to store and retrieve information were considered. Important though data and information handling are to an organization's information system, they are only one component. Modern developments allow the storage and use of expert knowledge as well. These are known as expert systems. It is the purpose of this chapter to explain the nature of expert systems and knowledge bases together with features of these systems that distinguish them from traditional information processing using file-based and database structures. It is important to treat (in some depth) the internal working of expert systems and the way that knowledge is stored in them. Unlike traditional information systems, where the business person or accountant will need a broad understanding of aspects of analysis and design but is little concerned with the technical implementation of the system, it is increasingly common for the expert to take a major role in the detailed aspects of the development of an expert system.

The chapter begins with an introduction to the role of an expert and the nature of expertise. This allows a definition of the basic ideas lying behind expert systems. More detailed coverage involves explanation of the important distinction between procedural and declarative knowledge. This is used as an introduction to the idea of the representation of knowledge in the form of rules and leads to an explanation of the basic components or architecture of an expert system. Various forms of knowledge representation are described, and their particular applications and limitations are highlighted. Reasoning with certain knowledge is dealt with by providing classical rules and methods of inference. The representation of uncertainty and its use in reasoning are also covered. The chapter as a whole acts as an introduction to the ideas behind expert systems.

17.1 Expert systems architecture

For many years, there has been a prediction of rapid growth in artificial intelligence (AI) in business as projects currently under development come to fruition. One of the greatest limitations of current information-processing systems is that their scope has been restricted to the fast and accurate processing of numeric and text data. Broadly speaking, this processing has involved numeric and algebraic functions on numbers, or various forms of insertion, deletion and retrieval of text. The processing is controlled by a program working on the numeric and text data. This mimics many tasks that were performed manually in the past. The accountant added debits and credits to arrive at balances, the scientist performed statistical tests on survey data, or the office clerk inserted or deleted data in files in cabinets. Other sorts of task, though, cannot be regarded as falling into these categories.

The doctor having a knowledge of diseases comes to a diagnosis of an illness by reasoning from information given by the patient's symptoms and then prescribes medication on the basis of known characteristics of available drugs together with the patient's history. The solicitor advises the client on the likely outcome of litigation based on the facts of the particular case, an expert understanding of the law and a knowledge of the way the courts work and interpret this law in practice. The accountant looks at various characteristics of a company's performance and makes a judgement as to the likely state of health of that company. All of these tasks involve some of the features for which computers traditionally have been noted – performing text and numeric processing quickly and efficiently – but they also involve one more ability: reasoning. Reasoning is the movement from details of a particular case and knowledge of the general subject area surrounding that case to the derivation of conclusions. Expert systems incorporate this reasoning by applying general rules in a knowledge base to aspects of a particular case under consideration.

What is an expert system? The short answer is that it is a computerized system that performs the role of an expert or carries out a task that requires expertise. In order to understand what an expert system is, then, it is worth paying some attention to the role of an expert and the nature of expertise. It is then important to ascertain what types of expert and expertise there are in business and what benefits will accrue to an organization when it develops an expert system.

An expert typically has a body of knowledge and handles that knowledge in its application to problems in a way not possessed by the layman. An expert:

- has a body of knowledge in a particular subject area;
- can apply this knowledge to problem situations, often in conditions of uncertain or incomplete information;
- can deliver effective and efficient solutions, such as the diagnosis of a problem, an assessment of a situation, advice, planning, or recommended courses of action and decisions;
- is able to provide explanations and justifications for these solutions;
- can provide information on the subject area of expertise;
- is able to identify his or her limitations in this subject area and know where to obtain further advice;
- can interact with a person requiring the expert's assistance;
- can improve their knowledge and expertise by learning.

For example, corporate tax specialists:

■ will have a body of tax knowledge on tax legislation and principles, together with the way that government taxation boards apply them;

■ will be able to apply this expertise in particular situations given corporate facts to, for instance, recommend ways of classifying corporate assets to minimize tax liability;

■ will be able to justify and explain their recommendations to government tax authorities and internal management in the organization for which the expert is acting as tax specialist;

■ will be able to answer specific tax enquiries;

■ will be aware of the limitations of their own tax expertise;

■ will be able to interact with those requiring tax advice at a level that takes account of the enquirer's level of knowledge and interests;

■ will be able to update their expertise in the light of new tax legislation or precedent.

Organizations have experts in many areas. A business organization will probably have general expertise in such areas as tax, accounts, marketing, production and personnel as well as specific expertise in the narrow area of its activity – for example, the design, production and retailing of motor cars. As well as 'high-level' expertise, there will be 'low-level' expertise. An example of this might be the knowledge possessed by a clerk of the way that an organization stores its records with cross-referencing and the handling of exceptions.

In order to justify the cost of an expert system, an organization will want to realize benefits. Among many possible benefits of an expert system are:

■ A cost-effective consultant system to aid or replace existing expertise within the organization. Being computer-based, expert systems perform consistently unlike human experts, who may have 'off days'.

■ An archive of specific skills that the organization possesses and on which it is dependent for its successful functioning – experts may leave or retire.

■ A training aid for 'future experts'.

■ A standard for expertise against which human experts can be compared.

The characteristics of an area of expertise that make it suitable for the design of an expert system are:

■ The area of expertise should involve the analysis of a complex set of conditions and the application of these to a specifiable area of knowledge that is amenable to computerized representation (see Sections 17.1.1 and 17.1.2).

■ The area of expertise is narrow and clear-cut and can be made explicit. It does not, for instance, involve the expert in using general knowledge or 'common sense'.

■ The expert's task typically takes between a few minutes and, say, three hours. Less than this and the use of computer input will slow the task; more than this and the task is likely to be too complex.

What is an expert system? We can return to this original question. Although a detailed answer is provided by the rest of the chapter, a brief answer follows from the previous considerations of the role of an expert and the nature of expertise. An expert system typically:

- incorporates expert knowledge in a particular subject area, usually by storing and representing this as rules or other representation forms (**knowledge base**);

- separates the general knowledge from the details of a particular case under consideration to which the knowledge base is applied (**particular context**);

- clearly distinguishes the knowledge from the mechanism of reasoning (**inference engine**);

- possesses an interactive user interface for providing explanations, justifications and questions to the user; and

- provides, as its output, advice or decisions in the area of expertise.

In addition, an expert system may be able to handle uncertain or incomplete information. It may also be able to learn – that is, modify its knowledge base or inference engine.

Expert systems have been developed and are currently being developed for a wide variety of areas of expertise in business. A few examples are:

- a system that provides advice to employers on the dismissal of employees;

- a system that provides advice on registration under the Data Protection Act in the UK;

- a system that develops investment plans for personal clients tailored to their needs;

- a system that aids auditors in providing an effective and complete audit of a company's accounts;

- a system that provides an assessment of a company's health from various perspectives such as the auditor, the trade creditor and the financier of loans.

Before embarking on the remainder of the chapter, a word of warning is appropriate. Vendors of software and systems sometimes describe their products as 'expert systems' for marketing reasons. The reader should be wary. As one software vendor of a major mainframe package explained:

> Our software has gone through various upgradings over the last ten years, but it is still essentially the same product. Ten years ago we called it a 'management information system', five years ago a 'decision support system' and now we sell it as an 'expert system'.

Expert systems are sometimes known as 'knowledge-based systems' or 'intelligent knowledge-based systems'. The architecture of a typical expert system is shown in Figure 17.1. Each of the parts is considered separately in the following sections in order to give an overview of the way an expert system works. Knowledge representation in the domain-specific knowledge base and the ways that inferences are drawn are also considered in more detail in Sections 17.2 and 17.3.

17.1.1 Domain-specific knowledge base

This is one of the two logically distinct components of the knowledge base. Domain-specific knowledge is the representation of the static expertise of the experts. As most experts are knowledgeable in limited areas, this is reflected in the term 'domain-specific'. An example of expertise might be how to interpret a complex tax law in such a way that it is most advantageous to a client. This is to be distinguished from general or common-sense knowledge, which we all have. The latter is often mundane. The fact that all objects fall to the ground when released, except if they are lighter than air or are fairly light and there is a strong wind blowing, is an instance of common-sense knowledge. Another example is that one might bring a bottle of wine, flowers or a box

Figure 17.1 Architecture of a typical expert system

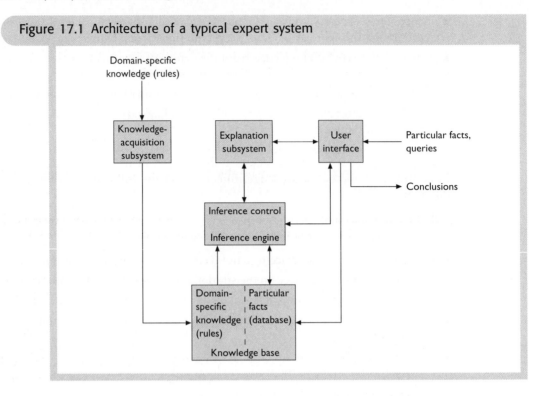

of chocolates to a friend's dinner party but not a plate of cold, uncooked liver. This latter sort of common-sense knowledge, although widespread among people, is most difficult to represent and use in reasoning in expert systems, because common-sense knowledge often involves a mixture of pictorial and verbal, general and specific, and uncertain and vague knowledge from many areas. It is linked to an understanding of the meanings of natural-language terms that surpasses that of any computer of today. Common-sense knowledge may be inextricably interwoven with moral beliefs, complex social attitudes and individual interests. All of this makes it difficult to represent such knowledge in a way that is accessible to automated reasoning. Common sense is widespread but not simple.

Declarative and procedural knowledge

Fundamental to any expert system is the assumption that much knowledge is declarative rather than procedural. To see the difference, it is illustrative to consider an example. The following is from a recipe for making moussaka:

> First slice the aubergines, pack into a colander and then sprinkle with salt. Place a plate on top and a large weight on the plate and leave for half an hour. Meanwhile, fry the garlic and onions in olive oil for about 5 minutes before adding the minced meat. In a basin, mix together the tomato puree, parsley and wine, season it with salt and pepper and when the meat has browned pour the mixture over it.

The knowledge contained in the above is largely procedural. With procedural knowledge, it is common to see statements such as '**DO** ⟨this⟩ . . . **THEN DO** ⟨that⟩ . . .' or 'meanwhile **DO** ⟨this⟩ . . . **UNTIL** ⟨that⟩ occurs'. The knowledge consists of actions or activities linked by temporal connections. Procedural knowledge can be easily incorporated into conventional programs, which execute code (activities) in the order in which they appear in the program. Cooking knowledge may still be beyond the computer of today, but numeric computation is procedural. In order to find the average of a set of numbers, the following recipe can be followed:

> Set a running total and count to zero. Take the first number and add it to the total and add one to the count. **DO** this with each successive number **UNTIL** there are no more numbers. **THEN** divide the running total by the count. The result is the average.

A computer program could provide a coded version of this requested set of actions. In contrast, declarative knowledge, illustrated in the following example, is rather different:

> **IF** the student has successfully completed level 1 of the examination **OR** has been exempted from level 1 by virtue of satisfying *any* of the conditions laid out in paragraphs 3 (a) to 3 (f) below, **THEN** the student is entitled to register for level 2 of the examination. A student registered for level 2 is exempt from examination papers 2.3 **AND** 2.4 **IF** he/she has obtained exemption from level 1 by virtue of satisfying the conditions 3(a) **OR** 3(b) below, **OR** satisfying 3(d) **AND** being in possession of an honours degree awarded by a British university **OR** accredited by the Council for National Academic Awards.

Here, the knowledge consists of propositions linked together by logical relationships. It is common to find expressions of the form 'IF ⟨such-and-such⟩ **THEN** ⟨so-and-so⟩ is the case' or '⟨so-and-so⟩ **UNLESS** ⟨this⟩ **OR** ⟨that⟩'. There is no sense in which one activity is performed before another. Rather, there is a set of conditions or area of knowledge that is declared.

Rules

It is often possible to represent this declarative knowledge in the form of rules. Figure 17.2 is an example of a set of rules representing declarative knowledge in the area of the assessment of a company's financial health. It is this set of rules that forms the domain-specific knowledge in the knowledge base.

Figure 17.2 Rules from a knowledge base dealing with a company's financial health

Rule 1   **IF** the quick ratio is higher than the industry average quick ratio
         AND the inventory turnover ratio is higher than the industry average turnover ratio
         THEN short-term liquidity is good

Rule 2   **IF** the debt to equity ratio is low
         AND the dividend cover is high
         THEN the medium-term insolvency risk is low

Rule 3   **IF** the short-term liquidity is good
         AND the medium-term insolvency risk is low
         AND EITHER the market is likely to expand
         OR the market is stable
         AND the company has a majority market share
         THEN the company is financially stable

The rules given in Figure 17.2 are often known as **if–then rules**. They have the form:

IF ⟨antecedent condition⟩ **THEN** ⟨consequent⟩

where the antecedent condition is any sentence or set of sentences connected by 'and', 'or' or 'not'. These are known as **Boolean operators** and give the structure of the rule. The simplest expert systems will treat expressions such as 'short-term liquidity is good' as simple and unanalysable atomic units. Their sole function is to be assigned a truth value (true or false). More complex systems might be capable of treating this expression as saying of the attribute 'short-term liquidity' that it has the value 'good' – it might have had the value 'poor' or 'average'. The presence of attribute–value pairs allows more complex reasoning to be undertaken by the system. This will be seen later in Section 17.2.1.

However, not all knowledge can be represented in the form of if–then rules. It has already been seen that some knowledge is procedural; also, much declarative knowledge cannot easily be cast into the if–then mould either. Any knowledge that relies on pictorial representation, such as the relative positioning of streets on a street map, cannot appropriately be represented as propositional knowledge and therefore not as if–then rules. Some declarative knowledge is best understood as knowing that certain entities have attributes; they inherit these attributes by virtue of being instances of other entities. It is unnatural to attempt to encode this in the form of rules. For example, salmon have fins by virtue of being fish, as do trout. Rather than represent this as if–then rules about salmon and trout separately, this knowledge can be represented as being facts about fish, which salmon and trout then inherit. Other suitable forms of representation such as semantic networks and frames are treated in Sections 17.2.3 and 17.2.4. However, for the explanation of the architecture of the expert system, a rule-based representation will be assumed.

The knowledge base may consist of several hundreds or even thousands of rules for complex areas of expertise. As a rough guide, it is convenient to class expert systems as small if they have between fifty and 200 rules and as large if over 1000 rules. With many fewer than fifty rules, the area covered is becoming so small that it will hardly qualify as expertise.

17.1.2 Knowledge-acquisition subsystem

The domain-specific knowledge in the form of rules, or some other chosen representational form, needs to be entered into the system. This is achieved by the knowledge-acquisition subsystem. In the simplest case, rules are entered at the keyboard. The rules are required to follow a specified syntax called the **knowledge-representation language** (KRL). As well as rules, other information can be added. For instance, in Figure 17.2, rule 1 requires that the quick ratio, a measure used in accounting, is higher than the industry average as a necessary condition that liquidity is good. When this rule is considered by the expert system in a later consultation, the system will attempt to determine the truth of that antecedent condition. It may be the case that whether the quick ratio is higher than the industry average or not is determined by further rules. Alternatively, the expert system may need a basic piece of evidence in order to establish the company's financial health, and the only way of finding this is to ask the user of the expert system a question. The exact text of the question can be specified when the rule is first input into the knowledge base. This may lead to the following representation in the KRL:

The quick ratio is higher than the industry average: **ASK TEXT** 'Is the quick ratio for the company higher than the average quick ratio for the industry as a whole?'

The user might require further explanation in order to be able to answer the question. The KRL can provide the facility for this. It is also clear that the condition is Boolean – TRUE or FALSE (or possibly UNKNOWN) should be assigned to the value of the proposition. All this can be incorporated, leading to the following full specification in the KRL:

The quick ratio is higher than the industry average: **ASK TEXT** 'Is the quick ratio for the company higher than the average quick ratio for the industry as a whole', **YES/NO**, **EXPLANATION** 'The quick ratio may be determined from the company's financial accounts and is given by the following formula:

quick ratio = ⟨current assets less inventory⟩/current assets'.

These rules and other details can be entered via a standard word-processing package. The text file is created and then compiled, the syntax is checked and the rules and other information are converted into a form suitable for storage in the knowledge base. Alternatively, the rules may be entered interactively during a rule-building consultation with the expert system. Each rule is checked for correct syntax as it is entered, and checks are made immediately to ensure that the rule is consistent with the existing rules. The process is analogous to interpreting a program in a high-level language rather than compiling, although this analogy should not be taken too far.

The methods of entry mentioned in the previous paragraph are typical of knowledge-acquisition subsystems associated with expert systems built from application packages called **expert system shells**. These are expert systems that initially contain no knowledge in their knowledge base. The knowledge is entered by the builders of the expert system.

The kind of knowledge acquisition just described is similar to rote learning. Just as scientific progress does not occur through rote learning of new rules (where do they come from?), so expert systems imbued with greater power may obtain knowledge in additional ways. Perhaps the most common is by deriving rules from a large number of cases. Given, for example, many cases of plant disease symptoms and other environmental conditions, together with the diagnosed disease in each case, a pattern connecting certain symptoms and environmental conditions with a particular disease can be established. The knowledge-acquisition subsystem scans details of these cases, often held on a conventional database, and derives this pattern in the form of rules, which are automatically generated and entered into the knowledge base. The process is called **rule induction**. Although automated machine learning is gradually being developed, there are still technical and theoretical difficulties that restrict its use to very specialized applications.

By far the most common method of acquisition is direct rule entry via the keyboard. To do this requires overcoming one of the major problems involved in building an expert system. That problem is to obtain the knowledge and represent it in the required form (for example, as a set of rules) when the knowledge originally resides in the mind of an expert and, as any psychologist will confirm, the way knowledge is represented to the human in the mind is still a mystery. The process of extracting the knowledge in the required form is called **knowledge elicitation**.

Knowledge elicitation

Although some expert systems are derived from source documentation, such as legislation, the vast majority of expert systems rely, partly at least, on expertise that is resident in the mind of an expert(s). It shows itself in behavioural terms only when required to perform a task. In the process of knowledge elicitation, this is extracted and displayed in a form suitable for incorporating into a computerized system.

The systems analyst relies heavily on interviewing personnel in an existing system in order to identify key tasks, information flows, data stores, and so on. This interview model has formed the basis of initial attempts at knowledge elicitation. However, even if the expert is willing to spend the considerable time and effort with the knowledge engineer in order to pass on the expertise, there are major obstacles to a smooth, orderly and exhaustive elicitation stage.

1. Many areas of expertise are highly technical, and unless the knowledge engineer is familiar with the area, he or she will have great difficulty in understanding and representing it correctly.

2. A knowledge engineer may attempt to become familiar with the domain by textbook research. Unfortunately, it is often the non-textbook heuristic approaches taken by experts, based on experience, that make their expertise so valuable. A little learning on the part of the knowledge engineer may be a dangerous thing. It can force the expert into the position of providing 'textbook' answers to questions asked from a textbook background.

3. An expert's time is precious, and knowledge elicitation is a lengthy task.

4. The expert may be a competent practitioner but may not be used to verbal discussion of the domain area in the manner required for knowledge engineering.

5. The chosen tool may affect the way that the engineer attempts to elicit the expertise. The expert, though, may not represent the knowledge internally in the form in which the engineer is attempting to extract it. This provides difficulty, and the expert may need to rethink the domain. However, this can be an instructive educational process for the expert. It forces valuable systematization and the adoption of new perspectives on the domain.

6. There is a temptation on the part of the expert to wish to discuss the more unusual and difficult areas that he or she deals with, whereas the primary purpose of the knowledge engineer is to concentrate on the central and often more mundane cases.

These problems have prompted the development of a number of knowledge elicitation techniques that go beyond the traditional interview.

Forward scenario simulation

This is rather like a structured interview in which the expert is given a series of hypothetical case study problems and asked how to solve them. The expert is required to explain what facts are being considered and how they are being treated as the problem is solved. The major advantage of this approach is that by a judicious selection of problems by, for example, another expert or even the expert subject of the elicitation process, the engineer can ensure a comprehensive coverage of the central types of problem in the domain area.

It is usual to conduct the interview on each problem in two stages:

1. Ask the interviewee to outline the task to be accomplished in solving the problem, including a description of the possible outcomes, variables and rules used.

2. Establish how general and how specific each of the discovered rules are.

Typical questions from the knowledge engineer might be:

- When do you do (such-and-such)?
- Why do you do (such-and-such)?
- Under what circumstances would this rule apply?
- Under what circumstances would this rule not apply?
- How did you establish (such-and-such)?

Protocol analysis

In protocol analysis, the knowledge engineer observes and probably audio/video tapes the expert in the course of performing tasks. These records are searched for key variables, rules and the order of approach taken during problem solving. This has one advantage over the structured interview in that the expert is not required to give explanations and justifications for every decision. The pressure that is present during the interview may generate spurious responses – experts do not like to say 'I just don't know why I did that' or 'It was no more than a guess'. However, unless all major types of case come up, protocol analysis techniques will not lead to a complete knowledge elicitation.

Goal decomposition

This is a set of techniques most suitable where the knowledge domain is structured in a hierarchy. The techniques derive from use in psychology. 'Laddered Grid' and '20 Questions' are two examples of goal decomposition. In the latter, the expert is confronted with an interviewer who has a set of hypothetical problems. The expert is provided with no initial information, and by a series of questions attempts to establish as much as possible about the problem. The types of question asked and the order in which they are put gives the knowledge engineer valuable insights into the way that the expert perceives the structure of the knowledge domain. This technique can only be used by an engineer with some familiarity with the domain.

Multi-dimensional techniques

These techniques provide some kind of map as to how the elements in a knowledge domain are put together where there are complex interactions. Many of these techniques also derive from the discipline of psychology, where they are used to build a model of the way that a person perceives the world. The techniques often involve determining ways in which two things are alike and different from a third. If this is repeated many times with different objects, a set of differentiating concepts that are important to the expert is established. Techniques such as repertory grid, factor analysis and multidimensional scaling fall into this category. Details of these may be obtained from the references at the end of this chapter.

Automated elicitation and acquisition

In the future, expert systems may be able to abstract general principles and rules applicable to knowledge domains directly from sets of given examples. However, the current state of the art is many years behind such developments, although primitive **induction** techniques are already used to infer straightforward rules governing a domain. Some expert system shells may have this induction facility, the aim being to by-pass much of the work of the knowledge engineer and produce working expert systems rapidly.

Figure 17.3 An automatic induction to provide a set of rules governing job selection

| CASE | ATTRIBUTES | | | DECISION |
	DEGREE CLASS	QUALIFICATION	EXPERIENCE	
I	I	YES	I YEAR	OFFER
2	3	YES	2 YEAR	REJECT
3	2	YES	2 YEAR	OFFER
4	I	YES	*	OFFER
5	2	YES	2 YEAR	OFFER
6	*	NO	*	REJECT
7	2	YES	3 YEAR	OFFER
8	3	NO	3 YEAR	REJECT
9	3	*	*	REJECT

(Note * = Unknown)

Rules
IF DEGREE CLASS = I **AND** QUALIFIED
   THEN OFFER

IF DEGREE CLASS = 2 **AND** QUALIFIED
    AND (EXPERIENCE = '3 YEAR' **OR** EXPERIENCE = '2 YEAR')
   THEN OFFER

IF DEGREE CLASS = 3 **THEN** REJECT

IF NOT QUALIFIED **THEN** REJECT

These shells typically work by requiring the expert (or some person) to select key attributes that are applicable to a task and then input a large number of instances of the task while giving the associated values of attributes and outcomes. The automated induction module of the shell is called up, and a set of rules is inferred. There are standard algorithms for this, and an example is given in Figure 17.3. Here, it is intended to determine the rules governing the selection of candidates for a post. Nine previous cases and their decisions lead to the four rules shown in the figure being inferred.

These systems will only be useful when theoretical issues surrounding induction have found algorithmic solutions. In particular:

■ How can an automated system decide upon the relevant attributes that are to be used in the induction, having been given a number of cases?

■ How can the system derive probabilistic rules governing attributes that take real-number values?

■ How can the system identify and ignore freak cases without upsetting the existing system of rules?

17.1.3 Case-specific knowledge base (database)

The other component of the knowledge base contains details relevant to a particular consultation of the expert system. An expert system used to diagnose a company's financial health will have permanent rules governing the factors that affect company financial health in general (domain-specific knowledge) but during use will have factual details on the company under consideration (XYZ Company). Details on XYZ will be stored in the case-specific knowledge base. The facts are either input directly by the user, for instance in response to a question, or taken directly from an external conventional database holding company data, or derived from the content of the factual knowledge base by reasoning with the rules.

The term 'database' is sometimes used to refer to the case-specific knowledge base. It must be realized that this is not the same use of 'database' as in Chapter 8 but refers merely to the store of case-specific data.

17.1.4 Inference engine

Given details of a particular case and general domain-specific rules, what conclusions can be drawn? The process of drawing conclusions is not a static one. It involves the application of sound methods of reasoning to evidence as it currently stands in the knowledge base.

The inference engine (or interpreter) applies the domain-specific knowledge base to the particular facts of the case under consideration to derive these new conclusions. Principles govern the work of the inference engine. Some of these concern the allowable types of inference that can be performed. The strictest inference principles are logically sound. That is, if we are given initial data as true, then the inferences drawn with the use of the principle must also be true. Some principles of inference, particularly those concerned with probabilistic or uncertain reasoning, do not meet this requirement.

In a rule-based system, the most common example of a sound inference principle is logical derivation by *modus ponendo ponens* (usually shortened to *modus ponens*). This is an obvious inference principle known to the ancients. A simple example of *modus ponens* is:

> Given rule *If* it is raining *then* the ground is wet
> Given fact It is raining
> Derived new fact The ground is wet

A similar though perhaps slightly less obvious inference is *modus tollendo tollens* (usually shortened to *modus tollens*). Using a weather example again:

> Given rule *If* it is raining *then* the ground is wet
> Given fact The ground is not wet
> Derived new fact It is not raining

In most formal systems, these can be shown to be logically equivalent forms of reasoning (specifically those systems in which we are entitled to assume the negation of an assumption if that assumption leads to a contradiction – another intuitively sound move known as *reductio ad absurdum*). However, some expert systems make use of *modus ponens* without *modus tollens*. This implies that they are unable to derive certain obvious and particularly useful conclusions from a given set of rules and particular facts.

Common inference principles for Boolean algebra given in Figure 17.4 (a) and (b) have already been considered, while (c) and (d) are trivial but important for those systems that allow antecedents of rules to contain conjunctions and disjunctions (as in rule 1 concerning short-term liquidity in Figure 17.2). They generate complex propositions from simple ones. (e) is known as the resolution principle and can be used to reduce a set of complex propositions to simpler ones, and (f) can be used to

Figure 17.4 Some inference principles for Boolean algebra: (a) *modus ponendo ponens*; (b) *modus tollendo tollens*; (c) conjunction introduction; (d) disjunction introduction; (e) resolution; (f) disjunction elimination

		Principle	**Example**
(a)	Rule	if A **then** B	**If** the creature has feathers **then** it is a bird
	Fact	A	the creature has feathers
	New fact	B	it is a bird
(b)	Rule	**If** A **then** B	**If** the creature has feathers **then** it is a bird
	Fact	not B	it is **not** a bird
	New fact	not A	the creature does **not** have feathers
(c)	Fact	A	it is a fish
	Fact	B	it weighs 10 kilograms
	New fact	A **and** B	it is a fish **and** weighs 10 kilograms
(d)	Fact	A	it is raining
	New fact	A **or** B	it is raining **or** snowing
(e)	Fact	(**not** A) **or** B	either it does **not** have gills **or** it is a fish
	Fact	(**not** B) **or** C	either it it is **not** a fish **or** it lives in water
	New fact	**not** A **or** C	either it does **not** have gills **or** it lives in water
(f)	Fact	(**not** A) **or** B	either it does **not** have gills **or** it is a fish
	Fact	A	it does have gills
	New fact	B	it is a fish

eliminate a disjunction. All expert systems will use some or all of these or their equivalents in the inference process.

These abstract inference principles need to be applied selectively in order to achieve a useful derivation of new facts during the consultation. At any given time, there may be many ways of proceeding from the set of rules and particular facts in the knowledge base. There must not only be principles for deriving new facts but also a way of choosing which principle is to be used at any moment. And given that, for example, *modus ponens* is chosen then which rules and existing facts should be used if there is more than one possible use? In short, there must not only be sound inference principles but also an inference control strategy for selecting which principles are to be applied to which rules in the knowledge base at a given time. ('Inference principles' has been used in the text to mean any method of inference. It is common elsewhere also to refer to these as 'inference rules'. This has been avoided as it may lead to confusion with rules held in the knowledge base that are domain-specific and provide empirical knowledge or definitions, such as in Figure 17.2. The matter is further complicated by the inclusion of inference rules in the rule base of some expert systems.)

An example of inference control is shown in Figure 17.5. This is a model of a very simple expert system illustrating the way that the inference engine dynamically interacts with the rule base and the fact base (database) to derive new facts. The inference engine is a set of activities that is incorporated into a computer program. The inference engine is procedural – the rules and facts are declarative.

The expert system attempts the identification of creatures based on certain characteristics such as whether they live in the sea, have stripes, eat meat, and so on. (No

Figure 17.5 Model of a simple expert system for classifying creatures

RULE BASE

(1) **IF** eats meat **THEN** carnivore
(2) **IF** suckles young **AND** warm-blooded **THEN** mammal
(3) **IF NOT** warm-blooded **AND** lives in sea **THEN** fish
(4) **IF NOT** carnivore **AND** striped **AND** mammal **THEN** zebra
(5) **IF** carnivore **AND** striped **AND** mammal **THEN** tiger
(6) **IF** mammal **AND** lives in sea **AND NOT** pinniped **THEN** whale
(7) **IF** fish **AND** striped **THEN** tiger fish
(8) **IF** pinniped **AND** mammal **THEN** seal
(9) **IF** hind flippers **THEN** pinniped

INFERENCE ENGINE

(1) Find all rules whose antecedents are satisfied by the database
(2) Ignore rules found in (1) whose consequents are in the database
(3) Execute lowest numbered rule remaining, **if** no rule **then** quit
(4) **Go to** (1)

DATABASE

Initial: suckles young, warm-blooded, lives in sea, hind flippers

	Pass 1	**Pass 2**	**Pass 3**	**Pass 4**
Rules relevant	2, 9	2, 9	2, 8, 9	2, 8, 9
Rule fired	2	9	8	
Database at end of pass	suckles young	suckles young	suckles young	suckles young
	warm-blooded	warm-blooded	warm-blooded	warm-blooded
	lives in sea	lives in sea	lives in sea	lives in sea
	hind flippers	hind flippers	hind flippers	hind flippers
	mammal	mammal	mammal	mammal
		pinniped	pinniped	pinniped
			seal	seal
				QUIT

claim is made for the sophistication of the system!) The inference engine works by executing instructions (1) to (4). As (4) is a **GOTO** instruction, the engine just loops until the exit condition is met in line (3).

Initial data is supplied on the beast to be identified. This is held in the database. In the example, the facts given are that the subject:

- is warm-blooded
- suckles young
- lives in the sea
- has flippers.

During **pass 1**, line (1) is executed and matches the data in the database with each rule in turn to establish whether the antecedent is satisfied. This results in rule 2 and rule 9 being selected. A check is made to ignore the rules that add nothing to the database, line (2). This leaves both rules still operative, so some method of resolving which rule to operate (or **fire**, as it is sometimes called) must be used. In the example, the simple expedient of executing the lowest-numbered rule is chosen – line (3). This is rule 2,

Figure 17.6 An intermediate representation of the knowledge base for the classification of creatures

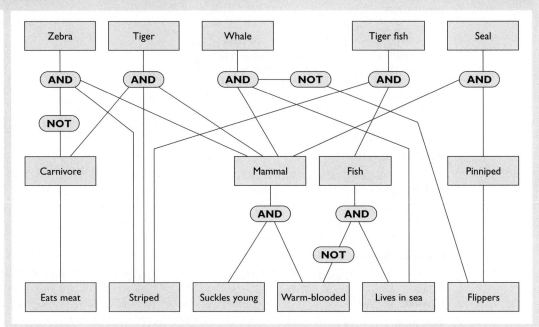

which allows the inference engine to derive the conclusion of the rule, 'mammal', and add it to the database. Line (4) is executed, returning control to line (1).

In **pass 2**, both rule 2 and rule 9 have their antecedents satisfied, but as 'mammal' is already in the database rule 9 is fired (line (3)) and 'pinniped' is added to the database.

In **pass 3**, rules 2, 8 and 9 have their antecedents satisfied (line (1)). Only rule 8 adds new facts to the database (line (2)). So rule 8 is fired (line (3)), and control is returned to line (1) (line (4)).

In **pass 4**, rules 2, 8 and 9 have their antecedents satisfied, but as their consequents are in the database no operative rules remain, and line (3) ensures that the process ends.

The rule base can be given an alternative representation, as in Figure 17.6. This representation highlights the logical connectives **AND**, **NOT** and **OR**. It also serves to establish a hierarchy of rules based on dependence. For instance, rule 8 can be seen to be dependent on rules 2 and 9. This kind of representation may be used when developing the knowledge base. Some people prefer it as they find it easier to work with a picture than the linguistic statement of rules.

A number of features are worth noting about the model in Figure 17.5:

1. The order of rules in the rule base is irrelevant to the final outcome. Reordering the rules might lead to facts being derived in a different sequence during the inferring, but on completion the same set remains in the database. This is characteristic of some, although not all, expert systems and corresponds to the fact that rules do not appear to be ordered in the human brain (except possibly by dependence).

2. The inference engine contains no domain-specific knowledge but only procedural rules for generating inferences. The rule base contains only domain-specific know-

ledge. Put another way, the inference engine could be used on a set of rules diagnosing a company's financial health – the strategy is the same. This feature explains why it is possible to have expert system shells.

3. Rules can be added to the rule base as more knowledge is incorporated. For instance, the following can be added:

Rule 10 **IF** warm-blooded **AND** feathers **THEN** bird

This does not require any other change in the rule base or the inference engine. In the latter case, the inference strategy works for nine or 900 rules. The knowledge base can grow. This would not be so easy if rules in the knowledge base were not purely declarative.

4. The expert system in Figure 17.5 is very primitive. This is not just because the rules are naive and cover only a fraction of the taxonomy of the animal kingdom. Rather, the inference control strategy (using *modus ponens*) is simple: given the antecedents of conditionals then derive the consequents. This strategy when applied repetitively is called **forward chaining**. Looked at from the point of view of Figure 17.6, it can be seen that given baseline facts, such as 'eats meat' and 'suckles young', the strategy amounts to moving forwards (upwards) through the chart until no more progress can be made. This may be unwieldy if there are a large number of rules and facts to be handled, and it is often better to adopt a different inference control strategy.

An alternative is to take a conclusion as a working hypothesis. In the case of Figure 17.6, this might be to take as the initial assumption that the creature is a tiger. The inference strategy is to look for rules that 'prove' that it is a tiger. If one of the rules is found (rule 5), the next step is to attempt to prove the antecedent – in this case that the creature is a carnivore, is striped and is a mammal. The inference control strategy will attempt to prove each of these in turn. To prove that it is a carnivore, it is sufficient to show that it eats meat; this does not depend on a further rule as a basic element. If the fact is not in the database, then the creature is not a carnivore and not a tiger. The inference strategy then selects another goal – for example, it is a whale – and repeats the entire backtracking process.

However, if 'eats meat' is in the database, then it can be proved that the creature is a carnivore. This is the first step to proving that it is a tiger. The inference control strategy then attempts to show that the creature is striped and then that it is a mammal. If either of these fails, the strategy is to move on to another goal as before. This involves backtracking from conclusions to attempt to establish the facts that would prove them, so the inference strategy is known as **backward chaining**.

5. There is no facility for adding data from the user once the system has started its processing. The typical expert will, in the course of a consultation, ask for further information to back up a line of reasoning that he or she is pursuing. Here, the system just proves all it can from the initial data using forward chaining. It might be argued that there is nothing wrong with this provided that all the relevant facts are given at the beginning. This is inappropriate, because the relevant facts may only be established as relevant in the course of a consultation. For example, in a medical expert system it is not of much relevance to know if a patient is a rock musician, accountant or shop assistant in diagnosing the cause of spots, a high temperature and a sore throat. However, matters change if the symptoms are deafness. To say that all the facts should be given initially if they are relevant to the proof of some conclusion (relevant to the diagnosis of some disease) is just not practical – there

are often too many, and only the expert knows which facts are relevant. In any case, the aim of an expert system is to simulate the behaviour and knowledge of experts, and they proceed by selective questioning having been given an initial set of facts. The vast majority of expert systems follow this approach. It is generally associated with inference strategies other than forward chaining.

17.1.5 Explanation subsystem

The explanation subsystem typically provides the following features.

HOW questions

An important feature of experts is that they are able to justify their conclusions. Indeed, it is this ability that leads us to have confidence in their advice. If a doctor concludes that a patient, X, has say, appendicitis, this conclusion may be justified by saying that:

> X's appendix has not been removed. The patient has a high temperature and vomiting, and the abdomen is sensitive to touch on the lower right-hand side. Under these conditions, a patient probably has appendicitis. This probability is further increased by the fact that none of the following range of foods has been eaten in the last 24 hours: shellfish, mushrooms, . . .

The doctor is providing an explanation of *how* these conclusions were reached. It is important that doctors can do this. If they could not, we would regard them as merely successful clairvoyants – that is, assuming they were right most of the time in their diagnoses.

Expert systems incorporate the possibility of *how* explanations in their explanation subsystem. The user of the system may at any stage interrupt the workings of the expert system to establish how a conclusion or intermediate derived fact has been derived. In the model system in Figure 17.5, after the consultation, the user might query the expert system with the keyboard input '**HOW** seal'. The expert system would respond:

> The conclusion 'seal' was reached because rule 8 applied '**IF** pinniped **AND** mammal **THEN** seal'. Rule 8 applied because 'pinniped' was derived using rule 9 '**IF** flippers **THEN** pinniped'. Rule 9 applied because 'flippers' was given initially. Rule 8 also applied because 'mammal' was derived using rule 2 '**IF** suckles its young **AND** warm-blooded **THEN** mammal'. Rule 2 applied because 'suckles young' and 'warm-blooded' were given initially.

The output given is typical of a response to a **HOW** question provided by an expert system. The proposition for which an explanation is being sought is treated by citing the rules in a backward line of reasoning, together with intermediate conclusions provided by these rules, until 'basic' facts are established – that is, those facts given initially or given in response to questions. The explanatory subsystem inserts expressions such as:

> The conclusion '. . .' was reached because rule . . . applied

in order to make the explanation more readable.

In a large expert system, the line of reasoning to a conclusion may be long and complex. It is usually possible to restrict the explanation facility to a shortened version.

WHY questions

Another form of question that is asked of the expert is a **WHY** question. The doctor may ask patient X whether they had eaten shellfish recently. The patient may wish to know why the doctor is interested. The doctor responds (perhaps rather insensitively):

I am trying to establish whether you have appendicitis. I have already established that you have a high temperature, vomiting and sensitivity to pressure in the lower right abdomen. This makes appendicitis possible. This possibility is increased if I can rule out the possibility of food poisoning. I can do this if you have not had one of a range of foods recently. Shellfish is one of this range.

Here the doctor is citing a possible diagnosis (conclusion) and explaining how the answer to the question will impact on the proof of this diagnosis. It is important that expert systems provide this possibility. It is achieved by means of a **WHY** question. The system in Figure 17.5 does not ask questions of the user during a consultation. However, imagine that it had this facility – no initial facts were given and it derived its conclusions by attempting to prove that the creature in question was each of the possibilities in turn. (This means that the inference engine cannot be identical to that in Figure 17.5.) Suppose further that the system is trying to prove that the creature under investigation is a whale. The expert system needs to establish, if it has not already done so, whether the creature is warm-blooded. The system will generate a suitable question to ask the user. In response, the user may type '**WHY** warm-blooded' at the keyboard. The **WHY** explanation facility provides the following on the screen:

I am trying to establish 'whale'.
'Mammal' is a necessary condition for a creature to be a 'whale', rule 6, and 'warm-blooded' is a necessary condition for a creature to be a 'mammal', rule 2.

Once again, text is inserted by the expert system to make the explanation more readable.

It is important to see that the explanation follows a template, and the rule numbers and the facts or potential facts are added in a standard way to the template. This means that the explanation facility would be of the same form even if the knowledge base were more complex or had a different subject matter.

Requests for further explanation

A third form of explanatory facility has been covered in Section 17.1.2. This is when the system is attempting to establish a fact by questioning the user. The question itself may need further explanation (what does the term 'quick ratio' mean in the question 'Is the quick ratio higher for the company than the quick ratio for the industry as a whole?'). This is provided by explanatory text added to the original text of the question. The explanation is optional, as it would be irritating and confusing to the experienced user to see large amounts of unnecessary additional text.

Consultation traces

A final explanation facility that may be provided generates a record of the inference paths taken by the system during a consultation. This is generally not so important to the user but may be of considerable help to the person building or testing the expert system. This trace is often graphic, showing the rules executed and the facts established in the chronological order of the consultation. For example, part of the graph of Figure 17.6 traversed during a consultation may be traced on the screen.

In summary, four forms of explanatory facility are generally provided:

1. **How:** how has a conclusion been established? What facts and rules were used in deriving it?
2. **Why:** why is a particular question being asked? What is the impact of the answer to the question on a proof to a conclusion?

3. **Further explanation:** provide more text accompanying the question as a further explanation.

4. **Trace:** provide a 'picture' of the consultation. Display the rules fired and the conclusions established in the order in which these events occurred.

Mini case 17.1

Expert systems

Tee Lim, the chief investment officer of AXA Rosenberg's Japan Small Cap Fund, does not venture out of his office in Tokyo to meet officials from companies that he is interested in investing in. Instead, he and his team rely solely on a computer program to pick stocks for them.

It may be a somewhat sterile strategy but it works. In the year to date, the Y15bn fund has had an absolute return of 41 per cent and has outperformed the benchmark Nomura Global Small Cap Index Japan by 48 per cent.

Mr Lim, a 16-year AXA veteran who became the CIO of the Japan Small Cap Fund in February, admits that he does not fit the mould of the traditional, peripatetic fund manager.

His fund has no researchers or analysts who contact companies. His staff, who primarily analyse statistics, rely solely on a computer program creatively called 'Expert System' to pick stocks.

This system, which brings to mind the character Hal from the movie *2001: A Space Odyssey* in its remarkable prescience, scours through 3,500 Japanese stocks to pick those that are undervalued. Kunio Noguchi, the fund's senior portfolio engineer who oversees its day-to-day performance, calls the relatively low share prices of good stocks the 'neglect effect'.

A low-risk, high-return portfolio is then put together, based on a company's fundamentals.

The process is entirely quantitative. The title of fund manager is shunned as there is no single individual who makes investment decisions using qualitative analysis.

Although last week's 5 per cent plunge in the benchmark Nikkei 225 average has left some wondering whether the recent stock market rally has lost steam, most foreign investors – including Mr Lim – remain bullish on the Japanese economy and its growth prospects.

'The words we hear regarding Japan's possible recovery are "guarded optimism",' says Mr Lim. 'Things seem to be recovering and we hope it will continue.'

The general elections in November are not a concern because Mr Lim believes it will simply result in a continuation of the status quo under prime minister Junichiro Koizumi.

He has no plans to re-weight the portfolio following the elections.

Adapted from: **Computers help track the 'neglect effect'**
By Mariko Sanchanta
Financial Times: 27 October 2003

Questions

1. How is the knowledge in this system acquired?
2. What evidence is there to suggest that this system does indeed exhibit intelligence?

17.2 Representation of knowledge

The ways that people represent their knowledge are rich and varied. There are pictorial representations, as in maps and diagrams; there are graphic representations showing relationships; and most common and most powerful of all, there are representations in natural language. This book is written in a natural language, English, and can be regarded as representing knowledge on various aspects of business information systems – their analysis, design and use. The only limits imposed in the representation are those governed by the rules of English and the amount of existing knowledge that is assumed to be possessed by the reader. English is a comprehensive natural language in terms of its vocabulary and its structure (the structure of a language is the set of its semantic categories, together with rules for assembling complex wholes such as sentences out of simpler parts – nouns, verbs, and so on). English is so rich that its rules have never been completely formalized. Attempts are being made, and success in this area is a prerequisite for the development of computers with genuine natural language interfaces. Large subsets of English have been formalized, although computers still have difficulty in treating idiomatic expressions. Few English representations adequately distinguish the fact that 'the whisky is good but the meat is bad' is not an example of 'the spirit is willing but the flesh is weak' (or so the joke goes).

The representation of knowledge used in Figures 17.2 and 17.5 has been very simple. If–then rules have been employed, together with the limitations that the constituents of these rules be simple sentences (bearers of truth and falsity and sentences made out of these by the logical connectives **AND**, **OR** and **NOT**).

Although knowledge representation in expert systems has not approached the power of expression of the English language, it has advanced beyond these simple structures. The next sections consider some of the limitations of these simple structures and the ways that they may be overcome using alternative knowledge representation techniques.

17.2.1 Attribute–value pairs

Imagine that the three rules in Figure 17.7 occur in an expert system that has been set up to deal with applications for credit cards. Part of the system determines whether the applicant's credit status is acceptable, while another part analyses the income to determine the type of credit card to which the applicant is entitled. The rules are simplified for the sake of the example.

If the representation is taken as being composed of complete propositions with no internal structure, then the fact that an applicant's income is £15,000 would not be applicable to these rules. 'Income = £15,000' does not occur as the antecedent to any of them. To ensure that rule 3 fires, the information 'income > £10,000' must be entered

---

Figure 17.7 Some rules governing entitlement to credit cards

Rule 1: If income > £30,000 **then** credit type = gold card
Rule 2: If income ⩽ £30,000 **and** credit status = OK **then** credit type = normal
Rule 3: If income > £10,000 **then** credit status = OK

as a unit in the database. But still neither rule 1 nor rule 2 has its antecedents satisfied. It is also necessary to add the fact 'income < £30,000' to ensure that rule 2 fires after 'credit status = OK' has been proved by rule 3.

The simple representation has the following disadvantages:

■ It is necessary to translate the details of the applicant, namely that income = £15,000, into the two facts 'income > £10,000' and 'income < £30,000' in order to ensure that the knowledge base works with the particular facts of the applicant who is the subject of the consultation. The level of income may be used in many other rules as well, but it is then necessary to make sure that income is rendered in the correct form to satisfy each.

■ The value of the attribute 'income' for the applicant is £15,000. Intuitively speaking, this is what should be entered. It should then be possible for the expert system to derive implied income statements such as 'income < £30,000' from this.

■ If the thresholds in the rules change, for example the critical income level in rule 3 is increased to £12,000, then the income fact as entered for an individual would need to be altered to take account of this.

These considerations lead to the attribute–value (A–V) pair as a common method of expressing knowledge in expert systems.

Applied to the rules in Figure 17.7, the A–V construction can be expressed as follows. There are three attributes – 'income', 'credit status' and 'credit type'. The value of 'credit status' can be 'OK' or 'not OK', the value of 'credit type' can be 'normal', 'gold card' or 'platinum card' (not shown), and the value of 'income' can be any number greater than zero. The user of the expert system inputs the value for the attribute 'income', which is £15,000 in this particular case. The expert system tests this value of income against the rules and assigns the value 'OK' to the attribute 'credit status' (rule 3) and 'normal' to the attribute 'credit type' (rule 2). The rationale behind the A–V representation is that much expert knowledge and reasoning concerns treatment of an example of an object type and its associated attributes where these attributes can have values. The credit card system is concerned with one type of object, a card applicant, and, for each consultation, one example of the applicant, say John Smith. There are a range of attributes of John Smith. Some have values that are entered into the system, whereas the values of others are derived using the rules.

Many common expert system shells work by using A–V pairs in an if–then rule format. It is uncommon, except in the simplest systems, to restrict the representation form to if–then rules containing conditions that are not capable of being further decomposed into constituents such as A–V pairs.

17.2.2 Object–attribute–value triples

Frequently, it is important to depict more than one object in an expert system. The attribute–value representation is then inadequate as all attributes are assumed to be of one object. This limitation may be overcome by using the object–attribute–value (O–A–V) model of representing knowledge. For example, the expert system that assesses a company's financial health may need to encode and work with information on each of the company's outstanding loans. Each loan will be treated as an object and will have attributes such as 'rate of interest', 'call-in date', 'amount', 'creditors' and 'redeemable', with values such as: '10%', '1 Jan 2004', '£1m', 'Federated Bank' and 'true'.

Figure 17.8 (a) A rule from MYCIN; (b) the representation of the rule as an object–attribute–value triplet

(a) RULE 85

If The site of the culture is blood, and
The morphology of the organism is rod, and
The Gram stain of the organism is Gram-neg, and
The patient is a compromised host

Then there is suggestive evidence (0.6) that the identity of the organism is
Pseudomonas aeruginosas

(b)

	Object	**Attribute**	**Value**
If	Culture	Site	Blood
	Organism	Morphology	Rod
	Organism	Gram stain	Gram-neg
	Patient	Compromised host	True
Then	Organism	Identity	*Pseudomonas aeruginosas*

Figure 17.9 O–A–V triplets representing two loans

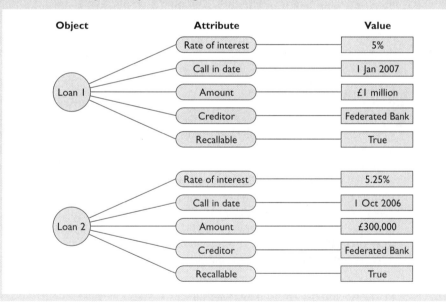

One of the earliest expert systems was MYCIN. This system was developed to aid doctors in the diagnosis and treatment of meningitis and bacterial infections of the blood. MYCIN is an example of a system that represents its knowledge as O–A–V triples within rules. Rule 85 is given in Figure 17.8(a), and its analysis using the O–A–V framework is given in Figure 17.8(b).

Object–attribute–values may be represented in diagrams. Figure 17.9 is the O–A–V triplet representation for two loans to a company. As a company may have many loans,

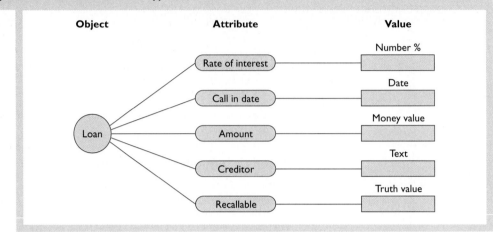

Figure 17.10 Structure of a typical loan

both may be present during a current consultation in Figure 17.10. The blanks indicate where the values of attributes will be added in order to depict an instance of the loan type. Figure 17.10 is the static representation of a generic loan. Figure 17.9 is the dynamic representation of instances of loans during a consultation. The working expert system can be thought of as filling these value slots during the consultation. Some will be filled by the user entering values; others will be entered as a result of the inference process.

17.2.3 Semantic networks

O–A–V triplets go some way towards representing the complexity of knowledge with which experts deal, but they are a long way from the flexibility needed to build models for all knowledge domains. O–A–V triplets are a special and well-defined limitation of the more general semantic network. If the subjects of objects, attributes and values are left and attention is focused on the network representation of Figure 17.9, then Figure 17.11 is arrived at. Here no distinction is made between the nodes (unlike Figure 17.9, where the different types of node have different semantic roles). There are, however, directed links between nodes. 'Has-a', 'is-a' and 'is-a-value-of' are the names of these directed links.

Figure 17.12 is an example of a general semantic network. Its formal composition is a network of nodes connected by directed links or arcs. There are well-known methods of representing this kind of structure at the physical level. Virtually no limitation is placed on what can be the content of a node or link, but it is usual to restrict the representation to the following:

Nodes

Nodes can be classified into the following categories:

1. Objects are generally represented as nodes. In the example in Figure 17.12, Anita Patel, John Smith and Jack Jones are all physical objects. Abstract objects are also placed in nodes. 40 is an abstract object. Some objects seem to fall between the two.

Figure 17.11 A semantic network representation of an O–A–V triplet

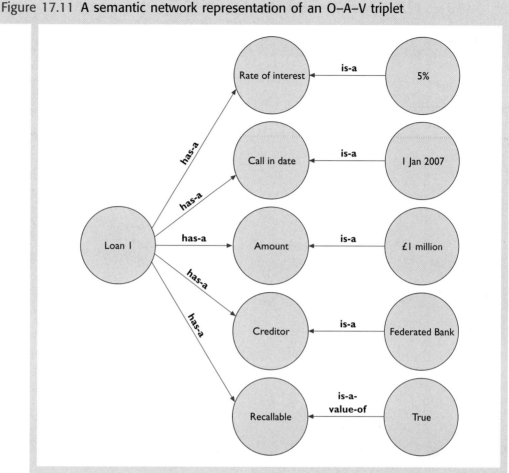

'Accounts department' names an object that is more abstract than Jack Jones but less abstract than the number 40. It is also represented as a node.

2. General terms such as 'employee' or 'accountant' are placed at nodes. These terms correspond to classes of individual objects. (In the terminology of data analysis and the development of the entity model covered in Chapter 13, these classes can be regarded as entity types, while the objects themselves will be entities, perhaps as some occurrence of an entity type shown in the figure.)

3. Attributes can be considered to be of two types. There are attributes that require values, and there are those that do not. 'Age' is an example of the former in that it needs a numeric value. 'Accounting qualification' and 'office' are attributes of 'accountant' and 'employee' respectively that do not require values in the illustrated semantic network. The distinction between attributes and objects is not always clear.

Generally speaking, those attributes that do not require values will rise to the highest possible level of abstraction associated with general terms. In the figure, it is a property of each employee that he or she has a company file. Therefore it is also a

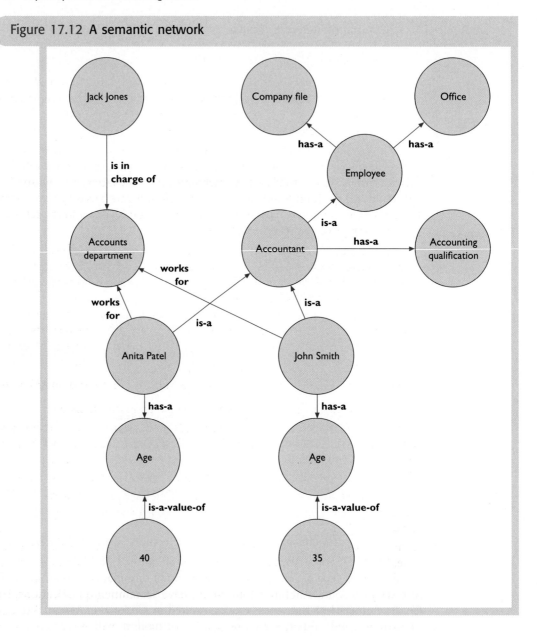

Figure 17.12 A semantic network

property of each accountant that he or she has a company file (because they are employees) and of both Anita Patel and John Smith that each has a company file (because they are accountants). It would be possible to associate the property individually with each object employee of the company – that is, with Anita Patel and John Smith – but this would waste space and miss the generality of the association of the property of having a company file with being an employee.

On the other hand, 'age' cannot rise through the hierarchy, because it requires a value. Although each employee has an age, it is not the same age. Age is really a function from the class of employees to the class of numbers.

Links

Links are one-way, directed connections between nodes. They generally fall into one of a number of categories:

1. 'Has-a' links relate attribute nodes to general-term nodes or to object nodes. They state that a general term has an attribute, such as an employee having an office or an accountant having an accounting qualification, or that an object has an attribute. Anita Patel has an age (40).

2. 'Is-a' links represent relations between object nodes and general-term nodes or between general-term nodes and other general-term nodes. In the former case, the relationship is similar to class (set) membership. In the latter, it is the subclass (subset) relationship. John Smith is an accountant and can be said to be a member of the class of accountants. The accountants are all employees, and the set of accountants is a subset of the set of employees.

3. Other links may be present. In the semantic network of Figure 17.12, the link between Anita Patel and the accounts department represents a relationship between two objects. The relationship is 'works for'. Similarly, Jack Jones is in charge of the accounts department – another relationship between two objects.

   Two types of link are of especial importance. Causal links are relationships between individual events or states and occur in many knowledge bases. Part links are also a common feature of the world and so appear regularly in semantic networks. (The dynamo is part of the engine, which is part of the car.)

Examples of common link/node structures and inheritance are shown in Figure 17.13.

Advantages: The advantages of semantic network representations are:

- They are extremely flexible. New nodes and links can be added as required. The lack of restriction on what the nodes and links mean makes it easy to add knowledge in a natural way.

- ⟨node: is-a link : node⟩ and ⟨node : has-a link : node⟩ correspond to common structures in English. Examples are Tweety is a robin (⟨object⟩ *is a* ⟨general term⟩), a robin *is a* bird (⟨general term⟩ *is a* ⟨general term⟩) and a bird *has a* beak (⟨general term⟩ *has a* ⟨attribute⟩).

- As mentioned earlier, it is possible to store information at the most abstract level possible. Nodes at lower levels inherit properties from nodes at a higher level through is-a links. In Figure 17.12, it can be inferred that accountants have company files and offices. Both Anita Patel and John Smith have accounting qualifications, company files and offices by virtue of is-a links. As well as minimizing redundant duplication of attributes, the inheritance corresponds to a natural way of reasoning in English.

- Semantic networks and inheritance hierarchies are closely linked to current artificial intelligence research into how humans store knowledge. Figure 17.14 is an example of the type of semantic net that Collins and Quillian (1969) used in an experiment to study memory. In general, if the subject of the experiment was asked 'Can canaries sing?' it took less time to answer than to answer the question 'Can canaries fly?' This in its turn took less time to answer than 'Can canaries breathe?' Collins and Quillian argued that information stored in the memory was stored at the most abstract level possible. This can be seen in the semantic network of Figure 17.14. The difference in response can be explained by the need to determine an inheritance in order to answer the question 'Can canaries fly?' but not to answer 'Can canaries sing?'

Figure 17.13 Some semantic network features: (a) common link/node semantic structures; (b) is-a and has-a inheritance

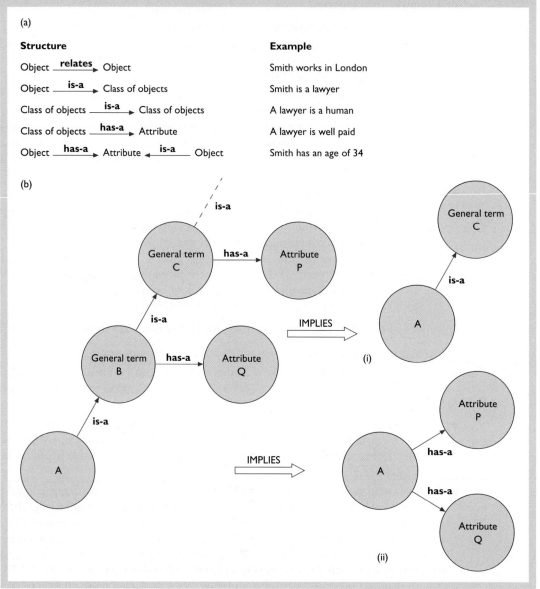

(a)

Structure	Example
Object ──relates──▸ Object	Smith works in London
Object ──is-a──▸ Class of objects	Smith is a lawyer
Class of objects ──is-a──▸ Class of objects	A lawyer is a human
Class of objects ──has-a──▸ Attribute	A lawyer is well paid
Object ──has-a──▸ Attribute ◂──is-a── Object	Smith has an age of 34

Semantic networks as a method of storage have some properties that simulate human knowledge storage and retrieval characteristics and to that extent are a useful representation technique.

Disadvantages: The disadvantages of semantic networks are:

■ The flexibility and simplicity of the structural constituents (links and nodes), as well as being assets, also imply that it is difficult to represent the difference between different semantic categories. For example, the structure ⟨⟨object⟩ *is a* ⟨general term⟩⟩

Figure 17.14 Semantic network hierarchy that explains human question response times

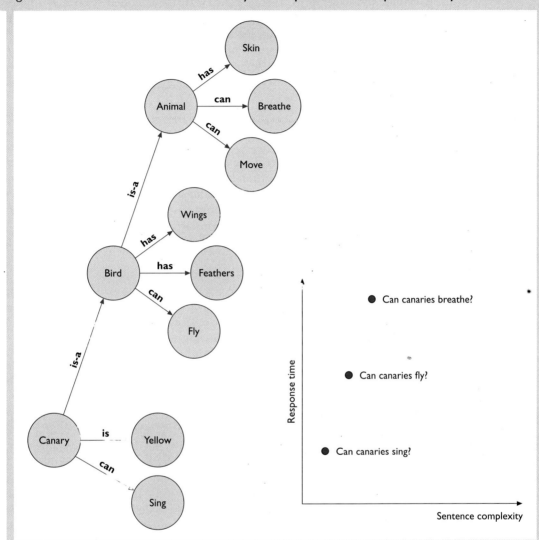

is represented in exactly the same way as ⟨⟨general term⟩ *is a* ⟨general term⟩⟩ by means of a ⟨node:link:node⟩ structure. This conflates the differences between the two structures. The difference is revealed in the way that they can be used to carry out inferences, or simply in the difference between '∈' and '⊆' of set theory. One of the aims of linguistic philosophy has been to analyse the semantic components of propositions into their constituent categories in order to represent meaning and facilitate inference. Simple semantic networks obliterate these distinctions.

■ They are particularly efficient as storage media for inheritance hierarchies, but as soon as exceptions occur semantic networks can become overly complex. In Figure 17.12, the has-a link connecting 'office' and 'employee' is a particularly convenient and efficient way of storing information that Anita Patel, John Smith . . . , all of whom are employees (as illustrated by the is-a link hierarchy), have offices. However, if there are exceptions, then these have to be encoded separately. Suppose, for instance, that John Smith is one of the few employees who does not have an office. This needs to be stored as a special property of John Smith with a has-a link so that the inheritance by John Smith of the 'office' property through the hierarchy is blocked. As long as there are a few exceptions, then a semantic network may be an advantageous storage representation, but once exceptions become common it becomes unwieldy.

17.2.4 Frames

Frames are an alternative way of representing knowledge. They use the basic idea of the object–attribute–value representation but build in refinements that overcome some of the limitations of the O–A–V form. The rationale behind frames is that experts represent their knowledge as various concepts (frames), which are interconnected. For instance, 'employee' is a concept that has various attributes, and 'storekeeper' is a connected concept, a type of employee, which will have more specific attributes than those of employee.

The use of frames can be understood by using the example in Figure 17.15. This is a frame for a long-term loan. The frame consists of slots in which entries are made for a particular occurrence of the frame type. The frame type can be thought of as an object type, the slots as attributes and the entries as attribute values. The frame is more developed than the O–A–V triplet in the following ways:

- The frame may have pointers to other frames. These pointers may indicate hierarchies of the is-a link sort typical of semantic networks or they may indicate other frames that have some bearing on the frame under consideration. In Figure 17.15, the 'long-term loan' is a kind of 'loan'. This corresponds to an is-a link.

- It is common for an expert to have incomplete knowledge of the facts of a particular case. What does the expert do? In many cases, the expert will assume that the missing information is typical for the kind of object under consideration – a 'best guess' philosophy. Frames allow this to be built into the description. In Figure 17.15, the 'rate of interest' of the loan needs to be specified. If it is not then a default is inserted – the current rate of interest. This may be a defined variable or may itself be another frame. Frames may point to other frames elsewhere. At any later stage, the default value may be overridden by known complete information being added. The 'type of repayment' also has a default value. In the case of particular long-term loans, it is unlikely that the default values will be used, but in many other business examples they will be an integral part of the representation.

- The difference between declarative and procedural knowledge was explained in Section 17.1.1. Although it is true that expert systems emphasize declarative aspects of knowledge, experts themselves will sometimes use procedures. When reasoning about a company's long-term loan structure, an expert may be required to calculate a future repayment against a loan. This is essentially a procedural task unless the repayment is found by simply looking up tables containing dates, rates of interest and loan amounts. Frames allow slot entries to be filled by the output of procedures, as in the 'repayment' slot in Figure 17.15. The frame contains in its specification the procedures to be called and under what circumstances. These procedures are defined in the knowledge base.

Figure 17.15 A frame for a long-term loan

ENTRIES

Frame type	long-term loan
Is-a-kind-of	loan

SLOTS   **DESCRIPTION**

Loan number	1348	Range: numeric
Amount	£300,000	Range: money value
Date acquired	12/06/2004	Range: date
Date repayable	12/06/2014	Range: date
Creditor	State Shire Bank	Text
Rate of interest	14%	Range: percentage
		Default: current rate of interest
Redeemable	Yes	Range: 'Yes', 'No'
		Default: 'Yes'
Type of repayment	Interest only	Range: 1 = 'interest only', 2 = 'interest plus principal'
		Default: 'interest plus principal'
Amount outstanding	£240,000	Range: money value
Repayment	£40,000	Range: money value
		If type of repayment = 1 **do** procedure *calc repayment 1*
		If type of repayment = 2 **do** procedure *calc repayment 2*

Generally speaking, it is best to speak of knowledge not as either procedural or declarative absolutely but as being represented as procedural (or declarative) for a particular purpose. Frames allow this flexibility in a way that O–A–V triplets do not. Figure 17.16 gives one procedural and two declarative representations of the same piece of knowledge. It uses a slightly extended version of the rules in Figure 17.7 covering the granting of credit cards.

17.2.5 Logic

Knowledge may also be represented in the form of logic. Philosophers since Aristotle have been interested in correct and incorrect forms of reasoning and have found that

Figure 17.16 Procedural and declarative knowledge

Figure 17.17 Representation of grandparent relations

Grandparent (x,y):-child (x,z) & child (z,y)

Child (George, Sarah)
Child (Sandra, Mary)
Child (George, Sandra)
Child (Sandra, James)
Child (Sarah, Ian)

valid reasoning conforms to various patterns of argument. In order to reveal these patterns, systems of formal logic have been developed as powerful symbolic representation tools. As expert systems are concerned with reasoning correctly in using knowledge, it is not surprising that formal logic has been an influence on the representation of knowledge. The influence of formal propositional logic has already been looked at. If–then rule representation using the Boolean logical connectives **AND, OR** and **NOT** is an example of this. The decomposition of the structure of the individual sentences involved in the rule may also be achieved using predicate logic.

An example of this is shown in Figure 17.17. The property of being a grandparent is defined in terms of being a child of a child. Individual facts are added to the database as illustrated. This form of representation facilitates drawing inferences according to the canons of classical logic. Each entry is either a rule defining a term or a fact.

The artificial intelligence language PROLOG is based on the predicate calculus. The expressions in Figure 17.17 are in a PROLOG-like form. The language contains within it its own inferential procedures. If 'grandparent (George,x)' were to be entered, a list of names satisfying the individual fact together with the rule definition of grandparent would be produced by the PROLOG system. PROLOG is forming the basis of the artificial intelligence kernel language of Japanese fifth-generation computers.

17.2.6 Knowledge representation – conclusion

The main forms of knowledge representation have been covered. Many expert systems allow a mixture of techniques, recognizing that each has its own area of suitability and limitations. The most general technique is the semantic network, of which frames, O–A–V triplets and A–V pairs are specializations. Most expert systems to date have employed O–A–V triplets together with production rules for the general knowledge base, although it is becoming increasingly common to use frames as well (especially as more low-cost expert system shells using frames are released on to the market). The influence of logic techniques has not yet been fully realized, although developments in this area are likely with the advent of Japanese fifth-generation computers.

17.3　Drawing inferences

The knowledge base contains domain-specific knowledge and particular facts. As can be seen from Section 17.2, these may be represented as production rules, object–attribute–value triplets, semantic networks, frames or statements in logic. The aim of an expert system is to apply the domain-specific knowledge to the particular facts to draw conclusions or give advice. It is the purpose of this section to sketch the ways in which this may be carried out. Principles of inference are considered, together with inference control strategies that apply these principles systematically, so ensuring that, wherever they exist, the expert system will arrive at proper conclusions.

17.3.1 Principles and methods of inference

Several principles and methods of reasoning are used in expert systems. Two of the most common are *modus ponens* and the resolution principle. These are now explained.

Modus ponens

The principle of *modus ponens* and the closely connected principle of *modus tollens* were considered in Section 17.1.4. They are basic to the understanding of most expert systems, as some reasoning in virtually any area of expertise is best captured using these principles with if–then rules. *Modus ponens* also reflects an obvious form of human reasoning (unlike *modus tollens*). It is so basic that even to question its validity has often been taken as evidence of a failure to understand the if–then construction and the words contained in it.

Figure 17.18 Truth tables: (a) a truth table for the logical connectives; (b) a truth table for *modus ponendo ponens*; (c) a truth table for the resolution principle

(a)

A	B	if A then B	A and B	A or B	not A	not A or B
T	T	T	T	T	F	T
T	F	F	F	T	F	F
F	T	T	F	T	T	T
F	F	T	F	F	T	T

(b)

	A	B	if A then B,	A	∴ B
*	T	T	T	T	T
	T	F	F	T	F
	F	T	T	F	T
	F	F	T	F	F

(c)

	A	B	C	not A or B,	not B or C	∴ not A or C
*	T	T	T	T	T	T
	T	T	F	T	F	F
	T	F	T	F	T	T
	T	F	F	F	T	F
*	F	T	T	T	T	T
	F	T	F	T	F	T
*	F	F	T	T	T	T
*	F	F	F	T	T	T

The strictest requirement on principles of reasoning is that these principles must lead to true conclusions when applied to true premises. Some principles dealing with reasoning and propositions were given in Figure 17.4. How do we know that these will meet this strict requirement? In other words, does proof from truth always lead to truth in these cases? To answer this, it is necessary to give meanings to the logical connectives.

Truth (T) and falsity (F) are employed for this task in Figure 17.18(a). The table can be read by looking at a combination of T and F for A and B together and then determining the given value for A and B joined by the logical connective. For instance, **IF** 'A' is true **AND** 'B' is false then 'A **OR** B' is true. The table defines the meanings of '**IF–THEN**', '**AND**', '**OR**' and '**NOT**'. Put another way, if a Martian had the concept of truth and falsity, then it would be able to understand the meaning of our words '**IF–THEN**', '**AND**', '**OR**' and '**NOT**' purely from these tables.

Figure 17.18(b) illustrates why *modus ponens* is a valid principle of reasoning. Here truth tables are used to assign T or F to each premise and to the conclusion in an inference. All possible combinations of truth and falsity are assigned to A and B. The truth value is then calculated for each premise and each conclusion. The requirement on a sound reasoning principle is that true premises lead to true conclusions. The starred line (*) is the only case where all the premises are true. Hernce the conclusion is true.

Resolution

The resolution principle is given in Figure 17.4(e) and is shown to be a sound principle of reasoning in Figure 17.18(c). Once again, the starred lines (*) represent cases where the premises are true. In each of these lines, the conclusion is true.

The resolution method is a systematic way of establishing whether a proposition can be proved from a set of if–then rules and other facts. Central to the resolution method is the resolution principle. Here is a simple example of the method in practice. The following is assumed:

(1) *If* it is raining *then* the road is slippery	**IF** A **THEN** B
(2) *If* the road is slippery *then* motor accidents increase	**IF** B **THEN** C
(3) It is raining	A

and we wish to establish whether the following can be proved:

(4) Motor accidents increase	C

The resolution method involves four steps.

1. Rewrite all if–then statements as or statements. The equivalence '**IF** A **THEN** B' and '(**NOT** A) **OR** B' is shown in Figure 17.18(a). (1) and (2) become (5) and (6):

(5) Either it is *not* raining *or* the road is slippery	**NOT** A **OR** B
(6) Either the road is *not* slippery *or* motor accidents increase	**NOT** B **OR** C

2. Assert the negation of the proposition under test – that is, assume the negation of (4) is true:

(7) Motor accidents do *not* increase	**NOT** C

3. Use the resolution principle (see Figure 17.4(c)) on (5) and (6) to derive (8):

(5) Either it is *not* raining *or* the road is slippery	**NOT** A **OR** B
(6) Either the road is *not* slippery *or* motor accidents increase	**NOT** B **OR** C
(8) Either it is *not* raining *or* motor accidents increase	**NOT** A **OR** C

Now use the disjunction elimination principle (see Figure 17.4(f)) on (3) and (8) to prove that motor accidents increase (9):

(8) Either it is *not* raining *or* motor accidents increase	**NOT** A **OR** C
(3) It is raining	A
(9) Motor accidents increase	C

4. Show that a contradiction has been reached between (9) and (7):

Motor accidents increase *and* motor accidents do *not* increase	C **AND NOT** C

so the supposition in (7) must be false, that is

Motor accidents increase	C

has been proved.

The resolution method always follows this four-step strategy. The resolutions in step 3 can be many and complex. The method is very important in expert systems because (1) it can be automated easily and (2) those expert systems that attempt to prove goals from sets of rules and facts (referred to in Section 17.1.4 as 'backward-chaining systems') can do so easily by asserting the negation of the goal to be proved and using the method to derive a contradiction.

The resolution method can handle expressions in the predicate calculus equally well, although it becomes more complex. This is important, as predicate logic is one of the standard representation techniques for the knowledge base.

17.3.2 Uncertain reasoning

So far, the principles and methods of inference that have been considered all deal with cases that involve certain truth or certain falsity, and the principles always lead from truth to truth. However, much human expertise is concerned with reasoning where propositions are not known with certainty, and conclusions cannot be derived with certainty, or with rules that are themselves perhaps not certain. Indeed, the presence of uncertainty in a real-life situation is for many people the chief reason for using an expert. As was mentioned at the beginning of this chapter, there are some who regard the handling of uncertain reasoning as an essential feature of an expert system.

1. An example of the first case of uncertainty mentioned might occur when a doctor attempts to diagnose the cause of fever-like symptoms. Neither the doctor nor the patient knows with certainty whether the patient has been in contact with a Lassa fever carrier from Nigeria. Probably not, but it is still a possibility and one of the factors that needs to be considered if the patient is suffering from some of the symptoms of Lassa fever.

2. An example of the second type of uncertainty concerns credit card applications. If the credit card applicant has an income of more than £30,000 per annum and a mortgage then the credit status is probably 'OK'. If it is known that the applicant has not defaulted on any other loans or credit card payments in the past then credit status increases to almost certainly 'OK'.

3. An example of the third case can happen on the frontiers of a discipline, where heuristic reasoning is carried out by experts using several rules, each of which may be doubted. This may happen where events are supposed, but not known, to be linked as cause and effect.

The implied format for each of these cases is:

(1) Probably A
(2) **IF** A **THEN** probably B
(3) Probably (**IF** A **THEN** B)

Some mixture of these may be present in the same case.

Reasoning with uncertainty is a treacherous area. Many plausible reasoning principles turn out to be ill founded. A student thought that the following was an acceptable reasoning method (note its similarity with the example used to explain resolution):

If it is raining *then* probably the road is slippery	**IF** A **THEN** probably B
If the road is slippery *then* probably accidents increase	**IF** B **THEN** probably C
It is raining	A

therefore

Probably accidents increase	probably C

The student thought again when the following instance of the reasoning method was provided:

If there is shortly to be an avalanche *then* probably it has been snowing recently	**IF** A **THEN** probably B
If it has been snowing recently *then* probably I will go skiing	**IF** B **THEN** probably C
There is shortly to be an avalanche	A

therefore

Probably I will go skiing   probably C

There are two major areas to be looked at with respect to uncertainty in expert systems. First, how is uncertain knowledge represented? Second, how is uncertainty handled in reasoning? The way that uncertainty is represented will impact on the way it is handled in reasoning.

Certainty factors

This is the method used in MYCIN and several other expert systems. Each proposition (or value associated with an attribute of an object) is assigned a certainty factor in the real number range −1 to +1. −1 indicates certainty that the proposition does not hold, +1 indicates certainty that it does, and 0 indicates ignorance.

There are different ways that reasoning using certainty factors may be carried out. One method is to regard the certainty factor of a pair of propositions to be the minimum of the two factors if they are connected by **AND** and to be the maximum if connected by **OR**, and to regard the certainty of the conclusion of an if–then rule to be the certainty of the antecedent multiplied by the certainty of the consequent. The rule normally has some threshold certainty associated with the antecedent. Below this, the rule will not fire. 0.20 is a typical threshold that is used in MYCIN. Consider the following example. Given:

A (certainty = 0.6)
B (certainty = 0.4)
IF A **AND** B **THEN** C (certainty = 0.9)

therefore

A **AND** B (certainty = min (0.6, 0.4) = 0.4)
C (certainty = 0.9 ∞ 0.4 = 0.36)

Necessity and sufficiency factors

The certainty factors in MYCIN's rules indicate how sufficient the evidence (antecedent) is for a conclusion (consequent). In many areas of expertise, the absence of evidence for a conclusion is often taken as indicating that the conclusion does not hold. The evidence is therefore necessary for the conclusion. So, as well as sufficiency factors there are necessity factors. PROSPECTOR is an expert system that contains rules with both of these factors. From PROSPECTOR:

> *If* there is hornblende pervasively altered to biotite *then* there is strong evidence (320, 0.001) for potassic zone alteration.

Without going into the exact meaning of these dual factors, the value of 320 indicates that the altered hornblende is highly sufficient for potassic zone alteration, but 0.001 indicates that the absence of this evidence does little to rule out the possibility. Necessity and sufficiency factors are particularly important where a condition may be associated with one of a range of circumstances.

Fuzzy sets

The use of fuzzy sets is a formal approach to inexact reasoning that diverges from the basic assumptions of classical logic. In traditional set theory, predicates such as 'is red' or 'is a bad debtor' are assumed to denote sets – the set of red things and the set of bad debtors. Each object in the world is either in the set or it is not. Thus Jones is in the set of bad debtors, whereas Smith and the Eiffel Tower are not. Fuzzy set theory, in contrast, interprets predicates as denoting fuzzy sets. A fuzzy set is a set of objects. Some objects are definitely in the set. Some are definitely not. And some are only probably or possibly in the set.

Uncertain reasoning – conclusion

Three forms of representing uncertainty and reasoning with uncertainty have been covered. This coverage is only superficial. The treatment that each gives to handling uncertainty is too complex for the scope of this book. References are given at the end of the chapter for the interested reader. There are a number of features that must be highlighted:

1. There is no one agreed method of handling uncertainty. This is not because of technical disagreement but rather reflects deep and theoretical differences of opinion. Moreover, there seems to be little basis for adjudicating between the competing views, as criteria for comparison are not agreed.

2. The strict requirement that sound principles of reasoning must lead from truth to truth cannot apply in cases of uncertain reasoning.

3. There may be no one (or even several) correct model of uncertain reasoning to be applied *in vacuo*. It may be the case that the way uncertainty is handled is domain-dependent. That is, although accountants, doctors and car mechanics use terms like 'probable', 'unlikely' and 'possible', these are used in different ways in different areas of expertise (domains).

4. Empirical research in each domain of expertise may indicate the models of inexact reasoning that are used there. These models can then be built into an expert system. Nowadays, even expert system shells may not impose predefined methods of handling uncertainty upon the expert systems builder. They allow the architect to design control over the way in which uncertainty is handled in the final expert system.

5. Some expert systems provide 'friendly' user interfaces that use terms like 'probable' and 'likely'. These will be working with some numerical model of inexact reasoning behind the friendly and uncomplicated façade presented to the user. In understanding how an expert system arrives at its conclusions, it is important to penetrate this mask.

6. Reasoning under uncertainty is, and will remain, one of the most important and controversial theoretical and practical areas in expert systems.

17.3.3 Inference control strategies

Using a principle to draw an inference will yield a new fact or probabilistic conclusion. In order to carry out a consultation, however, an expert system needs to draw many inferences. These cannot be made randomly or else the inference system will 'wander' logically around the knowledge area. Preferably, there needs to be some pattern or strategy to decide which inferences to draw at which time. The purpose of an inference control strategy is to determine this. The strategy used will obviously determine the performance characteristics of the expert system.

Forward chaining

This strategy takes the established current facts and attempts to use the rules (or whatever representation form the domain-specific knowledge base takes) to derive new facts. The new facts are added to the set of established facts, and the strategy then attempts to derive further new facts to add to this set. The system is said to be data-driven. This is most obvious in the application of *modus ponens*, where the antecedent conditions are among the set of established facts and the conclusions when drawn are added to this set. At any one time, it may be possible to use more than one rule to derive more than one conclusion. In order to resolve the conflict, the inference control strategy must decide between the competing rules. A simple way of doing this is to number the rules and fire the lowest-numbered rule that has its antecedent satisfied. More complex conflict-resolving techniques are used in larger systems. An example of a forward-chaining system has been given in Figure 17.5, the model expert system dealing with creature classification.

Forward chaining is a useful strategy if there are a large number of possible outcomes given a small number of values for the initial data. This characteristic of an application is typical of expert systems dealing with planning where relatively few basic constraints are given.

Backward chaining

By far the most common inference control strategy is backward chaining. This is used in MYCIN and all the major systems. In backward chaining, a goal is selected and the system establishes the facts that are needed to prove the goal. Each of the needed facts becomes a subgoal, and the system establishes the facts that are needed to prove these, which, in their turn, become sub-subgoals, and so on. Eventually, a basic proposition is reached. A basic proposition is a sub-sub . . . goal that does not depend on other facts.

There are now three possibilities. The proposition required is in the database, in which case the system will go on to establish, if it can, the other facts needed to prove the initial goal; the negation of the proposition is in the database, in which case the system will need to prove the initial goal, if it can, by a different route; neither the proposition nor its negation has been established. In this last situation, it is normal for the expert system to interrogate the user. The answer provided can then be used in the reasoning.

In a consultation with an expert, say a doctor, it is usual for the patient to volunteer information at the start of the session ('I have been feeling tired for a week with loss of appetite and a sore throat. I also have a bad headache, which comes in the evening. . . .') The doctor will use this initial information to select a most likely goal (diagnosis) and then seek to establish this by backward reasoning – performing laboratory tests, asking the patient particular questions, checking reflexes, and so on. This form of approach is quite common. Suppose that a client consults an investment adviser when seeking a planned portfolio. The client will start by proffering information such as the amount of money involved, why they wish to invest, what special requirements are needed (for example, lump sum capitalization in 15 years to pay for a university education), constraints (such as no wish to invest in companies involved in military hardware), and so on. The investment adviser will use this to select likely strategies, which will require further elicitation of facts from the client.

Both of these examples can be characterized by initial forward chaining followed by backward chaining. It is common for modern expert systems to allow this mix of inference control strategies.

Much research work is yet to be done on inference control strategies. These strategies become particularly important when dealing with large expert systems. The hundreds or even thousands of rules involved may use large chunks of computer processing during searching unless efficient control strategies are adopted. This is crucial with the current trend towards large multi-user expert systems in the areas of finance and insurance.

17.4 Intelligence and the Internet

The expert systems that have been described so far in this chapter represent one particular implementation of artificial intelligence. In general, they are tools designed within a particular problem domain and based upon a knowledge base limited by the expert knowledge acquired and stored. An example of their use is the assessment of insurance risk leading to selection of an appropriate policy.

Intelligent agents are another application of artificial intelligence. Unlike the bounded knowledge base servicing an expert system, the source data for an intelligent agent can be located on any traversable route on the Internet. Another distinguishing feature of intelligent agents is their need and ability to relocate from node to node across networks of computers and to communicate with other pieces of software such as other intelligent agents.

Intelligent agents

The quantity of information available through application of the Internet is already huge and continues to grow exponentially. The sheer amount of information available is itself becoming a prohibitive factor in effective and efficient searching.

The use of intelligent agents was introduced in Chapter 6. An intelligent agent is a piece of software that performs a task on behalf of the user; the task is invariably mundane or highly repetitive in nature and often concludes with a result or a suggestion.

Intelligent agents can be either closed or open in their activity. A closed agent operates in a particular system environment reacting to goal setting in this limited domain. A simple example is the desktop computer's own system agent, which checks internal performance, such as the degree of disk fragmentation, and makes recommendations for more effective operation of the system. An open agent, however, can interface with other intelligent agents and work cooperatively in a multidisciplinary environment. This environment is called an **agent society**. Many of the search agents that trawl websites for information operate in this collaborative way. Some work has already been undertaken to establish standards for communication between intelligent agents. An example is the development of a Java standard for intelligent agent applets, called **aglets**.

Functionality of intelligent agents

Intelligent agents appear in many forms. The range of functions that they carry out can be evaluated under three main headings:

1. **Autonomy:** While human interaction is essential at key stages of the activity of an intelligent agent, a desirable feature is that the agent can reach its goals without intervention. Similarly, when interaction with other intelligent agents occurs, autonomy in deciding whether and how the exchange of information is to take place is another distinguishing feature.

2. **Intelligence:** This is usually manifested by an appreciation of the agent's own environment. An ability to recognize features of the environment, to respond to changes in the environment and to modify the goal if appropriate are all desirable attributes. These characteristics confer intelligence on the agent's activity.

3. **Relocation:** An intelligent agent must be able to move effectively between nodes on a network and across the Internet using the autonomous characteristics and intelligence outlined above. Ease of travel is an essential feature.

Intelligent agents and the value chain

Examples have already been given in previous chapters showing the application of intelligent agents to business, particularly in the e-commerce arena. Applications are already available to enable consumers to compare prices and products, for businesses to interact with suppliers and retail outlets and to facilitate more effective electronic negotiations and transactions. In particular, the most effective applications have applied the intelligence to other problem domains to add value to the solutions provided. An example can be found in push and pull marketing.

The concept of push and pull technology was introduced in Chapter 6. Push marketing is characterized by the unsolicited approaches made by business systems to existing or potential customers. The combination of intelligent agent technology with data warehouses and sophisticated mining techniques has enabled customer relationship management to become far more focused and thereby more successful. The intelligent agent can locate potential customers; these customers can then be matched with existing profiles held in data warehouses. The net result is to cut down on the poor targeting often associated with unwanted, mass-distribution e-mail, often referred to as **spam.**

Intelligent agents that can assist in pull marketing are the best developed of these technologies. Web crawlers and gophers have a long history in the evolution of the web. Modern search agents are often called **bots.** The word is an abbreviation of **robot,** derived from the Czech word *robota* meaning *work.* Common uses are in locating the best price for a particular product, often achieved by employing the combining efforts of several existing search engines. Another example of the use of intelligent agents in pull technology is in the subscription to an information provider. Users request a particular service, such as news features about a particular topic or books of a particular style or by a named author. The intelligent agent supporting the marketing pull will search for relevant sites and download the required information in an ongoing fashion. As changes occur, the latest updates are constantly retrieved as long as the intelligent agent is active.

Summary

Expert systems are a rapidly expanding area in the application of artificial intelligence in business. It is estimated that investment in expert systems will continue to increase in the twenty-first century. Expert systems incorporate the expertise or competent skills of one or many experts. They do this in a way that separates the general knowledge of the expert from the particular details of a case under consideration. The expert system then applies this knowledge to the case and uses reasoning to come to conclusions, gives advice, makes planning decisions, or suggests analyses and diagnoses.

The main components of an expert system are the knowledge base, the inference engine, the explanation subsystem and the knowledge-acquisition subsystem. The knowledge base stores the domain-specific knowledge of the expert, together with particular data obtained during a consultation. The inference engine is responsible for dynamically applying the domain-specific knowledge to the particular case during use of the system. The explanation subsystem allows users to interrogate the expert system with requests as to *how* a specific conclusion has been derived or *why* a question is being asked. The knowledge-acquisition subsystem enables the entry of knowledge by the expert or generates general rules from a database of past cases by automated induction. The major problems in knowledge acquisition occur in the earlier stages of knowledge elicitation from the expert and the representation of this in a suitable form for the system.

The choice for the form of representation is an important one. Different forms have different areas of suitability. Rule-based representations are common in many expert systems, particularly small systems. This structure may be combined with the representation of attributes and values of objects (A–V pairs) in the rules themselves. If many objects are used in a system, it may be convenient to use an object–attribute–value representation strategy. Semantic networks provide a general way of representing the connections between various objects and concepts. Frame-based representations, in which concepts are modelled as frames with slots for attributes, are now becoming widely used. The ability for default values to fill the slots, references to procedures and the way that frames can be linked together, and in so doing model the interconnections between concepts, enable knowledge to be represented in a powerful way.

Different principles of inference can be used in different systems. Where the reasoning is concerned only with certainty there is some agreement about the constraints that inferences should meet. However, matters become more complex when, as is common with many areas of expertise, the luxury of a certain world disappears. The way that uncertain knowledge is represented interacts with the techniques of reasoning with uncertainty. Various approaches are common. Certainty factors, necessity and sufficiency measures and fuzzy sets have all been used. There is still a large area of disagreement about the representation and patterns of reasoning to be used with uncertain knowledge. It may be the case that what counts for adequate uncertain reasoning cannot be based on analytical or mathematical investigation but will rely on empirical research, which may deliver different results for different areas of expertise.

Inference control strategies ensure that the inference engine carries out reasoning in an exhaustive and efficient manner. Systems that attempt to prove selected goals by establishing propositions needed to prove these goals, which in themselves become secondary goals, are backward-chaining or goal-driven systems. This is in contrast to forward-chaining systems, which attempt to derive conclusions from established facts.

It is important for the business person involved in the development (and use) of expert systems to have an understanding of their components, the way that knowledge is represented in them and the forms of reasoning used. This is because it is likely that in the development of such systems they (the experts) will be more intimately involved than they would in the development of traditional information systems.

Intelligent agents can be used to enhance activities along the supply chain and help to add value. Agents can be either open or closed in operation. Examples are found in push and pull marketing, with the use of bots being the most common application.

Review questions

1. Briefly explain the following terms:

knowledge base	HOW question	has-a link
inference engine	backward chaining	inheritance hierarchy
inference principle	declarative knowledge	forward chaining
inference strategy	procedural knowledge	uncertain reasoning
if–then rule	object–attribute–value triple	certainty factor
knowledge-acquisition	frame	expert system shell
subsystem	semantic network	artificial intelligence
explanatory subsystem	is-a link	WHY question

2. What is meant by *reasoning with uncertainty* in the context of knowledge systems?

3. Using an example, explain the difference between *declarative* and *procedural* knowledge.

4. Explain the difference between a system that uses attribute–value pairs and a system that uses object–attribute–value triplets to represent knowledge. Give an example where it is necessary to use O–A–V representation rather than A–V representation.

Exercises

1. 'There is little difference between an expert system interrogating a knowledge base and a database management system accessing a database.' Do you agree?

2. Select a familiar task that requires the use of knowledge to be carried out successfully. Specify the central knowledge areas involved in performing the task and represent these as if–then rules. A partial example is now given:

Task: Decision on the purchase of a second-hand car.

Areas: (1) Is a car needed?
       (2) Is the car that is being considered sound?
       (3) Is the car that is being considered priced reasonably?
       (4) Can I finance purchase of the car?

if–then rules (Area 2)

(2.1) *If* the bodywork is sound
    and the engine is sound
    and the suspension is sound
    and the steering is sound
    and the general condition is satisfactory
    then the car is considered sound.

(2.1.2) *If* there is not knocking from the engine when idling
    and there is not blue smoke from the exhaust
    and ...
    and ...
    then the engine is sound.

3. Explain, using a simple example, what is meant by a *frame-based representation*. In what ways does a frame-based representation differ from a semantic network? Explain the advantages and disadvantages of a frame-based representation over:

(a) O–A–V triplets

(b) a rule-based representation.

4. (a) Explain what it is for a pattern of reasoning to be sound.

(b) Consider the following argument forms:

     (1) No As are Bs
         Some Bs are Cs
         ∴ No As are Cs

     (2) All As are Bs
         Some Bs are not Cs
         ∴ Some As are not Cs

     (3) Some As are Bs
         No As are Cs
         ∴ Some Bs are not Cs

     (4) Not all As are Bs
         Some Bs are not Cs
         ∴ Some As are Cs

     (5) Some As are Bs and some are not
         Some Bs are Cs and some are not
         ∴ Some As are Cs

     (6) All As are Bs
         No Bs are Cs
         ∴ No As are Cs

In each of these cases, decide whether the pattern of reasoning is sound. [Hint: Represent each predicate by a set drawn on a Venn diagram constructed to reveal the argument form. Attempt to produce a Venn diagram where all the premises are true yet the conclusion is false. If this can be done, the argument form is unsound. Why? See Figure 17.19.]

For unsound patterns of reasoning, suggest an English example where the premises are true and the conclusion false.

[Example for (1)

No women are men TRUE

Some men are doctors TRUE

No women are doctors FALSE]

Figure 17.19

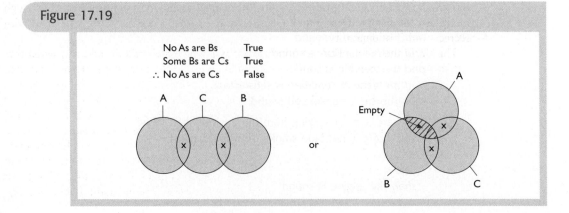

5. Explain the resolution method of proof. Why is it particularly applicable to backward-chaining strategies?

6. The resolution principle may be stated as:

   A **OR** B
   NOT B **OR** C
   ∴ A **OR** C

   Show that this is a sound principle by using a truth table.

7. Represent the following paragraph (taken from the main text of the chapter) as:

   (a) Boolean if–then rules
   (b) O–A–V triplets within rules.

   If the student has successfully completed level 1 of the examination, *or* has been exempted from level 1 by virtue of satisfying *any* of the conditions laid out in paragraphs 3(a) to 3(f) below, *then* the student is entitled to register for level 2 of the examination. A student registered for level 2 is exempt from examination papers 2.3 *and* 2.4 *if* he/she has obtained exemption from level 1 by virtue of satisfying the conditions 3(a) *or* 3(b) below, *or* satisfying 3(d) *and* being in possession of an honours degree awarded by a British university or accredited by the Council for National Academic Awards.

8. Are intelligent knowledge-based systems (expert systems) really intelligent in the sense that we use the word 'intelligent' to apply to human beings? If so, by virtue of what characteristics are they to be regarded as intelligent? If not, could a computer-based system be regarded as intelligent, and what would constitute the justification for applying the term?

9. 'Backward chaining is an efficient reasoning strategy when the number of goals is small relative to the number of rules to be considered. As technology advances, however, the increase in the speed of making inferences using facts and knowledge in the knowledge base will blur the importance of the distinction between forward and backward chaining as far as the user of the expert system is concerned.' Is this true?

CASE STUDY 17

Expert systems

Banking and finance are prime areas for investment in expert systems projects, although many of these have not yet come to fruition and the area is one naturally associated with secrecy and confidentiality.

The UK branch of the Bank of America acts as a 'wholesale' bank dealing only with other banks and companies. It has developed a small expert system dealing with the treatment of letters of credit. When a UK company makes an agreement to export goods to or import goods from another country, certain documents must be prepared and checked. These documents pass between the UK company, its bank, the overseas company, its bank, and sometimes other intermediary banks and agencies as well. This documentation is often quite extensive and may occupy a file more than an inch thick. The letters of credit contained need to be checked for completeness, accuracy, authenticity, correct cross-referencing, and so on. It is estimated that Britain loses in excess of £50 million per year through refused payments as a result of incorrect paperwork in this area. The checking of the letters, although

▶

mechanical, requires a great deal of obscure knowledge. The Bank of America requires that its employees have at least ten years' experience before allowing them to authorize payments of substantial sums of money involved in overseas trade. It takes up to two years to train junior clerks.

This seemed suitable as an expert system domain as the task was clear-cut, the expertise was at least worth archiving if not developing as a system for expert assistance, and there was a commitment from those involved, including the bank's head of marketing and development, for cash management and electronic banking services in the UK. Originally, it had been intended that the domain would cover the entire set of documents relevant to granting letters of credit, and it had been hoped that a system could be designed that would detect all the shortcomings in the supporting documentation. It soon became clear that this area was too large, at least for the bank's first attempt to build an expert system, so the domain was pruned by restricting the system to the seven most important documents. These included the invoice, certificate of origin, insurance certificate, drafts and the transportation documents.

It was decided to use an expert systems shell (Expert Edge) together with an experienced knowledge engineer and one expert – the head of documentary services at the bank. Expert Edge is a backward-chaining PC shell written in C. It took about six weeks of knowledge elicitation and six weeks of testing to arrive at a working system. There were 270 rules, perhaps a large number to count as a small system.

The knowledge elicitation began by developing a structure similar to a semantic network, although in the form of a tree (called a name tree). This had a root called 'discrepancy', with branches for each of the document types. Each of these also had branches. For instance, 'transportation document' had branches called 'signature', 'endorsement' and 'quantities'. The name tree is part of the knowledge base and is referred to during a consultation. The rules are either added via standard word-processed text in the knowledge representation language of the shell or are added through a facility of Expert Edge that prompts users for the various parts of a rule. This is simpler for 'uneducated' users as it avoids the need to master the syntax of the knowledge-representation language.

A number of problems were encountered in development. First, there was a shortage of available expert time. This was particularly noticeable in the testing stage of the system, and it was difficult to choose a comprehensive set of test examples. Second, there was a trade-off concerned with the use of technical terms. These terms are preferable as they have a precise meaning and they often aid conciseness in the final system. Unfortunately, however, their use makes the system less comprehensible to inexperienced users.

This is also connected with a third problem area. It was initially intended that the system be used as a training medium for the bank's personnel and that it be sold to outside import/export companies. Both of these aims required the use of different questions and recommendations, depending on the nature of the end user. For instance, a particular discrepancy should lead to a recommendation that the bank refuse payment if it is using the system but lead to the recommendation that the export/import company correct the inaccurate documentation if it is using the system. Much of the knowledge would be most naturally represented in tabular form, but the particular expert system shell had no facility for this, although interfacing with a desktop database package was possible.

A consultation with the system typically takes about 20 minutes and involves the system interrogating the user to obtain answers to yes/no, numeric or menu selection questions. There are no questions that require a text response. Complex calculations may be performed by the system during a consultation. Whenever a rule governing the correct use of documentation is found to be infringed an error message is displayed on the screen, normally detailing the type of error found and a recommended course of action. The system allows WHY questions, and it answers them by proceeding up the rule trees of dependent rules as far as the user wishes. Most trees are broad and shallow, reflecting the nature of the task – carrying out checks over a wide range of areas where each check does not exhibit much depth. As was explained earlier, the system covers only the seven most important documents. What happens if other documentation is involved? This is handled by the system asking the question as to whether the letters of credit require other documents. If the answer is 'yes', then the user is directed to a senior officer.

The system is now used for training purposes, and it is estimated that the previous training period of one and a half to two years can be reduced to about two weeks with the system – a substantial saving. The system always performs reliably and makes the user think about the task in a systematic way. It is simple to use; even the typist is using it. However, it is not being used as a live system. There are two reasons. First, the system is slower than the human being. The need to input data at the keyboard means that the time taken in a consultation is (slightly) longer than the average time taken for a manual check of the documentation. Second, and more importantly, the system has not, as yet, passed the test of confidence. Whether it does so subsequently depends on its performance in continued future use. The bank has been favourably impressed by its first expert system development and intends to continue with other developments if suitable domains are found. The main lessons learned by the participants in the process seem to be that it is necessary to establish that the chosen area is representable as a set of rules prior to the start of the project, that time should be made clearly available by the expert, and that the project should proceed with an interactive prototyping approach combined with clear checkpoints along the development trail.

Questions

1. What features of the handling of letters of credit lend this system to an expert system solution?

2. The system was developed using an expert systems shell. What is an expert systems shell? What advantages are there to developing a solution using a shell rather than a programming language such as PROLOG?

3. The expert systems shell used backward chaining. What is meant by this?

4. Explain how knowledge acquisition took place in this system.

5. The system allowed 'why' questions to provide an explanation of how a decision has been reached. Describe in general terms how this is accomplished by the explanation subsystem.

6. Define a semantic net. How might semantic nets have been used in developing this system?

7. What problems were encountered in implementing the system? Would you consider the project to have been a success?

References and recommended reading

Arnold M. and Rush D. (1987). An expert system approach to the appraisal of accounting software. *Management Accounting*, January

An introductory article illustrating an application of expert systems in appraisal. This can be read with no prior knowledge of expert systems.

Barr A., Cohen P.R. and Feigenbaum E.A. (eds) (1981). *The Handbook of Artificial Intelligence*, Vols 1 and 2. Los Altos, California: William Kaufmann

Beerel A. (1993). *Expert Systems in Business: Real World Applications*. Chichester: Ellis Horwood
This is a readable text that combines an introduction to theoretical aspects of expert systems with the practical knowledge and experience of an expert systems builder. The book also has case studies. Included is material on the relationship between corporate culture and expert systems, project management of expert systems and investment decisions on expert systems development.

Brighton H. (2003). *Introducing Artificial Intelligence*. Icon Books
This provides a straightforward and very readable background to AI.

Chorofas D.N. (1987). *Applying Expert Systems in Business*. McGraw-Hill
This is a readable text that sets expert systems within the context of management perspectives, decision support systems and the information centre. With chapter titles such as 'Expert systems and the industrialization of knowledge', this text provides a broader perspective within the organization to locate expert systems.

Chorofas D.N. (1998) *Agent Technology Handbook*. McGraw-Hill
This is a thorough coverage of the use of intelligent agents in networks and mobile computing. The book contains sections on reliability and diagnostics issues. The book is mainly business-focused, with relatively little complex technical content.

Cohen P.R. and Feigenbaum E.A. (eds) (1990). *The Handbook of Artificial Intelligence*, Vol. 3. Los Altos, California: William Kaufmann
These are invaluable reference books on all aspects of artificial intelligence.

Collins A. and Quillian M.R. (1969). Retrieval time from semantic memory. *Journal of Verbal Learning and Verbal Behaviour*, 8, 240–7

Harmon P. and King D. (1988). *Expert Systems*. New York: Wiley
An excellent introduction to all aspects of expert systems and their development. It is aimed at the intelligent reader from business rather than the computer specialist.

Negnevitsky M. (2001). *Artificial Intelligence: A Guide to Intelligent Systems*. Addison-Wesley
An accessible book which introduces the topic of AI and concentrates on the concepts without dwelling excessively on the mathematical foundations. The book describes the building of a system and the evaluation and selection of appropriate tools.

Newell A. and Simon H. (1972). *Human Problem Solving*. Englewood Cliffs, NJ: Prentice Hall

Parsaye K. and Chignell M. (1988). *Expert Systems for Experts*. Wiley
A comprehensive, readable exposition of the basic concepts used in expert systems. Although not specifically oriented towards business applications, this book provides one of the best introductions to the central ideas behind business expert systems.

Silverman B.G. (ed.) (1987). *Expert Systems for Business*. Reading, Massachusetts: Addison-Wesley
This provides a series of articles organized around such themes as expert support systems and integrating expert systems into a business environment. It is not an introductory text, although basic concepts in expert systems are introduced and explained early in the text.

Turban E. (1992). *Expert Systems and Applied Artificial Intelligence*. New York: Macmillan
This student text is a clear, comprehensive treatment devoted to applied expert systems. It also contains sections on natural language processing, computer vision, speech understanding and robotics.

Turban E. (2001). *Decision Support and Expert Systems*, 6th edn. Harlow: Longman Higher Education Division
This is a comprehensive textbook covering all aspects of DSS and expert systems from the perspective of a manager wishing to know about management support technologies. It has several case studies and chapter-end questions.

Wooldridge M. (2002). *An Introduction to Multi-agent Systems*. Wiley
Suitable for undergraduate and some postgraduate courses, this book provides a non-technical exploration of intelligent agents and multi-agent systems.

Index